Swimming Pool, Isola Nel Kantiere, July 1991. Photo: Massimo Sciacca

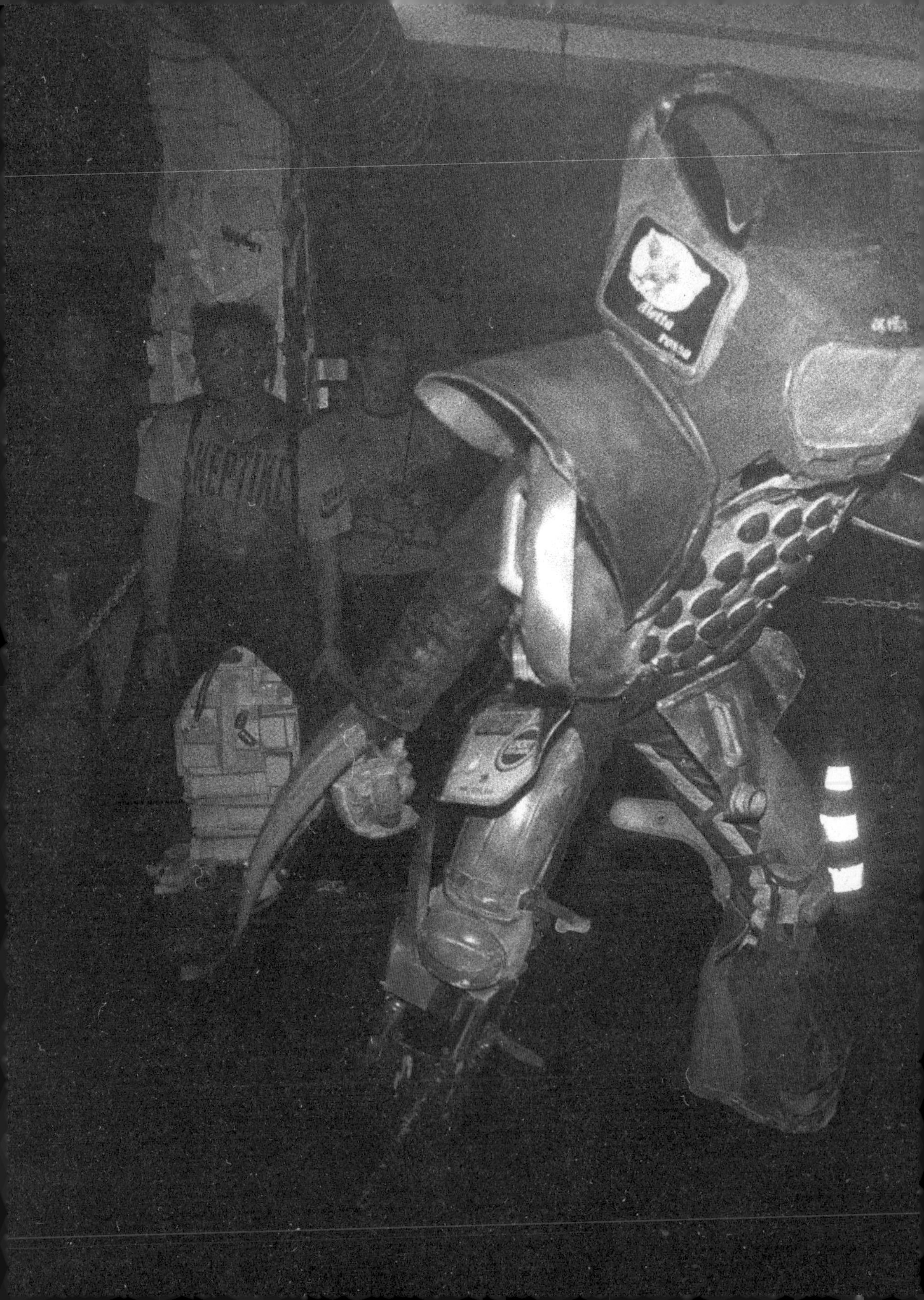

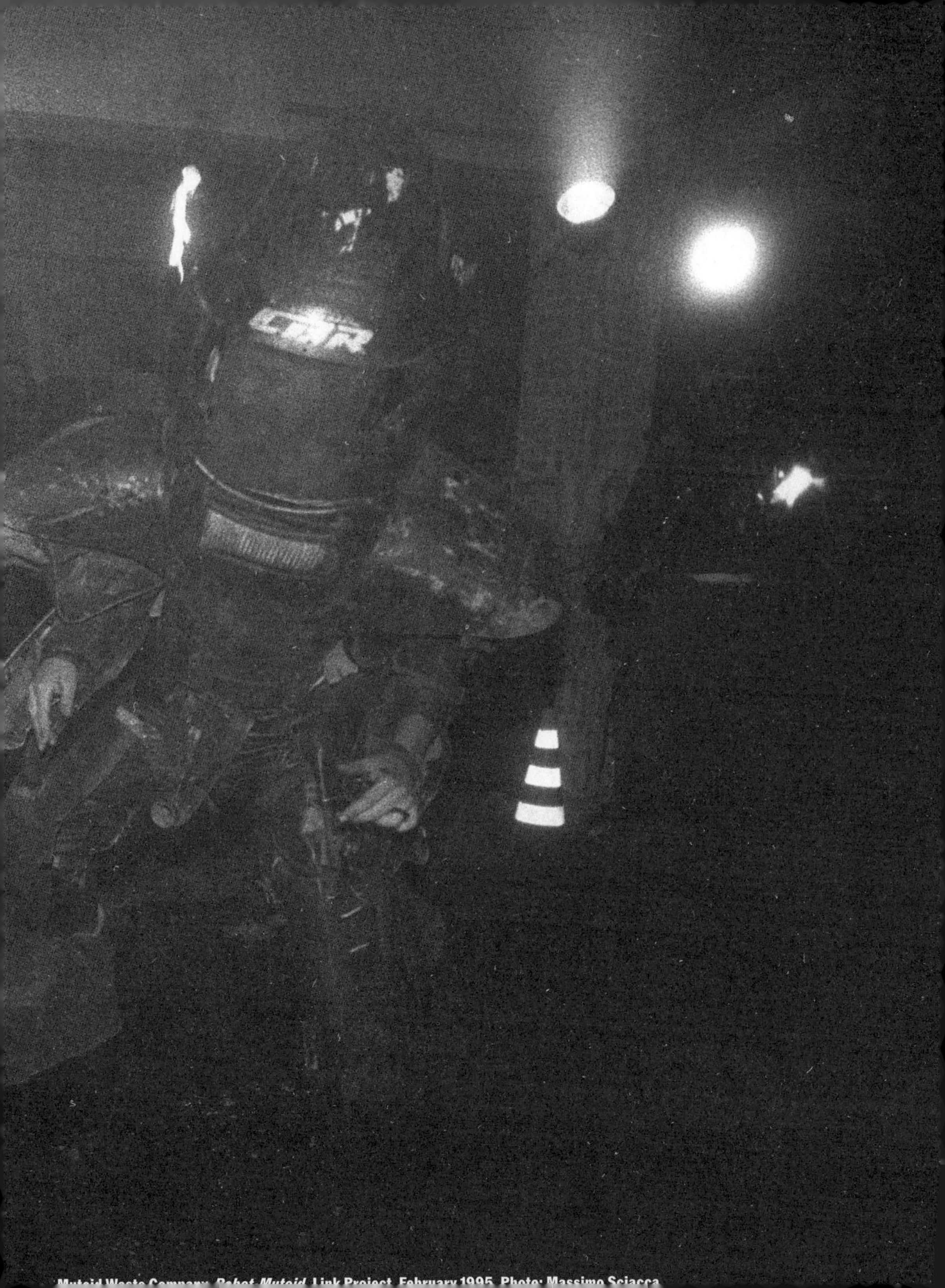

Mutoid Waste Company, *Robot Mutoid* Link Project, February 1995. Photo: Massimo Sciacca

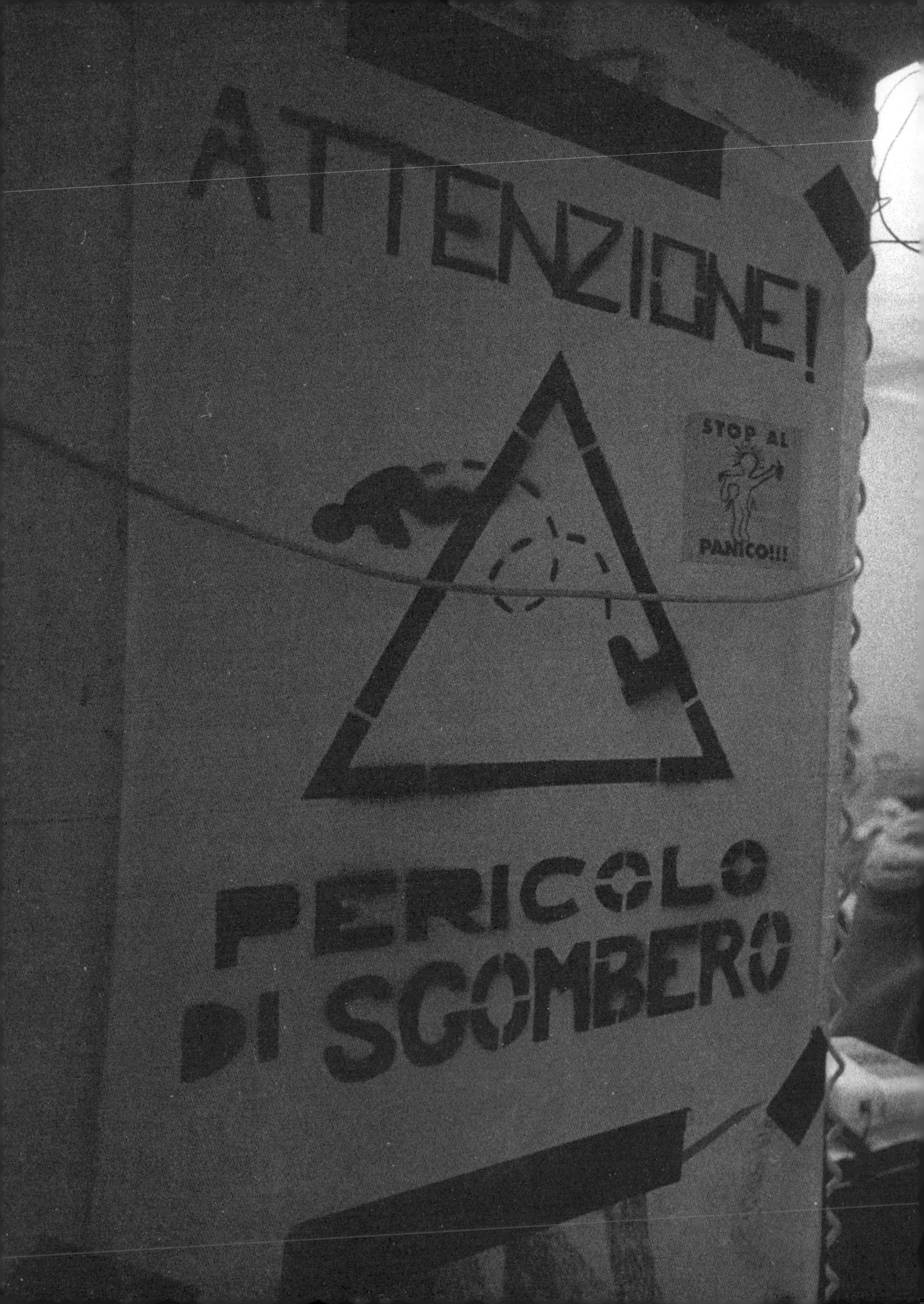

ATTENZIONE!
STOP AL
PANICO!!!
PERICOLO
DI SGOMBERO

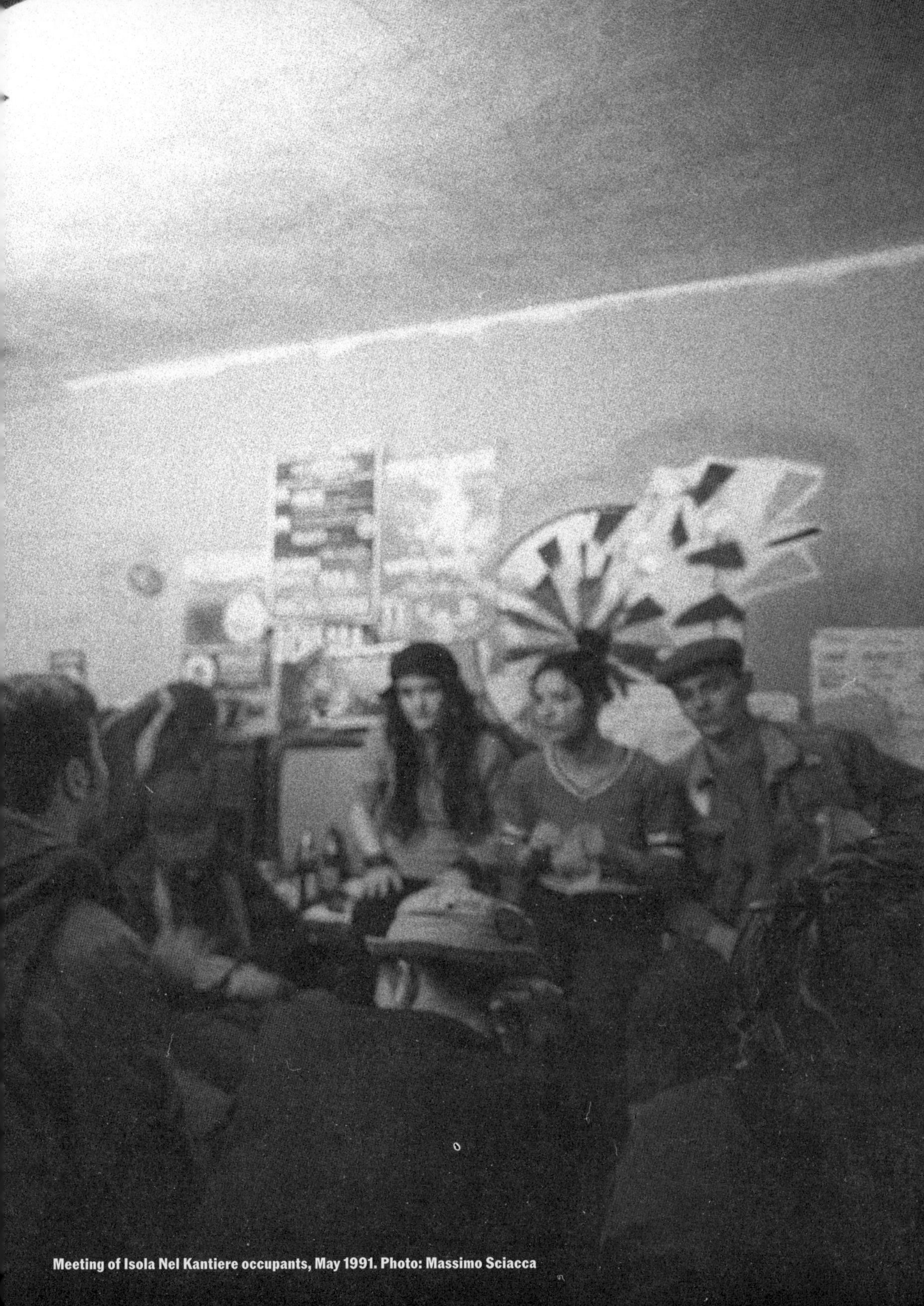

Meeting of Isola Nel Kantiere occupants, May 1991. Photo: Massimo Sciacca

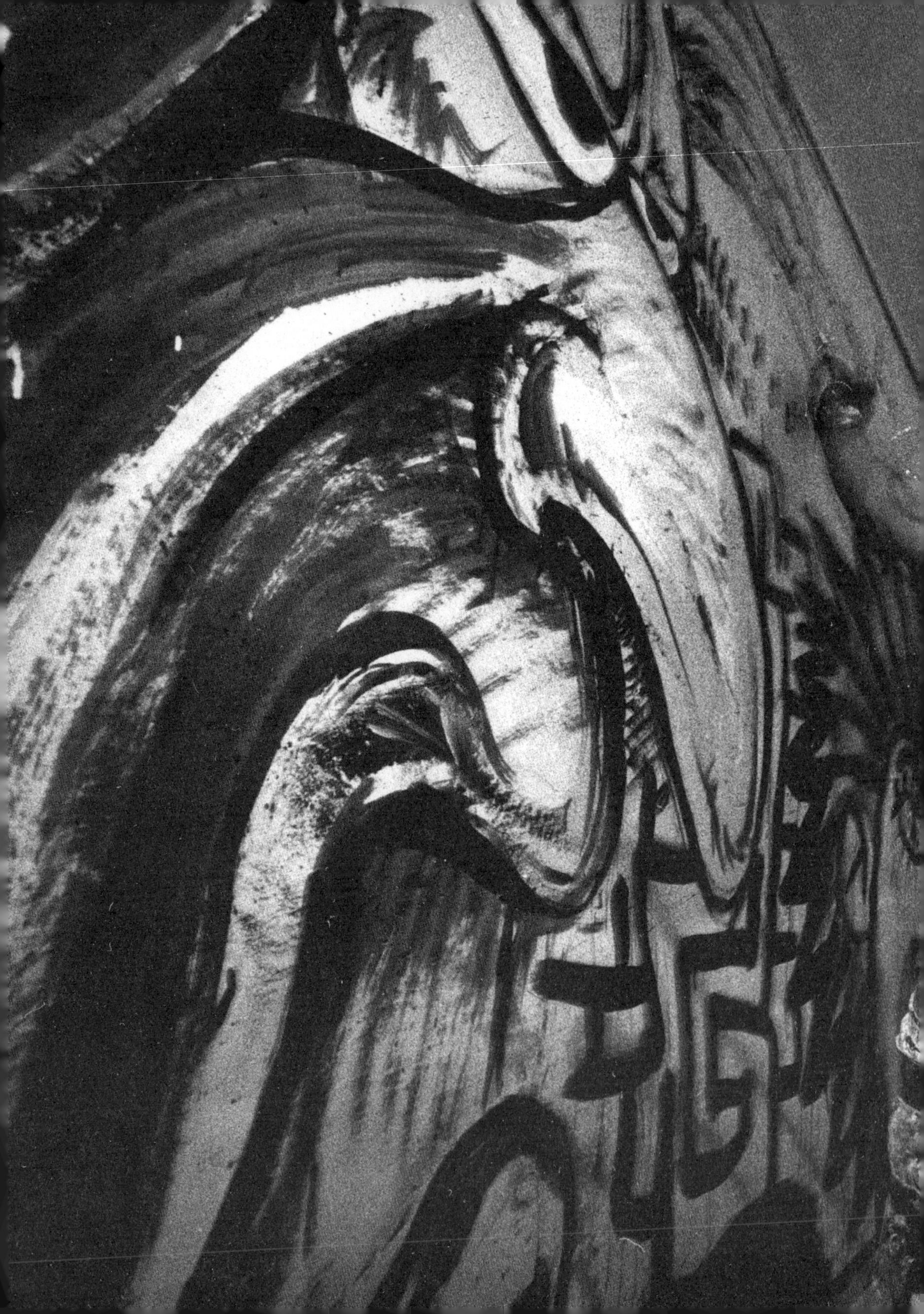

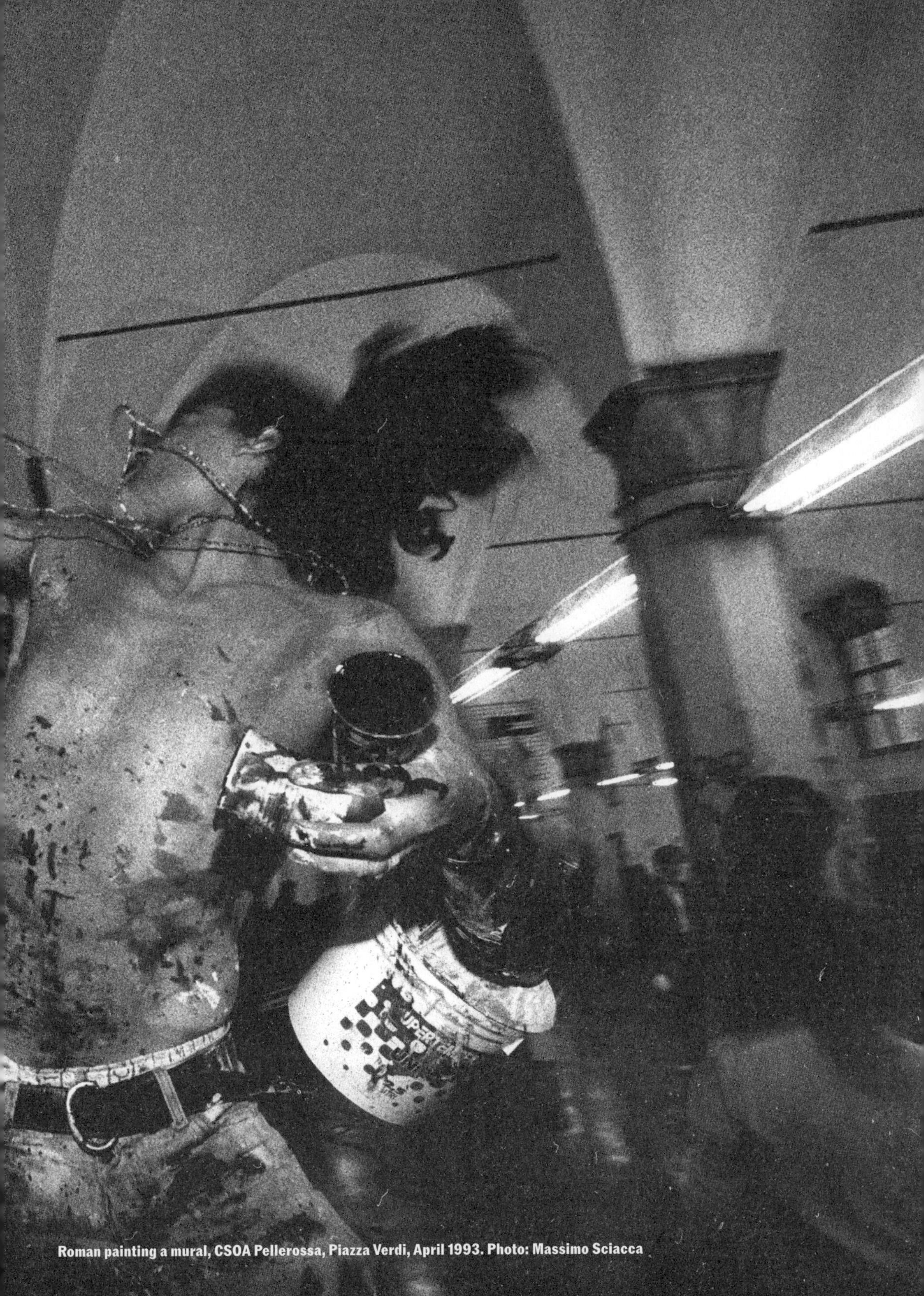

Roman painting a mural, CSOA Pellerossa, Piazza Verdi, April 1993. Photo: Massimo Sciacca

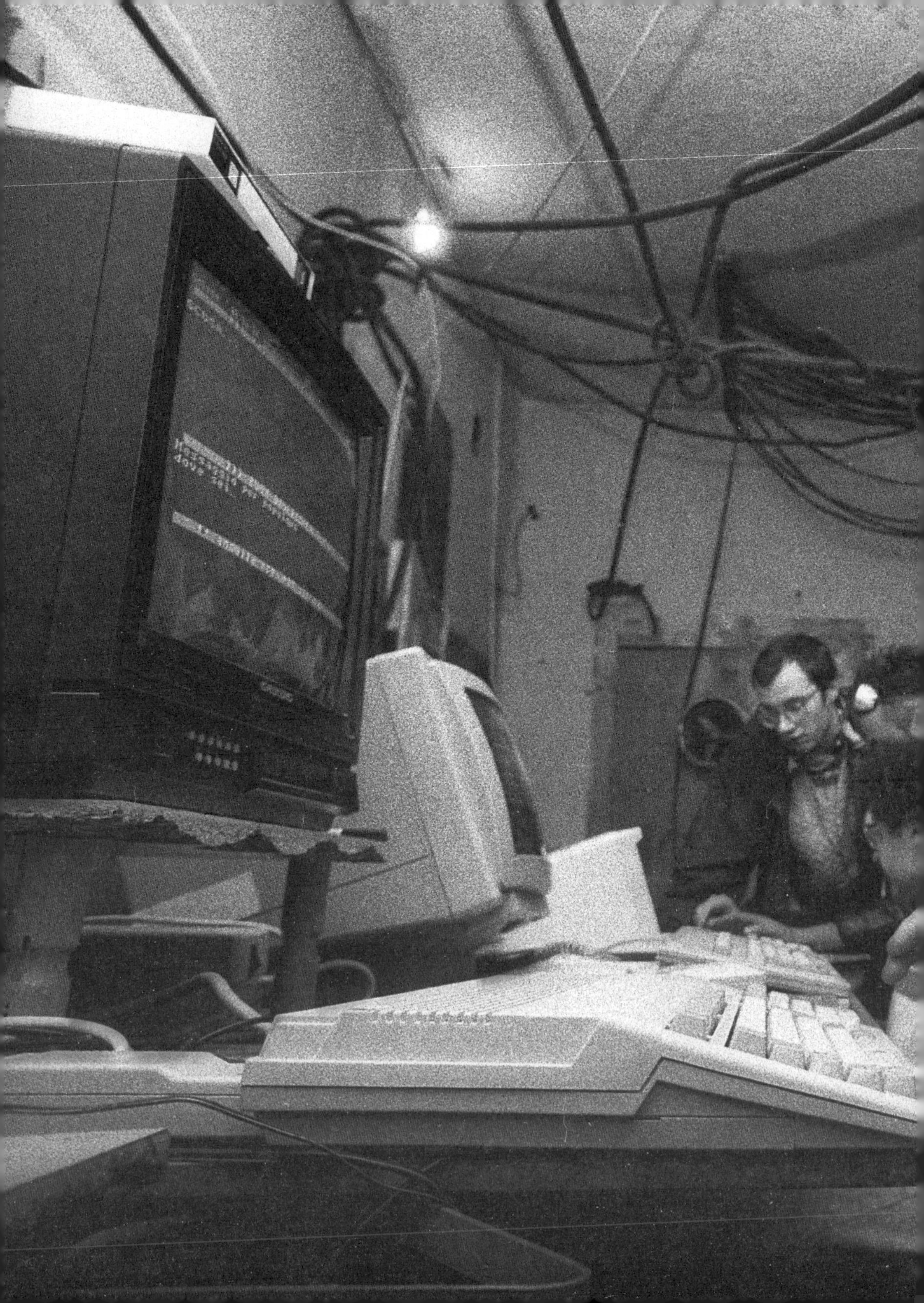

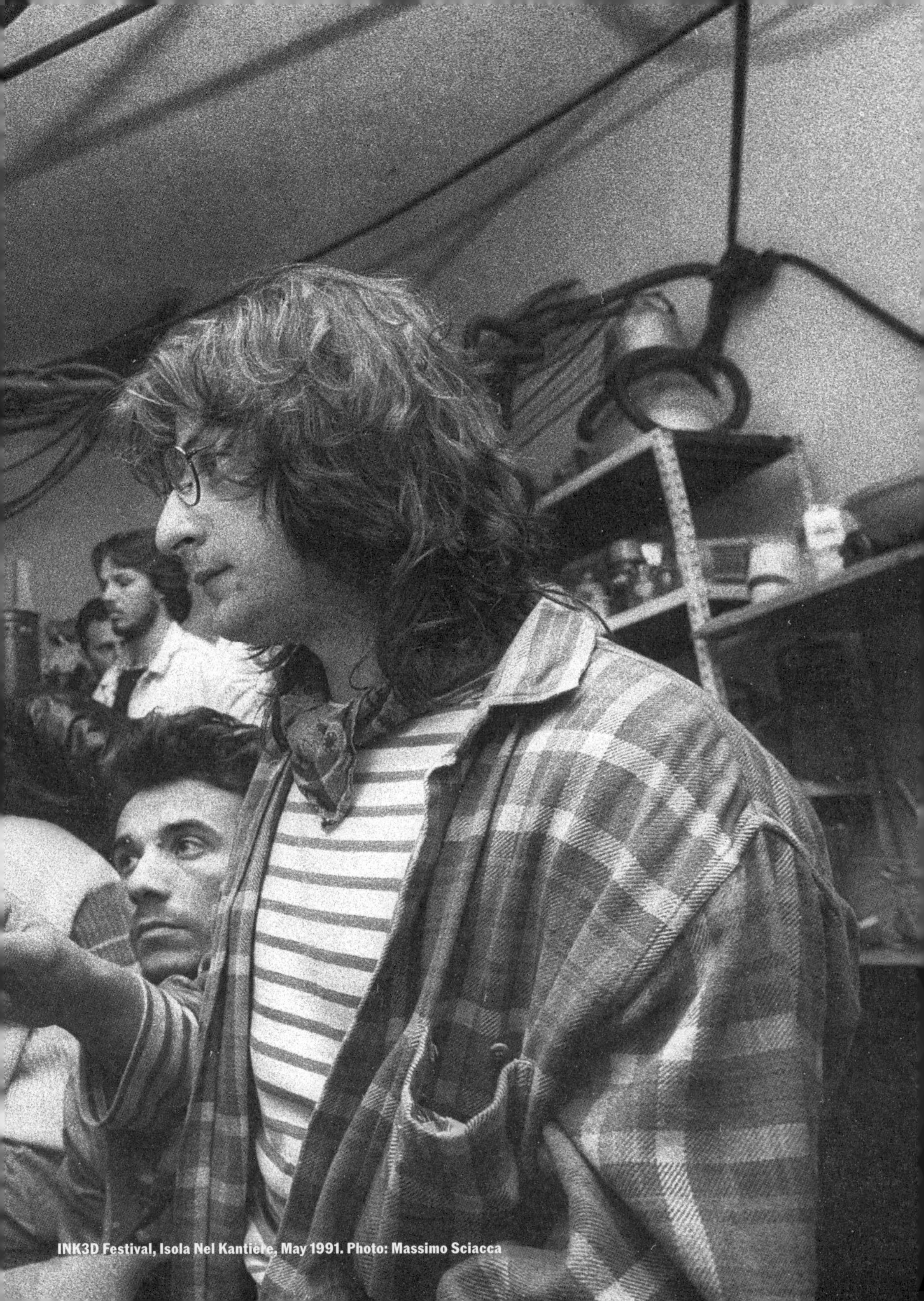

INK3D Festival, Isola Nel Kantiere, May 1991. Photo: Massimo Sciacca

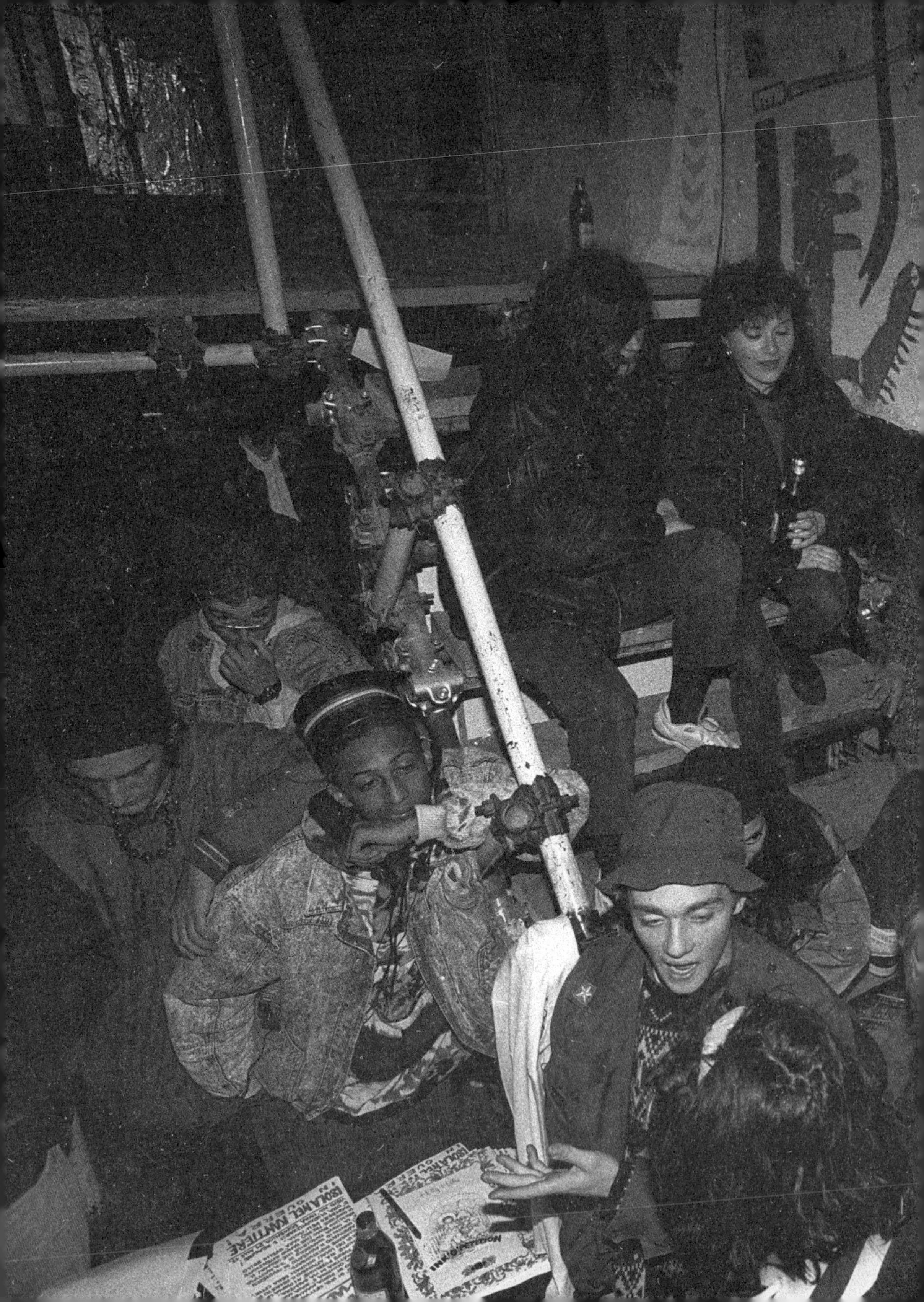

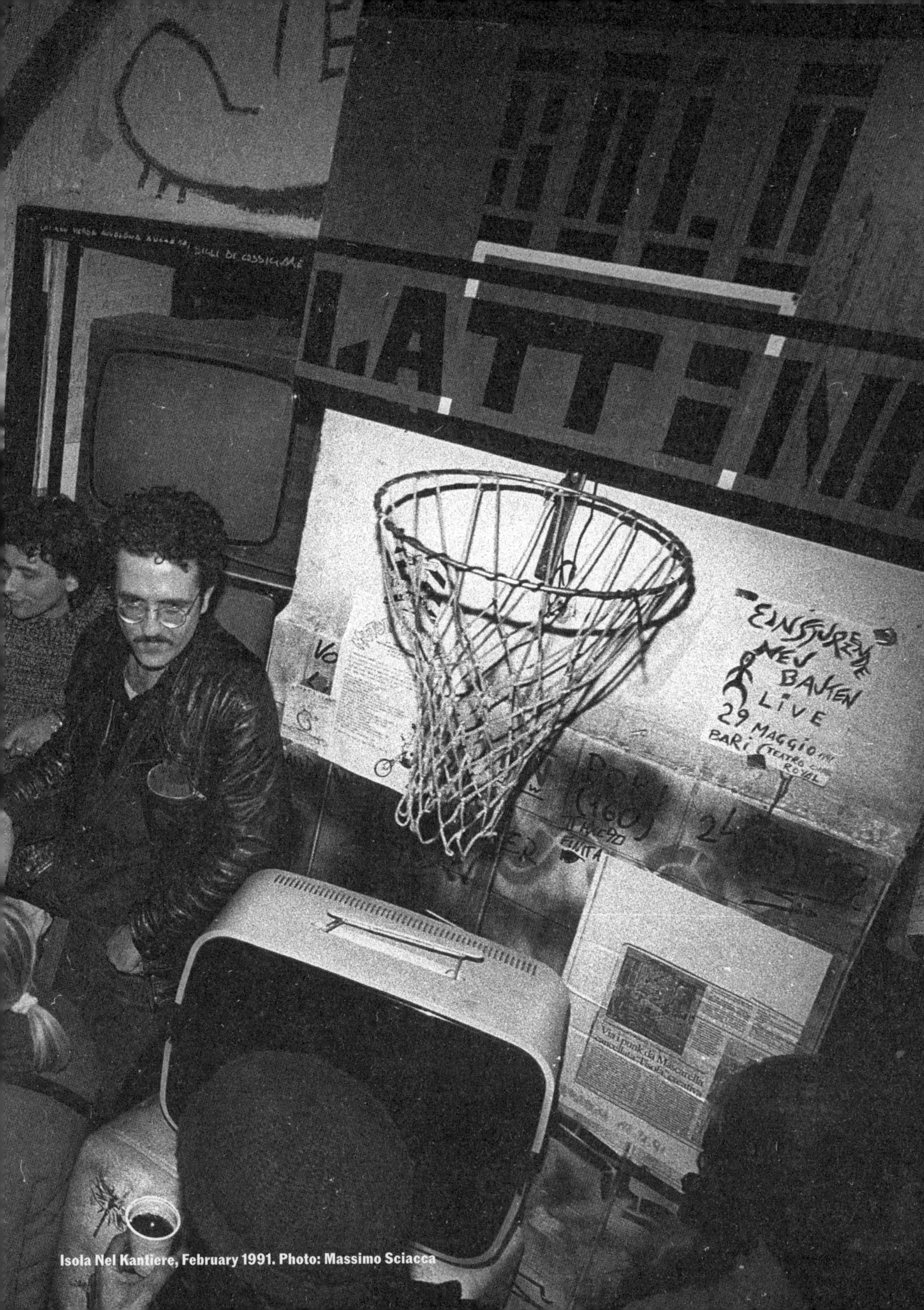

Isola Nel Kantiere, February 1991. Photo: Massimo Sciacca

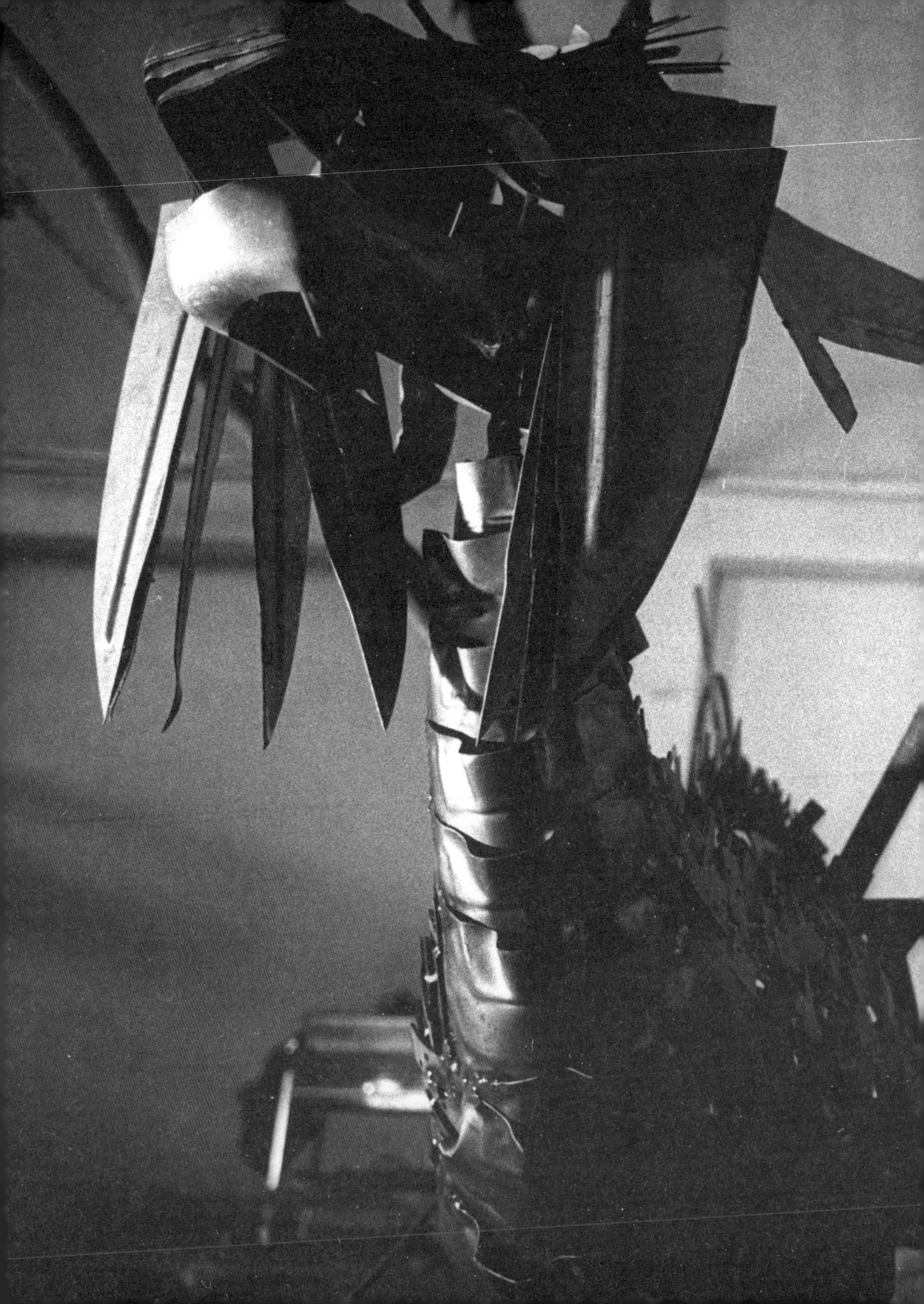

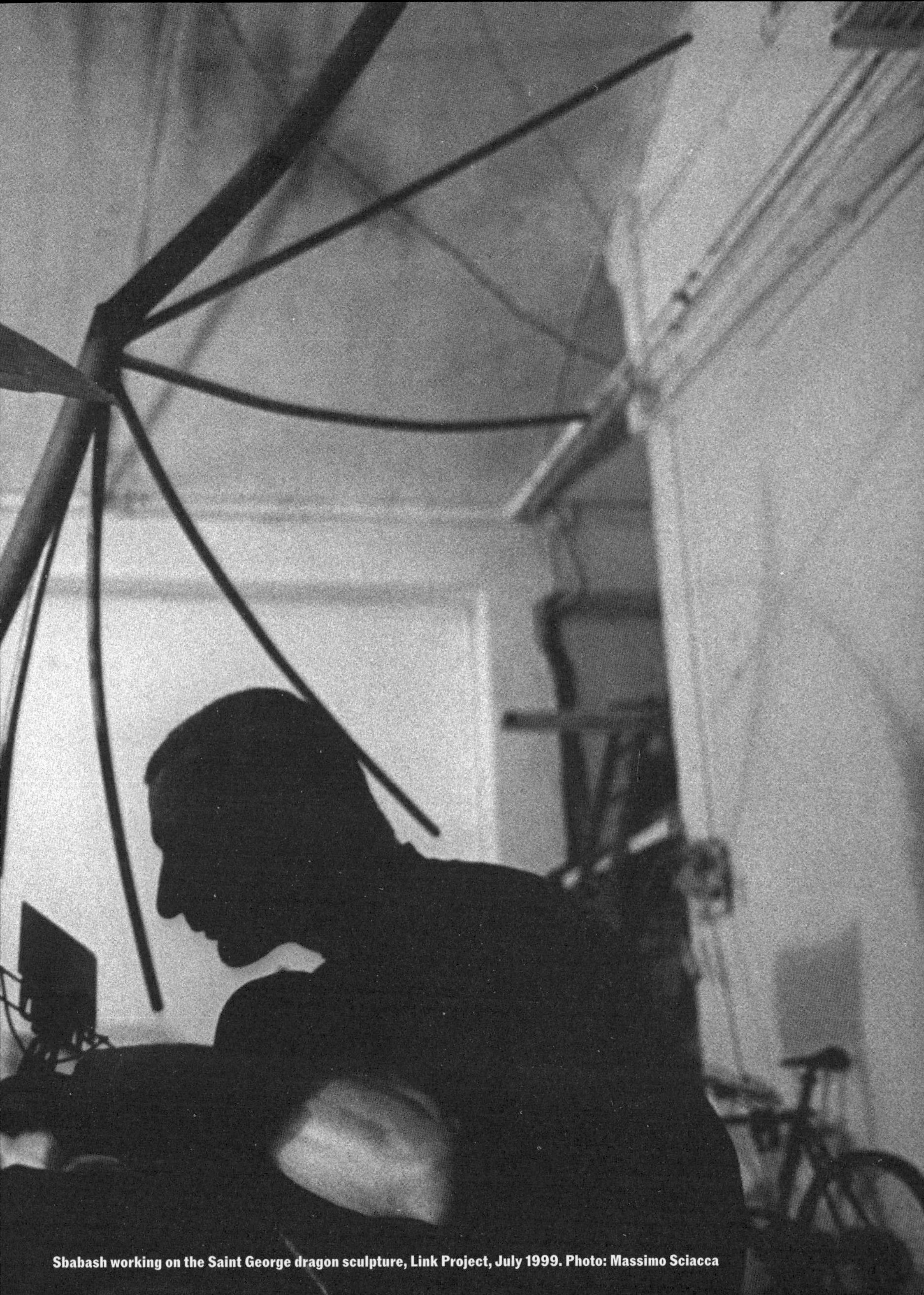

Sbabash working on the Saint George dragon sculpture, Link Project, July 1999. Photo: Massimo Sciacca

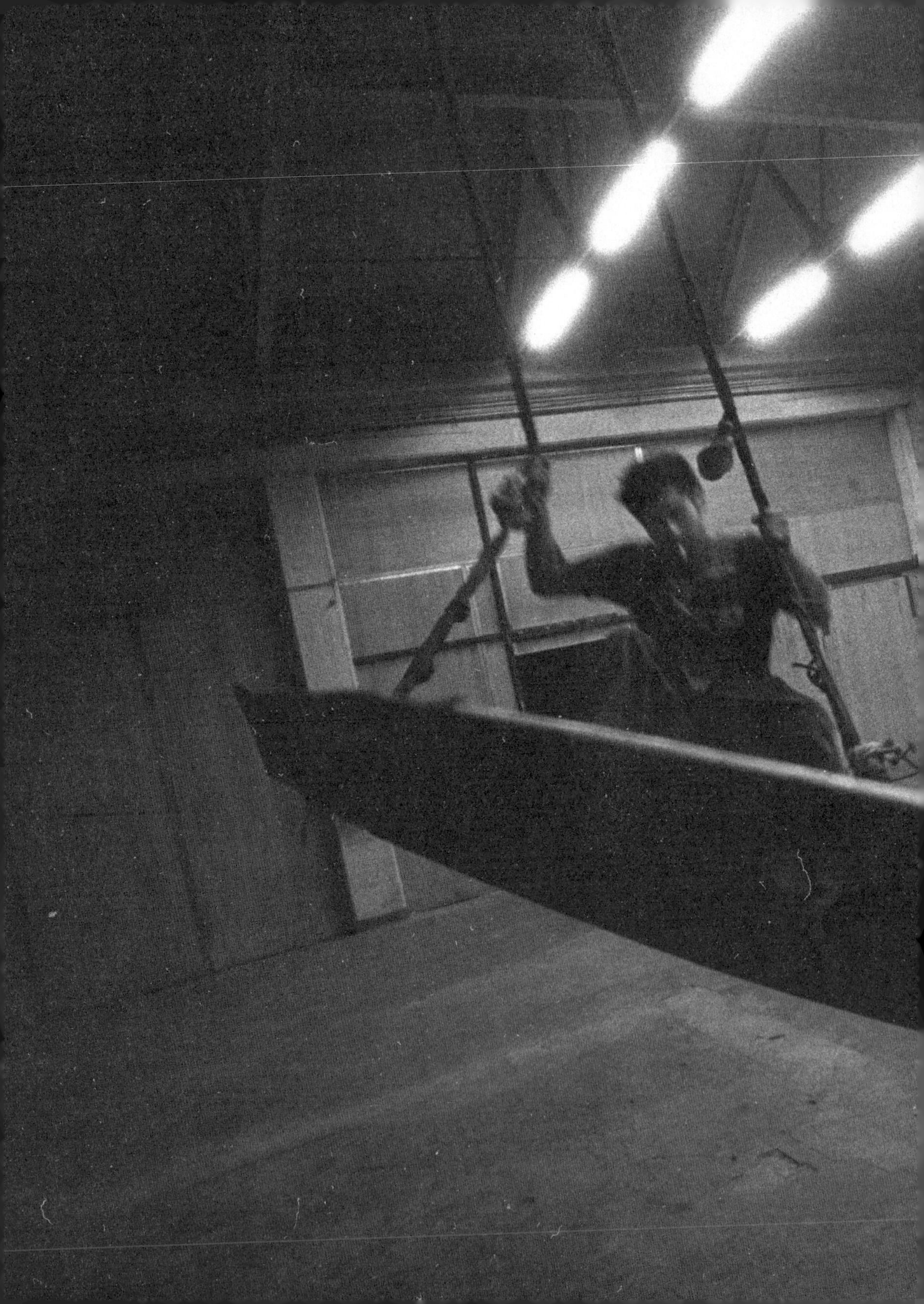

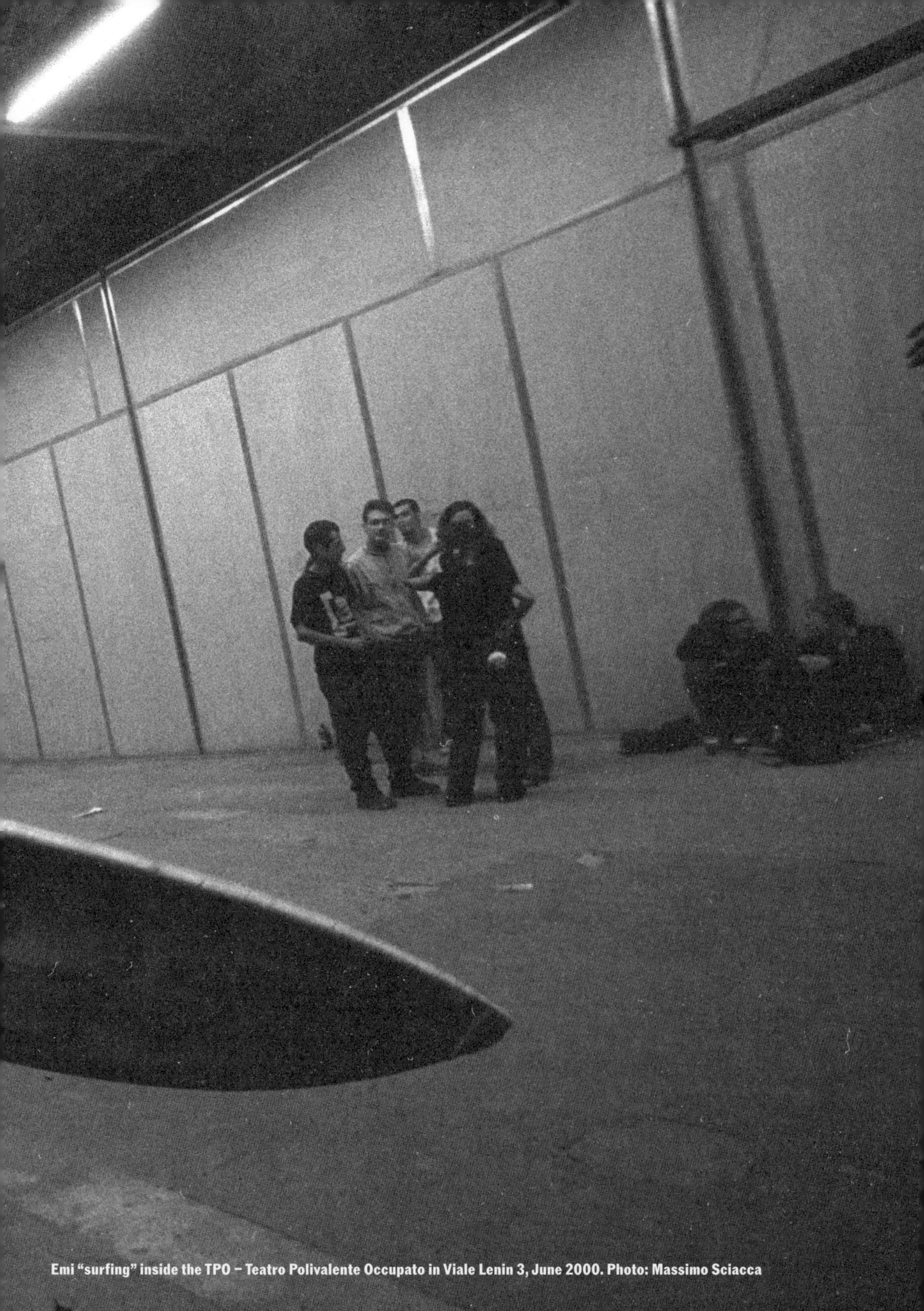

Emi "surfing" inside the TPO – Teatro Polivalente Occupato in Viale Lenin 3, June 2000. Photo: Massimo Sciacca

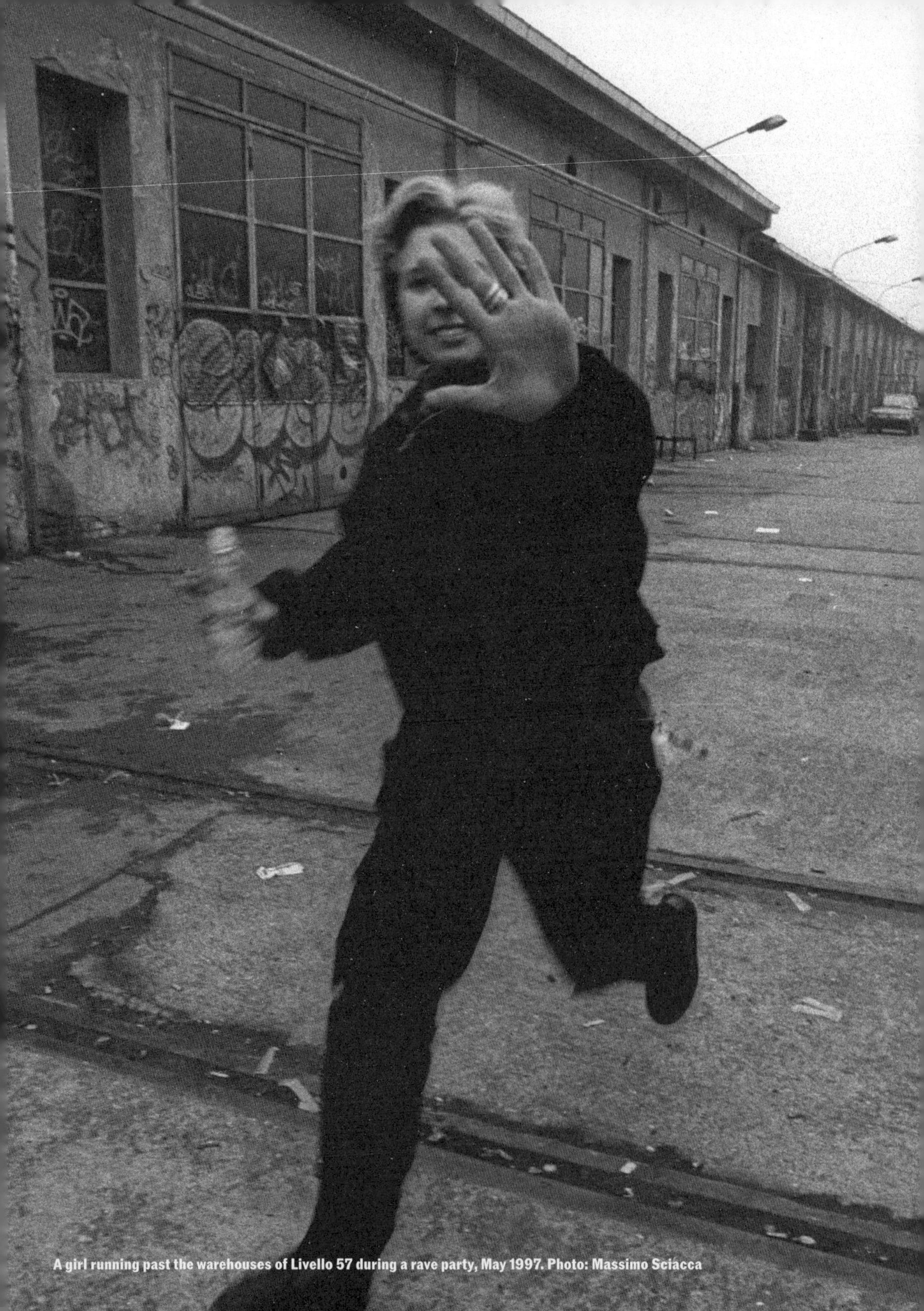

A girl running past the warehouses of Livello 57 during a rave party, May 1997. Photo: Massimo Sciacca

SKANK BLOC BOLOGNA

Alternative Art Spaces since 1977

Edited by
Roberto Pinto & Francesco Spampinato

Mousse Publishing

ESSAYS

ALTERNATIVE ART SPACES

ESSAYS

AMID POLITICAL COMMITMENT AND SPACES OF FREEDOM

The Importance of Being Alternative and Self-Managed

Roberto Pinto

Bologna played a key role in the artistic and cultural context of post-'68 Italy. Despite being only the seventh largest Italian city by population, it managed to bridge some of the distances that separated it from Rome or Milan through its own peculiar way of intervening in great depth on political-cultural issues, acquiring a weight and international standing that other Italian cities never achieved. To this end, the capital of the Emilia Romagna region exploited the historical role played by its university, which, in addition to fulfilling its institutional duties, also served as an incubator within which numerous waves of antagonist movements were founded or developed—as early as 1968, but especially in 1977 and then in the early 1990s—providing the cultural powerhouse of the city. Many of the promoters of the self-managed spaces we are dealing with here were part of such movements or often met within them, and came together with the intention of building a new society also—or sometimes principally—through their working together, without rules imposed from above and with the freedom to assert themselves. It was not only their common political militancy and attendance of the DAMS[1] or the Academy of Fine Arts that drove young people to put together this alternative cultural network. In fact, it is important not to overlook how the entire Bologna area has often been characterized by a focus on social inclusion and community development, which were also made possible thanks to a model of cooperative labor and enterprise that began in this region as early as the mid-nineteenth century.[2] This model, akin to that adopted in many of the independent spaces, developed more strongly in this territory than in other parts of Italy and is, to this day, a highly structured and widespread system.

An essential role in the growth and development of the cultural effervescence that characterized the city at the end of the twentieth century was therefore played by the widespread action of "associationism," or more generally, by collaborative labor. From formal unions recognized as legally constituted associations, or more simply setting out from a common interest—which often responded to the need to take over certain spaces (including through the illegal occupation of empty or temporarily unused spaces)[3] where to stage not only political actions but concerts, exhibitions, and theatrical performances—social centers,[4] alternative spaces, non-profit associations, and artist-run spaces proliferated, constituting the genuine backbone of the diffused creativity that emerged in Bologna throughout that period. Of course, the work performed by these independent and self-managed spaces was undoubtedly (at least percentage-wise) more incisive than what was being done in the rest of Italy.[5] Thus, such peculiar circumstances call for us to broaden our perspective of analysis so as to reread the Italian artistic situation at the end of the last millennium from a point of view at odds with the official version, that dominated by Arte Povera, the Transavanguardia, and all that ensued from them. This perspective instead aims to focus on a more political strand of artistic experimentation, which, although overlapping only occasionally with the official circuit of galleries and museums, built a parallel history that needs to be brought back to the surface.[6]

The political protests—especially post-'68—that started out in Bologna are therefore an essential element in understanding the role played by these spaces. The movements which then developed in 1977 in schools and universities emerged as a two-sided coin: one strictly political, structured according to the Marxist logic of the class struggle, and the other (equally important and over time destined for broader success) which prioritized political action among its objectives, deployed through the media and culture. An idea—in some respects utopian and shared by theorists, artists, and writers, such as Andrea Pazienza or Pier Vittorio Tondelli—still strongly rooted in the cultural scene of the day, and based on the belief that freedom also passed through the transformation of individuals, the conquest of broader personal autonomy and the chance to follow one's own desires. This is how Franco "Bifo" Berardi, one of the protagonists and theorists of the movement, explains it in a book with the emblematic title *1977: l'anno in cui il futuro cominciò* ("1977: The Year the Future Began"):

The year 1977 may thus be described as the point of separation between the industrial era with its great political, ideological, and state formations, and the ensuing one, that of the age of proliferating digital technologies, of the molecular diffusion of the transversal power devices. Within this framework, we also need to understand the conflicting relationship between the movement and the traditional left, which inherited its rituals and ideologies from the previous history of the industrial era. The rift may appear to have been one of the many, endless doctrinal and political disputes within the labor movement to be found throughout the history of the twentieth century [...], but it was not so. It was not one of the many dogmatic discussions in which hegemony over the Communist movement was disputed, because the Communist movement was founded on premises that the '77 generation did away with as soon as it constituted as a movement. [...] Schizoid imagination took the place of paranoid disciplinary representations: the '77 movement did not want to be obsessed with the political centrality of the state, the party, or ideologies. It preferred to disperse its attention, its transformative action, its communication amongst rather more diverse areas: forms of housing, drugs, sexuality, the rejection of labor, experimentation with ethically motivated forms of work, creativity. For all these reasons, the movement undoubtedly escaped the conceptual and political grip of the third-internationalist labor movement, whether in its reformist variant of the Italian Communist Party or in its Leninist revolutionary variant. The movement no longer had anything to do with those old stories.[7]

One of the symbols of that season was also the emergence of free radio stations, which flourished spontaneously and illegally throughout Italy until they were regulated by a 1976 constitutional court decree sanctioning the liberalization of the airwaves. Radio Alice[8] was certainly one of the most active, although its broadcasts were only on the air for just over a year, and it became a symbol of youth creativity, political activism, and the musical revolution of the day.[9] A genuine social media channel *ante litteram*,[10] as people could call in and interject live about anything they wanted, addressing political or musical issues, or more simply, recounting their problems or desires. Radio Alice also often managed to report live on the unfolding of political demonstrations and protests, and even clashes with the police. The last live broadcast of Radio Alice, before a long closure, was in fact the live testimony of police forcing entry into the historic headquarters in Via del Pratello, on March 12, 1977, which put an end to its broadcasting.[11] The repression of those street movements, narrated by several of the station's voices, clearly marked the progressive distancing of individual and creative research from the political plot, so clearly united prior to that moment.

Such political and cultural entanglement well outlines the historical moment we are reconstructing, and indeed, many of the spaces and communities that created them were in fact formed as a reaction to that season and the subsequent wave that came along in the early 1990s.[12]

Often, however, such signs of protest and youth activities clash with the inability of institutions to understand the needs and the many different sensitivities of that new generation. Existing structures mostly ignored these new forms of expression. It should be acknowledged, however, that the tendency to not valorize or even leave room for the young bearers of new artistic forms does not only concern the Italian scene and is not only characteristic of the closing decades of the twentieth century. Like other institutions whose task is to conserve, museums tend to remain bound up in their own heritage, their collections, and artists who are already known and appreciated. Many of the movements and artists now recognized as milestones in art history struggled to display their works back in the nineteenth century, and organized exhibitions in alternative spaces which provided them with the freedom to propose new readings. Just to name but a few cases, we might recall Courbet's Pavilion of Realism (and there are earlier examples as well), the first Impressionist exhibition in Nadar's studio, or the Salon des Indépendants: created to avoid the commissions that would grant access to other exhibitions, for only established artists accepted through official channels were guaranteed entry to the most prestigious stages. Nor did the situation change in the period of the historical avant-gardes, as Amelia Jones recalls, pointing out that even in the New York Dadaist milieu, dominant readings were always privileged:

> In art history, this tendency to privilege the cultural "victors"—those artists whose reputation has already been solidified or whose work in one way or another serves the purposes of the discourses that comprise the discipline and its institutional support structures (including the university, the museum, and the art market)—is even more striking, perhaps because of the strong ties between the discipline and the art market's penchant for, and commodification of, "unique" objects that seem inexorably to point to "unique" subjects as their makers and origins. In a mutually sustaining circuit of value, the art market and its institutional corollaries, the art gallery

and museum, draw on the insights of art-historical scholarship and art-critical writing to legitimate the value (economic and otherwise) of the objects they display, which in turn are the "object" of art history's narratives of progress and critique.[13]

Certainly, as mentioned previously, cultural activism arose not only against an art system that was too "academic" or too mercantile, but, above all, as a search for a space of social-political freedom in which to abandon old models to follow, rules to abide by, traditional concepts to preserve, in order to be able to experiment freely even while challenging the traditional notion of artist and work.[14] Herein lies the importance of independent spaces in Italy, and in Bologna in particular, this was much greater than the perception of them in the late twentieth century, as may be deduced from how little has been written about their activities[15] and how much still remains to be done in order to enhance not only the perception of their role but also all the experimentation that passed through their spaces. On the contrary, the centrality of their function, certainly bound up in a close relationship with the democratic processes of a culture built from the grassroots upward, is evidenced in the United States by numerous writings on the subject and even by exhibitions such as *Cultural Economies: Histories from the Alternative Arts Movement, NYC*, curated by Julie Ault at one of New York's most important independent spaces, The Drawing Center.[16] At this event, the American artist and theorist had the chance to explain:

> Invention and reinvention are always possible, despite the Right, despite the culture wars, despite temporarily curtailed government funding, despite the stealthy and speedy privatization of the public realm. Looking back, and ahead, at the tremendously rich environment of structures, venues, support, and community produced by initiatives answering (or not) to the name alternative, one finds infinite exemplary acts and art. The result is countless models for practices that try to, and in some instances do, effectively transcend and challenge the established system. The individuals who come together around ideas of cultural democracy, working experimentally and taking risks, offer examples for others to emulate and improve on.

A comment that would fit perfectly onto a description of those years of research in Bologna.

Staying in Europe, in order to study the impact of the new independent centers, in most cases ones run by artists themselves, it is worth mentioning "The Glasgow Miracle": a name used by Hans Ulrich Obrist to emphasize the importance held by a system that saw the Transmission Gallery as an example for research and production centers.[17] But perhaps more than any other city in Europe, it was Berlin—especially from the years immediately following the fall of the Wall and the reunification of Germany—that acknowledged the centrality of independent spaces. The identity established in West Berlin during the Cold War as a privileged meeting place for the youth scene and artistic experimentation extended immediately after 1989 to former East Berlin as well. There were numerous significant spaces and episodes, the most striking of which took its cue from Klaus Biesenbach's exhibition *Berlin 37 Räume*,[18] held in 1992 with the collaboration of the Kunst-Werke Institute for Contemporary Art (which he had co-founded the previous year).[19] It was indeed the Kunst-Werke, in fact, which began as an occupation of abandoned spaces, and which since 1998 has also hosted the Berlin Biennale, which over time has gained an important role in international programming. In Berlin and Glasgow, therefore, in contrast to Italy, small self-managed realities such as those mentioned above, by virtue of their undeniable public and service role for the city (and not only), were helped to grow with the direct or indirect contribution of local institutions that grasped their potential and accorded them trust and support. We are certainly talking about a culturally and economically different systems, but in Italy, by contrast, independent centers were at best tolerated and almost never helped.

In general, in post-World War II Italy, contemporary art developed more slowly than in other European countries. In terms of artistic production—think of Alberto Burri and Lucio Fontana, Arte Povera or international phenomena such as Maurizio Cattelan—there were undoubtedly major players, but Italian artists had greater difficulty in being acknowledged and supported than their European colleagues. A similar argument could be made for the art market: Italian collectors (from Giuseppe Panza di Biumo to Miuccia Prada, from Giuliana and Tommaso Setari to Achille Maramotti) have often played a key role in supporting the latest research, while galleries—such as Massimo De Carlo or Continua—have been able to open branches in other hubs of the art system, such as London, Paris, Hong Kong, or Shanghai over recent decades. However, if we focus on the cultural, political and social role that art has taken on in society, we must conclude that it has been almost irrelevant. The main problem, as pointed out by all those in the field, is related to the shortage (or indeed scarcity) of public investment designed to support the activities of museums and exhibition spaces and to commission art projects in public spaces, streets, or squares. The result of the chronic lack of funding has had a number of direct and indirect consequences. In fact, this policy is responsible not only for the absence of a network of institutions and the limited programming possibilities of the few existing exhibition and museum spaces, but also for the scarce and intermittent public interest in such activity. Even the cultural debate, in a world in which the role of images has become increasingly important, has consistently ignored the development of artistic research and the critical discourse related to it, partly due to a substantial lack of opportunities in which to present such investigations.

Despite the major role performed by the Venice Biennale and—albeit to a lesser extent—the Milan Triennale and the Rome Quadriennale, Italian museums dedicated to contemporary art are few and less well funded than those in other European countries. The National Gallery of Modern Art in Rome, founded—like the Biennale itself—at the end of the nineteenth century, has long been the only institution in terms of its continuity and role promoting recent artistic experiences,[20] but its international relevance is still very marginal compared to other major public or private European museums.[21] The opening in the 1980s of Castello di Rivoli and later the Centro Pecci in Prato[22] were isolated phenomena, and even the system of "civic galleries" (i.e. art spaces linked to and supported by individual cities) has rarely provided interesting programs on an international level.

It was only on May 28, 2010 that MAXXI – Museo nazionale delle arti del XXI secolo (the National Museum of Twenty-First Century Arts) finally opened, and while this inauguration may certainly be viewed as an effort to de-provincialize the Italian situation, with a building designed by the archistar Zaha Hadid dedicated to art and architecture, over its first ten years of operation it drew a total attendance of 3,328,000 visitors,[23] roughly the annual footfall of the Tate Modern or the Centre Pompidou. But the steady increase in visitors over the years underscores how important it is (also for the qualitative spillover into artistic production) for places of knowledge and experimentation to be created, even if only—paradoxically—to have something to discuss or criticize. For all these reasons, and because the Italian exhibition offerings of the late-twentieth century were presented in the context of private galleries, the art (and artists) that magazines dealt with was mainly what the art market was purveying at time, which in the 1980s and (partly) 1990s, was largely painting, penalizing experimentation that produced little from a commercial point of view, or those linked to any critique of the commodification of art.

Thus, Italy's rich artistic-cultural heritage, the one that every government in office claims to want to enhance, has never served as a driving force for investment in this sector; rather, at the ministerial (and more generally public) level, the lack of sufficient funds to conserve the existing archaeological and artistic heritage has been the recurring argument to justify a substantial lack of interest in contemporary art, which has long remained unsupported, lacking in institutions and with little legitimacy in school or university contexts.

It follows that the art system in Bologna—as well as in Italy—had to be built, at least initially, on a decidedly asymmetrical yet solid base made up largely of private galleries. In the 1980s, in fact, all around Italy a group of galleries opened that were much more aggressive and attentive to new forms of production. Above all, Milan played a central role in launching a new artistic generation that, following the experimentation of the 1960s (in which the activities of Galleria Notizie in Turin and Sargentini in Rome stand out), lacked any real points of reference. In Milan, therefore, galleries were opened that shifted the general focus toward more current and international artforms: alongside the historic Studio Marconi and Luciano Inga Pin's Diagramma, realities such as Le Case d'Arte, Studio Casoli, Massimo De Carlo, Studio Guenzani, and Fac Simile also opened, to which the spaces of Emi Fontana and Raffaella Cortese were later added, making the Milanese gallery structure one of the leading European systems in this regard. There was a similarly growing interest in Bologna as well: alongside Galleria de' Foscherari, established in 1962, several other commercial spaces, such as Studio G7, began to spring up from the 1970s onwards, despite not always achieving the commercial success and notoriety of their Milanese counterparts. Since 1974, thanks in part to the impetus of Arte Fiera,[24] there has been ever greater attention to new artforms. In addition to being a topical moment for the market, the fair event has thus played a major role in reducing the information gap with foreign countries and in configuring itself as a place of comparison for Italy, also through a series of collateral events, such as, for example, International Performance Weeks[25]—with interventions, among others, by Marina Abramović and Ulay, Hermann Nitsch, and Vito Acconci—organized in collaboration with the Galleria Civica, which also hosted most of them.

Despite this relative effervescence, albeit somewhat episodically, experiences related to performativity, relational art, digital experimentation, and all those borderline territories between dance, music, video, theater, and the visual arts have struggled to emerge in this panorama. In other words, whatever doesn't fall into the macro-category of "objects"—things to be produced, exhibited, sold and preserved—was almost never exhibited in museums and galleries, and thus such experiments rarely became the subject of critical debate. The many spaces in Bologna that developed over time, such as the neon for example, certainly opened their doors to young people—such as Maurizio Cattelan or Eva Marisaldi, who both held their first solo shows there—who were not only interested in making works understood in the traditional sense. There was a fairly similar situation with regard to contamination between visual and performing arts, which in Link Project, with a gaze also turned to innovative technologies, found one of the most important centers not only at the Italian level, but internationally.

Alongside this mode of construction of independent realities, more devoted to production and exhibition, we should also note the parallel development of spaces (as well as associations and institutions) that focused their attention on the need to promote artistic mobility, and which therefore focused on fostering it through independent spaces given over to providing temporary residencies for artists.[26] Nosadella.due was perhaps the most active place in this respect, standing out as an exchange center for international artist mobility and new production, which made it one of the Italian nodes of a very wide network. Moreover, we should not forget, especially if we think about the legacy of the '77 movements, that there were places which used their energies and spaces to build an alternative political outlook and a more inclusive and open culture, such as the Cassero, which since 1982 has been a "political circle fighting for the recognition of LGBTQIA+ people's rights"[27] in which workshops, art reviews and social gathering activities all find their place. The cultural and political model that these spaces offer has also been taken up by the new generation. Many of these activities are, in fact, still in place and their fruits have germinated in other independent spaces that embrace similar ideals and practices: one example is K.I.N.:[28] a network of independent realities founded in 2021 promoting synergies among thirteen different art spaces around Bologna.

The great social and cultural ferment of these alternative venues thus encouraged a form of active disruption[29] with respect to the system of official art and culture, and also led to the development of political and social proposals that offer an alternative to the monolithic structuring imposed by conventional systems of cultural management. By virtue of the very fact that these realities are based on principles of collaboration and participation, their programming has not always been regular and their economic management has not always had an established pattern: in most cases these spaces have become flexible structures, capable of transforming to suit the needs of individual projects or changing conditions. In these places, hierarchies are dictated by needs, and roles can be easily intermingled: an artist can improvise as a curator (or even editor, organizer, etc.) and vice versa; anyone can actively participate in the creative processes of works and actions that were customarily the exclusive preserve of the artist. Even the role of the viewer can change to that of active participant, and sometimes even that of the activist. In brief, that of independent spaces is a story that ushers in a form (and conception) of art that is now more relevant than ever. The latest edition of documenta,[30] curated by the ruangrupa collective, indirectly testifies to its importance and relevance.

1 The DAMS course began at the start of the 1970s with the aim of intercepting the need felt among the young generations to broaden the study of the arts, music, and performance. See Claudio Marra, Arianna Casarini, *NO DAMS. 50 anni del corso di laurea in discipline delle arti, della musica e dello spettacolo*, (Bologna: Pendragon, 2021).

2 See https://www.legacoopemiliaromagna.coop/storia-e-valori/.

3 Historical-critical research on art that goes beyond the limits of the current norms was carried out by Rebecca Zorach (ed.), *Art Against the Law* (Chicago: School of the Art Institute of Chicago, 2014), a volume issued as part of the *Chicago Social Practice History Series*, Mary Jane Jacob and Kate Zeller (eds.).

4 A series of stories on and around the social centers my be found in Serafino D'Onofrio and Valerio Monteventi, *Berretta Rossa. Storie di Bologna attraverso i centri sociali* (Bologna: Pendragon, 2011).

5 To investigate the spread of participatory practices in Bologna, see Roberta Paltrinieri, Giulia Allegrini, *Partecipazione, processi di immaginazione civica e sfera pubblica. I laboratori di quartiere e il bilancio partecipativo a Bologna* (Milan: Franco Angeli, 2020); and the later Roberta Paltrinieri (ed.), *Culture e pratiche di partecipazione. Collaborazione civica, rigenerazione urbana e costruzione di comunità* (Milan: Franco Angeli, 2020).

6 In this sense, there have been numerous attempts to reconstruct the most hidden Italian contemporary art scene. Among the others, see Cecilia Guida, *Spatial Practices. Funzione pubblica e politica delle arti nella società delle reti* (Milan: Franco Angeli, 2012); Emanuele Rinaldo Meschini, *Comunità, spazio, monumento. Ricontestualizzazione delle pratiche artistiche nella sfera urbana* (Milan: Mimesis, 2021); Jacopo Galimberti, *Immagini di classe. Operaismo, Autonomia e produzione artistica* (Rome: DeriveApprodi, 2023); but also the exhibition and ensuing catalogue by Lara Conte and Francesca Gallo (eds.), *Territori della performance: percorsi e pratiche in Italia (1967–1982)* (Rome: MAXXI, October 21, 2022–June 11, 2023).

7 Franco "Bifo" Berardi and Veronica Bridi (eds.), *1977 l'anno in cui il futuro cominciò* (Rome: Fandango Libri, 2002), 24–25; see also Franco "Bifo" Berardi, *Dell'innocenza. 1977* (Verona: Ombre Corte, 1997). Unless otherwise noted, all the original Italian text are here rendered in English by the translator.

8 Just how important in the common imagination the role played by this radio station was, constituting almost a founding element of a certain form of political and cultural action, can be seen from the fact that there are no less than two fiction films and a documentary with a narrative revolving around Radio Alice. In 1991, Renato De Maria filmed *Il trasloco*; in 2002 Guido Chiesa produced the documentary *Alice è in Paradiso*, and he returned to the theme two years later (with a script written together with the Wu Ming group) with the film *Lavorare con lentezza. Radio Alice 100.6 MHz.*

9 As for the musical vicissitudes of Bologna (and partly those of Radio Alice) see Oderso Rubini and Andrea Tinti (eds.), *Non Disperdetevi. 1977–1982. San Francisco, New York, Bologna, le città libere del mondo* (Milan: Shake edizioni, 2009).

10 Franco "Bifo" Berardi, in the introduction to *Skizomedia. Trent'anni di mediattivismo* (Rome: DeriveApprodi, 2006), explains that "The live phone call, as used by free radio stations at the time, pre-empted the network model, meaning that the explosion of internet at the start of the 1990s did not catch me off guard" (3).

11 The Radio remained closed for about a month and then reopened without the support of the founders, grappling with the accusation—later deemed to be unfounded—that they had directed the violent riots of the day before, which followed the killing of a student, Francesco Lo Russo, who died during clashes with the Carabinieri. For a bibliography on Radio Alice, see https://www.radioalice.org/libri.

12 Many testimonies in this regard (albeit largely in the musical field) are brought together in Rubini, Tinti, *Non Disperdetevi*, which mainly deals with the end of the 1970s; regarding the "Panther" student movement born in 1989, see Luciano Nadalini, *La Pantera a Bologna*, (Bologna: Agalev, 1990).

13 Amelia Jones, "New York Dada: Beyond the Readymade" in Leah Dickerman (ed.), *The Dada Seminars* (Washington: The National Gallery, 2005).

14 I recall that Umberto Eco, a teacher at DAMS, had recently written *Opera Aperta. Forma e indeterminazione nelle poetiche contemporanee* (Milan: Bompiani, 1962) (*The Open Work*, Cambridge Massachusetts: Harvard University Press, 1989).

15 For the history of the role of non-profit Milanese spaces, see Patrizia Brusarosco and Milovan Farronato, *Souvenir d'Italie. A Nonprofit Art Story* (Milan: Mousse Publishing 2010).

16 The exhibition was held in the Wooster Street venue from February 24 to April 6, 1996. For the occasion, a catalogue was also published, curated by Julie Ault in collaboration with the magazine *Real Life*.

17 See https://www.transmissiongallery.org/about; Hans Ulrich Obrist, "Ars (Artist Run Spaces)" in *...dontstopdontstopdontstopdontstop* (2006; Milan: Postmedia Books, 2010), 20–21.

18 The exhibition was on show for one week only (from June 14 to 21, 1992) in thirty-seven different houses in Augustenstrasse, with the collaboration of thirty-one different curators. See Klaus Biesenbach, *Berlin 37 Räume* (Berlin: Graetz, 1992).

19 The Kunst-Werke Berlin was founded by Klaus Biesenbach, Alexandra Binswanger, Clemens

Homburger, Philipp von Doering, and Alfonso Rutigliano in an abandoned industrial space at the start of the 1990s.

20 The official website of the museum still lays claim to its uniqueness on the scene: "This is the only national museum entirely dedicated to modern and contemporary art" (https://lagallerianazionale.com/museo).

21 Footfall at the Galleria Nazionale in 2021, partly because of the pandemic, was 81,021; in 2019 it was 190,604, of which 88,676 paying visitors: http://www.statistica.beniculturali.it/rilevazioni/musei/Anno%202021/MUSEI_TAVOLA9_2021.pdf; http://www.statistica.beniculturali.it/rilevazioni/musei/Anno%202019/MUSEI_TAVOLA9_2019.pdf. Comparisons with foreign institutions leave no room for interpretation: both the Tate Modern and the Centre Pompidou—apart from the Covid-19 period—constantly draw in over three million visits annually, although of course any in-depth assessment would also require a comparison between the sums of money invested in these institutions by their respective governments.

22 They opened respectively in 1984 and 1988.

23 Data provided by the then Minister of Culture Dario Franceschini, and the President of the Fondazione MAXXI, Giovanna Melandri, during a celebratory press conference.

24 Arte Fiera Bologna was the first modern and contemporary art fair in Italy and among the first in Europe. It first opened in 1974, shortly after that of Cologne (1967) and Basel (1970).

25 See Uliana Zanetti (ed.), *La performance a Bologna negli anni '70* (Bologna: Edizioni MAMbo, 2023).

26 On this topic, see Taru Elfving, Irmeli Kokko, and Pascal Gielen (eds.), *Contemporary Artist Residencies. Reclaiming Time and Space* (Amsterdam: Valiz, 2019). While on the Italian scene, see Caterina Angelucci and Giulio Verago (eds.), *Endless Residency. Un osservatorio sulla mobilità artistica* (Milan: Postmedia Books, 2023).

27 "Our story begins against the backdrop of the student uprisings of '77, when the homosexual liberation movements began to strip homosexuality of the imposed labels of an elitist vice, sensitivity and artisticness at all costs," https://cassero.it/chi-siamo/.

28 https://keepinnetwork.com.

29 See Richard Sennett, *The Uses of Disorder: Personal Identity & City Life* (New York: Knopf, 1970), as well as Pablo Sendra and Richard Sennett, *Progettare il disordine, Idee per la città del XXI secolo* (Rome: Treccani, 2022), in which the American sociologist notes: "The nice thing about living in a city is that you are free and no longer controlled by a *nomos*: a culture of proper behavior. I prefer there to be more people in the street making a noise than eyes monitoring them. It's a very different experience of the collective body. The former orders; the latter reunites. If there was something original in my book, it was the proposal for people to assemble, however disorderly their assemblies might have been" (163).

30 ruangrupa (ed.), *documenta fifteen* (Berlin: Hatje Cantz, 2022).

THE BOLOGNA MODEL

Alternative Art Spaces as Labs of Interdisciplinarity and Professionalization

Francesco Spampinato

> "Someone's got a question but there's
> Nothing left to do [...]
> The Skank Bloc Bologna keeping us all alive
> Something in Italy [...]
> Now they're livin' on a notion and
> They're working on a hope
> A Euro vision and a skank in scope."[1]
>
> Scritti Politti, "Skank Bloc Bologna," 1978

A founding song of British post-punk, "Skank Bloc Bologna," is also among the most illustrative of tributes with which intellectuals and artists during the 1970s from around the world heralded Bologna as a hotbed of political agitation and cultural innovation. The band that wrote it, Scritti Politti—a group of militant Marxists and art students from Leeds Polytechnic—took its name from Antonio Gramsci's *Scritti Politici* (1967), mispronouncing the title. Another example, in the same period, is the special issue of *Semiotext(e)* devoted to "Autonomia" (1980), which confirms the infatuation—in this case of the Downtown New York art community—with Bologna as the epicenter of the '77 Movement. Renato Zangheri, who as mayor of Bologna from 1970 to 1983 solidified its image as a progressive city, stated how Bologna was indeed "exemplary of the experience of a communist government in the West [...] a testbed for many ideas, parties, institutions, and also individuals."[2]

The spirit of that Bologna, which the nostalgics decry as now at least partly lost and gone, may still be sensed, even on the threshold of this first quarter of the new century, under the porticoes of the center as well as in the suburbs, in urban regeneration projects and in the mechanisms of a human community that, while seduced by the global logic of automation and virtuality—as made clear by the presence of excellent industries in the packaging and motor sectors, as well as being home to one of the five most powerful supercomputers in the world—still acknowledges the value of going slow, of proximity and exchange. This spirit is embodied in the alternative art spaces that proliferated in Bologna from the late 1970s onwards, a phenomenon that took on such distinctive characteristics here that we might refer to it as the "Bologna model." This volume aims to outline the genealogy of the phenomenon, going through the salient points—i.e. the art spaces—to reconstruct both micro- and macro-histories, digging up data, prizing open doors, and unearthing containers of precious visual documents.

Drawing on a definition made by Julie Ault, co-founder of the US collective Group Material, in an anthology exploring the phenomenon of alternative spaces in New York City from the 1960s to the 1980s, these:

> alternative enterprises shape and position themselves in relation to that for which they are an alternative: on understanding the relationships and interdependencies between profit and non-profit sectors of the cultural economy, how "mainstream" and "alternative" determine and influence one another, and how they blend.[3]

More generally, by alternative art spaces, we mean those venues independent of institutions and the market, more often than not initiated and managed by artists, configured as places for interdisciplinary experimentation but also as liberated spaces in which, through the arts, identity, as well as social and cultural codes may be redefined. This is a phenomenon with origins dating back to the advent of modernity, yet one consolidated during the twentieth century in the wake of the avant-garde movements, of subcultures and countercultures, institutional critique and a whole range of political, relational, participatory, and pedagogical artforms.

In this parable, which stretches from the Cabaret Voltaire in Zurich, where Dada first emerged in 1916, to the nomadic spaces initiated since the 2000s by the ruangrupa collective, from Jakarta to documenta fifteen, a decisive period was the 1960s. This decade saw the first signs of the crisis of representative democracy, hand in hand with what Jean-François Lyotard identified as a loss of faith in all the grand narratives of the past, namely the advent of postmodernism.[4] Alternative art spaces are thus nothing more than a reflection of a much larger process of rebalancing equilibria within post-industrial society. However, they played a decisive role in that society, while the arts also exerted a profound influence on the level of the imaginary. In other words, they have the power to propose changes in perspective and prefigure transformations, and it is in these spaces that the arts give form to stances and subjectivities that constitute an alternative to "official" society and that, in some ways, represent a tangible overturning of it.

In topographical terms, to map these spaces, we might recall Thomas More's imaginary island of *Utopia* (1516), situationist psychogeography, micronations and all those fictitious places that stimulate humanity to imagine that ideal places might exist—just, peaceful, and democratic. To remain linked to the era in which the phenomenon of alternative spaces takes shape, on the other hand, links may be made with a number of philosophical metaphors proposed in the sphere of structuralism, such as Gilles Deleuze's concept of "the fold,"[5] viewed as an indefinite zone of shade, but even more so that of Michel Foucault's "heterotopia," which refers to "something like counter-sites, a kind of effectively enacted utopia in which the real sites [...] are simultaneously represented, contested, and inverted. Places of this kind are outside of all places, even though it may be possible to indicate their location in reality."[6] The same goes for the alternative art spaces: they are places and perhaps even utopian ones, but they may also be identified with actual locations in the city.

And so what does the "Bologna model" consist of if not first and foremost its close relationship with the social and cultural fabric of the city in which it took shape? Inevitably, some basic features of the phenomenon are common to all alternative art spaces: inclusiveness, interdisciplinarity, and independence. What distinguishes the history of Bologna's spaces, if anything, is that they elaborated models of bottom-up professionalization in the most diverse fields of the arts, entertainment, and communications, sometimes in synergy with institutions and local government but never dependent on them. Unlike the evolution of this phenomenon in New York or certain Northern European cities, for that matter,

Bologna's spaces have never enjoyed public funding except on sporadic occasions. And yet, idealistically and heroically, they have been able to exist and endure, some for a few months, others for decades, training generations of professionals in what we now call the CCIs or Cultural and Creative Industries.

Although many of these spaces placed themselves in a conflicting relationship to the municipality, exacerbated during certain administrations more than others, there is no doubt that they all found fertile ground in Bologna, both socially and culturally. The University of Bologna served as a formidable incubator in this regard, particularly the DAMS: the innovative degree program in Disciplines of the Arts, Music and the Performing Arts founded in 1971 as an offshoot of the Faculty of Letters and Philosophy. Innovative teaching approaches took shape at the DAMS, looking toward the visual arts, music and the performing arts—understood as theater and cinema—from a contemporary perspective, hybridizing with sociology and philosophy, in light of the growing impact of the media and the transformations of the cultural and communication industries. Another source of energies flowing into the alternative spaces was the local Academy of Fine Arts, confirming the need on the part of young artists to overcome the solipsistic studio model in favor of more pluralistic creative dynamics.

Hybrid collective entities were generated within DAMS, arising from confrontation between visionary professors and students eager to put into practice the dream of *immaginazione al potere* ("power to imagination"): the motto of a counterculture that spread in Italy from the 1960s and throughout the following decade. An exemplary case was that of the Gruppo di Drammaturgia 2 coordinated by Giuliano Scabia, from which in 1972 came *Gorilla Quadrumano*—a street theater show that foresaw the active participation of the inhabitants of a variety of Italian neighborhoods, starting with Bologna's outlying Pilastro area. Another key example was that of the Gruppo A/Dams, responsible for the collective text *Alice disambientata: materiali collettivi (su Alice) per un manuale di sopravvivenza* (L'Erba Voglio, 1978), which in turn grew out of a seminar on Lewis Carroll held by Gianni Celati. Clearly, Celati and his students were interested not only in the psychedelic dimension of the Wonderland in Carroll's novel, but also in the fact that the rabbit hole Alice falls into leads her into a true heterotopia.

Thanks to initiatives like these, in the classrooms and corridors of Strada Maggiore and Via Guerrazzi (then the headquarters of the DAMS), what many began to call the creative wing of the '77 Movement took shape. The carnivalesque performances of the Indiani Metropolitani during marches, the murals, and so the "Mao-Dadaist" counter-information initiatives set off by Franco "Bifo" Berardi—the soul of the Movement—namely Radio Alice (that's right, the same Alice!) and the magazine *A/traverso*,[7] were affected by a countercultural temperament somehow also inspired by DAMS professors: Scabia, Celati, Umberto Eco, Renato Barilli, Luciano Anceschi and many other "undisciplined" intellectuals. The influence of the DAMS was not limited to the origins of the phenomenon we are dealing with, but may still be felt to this day, and it is from this awareness, and in part a sense of responsibility, that the research underlying this volume took shape within the DAMS itself as well as other degree courses in the current Department of the Arts of the University of Bologna.

The first spaces with which this review opens, La Tregenda and Traumfabrik, already had a number of characteristics of the "Bologna model." Both founded in 1976, the former lasting a few months and the latter seven years, they were workshops of interdisciplinary practices arising from a spontaneous transposition of life into art and vice versa. The founders of La Tregenda, a basement on Via San Vitale, made the radical choice to open the space to women only, in line with the feminist fringe of the Movement. The Traumfabrik, or "dream factory" in German, on the other hand, was an apartment at Via Clavature 20—proof of how inseparable the intertwining of art and life was—illegally occupied by Filippo Scozzari, Gianpietro Huber, and Dadi Mariotti. In a city that in 1977 was marked by the killing of a student, Francesco Lorusso, the Convention Against Repression and "tanks" rolling down the streets below Bologna's two towers, in La Tregenda and the Traumfabrik, the Movement was exploring new forms of expression, underlining to the city's contradictions and exploring how to overcome them.

The Traumfabrik was a pioneering example of the "Bologna model," as a gathering center and multifunctional workshop connotated by its rejection of the dominant market and cultural logics. Bands such as the Centro d'Urlo Metropolitano, soon to be renamed Gaznevada, and the Stupid Set were formed at the Traumfabrik, as well as the Grabinski collective, which produced proto-music videos and multimedia installations for them, allegorizing television broadcasts and video surveillance systems. Scozzari and Andrea Pazienza, then a DAMS student, produced some of their most important comic book works here, but then at the Traumfabrik "everyone drew, and wildly so,"[8] as Scozzari recalls in one of his memoirs: illustrations, collages, storyboards for comics and films. Produced under the influence of drugs, these works on paper, together with Emanuele Angiuli's photographs, today represent a key corpus for reconstructing the epic nature of what was a totalizing space, a true counterweight to the contemporary art system of the day.

What made the Traumfabrik a prototype of Bologna's alternative spaces were not only its political dimension (as part of the '77 Movement milieu), its interdisciplinary approach to the arts and its art/life nexus, but also its connotation as a workshop of professionalizing activities based on hybridization. In addition to the Grabinski's unclassifiable intermedia productions, other examples were the graphic activities and editorial projects of the Topographic collective, which saw the frequent collaboration of Anna Persiani, from record covers and playbills to full-fledged magazines such as *L.U.X. Electric!* and *Musica80*. In this regard, we must also mention other revolutionary magazines that, although founded elsewhere, saw the involvement of Traumfabrik members—Scozzari first and foremost—namely *Cannibale* and *Frigidaire*, not to mention the vast range of musical projects. But rather than being subservient to the dominant consumerist culture, these examples of professionalization ended up, partly unconsciously, infiltrating it and eroding its foundations from within.

Bifo himself acknowledged their importance as a way of overcoming the Movement's betrayed dreams, as he wrote in *A/traverso* in 1981:

> A generation of proletarian experimenters is defined in "artistic" terms, for art is viewed both as a metaphorical and an experimental arena. A metaphor for social and technological concatenations that exceed the existent and thus outline the organization of knowledge and production that the existent aims to destroy. [...] Think back to '77 in Bologna: we had accumulated experimentation for years and spent it all in revolt. Today it is a matter of reversing the process.[9]

This issue of the magazine, subtitled "Game Over," was devoted to sound and visual experiments with interventions by Grabinski and Renato De Maria, one of the members of the group, who in time would be confirmed as the only one, along with Scozzari, to turn the Traumfabrik experience into a profession, going on to embark on an honorable career in the cinema industry.

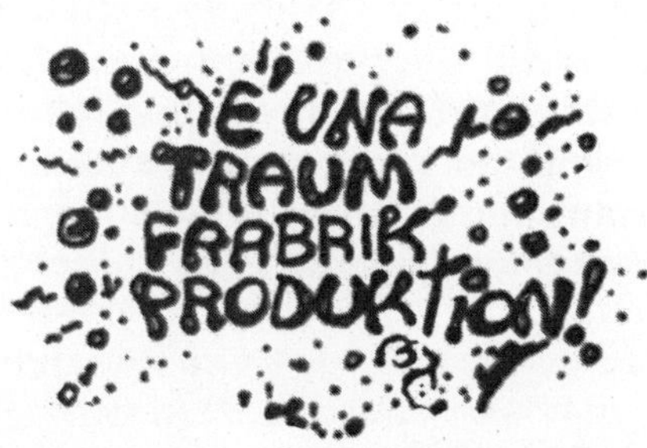

Some initiatives that sprung up within Traumfabrik took the form of pseudo-businesses starting with a sort of trademark, "Traumfabrik Productions," which appeared on Gaznevada flyers, on Pazienza's *Pentothal* comic boards (1977–1981), and in Topographic's art direction projects [Fig. 1]. Most of the bands formed in Via Clavature found support from Italian Records, a label headed by Oderso Rubini born out of the Bologna-based Harpo's Bazaar cooperative, a forward-thinking example of bottom-up production that made Traumfabrik's bands the finest examples of the Italian new wave. As the newspaper *l'Unità* wrote, Harpo's Bazaar "...attempts to position itself competitively with the big record monopolies rather than demonizing them. [...] The result is a thriving business that has gained cultural credibility even with local authorities."[10] The idea was to make self-recording a business model with a political-cultural matrix, leveraging the energies of the local territory.

In the sphere of punk and post-punk culture, independent record initiatives represented a counterbalance to the pop music giants, not only in terms of style and content, but especially because of the artists' need to maintain autonomy from the mass market. Scritti Politti themselves in 1980 published *How To Make a Record*: a do-it-yourself discography manual imbued with militant messages. More than the United Kingdom, however, greater affinities bound the Bologna art community to that of New York, which gravitated around *Semiotext(e)* and the No Wave scene.[11]

On the Bologna front, bridging the gap were the aforementioned Bifo and De Maria, along with Francesca Alinovi and Mariuccia Casadio, a DAMS researcher and former DAMS student, respectively. Edit DeAk, Diego Cortez, Lydia Lunch, Jean-Michel Basquiat, Arto Lindsay, and Keith Haring, on the other hand, were among the New York curators and artists involved in Bologna's International Performance Week, as well as participating in concerts, record productions, and exhibition projects in the city.

Coinciding with what was happening in some downtown Manhattan nightclubs such as the Mudd Club and Club 57, inside the cold storage room of a former slaughterhouse in Borgo Panigale, on the immediate outskirts of Bologna, Segreto Pubblico came into being. In 1981, Bifo organized a performance version of "Game Over" there, staging the Beijing trial of the Gang of Four in an arcade setting. Marking Segreto Pubblico's short history, however, were two exhibition projects in the form of parties, both in 1982. For *Frontiera Party*, curated by Alinovi, the space was transformed into a prehistoric environment in a postmodern key, with murals by Ivo Bonacorsi, colorful cocktails served by a group of artists linked to neon—another recently formed alternative space in the city—and a performance by a band with the exotic name of Eterodattili. The other project was the *Grabinsky TV Party*, an environment characterized by the eerie presence of surveillance cameras and screens, yet likewise aimed at entertainment: life as a party, art as an allegory.

With Segreto Pubblico, two other key elements of the "Bologna model" were consolidated: the space that becomes an immersive environment thanks to audiovisual set-ups and installations, and the possibility of combining a partisan stance with music and dance, viewed as tools for liberating bodies, without running the risk of the disengaged hedonism to which the postmodern lifestyle is usually attributed. Far from disengaged, in fact, were the collective initiatives that, following the historical examples discussed so far, sprang up in Bologna in the late 1980s and early 1990s, in particular Isola Nel Kantiere, Livello 57, Link Project, and TPO – Teatro Polivalente Occupato. These were social centers that emerged out of illegal occupations (except in the case of the Link) of disused buildings, run by non-profit collectives: a model that drew on the tradition of the *Case del Popolo* ("People's Houses") of working-class and socialist origin to reflect the international phenomenon of house squatting that was gaining force at the time within anti-capitalist and anti-globalization movements.

According to Serafino D'Onofrio and Valerio Monteventi, who provided valuable interpretative keys to the phenomenon discussed here with their 2011 book *Berretta Rossa*, these spaces were "workshops of politics and culture, forges of struggles and alternative forms of entertainment, but also, first and foremost, aggregations of individuals who decided to adhere to a common set of values."[12] And again, "genuine factories of post-industrial work, places of innovation and creative production, where trends and communicative models were elaborated on which the Milanese, Roman, and perhaps international industry then proceeded, adopting energies that had been unleashed right here in Bologna."[13] Also in this phase, the approach in artistic terms was broadly interdisciplinary and devoted to the exploration of convergences between visual, performance, and media languages that were direct extensions of a subcultural lifestyle matrix, i.e. tools that allowed a group of individuals to identify with a culture alternative to that of the mainstream.

The subculture *par excellence*—punk—in its most hardcore declination, was behind the birth of Isola Nel Kantiere: a squat also known simply as Isola or I.N.K., inside a building behind Via Indipendenza and the Arena del Sole Theater. Riccardo Pedrini, guitarist for the Bologna-based band Nabat, wrote that for him "being punk meant severing relationships with much of the so-called surrounding world. [...] It was a very strong tension toward an elsewhere, whether political, social or stylistic, musical or behavioral, or all of these things rolled into one."[14] At the Isola, this seems to be the assumption, although punk and hardcore—here also performed by international figures such as Fugazi, Henri Rollins, and NOFX—soon gave way to a new subculture: hip hop. Like punk, hip hop is an interdisciplinary movement, covering music, graffiti, dance, self-publishing, and media. And like punk, hip hop was also imported to Italy from other countries and other cultures, yet declined here in original ways.

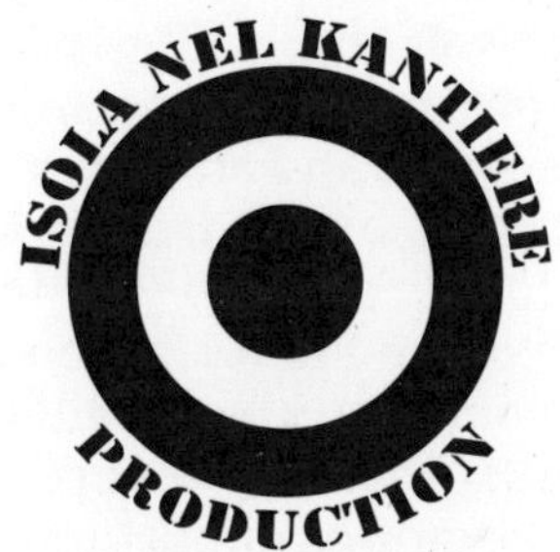

Isola Nel Kantiere became a cradle of Italian hip hop thanks to the founding of collectives such as Isola Posse All Stars to which we owe "Stop al Panico" (Stop the Panic, 1991), an unmatched archetype of homegrown rap, and bearer of the "Isola Nel Kantiere Production" trademark [Fig. 2]. The song served as a sounding board at the time for the Pantera student movement's distrust of institutions and the climate of terror generated in Bologna by the Uno Bianca massacres. With Isola Nel Kantiere, Bologna became the epicenter of a new movement of civil disobedience, also reinforced, like in '77, by artistic tactics. The line from "Stop al Panico" that best describes this sentiment is the one sung by DeeMo, one of the group's rappers: "Bologna is red with shame and blood, no longer dreaming. Years and years of bullshit names like 'the happy island' have done nothing but damage. Bologna is just the asshole of the world. Those who have taken, have taken, and those who have given now are going down."[15] Like with Alice, once again going down a hole, moving on to another heterotopia.

Isola Nel Kantiere was evicted in 1991, the same year British computer scientist Tim Berners Lee published the first website, thus making available to humanity access to the still unexplored universe on which we now largely depend, i.e. the internet. Of the web, understood then as a

Fig. 2   Isola Nel Kantiere Production trademark from the vinyl release of Isola Posse All Stars, "Stop al Panico," 1991 space of potential and for re-imagining society, the alternative spaces of those years were a tangible expression. A version of the concept of heterotopia updated to the novelties of the current era was that of T.A.Z., or Temporarily Autonomous Zones, developed by Hakim Bey also in 1991. These are places that for a limited period become independent from the social, political, and cultural context, in which the arts play a key role. Indeed, according to Bey:

> The TAZ is the only possible "time" and "place" for art to happen for the sheer pleasure of creative play, and as an actual contribution to the forces which allow the TAZ to cohere and manifest. Art in the world has become a commodity; but deeper than that lies the problem of re-presentation itself, and the refusal of all mediation. In the TAZ art as a commodity will simply become impossible; it will instead be a condition of life.[16]

In early 1990s Bologna, examples of T.A.Z.s were not only the spaces but also the areas of the city where the germs grown in their labs were then spread virally. We might think of the carnival processions and techno parades organized by Isola or Livello 57, capable of temporarily piercing the urban fabric—the squares, parks and porticoes—with autonomous rivers of floats, loudspeakers, signs, and anthropomorphic creatures made from recycled materials, perhaps by the British Mutoid Waste Company that initially made its home in Bologna and then in the nearby Romagna region. Alongside these anonymous art forms, conceived as tools of counter-discussion, exploratory missions were launched online. Isola, Livello 57, and Link all set up workstations with personal computers hooked up to the Internet, and offered various opportunities for discussion on the pivotal themes of cyberpunk culture, from BBSs to counter-information, from virtual reality to Net.Art, before the internet was irrevocably privatized and our subjectivities swallowed up by social media.

In the aftermath of the eviction of Isola Nel Kantiere, the Damsterdamned collective—which at the time of the Pantera ran the cultural programming of the occupied DAMS in Via Guerrazzi—along with other associations and groups, was at the center of negotiations with the Municipality of Bologna to find a new space. The choice fell to the former warehouse of the Farmacie Comunali on Via Fioravanti, behind the train station, where the Link Project came into being. A quintessential example of the Bologna model, the energies of Bologna's alternative art community shaped a cultural factory at Link, split into divisions with specific tasks, as outlined in an "organizational chart" on the first page of the second issue of its namesake magazine [Fig. 3]. The generic headings shown in the diagram correspond to professional entities such as Officine Alchemiche (displays), Opificio Ciclope (multimedia productions), Loew & Associati (graphics department), and others responsible for theatrical, musical, visual arts-related, film-related, and service-related programming, etc.

Today, Link's inhouse magazine provides a valuable benchmark for understanding the multipurpose and interdisciplinary nature of the center, which, as Daniele Gasparinetti—a key figure in Link's history—recalled in a recent text, was conceived as:

> world-of-editorials (a world-of-relationships), to create a "living magazine." The editorial teams were the minimal units of connection, comparison and ordering the ranks. [...] this was not the family (father-mother-offspring), but a dialectical process that could take on many forms of combination. Whatever went beyond these accounting units was already an "assembly." [...] Assemblies represent the places of confluence-divergence, and are the organs of non-totalizability.[17]

Gasparinetti's words, however, also reveal a contradiction in terms of alternative spaces: while these experiences rest on dynamics of sharing and collectivization, they are also incubators of divergences and frustrations that jeopardize their subsistence and also risk spoiling the memory of them.

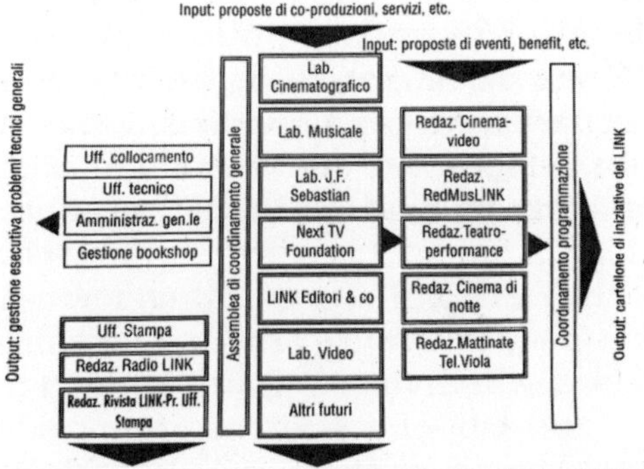

Electronic culture, in its most diverse forms, was what held Link together, and thanks to permanent installations and temporary sets, was configured as an immersive and intermedial environment, drawing on the convergence of sound, light, and screens. Music programming—the main economic lifeline—included performances by exponents of "historical" genres, from post-punk to hip hop to techno, along with the finest representatives of genres at the time such as IDM, post-rock and trip hop. Monographic reviews were devoted to protagonists of experimental cinema and video art, including Marcel Broodthaers, Chris Marker, Bill Viola, Gary Hill, and the Italian collective canecapovolto. Theatre experimentation played a prominent role, with performances by Italian companies such as Socìetas Raffaello Sanzio, Kinkaleri and Teatrino Clandestino. Through meetings and articles in the *Link Project* magazine, these alternative products of the culture industry were also contextualized and discussed by artists and academics.

The Link represented a watershed moment, not only because it systematized elements that had already emerged in previous spaces—as a hotbed of interdisciplinary and professionalizing activities, an engine of subcultural energies, and an all-encompassing space—but also because of its ability to weave relationships, however unstable, both with the public administration (which legitimized its existence) and with academia, the art system, and the culture industry. Regarding the art system, many previous spaces had ignored or opposed such attempts. The first initiative of Isola Nel Kantiere, for example, was the *manifestazione dei rubinetti* (the "faucet event"): a contestation of the Biennial of Young Artists from Europe and the Mediterranean, the fourth edition of which was organized by the City of Bologna in 1988. Armed with faucets, a group of "islanders" paraded through the streets of the city center to lament how, once the Biennial was over, the administration would again "turn off the taps" of art funding.

Other spaces founded prior to the Link, however, had demonstrated a capacity for dialogue with the city's contemporary art world, becoming places where artists had the opportunity to experiment with the techniques and languages of the visual arts but without necessarily being caught up the logic of commodification. This was the case with neon and Il Campo delle Fragole, the former a space dedicated primarily to expressions of a conceptual and relational nature, the latter more interested in painting and installation practices. Both these spaces and the artists behind their activities participated in gallery exhibitions and institutional initiatives, also establishing a relationship with the local Arte Fiera. Founded in 1974, Arte Fiera was one of the first fairs dedicated to contemporary art on an international level, and contributed to the perception of Bologna as a place of innovation also in terms of its cultural economy. Today as part of Arte Fiera, both for-profit and non-profit organizations contribute synergistically to a dense program of events known as Art City.

For several years, within the Link, during the days of Arte Fiera, former DAMS student and artist Luca Vitone organized Incursioni: an exhibition project that included installations, performances and meetings, reminding the art fair-goers that art can be a process without becoming a product. Several festivals dedicated to hybridizations between the visual arts and other expressive languages were also held at Link, such as Hops! and Suoni visivi e immagini sonore ("Visual sounds and sonic images"). The former was presented as a project "...in which borderline productions and interstitial zones coexist, hosting in turn *sui* or *sub generis* research: representative creative splinters of the contemporary world, rarely brought to the same playing field outside their respective aesthetic niches." [18] From these experiences and a group of Link members the Netmage. International Live Media Festival would later emerge, constituting an exhibition dedicated to contamination and convergence between the visual and the musical in both performances and intermedial projects, traveling year after year to various venues throughout the city.

The festival phenomenon, which alone would merit dedicated research and a volume of its own, developed considerably in Bologna from the 1990s onward, as an extension of activities emerging in alternative spaces or by associations and organizations linked to them. In particular, as Paolo Magaudda argues, festivals were the result of "a certain degree of 'institutionalization' of some of the city's social centers, which also goes in the direction of normalizing the cultural offerings. The subsidy of institutions altered certain experiences of extreme rupture into centers of cultural production."[19] In addition to Netmage, think of the Gender Bender festival produced by the Cassero, which for more than two decades has boasted leading international and interdisciplinary artistic programming with a focus on issues of gender identity. Also normalizing their cultural offerings, there are several spaces still active today, modeled on neon and Il Campo delle Fragole and devoted primarily to the visual arts, such as Adiacenze and Ateliersi.

In New York, billed as the place of choice for alternative art spaces, these experiences enjoyed substantial grants from the state and private individuals. Some spaces founded in the 1970s became full-fledged institutions, such as the New Museum of Contemporary Art and PS1, now a branch of MoMA. In Bologna, on the other hand, this support was limited to a handful of initiatives or concerned the concession of spaces owned by the municipality. The case of Cassero is of particular importance, as it was the first space run by a homosexual association in Italy to have been legitimized by the public administration through the concession of its own venue. The principle of intersectionality, i.e. the inclusion of usually discriminated and marginalized groups, with a focus on the LGBTQIA+ community, is another fundamental character of Bologna's alternative spaces, especially Cassero, TPO, and Atlantide. Unlike the former, however, the tales of the other two have been marked by a series of conflicts and evictions.

In brief, the following may be referred to as the fundamental characteristics of the "Bologna model," variously applicable to the alternative spaces for art that were the subject of this research:

- Bologna's fame as a place of political ferment and cultural innovation
- links with the city's academic milieu, particularly DAMS
- the convergence between life, politics, and artistic production
- an experimental nature, which made of them labs of interdisciplinarity
- a role as bottom-up incubators of professionalization in relation to the CCIs
- a totalizing dimension through immersive and intermedial environments
- a degree of independence from institutions and the market
- the development of subcultural art practices
- their ambiguous/synergistic/conflictual relationship with the art system
- their ambiguous/synergistic/conflictual relationship with the public administration
- and the principle of intersectionality and inclusion, determining their social value

Rather than spaces to be found *elsewhere*, this research shows how these are *in between* spaces, and ones that produce *in between* initiatives, events, projects, and subjectivities. Not by coincidence, some of the keywords recurring in the exploration of this phenomenon share the prefix "inter-," which indeed points to a midway position or a relationship of reciprocity: interdisciplinary, intermedial, intersectional, to which we might add interstitial, intertextual and other terms that allude to being in the middle. In the middle of just what, exactly? In the middle of the processes of signification, in the midst of the mechanisms of meaning-creation as part of the cultural economy and the media, in the gray areas where artistic production and communication blur, and in the crossover between art and life. The value of these spaces, therefore, lies precisely in their position, both in the city but at the same time as part of the very fabric that determines its way of operating, like distorting mirrors in which the arts allow the codes of postindustrial society to be redefined.

1 Extracts from the text of the song "Skank Bloc Bologna" by Scritti Politti, St. Pancreas Records, Leeds, 1978.

2 Renato Zangheri, *Bologna '77. Comunisti, potere, dissenso: analisi di un'esperienza dal vivo. Intervista di Fabio Mussi* (Editori Riuniti: Rome, 1978), 14, 101.

3 Julie Ault, "For the Record" in *Alternative Art New York, 1965–1985* (University of Minnesota Press: Minneapolis, 2002), 4.

4 See Jean-François Lyotard, *La condition postmoderne: rapport sur le savoir* (Les Éditions de Minuit: Paris, 1979).

5 See Gilles Deleuze, *The Fold. Leibniz and the Baroque* (Athlone Press: London, 1993).

6 Michel Foucault, "Des Espace Autres," in *Architecture / Mouvement / Continuité*, Paris, October 1984, n.p.

7 See Klemens Gruber, *L'avanguardia inaudita. Comunicazione e strategia nei movimenti degli anni Settanta* (Costa & Nolan: Genoa, 1997).

8 Filippo Scozzari, *Prima pagare poi ricordare. Da 'Cannibale' a 'Frigidaire.' Storica di un manipolo di ragazzi geniali* (Coniglio Editore: Rome, 2007), 58.

9 Franco "Bifo" Berardi, "Il movimento. La sperimentazione", *A/traverso* (Summer 1981).

10 Filippo Bianchi, "Un business chiamato movimento. La felice esperienza della cooperativa bolognese 'Harpo's Bazaar,'" *l'Unità*, April 22, 1981, in Oderso Rubini and Anna Persiani (eds.), *Pensatevi Liberi. Bologna Rock 1979* (Beatstream: Bologna, 2019), 81.

11 See Francesco Spampinato, "No Bologna No New York: il network No Wave tra le due città 1977–1983," in Uliana Zanetti (ed.), *La performance a Bologna negli anni '70* (MAMbo – Museo d'Arte Moderna di Bologna: Bologna, 2023), 184–93.

12 Serafino D'Onofrio and Valerio Monteventi, *Berretta Rossa. Storie di Bologna attraverso i centri sociali* (Pendragon: Bologna, 2011), 10.

13 Ibid., 28.

14 Riccardo Pedrini, *Ordigni. Storia del Punk a Bologna* (Castelvecchi: Rome, 1998), 91.

15 Original italian lyrics of the song: "Bologna è rossa di vergogna e sangue, non sogna più. Anni e anni, anni di cazzate tipo 'isola felice' non han fatto che danni. Bologna è solo il buco del culo del mondo. C'è chi ha avuto, ha avuto e chi ha dato e va a fondo." Isola Posse All Stars, "Stop al Panico," 12" vinyl, Isola Nel Kantiere Production, 1991.

16 Hakim Bey, *T.A.Z.: The Temporary Autonomous Zone, Ontological Anarchy, Poetic Terrorism,* The Anarchist Library, https://theanarchist-library.org/library/hakim-bey-t-a-z-the-temporary-autonomous-zone-ontological-anarchy-poetic-terrorism; *Zone Temporaneamente Autonome* (Shake: Milan, 2007), 116.

17 Daniele Gasparinetti, "Knil/Link. An inversion of the Link in Transhistorical Form," *Quaderni d'arte italiana*, No. 2 (Rome Quadriennale and Treccani: Rome, 2022), 107.

18 Description of the Hops! festival, on the occasion of its first edition, in the pages of *Link Project* magazine (January–February 2000), text unsigned, n.p.

19 Paolo Magaudda, "Sottoculture e creatività urbana. Le traiettorie, i luoghi e i miti della cultura giovanile a Bologna," in Piero Pieri and Chiara Cretella (eds.), *Atlante dei movimenti culturali dell'Emilia-Romagna 1968–2007: III. Arti, Comunicazione, Controculture* (Clueb: Bologna, 2007), 52.

THE SMELL OF THE ABSOLUTE PRESENT

It Wasn't Bologna after All

Andrea Lissoni

One image is not enough; there are too many of them. Not even a sound, too much sound, too many sounds. Of course there is a smell, a very specific one: that of the day after. This is not Bologna after all; it's the Link Project, from the steps of the station underpass, you head in the opposite direction to where everyone else goes, toward Bolognina instead of the center of town. The smell has remained there and it very occasionally resurfaces: that of smoke, bodies—human or otherwise—cars, beer, and lots more besides.

Bologna was a key hub for me. It was the place where everything I was passionate about took place. Everything that represented the absolute present was there, and I couldn't miss it. After fifteen years as a reverse commuter—traveling to Bologna for the weekend and not on workdays—I might say I never really knew it.

But what was the absolute present? It was the perception of a condition, that of being connected, being in the world, being in the flow, being part of an epochal revolution that was taking place by helping to share it locally, spreading it around, imagining how it might germinate further. For me, this was Bologna. Certainly a specific Bologna, that of the Link, of the Cassero first of all, and then of festivals such as Netmage, F.I.S.Co., and for completely different reasons, also that of the Cinema Ritrovato. Bologna between about 1996 and 2013.

Only by going back again and again, other key trajectories emerged: the presence and importance of Bifo, the commonly adopted line of post-factory worker thought, the extraordinary and I might say unique network of heterodox performance realities scattered across Romagna, between Cesena, Ravenna, Rimini and Riccione, aggregators and diffusers of splinters of Anglo-Saxon audiovisual culture, such as the Riccione TTV Festival, the links with Florence and Prato, especially with CPA, and with Kinkaleri, Virgilio Sieni and Ogino:knauss in particular. And then there was neon, later known as campobase.

I remember going there on Saturdays, before dinner, and each time encountering something extremely sincere, restrained in form, often emotionally charged, never dramatic, never smarmy, never modest in the breadth of gesture or the extent of conceptual scope. Something different yet strangely familiar. Substantially unlike what I might encounter in Milan, the heterodox liveliness of Viafarini, the energy of elsewhere and the never before perceived of Emi Fontana, the elegance of Guenzani, the ambitious provocation of De Carlo, or the light visionariness of Horatio Goni's Fac-Simile. Neon gave the impression of a community to which all who entered belonged automatically, without scrutiny or evaluation, which artists would offer their works to without mediation, compromise, strategy, or skin.

In the bowels of the Link, next to the bookstore—Modo Infoshop, an essential reference for the culture of the day—before that smell formed, there were the dinners, where everyone (artists, technicians, workers, and collaborators) would all meet. I think back to it as a unique and extraordinary moment, partly a missed opportunity, due to my over-commitment, the density of conversation, and my shyness.

Of course, there must have been a first trip. But how did I end up there, and why? I was studying modern art at the University of Pavia, in the wake of the student movement La Pantera and the inter-university connections via fax, and the most interesting experiences were taking place at the intersection between on and offline, and I was following them by commuting on buses and trains: in Milan and hanging out at Calusca and Conchetta, looking toward "Gomma" Guarneri and Raf Valvola, reading the whole of *Decoder*, ShaKe publications, the Interzone series, avidly devouring everything by Gibson, Haraway, Lanier, and Sterling. I was listening and dancing to everything that had never been heard before and that was happening at that time: electronic in general, via jungle, broken beat, trance, distorted hip hop, trip-hop, illbient, but also the new indie scene and all its roots. I had worked on Studio Azzurro for my thesis, and there I had come across a network of people who would accompany me everywhere, among those festivals where I always helped out (Taormina Arte Video, with Valentina Valentini, who had previously tutored my thesis) and others where I moved among the few specialists. In Milan there was Invideo, but that wasn't enough: the real energy came from Mudima, where through the formidable program dedicated to presenting the protagonists of Fluxus, I was starting to see radically unconventional forms of art, performance, music, and video rigor in form, freedom in behavior. I had helped out and collaborated with then lively Progetto Giovani, driven by the dedicated motivation in the quality of Roberto Pinto's international voices, especially through the series of meetings known as *La generazione delle immagini* ("The Generation of Images"). In Pavia, while having breakfast at the Student House, I had made a habit of reading *Il Manifesto*, devoured *Alias*, but I could never miss Ninì Candalino's Friday column on electronic visions. That was where I came across the name Damsterdamned and began to follow the first waves being issued from Bologna, until they formed into genuine signals and, later, entanglements. Various collectives that had started out within DAMS (and beyond) were coming together—so I read—and the Link was being founded.

I was increasingly involved in video art, fascinated by the formidable transition that was revolutionizing the tradition of analog and electronic culture at the same time, dissolving them both into the digital. I was working in Paris at the New Media Department of the Musée National d'Art Moderne/Centre Georges Pompidou on a fellowship program, and all I dreamed of was to see an experimental museum situation—one of research but also of production—emerge in Italy as well. It seemed unthinkable in a country where the institutions were so staid. The only signs of life came from Bologna, from the Link, inevitably, which was not only dedicating original evenings to heterodox, extreme, underground film and video works on a regular basis, but also seemed to be programming more and more art and, in particular, artists' film and video. Link was also home to Rifrazioni: a distribution house for art and artists' videos with a very unusual catalogue, featuring a strong bond with the German scene and the countercultural artworld more generally, co-directed by Daniele Gasparinetti and Rainer Bumke, also active as a producer at Studio Azzurro. I think the first physical step was my attraction to Romeo Castellucci/Socìetas Raffaello Sanzio, in the fall of 1995, still during my military service, when I first entered the nocturnal world of the

Link and was swept away by it forever. At that time, Aphex Twin had played his first gig in Italy there, and my world changed forever. I remember coming across the name Raphael Montañez Ortiz for the first time: an artist who would accompany me for twenty years until I finally met him in New Jersey. And Jürgen Reble, with whom we would later collaborate. But, equally important was coming across works and names like Nan Goldin, Rebecca Horn, Angela Melitopoulos and, not surprisingly, Emi Fontana.

I think I dwelt on Montañez Ortiz and Reble because in a sense for me they represented the soul of the Link, or rather, its image: that approach based on cutting, pasting, recombining and generating new life and a world of alchemical transformation, one based on the alteration of matter, on alchemy. A visionary artist who had founded the Barrio Museum in New York, a leading figure at the *Destruction in Art Symposium* in London in 1966, a revolutionary in the history of video, a key figure in the cut 'n' mix aesthetic, a joyful but rigorous practice that we would adopt as a curatorial philosophy. An experimental filmmaker who knew no bounds, be it of the movie theater—he mostly produced expanded cinema performances—or of the treatment of the film spools, which he would retrieve second hand, dye, bury, hide among the trees or leave exposed to the elements, and then share its alterations in unforgettable and ever-changing projections, often cooperating with electronic musician friends like Thomas Köner.

The plunderphonic souls of Montañez Ortiz, Dara Birnbaum, Alberto Grifi, Chris Cutler, Terre Thaemlitz, Coldcut and others were spontaneously programmed among video, film and especially music, interspersed with abstract, visionary, alchemical and drifting worlds: together, in 2000, on the occasion of Bologna European Capital of Culture, they would generate the first version of the Netmage festival (the title came about as the answer to the question "what are images in the age of the net?"), the life of a still small creative-curatorial post-Link community, which we titled Media Magica, sowing seeds for a new community, this time ambitiously international. While Bologna seemed to be gaining clout on the arts scene—the MAMbo was opening in new buildings right next to the Magazzini del Sale, home to the vibrant Cassero LGBTQIA+ Center and a stone's throw from the Cineteca, potentially a unique creative district in Italy—with a symbolic peak in energy prior to Arte Fiera, before Artissima took an explicitly curatorial turn in the mid-2000s, also at the Link Luca Vitone had first started Incursioni during the days of the Fair, later inviting me to co-curate Hops!: the underlying vision was to present everything that would not find space at the Fair, offering a nocturnal and especially performative alternative, always and urgently with a special focus on the most restless local or budding Italian realities, first and foremost those who came across as a passionate and curious audience. One line would remain in F.I.S.Co., the international contemporary performance festival conceived and led by Silvia Fanti, which since 2000 had been turning the tables on the Italian scene, combining the "local" excellence of Kinkaleri and mk with restless artists and then fellow travelers such as Jérôme Bel, Myriam Gourfink, Maria Hassabi, Xavier Le Roy, and Eszter Salamon. In all this, the various artists and practices were almost endless, to the point of generating new paradigms, from VJing to Live Media.

Subsequent memories are associated with seeking and finding spaces. A permanent one, Raum, a selective attractor of heterodox research practices, in actual fact a permanent hub of eclectic education offering excellent results, seen from an international perspective, and thus perhaps the first real independent arts center in Italy. And many temporary venues, especially for Netmage: unfamiliar gardens, undergrounds, underpasses, tunnels, buildings in transformation, former theaters, disused cinemas, railway yards, municipal buildings, right up to the installation in the central and majestic Palazzo Re Enzo.

This annual pilgrimage, which I embarked upon with great reverence, corresponded in my memory to the image of "renewed recovery" that I was so familiar with, and which in fact forever shaped me. A recovery of precious sources in which, indeed, "to seek, locate, select, and recombine, while welcoming, listening, and alchemically transforming," had by then become a vision of cultural programming, if not already of life itself.

Memories are ones of exploration, of dampness, wet floors, puddles, a lack of light, that stuffy smell, and then finally a few days of pure magic.

That pure magic of yet another memory, one no longer personal, but of the future, that musician Caterina Barbieri recently shared with me. One late afternoon when she was very young, passing by Piazza Maggiore on her bike on her way back from class at the conservatory, Caterina saw Palazzo Re Enzo lit up from inside with lights and colors like she had never seen before: the curiosity, the entrance, the sounds, the number of people, and a duo of girls playing electronic music sitting on the floor. They were the Byrne sisters, the Ectoplasm Girls: a very young Swedish electronic noise art duo. For Caterina, Netmage was the spark: two girls playing in front of a focused audience at a festival midway between art and electronic music: she could definitely do that too.

And so as of now, is my most poignant memory of Bologna, these fragments of the past coupled with visions, with dedication and a sense of transformation grounded in a potential ever-ready to be triggered. And after all, this is also the premise on which the summer days of Cinema Ritrovato are based: an event that inhabits the district but which has long transformed Piazza Maggiore into an international platform of outright quality and importance.

And by the way, I came across the closing English-language statement/ open letter to all those involved in the Link Project, and I think an excerpt says more than anything about that period and represents the subterranean waterways that my memories still float along:

> The Link Project has certainly been something more than just a cultural association, both in a formal way and at a more substantial level.
> We believe that it has represented a very important stage in Bologna's cultural life, having had the capability to go well beyond its original role.

It is not yet possible to summarize in a few lines what the whole experience was about, either from a personal point of view nor from any other perspective, be it long-term and historical.

It certainly turned out to be a vital experience. An organism, for better or worse, invaded by thousands of streams and currents of thought. This was its strange energy.

We are dealing with an energy that surely has not failed and will not fade now with the close of its historically associated structure. The nature of vital worlds has this prerogative: extinction followed by rebirth.

It may have been paradoxical to institutionalize this experience by crystallizing its features.

Networks have fortunately become realities on a wide scale. Perhaps this was paramount in our minds when we undertook this route years ago.

Another series of ups, then, because it is in this cycle of rebirth and renewal, which we have wanted to believe in, that we chose to involve ourselves and others on this strange adventure.

We want to thank all the people who, for different reasons, have participated and were connected with the project.

We wish all Link-thinkers a very exciting future.

More darkness and artificial light than sunlight, more strange smells than crisp air, more hyperactivity and conversation than thought and contemplation, more action than documentation, more decisive actions than gradual drifts. Transformation. And so much more.

INDEPENDENT DISPLAY SPACES FROM A GENDER PERSPECTIVE

Lara De Lena

With this essay, we set out to analyze the feminist dimension of the Bologna spaces in relation to the Italian context, the role of women within them, and more generally, within the institutional and non-institutional artworld between the 1970s and 1990s.

As Linda Nochlin argues,[1] art is always the result of a social situation, both in terms of the evolution of the artist and the nature and quality of the work itself. Her 1971 intervention in *ARTnews*, provocatively titled "Why Have There Been No Great Women Artists?," denounces the absence of the female component in art history, caused by the persistence of falsely universal criteria of judgment that have always ignored women artists and all their forms of creativity. Although there is no style recognizable as feminine per se, according to the American scholar, something unites successful female artists: the sense of guilt for having broken free of the web of social expectations, since—inevitably—everything that is habitual also seems natural.[2]

As Maria Antonietta Trasforini recounts, the art dictionaries produced in the 1950s mention almost no female artists, while from the 1970s the numbers increase considerably: there are about 500 mentioned in 1976, rising to 21,000 in 1984.[3] The rediscovery of forgotten women artists of the past is thus accompanied by a blossoming of women artists working in the contemporary sphere. The neo-feminist push shook up the world of art and culture, and led to what Chiara Zamboni refers to as a "radiant moment,"[4] in which there is a shared sense of urgency for a new language that adopts words and that, as Mariella Pasinati notes, may "...subvert the male gaze on women, on art, on the world, in order to assert its own, autonomous vision."[5]

In Italy, the first step in the direction first undertaken by Nochlin came a few years later, in 1976, thanks to the artist Simona Weller, who wrote *Il complesso di Michelangelo, ricerca sul contributo dato dalla donna all'arte italiana del Novecento* ("The Michelangelo Complex: Research into the Contribution Made by Women to Twentieth-Century Italian Art") for the publisher La Nuova Foglio Editrice in Macerata. In this text, Weller aims to dismantle the atavistic sense of inferiority of women artists in relation to male creative genius, and she does so through a field survey, a sort of census on the professional and social condition of women working in the artworld in Italy. In the spring of the following year, the book would lead to an exhibition of the same title at the gallery in Via Giulia in Rome, which presented the work of forty Roman women artists in chronological order, from the early twentieth century up to the most recent trends of the 1970s.[6] As Weller's operation shows, while for male artists there was a certain ease in gaining visibility and recognition in institutional and academic spaces, for women access to exhibition opportunities was more problematic. While it is true that, as Virginia Woolf argued, "A woman must have money and a room of her own if she is to write fiction,"[7] to enter the artworld as a protagonist, she instead needs to step out of the domestic space and conquer exhibition spaces, the press and critical debate, all while maintaining social credibility and authority. But how can female artists, critics, and curators conquer spaces if they find every entrance barred by a longstanding and diehard male hegemony?

We need to start somewhere, and this may be done from the interstices, from minor realities and sporadic yet fundamentally enlightened outlooks. The independent circuits, in this context, become a place of expression and visibility for women artists: less institutional, more informal and anti-hierarchical, they offer a welcoming and inclusive environment in which to share experiences and support each other in the struggle for emancipation, as much in art as in society at large. At an early stage, the data were certainly not encouraging. In the context of the Bologna scene, it is worth mentioning that even in the case of realities such as Galleria Studio G7 and Studio Cavalieri—founded by pioneers such as Ginevra Grigolo and Adriana Cavalieri, who entered the world of private galleries in the early 1970s not without a certain degree of difficulty—the presence of women in exhibitions appears to be rather meager: between fifteen and twenty percent of the many artists who have exhibited there over the years. And we are talking about virtuous examples linked to the world of Bologna's private galleries, places that have always addressed an international market rather than local collecting, and that have promoted the most innovative of approaches, even in the case of works that are not easily commodified.

In the storm of the Bologna feminist movement, amid militant, playful and provocative approaches, the 1970s saw the proliferation of street performances and small publishing phenomena, such as the single issue of the Dada-esque fanzine *Siamo isteriche...*, published in 1976 by the Collettivo femminista bolognese, as outlined in the documentary *Io sono femminista!*, made in 2019 by Teresa Rossano and promoted by the "Francesco Lorusso—Carlo Giuliani" Movement Documentation Center in Bologna.[8]

Throughout these years, independent spaces run by women, such as La Tregenda and the Librellula bookstore, popped up around the city. Founded in 1976 by Syusy Blady, La Tregenda was very short-lived (about six months), but it still managed to create high-level cultural evenings, offering music, theater, and performance, to which only women had access. As the founder says, "We were organizing shows and parties, and the space was the upshot of my previous political and feminist experience. We tried to develop a place where women could meet, become self-aware and develop [...] their creative vein."[9] The contribution of Librellula was also fundamental: a historic women's bookstore in Bologna, established in March 1977 in Strada Maggiore by a group of women belonging to the experience of the Bolognese feminist collectives, which in the same year of its opening staged the Festival del teatro femminista ("Feminist Theater Festival")—among the first cultural events for women—holding presentations and debates on group productions arising from groups of self-awareness, such as *Equilibrismi*: a documentary and photographic collection linked to crossdressing as a form of discovery, which Donatella Franchi worked on with her own collective between 1977 and 1981, yet which, for a number of reasons, would never be published.

These were operations devoid of any idea of authorship, in which every form of creativity was embraced without hierarchies of value.[10] In the meantime, on institutional circuits there was still great unwillingness to talk about female art: emblematic is the case of the famous exhibition *L'altra metà dell'avanguardia*, proposed by Lea Vergine to Franco Solmi for the GAM in Bologna as early as 1975, and which would instead see the light only in 1980 in Milan.[11]

The encounter between art and gender issues often leads to conflicts and contradictions: while always reasoning from a perspective of difference and contextualizing each experience and trend, it is a fact that, for the most part, female artists working in the years of the struggles for emancipation differed from male artists in the themes that characterize their work, tending to focus more on women's experiences and including themes related to gender identity, social issues and women's traditional roles in society.[12] Suffice to think of the ways in which the artist's own body is expressed, exposed (or lacerated) in works such as those of Renate Bertlmann, Gina Pane, or Marina Abramović: artists who went on to the International Performance Week and who were certainly sources of inspiration for the Bologna art community and for the emergence of new practices around the city. A fairly recent example of how they contributed to a gendered reading of performance is *Significato*: the inaugural action of the Musée de L'OHM, founded by Chiara Pergola in 2009, in which the work "becomes" Abramović's body in the renowned performance *Rhythm 0* (1974).[13]

Built on the limits of physical, psychological and emotional resistance, in these kinds of operations, the use of the body serves to reveal the ambiguities of its reading in the social sphere and the direct relationship between art, desire, and violence. It is these themes that find space and become the medium of these female artists who—united by the same sociopolitical substrate—simply seek to give voice to their personal experiences, asking questions about themselves, their identity, and their place in society. According to Raffaella Perna, at the time, the women artists "employed the body not only as an expressive vehicle, but as an active tool of political action, generating a symbiosis between ethics and aesthetics aimed at a complete redefinition of the very concept of gender."[14]

Let's take a step back. In the 1960s and 1970s, as is well known, Italy was a hotbed of feminist movements. As Fiamma Lussana notes, feminism in Italy was a social and cultural phenomenon in opposition to the political context in which it was couched. The women's political organizations that emerged during the Resistance, along the lines of a trend shared with many of the American and European feminist movements, promoted formal equality between the sexes and, as a result, enforced laws to protect women: an example is Law 1204 of December 30, 1971, which foresaw reduced hours and specific tasks for female workers and mothers. These kinds of measures, for Italian feminists, served only to legitimize a male political order that was "neutral and universal by definition"[15] and which endorsed already-engrained stereotypes, imprisoning women in their conventional social roles. It was not until the second half of the 1970s that feminist collectives began to approach institutions and the radical left, not without difficulties and irreconcilable stances.[16] The equality/standardization binomial is the basis on which Italian feminist movements were declined in that period, even in the sphere of artistic research (and its criticism). However, we are not talking about a common but rather an antithetical line, at least in most cases.

Carla Lonzi—to take the best known and most emblematic example—exemplifies a radical discontinuity between art and feminism, both through her writings (from which the repressed link between the two inexorably emerges) and in her decision to abandon art criticism in favor of social engagement. According to Giovanna Zapperi, in Lonzi's view, "the autonomy of the feminist subject is based on the rejection of culture as an ideology and form of power that encompasses all aspects of social relations, particularly in terms of how they help to imprison female subjectivity within a set of roles and identities."[17] The Rivolta Femminile collective and its sister publishing house Scritti di Rivolta Femminile—which the critic founded in Rome in 1970, together with Elvira Banotti and Carla Accardi—emerged from the difficulty (and ensuing frustration) of the three to manage to position themselves exclusively and professionally in the artworld, and promoted the radical rejection of dominant notions of creativity as a liberating practice for women.[18]

In her professional role as an art critic, Lonzi developed a growing impatience with the detachment, paternalism and notion of authority characteristic of her male colleagues. This rejection had already been externalized years earlier in the article "La solitudine del critico" ("The Loneliness of the Critic") published in *Avanti!* in 1963, which led her to take an interest in artists understood as people rather than merely in the works they produced.[19] Participation—as with the interviews in *Autoritratto* ("Self-Portrait," 1969)—thus becomes a means to allow her to transcend the role of the passive observer, a spectator excluded from the creative process who can be ambivalently identified with both critic and woman, since, as Donatella Franchi observes, in the patriarchal society on which the artworld also feeds, "The woman has the role of the neutral counterpart *par excellence*. She witnesses the creative gestures of the man who needs her as a mirror of his creative self without acknowledging hers, and she seeks the male partner, the male artist, as her true interlocutor."[20]

Yet why is it so hard for women to achieve the same notoriety and credibility as their male colleagues? What creates this gap between the two genders? This, as we know, is still openly debated. It is interesting, for example, that Emanuela De Cecco draws attention to how in the 1970s the privileging of more participatory manifestations in art disadvantaged women, when it is precisely thanks to them that relational and collective art practices have flourished for decades. We may now say that while art leans ever less toward a unilateral view of the world in favor of a multiplicity of visions in relation to each other, this is thanks to the presence of women, to their perseverance in practices focused not only on the final result, but which valorize an ever-shared path. At the same time, we might also say that, in that same period, a certain part of art bound up in behavior became highly politicized, drawing on aspects of "spectacularity," creating a gap with the expression of subjectivity and introspection to the total disadvantage of women artists, especially those who used typically feminine and affective themes, media, and materials.

This prejudice, which has always been rooted in a reading that De Cecco believes to be still bound up in that of Vasari—i.e. based on an interpretation of art history from the point of view of the "genius"—caused a veil of censorship to fall over the work of female artists, the significance of which was reevaluated only in retrospect (as was the case, for example, with Maria Lai and Marisa Merz). The scholar writes:

> The climate of the 1970s, transferred to the sphere of art, privileged artists interested in involving the public, working on the social dimension and opened to women artists, by culture and tradition more sensitive to the subjective sphere: two paths both fraught with pitfalls. Women artists interested in the dynamics of personal experience and the everyday dimension were relegated to a secondary role; others, on the other hand, opted for issues related to their own role in society, shifting their interest more to the contents than to the linguistic development of their work.[21]

In short, at the time there was no getting away from the "Michelangelo complex" Simona Weller spoke of. No path was safe for women artists, and feminism, in its complex declination, proved to be the other side of the ostracism to be fought to find one's place in the world.

Decidedly less antagonistic and repulsive positions than Lonzi's and ones more inclined to favor "gendered" art were represented in that decade by influential female protagonists of art history. Among them, it is worth mentioning the gallery owner Romana Loda and the artists Anna Oberto and Mirella Bentivoglio (although the list is much longer), among the most active promoters of feminist art, and who are credited with theorizing and staging exhibitions of only women artists that, regardless of the public and critical response, were able to highlight the strong gap between the male and female presence on the art scene at the time, at a historical moment when—unlike the Anglo-Saxon world, already familiar with Women's Studies—any theoretical debate on the subject was almost entirely lacking in Italy. Loda, a gallerist and curator from Brescia, is unfortunately still largely unknown, and the subject of only a handful of mentions in critical activity related to such themes (among these, the interest shown in recent years by scholars such as Perna stands out).[22] Lea Vergine herself reports that she got the idea of devoting herself to a rereading of art history from a woman's perspective from her, as she told Ester Coen in 2001: "I began to pay greater attention to women's work when at an exhibition held by Romana Loda in Brescia, a historical exhibition, someone—perhaps Boetti's wife—said to me 'you have written so much about women artists—why don't you take a serious look at this issue?'"[23]

The exhibition Vergine is referring to here is *Magma. Rassegna internazionale di donne artiste* at Oldofredi Castle, near Brescia, in three editions between 1975 and 1977. In the catalogue of the third edition, the curator defines this exhibition and the previous one, *Coazione a mostrare* (1974), not to be considered merely as exclusively feminist exhibitions, since the women artists involved had to meet precise selection criteria. On the other hand, Bentivoglio underlines she is not against feminist exhibitions but simply warns of their greatest risks.[24] The "pink ghettos" issue is a nodal point here. As already mentioned, since women artists at the time were precluded from an active role in the institutional artworld and thus from any full recognition of their work, the reaction to this censorship makes their relationship with the movement related to the emancipation of women very complex and, paradoxically, often distances them from it. Thus, the rejection of a gendered reading in art prevails on the part of some women artists who fear thus being cut off from higher-level artistic debates. For example, this is the case of the exhibition curated by Bentivoglio in 1972 at the Centro Tool in Milan, entitled *Esposizione Internazionale di Operatrici Visuali* ("International Exhibition of Female Visual Workers"). Anna Oberto was asked to write an introductory text to the exhibition, published as a postcard text in the tenth issue of the magazine *Ana Eccetera* as part of the "Anacultural Feminist Manifesto." As the author says:

> Ugo Carrega of the Centro Tool in Milan had long been thinking of hosting a women-only exhibition. When in 1971 Bentivoglio proposed this extraordinary collection of works by international women artists to him, Carrega, who had been our editor, asked me to write an introductory text. With the title "Why an exhibition of only women?," it was an opportunity to declare my (ideological) attitude toward art as a bargaining chip, against the marginalization of women in culture, and also my elaborations on women's language, paralleling the political movement of women's liberation that was beginning to surface at the time with the liberation from male-coded language of new visual writing to signify one's identity.[25]

Despite the fact that *Esposizione Internazionale di Operatrici Visuali* was perfectly in keeping with the desire to raise awareness of the issue of discrimination against women artists, it was contested by them, and a fair part of those called upon to exhibit declined the invitation and labeled the exhibition as "sexist," claiming—as Anne Marie Sauzeau Boetti reported—that "art can be good or bad, but it has no gender."[26] Although what these women artists objected to is true, it is appropriate to contextualize that statement through what US feminist critic Lucy Lippard wrote in 1976:

> "My art has no gender" is a common statement. Of course art has no gender, but artists do. We are only now recognizing that those "stereotypes," those emphases on female experience are positive, not negative characteristics. It is not the quality of our femaleness that is inferior, but the quality of a society that has produced such a viewpoint.[27]

Bentivoglio's project was later replicated in several galleries in Italy, at Columbia University in New York, and at the São Paulo Museum of Art in Brazil, until it landed at the 1978 Venice Biennale with the exhibition *Materializzazione del linguaggio* at the Magazzini del Sale at the Zattere in Venice, where the work of eighty Italian and international women artists was presented. According to Arianna Di Genova, there Bentivoglio "claimed the primogeniture of women in shaping the world, in enshrining reality through manipulation and semantic capacity. In the very special exhibition, she grafted the women artists' experiments onto graphic transcriptions and anonymous evidence, proceeding toward the recognition of a 'metalanguage' underpinning women's production."[28] The exhibition at the Biennale was plagued with troubles: there was little time to organize it, difficulties in the reception of the works to be exhibited (particularly from the Soviet bloc, from where works by emerging women artists had been sent, and through which the curator intended to give voice to those living a situation of repression) and it also suffered from the choice of a venue somewhat off the beaten track. Moreover, critics tended to ignore it because of its supposedly "separatist" nature. In actual fact, the experience marked a milestone toward the evolution of female incidence in the artworld, for it was the first recognition granted to militant women artists in institutional spaces and circuits. It is no coincidence that she was recently honored by Cecilia Alemani in the 2022 Venice Biennale, *The Milk of Dreams*, when an anastatic reprint of the 1978 catalogue was also published.[29]

After the 1970s, we come to what Bentivoglio herself called "the reflux decade."[30] Indeed, in the 1980s, the feminist theme seemed to grind to a standstill. As Francesca Della Ventura notes:

> With the dissolution of the second feminist wave and the political changes that took place in the late 1970s and early 1980s—not only in Italy with the consolidation of Bettino Craxi's Socialist Party, but also in the rest of present-day Europe, with François Mitterrand in France, Margaret Thatcher in England, and Helmut Kohl in Germany—the issue of the active participation of citizens (including women) in politics was seen to take a back seat, and as a result, the artistic research that had been nourished by social contestations over the previous decades also diminished, especially from a feminist perspective.[31]

Compared to the previous decade, this was a historical period that changed the course of many aspects of artmaking. In particular, in institutionalized exhibition spaces, the balance between critics, curators, gallery owners and artists altered (to the distinct disadvantage of the latter). The art critic became rolled into one with the product he intended to sell to the public, making it an emanation of himself: an example of this is the article that Achille Bonito Oliva published in November 1979 in *Flash Art*, identifying himself with "his" Transavanguardia, just as Gustave Flaubert identified himself with Madame Bovary ("La Transavanguardia ç'est moi!"). The planetary success of his project can only confirm that, at that time, this was still the right formula in market terms, given the demise of ideological art and the onset of Reaganist hedonism. If the Transavanguardia was the upshot of a "morganatic" marriage between Pablo Picasso and Marcel Duchamp, heaven forbid what women might possibly have had to do with it.

However, the 1980s represent more than just a step backward for Gender Studies. Non-profit spaces once again manage to put their alternative onto the streets, and in this context, Bologna was a pioneer. Also thanks to the contribution of student movements and a cooperative municipal administration, around the turn of the 1980s, the city experienced a period that was as difficult in political and social terms as it is magical in the construction of a sort of urban mythology that sees it as the crossroads of the most innovative cultural manifestations. Founded in 1978, Cassero was one of the first alternative centers in Italy, establishing itself as an important meeting and support point for the LGBTQIA+ community in Bologna and beyond.[32] In 1980, its granting of an official venue in the city thanks to Mayor Renato Zangheri was an unprecedented moment, marking the abandonment of a state of invisibility which the LGBTQIA+ community had always been accustomed to. As Daniele Del Pozzo recalls, "The militants publicly displayed their identities and desires—in the squares, in the newspapers, and in the offices of the city hall—putting their faces and bodies into it. This conscious, public and political use of one's body did not arise by chance and no doubt descended from earlier feminist demonstrations."[33]

Born as a place of refuge and solidarity for LGBTQIA+ people in the face of prevailing discrimination and ostracism, the Cassero was also an active reference point on the role of prevention and against the stigmatization of AIDS, when the issue was still shrouded in the censorship of bourgeois respectability. From the outset—and this is not a minor aspect— it also had a documentary role: the construction of an archive and library proposed very early on in the minutes of the board meetings, reflecting an iron will to tell a story within a story in which citizens could mirror themselves. "Today we talk about decolonization," says Sara De Giovanni, "but there was an attempt even then, in some way, to decolonize the city's cultural contexts from a hetero-normative notion."[34] This Bolognese reality, the first and only one of its kind in Italy, effectively used culture to bring citizens closer to what until then had been considered only a minority, a nomadic reality that was slowly gaining its place within the city walls. It would take two years for the LGBTQIA+ community to expunge its historic headquarters in the gates of Porta Saragozza: it would do so in grand style on July 26, 1982, with an inaugural parade made up of rings, the distribution of candy, and a memorable dance on the terrace with Sandra Soster, then the city's Councilor for Culture.

As Stefano Casi noted, "The birth of the Cassero occurred on the wave of that imaginative, alternative, voluntaristic and sometimes bungled thinking of the 1970s, but it already contained the sense and object of what has only in recent years become increasingly clear: the return from insurrection to integration, both as an idea and as a goal."[35]

In Bologna in 1981, the neon gallery was also founded on the idea of a group of young students as an independent exhibition space that, over its thirty-year history, created an unparalleled model of cultural exchange and promotion outside institutional circuits (and logics). Despite feeling the brunt of "post '77" Bologna, from the very beginning, neon managed to turn to the present, always veering toward experimentation. More than just a gallery, it was a true community in which artists, critics, curators and collaborators interacted on the same level. Gino Gianuizzi, one of the creators of the project, tells how it all came about through friendship with Stefano Delli, Valeria Medica, Antonia Ruggeri, and Maurizio Vetrugno, "because we liked each other and loved spending time together, and so imagining a shared place and project seemed an exciting prospect."[36] Neon immediately became a sounding board for many emerging artists, including female voices later established in institutional exhibition circles as well. This was the case of Eva Marisaldi, Antonella Mazzoni, Patrizia Giambi, and Mili Romano, among others, not to mention the critic Francesca Alinovi who served—in the words of its founder—as a "catalyst," right from the foundation of the space up until her untimely death. As Gianuizzi states, "Francesca entered neon on the day of the opening and we immediately felt a liking for each other. She sensed the same air she had breathed on her first trips to explore the New York scene."[37] And Alinovi would be followed by many curators over the years.[38]

As far as women artists are concerned, it was Marisaldi in particular who had a sort of partnership with neon: she first participated in 1987, while still a student at the Academy of Fine Arts in Bologna, in a series of group shows dedicated to the new generations of Italian and international artists, with which neon inaugurated its new season following the move to its new headquarters in Via Avesella. In 1990, she held her first solo show, *ee*, curated by Roberto Daolio, and with the latter, who had also been her professor at the Academy, she participated the following year in the exhibition *Nuova Officina Bolognese* at the GAM in Bologna, presenting the installation *Scatola di Montaggio*: a work that has remained emblematic for the peculiar ways used by the artist to narrate the difficulties in and, at the same time, the urgency of communicating with others.[39] In 1993, in the neon spaces, Marisaldi made *La portata umana è nulla* ("The human reach is nothing"), producing a three-meter-deep well set between the two floors of the gallery filled with quicksand. An installation as daring as it is evocative, proving once again how this exhibition space was ready to "take risks," creating situations on the edge of safety, disorienting yet extremely suggestive. For Elisabetta Modena, who gave an enthusiastic account of it in the catalogue *NO, NEON, NO CRY*, observing this abyss within an exhibition space "represented a fundamental moment, not only in the history of the artist and the gallery, but also in that of Italian art."[40]

The forms of expression with which this artist and colleagues of her generation operated led on to the typical climate of the 1990s, given by the overcoming of postmodern aesthetics in favor of a return to the object and interest in mass-media communication. In Gianni Romano's words, "Since the many artistic movements that came to the fore in the early-twentieth century were characterized by a desire to break with the past, the non-movements of the late-twentieth century seem to be characterized by a decisive desire to open up to the future."[41] Also in progress was the theoretical debate between art and feminism, which on the eve of the new millennium finally began to institutionalize studies on women artists, albeit with all the difficulties that academia has always had with novelties. In Bologna, these were the days of artist-run spaces, independent, non-profit venues with a hybrid nature, such as Il Graffio on Via Sant'Apollonia, frequented by feminist self-awareness groups since the late 1970s and run from 1994 onwards by artist and lecturer Anteo Radovan. Until its closure in 2002, Il Graffio was a training ground for up-and-coming artists, often students at the Academy. Among them was Claudia Losi, an artist and curator with a multidisciplinary approach who addresses issues related to nature, the body and the female sphere. In perfect harmony with the creatives of the previous two decades, the artist adopts participatory practices and uses organic materials such as wool, fur or leather to investigate relationships with private spaces and intimate places. Like other women artists of her generation (I am thinking here of Sabrina Mezzaqui, with whom she shared the experience of Il Graffio), Losi challenges cultural and social conventions and fosters reflections on femaleness and its relationship with nature and the surrounding environment.

The projects carried out by women artists in this space are often based on the idea of exchange as a form of liberation, just as happened in feminist self-awareness circles. An example of this is *Andata e Ritorno*, a group exhibition created on the occasion of Bologna 2000 European Capital of Culture: conceived by Federica Manfredini and Donatella Franchi in 1997, this female "mail art" in which a packing box travels between female artists who use it to exchange works, was a useful experience in terms of interweaving relationships with female artists from other cities.

The cultural associations and artist residencies Nosadella.due headed by Elisa Del Prete,[42] and Novella Guerra by Annalisa Cattani have also always favored discursive rather than object-based practices and shared creative processes, such as *To walk is easy. Just go*, for Art City Bologna in 2014, at the conclusion of South African artist and activist Kyla Davis's residency program on issues of social and environmental justice. This type of approach to artistic production, accepted at long last, demonstrates that through the breaking down of the established categories that had hegemonized previous decades, the diversity and heterogeneity of women's voices is fostered once more, and they again look to the activism of those who preceded them. However, feminist discourse is no longer the one practiced in the years of social contestation, and while building on the thinking of the generations from two decades earlier, it is being put back into play by looking at the present, at globalization and the prevailing forms of hybridization from which expressivity can no longer be disregarded. At last, speaking of genres as the result of superstructures, and thus without denying or emphasizing them, we can look more transparently at women's artistic production and make the words of artist Mona Lisa Tina our own:

> Artistic approaches and the expressive potential of women's art, as we know, are as numerous as women artists themselves. What is interesting is that the critics of feminism, who prefer to avoid the debate about the mechanisms of society and the "war" between the sexes, argue that "good art" has no gender; on the contrary,

contemporary critics emphasize that gender, which always has a role, should not be considered a given but a social superstructure. Perhaps none of the views has or has had such a major influence on the awareness and emotional and psychic mechanisms that drive a woman *to be* an artist and not *to become* an artist.[43]

1   Linda Nochlin, "Why Have There Been No Great Women Artists?," *ARTnews* 69, No. 9 (January 1971).

2   For a rereading of Nochlin's text, see the preface by Maria Antonietta Trasforini to the Italian edition *Perché non ci sono state grandi artiste?*, trans. by Jessica Perna (Rome: Castelvecchi, 2015); see also Giovanna Zapperi, "L'Arte non è neutra," *Il Manifesto* (February 27, 2015): https://ilmanifesto.it/larte-non-e-neutra.

3   Maria Antonietta Trasforini, "Lontane da dove. Artiste fra centri e periferie nei mondi dell'arte," in *Arte-mondo. Storia dell'arte, storie dell'arte*, Emanuela De Cecco (ed.) (Milan: Postmedia Books, 2010), 48.

4   Chiara Zamboni, "Momenti radianti," in Luisa Muraro, Wanda Tommasi, Chiara Zamboni, *Approfittare dell'assenza. Punti di avvistamento sulla tradizione* (Naples: Liguori, 2002), 171–85.

5   Mariella Pasinati, "Grandi artiste, ipotesi di genealogie femministe," *Letterate Magazine, SIL – Società Italiana delle Letterate*, No. 104, (August 4, 2014), https://www.societadelleletterate.it/2014/07/5995.

6   See Laura Iamurri, "Femmes artistes italiennes du XXe siècle: Il complesso di Michelangelo, Roma 1977," *Artl@s Bulletin* 8, No. 1 (Spring 2019), https://core.ac.uk/reader/220148380.

7   Virginia Woolf, *A Room of One's Own* (London: Hogarth Press, 1929). The reference to the English writer, now a cornerstone of feminism, is not accidental, for it concerns the relationships between writing and the visual arts that emerge from collective practices. The conversation circles that Woolf, her sister, the artist Vanessa Bell, and the two brothers Thoby and Adrian Stephen held in their London drawing room in the early twentieth century were a form of avant-garde art in stark contrast to other coeval movements, and represented an example of mutual listening without gender hierarchies, understood both as male and female genders and as hierarchies of artistic forms of expression. See Donatella Franchi, "La novità fertile," in *Matrice. Pensiero delle donne e pratiche artistiche*, Donatella Franchi (ed.) (Milan: Libreria delle donne di Milano, 2004), 13–32.

8   See the interview with the director in: Serenella Calderara, "Perché dire 'Io sono femminista' fa ancora paura," in *Left*, (October 30, 2019): https://left.it/2019/10/30/perche-dire-io-sono-femminista-fa-ancora-paura/. On the topic of hysteria, see also Maria Antonietta Trasforini, "Costruzioni nell'isteria," in Uliana Zanetti (ed.), *Autoritratti. Iscrizioni del femminile nell'arte italiana contemporanea*, exhibition catalogue (Bologna: MAMbo, 2013), 139–41.

9   Oderso Rubini, Andrea Tinti (eds.), *Non disperdetevi. 1977–1982. San Francisco, New York, Bologna, le zone libere del mondo* (Rome: Arcana Libri, 2003), 326.

10 The activities of feminist self-awareness centers at the time revolved between Librellula, the Bologna Centro di documentazione delle donne (Women's Documentation Center, CDD) and the Milan Libreria delle donne (Women's Bookstore). Currently, the CDD is located at Via del Piombo 5 in Bologna, and includes the Italian Women's Library, the Women's History Archive and the Center for Political and Cultural Initiative. It has existed under an agreement between the Associazione Orlando and the City of Bologna since 1983. The Women's Bookstore, on the other hand, is located at Via San Felice 16/a and is run by the feminist and transfeminist association Non Una di Meno Bologna.

11 See Maria Antonietta Trasforini, "Luoghi del femminismo, sconfinamenti e azioni 'performative.' Bologna anni '70," in *La performance a Bologna negli anni '70*, Uliana Zanetti (ed.) (Bologna: Edizioni MAMbo, 2023), 226–35.

12 On the theme of the difficulty for women artists operating during the years of social struggles between art and feminism, see Maria Antonietta Trasforini, "A paso distinto. Arte y feminismo en Italia desde los años setenta," *MODOS: Revista de Història da Arte* 7, No. 2 (May 2023); the interview with the artist Suzanne Santoro in Marta Seravalli, *Arte e femminismo a Roma negli anni Settanta* (Rome: Biblink, 2013), 217–24.

13 The action *Significato* took place at the neon> campobase gallery in Bologna on September 29, 2009. For the occasion, those present were offered cutting instruments (currently held in the vaults of the Musée de l'OHM) with which to intervene on the surface. For a description of the intentions of the artist, see Chiara Pergola, "La forza fisica. Per un#arte femminista globale," *Manastabal. Femminismo materialista* (October 27, 2019): https://manastabalblog.wordpress.com/2019/10/27/la-forza-fisica-per-un-arte-femminista-globale/.

14 Raffaella Perna, *In forma di fotografia. Ricerche artistiche in Italia dal 1960 al 1970* (Rome: DeriveApprodi, 2009), 71.

15 Fiamma Lussana, *Il movimento femminista in Italia. Esperienze, storie, memorie* (Rome: Carocci, 2012), 33.

16 Especially with regard to the theme of abortion linked to Law 194, see Raffaella Perna, *Arte, fotografia e femminismo in Italia negli anni Settanta* (Milan: Postmedia Books, 2013), 7–11.

17 Giovanna Zapperi, "Dialoghi tra creatività e femminismo: letture di Carla Lonzi nell'arte contemporanea," *Narrativa*, No. 37 (2015): 53, http://journals.openedition.org/narrativa/970.

18 Anne Marie Sauzeau Boetti sets out from the same presuppositions as Carla Lonzi, but comes to a different conclusion only a few years later: in her view, the creative power of the woman artist in fact implies the betrayal of the expressive mechanisms of male patriarchal culture, and thus leads towards its radical resignification. See Anne Marie Sauzeau Boetti, "Negative Capability as Practice in Women's Art," *Studio International* 191, No. 979 (1976): 24–25.

19 See Laura Iamurri, *Un margine che sfugge. Carla Lonzi e l'arte in Italia 1955–1970*, (Macerata:

Quodlibet Studio, 2016); Mariasole Garacci, "Sputare sulla critica d'arte. Carla Lonzi e il soggetto imprevisto contro la dialettica," *OperaViva*, (September 19, 2016): https://opera-vivamagazine.org/sputare-sulla-critica-darte/.

20 Franchi, "La novità fertile," 28.

21 Emanuela De Cecco, "Trame: per una mappa transitoria dell'arte italiana femminile degli anni Novanta e dintorni," in Emanuela De Cecco, Gianni Romano (eds.), *Contemporanee. Percorsi e poetiche delle artiste dagli anni Ottanta a oggi* (Milan: Postmedia Books, 2009), 16.

22 See Raffella Perna, "Mostre al femminile: Romana Loda e l'arte delle donne nell'Italia degli anni Settanta," *Ricerche di S/Confine* VI, No. 1 (2015): 143–54.

23 Ester Coen, *Schegge. Lea Vergine sull'arte contemporanea. Intervista di Ester Coen* (Milan: Skira, 2001), 38. I am interested in drawing attention to Lea Vergine's mention of the artist Alighiero Boetti's wife: this is the aforementioned Anne-Marie Sauzeau, who was engaged in those years in the investigation and promotion of female production, interests that are not coincidentally reflected in some of her husband's works, such as *Maschio Femmina* (1973–74), in which the investigation of sexual difference distances him from the "masculine" themes and approaches customary at the time. Boetti's tendency to work collectively and to outsource the factual production of his works is also in line with his rejection of the stereotype of the artist-genius in favor of a vision of the artistic operation as a social phenomenon.

24 See Romana Loda (ed.), *Magma: rassegna internazionale di donne artiste*, exhibition catalogue (Iseo: Castello Oldofredi; Verona: Museo di Castelvecchio, 1975–77).

25 Anna Oberto, Raffaella Perna, "Dare corpo alla parola. Intervista ad Anna Oberto," *OperaViva* (July 18, 2016): https://operavivamagazine.org/dare-corpo-alla-parola/.

26 Sauzeau Boetti, "Negative Capability as Practice in Women's Art," 24.

27 Lucy Lippard, *From the Center. Feminist Essays on Women's Art* (New York: Dutton, 1976), 147–48.

28 Arianna Di Genova, "Mirella Bentivoglio, il corpo delle parole," in Maura Pozzati (ed.), *Artiste della critica* (Mantua: Corraini Edizioni, 2015), 50.

29 The artist's presence at the Venice Biennale 2022 was part of the capsule called *Corpo orbita*, in which Cecilia Alemani featured the work *Storia del monumento* that Mirella Bentivoglio produced with Annalisa Alloatti in 1968. The work consists of a folder of six lithographs defined by the artist as the very symbol of the "fall of the fetish," understood as the masculine logos symbol.

30 *Post Scriptum. Artiste in Italia tra linguaggio e immagine negli anni '60 e '70 (VIII Biennale Donna di Ferrara)*, Anna Maria Fioravanti Baraldi (ed.), exhibition catalogue (Ferrara: Padiglione d'Arte Contemporanea, 1998), 4.

31 Francesca Della Ventura, "Gli anni Ottanta e il lento revisionismo dei femminismi: l'Italia transavanguardista e la *Subkultur* tedesca," *Flash Art* (May 20, 2021): https://flash---art.it/2021/05/gli-anni-ottanta-e-il-lento-revisionismo-dei-femminismi/.

32 See Stefano Casi (ed.), *Teatro in delirio: la vera storia del K.G.B. & B.-Kassero gay band & ballet*, *Quaderni di critica omosessuale*, No. 7, Cassero Documentation Center, Bologna, 1989; for a reconstruction of the history of the Cassero, see also the documentary produced by Andrea Adriatico in 2015, *Torri, checche e tortellini. Appunti per una storia senza storia dell'omosessualità del '900*.

33 "Il Cassero. Performare il genere, conversazione con Sara De Giovanni e Daniele del Pozzo," in Zanetti, *La performance a Bologna negli anni '70*, 330.

34 Ibid.

35 Stefano Casi, "Le checche di Bologna che cambiarono la storia," *casicritici* (June 14, 2015): https://casicritici.com/2015/06/14/le-checche-di-bologna-che-cambiarono-la-storia/.

36 Valentina Rossi, "Gino Gianuizzi racconta la galleria neon e la mostra che ne ripercorre la mitica storia," *ZERO Bologna* (July 20, 2022): https://zero.eu/it/persone/gino-gianuizzi-neon/.

37 Gino Gianuizzi, Eleonora Mariani (eds.), *NO, NEON, NO CRY*, exhibition catalogue (Bologna: MAMbo, 2022), 5.

38 Out of around 300 events, including actions, shows and series, in the complete list available in the chronology at the end of the catalogue, eighty-three curators are listed.

39 A significant recollection of this work is given by collector Giorgio Fasol, who had come into contact with the artist precisely through neon and who purchased the work. See Gianuizzi, Mariani, *NO, NEON, NO CRY*, p. 99.

40 Ibid., 137. On the work of Eva Marisaldi, see also Elisabetta Modena, "Eva Marisaldi, Dopolavoro. Frammenti di realtà al Premio Suzzara (1948–2013)," *Ricerche di S/Confine* VII, No. 1 (2016), 110–30.

41 Romano, "Pratiche mediali nell'arte delle donne: 1977–2000," in De Cecco, Romano, *Contemporanee*, 46.

42 Over the course of its decade of activity (between 2006 and 2016) Nosadella.due brought more than sixty artists and curators to Bologna and offered events, performances, workshops, screenings, and lectures focused primarily on the processes the artwork undergoes prior to its finalization. See http://www.nosadelladue.com.

43 Mona Lisa Tina, "Il linguaggio transgender dell'arte e il suo eterno femminino," in Lori Adragna, *Il corpo delle donne #1 [Archivio di una curatrice di performance]* (Rome: Inside Art Autori, 2018), 117.

THE STAGING OF INDEPENDENCE

Davide Da Pieve

The love-hate relationship that so-called independent spaces have with official institutions could be the lowest common denominator of a broad and multifaceted—though still rather understudied—category. Whether it is a feeling more akin to hatred or love matters little, for in both cases, it gives rise to the kind of rapport that determines the *raison d'être* of these places that, the closer we try to observe, the less they seem to us to be truly independent and detached from the intricate fabric on which artworlds grow. Starting from the way of "being, talking and gesticulating" of the independent spaces in Bologna and of those who frequented them between the 1970s and the start of the new millennium, on the basis of the sociological approach elaborated by Erwin Goffman,[1] this text will present a number of theories and results arising from the study of the interaction between the various groups that animated some of these spaces, in order to try to understand what their role was in society and, in particular, in the artworld. Such an exercise is particularly complex because the sources available to us are few and far between: indeed, the present volume aims to go about systematically filling this great void, until now only partially filled thanks to the documentary videos made by Emanuele Angiuli[2] and to a limited number of publications and exhibitions. Our sources consist largely of personal accounts, self-produced film and VHS footage, unable to provide us with a complete and truthful picture as they are inevitably incomplete. One of the most interesting and original aspects of this research consists precisely in having to deal with unusual documents typical of that historical period—such as flyers, hand-drawn posters, pamphlets, and fanzines—through which the climate of the time may be sensed both visually and linguistically, but which still leave numerous questions to be answered through the reconstruction of events.

Very few of these places have maintained orderly archives, especially those dating back to the pre-digital period. Take, for example, the Traumfabrik: a house occupied in April 1976 that, within a few years, had become a point of reference for many in the city and to which, in 2007, an exhibition was dedicated in the spaces of neon—at that time already neon>campobase—thanks to the fortuitous discovery of a box containing four hundred drawings produced by those who had passed through the place. "One morning, Piera [Zaganelli] comes into the office and hands me a box with the words *Disegni di Huber* ['Drawings by Huber'] written on it in marker, and tells me that Alessandra Andrini gave it to her," declares Gianpietro Huber, one of the main protagonists of the space along with Filippo Scozzari and Giorgio Lavagna, in the excerpt of an article.[3] With this box, "the TRAUMFABRIK file was reopened. The creative chaos of Via Clavature 20, [...] in which Huber and Lavagna bring the project back to life by making it available to a new generation of creative extremists,"[4] reads the closing passage of the press release of the exhibition staged by neon>campobase.

These two short quotes show us that in some cases even the founders of the spaces are not aware of the whereabouts of their materials, but more importantly it makes us realize how much the texts accompanying the exhibitions fuel a certain narrative that, inevitably, influences the perception and meaning of what we observe: for example, what exactly is a "creative extremist"?

In this study, we will not adopt an ontological approach; rather, we will try to understand how such definitions contribute to the creation of the role of these spaces, and what influence such meanings exert on the perception of the artistic activities they offer. The focus will therefore be on the mediating materials produced by Bologna's independent spaces: we will not limit ourselves to the materials accompanying the exhibitions, but we will turn to all that documentation—predominantly textual in our case, but which may also be non-textual, as in the case of videos, audio recordings, etc.—available and produced by exhibition spaces primarily for promotion purposes, and which inevitably adds meaning and enriches the audience's experience within the space.

In the above-cited case, in the short press release text launching the Traumfabrik exhibition from neon>campobase, we are confronted with what Jérôme Glicenstein refers to as "constituent mediations," that is, "all the preliminary writings that lead to the staging of an exhibition"[5] and that influence the perception of its content. Howard S. Becker previously noted how all cultural workers contribute to the creation of the artwork, especially from a practical point of view.[6] Through a focused reflection on mediation, we come to realize that the role a space plays in society and especially the type of interaction it has with institutions also contributes to the construction of the meaning of what it presents and exhibits.

The first moment in which a space is expressed, what we might call its initial "constituent mediation," is inevitably the document related to its foundation. To set out in search of such a document is to find oneself faced with something different depending on the type of space that produced it. In fact, there are two possibilities: in the case of occupied spaces, most likely, we will be dealing with documents that have no legal value, ephemeral testimonies produced by the occupants (pamphlets, fanzines, posters, banners, etc.); on the other hand, if we are dealing with a space to which an association belongs, we must take into account that the latter, in order to be defined as such and stand out from what is called an "informal group," can only be constituted through a public deed.[7] Clearly, to the materials left by the founders a whole corollary of sources from outside may be added, such as newspaper articles, interviews, memoirs, research and studies conducted retrospectively, through which specific dates and facts may be traced.

It is important to dwell on the nature of the mediation documents because, for example, neon as a cultural association had to draw up a deed of incorporation,[8] entailing the constitution of a formal group and consenting to a whole series of legal aspects to be respected. Another detail that should not be overlooked is that, thanks to this document, we know for sure that Gino Gianuizzi, Valeria Medica, Stefano Delli, Antonia Ruggeri, and Maurizio Vetrugno were the founders of the space and that the first three were members of the steering committee—information that is important for historical reconstruction purposes, but also useful to understand who had legal responsibility for the venue. This kind of documentation obviously does not exist in the case of occupied spaces and, indeed, the dynamic of responsibility is totally upturned: those who occupy tend to mask their identities because they are doing something clearly illegal. Hence, the artists who exhibit in these spaces are also infringing the law in some way. The definition of "creative extremist" might perhaps now already be clearer, since, as the Traumfabrik was an occupied house, this binomial indicates not only a particular kind of creativity from an aesthetic point of view, but also the incidence of the peculiarities of the space in the kind of creativity that went on there.

Beginning with these aspects—in some ways taken for granted, but fundamental in order to get to the heart of the arguments that we intend to address—the role that an occupied space plays is certainly very fascinating, absolutely authentic and genuine, for in the name of their urgencies and ideals, people are willing take a clear stance and put themselves at some degree of risk, consistently drawing on words such as "independence," "autonomy," or "alternative." More specifically, it is possible for such spaces to take on this role of genuine independence because they are organized through the formulation of constitutive rules, i.e., each responds to its own law and not to that of the state. As John Searle explains, the rules of chess—and, more generally, the rules devised for a game—are instituted specifically for that particular purpose, and are thus definable as constitutive rules; unlike normative rules, on the other hand, i.e. those that configure something that already has its own stable manner of functioning.[9] Despite the fact that cultural associations, just like museums and galleries, have the power to constitute their own internal regulations and to grant wide margins of autonomy to the artists and subjects hosted, organizing themselves internally however they prefer (even on the basis of the number of staff and their own needs), in Italy their functioning remains governed by the Civil Code: they are therefore obliged to conform to pre-constituted legal rules, which partially define their entity, identity, and role. For example, cultural associations have a number of obligations and limitations in relation to commercial activities,[10] compliance with or control over which may depend on numerous factors.

The real differences between these two types of places (legal and illegal) lie not so much in the degrees of artistic freedom that can be expressed within them, but rather in the expressions or *façade* that each of these places offers of itself, and thus in the way they are perceived by the public.

In this regard, it is interesting to read that one of neon's founders, Gino Gianuizzi, states: "When we decided to start neon, we didn't really know what we wanted to do,"[11] and that neon corresponds to "a Dadaist/situationist/anarchist action."[12] Dede Auregli recalls "that small but very alternative space,"[13] and it's very easy to find evidence of this kind among the pages of the catalogue of the exhibition *NO, NEON, NO CRY*, held at MAMbo – Museo d'Arte Moderna di Bologna in 2022, or in older publications dedicated to "places of opposition."[14] Neon is outlined for all intents and purposes as an alternative and independent place, both in terms of attitude and artistic proposals.

Angelo Candiano recalls that:

> there was a need for new exhibition spaces to give voice to our generation, one that could critically dissent from certain stereotyped and obsolete positions, while deploying a constructive outlook and in any case adhering to a decidedly altered reality. It was the very recently founded neon gallery in Bologna, along with a handful of others in Italy, that served this function.[15]

This quote is very interesting because it highlights the sense of rupture of this place and, at the same time, it is one of the few texts in the MAMbo exhibition catalogue that talks about neon as a "gallery." In fact, by around the start of the 1990s neon had begun to be defined as a gallery. One of the many reasons for such acknowledgement comes from a series of ambiguous participations that saw neon "take part in Art Basel, Art Frankfurt, Arte Fiera, Artissima, etc."[16] Primarily, it was clearly its participation in Arte Fiera in Bologna in 1990[17] that altered the perception and role of the space. The approach was evidently unlike that of a traditional gallery:

> We would set off in a camper van, loading up both works and artists, and once we arrived in Basel, the camper would become a base for other artists. We imagined the fair as a place to establish relationships and not as an articulation of the market system. [...] Being inside the system meant inserting elements of disruption, without playing by its rules. Needless to say, it was a losing game.[18]

Participation in such events led to neon being "featured among the top galleries in one of *Flash Art*'s periodical rankings, included in a Rai documentary dedicated to the most interesting Italian art galleries," proposing "artists who then go on to enter the orbit of commercial galleries."[19] This proximity to the market, although indeed very particular and never really commercial, earned neon legitimacy in the artworld, despite its proposal of then-unknown young artists and the urgent need to approach the artworld in a new and alternative manner.

Leaving aside value judgments for the moment, we would just like to point out that, contrary to what we have just seen, there is no record of an occupied space participating in art fairs. This is not because the youth of the occupied spaces were less deserving but, most likely, both because the occupiers had no such desire to do so, and because it is easier for a place that lives on the fringes of legality to create its *own* fair with those who share the same rules of the game—with those we might define as being from the "same circuit"—rather than setting up, becoming institutionalized and having the chance to be invited to join an official fair circuit. Such a sudden change would inevitably devalue the *self*—as Erving Goffman puts it[20]—i.e. the personality, the *façade* and thus the role of an occupied space.

And so is this the crossroads shared by many of these occupied spaces: to remain within their own circuit, and thus detached and "absent" from within the artworld? Or to bow down, accept its rules and see their alternative demands legitimized in order to establish new recognized practices?

Of course, there is no single answer to such questions. As recalled by DeeMo, one of the occupants of Isola Nel Kantiere, a space set up inside the construction site of the Arena del Sole Theater, where in 1991, after three years of intense activity, two possibilities had emerged:

> The first was to accept the proposal of the municipality, to take over a space, submitting to its rules, thus becoming institutionalized, founding a cultural association, complete with names, references, etc. Of course, many people rejected the idea of becoming institutionalized out of hand. The alternative was to occupy another space. Isola didn't exactly split in two over the issue, but some Isola members took up the municipality's offer together with others who had become affiliated with the DAMS circles, etc., and opened the space that would later be known as the Link [Project].[21]

From these words, one might think that the following experience, that of Link Project, was an institutionalized entity and therefore less interesting, with a devalued sense of self.

In the editorial of the first volume of the *Link Project House Organ* pamphlet published in 1994—the communication channel through which Link Project would inform its public throughout its existence—we read, "absence of inauguration, of that moment between officialization and the social ritual [...]. Let us speak instead of the initial act of the will to exist [...]. Not a social center, not even a cultural center, much less a youth or post-adolescent or post-senile center. We could speak of a five-year plan, yes of those that were used 'in the good old days.'" They go on to write in the conclusion, "[The birth of the Link Project] is an act of will, we might add, toward the bureaucratic monster with which we ended up being confronted. An act that does not reflect a concluded idea, a precise stance that situates us against the already saturated landscape of cultural-behavioral consumption in Bologna and throughout Italy."[22]

Already in these first few lines, we find all the contradictions and ambiguities necessary for the creation of a very strong and unpredictable personality, which hints at a character that is anything but subject to the few—but decisive—rules that a cultural association must respect. The "self" of this place, according to Goffman's theories, may still be grasped through the unintended aspects of an expression, elements that provide us with a more realistic notion of our interlocutor. As the Canadian sociologist explains:

> Knowing that the individual [spaces in our case, or the identity of a collective] is likely to present himself in a light that is favourable to him, the others may divide what they witness into two parts: a part that is relatively for the individual to manipulate at will, being chiefly his verbal assertions, and a part in regard to which he seems to have little concern or control, being chiefly derived from the expressions he gives off.[23]

The authors of the editorial deny being the product of all the best-known venues at the time, and it is worth noting that all the spaces that appear in the list lay some claim to institutional legitimacy. By contrast, occupied spaces are not mentioned: it is clear that the Link Project is no longer one of them, for there is an agreement between the City of Bologna and the founders,[24] but the failure to mention occupied spaces among the things the Link Project is not "alludes to" a touch of aversion toward the institutional model and, perhaps a willingness to continue pursuing the ethos of the occupied space despite agreements with institutions.

Instead, Link Project would seek to open a third way, in both artistic and political terms. In the Link Project, there is a genuine refusal to hold art exhibitions in the traditional sense and, at the same time, an urgency to open up to happenings and relationships in order to bring to life a unique form of programming, in which space was given over to artists and productions that did not occur in other Bolognese or even Italian venues. The Link Project, drawing on the model of occupied spaces, nevertheless manages to behave as a constitutive and foundational space of new experiences, struggling throughout its years of activity with the administration, with the attempts made to impose rules on it and, indeed, even with itself. It is an alternative and socially recognized institution that cannot digest aspects that it is uncomfortable with, for "the increasingly central problem of identities is one of great substance. They precipitate. [...] But how can substance and lightness be coupled? [...] How not to lose all the substance, cleansing it of what is really unpleasant about it, bound up with the issue of identity, of the clan, of sub-ethnic caste affiliations...."[25]

Reading these words, the other issues of the pamphlet, and aware of the caliber of the experiments and activities proposed at Link Project, we may end up thinking that, paradoxically, the role of an occupied space is much more connoted than that of an associative space, for despite what we might expect, it possesses much more rigid boundaries, a clearer social role and is in so many ways endowed within its own definition, urgencies, and needs: its die-hard identity affords much less room for change. Associative spaces, on the other hand, are heterogeneous spaces *par excellence*, insofar as they may negotiate with and hybridize the definitions they prefer, in exchange for adherence to some basic and loosely defined rules.

An alternative stance is also found in the language adopted by the Link Project, which speaks of itself in the first person plural, as if the space always spoke on behalf of a collective, somehow thus becoming an entity in its own right. It is difficult to find similar documents for museums and galleries of the time, which mostly produce room texts or catalogues, and more rarely editorials in which they tell their own stories. In any case, galleries and museums are very different places of work, which can have very long histories, and are therefore often separate entities from the people who work there. In the Link Project texts, on the other hand, we sense that the people—or rather the collective intelligence that leads it—is at one with the space: "we have made," "we are...."[26]

This overlap between the place and the people who run it is actually a rather common phenomenon among these kinds of spaces, certainly occurring more frequently when they are directed for many years by the same figure. For example, suffice to quickly browse through the recent exhibition catalogue *NO, NEON, NO CRY* to see that such "personification of space" is not limited only to texts: "I discovered not long ago that 'Gino-Neon,' as he was called by everyone, is in actual fact Gino Gianuizzi,"[27] declares Giorgio Fasol, and indeed, Alberto Balletti of the Balletti e Mercandelli duo uses the same binomial: "'Gino Neon' is still synonymous with freedom for me," with an implicit reference to both person and space.[28] Elisa Del Prete also recalls that "neon and 'Gino' were used almost as synonyms,"[29] and even Gianuizzi himself affirms that "talking about neon is paramount to talking about me."[30]

At this point, we notice that among all these places there are as many differences as there are similarities. Neon is very unlike the Link Project, but despite this, the two realities have at least four elements in common (and perhaps even more): they are both cultural associations; they have spaces assigned by the municipality; youth participation (both among the organizers and in the audience) is central; both try to place themselves outside the artworld, while being more or less aware that they are not.

This latter aspect is perhaps the key element to understanding the centrality of the experiences of these two spaces, and how thanks to them, we may perhaps speak of a sort of a "Bolognese model" for the development of Italian and perhaps even foreign alternative spaces. This collision, this clashing encounter, all this love and hate was to make it increasingly common from the 1990s onwards for independent and alternative spaces dedicated to art to stipulate agreements with public administrations, while declaring themselves independent. The role of such spaces is increasingly characterized through their dialogue with the artworld yet, at the same time, a rejection of the latter.

In his book *La vita quotidiana come "gioco di ruolo,"* Giovanni Balducci states that "the social life of the individual, according to Goffman, would take place, therefore, precisely between the frontstage and backstage, so the 'social actor' is called upon not to confuse the two contexts, as this might engender misunderstandings about his/her 'role' and, even, a 'devaluation' of his/her own 'self.'"[31] Perhaps therein lies the ultimate difficulty in describing and grasping the behavior (and the very nature) of alternative spaces within society: these are simultaneously actors and spectators of the artworld, entities with an ambiguous nature insofar as their *façade* embodies an unresolved contradiction that may be more or less evident. As early as 1995, in a Link Project pamphlet, awareness of this conflict is made explicit in a passage by Teatrino Clandestino: "[...] but it's not that I want to reintroduce notions of unawareness which are now all too aware of being so, nor to justify theories of anti-theory—we have come here in pursuit of our anachronism, of our romanticism, as we are pathetically duped by the illusion of grasping the sublime."[32] Perhaps the only way forward is to be illuded, to continue to struggle and not to lose that institutional drive capable of expanding a city's cultural programming and, perhaps, making this society a better place.

Beyond good intentions and hopes, we may thus sense a clear and genuine mutation, a transformation of the role of independent spaces through ruptures created within the implicit traditions or habits that characterize the role of any social actor.

The habits of a social actor—what Goffman refers to as "routines"—are those implicit elements that make us associate the self with a certain category or behavior: a haircut, for example, may make us think that the person follows a certain fashion. The multifacetedness that characterizes independent spaces, in conjunction with the rise of increasingly overt neoliberal policies, meant that a self-managed space moving from the grassroots may be somewhat overlaid and confused with the liberal ideal of individual self-assertion. We may certainly detect a general devaluation of the more idealistic selves and that, most likely, acting independently and alternatively should now be viewed more as a *style* than an *urgency*, a way of posing and presenting things, a very specific role to be played within society rather than as a parallel artistic circuit in which practices are presented as deviant from the way institutions and the dominant hegemony want things done.

The limiting and paradigmatic case of this hypothesis comes from the numerous instances in which institutions have begun to use the binomial "independent spaces" as a label, as if it were a musical genre, rather than an alternative or even adverse ideal to the institutions themselves. In 2003, the Italian Ministry of Culture, then headed by Giuliano Urbani, launched the project *Luoghi del Contemporaneo* to "map and promote the network of contemporary art spaces in Italy."[33] In 2012, under then Minister Lorenzo Ornaghi, the project was radically updated by the Architecture and Contemporary Art Service of the General Directorate for Landscapes, Fine Arts, Architecture and Contemporary Art, and was made available online.

> With this new platform, the General Directorate for Contemporary Creativity aims to recount the changes that have taken place in the geographical distribution of the *Luoghi del Contemporaneo* ("Contemporary Places"). At the same time, the mapping was carried out, organizing the various places on the basis of a typological subdivision that—in addition to the already traditionally recognized spaces—includes independent spaces, corporate museums and a selection of artistic interventions in public and urban spaces.[34]

The short circuit is as glaring as it is interesting and disastrous. To this day, we can consult the platform and see that in the files of Bologna's independent spaces—which include Raum, Adiacenze, Localedue, and Gelateria Sogni di Ghiaccio—three times out of four the word "youth" is stated, but in no case the word "independent." Such an operation merely legitimizes the existence of these places, downplays elements of their "self" and treats them merely as important places for young people and the potential for cultural innovation they bring. As the tradition of such places dictates, it must be young people who go through them, yet legitimizing them and treating them as independent at the same time means perhaps elevating them to official spaces of the precariat: places midway between artistic experimentation and the search for professional recognition. Such an action had something of boomerang effect with regard to the role of these realities, especially for those run and founded by younger people, as legitimizing them in this way probably led to creating internal competition among independent spaces, where autonomy is something more akin to a behavioral style, a label to be proud of, rather than a necessity or a *raison d'être*.

In fact, independent spaces were involved in and invited to official fairs (such as at ArtVerona[35]) and allowed to display their pure and uncorrupted *façade*, despite being presented within the cage of independence. Interestingly, in this manner, the typical stance and approach of occupied spaces re-emerges—i.e. creating their own circuit—but in a completely opposite manner: not a way of acting aimed at self-liberation through the establishment of new rules of the game, but, on the contrary, joining someone else's game, embracing the instrumentalization and transformation of an ideal into a label or mere stylistic exercise.

The comparison with music is exemplary in terms of showing how the role of independent or alternative spaces, whatever they may be, also allows artists and their own achievements to acquire a certain status or absorb a certain style from all the linguistic and symbolic mediations surrounding them. Take for example Aphex Twin, a musician who played a live show also in the spaces of the Bologna-based Link Project in 1995,[36] and who today is a world-renowned artist and brand. The British musician, who grew up professionally between his room and London, the underground city *par excellence*, was able to bring his experimentation to the fore without ever losing that sort of stigma and alternative style, so much so that he himself became the emblem of such an attitude. Despite his enormous success, Aphex Twin will always be part of that underground and alternative world that he in actual fact abandoned conceptually with his first planetary success, in 1992, when he cast the logo of his project all over the world, transforming himself into a brand—just as artists such as Jeff Koons or Damien Hirst were doing at the time, or various other personalities, from Michael Jordan to Puff Daddy, as listed by Naomi Klein in her book *No Logo*.[37]

Perhaps it would be more appropriate to say that independent spaces are places that believed they were such by playing that role in society to perfection, until they realized that their own experimentation and urgencies were interacting with those very dynamics by feeding the very system they wanted to shy away from. As a result, such an approach became a stylistic exercise capable of making people perceive not only a given place, but also everything presented within it, as something capable of maintaining the illusion of being recognized while standing outside the artworld.

Art, whether rooted in museums or outside of them, is itself a commodity—whether material or immaterial—that needs to be acknowledged: being artistic is the status that an object may acquire or lose.[38] Thus, legitimization is a double-edged sword: on the one hand, it lets your experiments be taken seriously; on the other, you risk devaluation as you become part of what you initially eschewed.

Perhaps the importance of the role of alternativists or independents is to be found in their ability to be institutional epicenters of artistic and social novelty, forges of experimentation that lay bare pressing issues that often also renew the way institutions act and behave. In the ability to open up new utopias and horizons lies perhaps the key to independent spaces, in their ability to break boundaries, go beyond genres and above all beyond the idea of preservation, choosing instead to renew and progress. In the second issue of *Link Project* magazine,[39] a passage granted to the Usmis editorial staff for the presentation of its project and Friuli-based space Cjanive—one mindful above all of immigration issues as well as artistic ones—in fact states: "We cannot change the world, or even save it, but from what is lost, we can head toward the impossible." We are thus faced with two sides of the same coin: if a hegemonic art-world did not exist, neither could its alternative.

1 Erving Goffman, *The Presentation of Self in Everyday Life* (1956) (London: Penguin Books, 1990).

2 I refer in particular here to: *Traumfabrik – Via Clavature 20* (2009), *Piccolo gruppo in moltiplicazione* (2015) and *NEON 1981–2011* (2017).

3 Valerio Vigliar, "La Fabbrica dei sogni nella Bologna '77," *XL Repubblica* (February 20, 2012): https://videodrome-xl.blogautore.repubblica.it/page/111/.

4 *Traumfabrik*, exhibition press release, Bologna: neon>campobase, 2007, available at https://1995-2015.undo.net/it/mostra/58634.

5 "[…] médiations constituantes […] tous les écrits préalables conduisant à la réalisation d'une exposition." Jérôme Glicenstein, *L'Art contemporain entre les lignes* (Paris: PUF, 2013), 11.

6 Howard S. Becker, *Art Worlds* (University of California Press: Berkely and Los Angeles, 1982).

7 A public deed for the constitution of a cultural association in the 1980s had to be registered with a notary public; today, it is sufficient to register it with the Inland Revenue Agency.

8 The deed of incorporation of neon is a document that I managed to view thanks to Gino Gianuizzi, who keeps it in his own private archive.

9 See John Searle, *Speech Acts* (Cambridge: Cambridge University Press, 1969); and John Searle, *The Construction of Social Reality* (New York: Free Press, 1995).

10 See articles 14–42 of the Italian Civil Code, which outline the discipline of associations, foundations and committees, both those officially recognized and otherwise.

11 Santa Nastro, "Neon a Modica. La storia della gloriosa galleria bolognese in mostra a LaVeronica", *Artribune* (December 29, 2018): https://www.artribune.com/arti-visive/arte-contemporanea/2018/12/neon-a-modica-la-storia-della-gloriosa-galleria-bolognese-in-mostra-a-laveronica/.

12 Ibid.

13 Gino Gianuizzi, Eleonora Mariani (eds.), *NO, NEON, NO CRY*, exhibition catalogue (Bologna: MAMbo, 2022), 23.

14 In this regard, see the section "Indirizzario e elenco di alcuni luoghi delle opposizioni," in Tommaso Tozzi, *Opposizioni '80. Alcune delle realtà che hanno scosso il villaggio globale* (Milan: Edizioni Amen, 1991), 287.

15 Ibid., 56.

16 Ibid., 5.

17 Ibid., at the end of the book there is a complete list of neon's appearances at art fairs.

18 Ibid., 5.

19 Ibid.

20 Goffman, *The Presentation of Self in Everyday Life*, 32.

21 Sonia Garcia, "Spazi di comunione: Isola Nel Kantiere," *Vice* (October 12, 2015): https://www.vice.com/it/article/6exq3k/spazi-comunione-isola-nel-kantiere-deemo.

22 "Tanto per cominciare…," *Link Project House Organ*, No. 1 (April–May 1994): 1.

23 Goffman, *The Presentation of Self in Everyday Life*, 18.

24 The convention stipulated between the Municipality of Bologna and the Link Project is a document that I was able to view thanks to Daniele Gasparinetti and Silvia Fanti, who keep it in their own private archive.

25 "Tanto per cominciare…," *Link Project House Organ*, No. 1: 1–2.

26 Ibid.

27 Gianuizzi, Mariani, *NO, NEON, NO CRY*, 99.

28 Ibid., 25.

29 Ibid., 83.

30 Ibid., 11.

31 Giovanni Balducci, *La vita quotidiana come "gioco di ruolo." Dal concetto di face in Goffman alla labeling theory della scuola di Chicago* (Milano: Mimesis, 2021), 42.

32 Teatrino Clandestino, "L'idealista magico," *Link Project House Organ*, No. 13 (1997): 6.

33 https://luoghidelcontemporaneo.beniculturali.it/progetto.

34 Ibid.

35 Claudia Giraud, "10 anni di indipendenti: ecco i progetti di 14 project space italiani selezionati per ArtVerona," *Artribune*, (August 15, 2019): https://www.artribune.com/arti-visive/arte-contemporanea/2019/08/10-anni-di-indipendenti-ecco-i-progetti-dei-14-project-space-italiani-selezionati-per-artverona/.

36 "Rephlex -Rephlex -Rephlex …… loop rave," *Link Project House Organ*, No. 5 (1995): 30.

37 Naomi Klein, *No Logo* (New York: Knopf Canada, 1999).

38 Nigel Warburton, *The Art Question* (Routledge: Abingdon, 2002).

39 Usmis, "Benandants electronics," *Link Project House Organ*, No. 2 (1994): 17.

ALTERNATIVE ART SPACES

La Tregenda

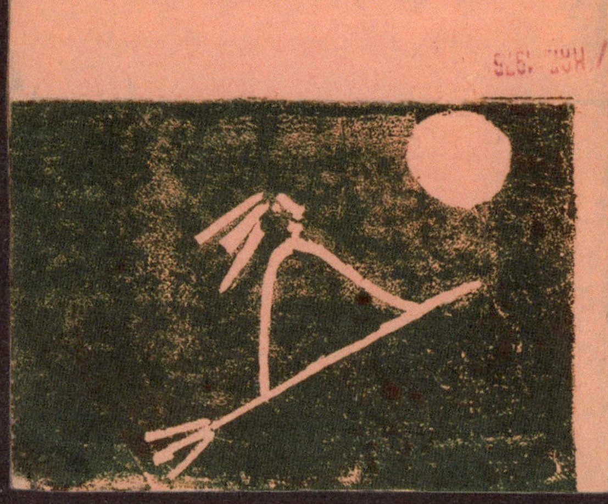

La Tregenda membership card, 1976

Maurizia Giusti (Syusy Blady) and Antonietta Laterza with her daughter Vanessa, 1976

1976–1977

La Tregenda was one of the first and rare spaces in Italy to be open to women only, who could meet, become self-aware and express themselves through the arts, in line with both the feminist and creative wings of the 1977 Movement. It was based in one of the "historic" cellars on Via San Vitale frequented by creatives of all sorts, including musical groups such as the Skiantos who had a rehearsal room there. In the few months of operation, several events related to multiple forms of artistic expression were organized at La Tregenda: exhibitions, performances, meetings and film screenings. It also hosted performances by established artists such as ethno-musical and folk singer-songwriter Giovanna Marini, jazz musician Patrizia Scascitelli and dancer Valeria Magli. However, the space was also open to hard-to-classify contributions proposed by anonymous female visitors, including the surreal installation of an adult-sized baby's cradle, where it was possible to lie down and sleep. La Tregenda strongly pursued a model of autonomy and self-management, being able to rely only on forms of self-financing and the voluntary collaboration of its home community.

The peculiar feature of this space—and the aspect that still makes it a radical and unrepeatable model of political and cultural autonomy—was its exclusive allocation to a women-only audience. Men were granted access only on rare occasions, including a Carnival party, remembered by the founders as a time of liberation and lightheartedness, as opposed to the angry attitude of absolute separatism pursued by the more extreme wing of the feminist movement.

La Tregenda closed in 1977, when the suppression of the Bologna Movement by local government and law enforcement ended an era of experimentation in which political and behavioral instances took shape and found their own voice through the arts.

ADDRESS Via San Vitale 13, Bologna. FOUNDERS Maurizia Giusti (Syusy Blady), Antonietta Laterza, Anna Rita Dall'Olio, Fioretta Fabbri. COLLABORATORS Nadia Gabi, Patrizia Scascitelli, Giovanna Marini

Traumfabrik

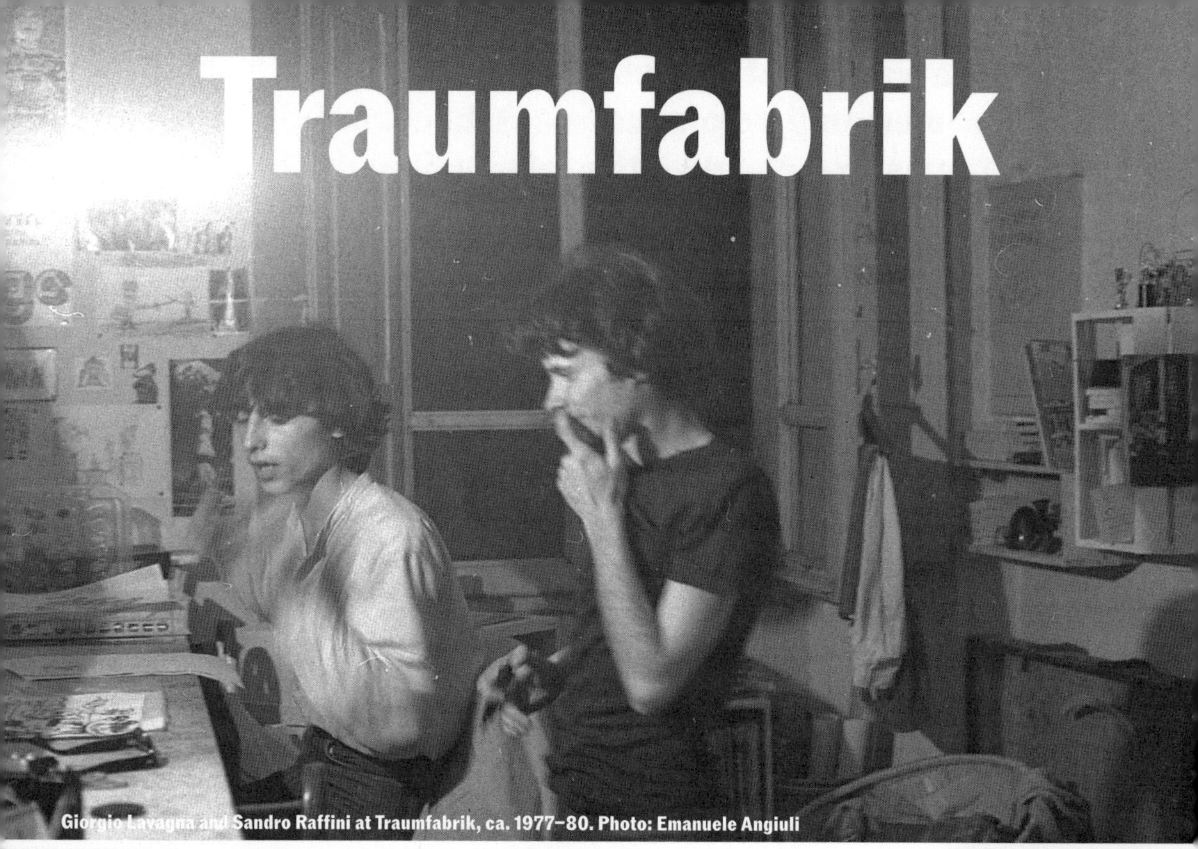

Giorgio Lavagna and Sandro Raffini at Traumfabrik, ca. 1977–80. Photo: Emanuele Angiuli

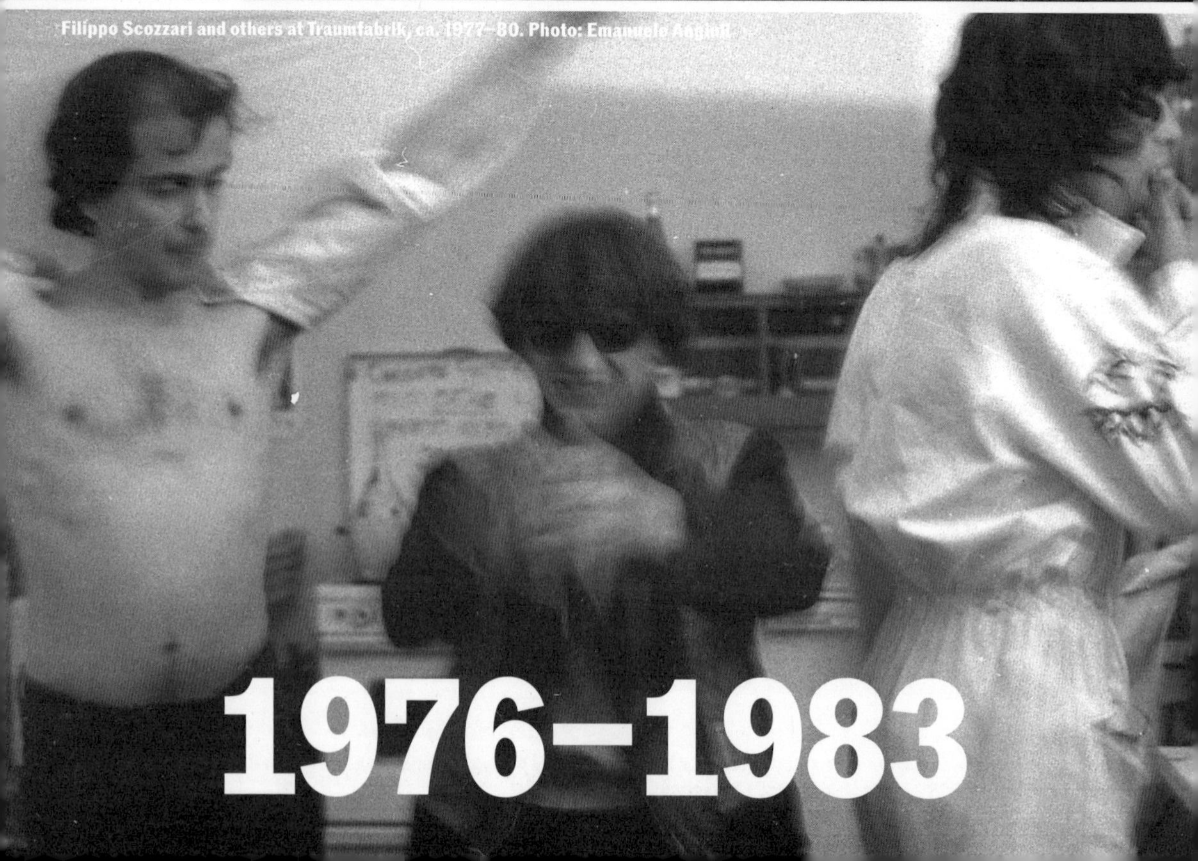

Filippo Scozzari and others at Traumfabrik, ca. 1977–80. Photo: Emanuele Angiuli

1976–1983

An emblematic experience of Bolognese creativity around the turn of the 1980s, Traumfabrik gathered the essence of a generation betrayed by the unfulfilled promises of the 1970s revolution and dazzled by the glories of the hedonistic 1980s.

The "dream factory" was founded by Gianpietro Huber, Filippo Scozzari, and Dadi Mariotti in 1976 inside an apartment they had occupied on Via Clavature, in the city center's *Quadrilatero* area, imagined as a place to escape from the impositions of society, perceived as outright cages of creativity. Over its seven years of activity, Traumfabrik did not offer exhibitions or performances, but became an open meeting space in which to have fun by playing and listening to music, making experimental films and drawing, constituting a heterotopia shared with friends and comrades of the Movement, a workshop of alternative cultural productions.

Fitted out by Huber with salvaged furniture and objects, the apartment on Via Clavature came across as a multifaceted space of creation, whose frequent visitors included some of the leading exponents of New Italian Comics such as Scozzari and Andrea Pazienza. Others were involved in post-punk bands such as Gaznevada, Stupid Set and Confusional Quartet, also collaborating with Harpo's Bazaar, later Italian Records, working on their record covers and flyers. Coming together under the acronym Topographic, some of them published issue zero of the magazine *L.U.X. Electric!*, and contributed to the graphics and editing of the early issues of *Musica80*. Others, under the name Grabinski, embarked on experimental audiovisual production consisting of proto-videoclips and multimedia installations based on the use of found footage. Several members of Traumfabrik were involved in the IV (1980) and VI (1982) International Performance Week in Bologna: an event curated by Francesca Alinovi, Renato Barilli and Roberto Daolio. Other than that, there were few instances when their work was presented within the context of contemporary art.

In addition to comics, record covers, flyers and fanzines, Traumfabrik's fruitful cultural production included a number of objects made by modifying recycled materials and hundreds of works on paper: drawings, watercolors, collages, and photomontages. After passing from one basement to another, all that remains of that corpus is a box of works on paper, "saved" by an artist, Alessandra Andrini, who although she had not participated personally in the events of Traumfabrik for age reasons, discovered she was the sole custodian of this precious find, and immediately named it "exhibit 1"—the contents of which were presented at the neon gallery in Bologna in 2007.

The spread of heroin and the spread of a Hepatitis C epidemic heavily influenced the decay of the Traumfabrik, whose story ended with eviction from the building in 1983. Of that experience, as spontaneous as it was heroic if we consider its longevity and self-supporting dynamics, a number of protagonists have told their own tales, such as Scozzari in his memoir *Prima pagare poi ricordare* ("First Pay Then Remember," 2004) and Emanuele Angiuli of Grabinski with the documentary *Traumfabrik Via Clavature 20* (2009), but it is "exhibit 1" that is the real legacy of the dream factory, and only its study and valorization will be able to do justice to this experience as a pioneering example of a liberated artistic space and a place for rethinking art, approached in an interdisciplinary and democratic way.

ADDRESS Via Clavature 20, Bologna. FOUNDERS Gianpietro Huber, Filippo Scozzari, Dadi Mariotti. COLLABORATORS Emanuele Angiuli, Renato De Maria, Anna Gozzi, Giorgio Lavagna, Ciro Pagano, Andrea Pazienza, Alessandro Raffini, Sandra Zabbini

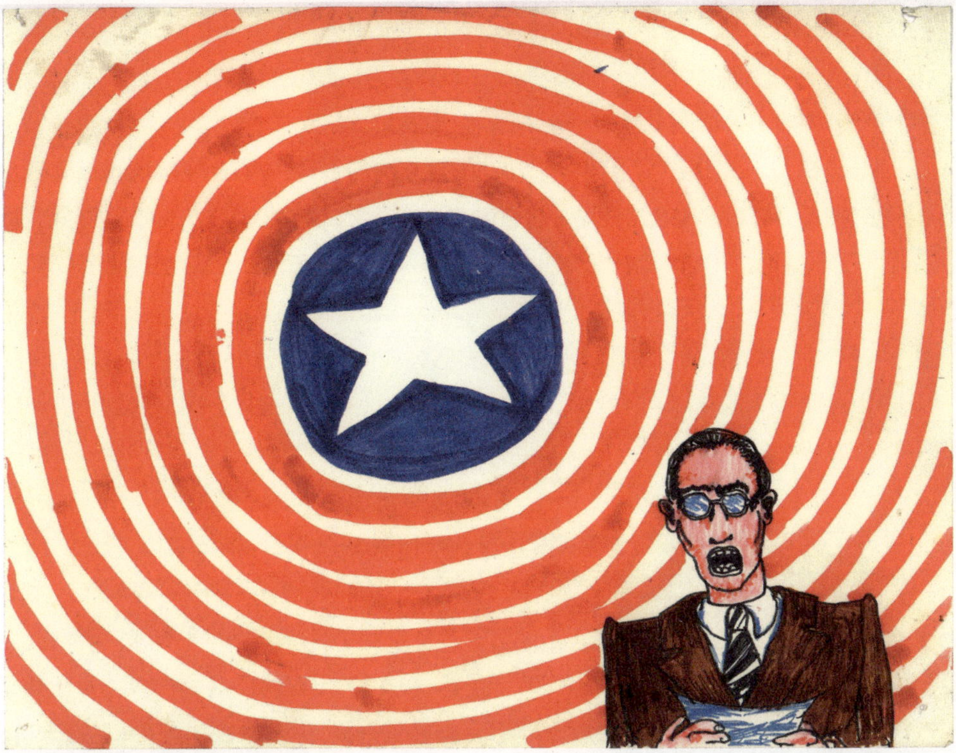

Giorgio Lavagna, *Untitled*, ca. 1976–80

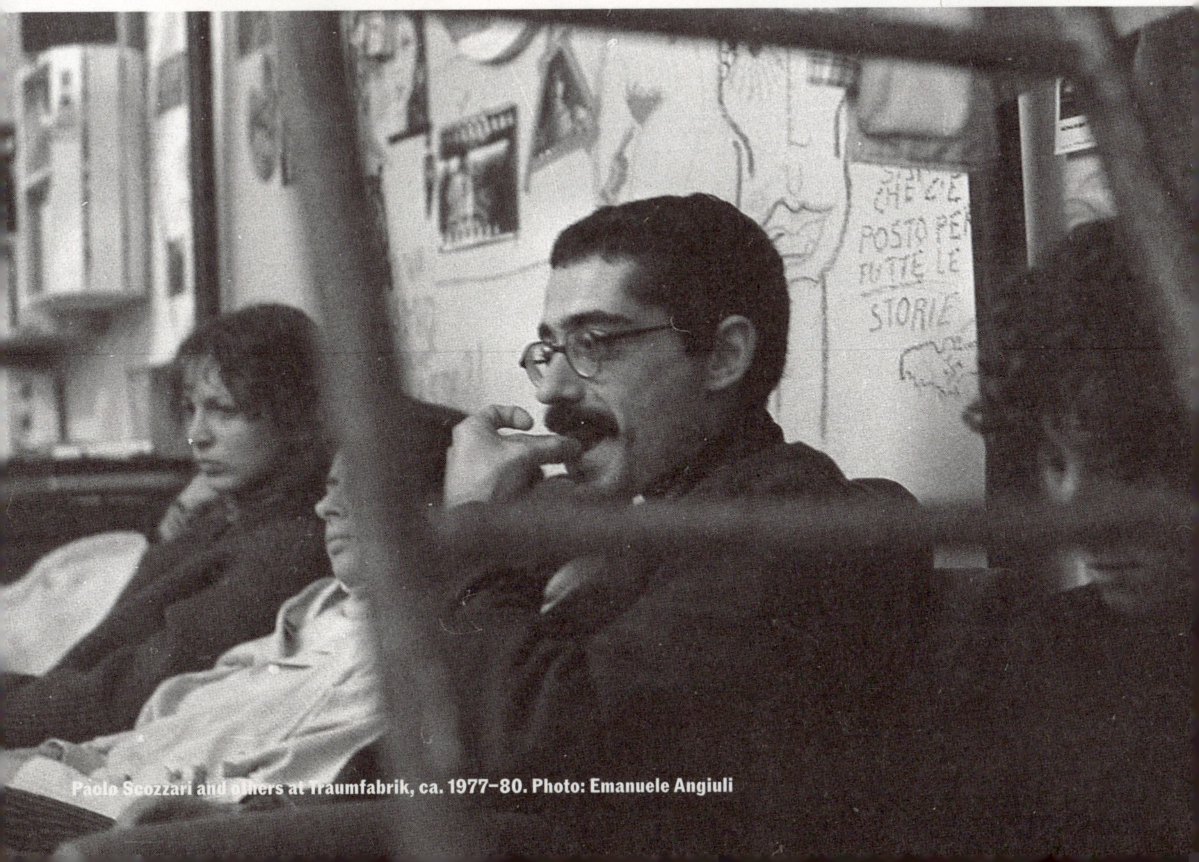

Paolo Scozzari and others at Traumfabrik, ca. 1977–80. Photo: Emanuele Angiuli

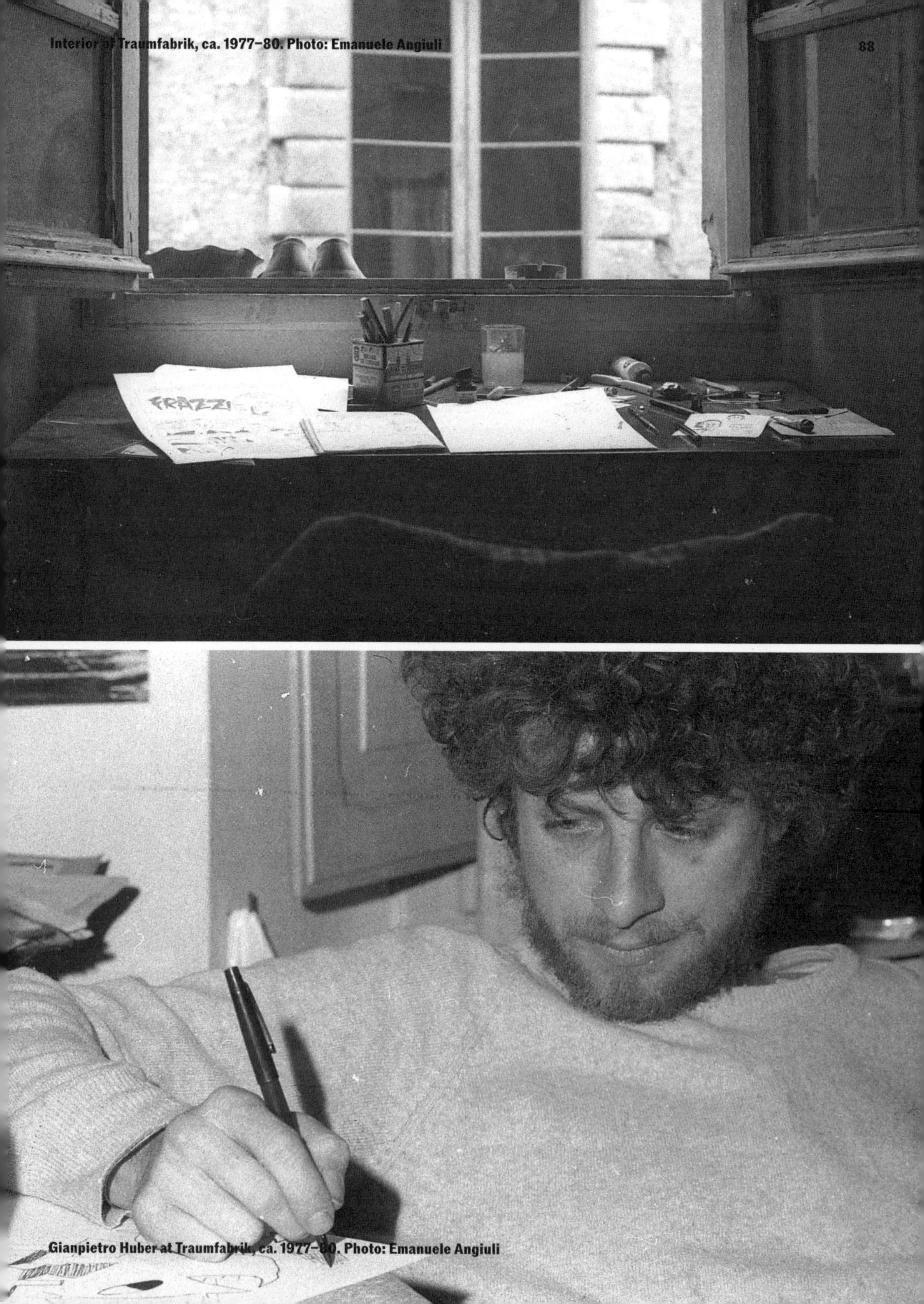

Interior of Traumfabrik, ca. 1977–80. Photo: Emanuele Angiuli

Gianpietro Huber at Traumfabrik, ca. 1977–80. Photo: Emanuele Angiuli

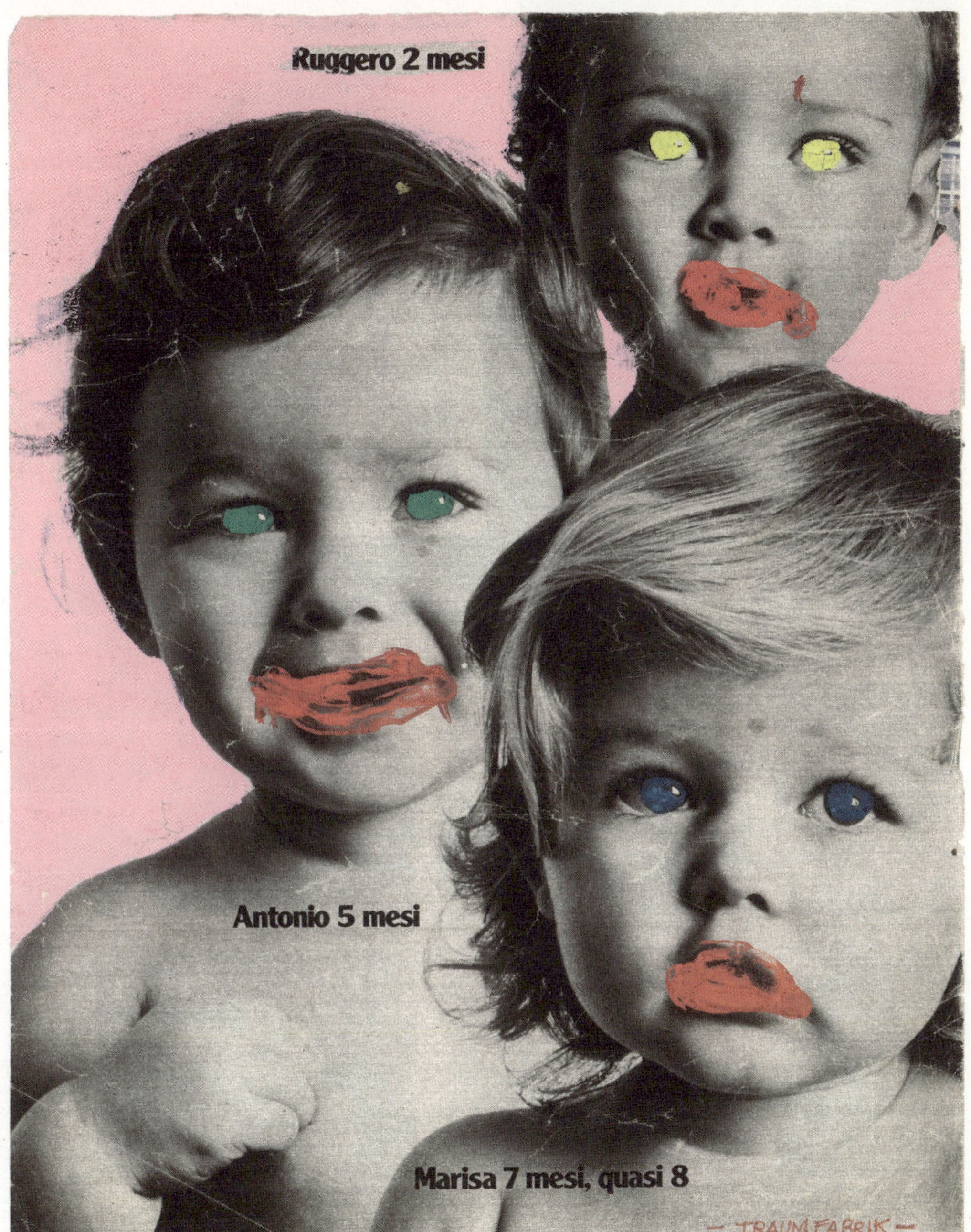
Ruggero 2 mesi
Antonio 5 mesi
Marisa 7 mesi, quasi 8
— TRAUM FABRIK —

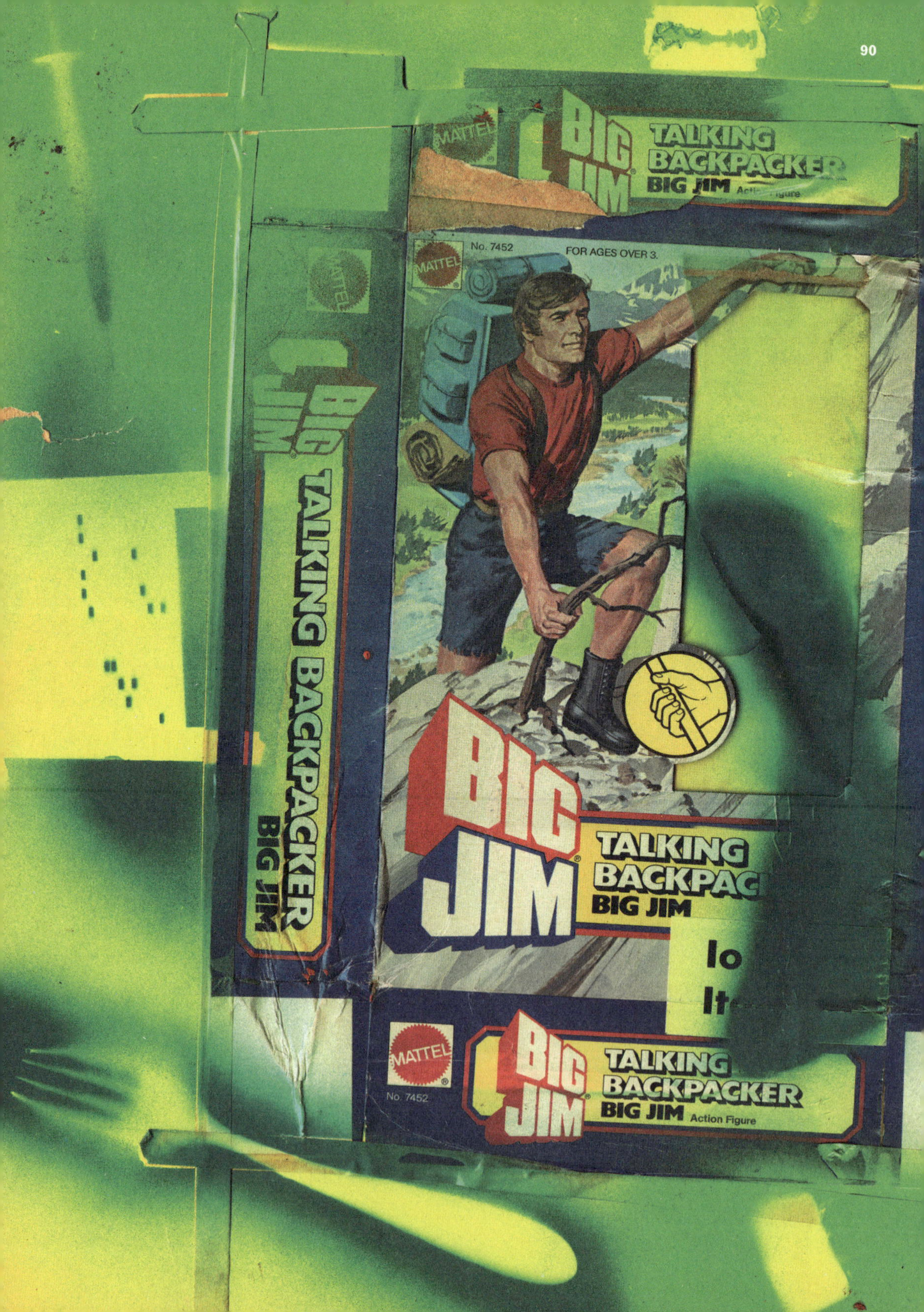
MATTEL
BIG JIM
TALKING BACKPACKER
BIG JIM Action Figure
No. 7452
FOR AGES OVER 3.
MATTEL
BIG JIM TALKING BACKPACKER BIG JIM
BIG JIM
TALKING BACKPACK
BIG JIM
lo
lt
MATTEL
No. 7452
BIG JIM
TALKING BACKPACKER
BIG JIM Action Figure

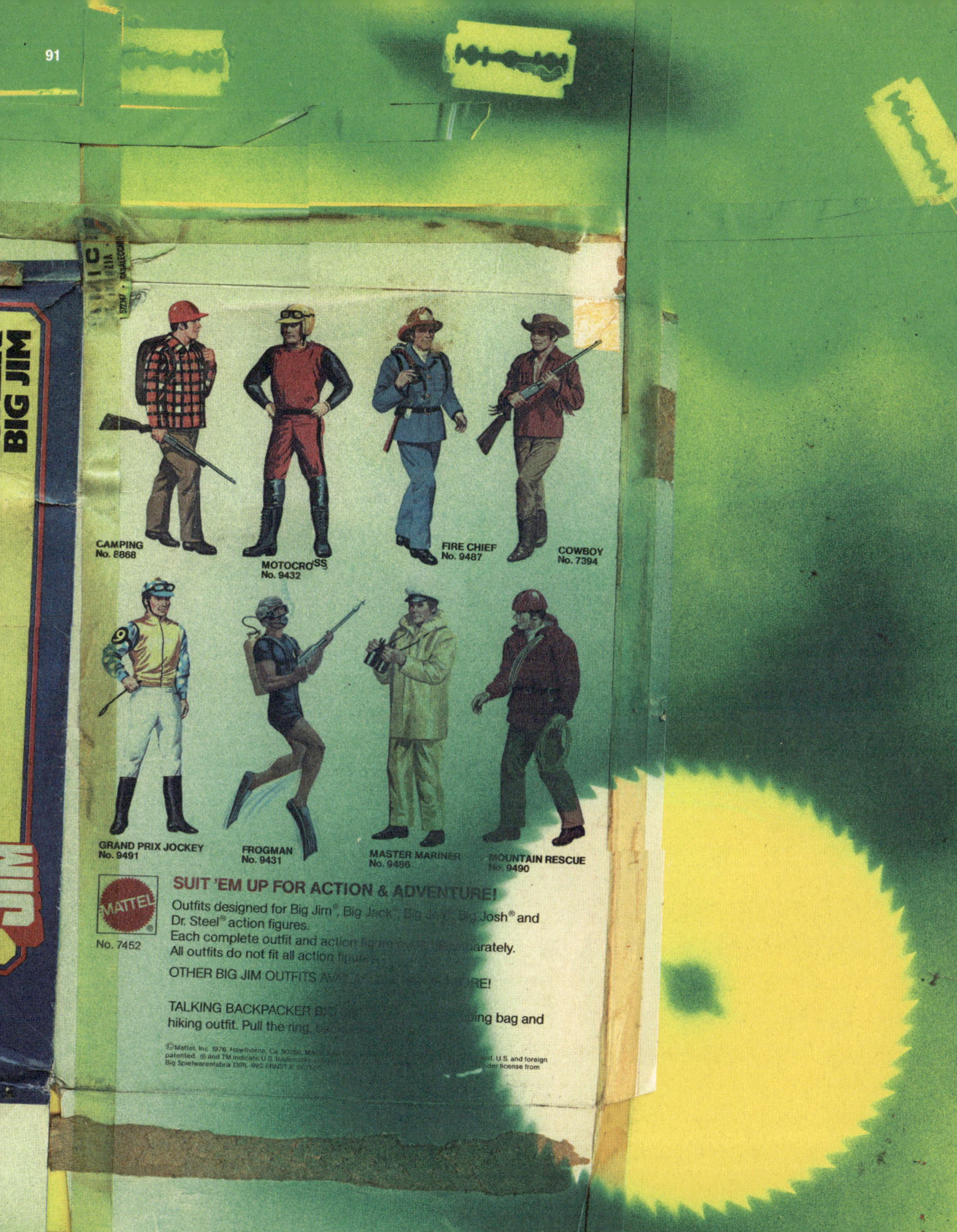

Gianpietro Huber, *Untitled*, ca. 1976–80

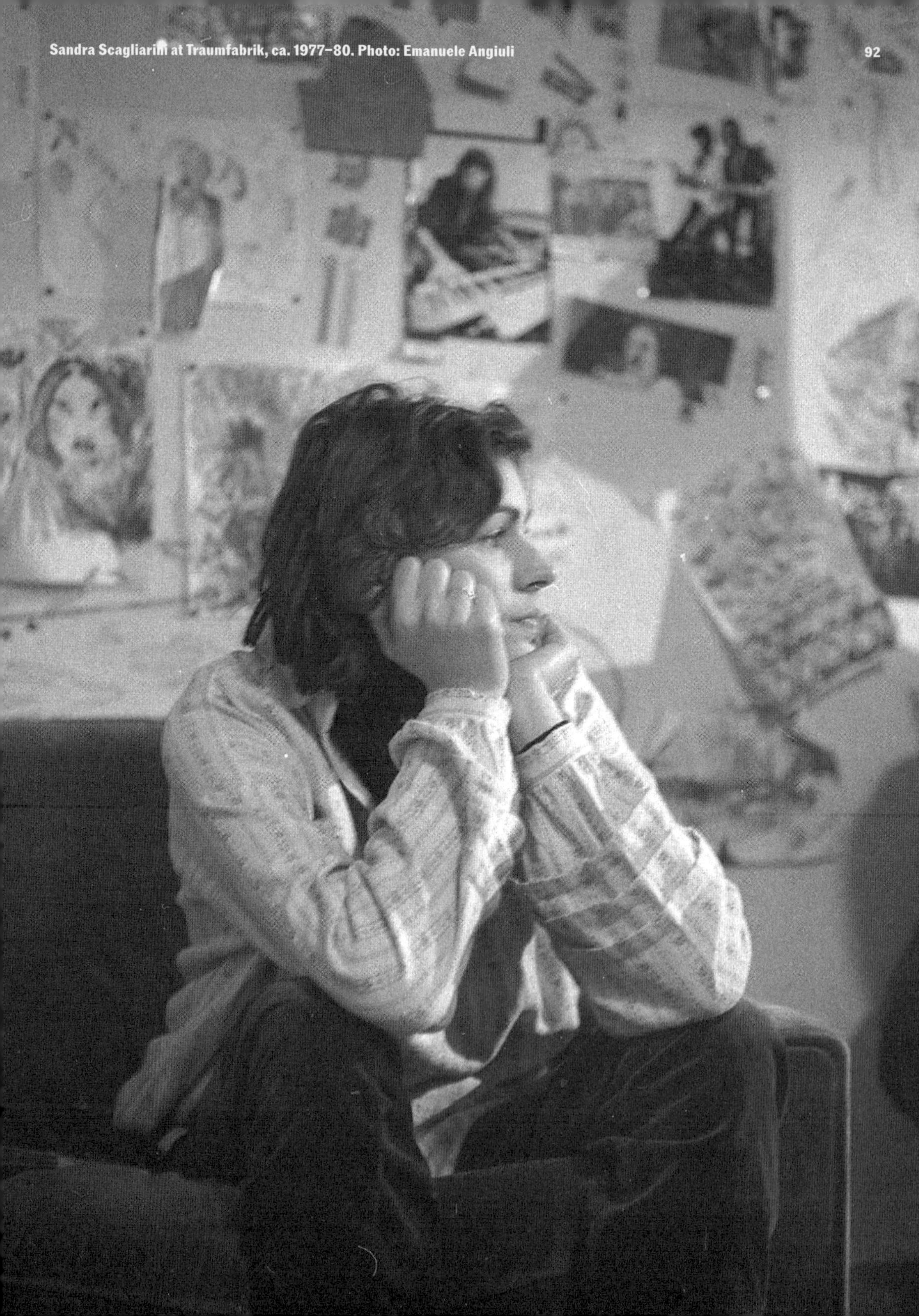

Sandra Scagliarini at Traumfabrik, ca. 1977–80. Photo: Emanuele Angiuli

 Roberto "Freak" Antoni on the Traumfabrik terrace. Stills from Renato De Maria's video *Trilogy of Banal Life: Waking Up in the Morning*, 1980

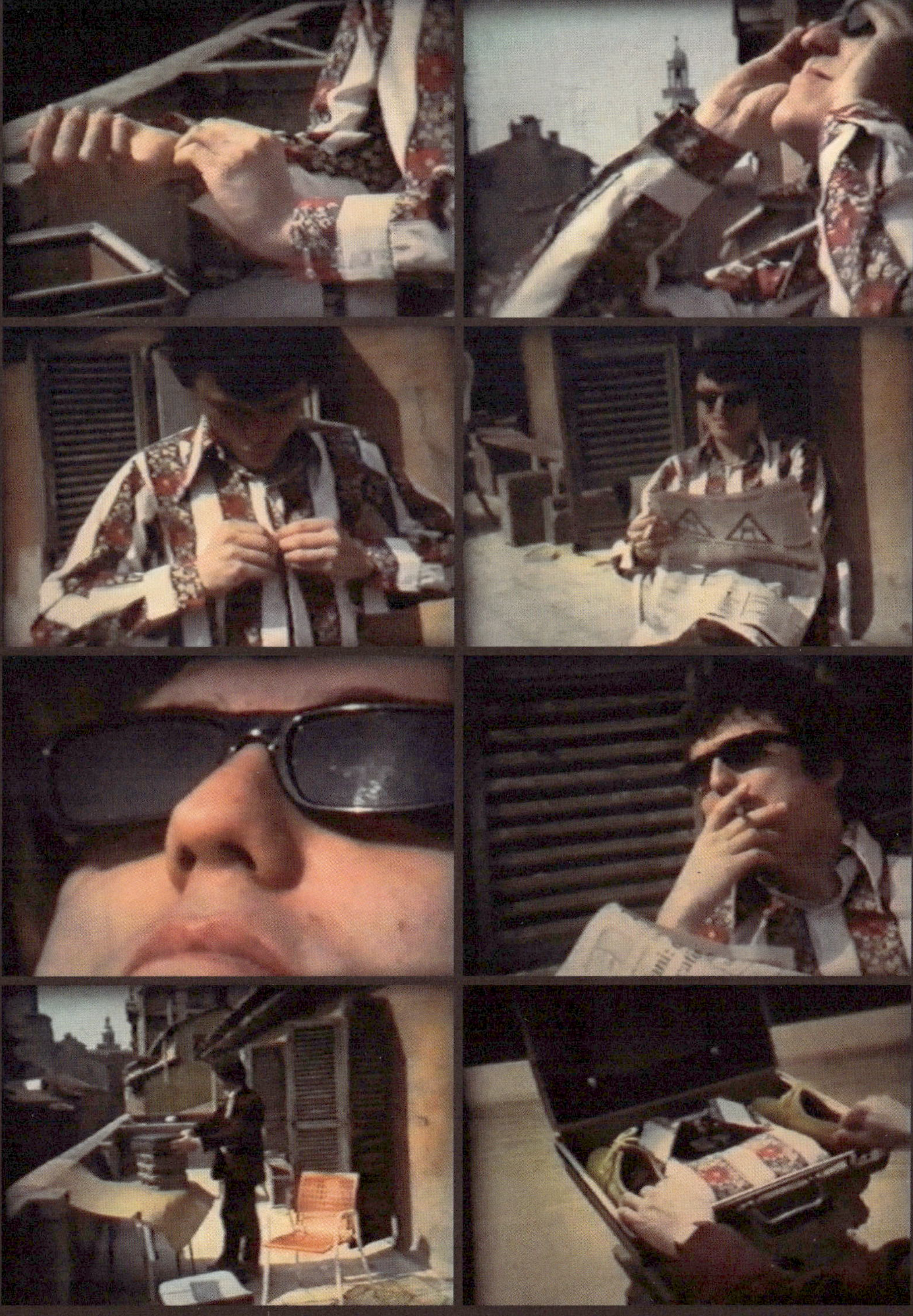

neon

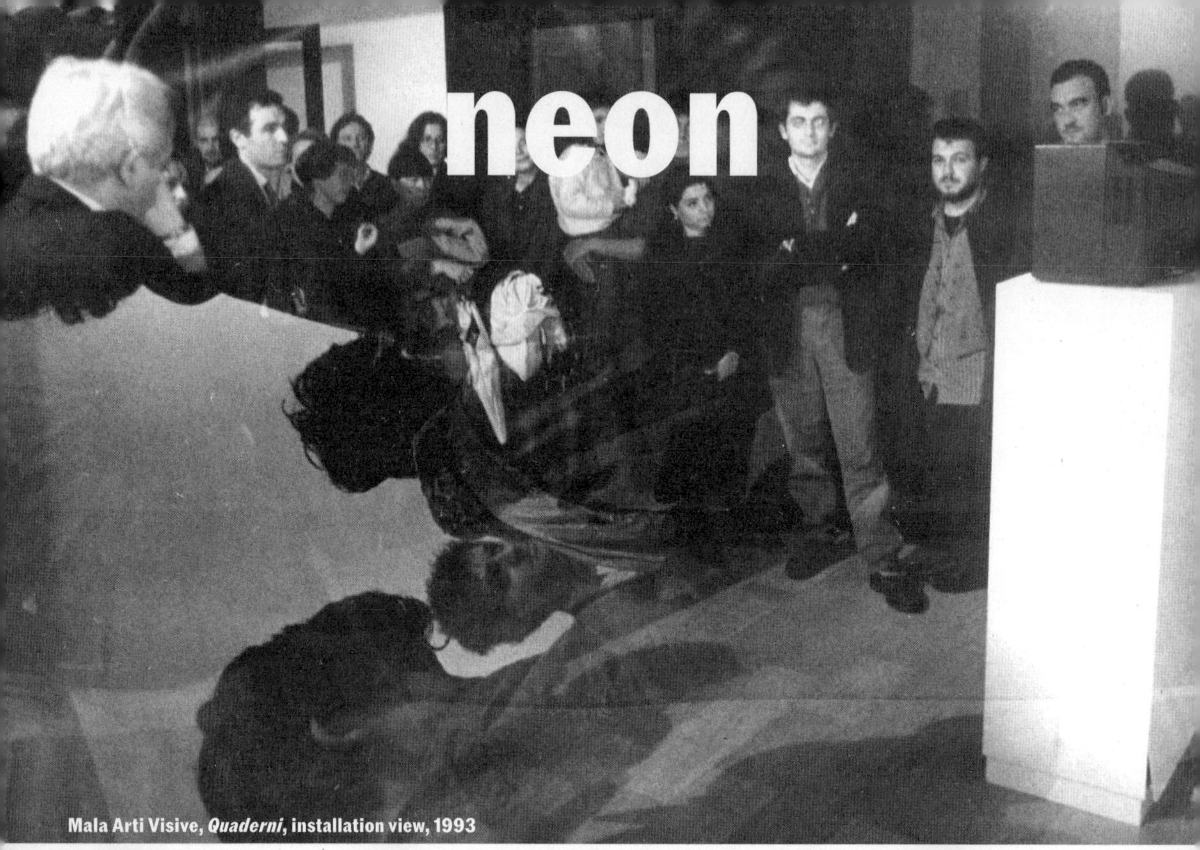

Mala Arti Visive, *Quaderni*, installation view, 1993

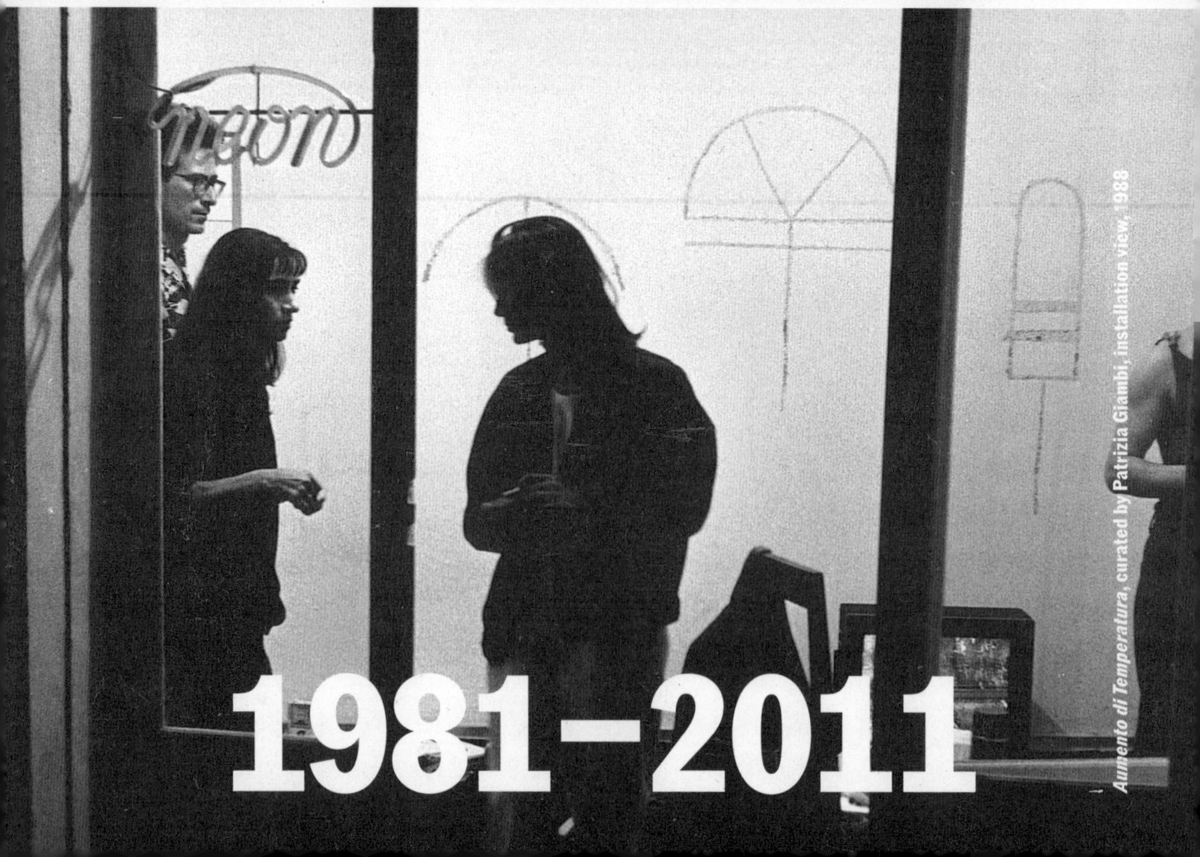

1981–2011

Aumento di Temperatura, curated by Patrizia Giambi, installation view, 1988

The desire to open a space for dialogue about art within which to propose innovative practices and question the status of works, artists and the system led Gino Gianuizzi, Stefano Deli, Antonia Ruggeri, Valeria Medica, and Maurizio Vetrugno to found neon in 1981. Originating as an open experiment based on the confusion between the roles of artist, gallerist, and critic-curator, both with a punk spirit and situationist, neon's initial thrust was characterized by a desire to inoculate disruptive elements into a sclerotized system. Numerous projects in the early years were entrusted to Francesca Alinovi, a scholar and curator capable of catalyzing insights and energies of international scope into activities of local origin, as in the case of Enfatismo: an artistic micro-movement she theorized and that remained active until 1983, the year of her death. After a few years of hiatus, neon resumed activity in 1987, seeing Gianuizzi and, later, Roberto Daolio involved in particular, who shared a focus on emerging artists. From its original headquarters in Via Solferino, neon changed name and location several times—even founding two locations in Milan in its latter period of activity—but never failing in its desire to support artists mostly at the start of their careers.

The absolute freedom from the conventions of the commercial system of contemporary art resulted in a disjointed activity that was difficult to frame, in which the artists exhibited were mainly related to conceptual art, but also to performance and video experiments. Initially, Gianuizzi invited artists with whom he had empathetic relationships such as Marco Lavagetto, Fathi Hassan, Maurizio Cattelan, and Croce Taravella. Later, with Daolio, neon became the gallery for young emerging artists, exhibiting Roberto Orlandi, Antonella Mazzoni, Eva Marisaldi, Alessandro Pessoli, Luca Vitone, and Monica Cuoghi, among others. After moving to the Via Zanardi venue, neon>campobase became particularly interested in sound research and video experimentation, offering a continuous flow of events capable of constituting itself as a permanent laboratory of research and confrontation.

In institutional contexts—such as, for example, those of the contemporary art fairs in which the space participated from time to time—neon represented a disruptive element that did not abide by codified rules, adopting a situationist attitude. Public funding from institutions that did not recognize its potential was rare, but neon was mainly interested in establishing an osmotic relationship with the city, as is clear in the two projects *Container* and *Fuori contesto* that proposed direct interventions in the city environment. Neon's audience consisted of a community of artists, students from the city's Academy of Fine Arts and DAMS, and, in later years, a few brave collectors.

The neon experience ended in 2011 due to increasing financial problems and a lack of interest in becoming a full-fledged commercial art gallery.

ADDRESS neon: Via Solferino 41/a, Bologna (1981–91); Via Avesella, Bologna (1991–96); Via Bersaglieri, Bologna (1997–99) | neon>field: Via Zanardi 2/5, Bologna (2000–11) | neon>projectbox: Corso Garibaldi 42, Milan (2002–04) | neon>fdv: Fabbrica del Vapore, Milan (2006–09) FOUNDERS Gino Gianuizzi, Stefano Delli, Valeria Medica, Antonia Ruggeri, Maurizio Vetrugno COLLABORATORS Francesca Alinovi, Roberto Daolio

Gino Gianuizzi and Maurizio Vetrugno, *Il Risaltante*, installation view, 1981

Maurizio Cattelan, *Torno Subito*, **installation view, 1989**

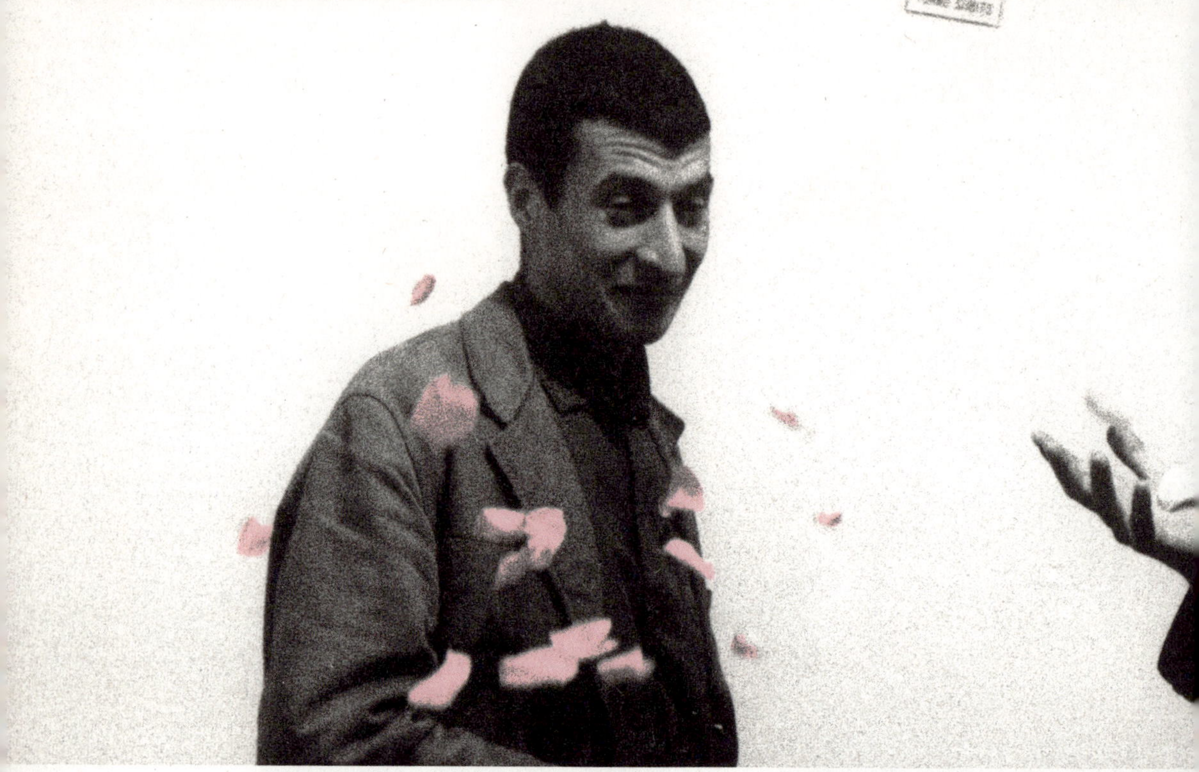

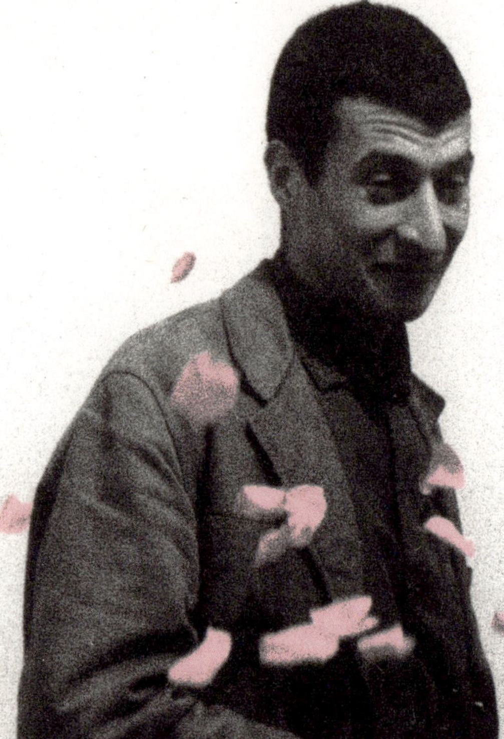

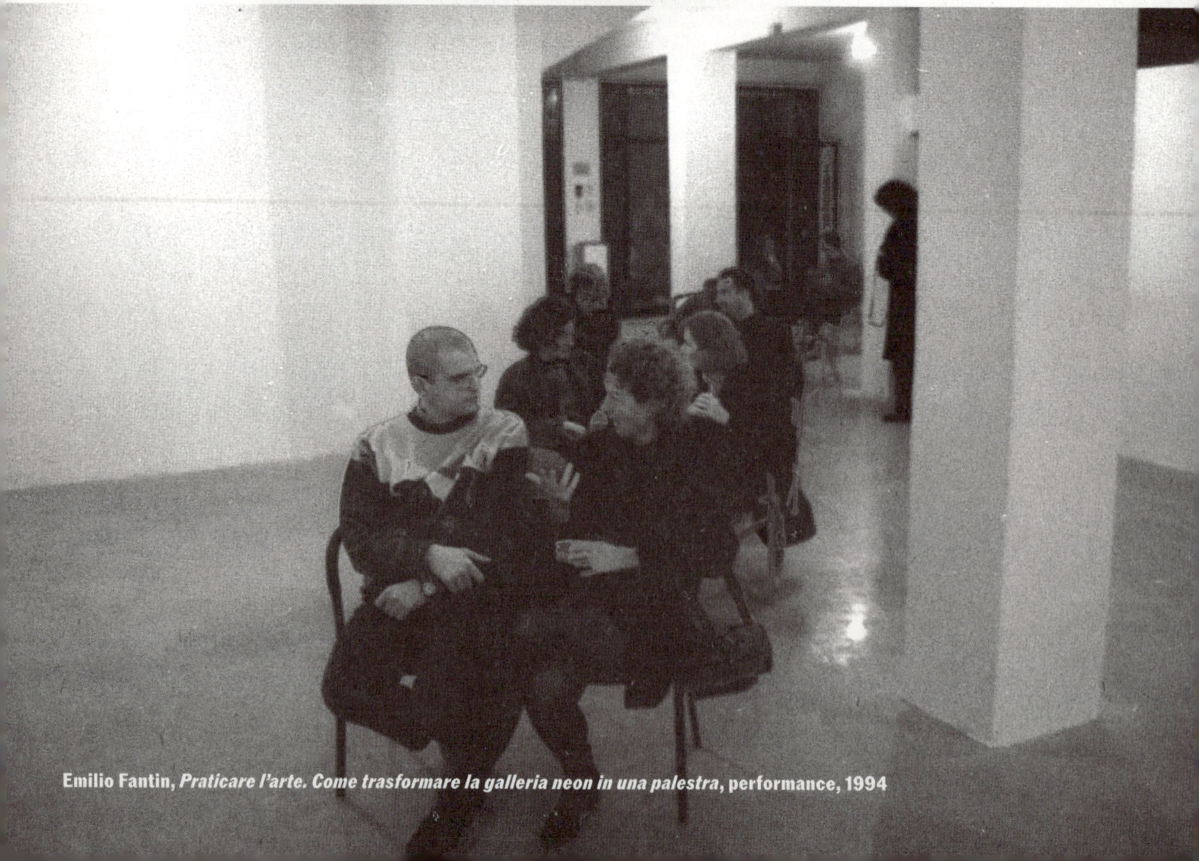

Emilio Fantin, *Praticare l'arte. Come trasformare la galleria neon in una palestra*, **performance, 1994**

   Maurizio Finotto, *Gunther Solo's Night*, performance, 1997

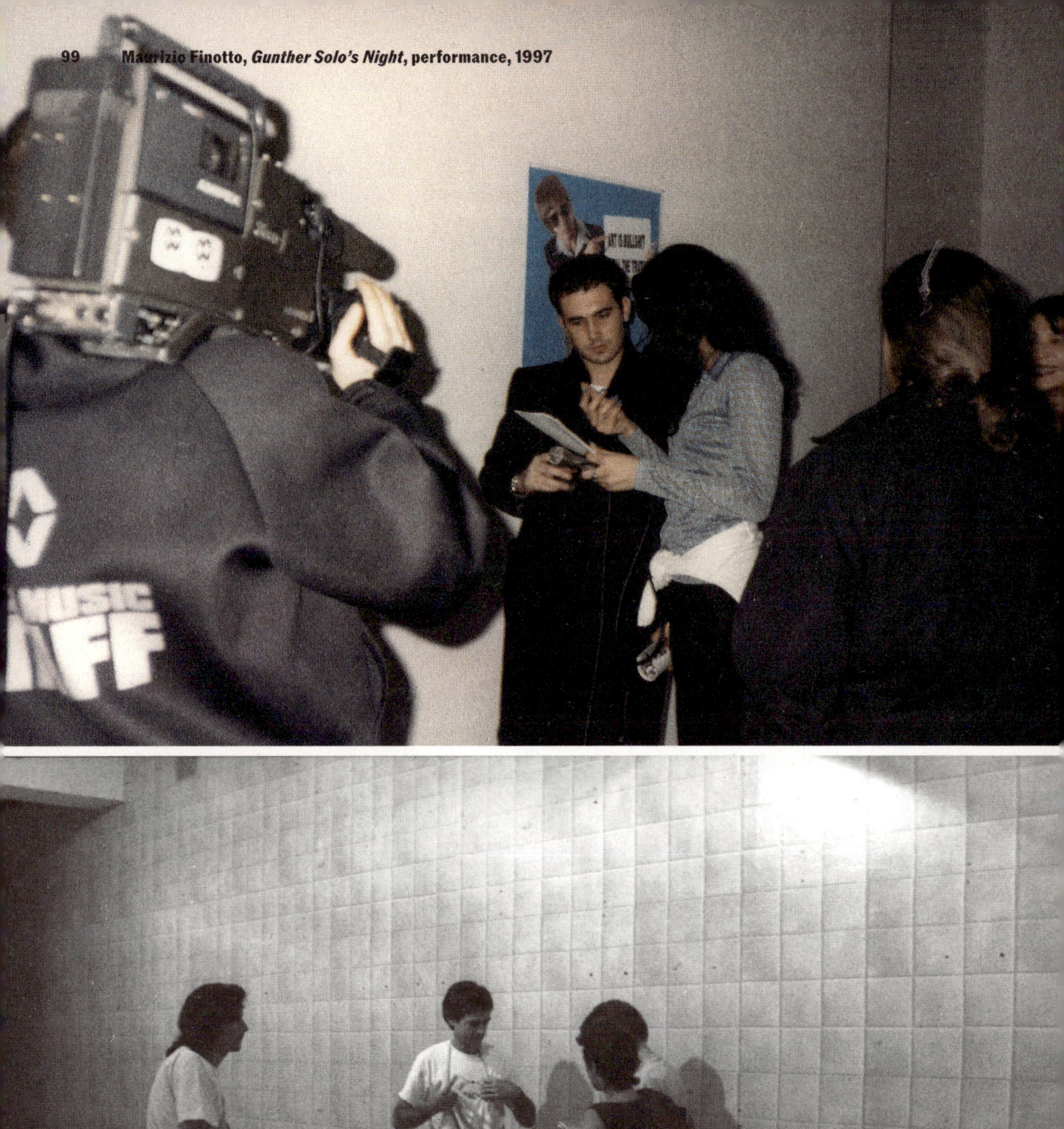

Alessandra Tesi, *Tic de l'esprit*, installation view, 1997

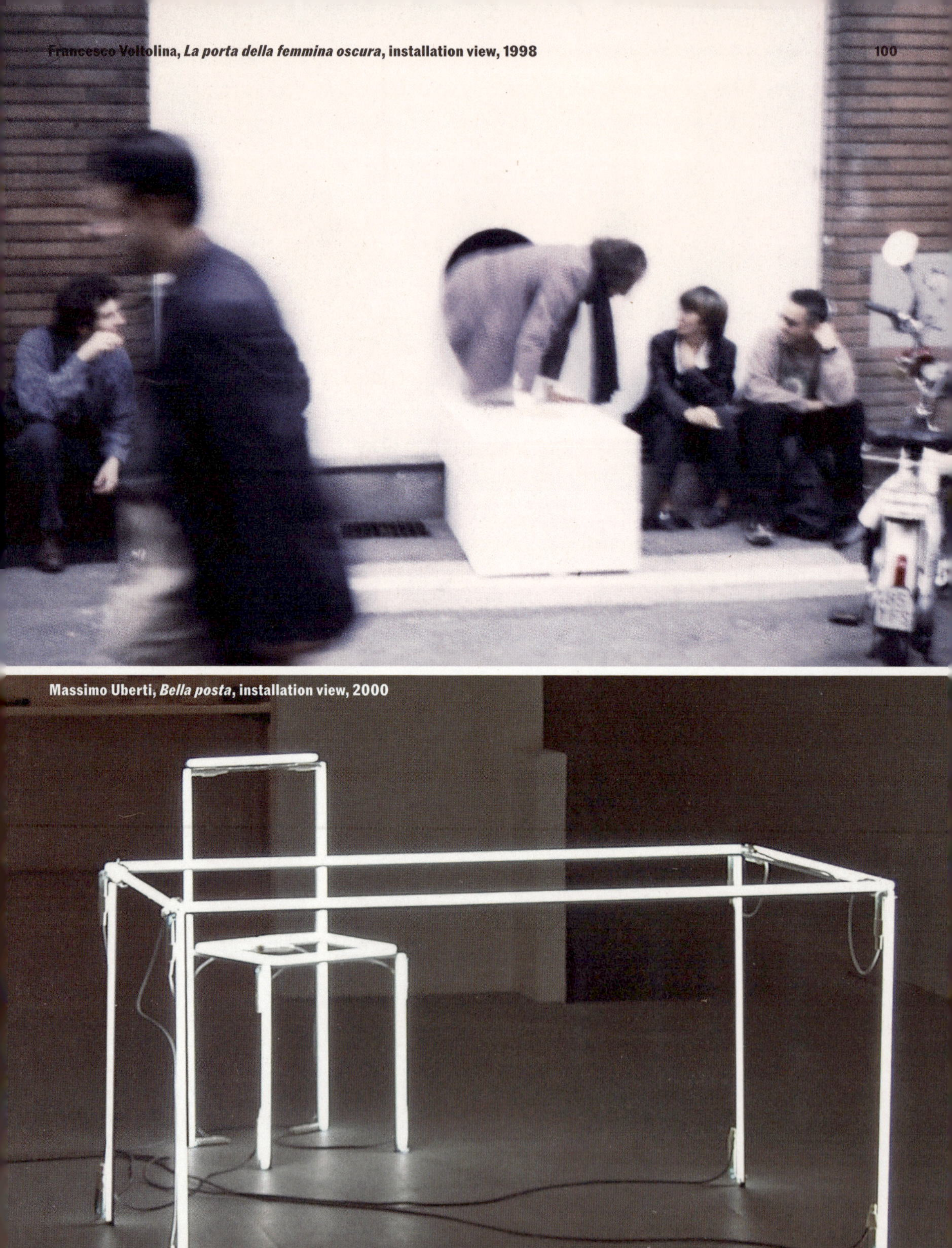

Francesco Voltolina, *La porta della femmina oscura*, installation view, 1998

Massimo Uberti, *Bella posta*, installation view, 2000

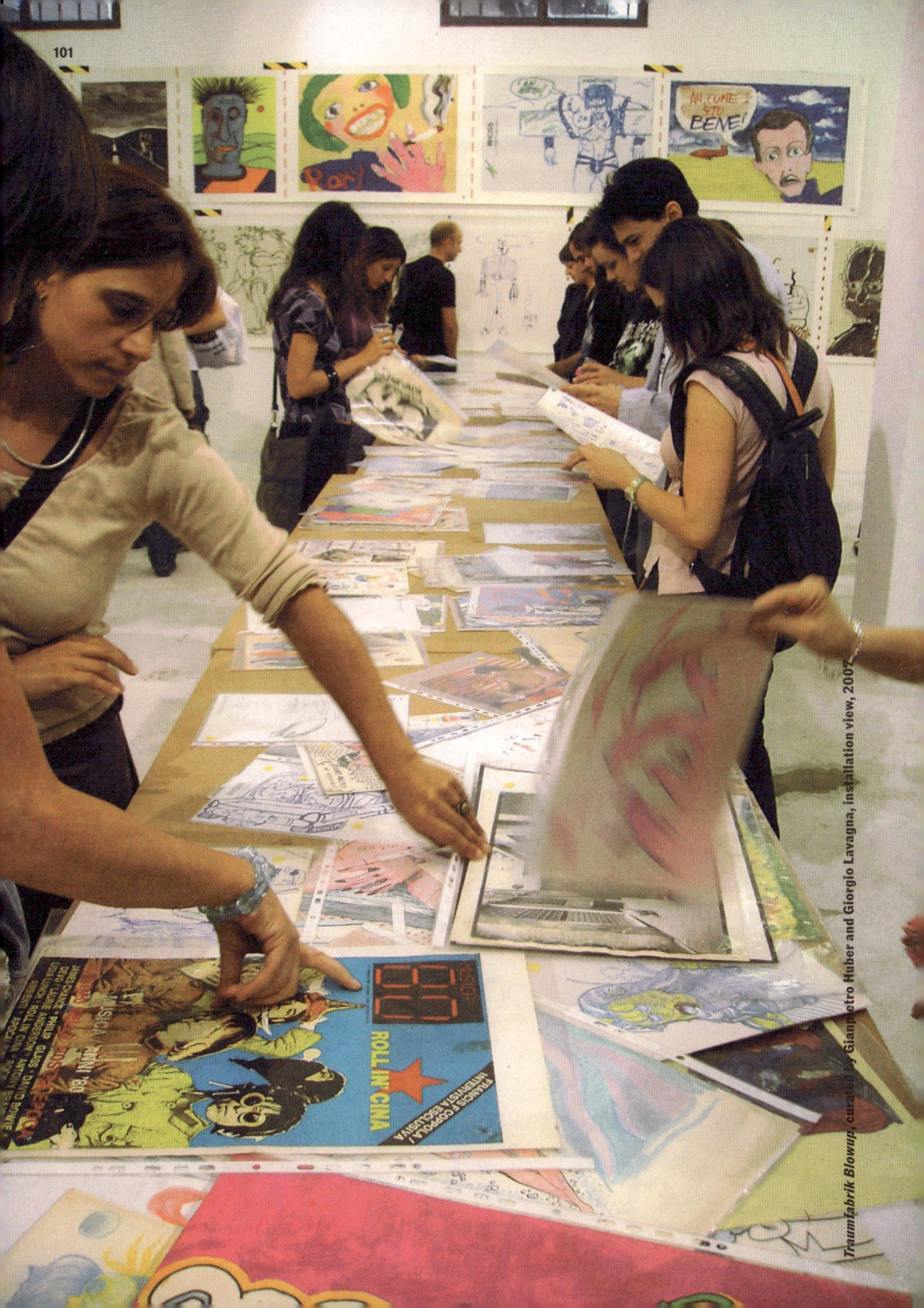

Traumfabrik Blowup, curated by Gianpietro Huber and Giorgio Lavagna, installation view, 2007

Segreto Pubblico

1982–1985

Segreto Pubblico was born from the bond of friendship between Ginetto Campanini and Francesco Tabarrini, both of whom moved to Bologna in 1982 after a period of study in Trento. A place of experimentation and research, this space aimed to develop viral contaminations between various artistic and performative languages. The first venue was the old icehouse of a slaughterhouse in the Bologna suburb of Borgo Panigale: an unusual and fascinating space whose conformation lent itself in particular to sound experimentation. The dome of the interior of the icehouse, in fact, served as a sound box, incurring a slight delay in the propagation of sound. Later, the need to transform Segreto Pubblico into an economically viable reality led the collective's members to move from the suburbs to the center of Bologna, to a new, more functional venue on Via San Carlo.

The cultural program featured events, exhibitions, performances, and reviews of music, theater, and poetry, and aimed to open the world of contemporary art to new input, thanks in part to the involvement of exponents of the city context such as Francesca Alinovi and Gino Gianuizzi and various protagonists from other Bologna spaces such as Traumfabrik and neon.

Of particular interest were two 1982 art projects presented in the form of parties, a model—that of the party—which responded to the hedonistic instances typical of the postmodern era, in line with a trend characteristic of the downtown New York art scene at the time. For *Frontiera Party*, curated by Alinovi, the space was covered with graffiti of a tribal nature by Ivo Bonacorsi—flowers and dinosaurs—while the art rock band Eterodattili performed on stage. For the *Grabinsky TV Party*, on the other hand, the audiovisual experimentation group Grabinski, which had originated within the walls of the Traumfabrik, placed a camera at the base of the staircase leading to the venue, recordings of which feature a long line of the typical patrons of Segreto Pubblico, including Jean-Michel

Basquiat, a friend of the group and often in Bologna at the time. The space also hosted post-punk musical performances with up-and-coming Italian bands, such as neon, and figures from the New York scene such as Steve Piccolo, as well as a performance project curated by Franco "Bifo" Berardi based on the transposition of the "Game Over" issue (1981) of his magazine *A/traverso*: a staging of the Beijing trial of the Gang of Four in an environment characterized by the presence of four arcade games.

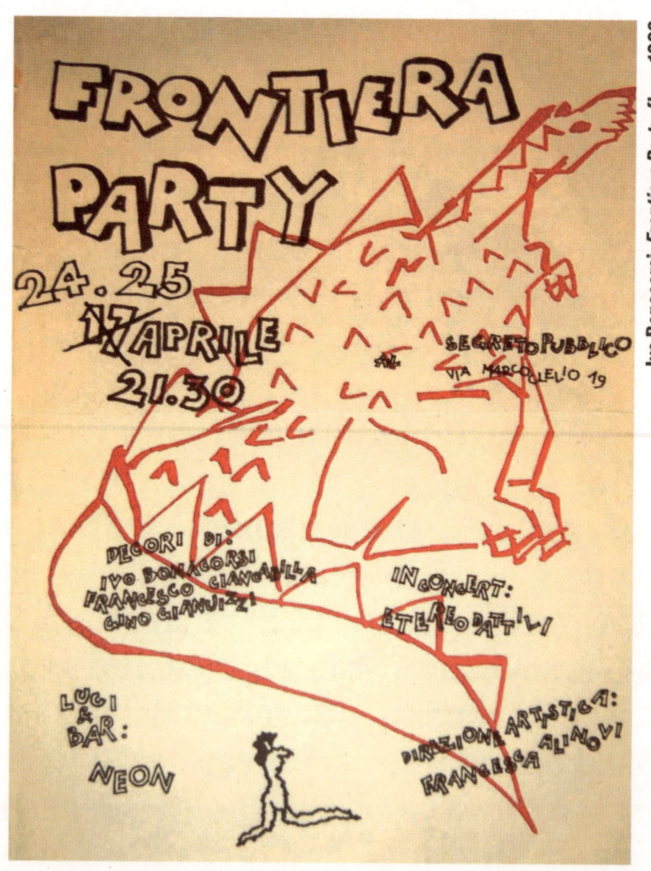

Ivo Bonacorsi, *Frontiera Party*, flyer, 1982

ADDRESS Via Marco Celio 19, Borgo Panigale (1982–84); Via San Carlo 5, Bologna (1984–85). **FOUNDERS** Ginetto Campanini, Francesco Tabarrini. **COLLABORATORS:** Marco Coppi, Sebastiano de Pascalis, Amos Masè, Claudia Morettini, Fabrizia Poluzzi

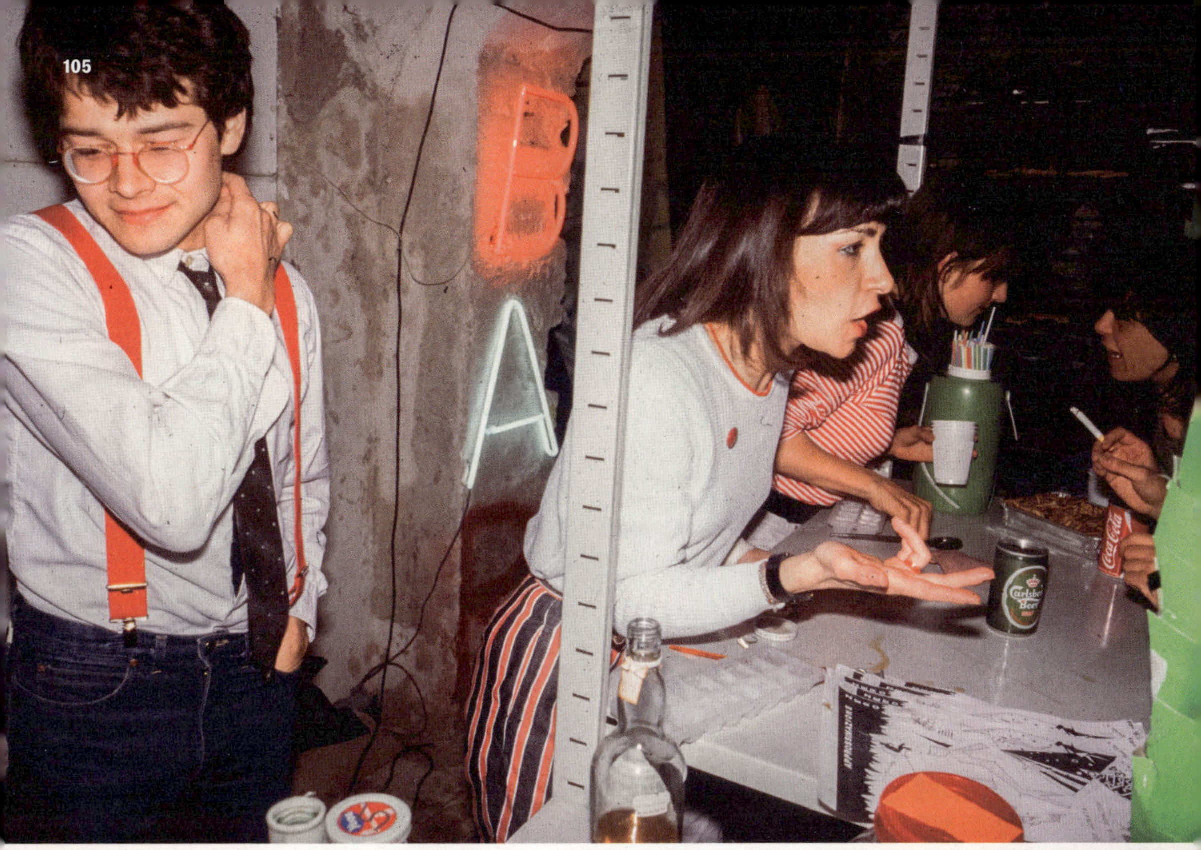

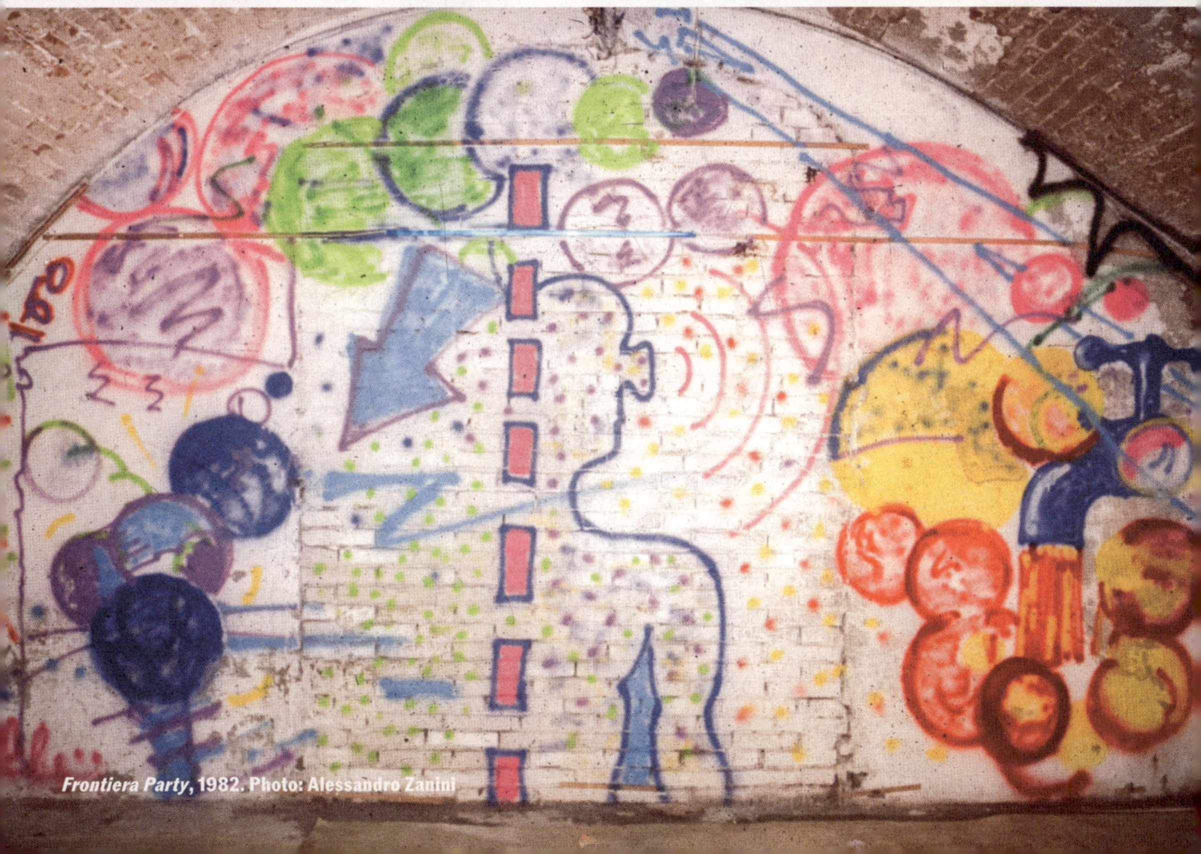

Frontiera Party, 1982. Photo: Alessandro Zanini

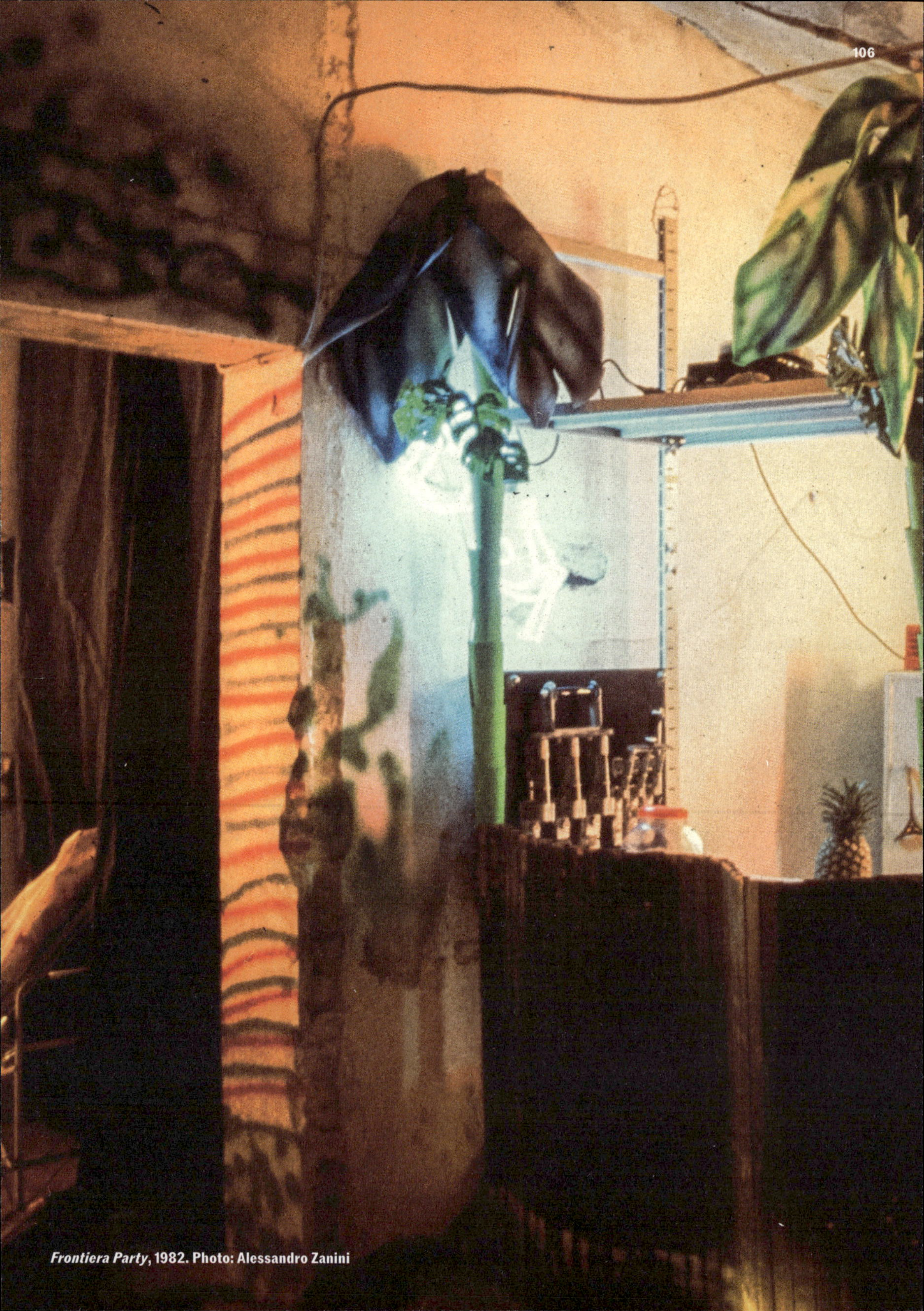

Frontiera Party, 1982. Photo: Alessandro Zanini

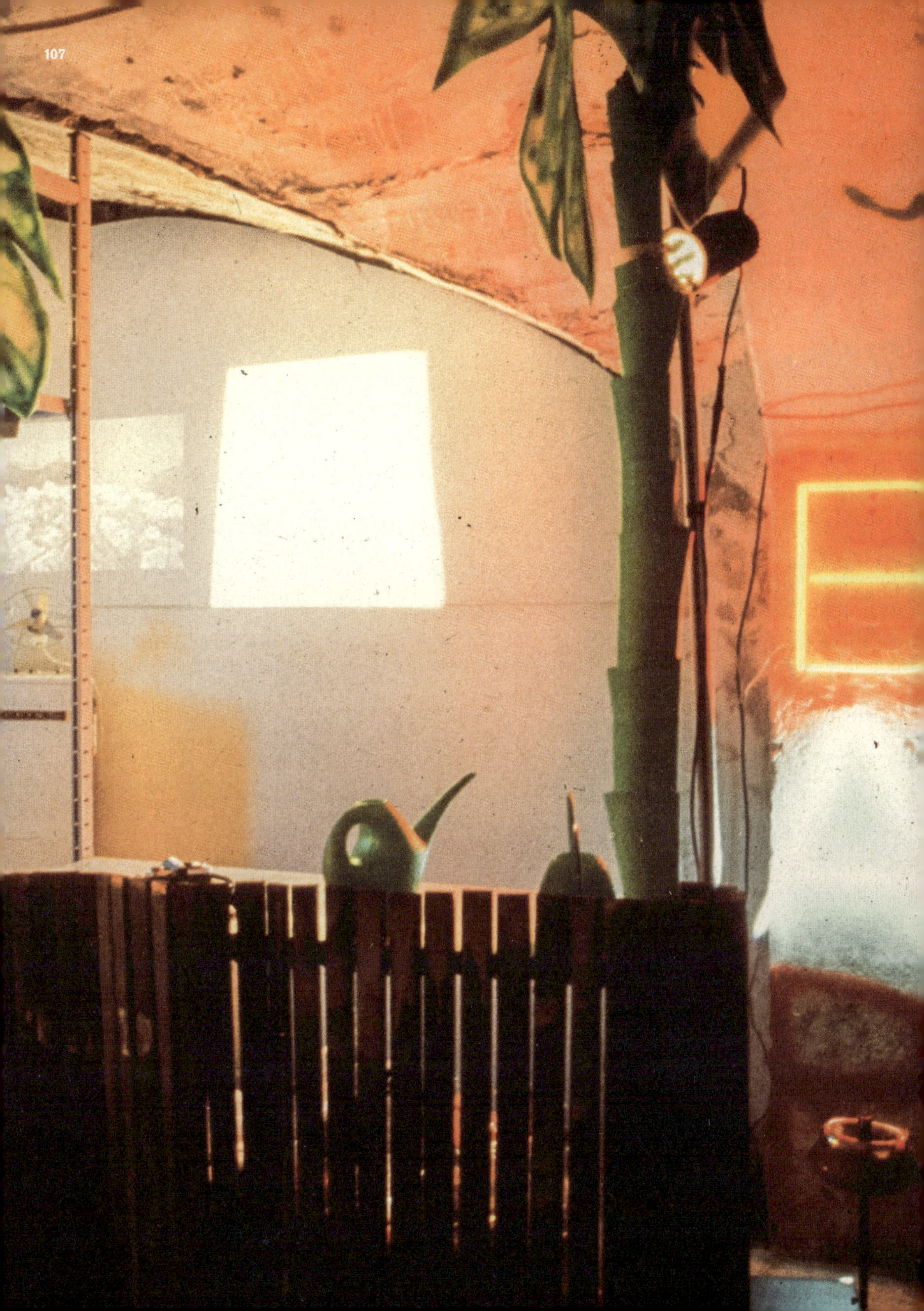

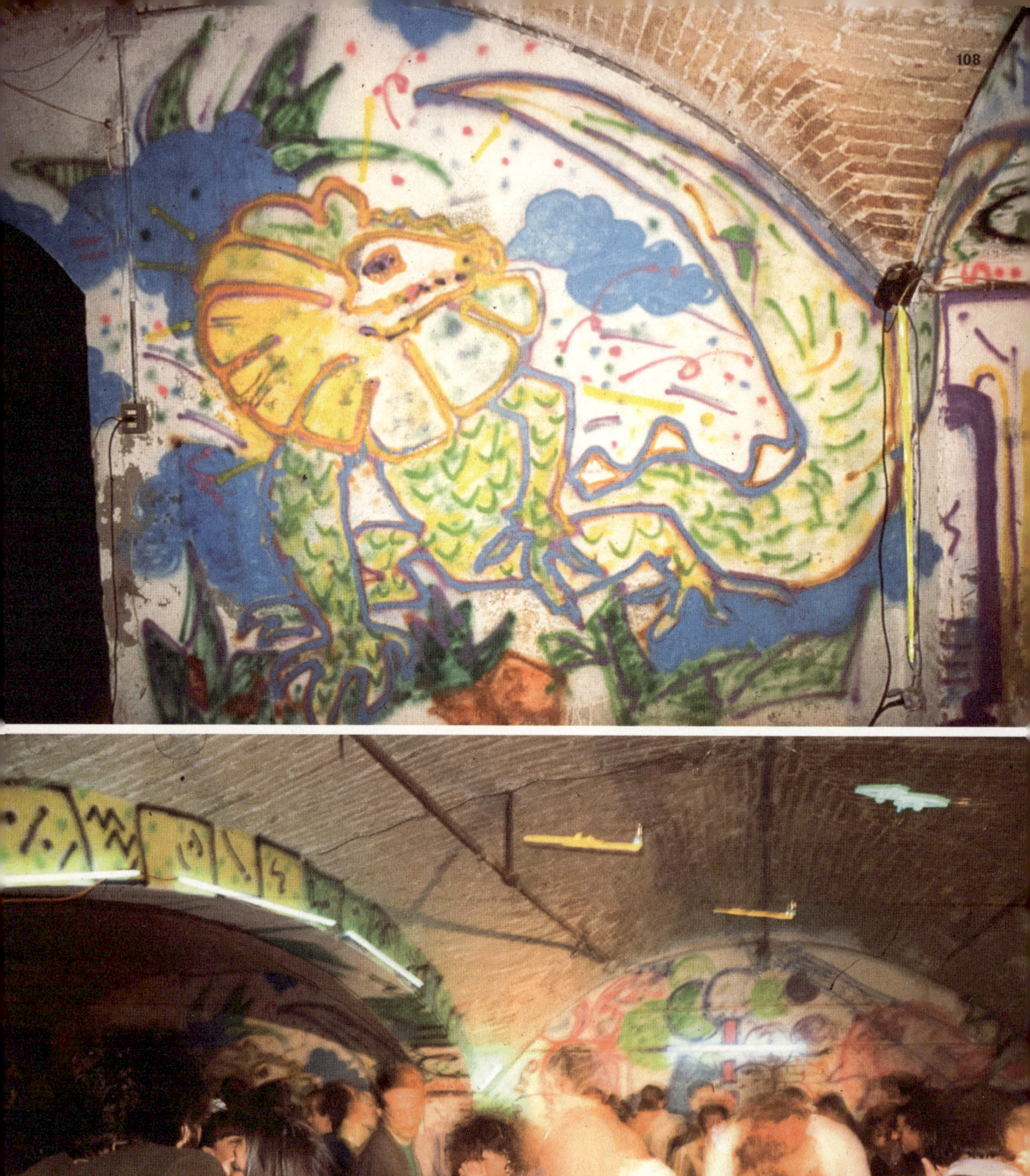

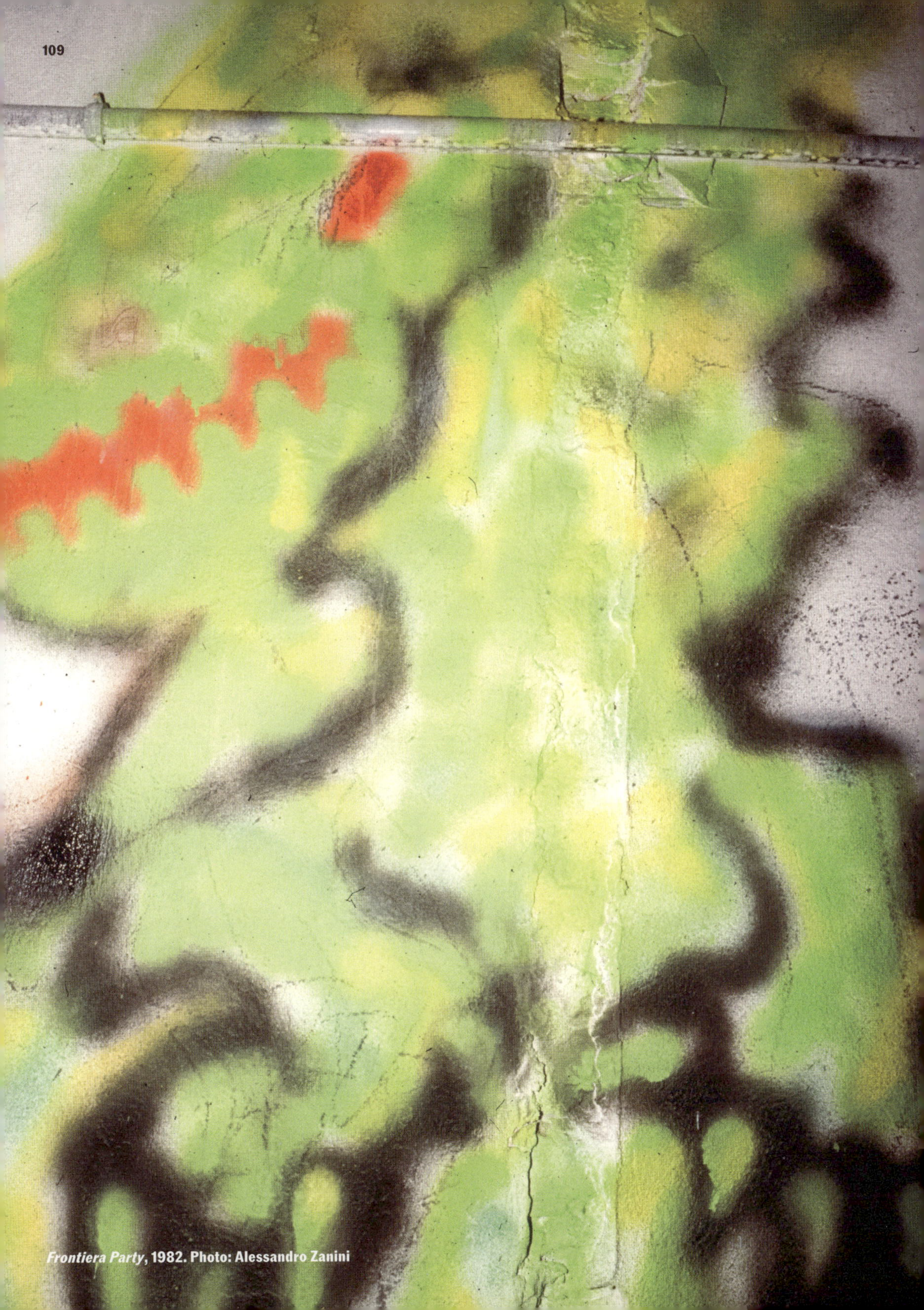

Frontiera Party, 1982. Photo: Alessandro Zanini

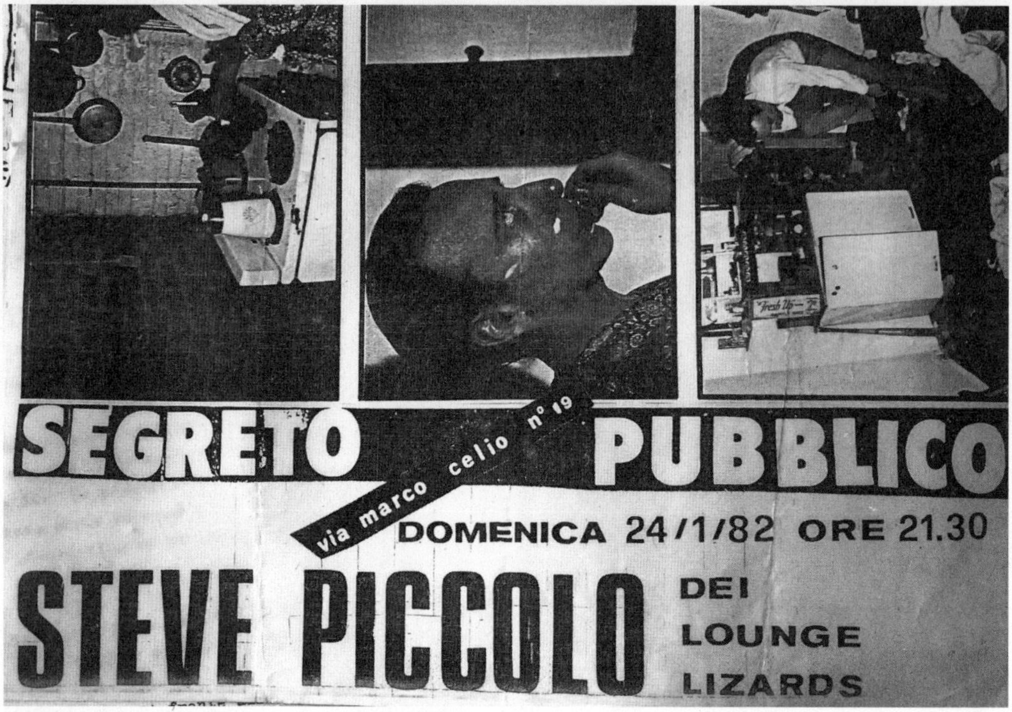

Steve Piccolo, live performance, flyer, January 24, 1982

The Grabinsky TV Party, flyer, March 13, 1982

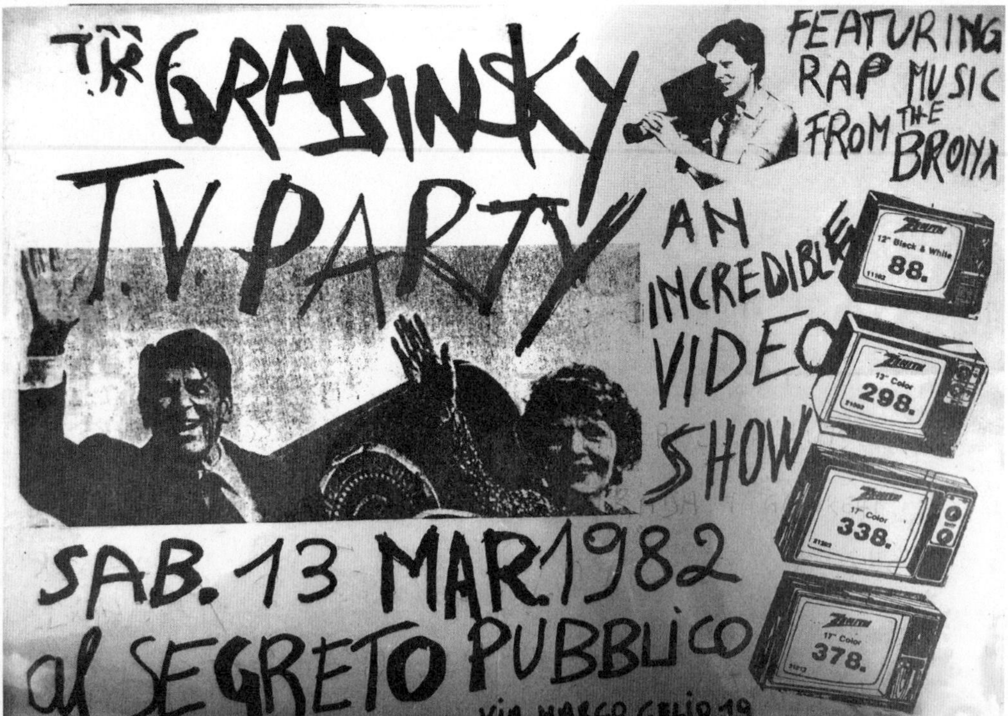

Grabinski, *The Grabinsky TV Party*, stills from a video camera placed at the entrance of Segreto Pubblico, 1982

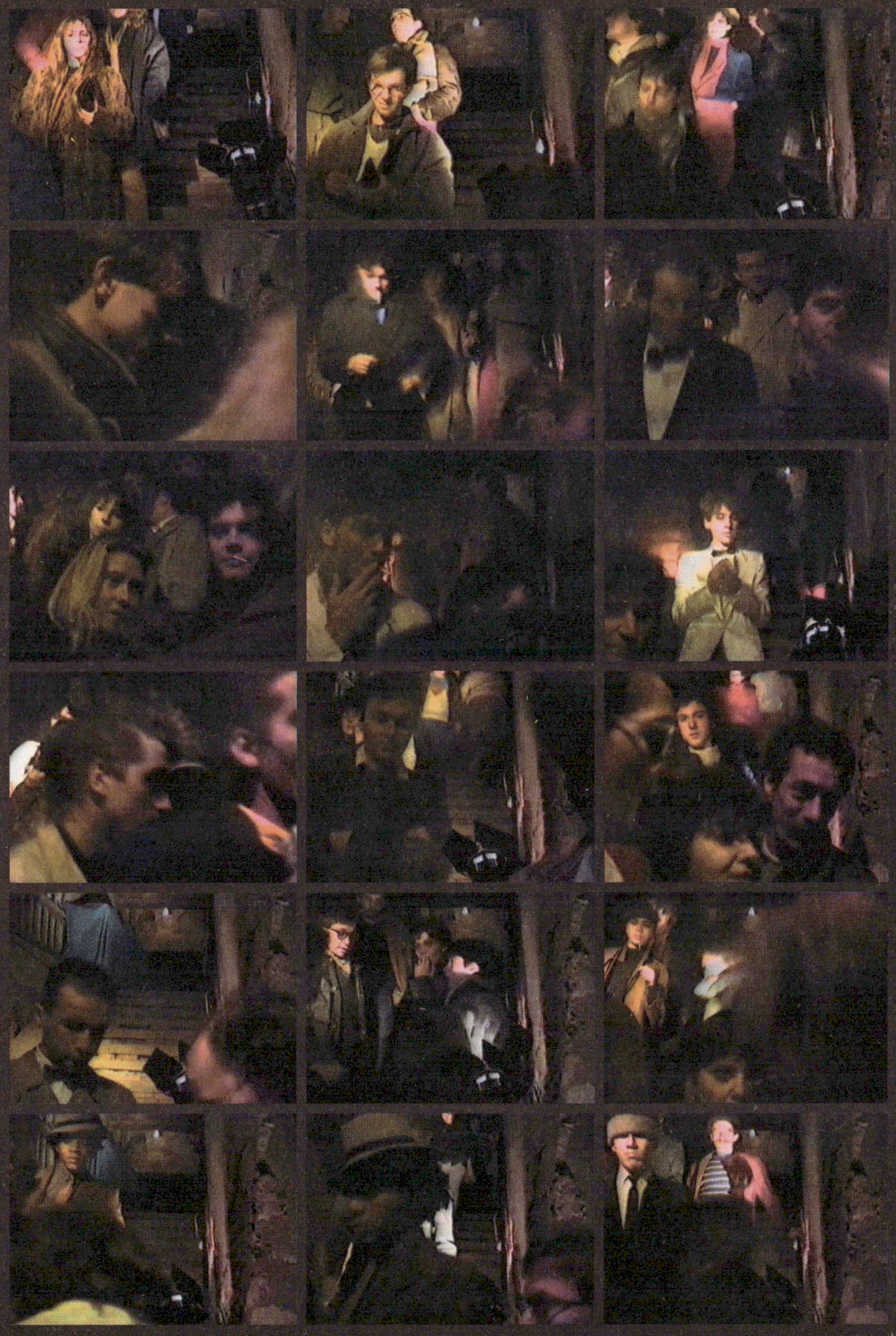

Cassero

1982–ongoing

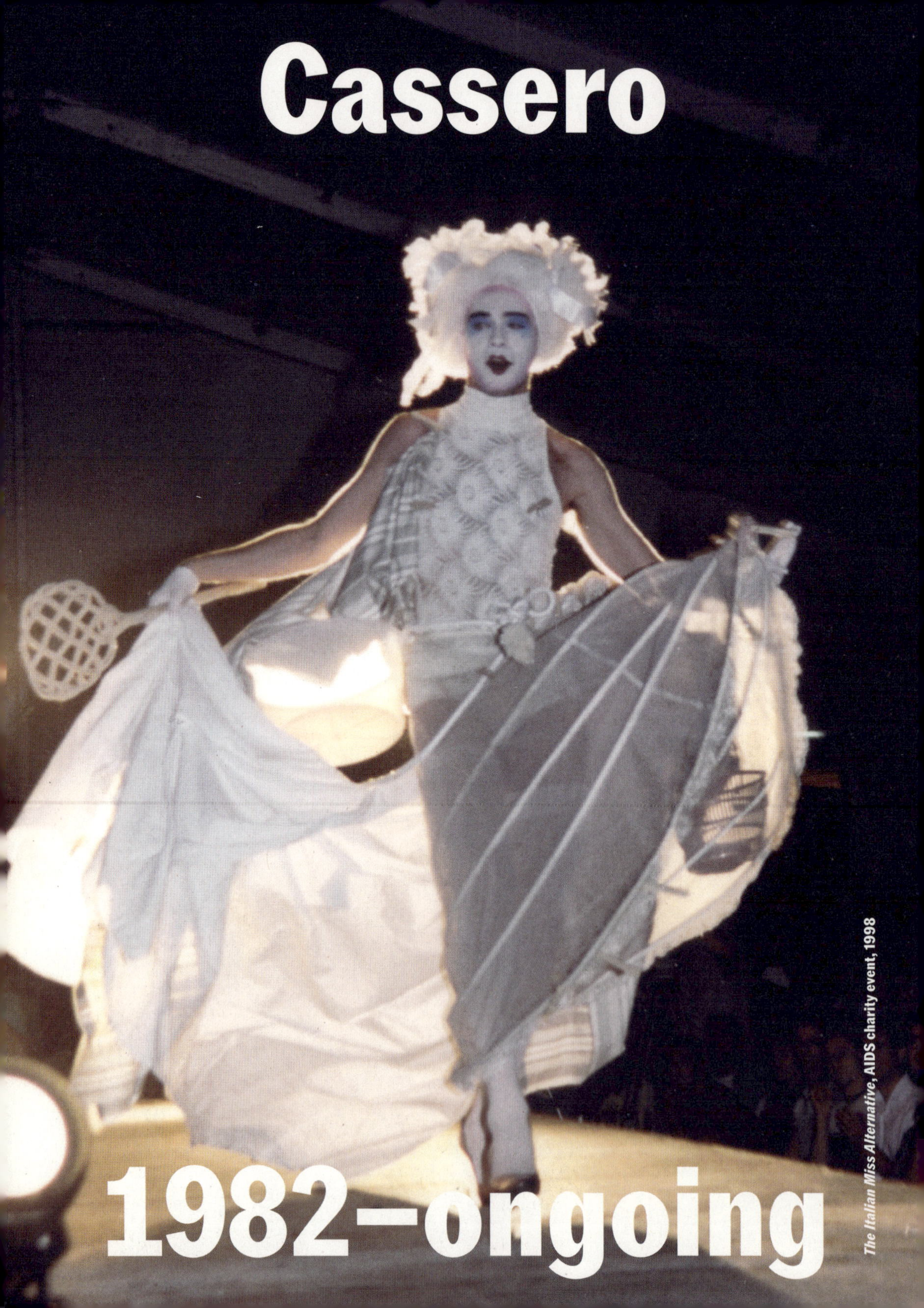

A multipurpose space that has become a symbol of the political and civil claims of the LGBTQIA+ community nationally and internationally, the Cassero has always been a promoter of cultural programming of extreme importance on an artistic and social level.

In 1982, a milestone date for the city of Bologna and for Italy, Mayor Renato Zangheri assigned the Cassero di Porta Saragozza—one of the small towers in the ancient city walls of Bologna—to the Circolo XXVIII Giugno, a homosexual group that had already been active for several years in the Emilian capital: thus Cassero was born. It was the first time in Italy that a public administration recognized social and cultural value to an openly homosexual association, assigning it a city-owned venue. The council made this decision despite the discontent of the Bologna clergy and part of the citizens, opposed to the fact that this kind of reality might be given a home in a building originally dedicated to the Madonna di San Luca. The visibility of the circle and the scope of its activities increased in 2002, with the relocation of Cassero to the Manifattura delle Arti at the Salara del Parco del Cavaticcio, at the behest of center-right mayor Giorgio Guazzaloca, who thus wanted to symbolically return the Cassero di Porta Saragozza to the religious community, considering the centrality of the building during the procession dedicated to the Madonna.

Born out of a minority need and identity claims, since its early years, Cassero has had a cultural and artistic approach significantly linked to the political and social sphere of the LGBTQIA+ community. Various initiatives over the years have enabled the circle to increase its social and cultural weight through art, music, theater, cinema, literature, and the performing arts, all forms of artistic expression given space through events of an interdisciplinary nature such as the Festival del Cinema Gay e Lesbico di Milano e Bologna, Blowing Bubbles, the Libera Università Omosessuale, the Gender Bender festival,

Teatro Arcobaleno, and Performing Gender. Despite the fact that its forty years of activity—and particularly the last two decades—have been characterized by intense relationship-building and networking with other citywide, national, and international entities, Cassero has always maintained an aspect of independence understood as autonomy in decision-making. It is precisely this freedom that still allows Cassero to address a diverse audience, one that has become post-identitarian over the years, insofar as it is not composed solely of people belonging to the LGBTQIA+ camp but to the broader community, including the arts audience.

The Cassero's cultural events in fact respond to the need to provide alternative readings to the mainstream ones proposed by the mass media, proposing non-stereotypical outlooks. Cassero today maintains a politically and culturally prominent position nationally and internationally because of its ability to change and adapt to the new needs of society, making art a political and identitary tool of liberation.

ADDRESS Porta Saragozza, Piazza di Porta Saragozza 2/a, Bologna (1982–2002); Salara del Parco del Cavaticcio, Via Don Giovanni Minzoni 18, Bologna (2002–). FOUNDERS Samuel Pinto, Beppe Ramina, Diego Scudiero, Antonio Frainer, Claudio Fuschini, Valerio Cacciari, Luciano Pignotti. COLLABORATORS Stefano Casagrande, Bruno Pompa, Mauro Copeta (Wawashi), Sara De Giovanni, Daniele Del Pozzo, Mauro Meneghelli

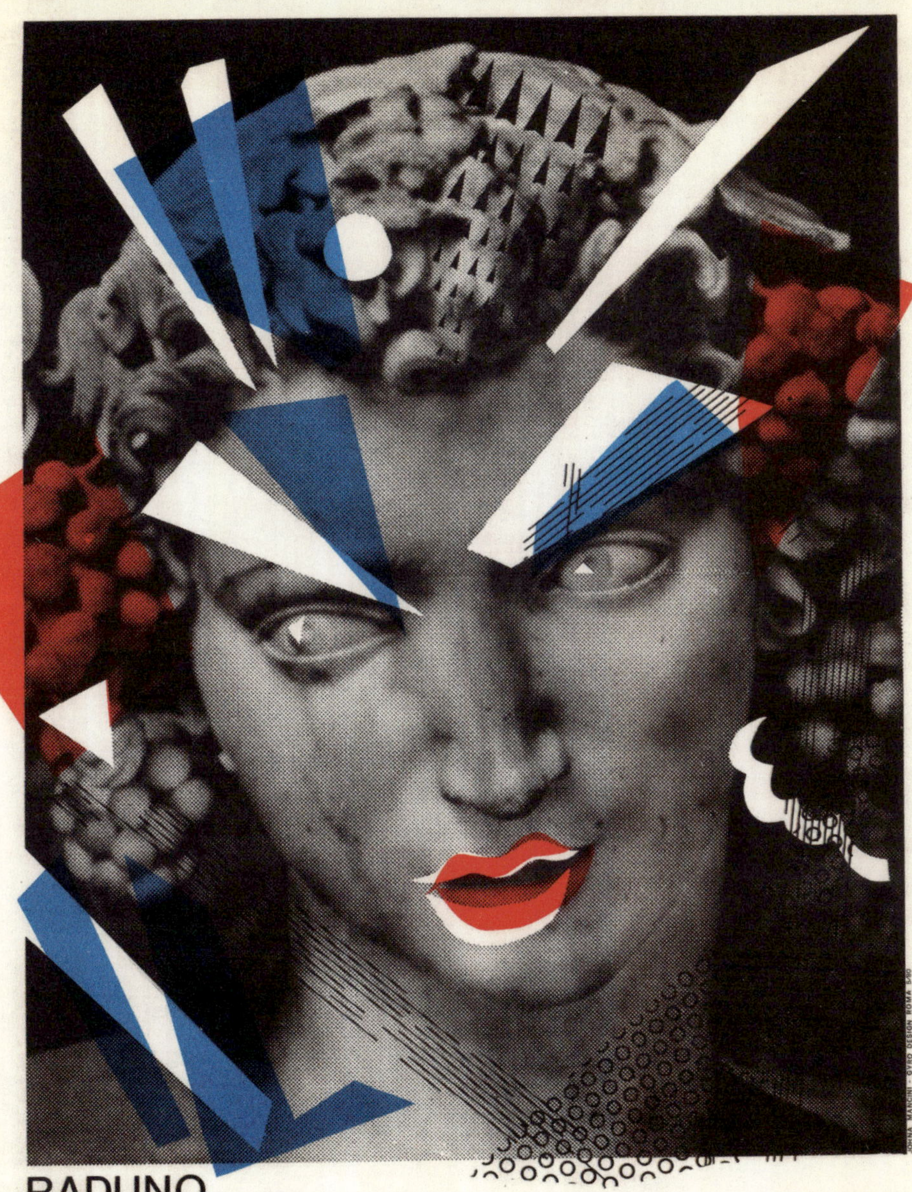
ORGOGLIO OMOSESSUALE
RADUNO
Bologna, ven. 27; sab. 28; dom. 29 Giugno
PUNTO DI RIFERIMENTO/ INCONTRO: SALONE DEL PODESTÀ P.za MAGGIORE
Comunicato stampa- Benvenuto- Mostra fotografica- Teatro.
Corteo ore 14/15- Performances in P.za Maggiore- ore 21/24 Serata danzante & tante altre iniziative.
Incontro/riflessione nel salone del podestà sulle giornate trascorse- Giochi ecc. ecc. . . . .
PER INFORMAZIONI TELEFONARE AL N° 051/551389

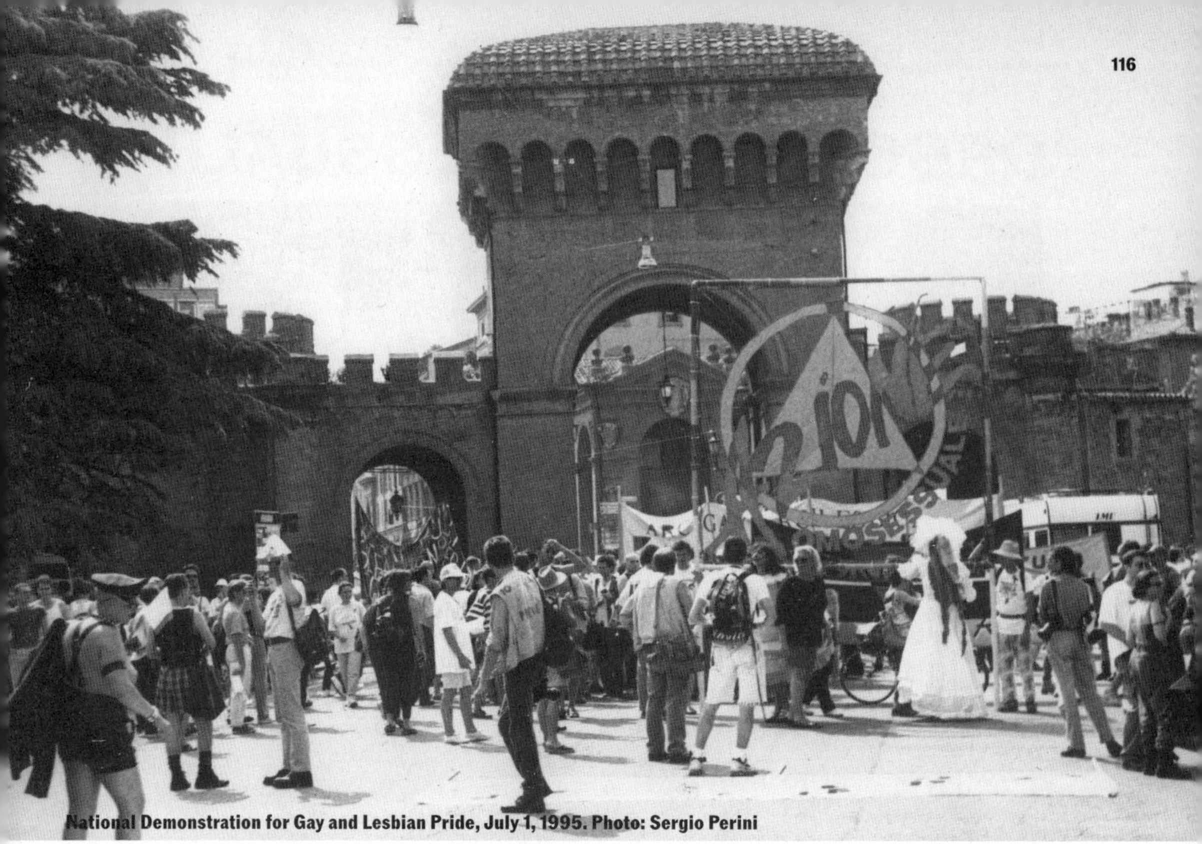

National Demonstration for Gay and Lesbian Pride, July 1, 1995. Photo: Sergio Perini

Inaugural parade for the opening of the Cassero in Porta Saragozza, June 26, 1982

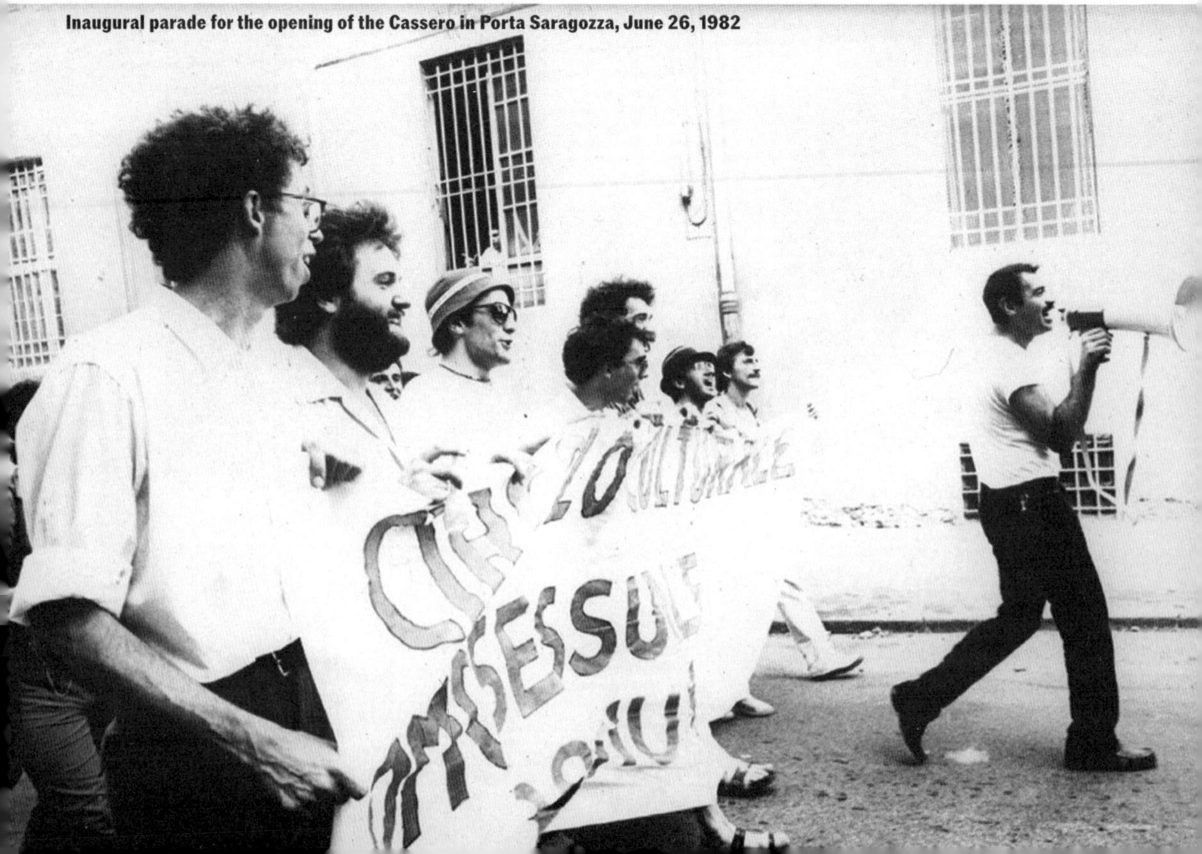

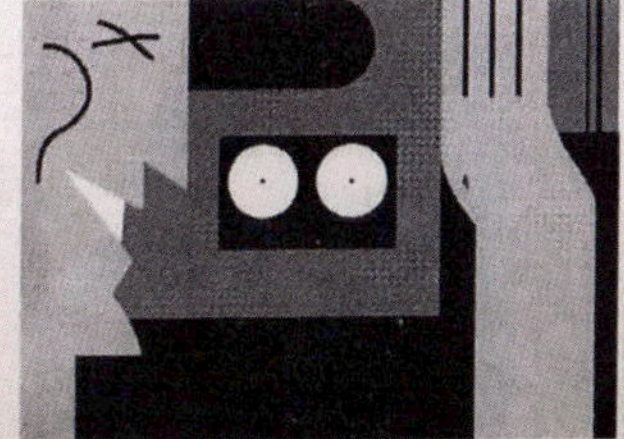
Blowing Bubbles
93
International Video Competition on Aids

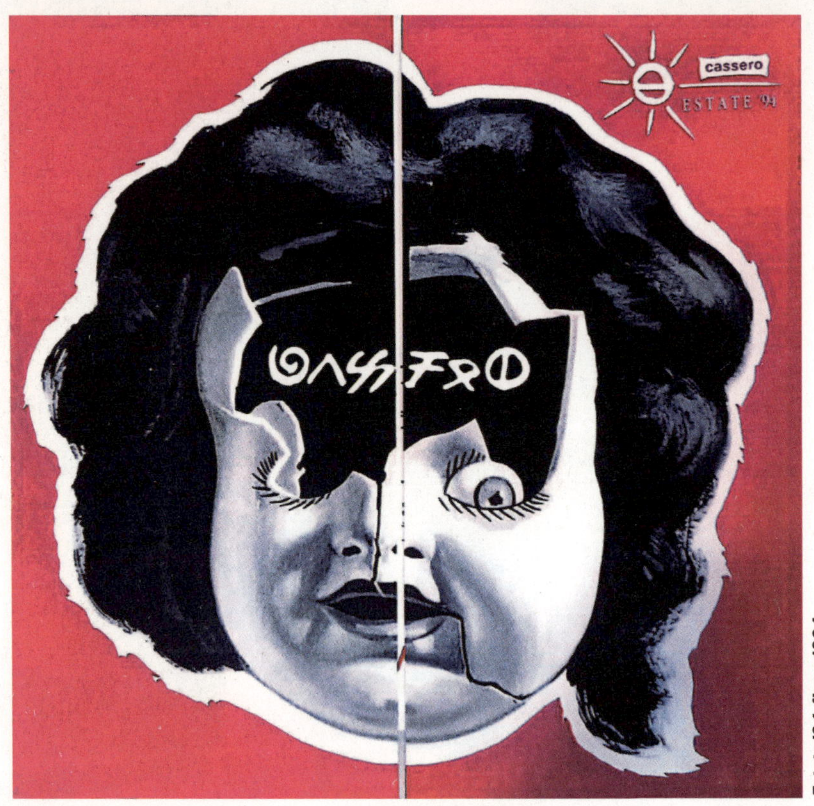

Estate '94, flyer, 1994

Perversailles, flyer, 1989

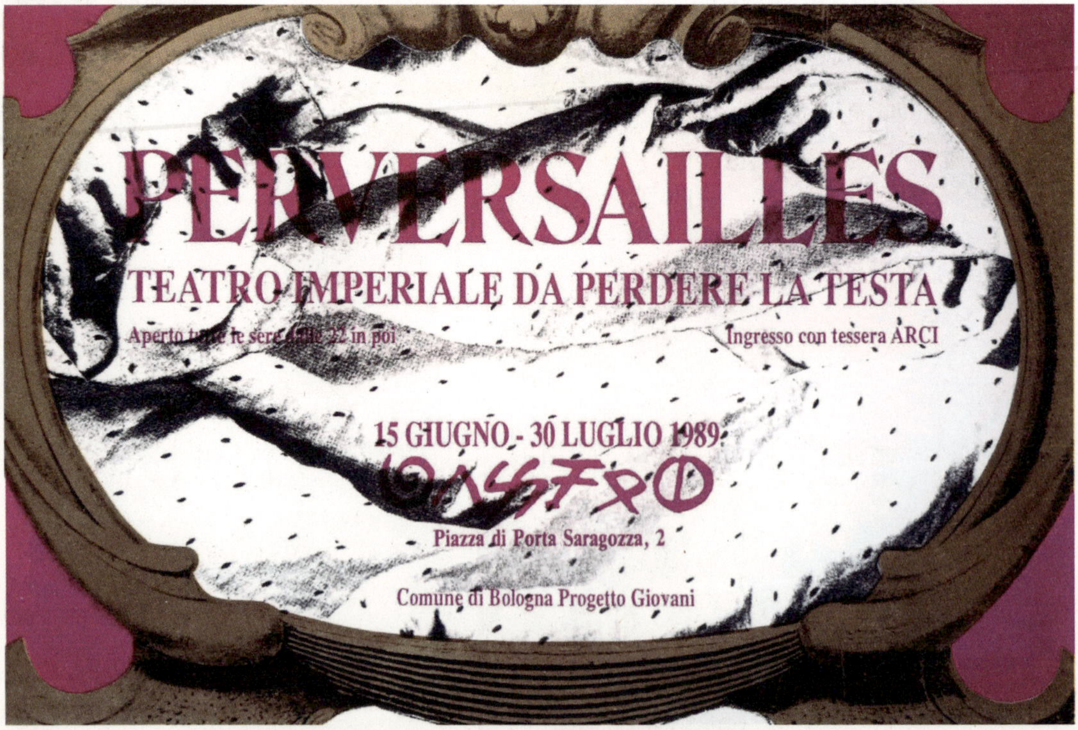

  Daniele Ninarello and Performing Gender, *Crowded Bodies*, **Gender Bender festival, June 18, 2023**

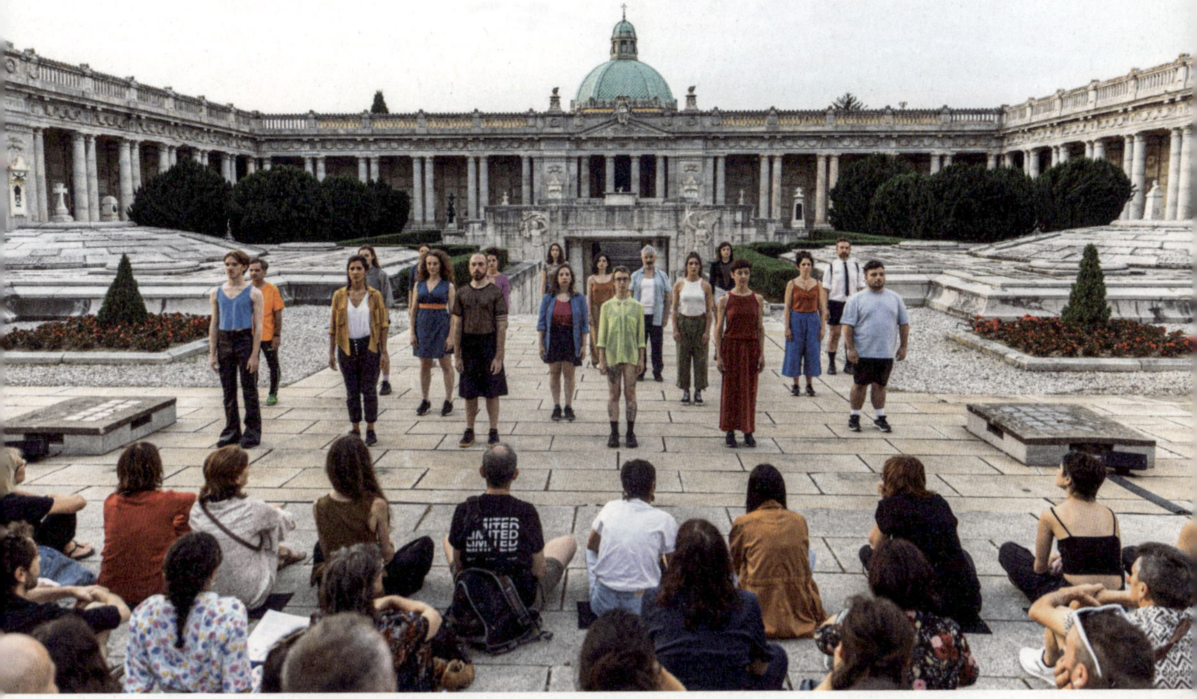

Le unioni civili non ci coglieranno di sorpresa, **flyer, 1994**

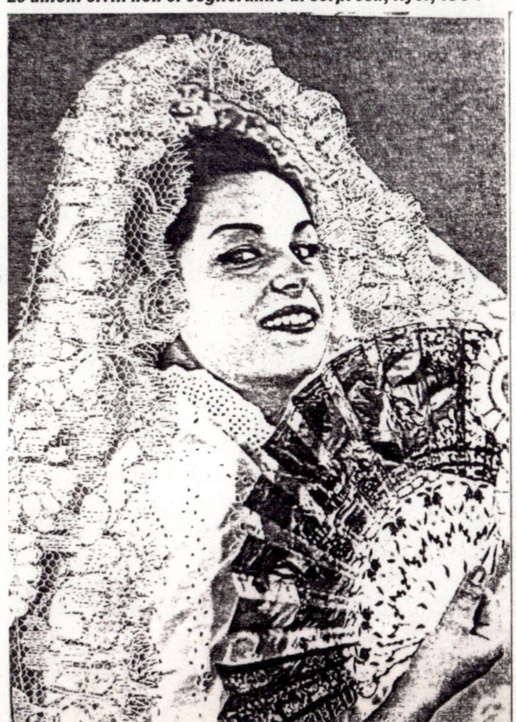

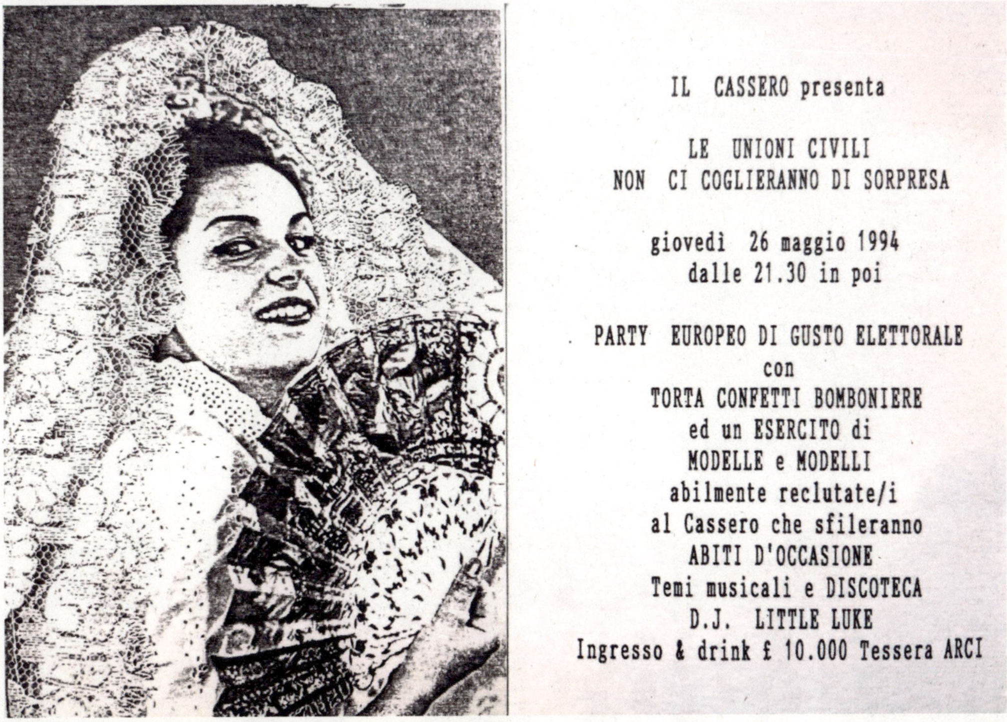

IL CASSERO presenta

LE UNIONI CIVILI
NON CI COGLIERANNO DI SORPRESA

giovedì 26 maggio 1994
dalle 21.30 in poi

PARTY EUROPEO DI GUSTO ELETTORALE
con
TORTA CONFETTI BOMBONIERE
ed un ESERCITO di
MODELLE e MODELLI
abilmente reclutate/i
al Cassero che sfileranno
ABITI D'OCCASIONE
Temi musicali e DISCOTECA
D.J. LITTLE LUKE
Ingresso & drink £ 10.000 Tessera ARCI

Nowall

1985–1988

Nowall (No wall/Now all) was founded in 1985 inside a building previously occupied by the Arci Circle on Via delle Moline 2. The spacious venue consisted of two rooms, on the ground and second floors, yet cultural projects sometimes contaminated the outside of the venue. Decisions were made collectively, while the organization of events was entrusted to individual members who had full decision-making powers, although Alberto Masala was responsible for the artistic directorship. The space was financially supported by revenues from the bar as well as external sponsorships. With time and the advancement of the projects, in addition to the support of Arcimedia, relations with the Department of Youth Policies of the Municipality of Bologna were also established.

Nowall's activities were inspired by a number of European and US neo-avant-garde art movements, such as the Beat Generation, Fluxus, Parisian Art Brut, and the Amsterdam Provos, but also by contemporary practices such as Neoexpressionism and Berlin Punk. In 1986, Nowall joined the international network of independent cultural centers Trans Europe Halles. In collaboration with this network, events were produced including two editions of the Festival d'Art Room, which brought together various research situations focused on new poetics and cultural actions from the social context, two editions of the Biennial of Young Artists from Europe and the Mediterranean, an edition of the AFA Festival, and the exhibitions *Landjuveel* (1987) and *Berlino Capitale europea della cultura* (1988).

Rereading Nowall's experience today, a clear alignment with the spirit of post-punk culture emerges, even considering the focus on performance practices, gender identity issues, interdisciplinary approaches and the decadent and at times nihilistic aesthetics typical of goth culture.

ADDRESS Via delle Moline 2, Bologna. FOUNDERS Alberto Masala. COLLABORATORS Fabio Leopardi, Barore (Salvatore) Molinu, Donatello Argiolas, Leo (Heliodoro) Martin Peña

THE ETERNAL

performance di fabio ciriachi

CON: FEDERICO CASTELLI, SUSANNA COUVERT, FABIO CIRIACHI

TESTI DI: OSCAR WILDE

USICHE DI: SIOUXIE AND THE BANSHEES, THE DAMNED, JOY DIVISION, JOHAN SEBASTIAN

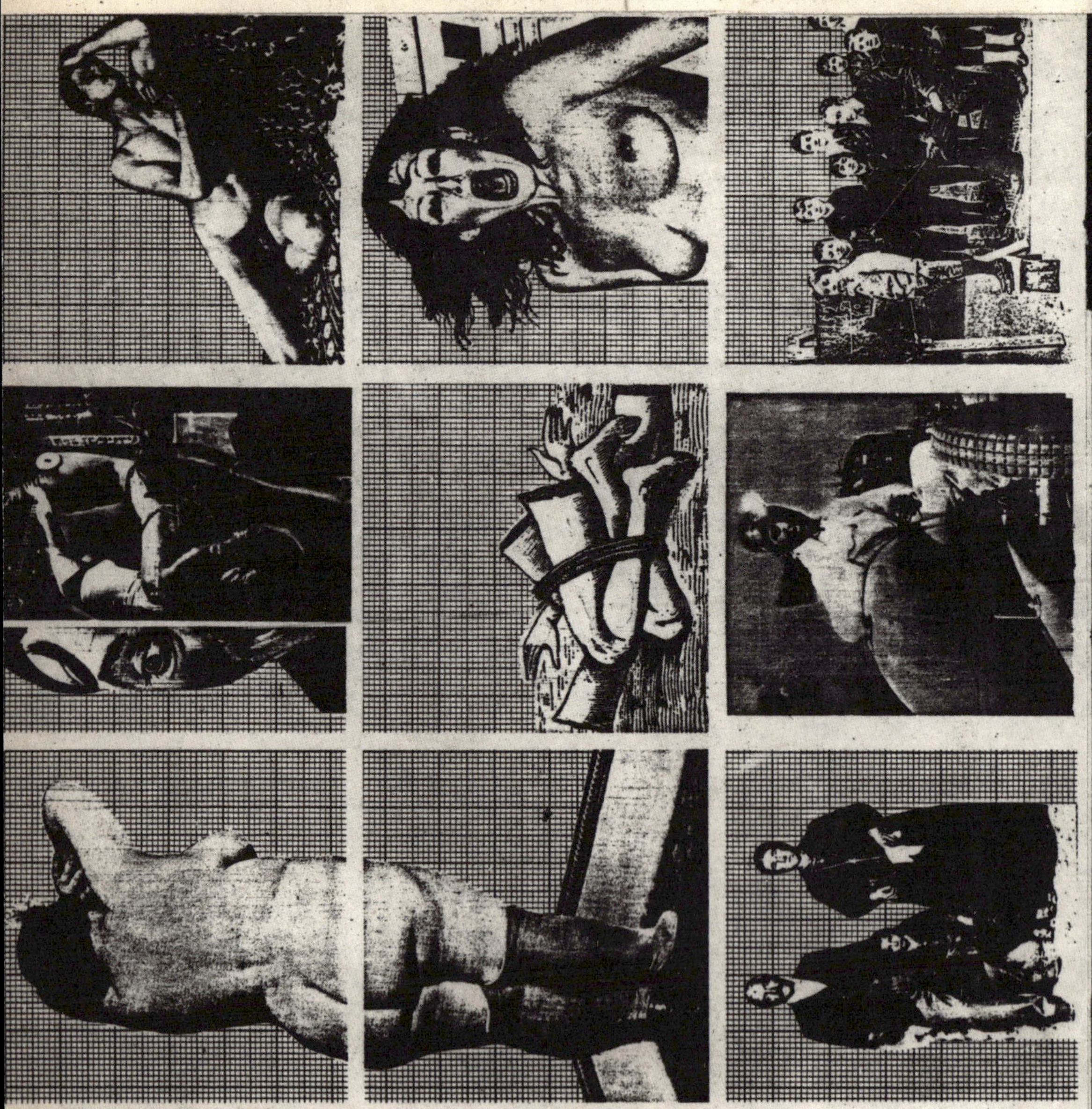

Fabio Ciriachi, *The Eternal*, flyer, 1985

   Michelle Probert, *Style Factory*, flyer, 1985

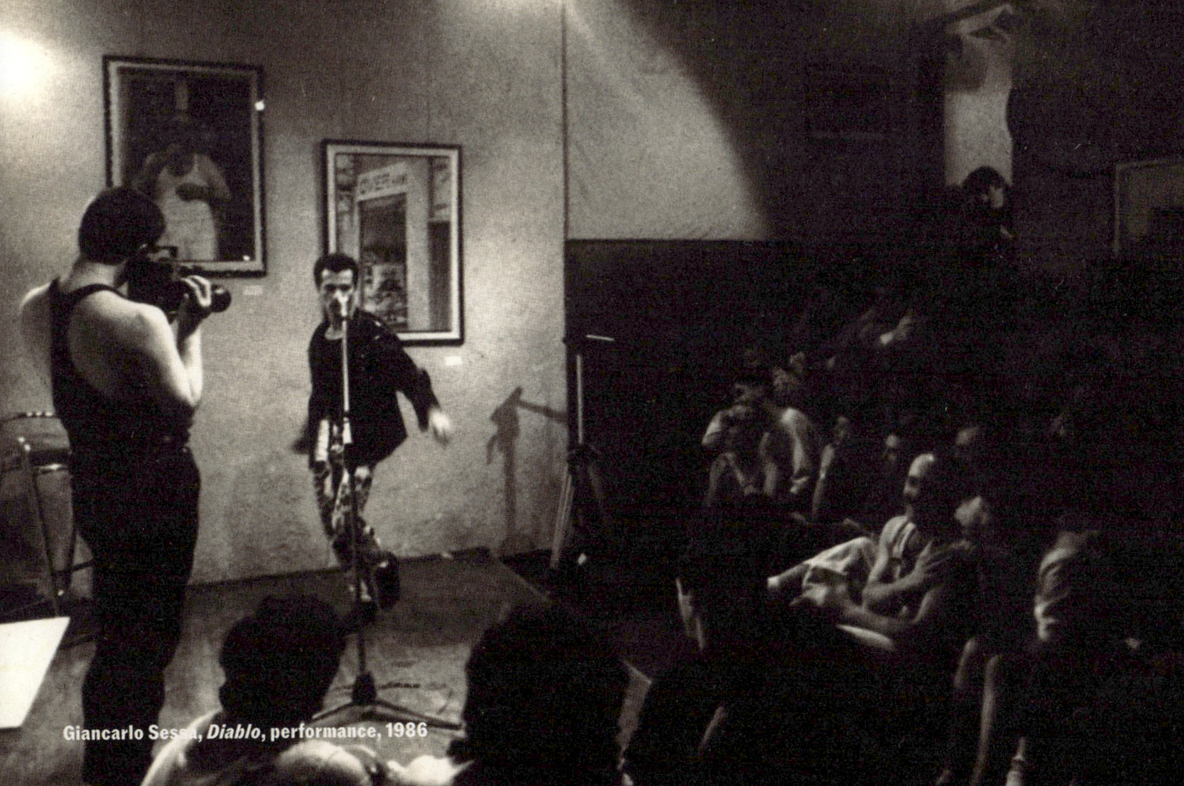

Giancarlo Sessa, *Diablo*, performance, 1986

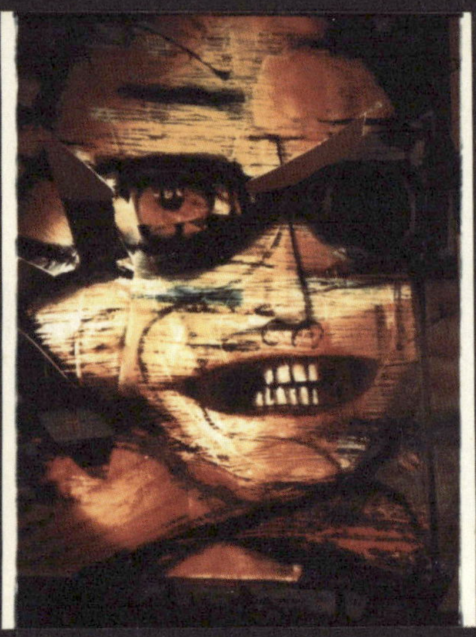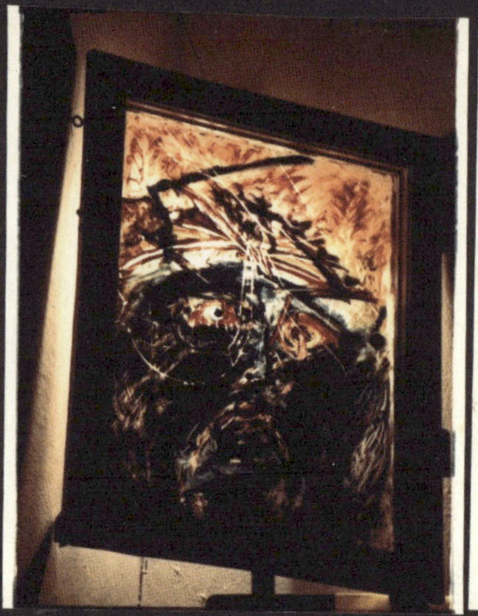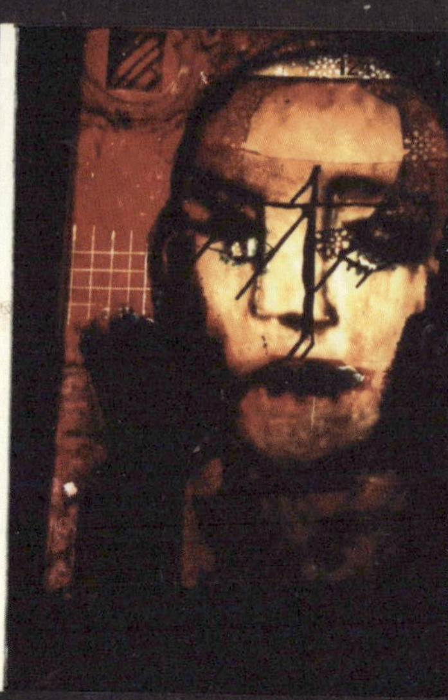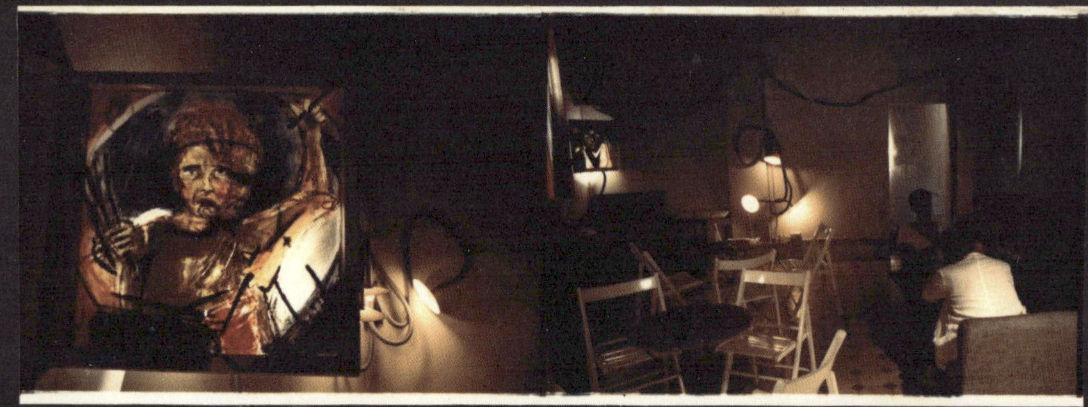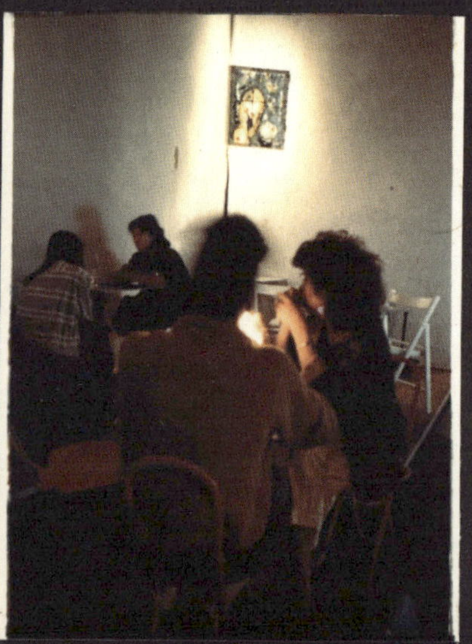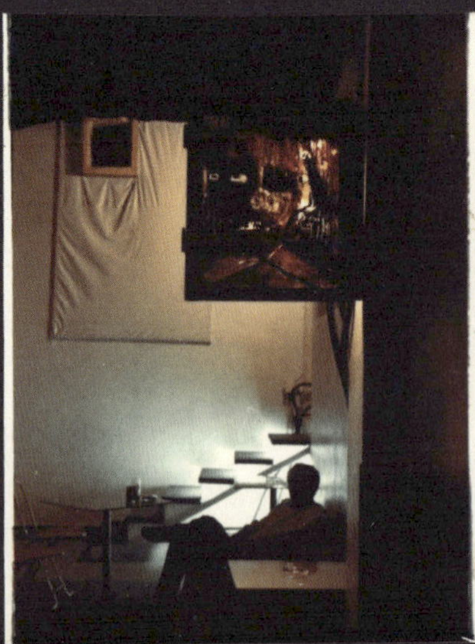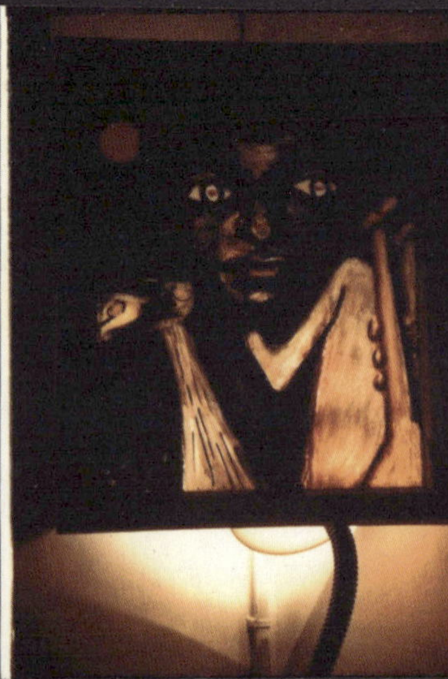

Oliver Richter, *Berliner Fenster*, installation view, 1985

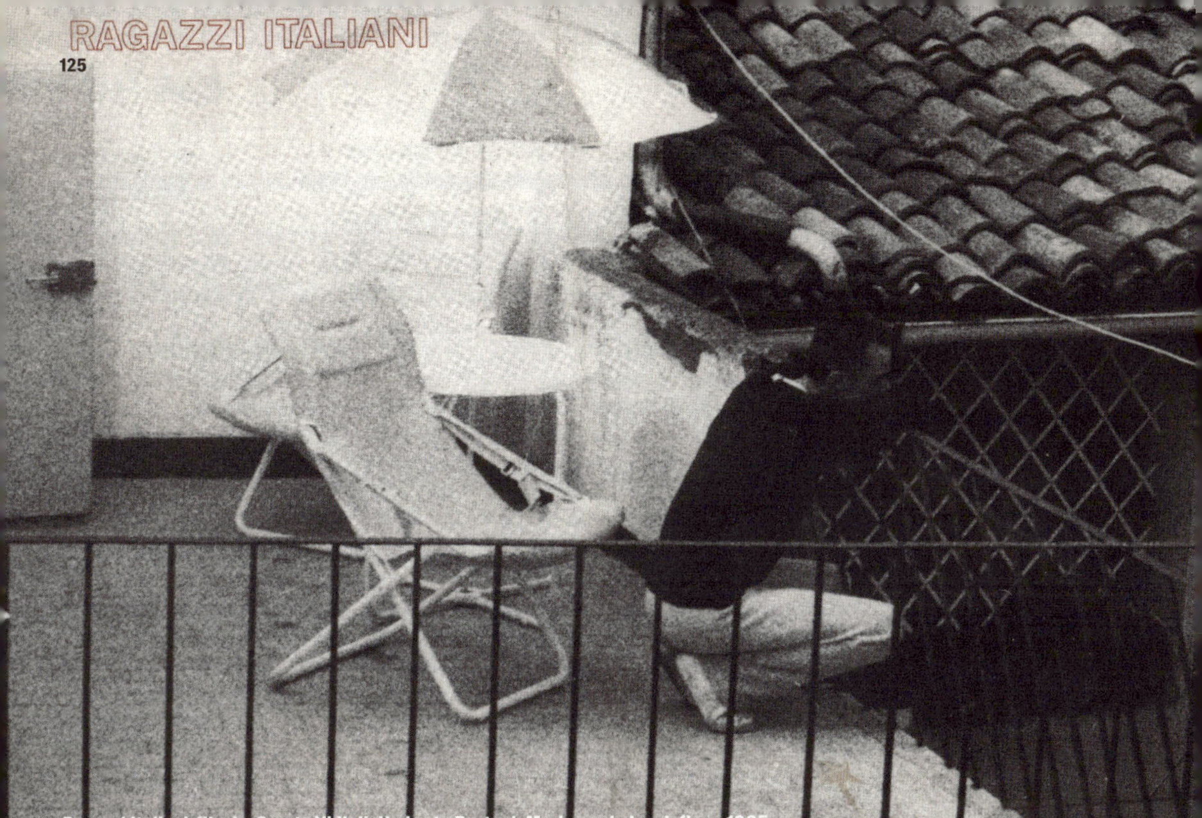

Ragazzi Italiani, film by Oreste Vidioli, Umberto Bertani, Mariagrazia Iacci, flyer, 1985

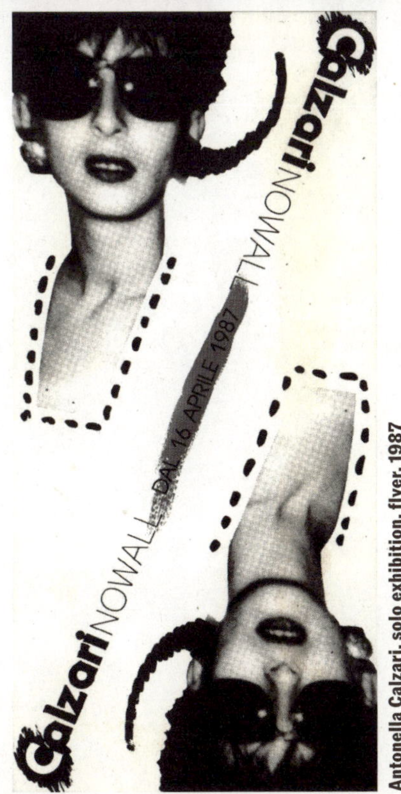

Antonella Calzari, solo exhibition, flyer, 1987

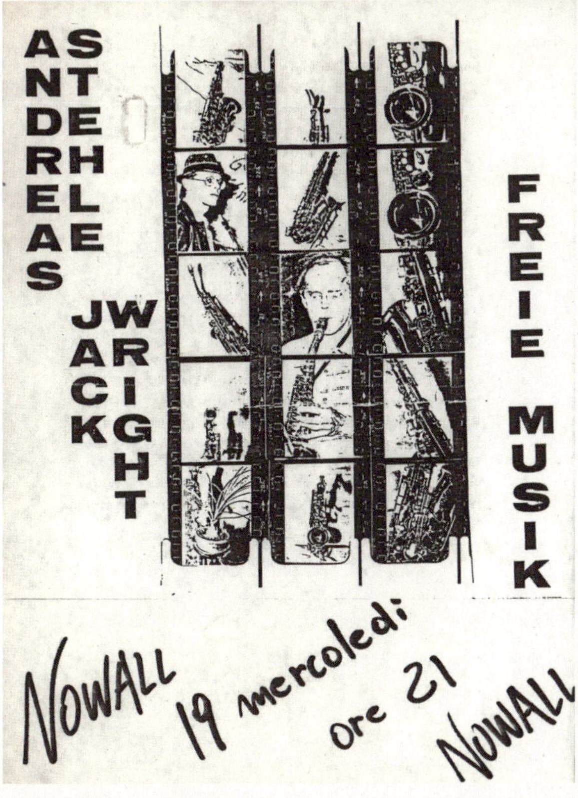

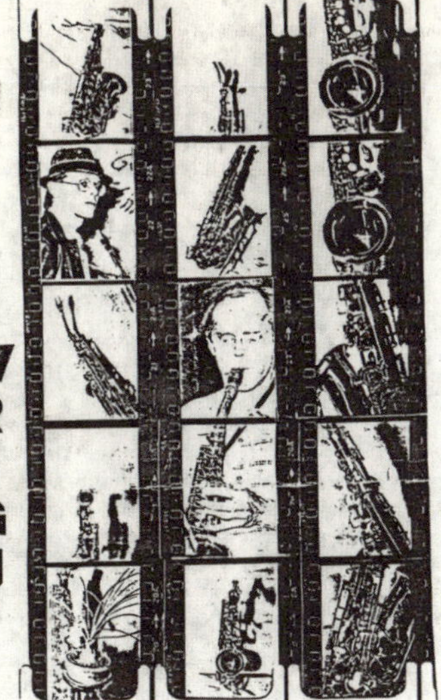

Andreas Stehle and Jack Wright, *Freie Musik*, flyer, March 19, 1986

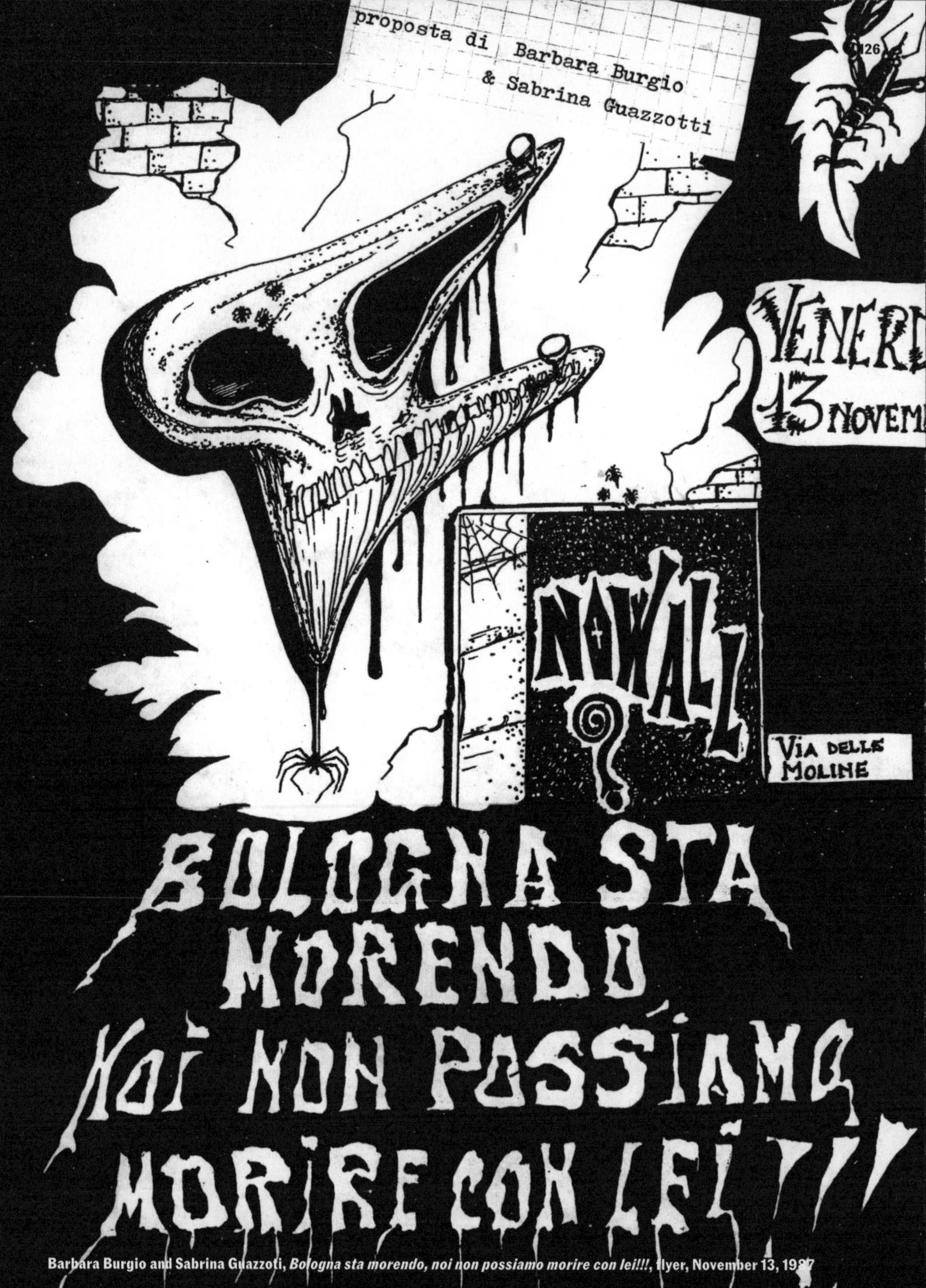

Barbara Burgio and Sabrina Guazzoti, *Bologna sta morendo, noi non possiamo morire con lei!!!*, flyer, November 13, 1987

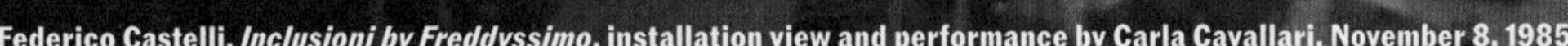

Federico Castelli, *Inclusioni by Freddyssimo*, installation view and performance by Carla Cavallari, November 8, 1985

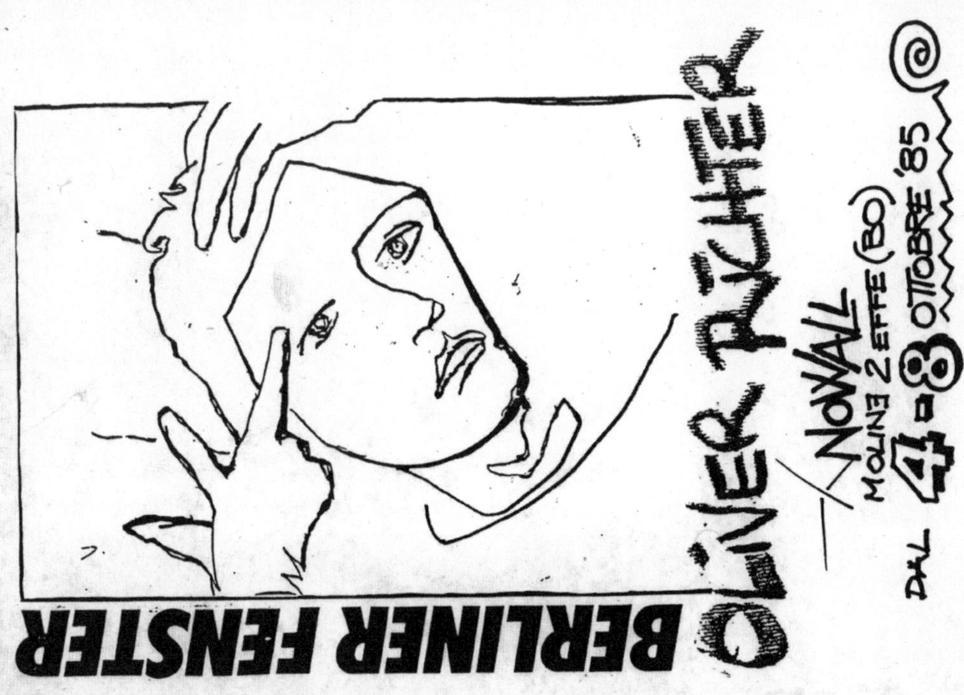

Oliver Richter, *Berliner Fenster*, flyer, 1985

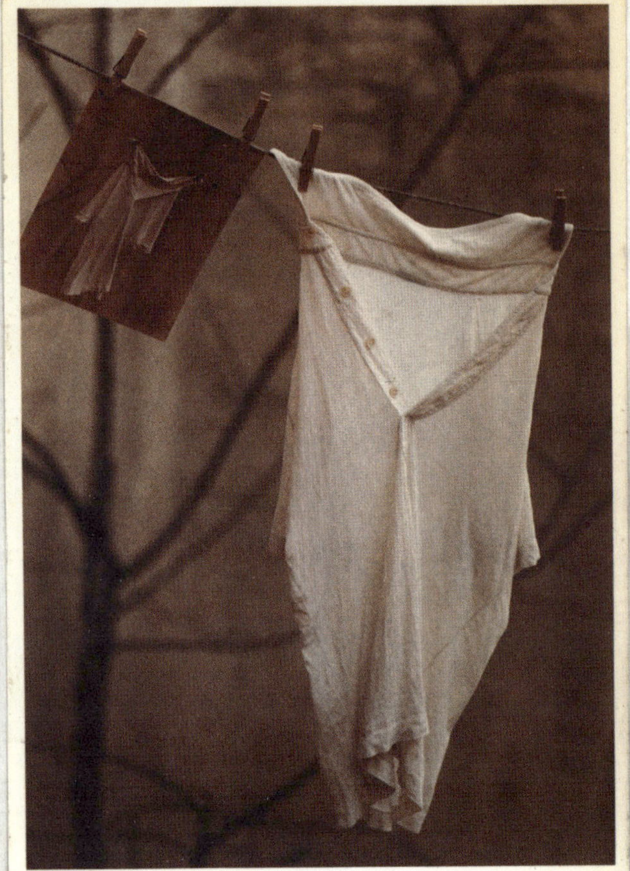

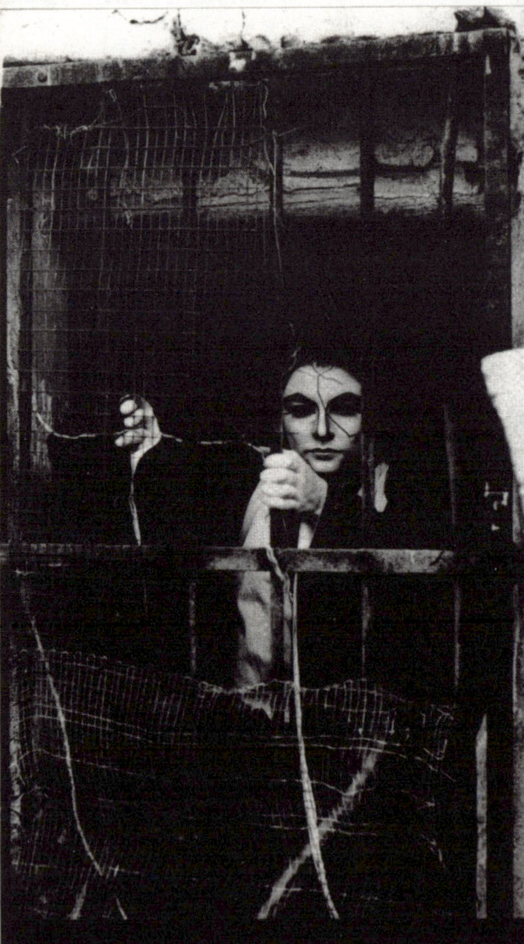
dalle finestre alle finestre
personale fotografica di
mimma giovinazzo
ore 21,00
5 - 13 dicembre 1986 - nowall

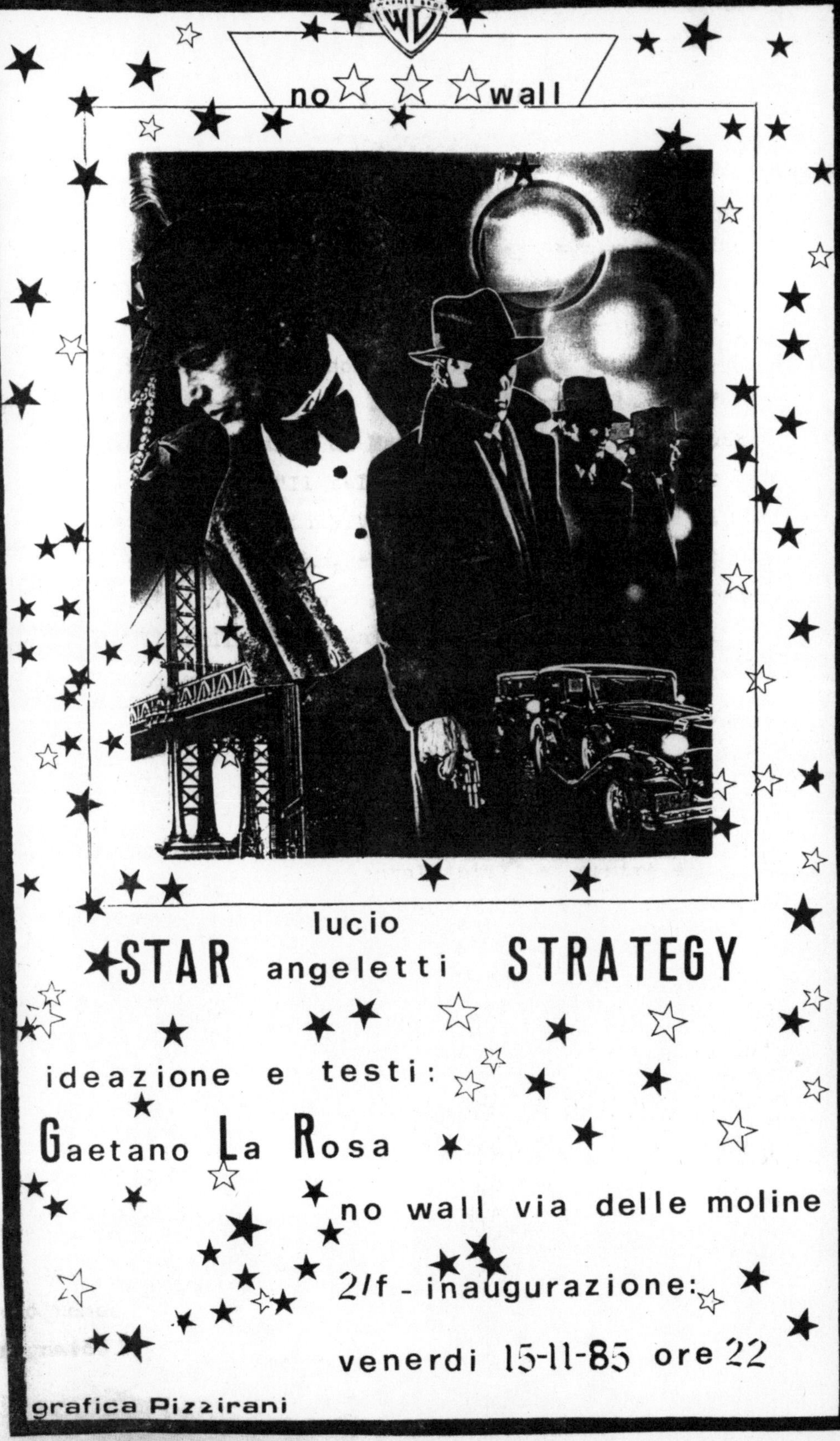
no wall
STAR
lucio
angeletti
STRATEGY
ideazione e testi:
Gaetano La Rosa
no wall via delle moline
2/f - inaugurazione:
venerdi 15-11-85 ore 22
grafica Pizzirani

Isola Nel Kantiere

Interior of Isola Nel Kantiere, 1991. Photo: Gianluca Perticoni

Creative workshops, 1991. Photo: Gianluca Perticoni

1988–1991

Within the Bolognese punk scene of the mid 1980s, from a nucleus linked to the anarchist center of Porta Santo Stefano and the squatters responsible for the occupation of a number of houses in Via Galliera, there arose the need to give life to a self-managed cultural space that reflected the political demands of a new generation that aimed to shape its dissent through the arts. Although the anarchist-inspired punk scene was at the origin of Isola Nel Kantiere, this space eventually became an incubator for Italian rap.

The discovery of a former ceramics warehouse overlooking Piazzetta San Giuseppe, behind the Arena del Sole Theater and the busy high street, Via dell'Indipendenza, equipped with an acoustically isolated basement particularly suitable for musical performances, led to the founding of I.N.K. in September 1988. Isola took shape on the model of similar initiatives, such as Virus in Milan and numerous other occupied spaces in Berlin, Amsterdam, and Copenhagen.

Within the collective, a series of roles were immediately outlined on the basis of individual skills: technician, graphic designer, promoter, cook, etc. The organization was run horizontally and the only decision-making body was the assembly.

Isola opened with a protest at the Biennial of Young Artists from Europe and the Mediterranean, based in Bologna that year, demonstrating the collective's disinterest in dealing with the official art system, if not on confrontational terms. On the contrary, the group immediately entered into relations with an international network of record labels and punk, hardcore, and industrial bands from the United States, Germany, and the Netherlands who were interested in playing in self-managed spaces. In this regard, mention should be made, for example, of performances by Henry Rollins, Fugazi, and Test Dept.

Independence from public institutions and the logic of commercial production was a fundamental aspect of Isola Nel Kantiere, which was expressed mainly through the self-production of records, fanzines and interdisciplinary artistic activities, from curated movie programs to graphic design and graffiti; from sculptural operations based on the use of discarded materials to multimedia projects.

The do-it-yourself and anti-authoritarian spirit of punk was soon channeled into a new set of creative energies, notably the earliest hip-hop jams in town, where Isola Posse All Stars members developed their own brand of rapping, among the first in Italy to use the Italian language to rap. They were a crew formed inside Isola Nel Kantiere, and it was here that they came out with the song-manifesto "Stop al Panico" (1991), as the soundtrack for a massive demonstration against the forceful eviction of social spaces underway in Bologna at the time, in a social climate influenced by the Uno Bianca massacres. Pioneers of Italian hip hop and related genres such as raggamuffin who made their debut at Isola include members of Sud Sound System, DeeMo, Deda, Gopher D, and Papa Ricky.

The life cycle of Isola was a short one, but full of cultural initiatives and events. The final months were characterized by more articulated proposals, such as the three-day INK3D, and by public events in the streets of Bologna's town center aboard mobile sound systems, succeeding in bringing the contents and spirit of the occupied space to the outside world. Isola Nel Kantiere was evicted in 1991 at the behest of the Department of Culture, and the space was earmarked as a loading dock for the Arena Del Sole, despite a proposal to change the design submitted to the City Council by the collective in collaboration with an architect.

ADDRESS Piazzetta San Giuseppe 8, Bologna. FOUNDERS I.N.K. COLLABORATORS I.N.K.

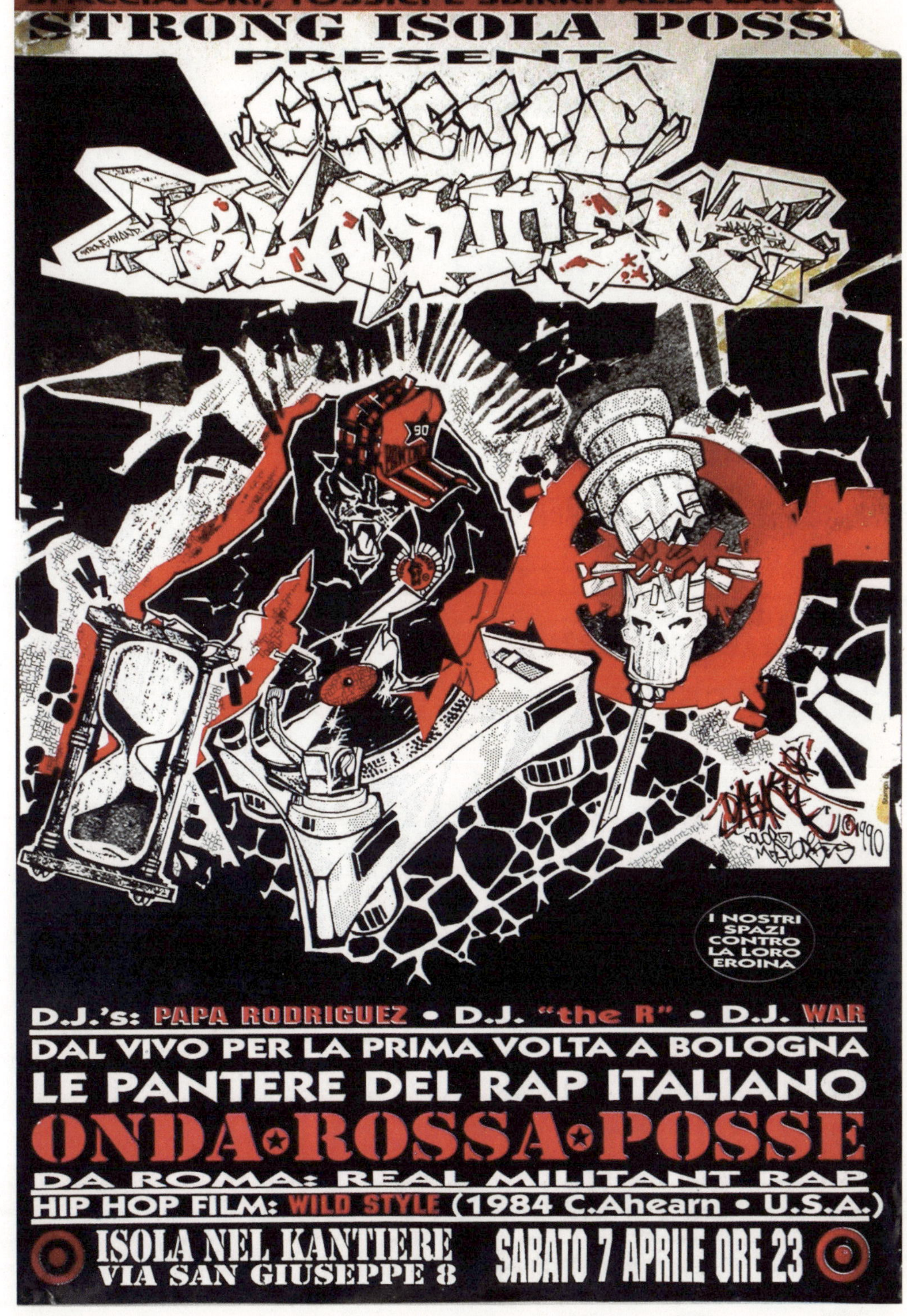
SPACCIATORI, TOSSICI E SBIRRI: ALLA LARG
STRONG ISOLA POSSE
PRESENTA
GHETTO BLASTERS
I NOSTRI SPAZI CONTRO LA LORO EROINA
D.J.'s: PAPA RODRIGUEZ • D.J. "the R" • D.J. WAR
DAL VIVO PER LA PRIMA VOLTA A BOLOGNA
LE PANTERE DEL RAP ITALIANO
ONDA ★ ROSSA ★ POSSE
DA ROMA: REAL MILITANT RAP
HIP HOP FILM: WILD STYLE (1984 C.Ahearn • U.S.A.)
ISOLA NEL KANTIERE
VIA SAN GIUSEPPE 8
SABATO 7 APRILE ORE 23

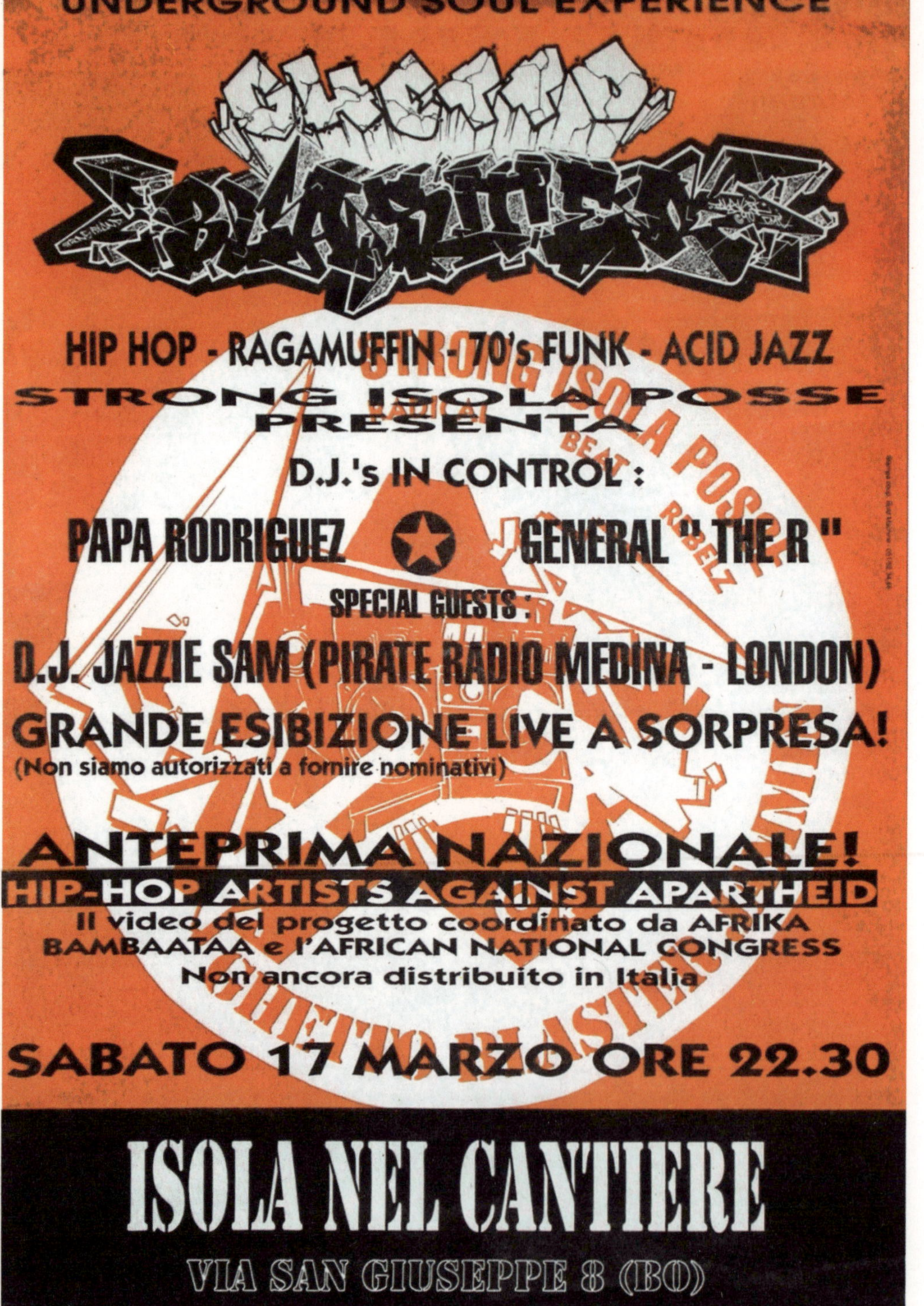
UNDERGROUND SOUL EXPERIENCE
GHETTO BLASTERS
HIP HOP - RAGAMUFFIN - 70's FUNK - ACID JAZZ
STRONG ISOLA POSSE
PRESENTA
D.J.'s IN CONTROL :
PAPA RODRIGUEZ
GENERAL " THE R "
SPECIAL GUESTS :
D.J. JAZZIE SAM (PIRATE RADIO MEDINA - LONDON)
GRANDE ESIBIZIONE LIVE A SORPRESA!
(Non siamo autorizzati a fornire nominativi)
ANTEPRIMA NAZIONALE!
HIP-HOP ARTISTS AGAINST APARTHEID
Il video del progetto coordinato da AFRIKA
BAMBAATAA e l'AFRICAN NATIONAL CONGRESS
Non ancora distribuito in Italia
SABATO 17 MARZO ORE 22.30
ISOLA NEL CANTIERE
VIA SAN GIUSEPPE 8 (BO)

Papa Ricky, 1991. Photo: Gianluca Perticoni

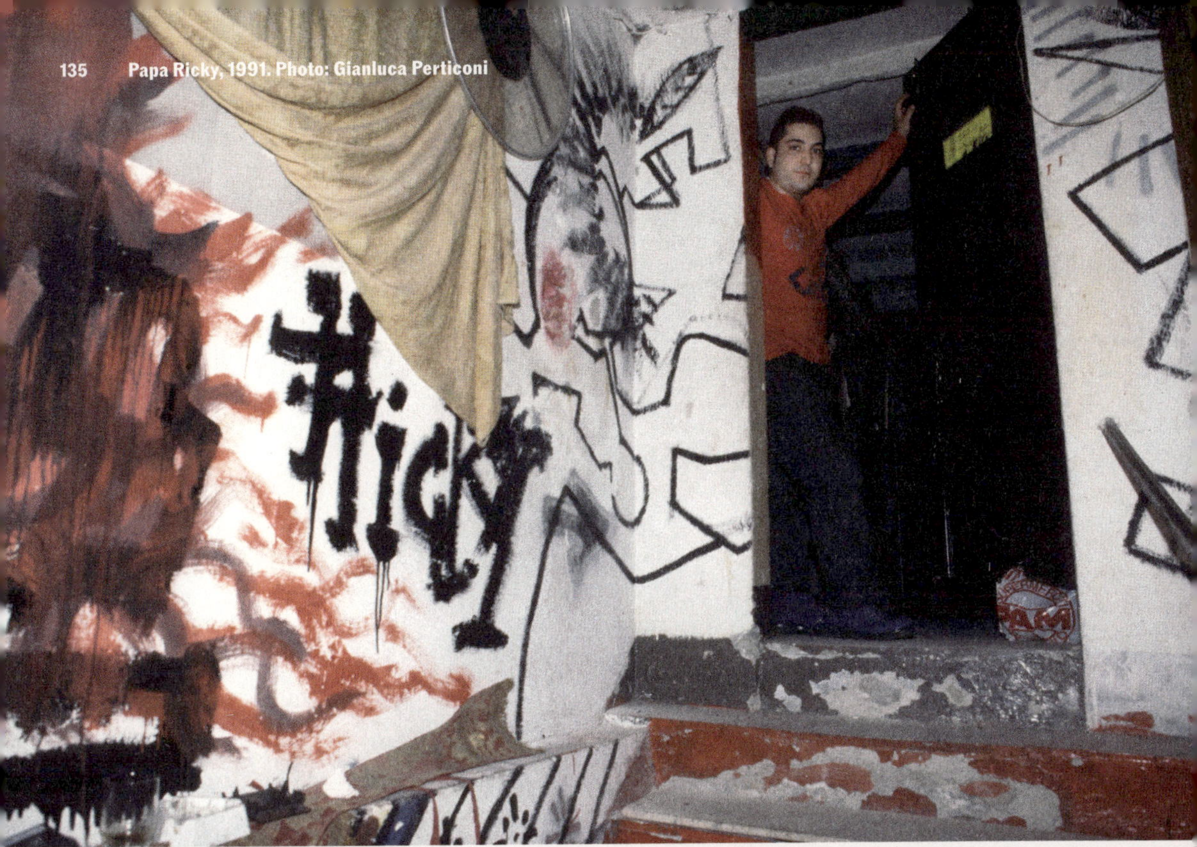

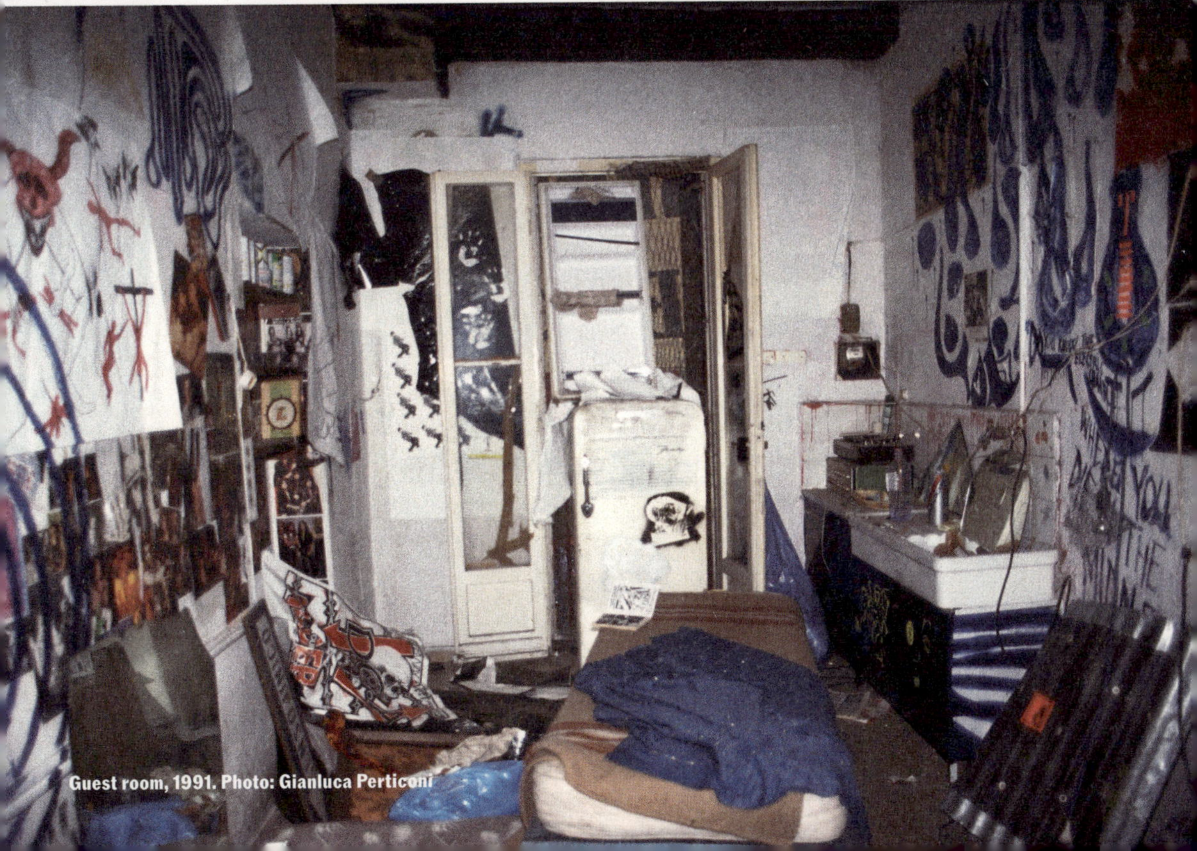

Guest room, 1991. Photo: Gianluca Perticoni

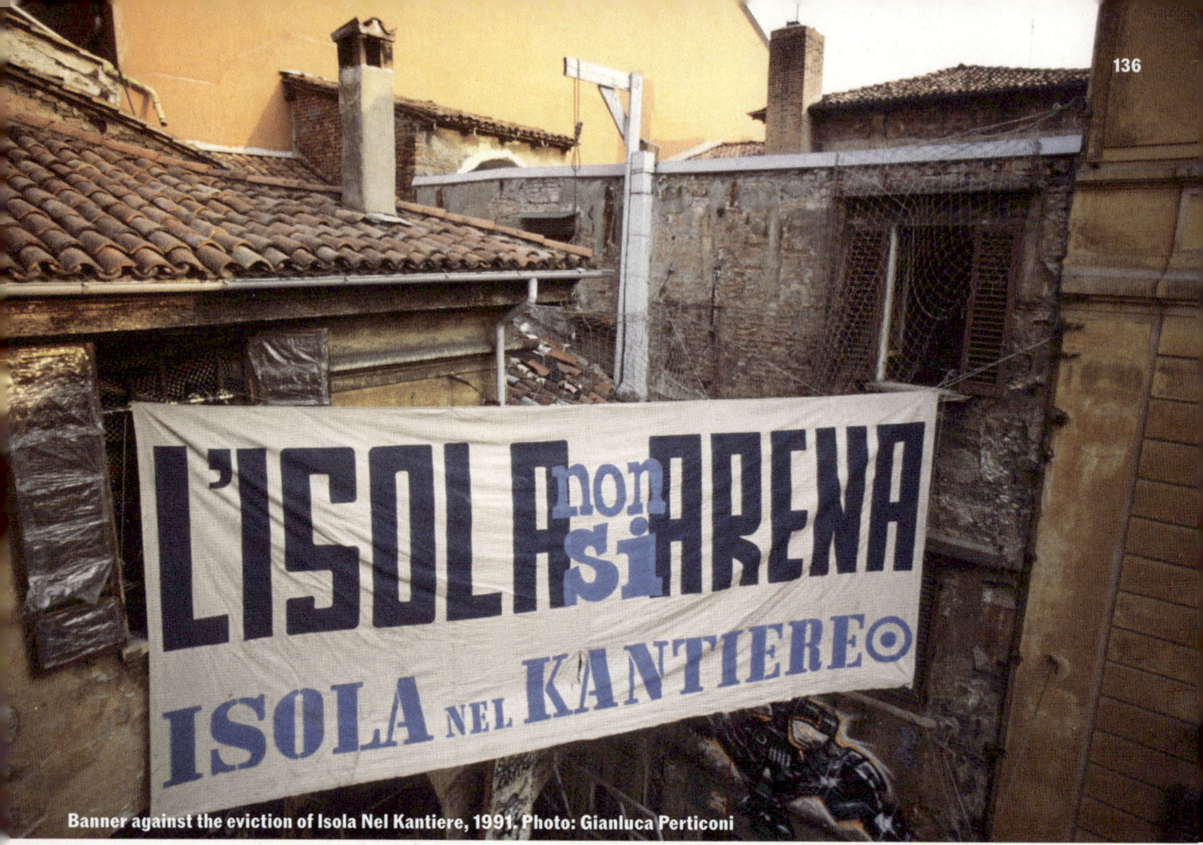

Banner against the eviction of Isola Nel Kantiere, 1991. Photo: Gianluca Perticoni

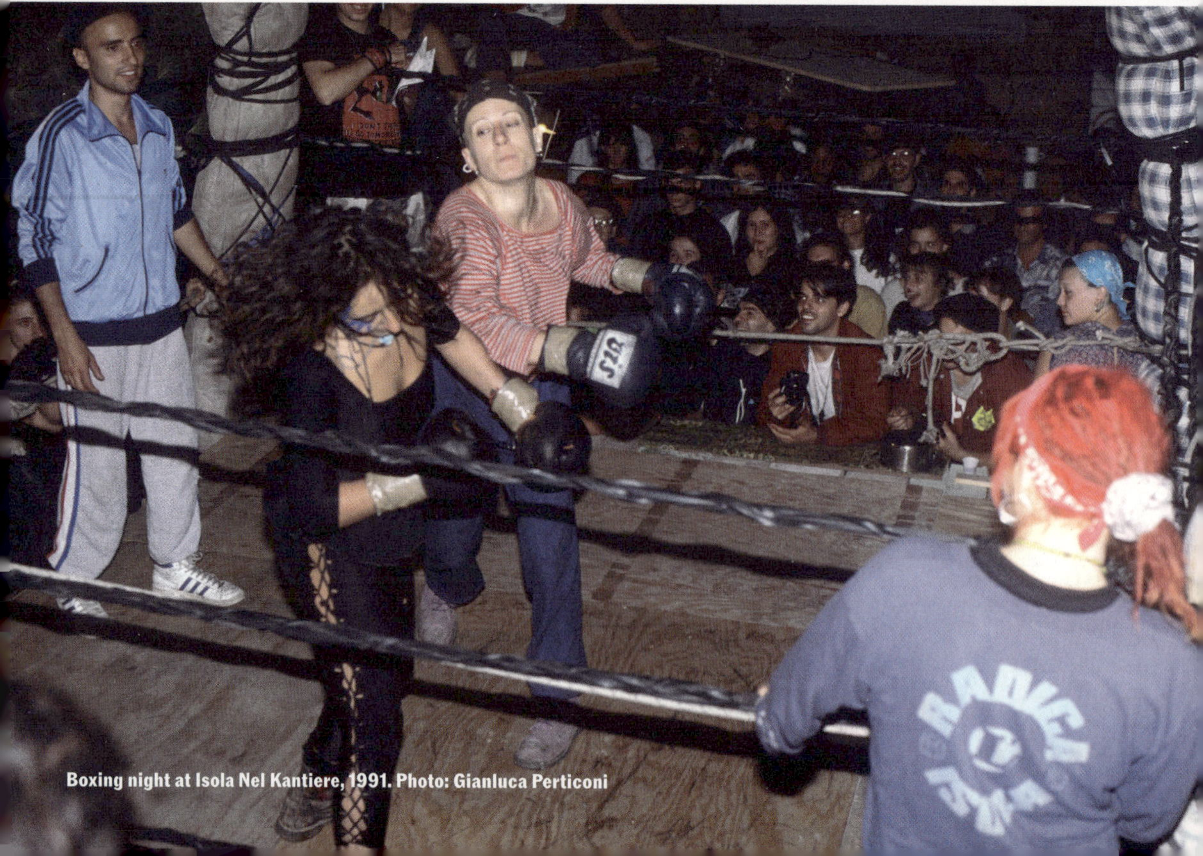

Boxing night at Isola Nel Kantiere, 1991. Photo: Gianluca Perticoni

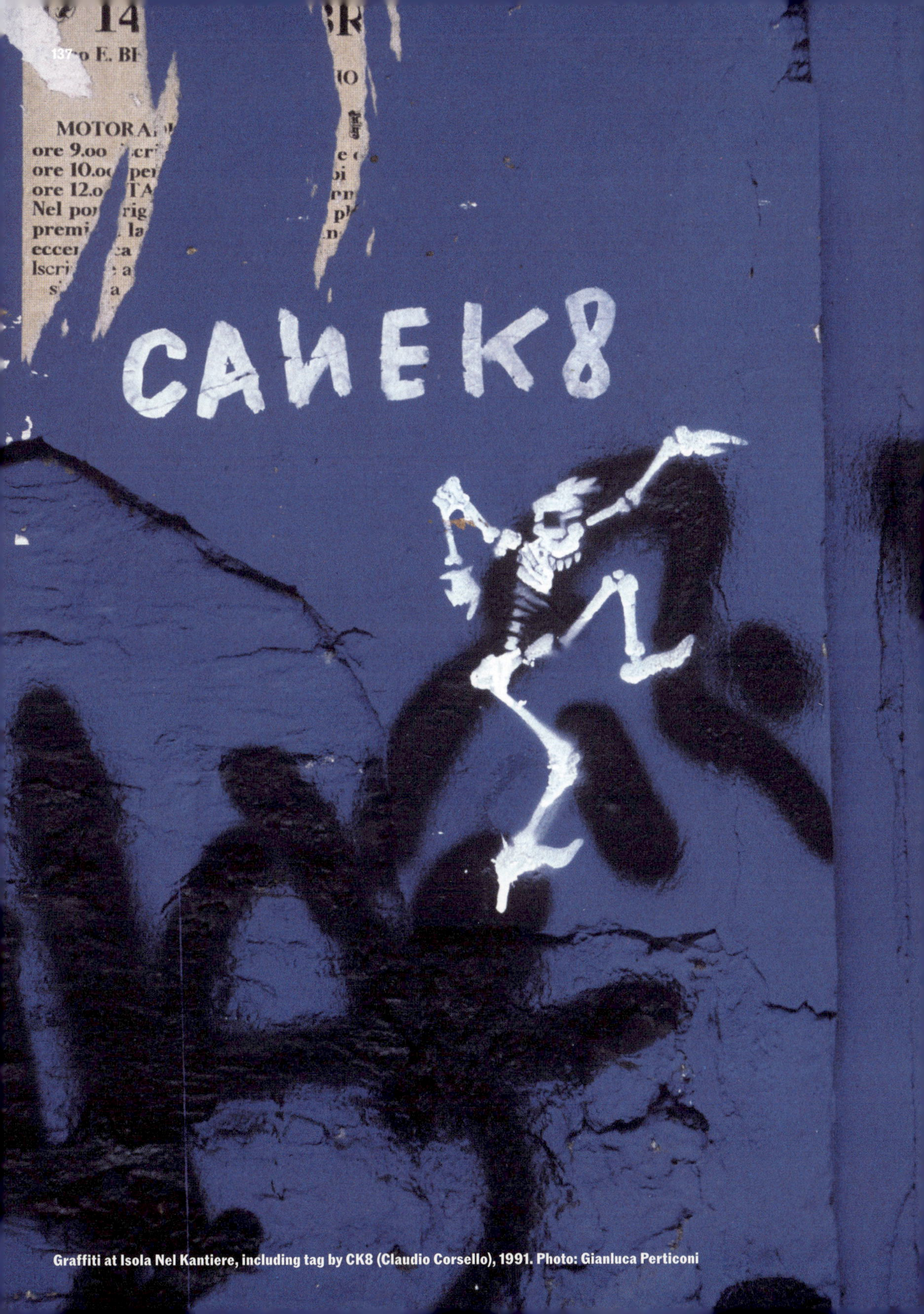

Graffiti at Isola Nel Kantiere, including tag by CK8 (Claudio Corsello), 1991. Photo: Gianluca Perticoni

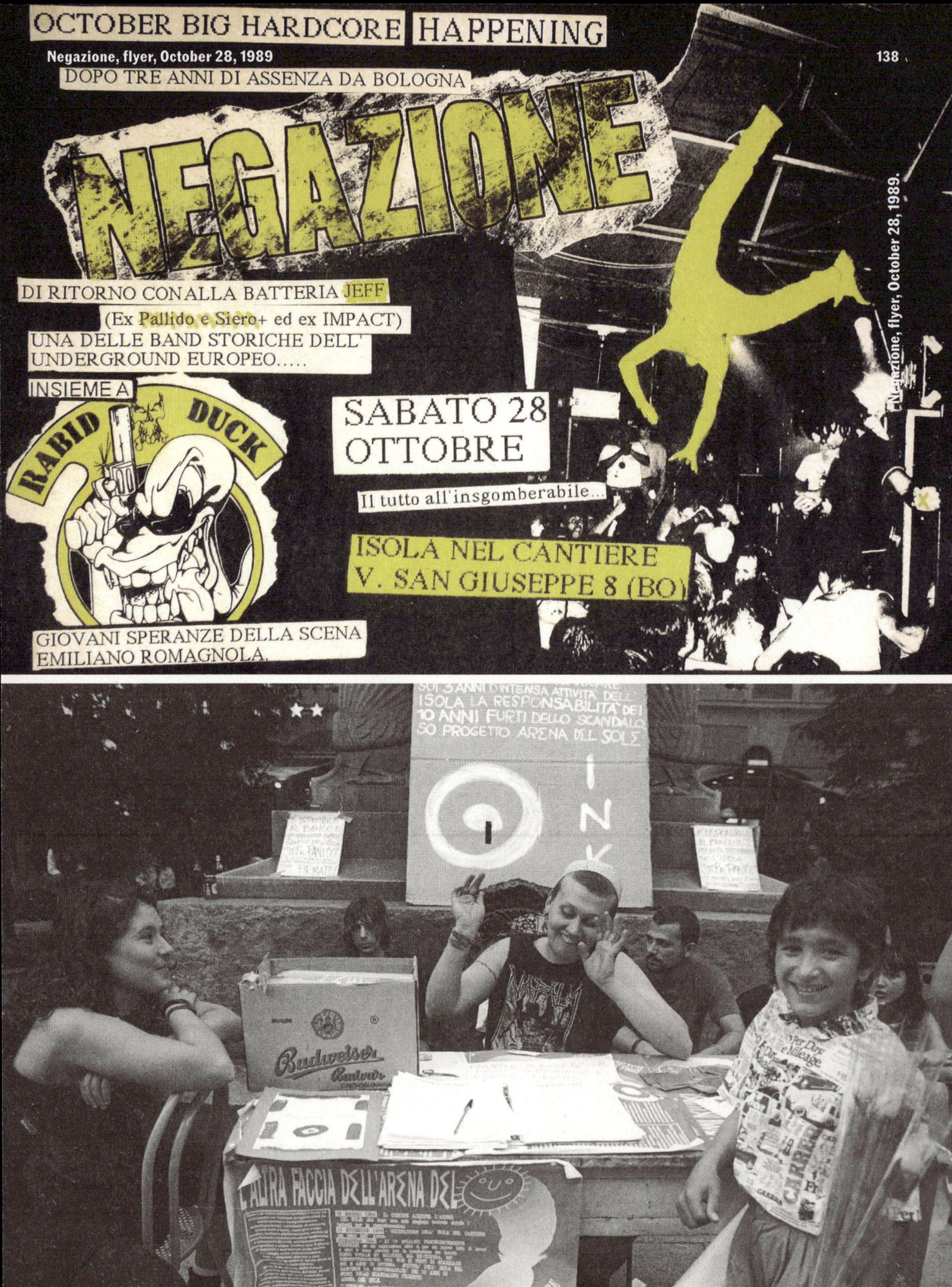

Negazione, flyer, October 28, 1989.

138

Petition against the eviction of Isola Nel Kantiere, Via dell'Indipendenza, 1991. Photo: Gianluca Perticoni

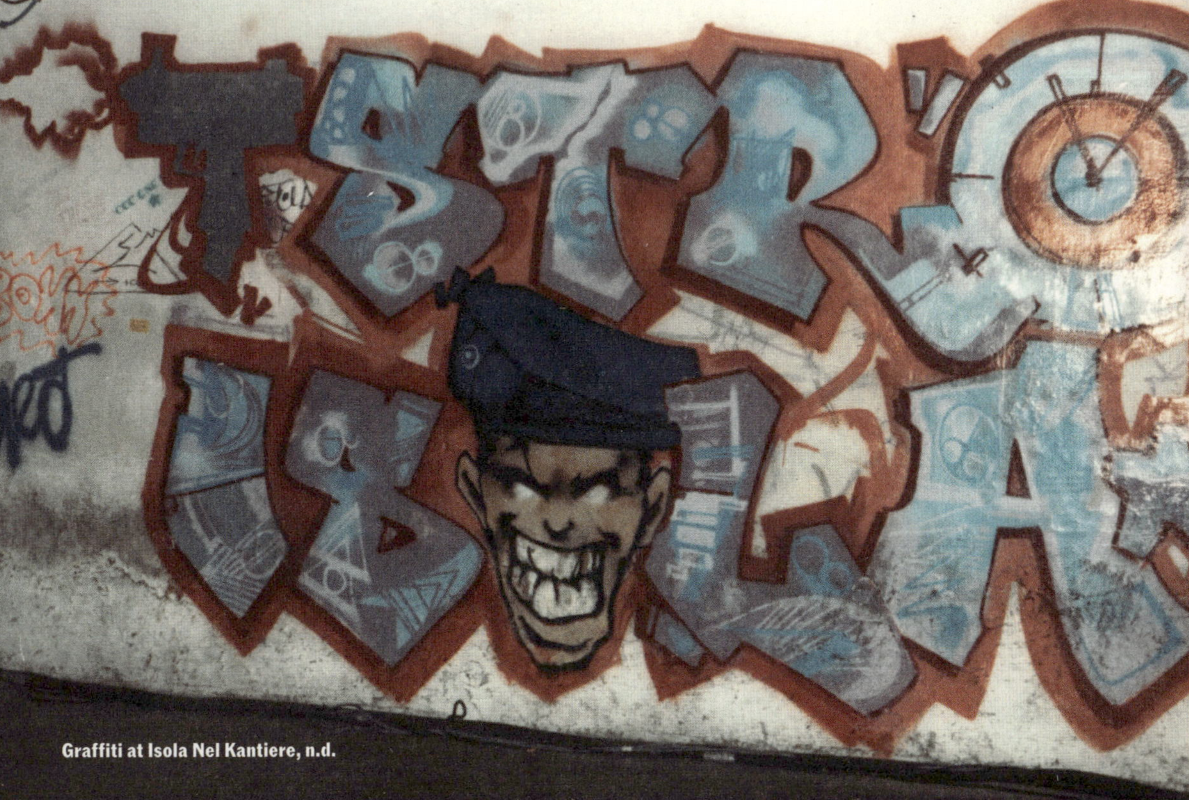

Simone Bellotti in front of the protest banners against the eviction of Isola Nel Kantiere, 1991. Photo: Gianluca Perticoni

Graffiti at Isola Nel Kantiere, n.d.

Depot

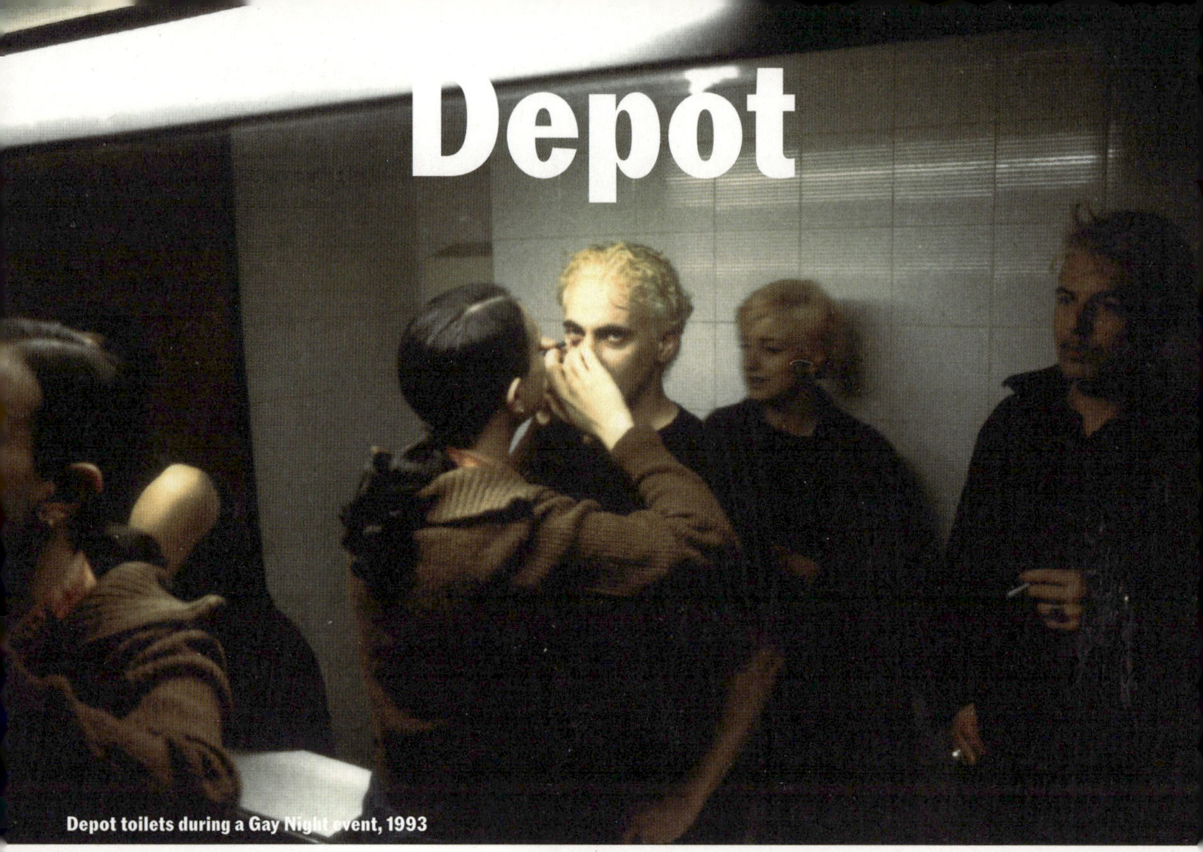

Depot toilets during a Gay Night event, 1993

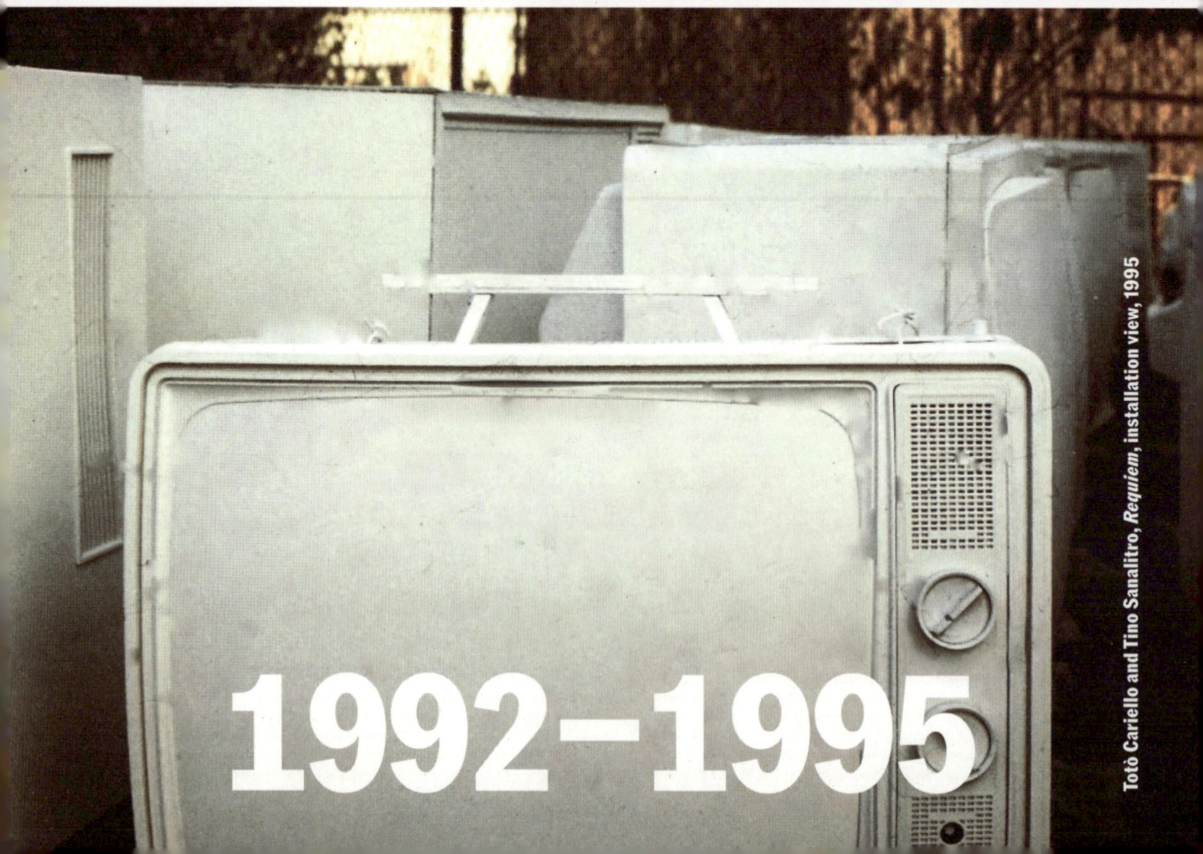

1992–1995

Totò Cariello and Tino Sanalitro, Requiem, installation view, 1995

Depot's activity, also known as Depot and Hip Hop Gallery, although there were no obvious ties to hip hop culture, sought to propose a new approach to culture by subverting the elitism and commercial dynamics that characterize the art world.

During its three years of activity, Depot organized exhibitions on a weekly basis inside a bar on Via del Pratello, involving emerging artists and in collaboration with scholars and curators active in the city such as Silvia Grandi, Michele Mariano, Roberto Daolio, Gino Gianuizzi, Guido Molinari, Vittoria Coen, Gilberto Pellizzola, Valerio Dehó, and Claudio Marra. The exhibition projects focused on experiments in performance, video art, and installations.

One of the most ambitious projects was the open-air exhibition *ARS LUX* (1995), which involved Roberto Daolio, Giacinto di Pietrantonio, Gabriele Perretta, Roberto Pinto, Gianni Romano, Marco Senaldi, and Silvia Grandi. It was a traveling exhibition consisting of 150 works by artists from all over the world, printed on PVC and placed on light platforms used for advertising, exhibited in seventeen Italian cities over three months.

The Depot adventure, an innovative cultural reality emblematic of the Bolognese fervor of the early 1990s, ended in 1995 due to noise pollution issues.

ADDRESS Via del Pratello 13/a, Bologna. FOUNDERS Ioannis Kopsinis COLLABORATORS Silvia Grandi, Nicola Ferrari, Michele Mariano, Guido Molinari, Roberto Daolio, Gino Gianuizzi, Vittoria Coen, Gilberto Pellizzola, Valerio Dehó, Claudio Marra

Milton Manetas, solo exhibition, flyer, design by Grafton9, 1993

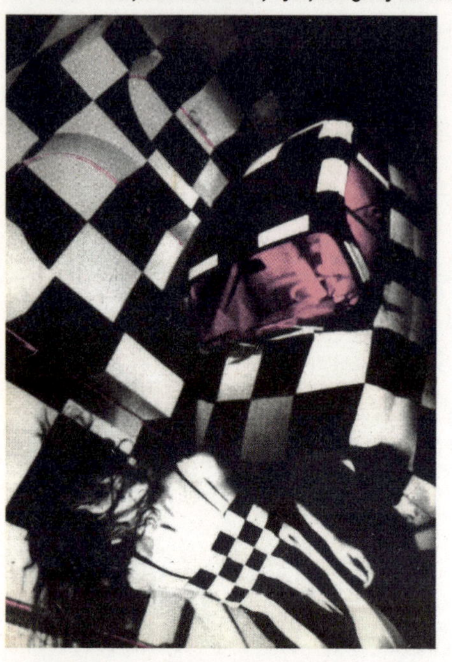

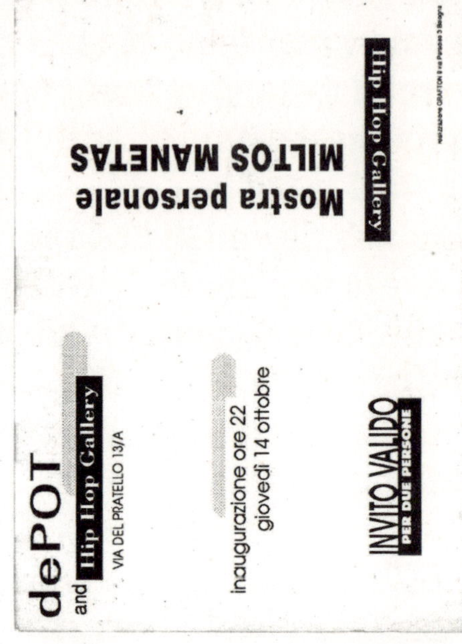

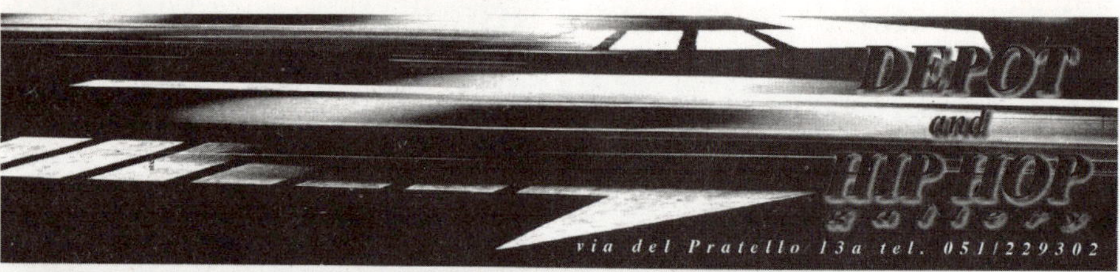

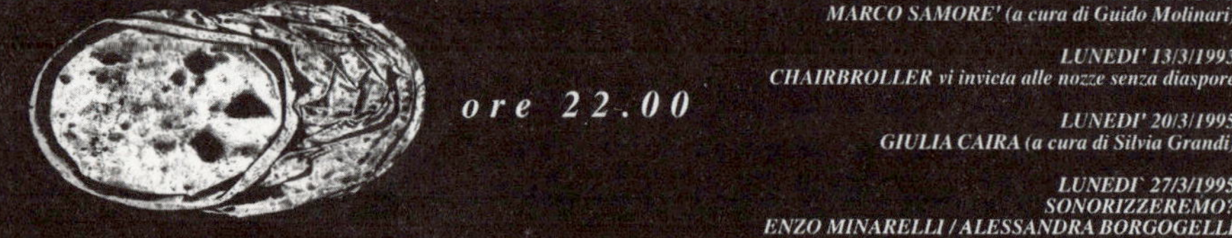

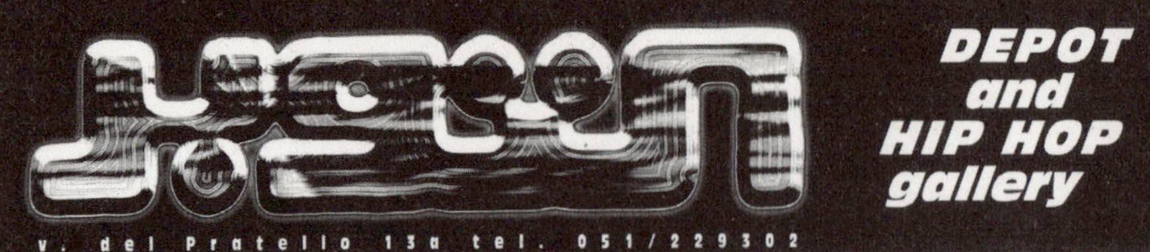

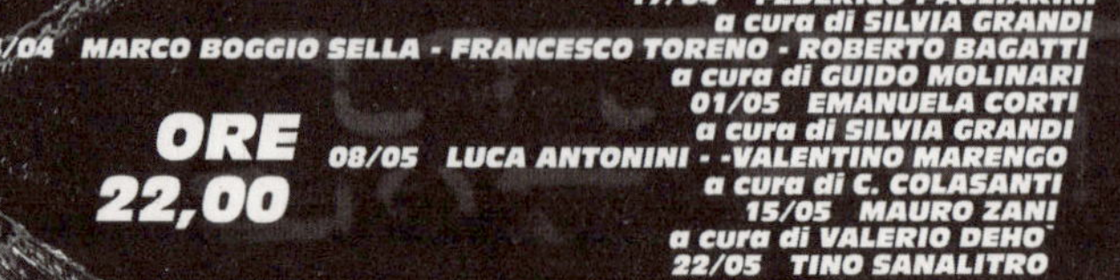

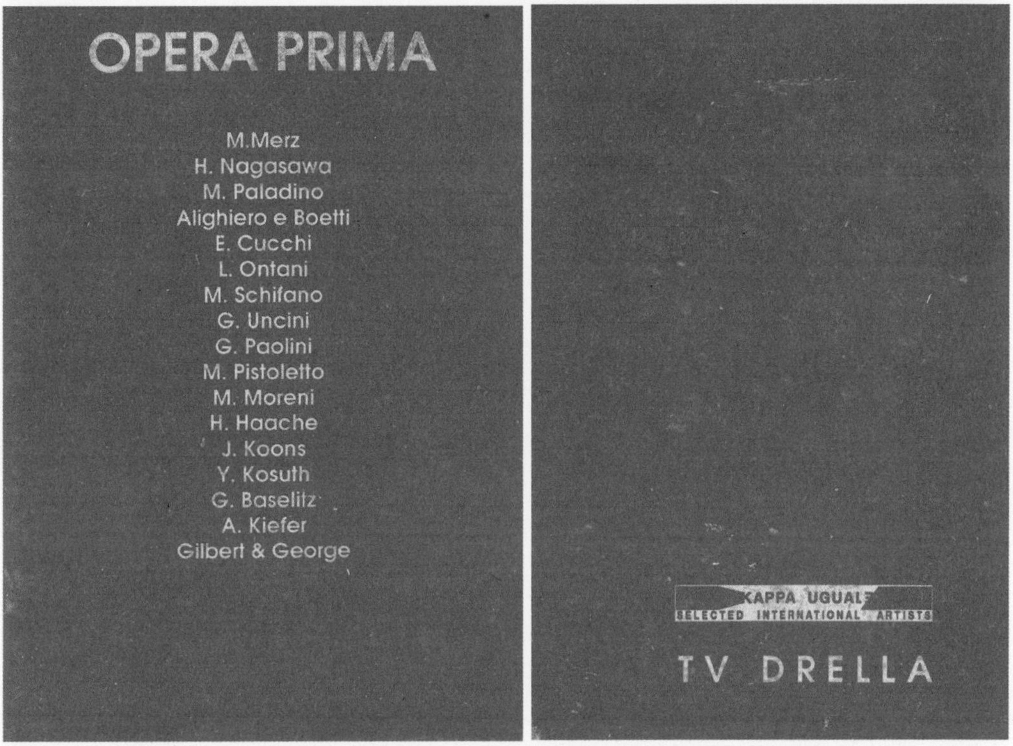

OPERA PRIMA

M.Merz
H. Nagasawa
M. Paladino
Alighiero e Boetti
E. Cucchi
L. Ontani
M. Schifano
G. Uncini
G. Paolini
M. Pistoletto
M. Moreni
H. Haache
J. Koons
Y. Kosuth
G. Baselitz
A. Kiefer
Gilbert & George

KAPPA UGUALE
SELECTED INTERNATIONAL ARTISTS

TV DRELLA

Opera Prima, edited and designed by Ioannis Kopsinis, publication, 1994

Opera Prima, curated by Ioannis Kopsinis, installation view, 1994

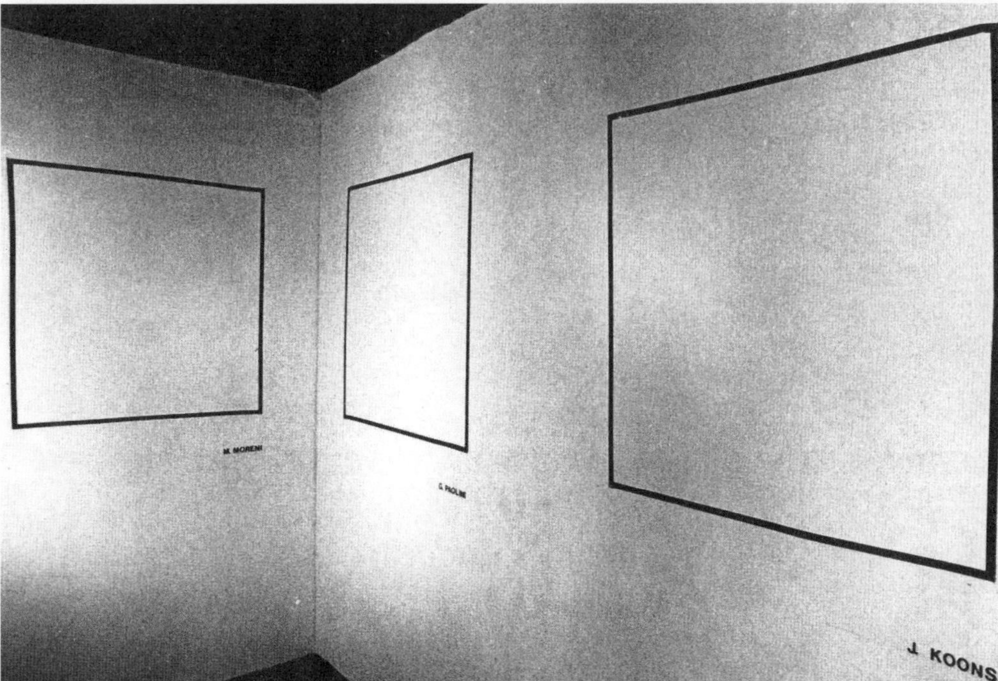

Il Campo delle Fragole

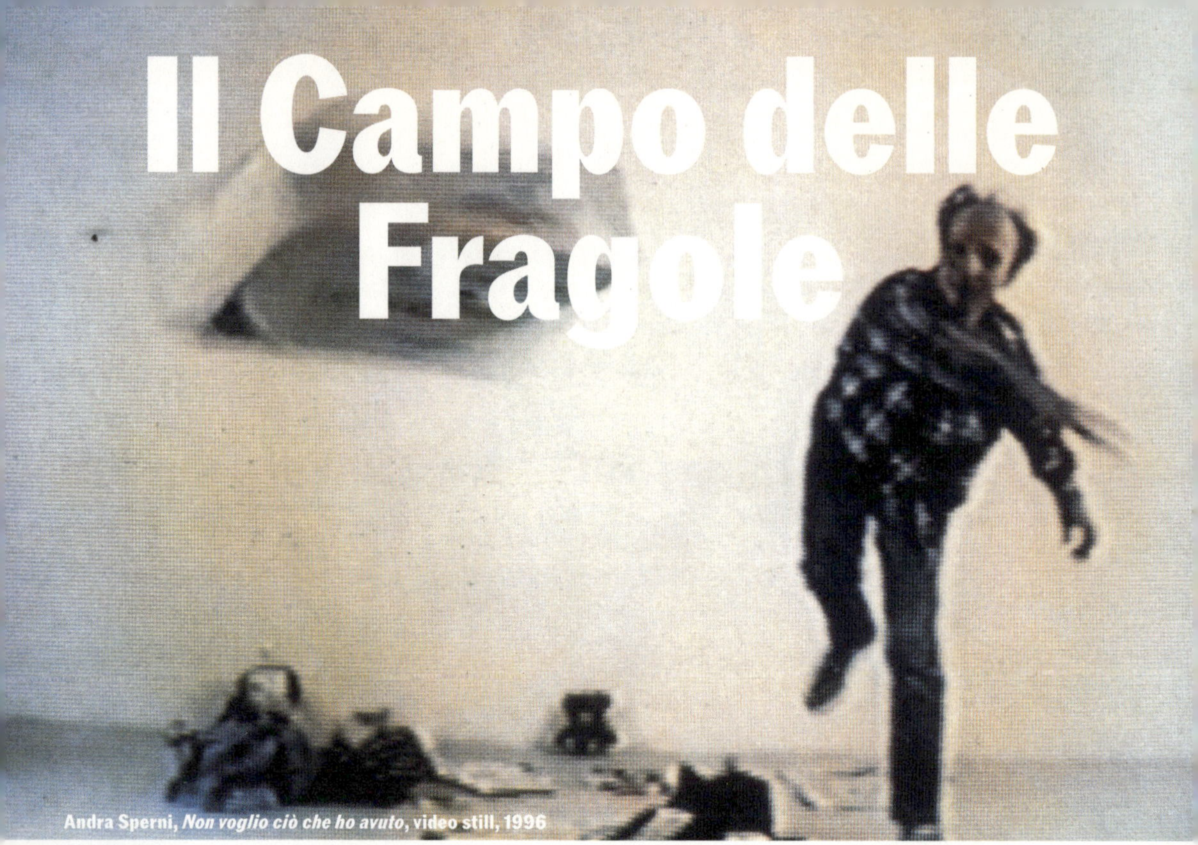

Andra Sperni, *Non voglio ciò che ho avuto*, video still, 1996

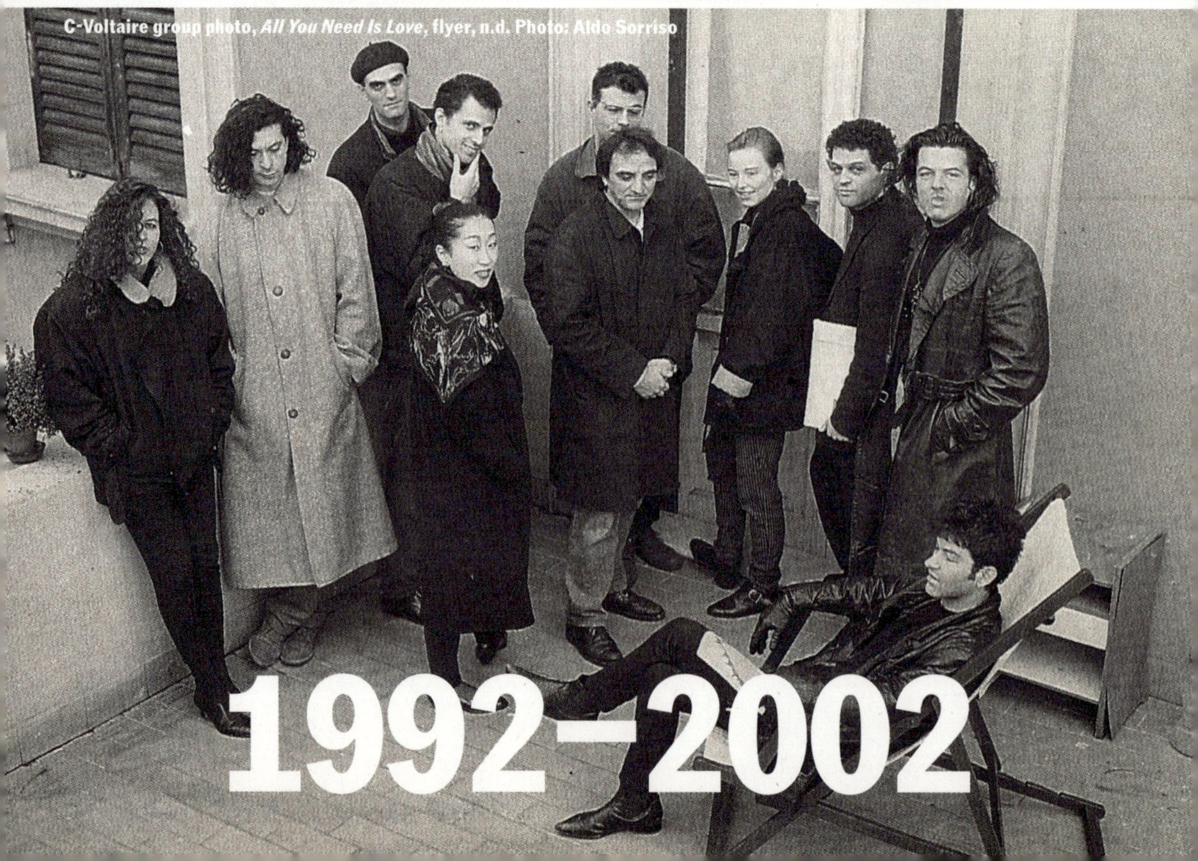

C-Voltaire group photo, *All You Need Is Love*, flyer, n.d. Photo: Aldo Sorriso

1992–2002

Il Campo delle Fragole was founded by a group of visual artists and curators called C-Voltaire, to fill the lack of a space in which to exhibit their works and in which they could discuss and plan events, without having to deal with commercial dynamics or individualist logics of affirmation and recognition. The members of the group formalized the idea of opening a space in the face of experiences of collaboration and dialogue that had seen them involved within La Vereda tavern: a meeting place frequented by various members of the Bologna art community.

Coordinator of the space was Tiziana Ramponi, who was joined at certain times by Luisa Castagnoli, but Il Campo delle Fragole saw the participation of all C-Voltaire members. Decisions were made in a circular fashion; proposals were discussed together and implemented through collective collaboration. Roles were never defined, and it is interesting to think about how visual artists found themselves taking on the role of curators or working on communication and cultural promotion projects that until then were outside the traditional training typical of the artist.

With the move to the Via Polese location, which was larger than the previous one on Via del Pratello and spread over two floors, Il Campo delle Fragole began to host painting and sculpture exhibitions, installations, performances, music, theater, cabaret and dance events, meetings, readings, and film reviews. Ramponi dealt carefully with the relationship with critics and curators, sometimes with the support of Luigi Mastrangelo. Artists and projects were chosen collectively, based on personal relationships of the group or by activating collaborations with similar spaces in other cities such as Rome, Turin, Milan, and Trieste.

Independence was a key element in having design space and freedom in artistic expression, cultural programming choices, and collaborations with other realities inside and outside Italy.

The importance of C-Voltaire in the local and national context was acknowledged by several critics who reviewed its activities in major contemporary art magazines, and by researchers and professors from the Academy of Fine Arts and DAMS who collaborated on various projects. Among Il Campo delle Fragole's most important productions are the twelve editions of Exit, sponsored by the City Council and Arci, which led to the organization of annual exhibitions in various places in the city throughout the days of Arte Fiera.

The main economic sources were self-financing, with external donations and sporadic forms of institutional sustenance (including collaboration with the Arci for the printing of catalogues), but above all the proceeds from the bar located within the space.

Il Campo delle Fragole's experience came to a natural end, at the conclusion of a personal evolution that prompted the members of C-Voltaire to pursue their work individually. This independent space is remembered in Bologna history for its ability to operate within and outside the art system, in opposition to schools, trends and the entrepreneurial nature of mainstream art.

ADDRESS Via del Pratello 58/a, Bologna (1992–95); Via Polese 7/2a, Bologna (1995–99); Via Giuriolo 7, Bologna (1999–2001); Via Marco Polo 21/12, Bologna (2002). FOUNDERS Karin Andersen, Totò Cariello, Yumi Karasumaru, Ioannis Kopsinis, Stefano Marchesini, Michele Mariano, Luigi Mastrangelo, Tiziana Ramponi, Gianni Pedullà, Squp. COLLABORATORS Lino Baldini, Bruno Benuzzi, Pier Luigi Capucci, Luisa Castagnoli, Roberto Cascone, Claudio Cerritelli, Claudia Colasanti, Loretta Cristofori, Roberto Daolio, Valerio Dehò, Edoardo Di Mauro, Roberta Fanti, Nicola Ferrari, Alessandro Frigau, Eugenio Gazzola, Roberto Grandi, Silvia Grandi, Gianni Gosdan, Gabriele Lamberti, Mariella Mastri, Fabiola Naldi, Pascal, Gilberto Pellizzola, Gabriele Perretta, Michael Perricone, Antonio Picariello, Bruno Picariello, Jennifer Ramsey, Roxy In The Box, Alice Rubbini, Leonardo Santoli, Elena Savigni, Peter Weiermair, Irene Zangheri, Sabrina Zannier

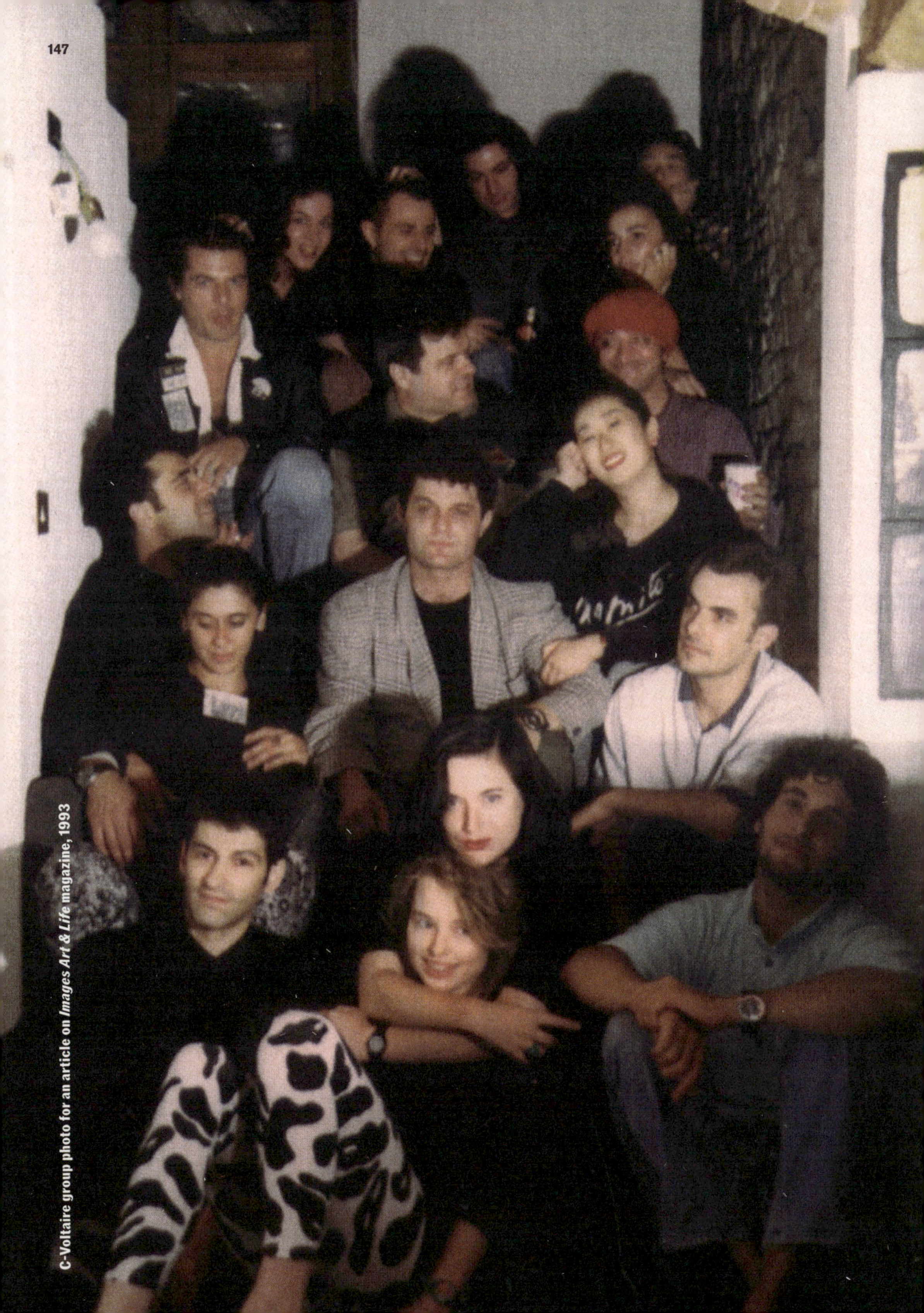

C-Voltaire group photo for an article on *Images Art & Life* magazine, 1993

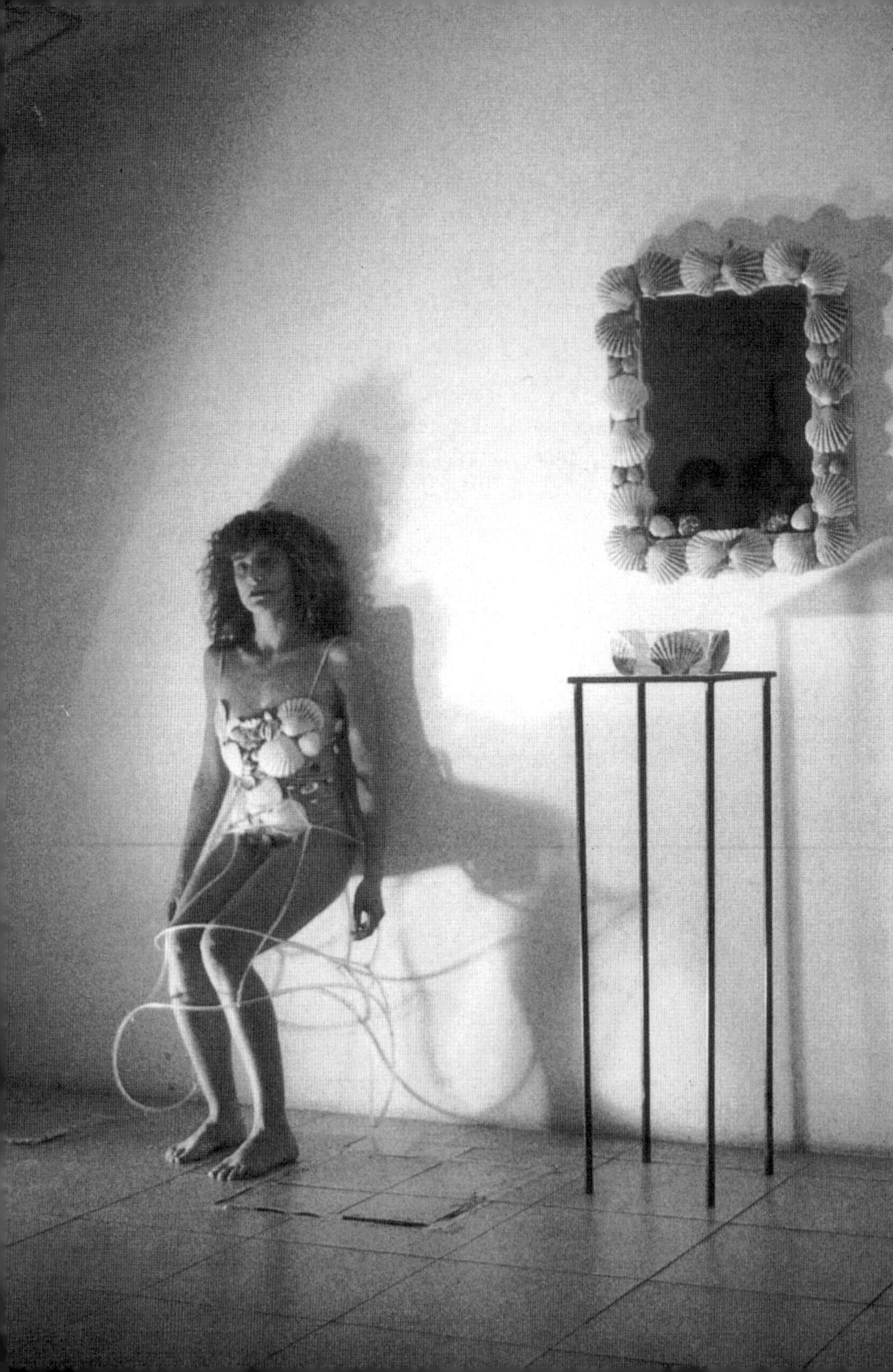

Sqap, *Untitled,* performance, 1997. Photo: Mathias Gumprich

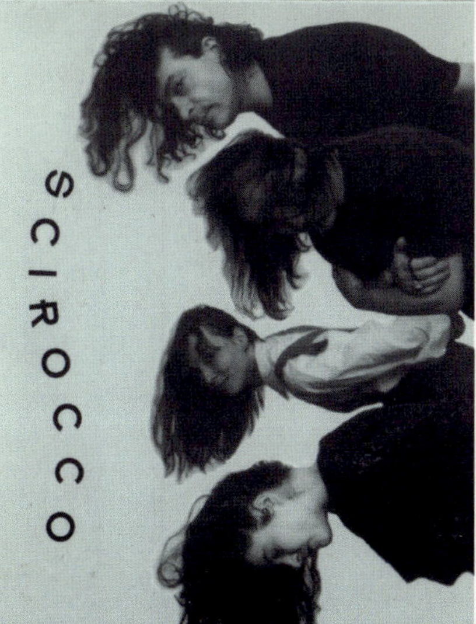

Scirocco, flyer, 1995

Siamese People, flyer, 1996

Il Campo delle Fragole, logo, n.d.

C-Voltaire Manifesto, n.d.

C-VOLTAIRE

C-VOLTAIRE E' LA GRANDE NOVITA' DELLA SCENA ARTISTICA BOLOGNESE, E' LA "SOCRATICA LEVATRICE" DELLA NUOVA ARTE.

C-VOLTAIRE E' UN ATTEGGIAMENTO RISPETTO AL MONDO.

GLI ARTISTI DEGLI ANNI '70 ERANO IPOCRITI, QUELLI DEGLI ANNI '80 CINICI, GLI ARTISTI DI C-VOLTAIRE RIVENDICANO SEMPLICEMENTE IL DIRITTO ALLA PROPRIA ESISTENZA IN QUANTO TALI.

PRATICARE L'ARTE PER C-VOLTAIRE VUOL DIRE SOTTRARSI AI RITMI DELLA PRODUZIONE TOTALE.

C-VOLTAIRE AMA LA VITA. PER QUESTO E' CONTRO LA MAFIA E CONTRO L'EROINA, ANTIRAZZISTA E CONTRO LE LEGHE.

C-VOLTAIRE E' DENTRO E FUORI IL SISTEMA DELL'ARTE. E' DENTRO PERCHE' IL RISTRETTO MICRO-AMBIENTE CULTURALE COSTITUISCE IL CIRCUITO DI SMERCIO E CONSUMO DELLE OPERE, E' FUORI PERCHE' L'ARTE DEVE INVADERE I LUOGHI DI MASSA, LA STRADA, DOVE PUO' ESSERE TRANQUILLAMENTE CONSUMATA DA TUTTI, DOVE ESSA SI FONDE CON LA VITA, DOVE VIVE DIRETTAMENTE NELLA PELLE DI CHI LA PRATICA E DI CHI LA FRUISCE, E NON E' SOLO MERA SPECULAZIONE INTELLETTUALE O COMMERCIALE.

C-VOLTAIRE E' NEO-SITUAZIONISTA, VUOLE DISTRUGGERE E RIFONDARE.

C-VOLTAIRE E' CONTRO IL TOTALITARISMO DELLE SCUOLE E DELLE TENDENZE. LO STILE DI OGNI SUO ARTISTA E' POETICAMENTE DIFFERENTE DALL'ALTRO.

LO STILE PER C-VOLTAIRE E' L'INESORABILE BISOGNO DI DISTINGUERSI, E' IL MEZZO PER SINTETIZZARE LA PROPRIA ESISTENZA.

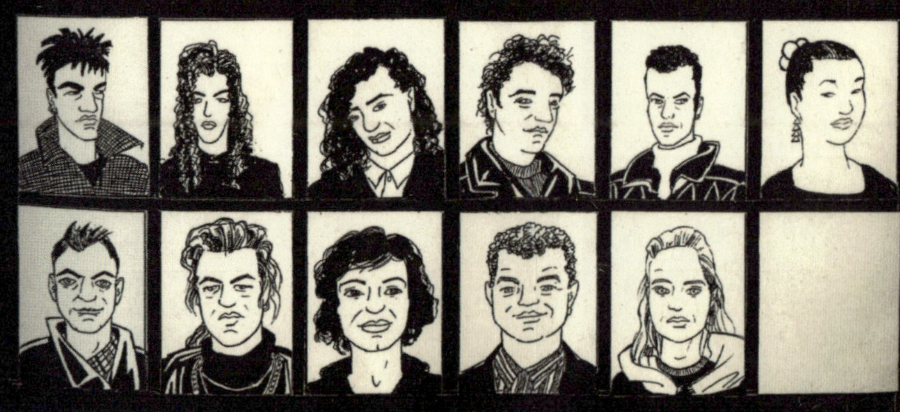

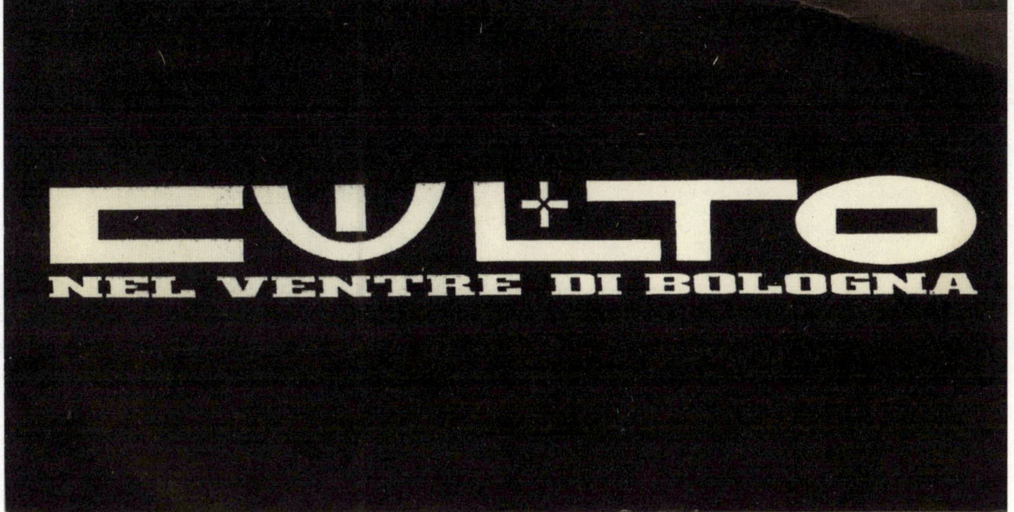

Cover, flyer, 1991

Culto, flyer, 1992

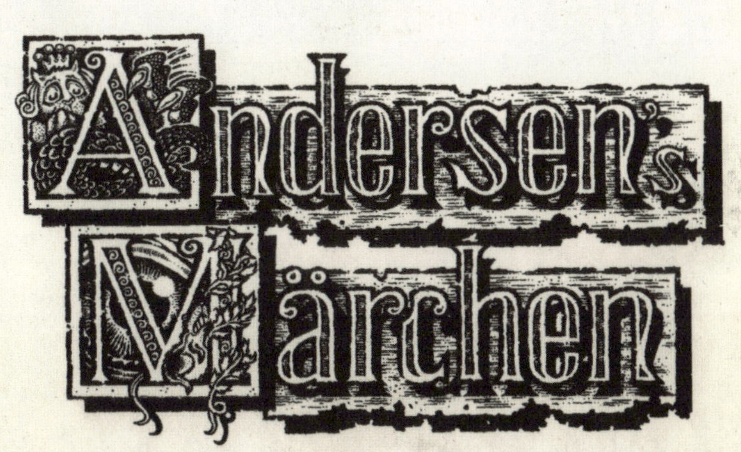

Karin Andersen, *Märchen*, flyer, 1995

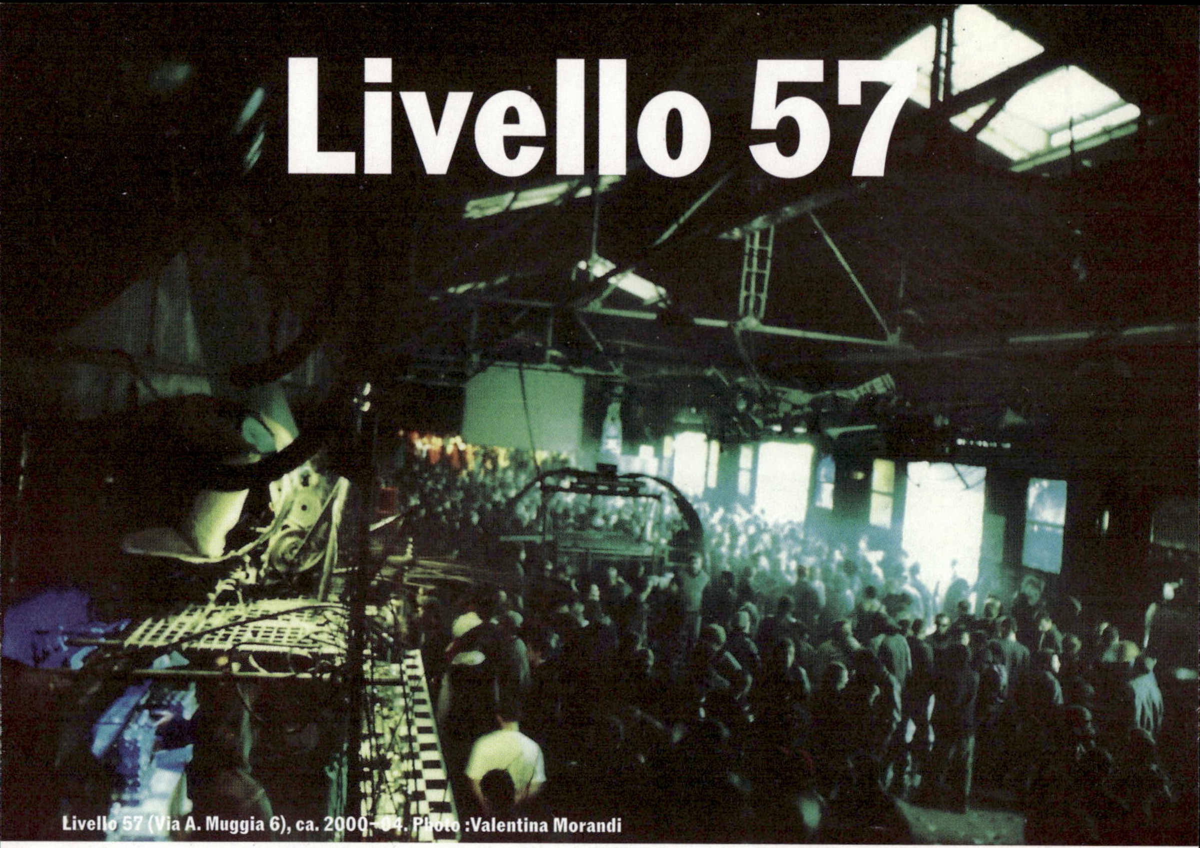

Livello 57

Livello 57 (Via A. Muggia 6), ca. 2000–04. Photo: Valentina Morandi

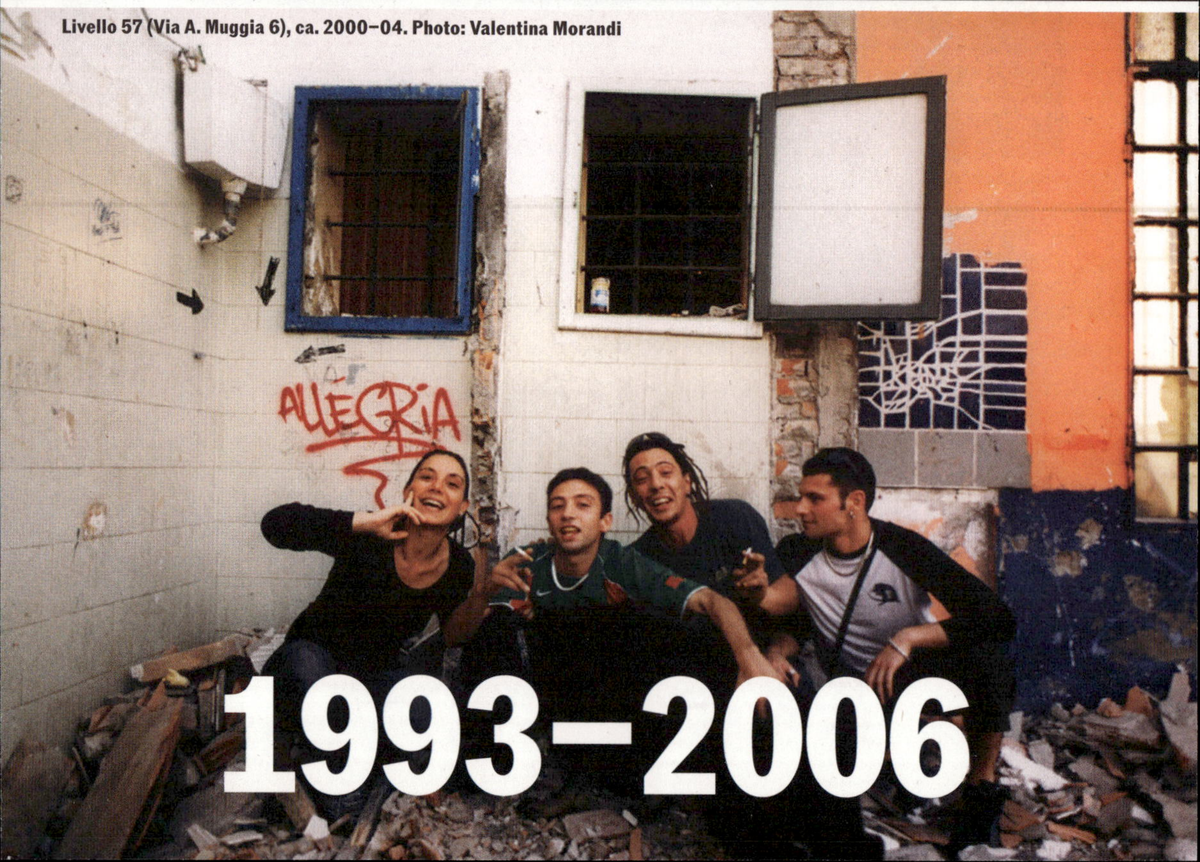

Livello 57 (Via A. Muggia 6), ca. 2000–04. Photo: Valentina Morandi

1993–2006

Livello 57 was founded in the early 1990s, at a time when Bologna was characterized by the presence of various other self-managed social centers. A place for experimentation with new forms of coexistence aimed at overcoming the normality codified by mass culture through art and sociality, much of the activities proposed by Livello 57 were related to cyberpunk and hip hop culture. The social center was started inside an occupied building on Via dello Scalo by former members of the Pellerossa social center (recently vacated from its Piazza Verdi location), several off-site university students belonging to the Pantera movement, and figures involved in Radio K Centrale and the Grafton9 publishing project, the latter now a valuable organ of archiving and dissemination of underground and self-produced cyberpunk publications from that period.

Cultural programming ranged from the organization of highly participatory collective events such as the Festa della Semina ("Sowing Party") and the Street Rave Parade Anti-proibizionista ("Anti-Prohibitionist"), to the production of fanzines, to self-produced records such as the *Livello 57 Zona a Rischio* project. The space quickly came to represent a place of liberation and a fervent center of experimentation in the fields of music, performing arts and graffiti art, although events were rarely presented as exhibitions or as cultural activities, because labeling them as such would have dampened their spontaneous and unconventional character.

In its most characteristic location, the one on Via Muggia, under the bridge on Via Stalingrado and adjacent to the railroad tracks, the presence of a skateboard ramp—one of the largest in Italy—was central, confirming the disobedient nature of this practice in those years, as well as the long horizontal walls that bordered the complex and became the support for works created by leading Italian and international graffiti artists.

In 1995, in the light of the need emerged to carry out an awareness-raising project on the conscious consumption of drugs, Livello 57 proposed the Laboratorio Antiproibizionista, which became known as a space for political elaboration on drugs and their consumption, the first in Italy to produce information pamphlets on new synthetic drugs such as ecstasy and ketamine. Despite a brief phase of dialogue initiated by center-right mayor Giorgio Guazzaloca in 1999, Livello 57's relationship with city institutions became one of a conflictual nature. In fact, its existence came to an end on July 25, 2006, following the judicial seizure of the site on Via Battirame (its final location) self-managed by the social center, on charges of being a place for the production and distribution of drugs.

ADDRESS Via dello Scalo 21, Bologna (1993–95); Via A. Muggia 6, Bologna (1995–2004); Via del Battirame 11, Bologna (2004–06). FOUNDERS Rosella Chirizzi, Rosario Picciolo, Oberdan Cappa, Salvatore Fiorentino. COLLABORATORS InfoShock NoCopyright, Grafton9, Radio K Central, Lab57, M.d.M.A Antiprohibitionist Mass Movement, Mutoid Waste Company, Zero, Alchemical Workshops, TeknoMobilSquad, Autonomous Astronaut Association, Flammenraum, Luther Blissett, Living Theatre

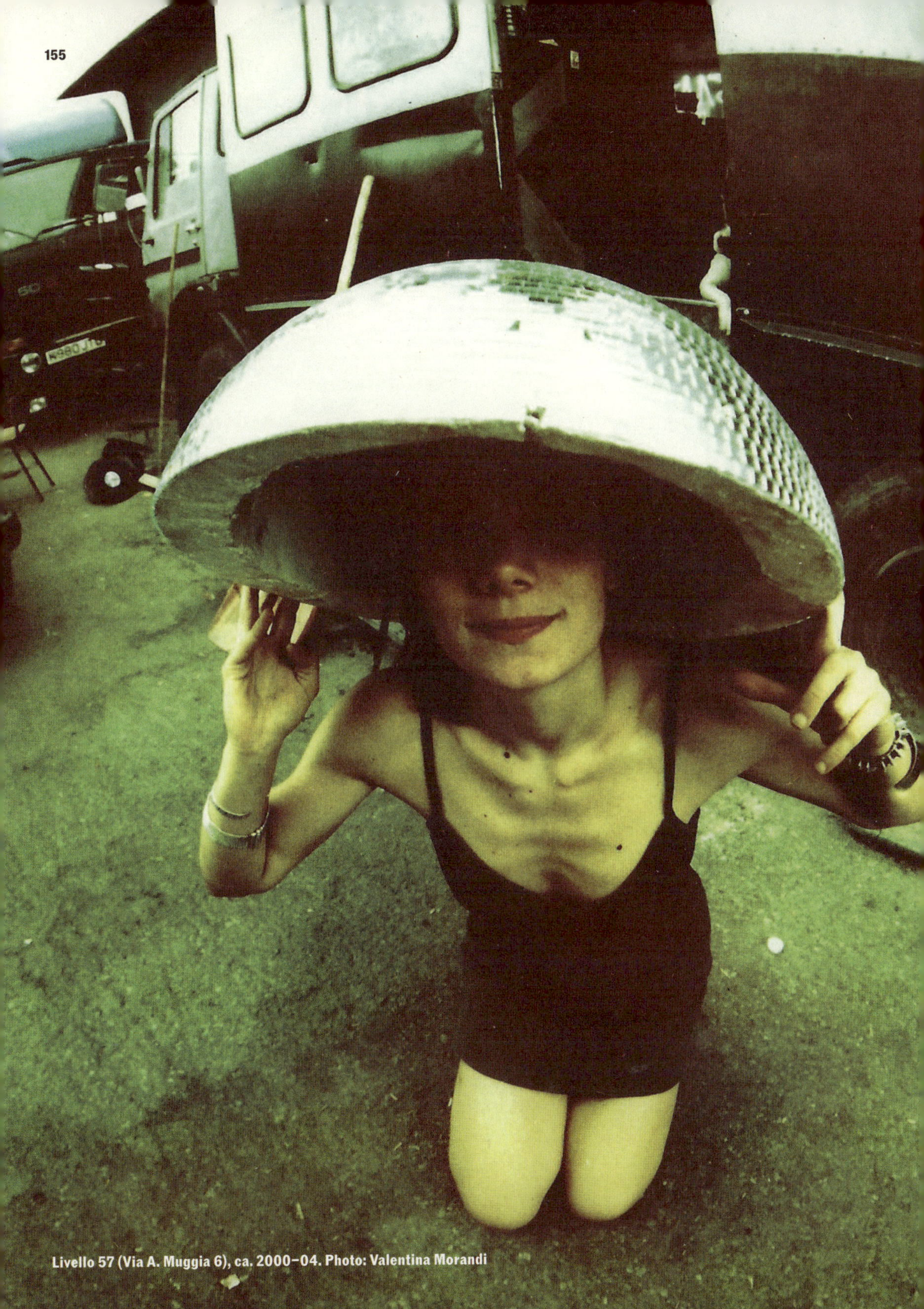

Livello 57 (Via A. Muggia 6), ca. 2000–04. Photo: Valentina Morandi

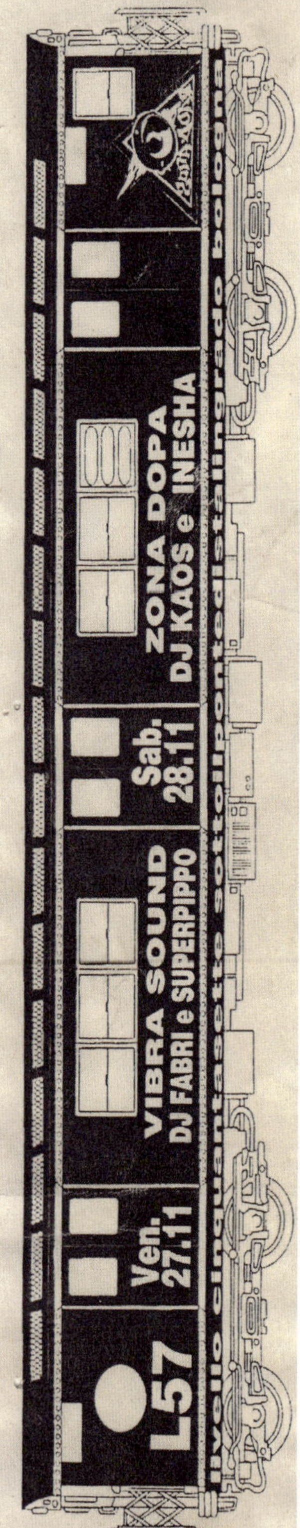

Vibra Sound and *Zona Dopa*, flyer, 1988

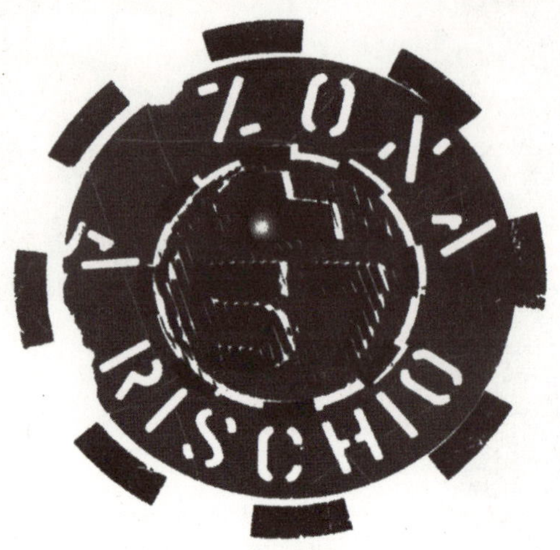

L57 Zona a Rischio, logo from the booklet *Depot-Link-Livello 57*, 1995

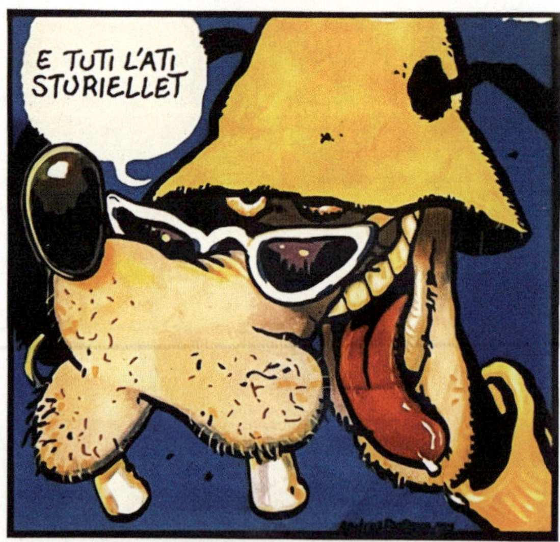

Movimento di Massa Antiproibizionista, poster, design by Mitch (Michail Mauracher), 2002

  Street Rave Parade Antiproibizionista, June 21, 1997. Photo: Giorgio Di Trapani

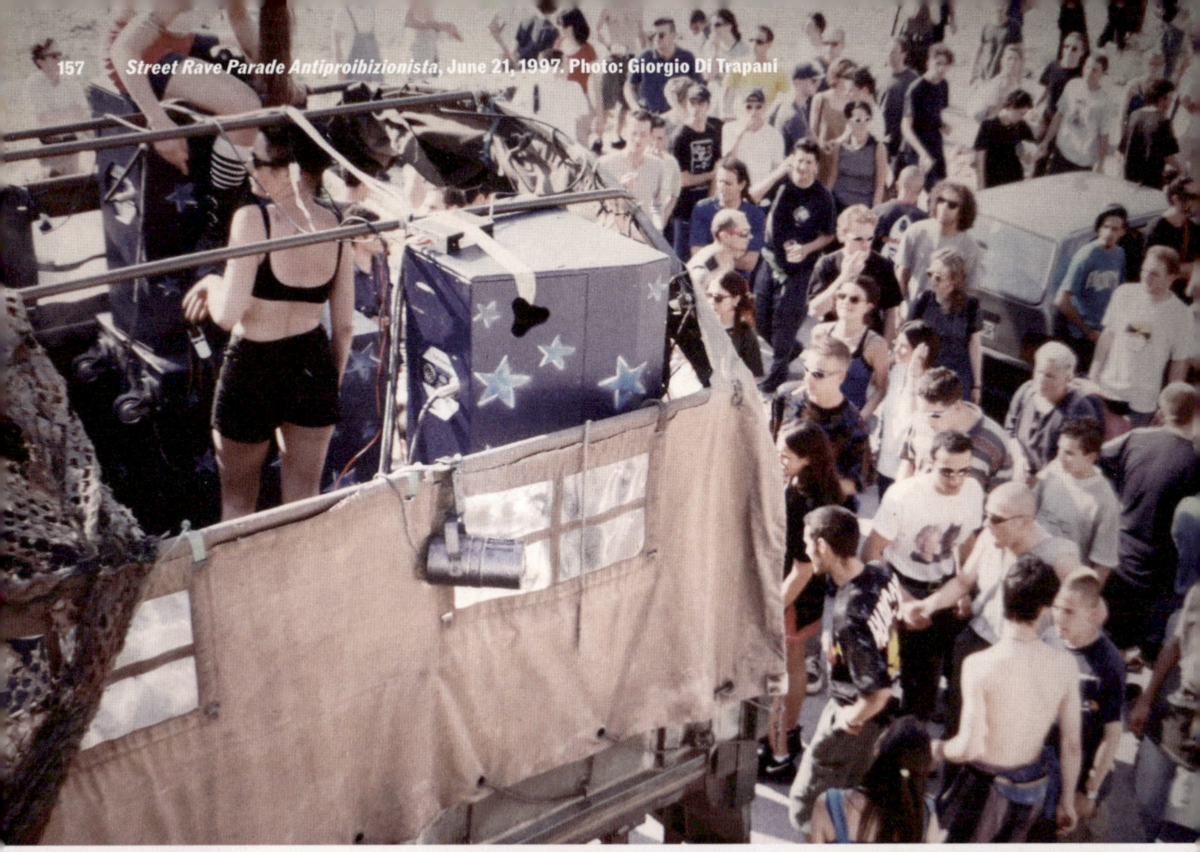

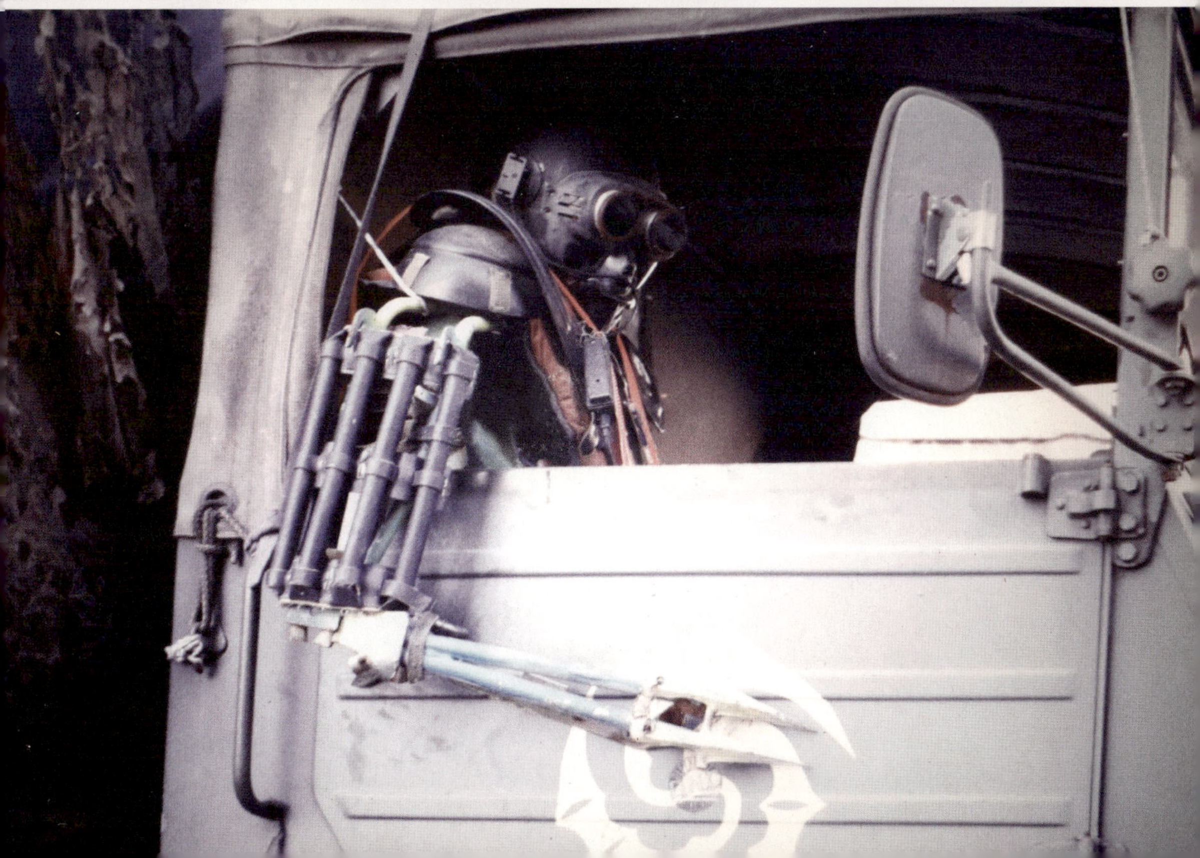

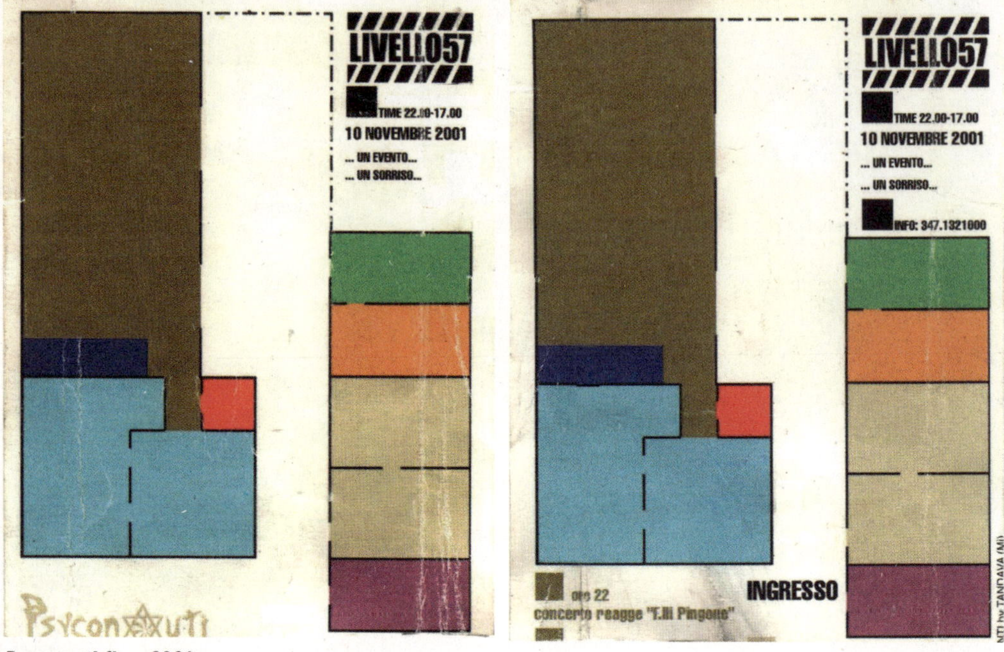

Psyconauti, flyer, 2001

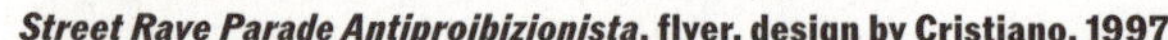

Street Rave Parade Antiproibizionista, flyer, design by Cristiano, 1997

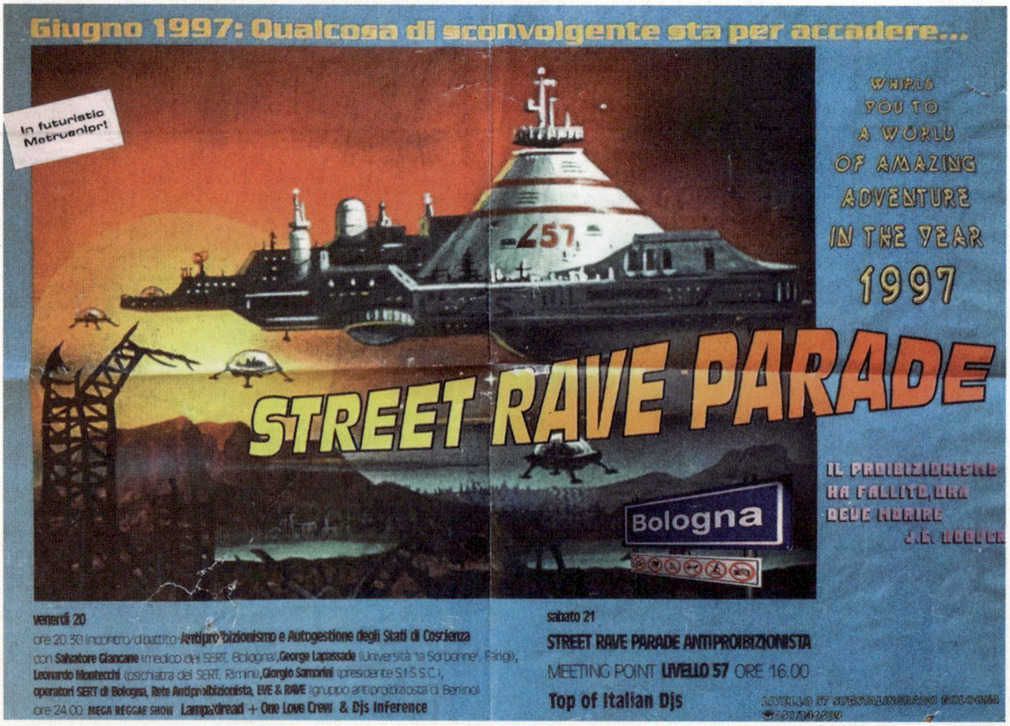

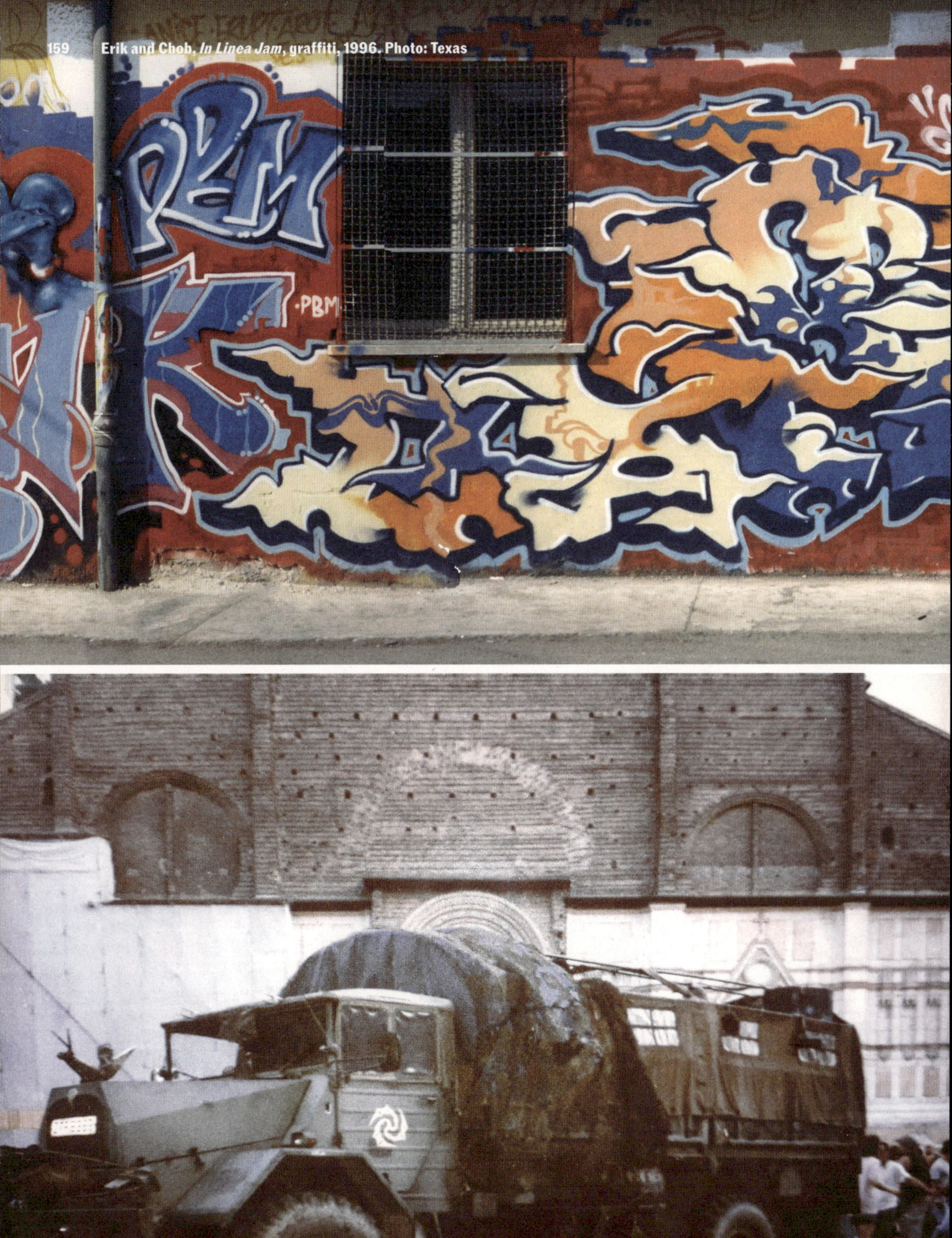

Erik and Chob, *In Linea Jam*, graffiti, 1996. Photo: Texas

Street Rave Parade Antiproibizionista, June 21, 1997. Photo: Giorgio Di Trapani

Link Project

Granular Synthesis, *POL*, Netmage festival at Link Project, November 2000. Photo: Gianluca Perticoni

Flava Break Dance, 1998. Photo: Gianluca Perticoni

1994–2001

Link Project, also known as Link, was born in 1994 following the authorized occupation of the Farmacie Comunali warehouse at Via Fioravanti 14, behind Bologna train station. The collective established there was made up of figures who had participated in previous experiences such as Isola Nel Kantiere and the Pantera movement. Founded at the conclusion of a cycle of illegal occupations and histories of conflict with local administrations, the Link's affairs enjoyed an unprecedented level of dialogue with the institutions.

Cornerstones of the collective's spirit of independence were self-determination and self-construction, starting with the way the space was transformed internally. In keeping with the post-industrial aesthetic that characterized nightclubs in Berlin and London in those years, a group of artists shaped interiors and sculptures by reusing waste material, particularly scrap metal.

The work, the managerial aspects of which were discussed and planned democratically during weekly assemblies, was organized into various subgroups that focused on different aspects of the activity, proposing a varied schedule of events. The space also housed various self-production workshops, which later became production houses specializing in various artistic languages, from video to graphic design to music (Opificio Ciclope, Loew, Officine Alchemiche, Century Vox Records, Massimo Volume, Fastilio, Splatterpink, Notte Vidal, TurbanZ, and Shado).

More than exhibition projects in the traditional sense, Link's activities were characterized by an interest in performance and multimedia practices, often the result of an interdisciplinary approach. Whether it was immersive installations, live sets with a musical matrix or relational theater productions, the interweaving of the arts and the intermedial use of multiple technological devices were characteristic elements of Link's offerings. At the center of interest of the space, in fact, was electronic culture, rethought—in the heyday of its mass diffusion—as an instrument of liberation and emancipation of the individual. The fulcrum of the Link was, not surprisingly, an Internet point where free access to the web was guaranteed at a time when the web was still looked upon with a sense of utopian awe. The entire environment was conceived as a place of happenings and relationships where artists had the opportunity to experiment with and question the parameters of their own activity.

Link was economically independent, self-financing itself through admission tickets, the bar, and the bookshop. Of particular appeal were the DJ sets and musical performances, mainly related to the electronic music of those years and to musicians and producers from the UK and Germany, from Aphex Twin to the new Berlin scene. Link was an extraordinary laboratory of innovative and interdisciplinary cultural experimentation, untethered from the usual commercial logic. A useful tool to understand what this place represented is the magazine of the same name produced within it, but its real spin-offs concern the professionalization of many people who today work in the cultural, technical, administrative, management and creative fields in Bologna and the rest of the world, figures for whom this space was a genuine school.

Link closed in 2001 and the complex was razed as part of a neighborhood redevelopment project. In 2004, several members of the Link Project started Link Associated, establishing themselves in a new location and offering almost exclusively music programming with a focus on various forms of electronic dance music.

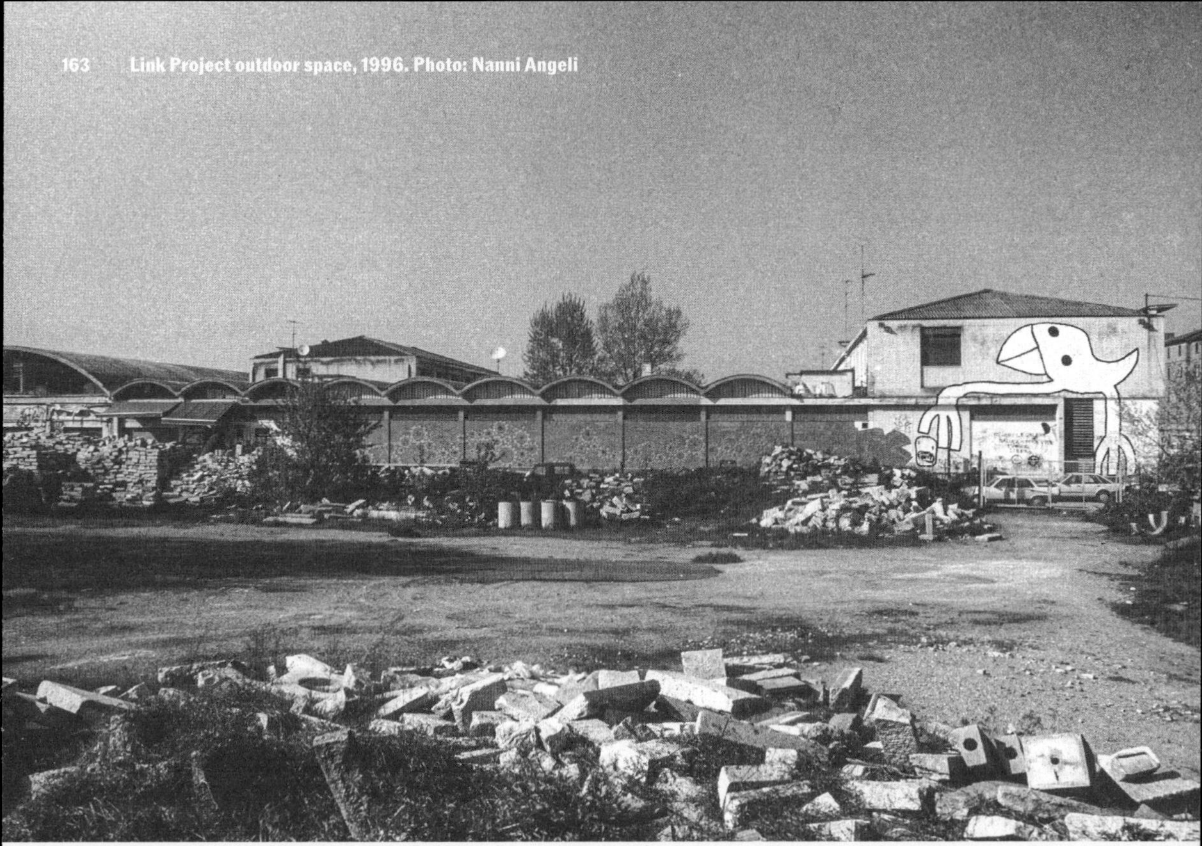

Link Project outdoor space, 1996. Photo: Nanni Angeli

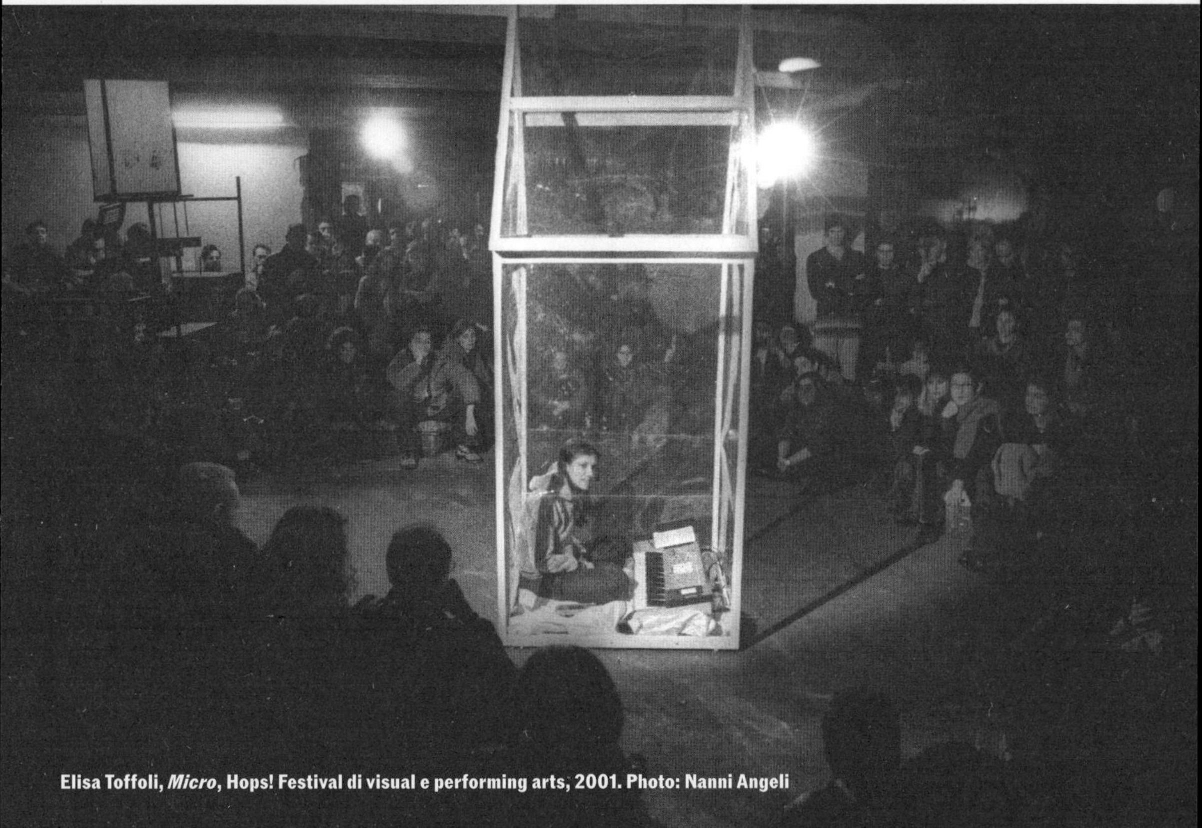

Elisa Toffoli, *Micro*, Hops! Festival di visual e performing arts, 2001. Photo: Nanni Angeli

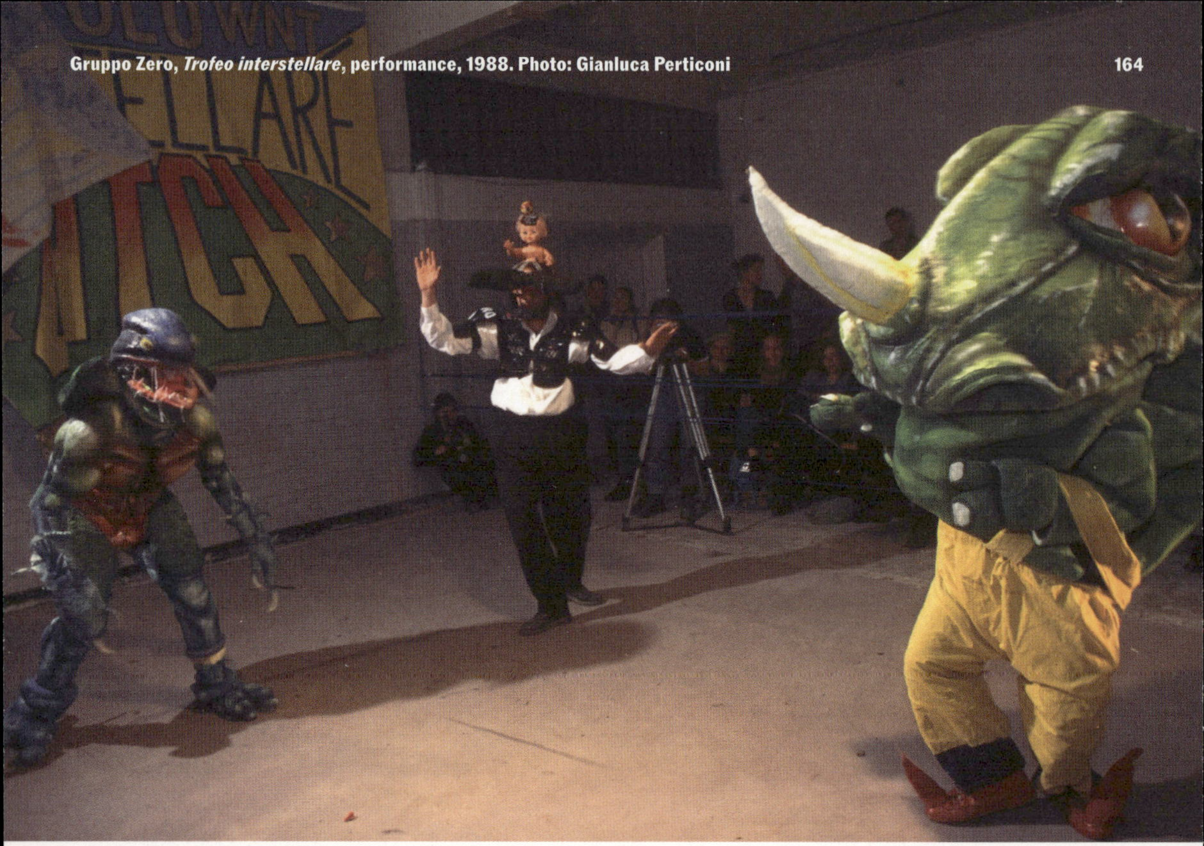

Gruppo Zero, *Trofeo interstellare*, performance, 1988. Photo: Gianluca Perticoni

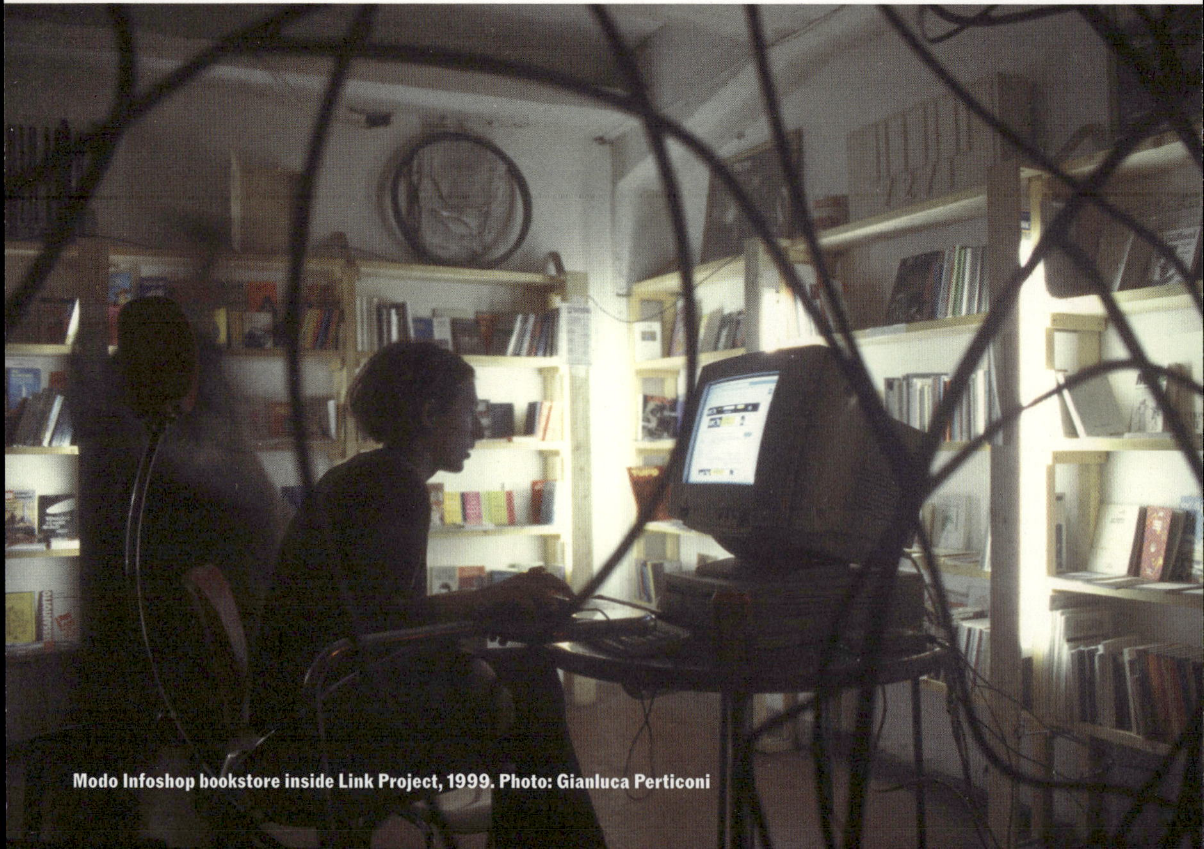

Modo Infoshop bookstore inside Link Project, 1999. Photo: Gianluca Perticoni

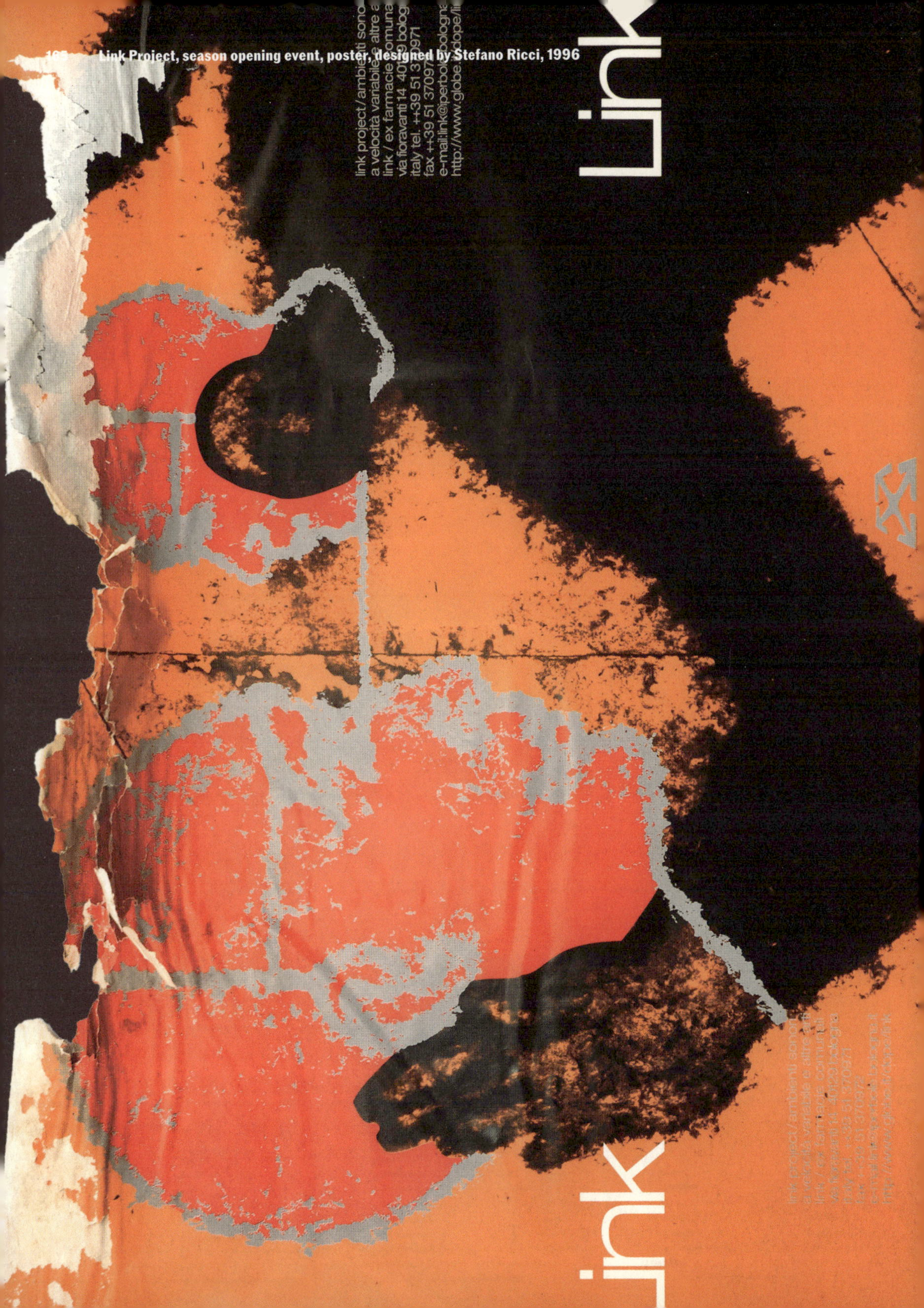

165 Link Project, season opening event, poster, designed by Stefano Ricci, 1996

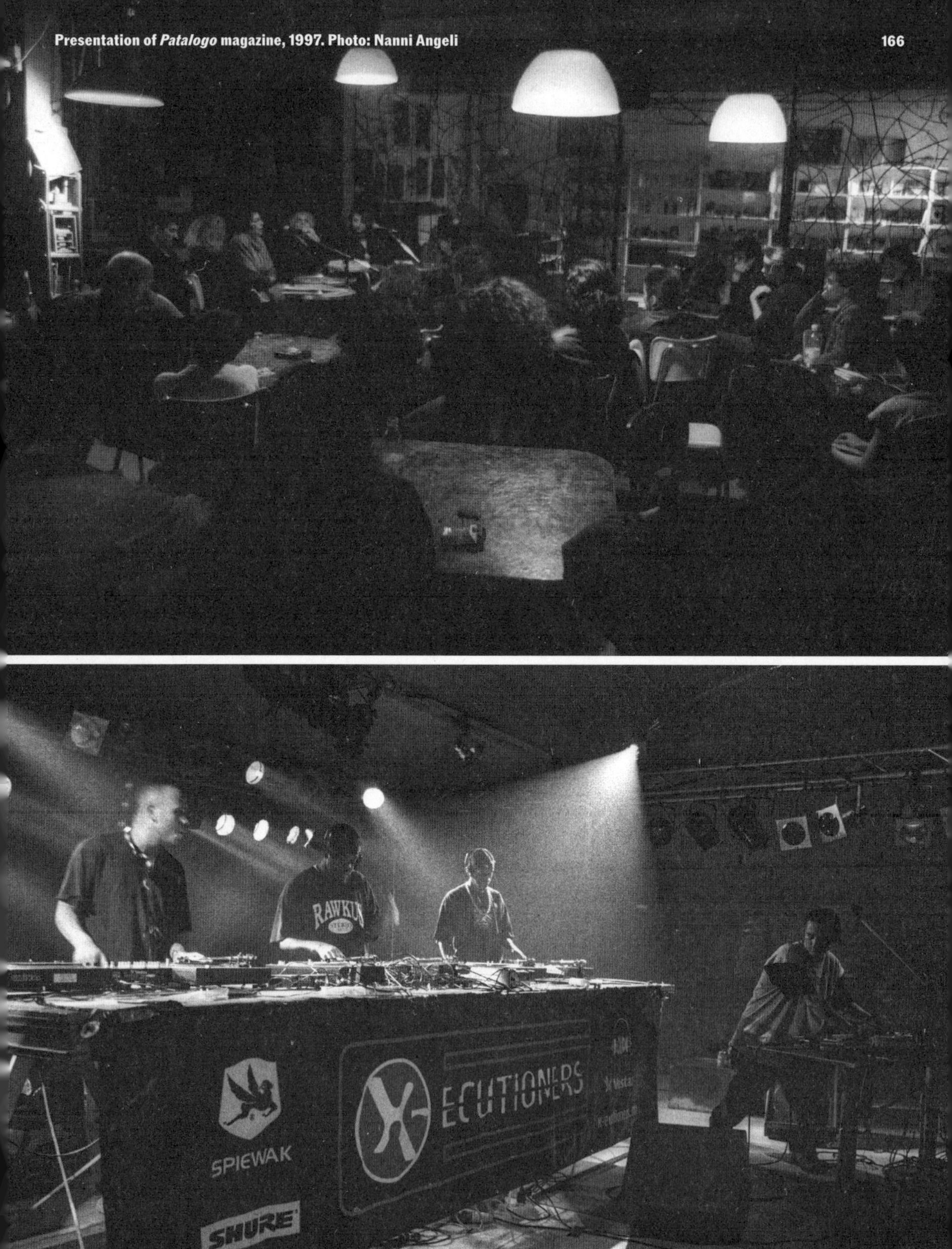

Mike Patton vs The X-ecutioners, performance, AngelicA festival, 2000. Photo: Nanni Angeli

distorsonie

festival di musica dance elettronica innova[tiva]

1° convention nazionale v-[...]

gio 8 aprile

DAVID CHAZAM (BNO Records, Paris F)
WANG INC. (sonig Rec, D)
BEAT ACTIONE (Dj Ilo & Cdj Peak Nick, I)
DAVID CALÒ (Morphine, I)

ven 9 aprile

DEAN ROBERTS (Mille Plateaux rec., I)
ENTROPIA/AMP-TEK (Ecletic rec., I)
STARFUCKERS (Lessness rec., I)
RECYCLE (Wot 4 rec., I)
MARTIN PATERSON (Wot 4 rec., uk, I)

sab 10 aprile

ANDI MADDOCKS JEGA (Skam rec., UK)
ROB-HALL GESCOM (Skam rec., UK)
FREEFORM (Skam-Warp rec., UK)
2ND GEN (Nova Mute, UK)
R.E.F./Roman Electronics Fighters
(Benedetti, Passaroni, Durante)
(Kiloton, W.W.F., Weird Uncle Betty, Alex D Steak)
dune records live up

PIXELL TRIBE PR[...]

www.linkproject.org

[...]4 bologna italy tel 051 570971 fax 051 570972

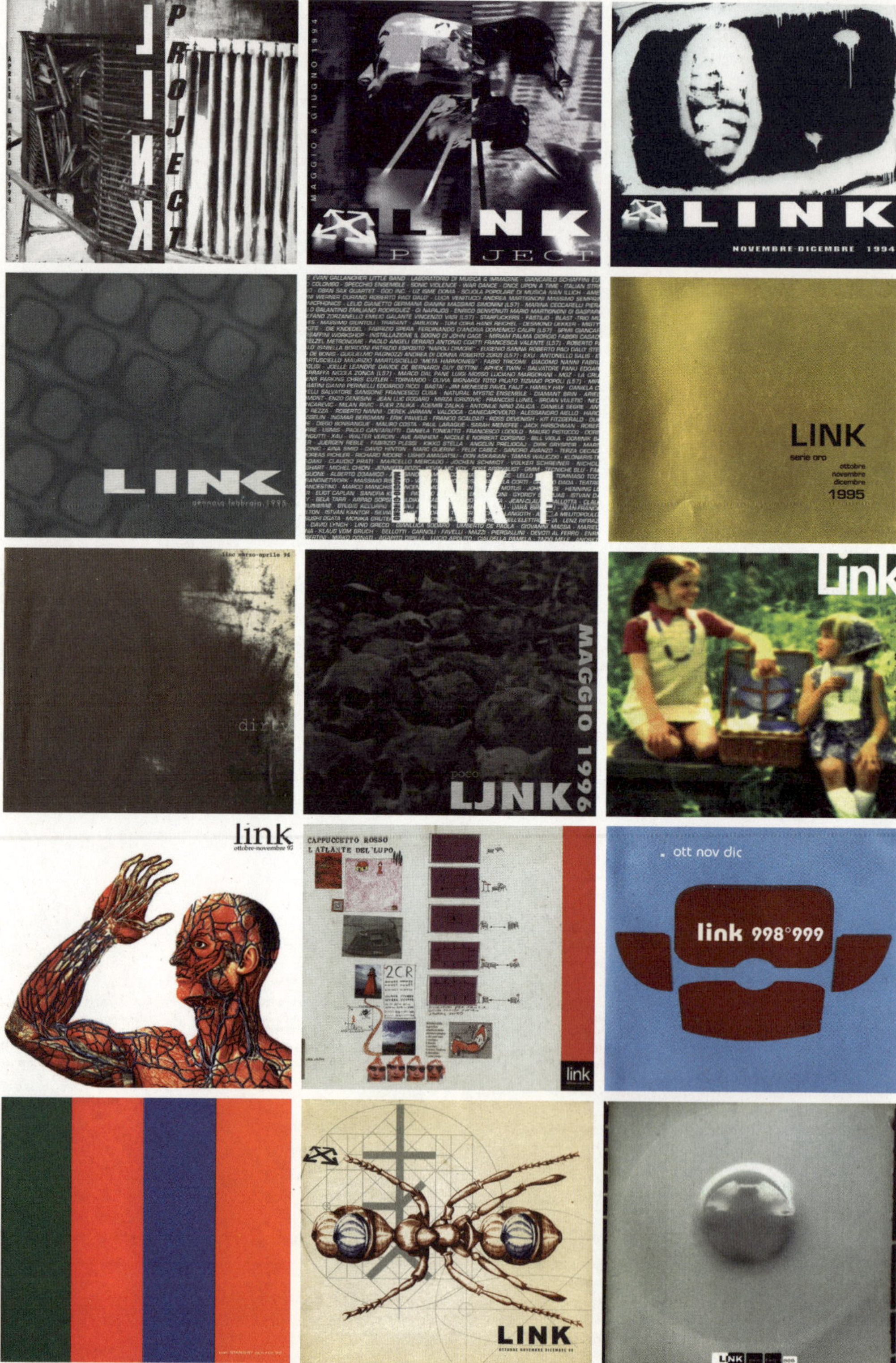

Marcel•lí Antúnez Roca, *Epizoo*, mechatronic performance, 1997. Photo: Gianluca Perticoni

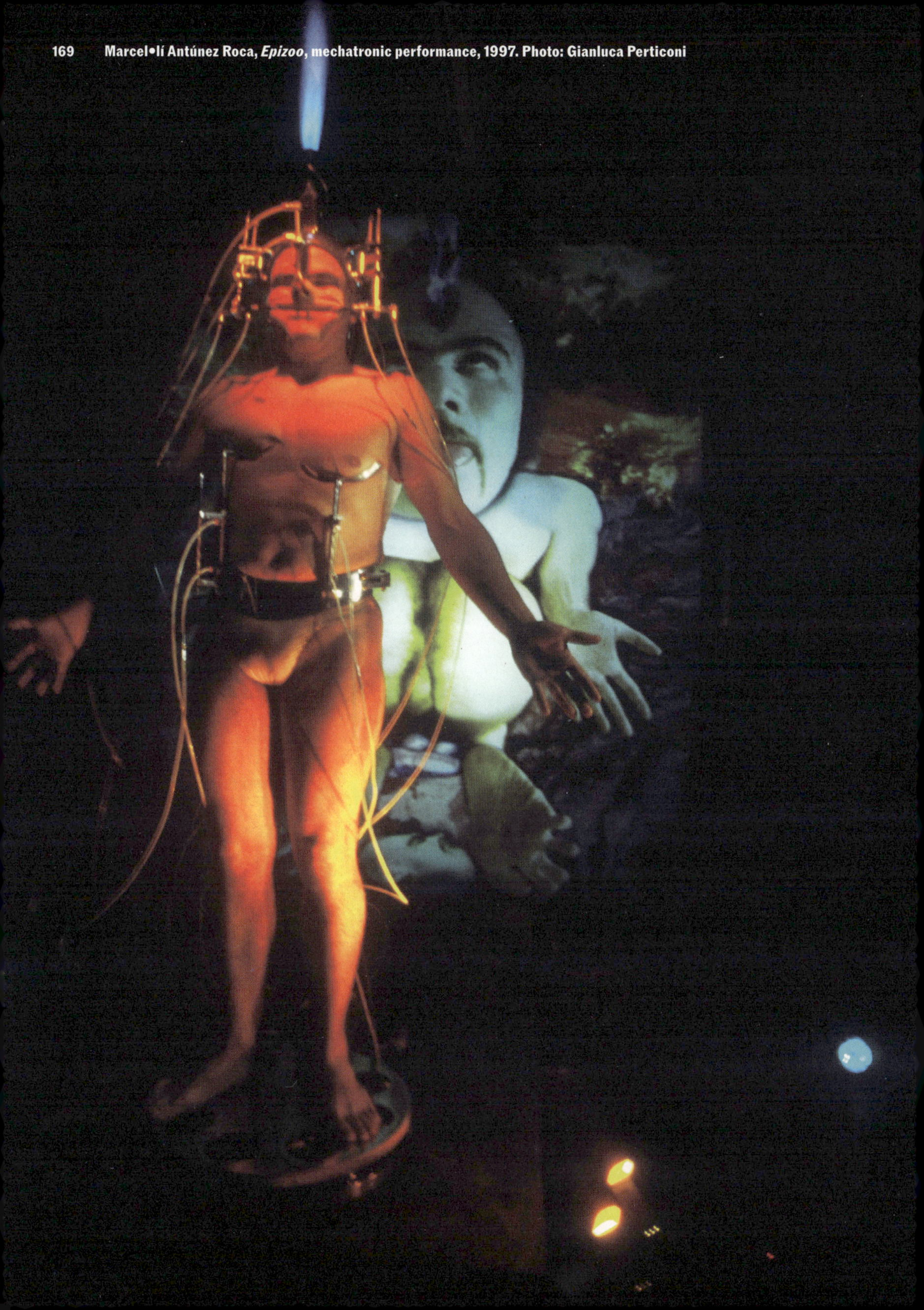

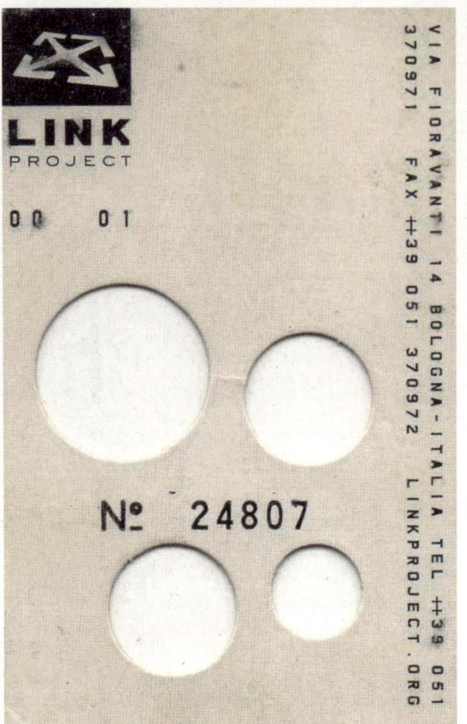
LINK
PROJECT
00 01
№ 24807
VIA FIORAVANTI 14 BOLOGNA-ITALIA TEL ++39 051 370971 FAX ++39 051 370972 LINKPROJECT.ORG

CODX
№ 3063
LiNK 998°999
tel 051370971
www.comune.bologna.it/iperbole/link
fax.051370972
e mail link@iperbole.bologna.it

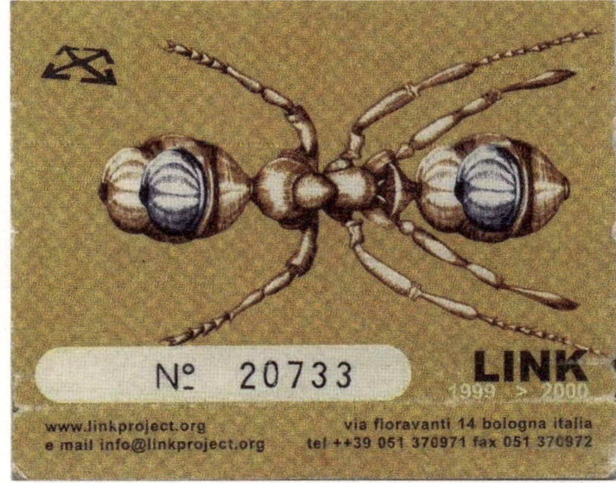
№ 20733
LINK
1999 > 2000
www.linkproject.org
e mail info@linkproject.org
via floravanti 14 bologna italia
tel ++39 051 370971 fax 051 370972

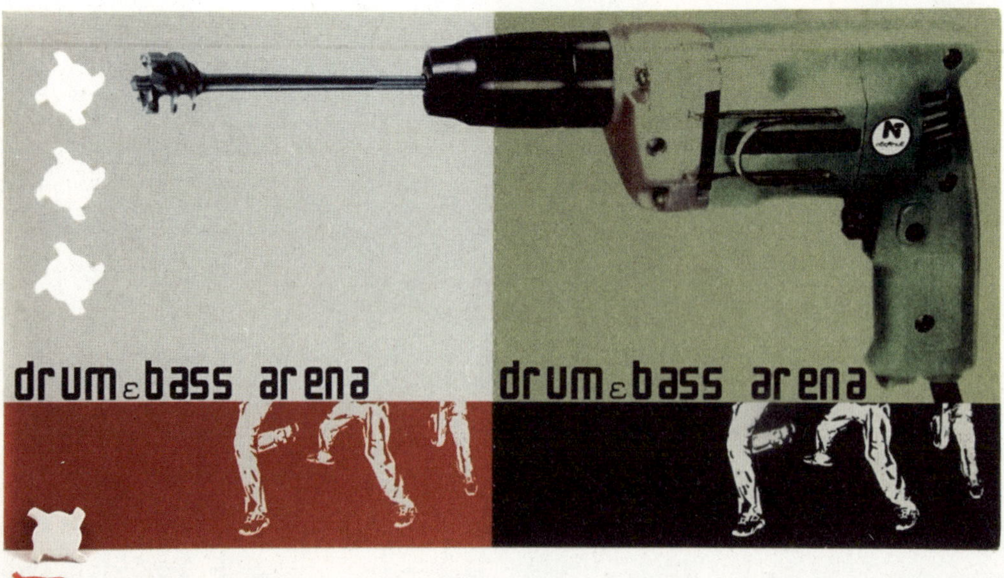
drumεbass arena
drumεbass arena

 Gruppo Zero, S/M night, 1998. Photo: Gianluca Perticoni

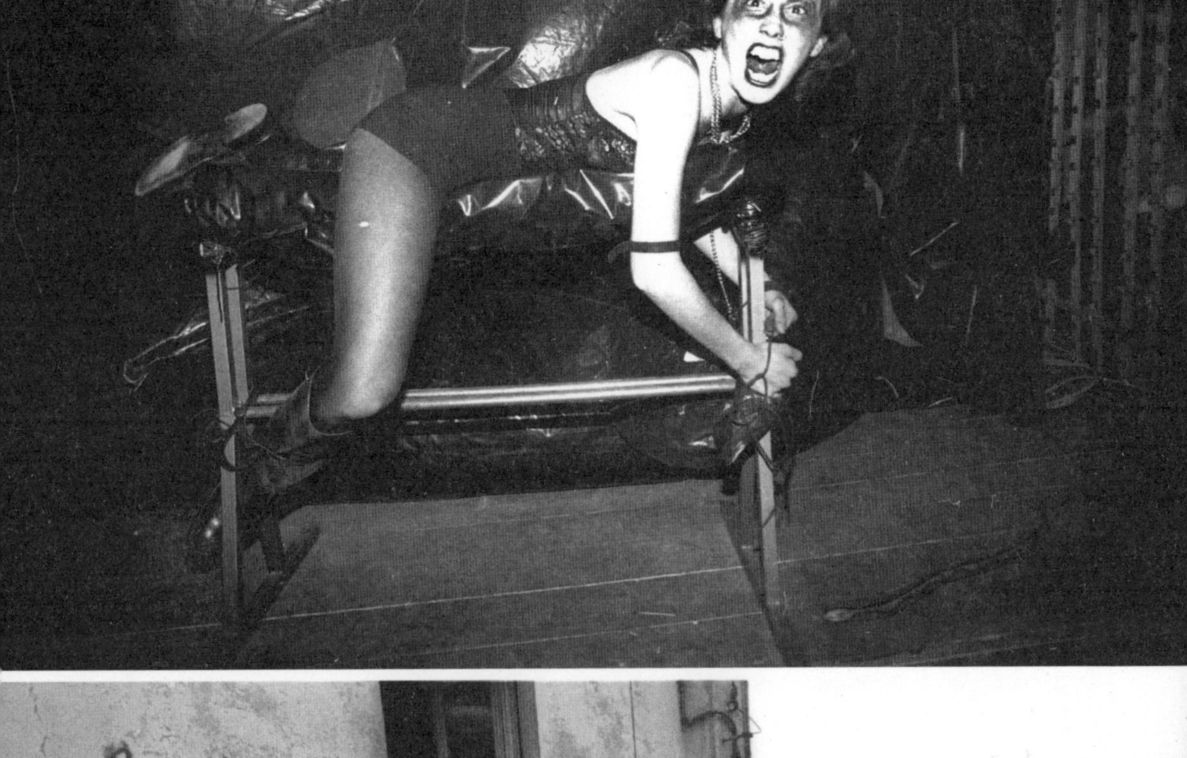

Simone Bellotti with his artworks, 1996. Photo: Gianluca Perticoni

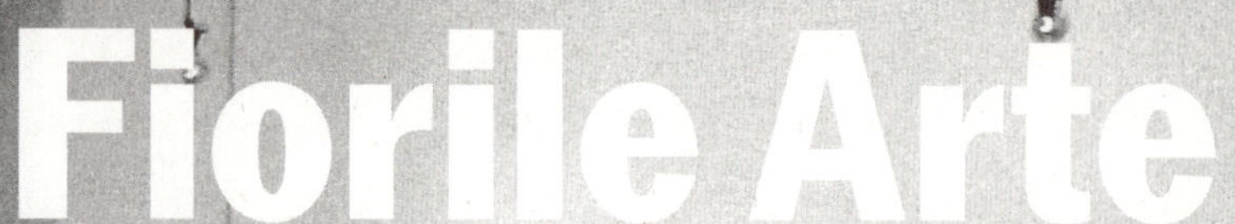

Fiorile Arte

Liuba, *Vie d'uscita*, performance, 1999

Franco Pappalardo, *Hard'Arte*, installation view at Fiorile Arte, 2001

1995–2005

This small four-by-five-meter space on Via Nosadella hosted exhibitions by both emerging and well-known artists. The founders, Mariangela Bacega and Patti Campani, were responsible for the artistic direction and management of the space, but choices were made in unison with the various collaborators involved from time to time. The audience was heterogeneous, consisting of both people in the field and individuals from outside the art world who happened to be passing in front of the space on this characteristic street in downtown Bologna.

Fiorile was in contact with several local associations and realities such as the Arci circuit, Osteria del Montesino and the C-Voltaire collective, responsible for Il Campo delle Fragole. Over the years, there were several collaborations with curators including Roberto Vitali, with whom Campani produced the radio program *Kactus*, Edoardo Di Mauro, Valerio Dehò, and Gabriele Perretta. The municipality gave the space sponsorship of some of the activities, but in economic terms the association relied on self-financing.

After the closure of the space, brought about by financial and organizational difficulties, Campani would continue to curate exhibitions in various spaces under the name Fiorile+.

ADDRESS Via Nosadella 37/d, Bologna. FOUNDERS Mariangela Bacega, Patti Campani. COLLABORATORS Roberto Vitali, Edoardo Di Mauro, Valerio Dehò, Gabriele Perretta

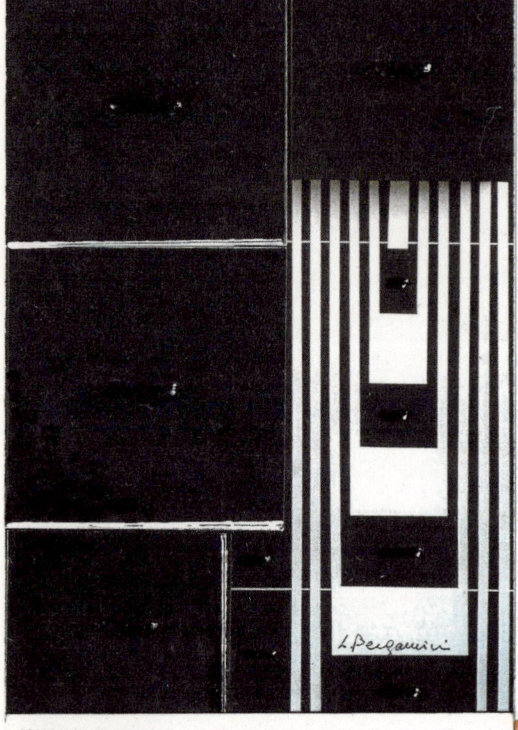
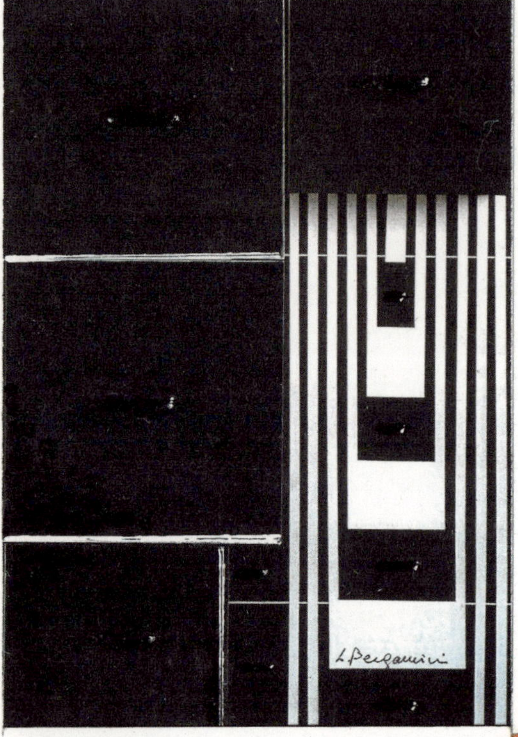

L.Bergamini

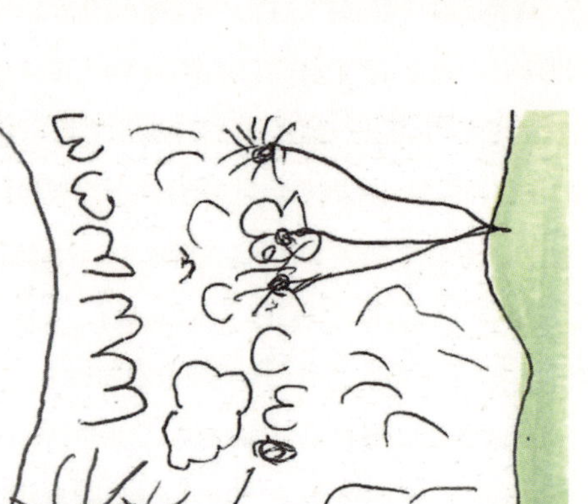

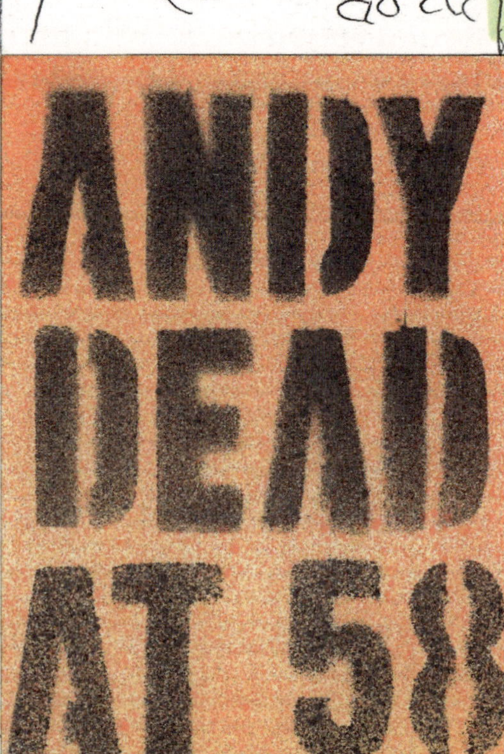
ANDY DEAD AT 58

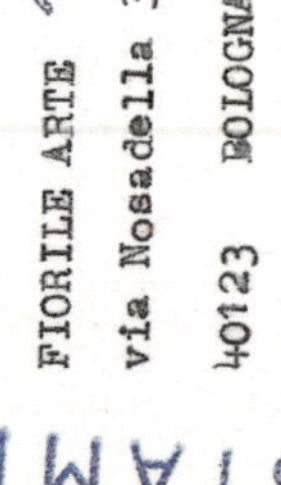
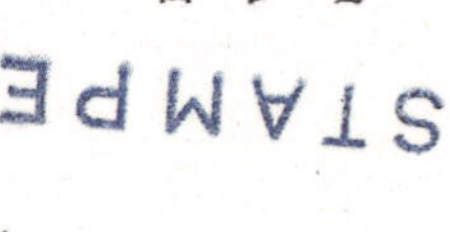
FIORILE ARTE
via Nosadella 37/D
40123   BOLOGNA
STAMPE

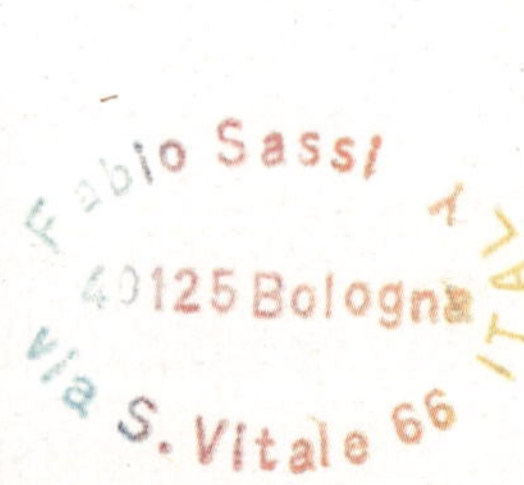
Fabio Sassi
40125 Bologna
via S. Vitale 66   ITALY

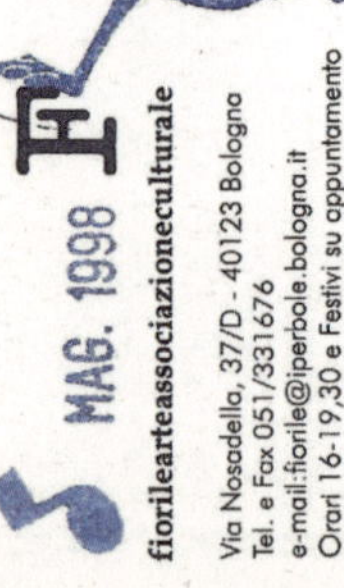
8 MAG. 1998
fiorilearteassociazioneculturale
Via Nosadella, 37/D - 40123 Bologna
Tel. e Fax 051/331676
e-mail:fiorile@iperbole.bologna.it
Orari 16-19,30 e Festivi su appuntamento

finto
ri
attoni
Case

noreggia
rmai

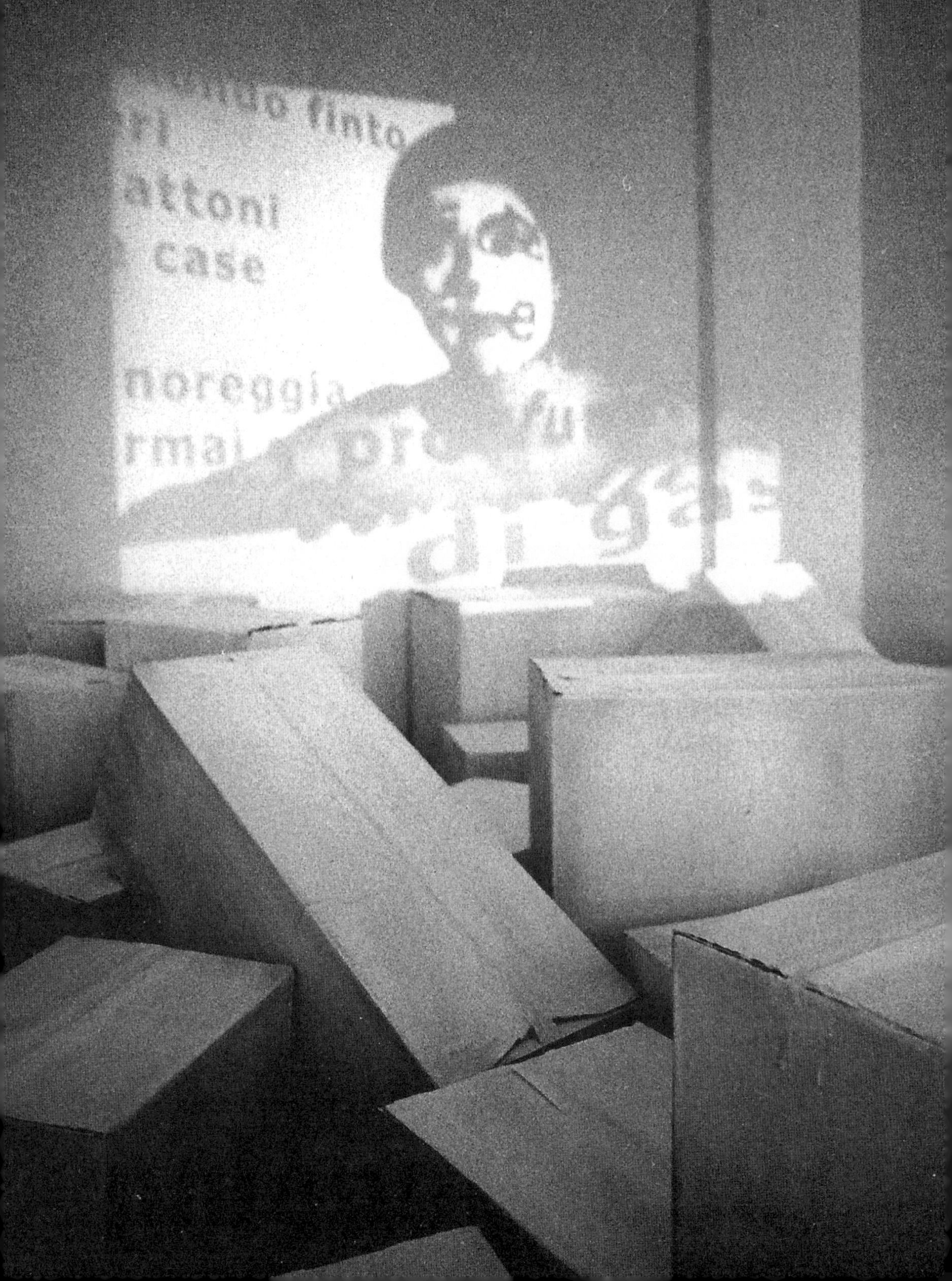

TPO

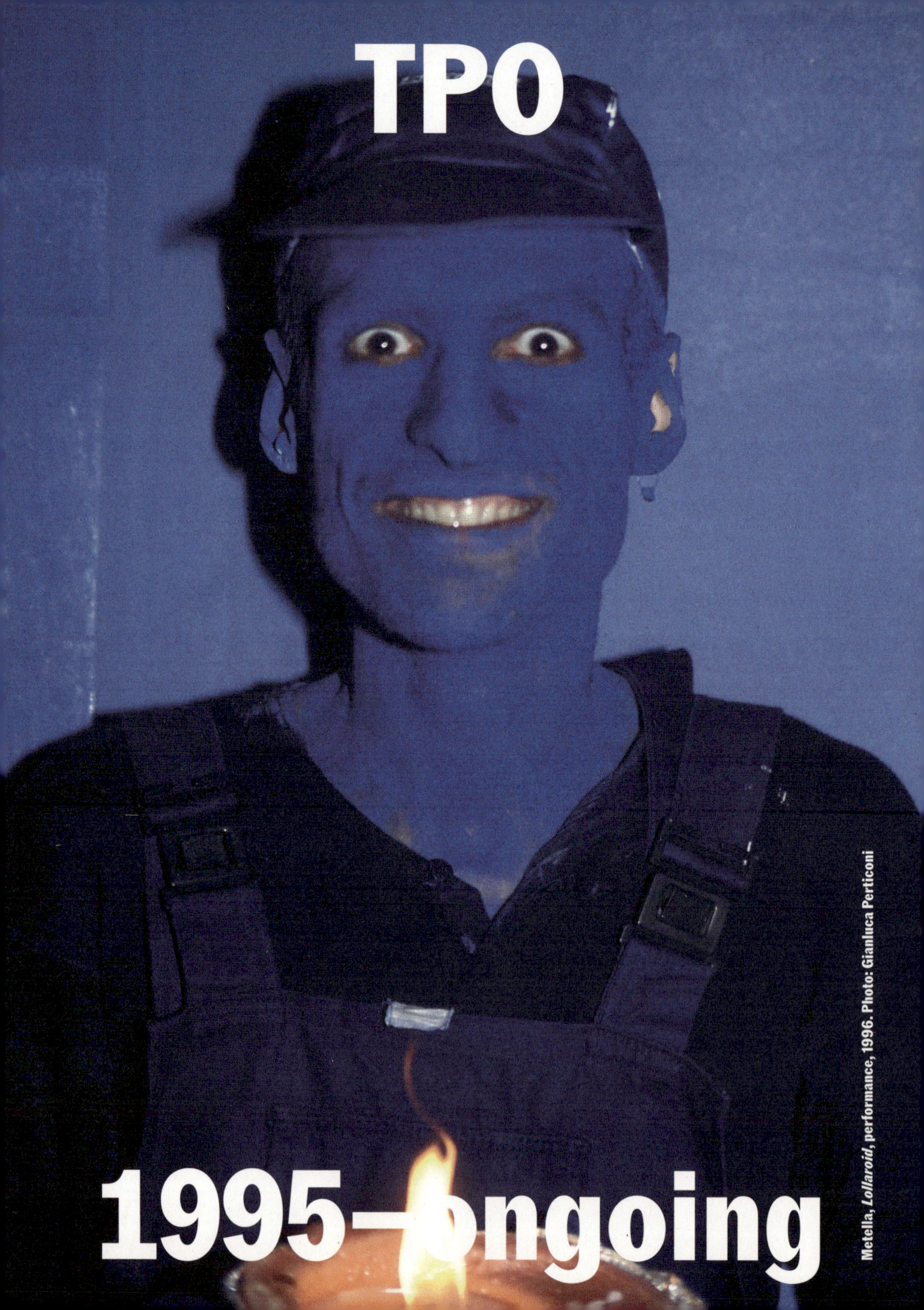

1995–ongoing

The origins of Teatro Polivalente Occupato, better known by the acronym TPO, date back to an assembly held inside the Radio K Centrale headquarters in 1995, in which a group of young theater figures talked about creating an open, experimental space. This space became a reality a few months later, on November 6, 1995, when a number of independent acting companies—including Amadossalto, Teatro dell'Infetto and the Teatro Situazionautico Luther Blissett—came together under the label of Teatranti Occupanti, and invaded the Teatro di Scenografia on Via Irnerio, owned by the Academy of Fine Arts of Bologna, designed by sculptor and architect Farpi Vignoli thirtyfive years earlier and largely unused up to that time.

Since its inception, the TPO has characterized itself as an inclusive, widespread and participatory social center, anti-fascist and anti-sexist by nature. The various figures and groups that have participated have asserted rights to free expression through declarations, demonstrations and innovative and often provocative cultural programming, according to an idea of art as a tool for social construction and a critique of systems of power. TPO is, in fact, a laboratory of expanded cultural practices and interdisciplinary languages, as well as a space for widespread knowledge and cooperation.

From its first year of activity, the occupation met with the approval of several Academy professors, including Concetto Pozzati, at the time culture councilor of the City of Bologna, as well as Vignoli himself, who was enthusiastic about this unexpected use of the building he designed. The relationship with other realities in the area always proved fruitful, especially in relation to spaces and organizations that are close in terms of identity and similarly devoted to independent artistic production.

There has never been a rigid organization of events and internal cultural programming, and any major management or political decisions are made at regular meetings. Being independent is still expressed in the maximum freedom of action both in programming and the political positions of the association, but also in economic terms, considering that TPO's activities are largely self-financed.

TPO's cultural programming has always been extremely diverse and manages to accommodate different audiences attracted to specific events, who within this space know they can find multidisciplinary offerings. Over the years, the TPO has offered performance and music projects, film screenings, festivals, meetings and workshops in the areas of theater and audiovisual media, following an interdisciplinary approach and a vocation for multimedia. Of particular importance was TPO's role in the emergence of a new wave of avant-garde theater In the 1990s, with projects by groups such as Motus, Teatrino Clandestino and Fanny & Alexander, among others.

TPO remained in the Via Irnerio location until 2000, when pressure from the Academy of Fine Arts and the policies of center-right mayor Giorgio Guazzaloca led to the venue's eviction and relocation to the former Euraquarium on Viale Lenin, an abandoned industrial complex. The move to the new location, outside the center of Bologna, caused a split in the original group that was not to heal. Forced to leave the Viale Lenin building, demolished to make way for a residence and parking lot, TPO has been based at Via Casarini 17/5 since 2007.

ADDRESS Bologna Academy of Fine Arts Scenography Theater, Via Irnerio (1995–2000); former Euraquarium, Viale Lenin 3, Bologna (2000–07); Via Casarini 17/5, Bologna (2007–). FOUNDERS Riccardo Paccosi, Bettina Cottone, Elena Lolli, Francesco Carta, Marco Morri

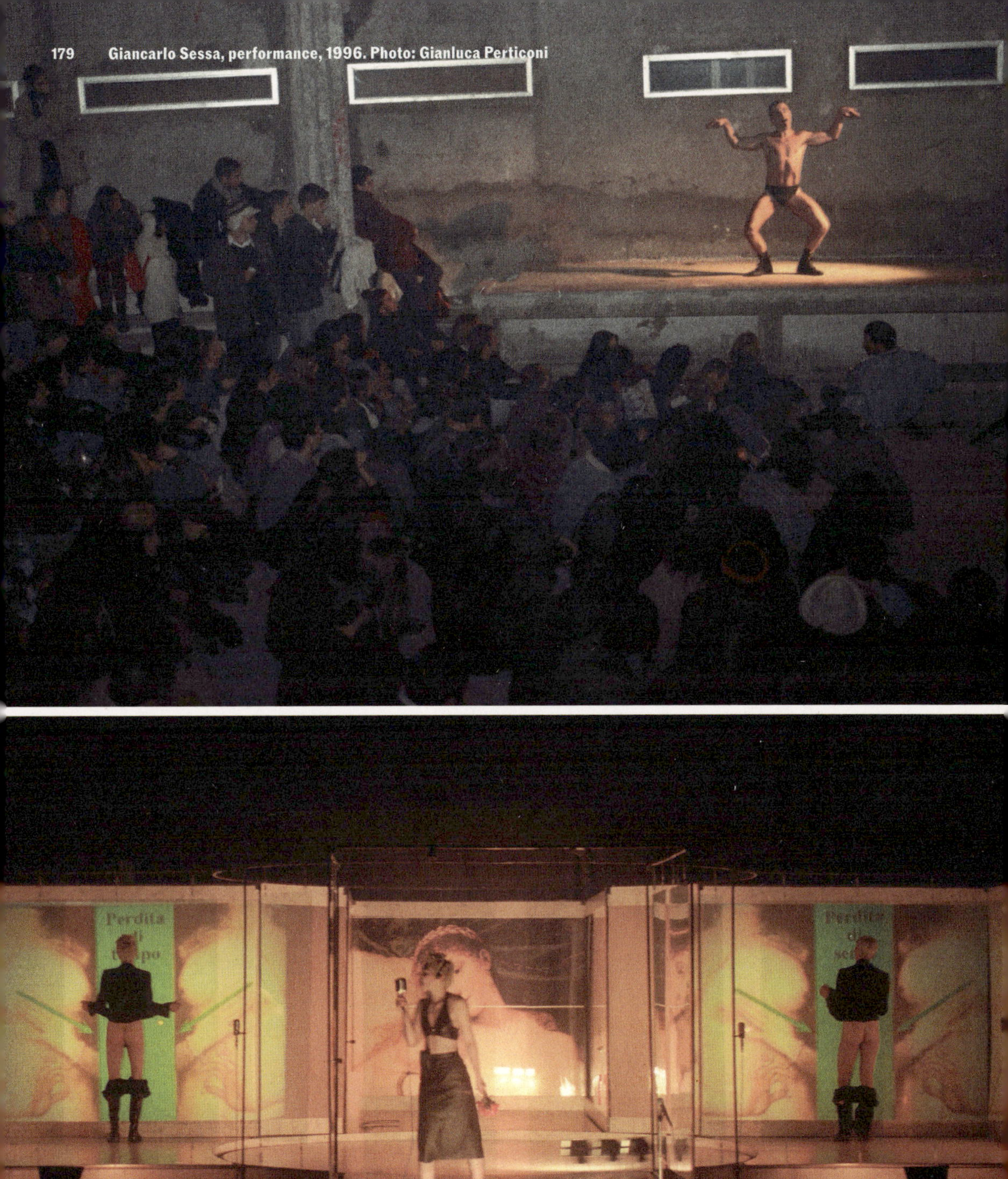

Motus, *O.F. ovvero Orlando Furioso*, performance, 1998. Photo: Gianluca Perticoni

TEATRO POLIVALENTE OCCUPATO

LUOGO NEGATO ALLA COLLETTIVITA' ABBANDONATO ALL'INCURIA E ALLA TOTALE ROVINA DA TRENT'ANNI .

GLI OCCUPANTI PONGONO IN ESSERE LA GIUSTA NECESSITA' DI DESTINARLO AL SUO RUOLO SPERIMENTALE POLIVALENTE.

DAL SEI NOVEMBRE GIA' CINQUE MESI FA' E' STATO MESSO IN MOTO IL PROGGETTO DI TEATRO POLIVALENTE E LABORATORIO CREATIVO.

SI SUSSEGUONO AUTOPRODUZIONI; TEATRALI, MUSICALI DI ARTI PLASTICHE E VISIVE, VI SI SVOLGONO ATTIVITA' LABORATORIALI, STAGES, MOSTRE, INSTALLAZIONI, CONCERTI, INIZIATIVE DI SOLIDARIETA'.

ABBIAMO APERTO UN CONFRONTO SINCERO CON TUTTE QUELLE REALTA' CITTADINE INTERESSATE ALLA COSTRUZIONE DI UN PERCORSO COMUNE.

IL TEATRO E' UN CANTIERE CREATIVO RESTAURO E RISTRUTTURAZIONE SONO IN ATTO, AL FINE DI SVILUPPARNE LE POTENZIALITA' .

PRATICARE L'AUTOGESTIONE E L'OCCUPAZIONE SIGNIFICA AUTODETERMINARE IL PROPRIO SPAZIO E TEMPO, PER SOCIALIZZARE COINVOLGENDO OGNI SOGGETTO NELLE FINALITA' CHE COLLETTIVAMENTE VENGONO DETERMINATE.

IL RUOLO CENTRALE DELL'ASSEMBLEA E LA GESTIONE COMUNE, SONO I PRINCIPI CARDINI CONTRO OGNI FORMA DI DELEGA E PASSIVITA'.

IL TENTATIVO DI CREARE IL "MOSTRO = OCCUPAZIONE "ATTRAVERSO CERTA STAMPA ALLARMISTA DI PROFESSIONE LOBBISTA E ALTRI ATTACCHI PIU' O MENO EVIDENTI, AL FINE DI CREARE LE CONDIZIONI PER LO SGOMBERO, HA UNA SOLA RISPOSTA; IL TEATRO POLIVALENTE OCCUPATO RIMANE NON UN PROBLEMA DI ORDINE PUBBLICO, MA DI ORDINE STRETTAMENTE POLITICO CULTURALE .

T.P.O. V. IRNERIO 45

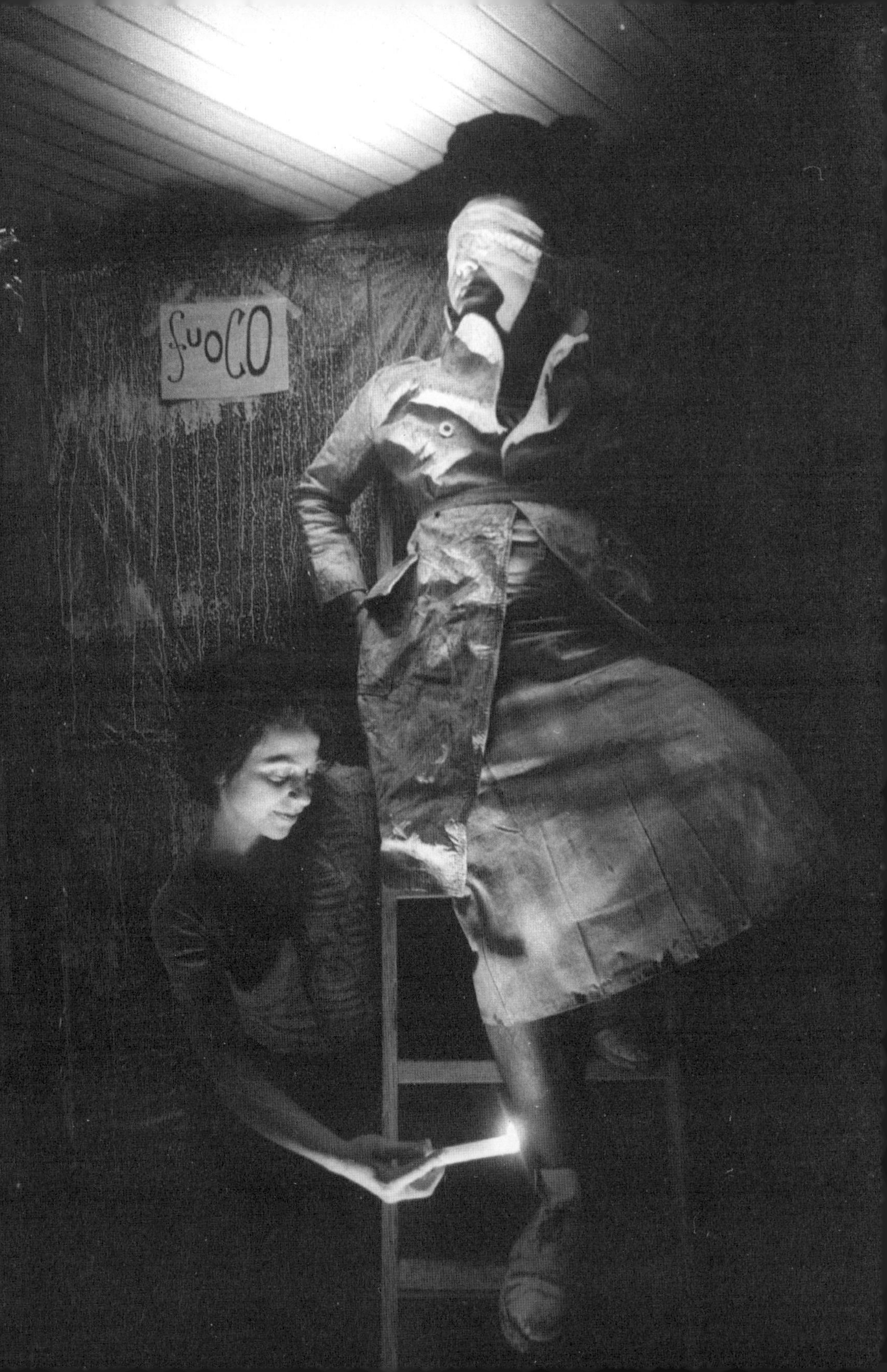

fuoCO

Installazioni Viventi: Acqua–Vento–Fuoco–Terra, performance, 1996. Photo: Gianluca Perticoni

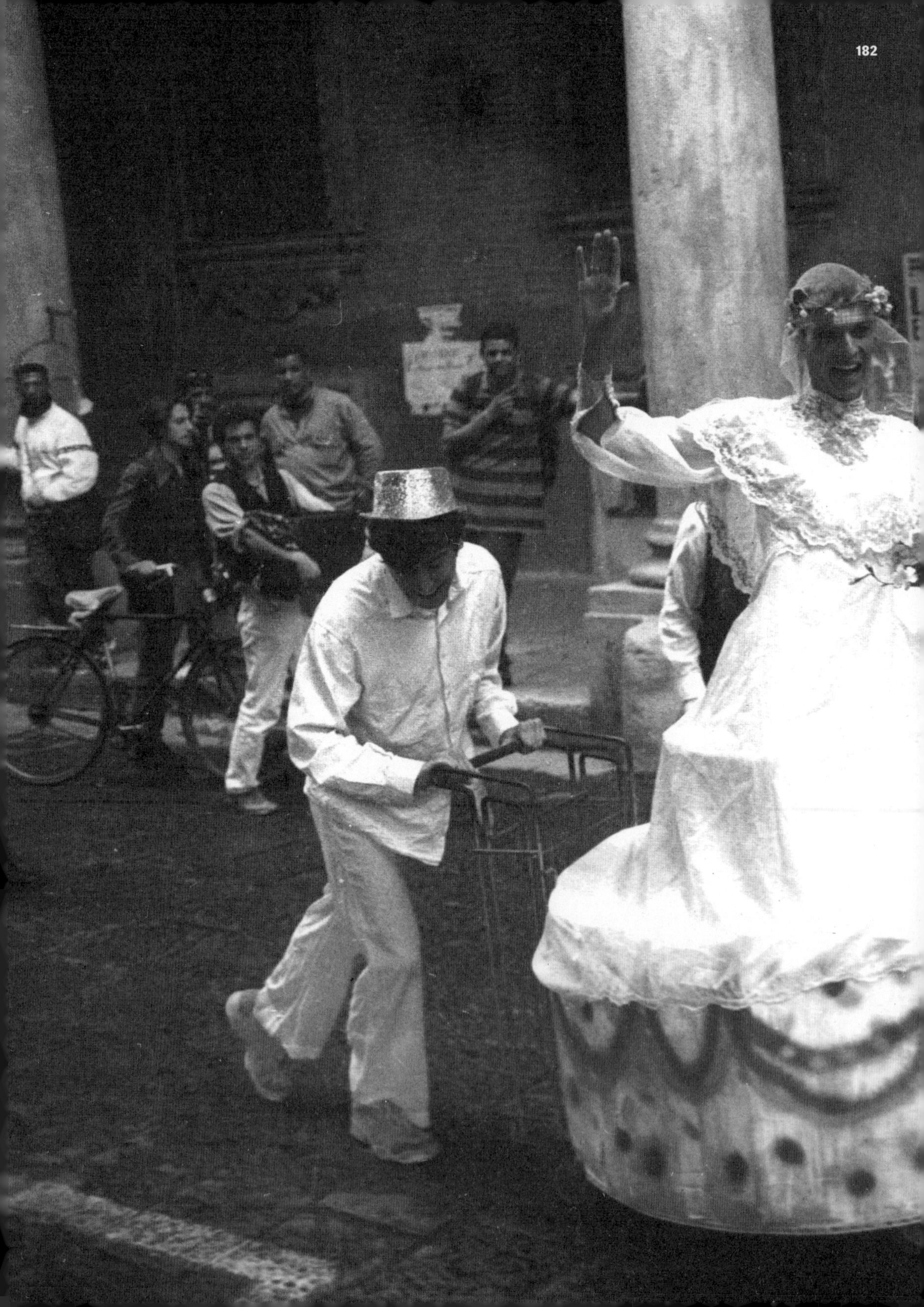

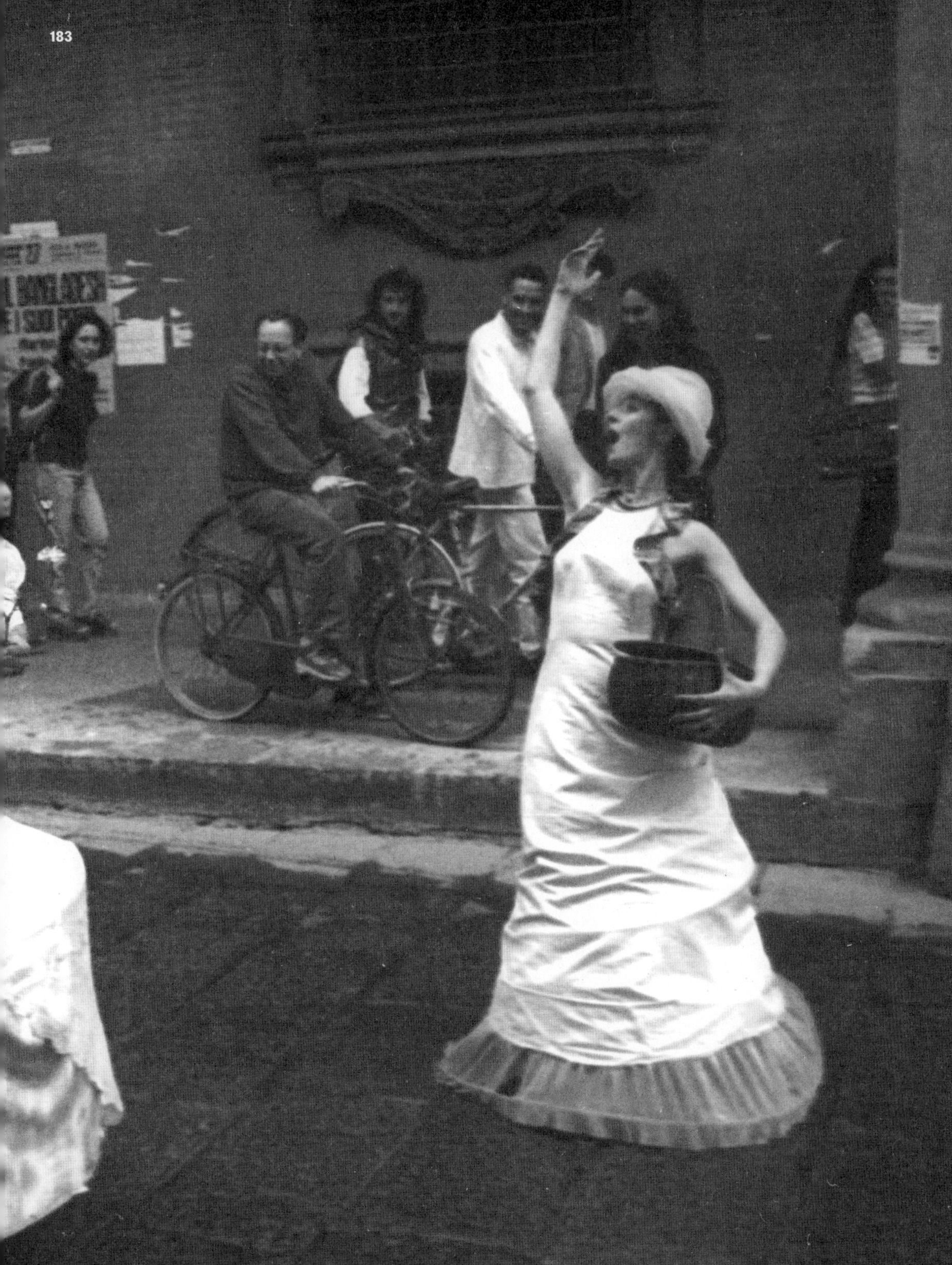

Teatro Situazionautico Luther Blissett, public performance, 1998. Photo: Gianluca Perticoni

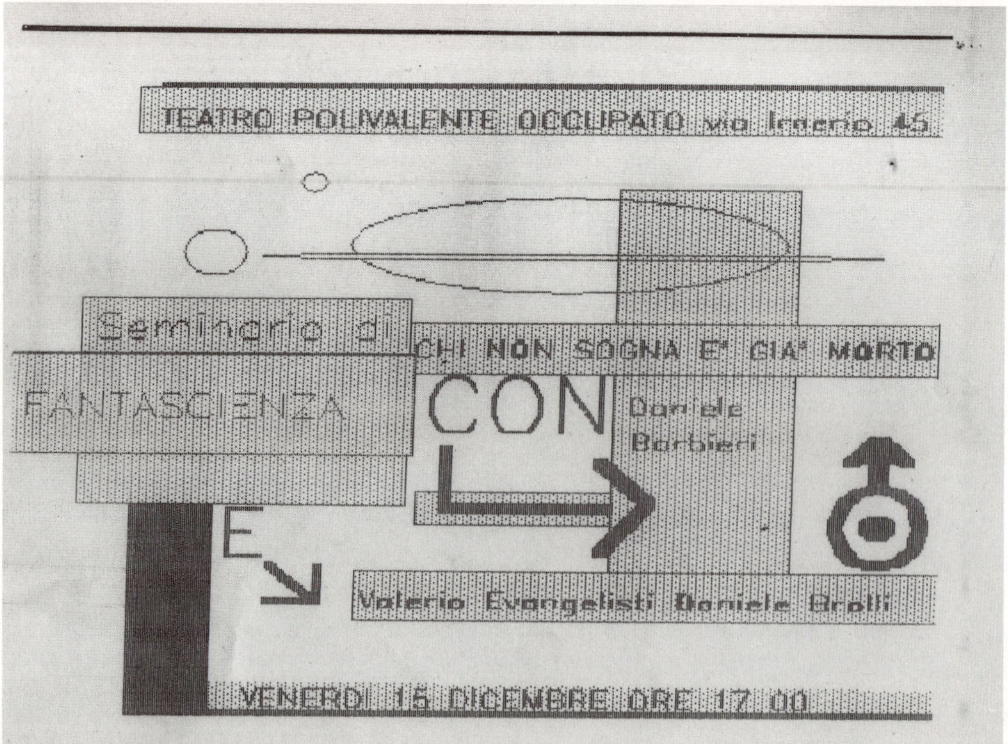

Daniele Barbieri, Valerio Evangelisti, Daniele Brolli, *Seminario di Fantascienza – Chi non sogna è già morto*, flyer, 1995

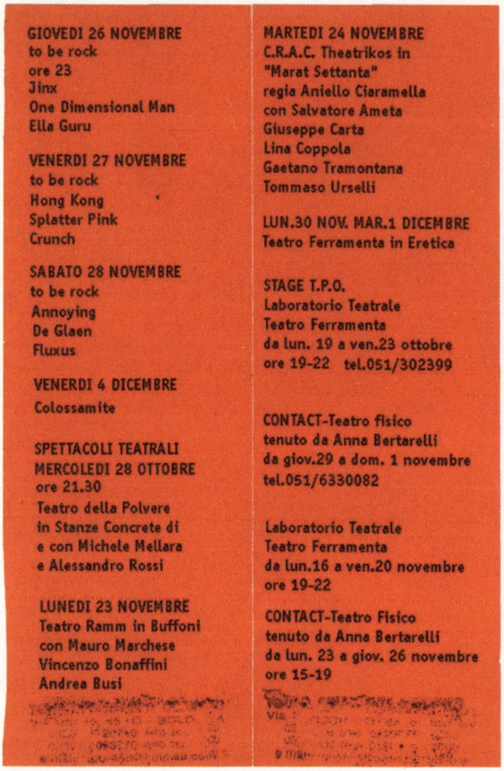

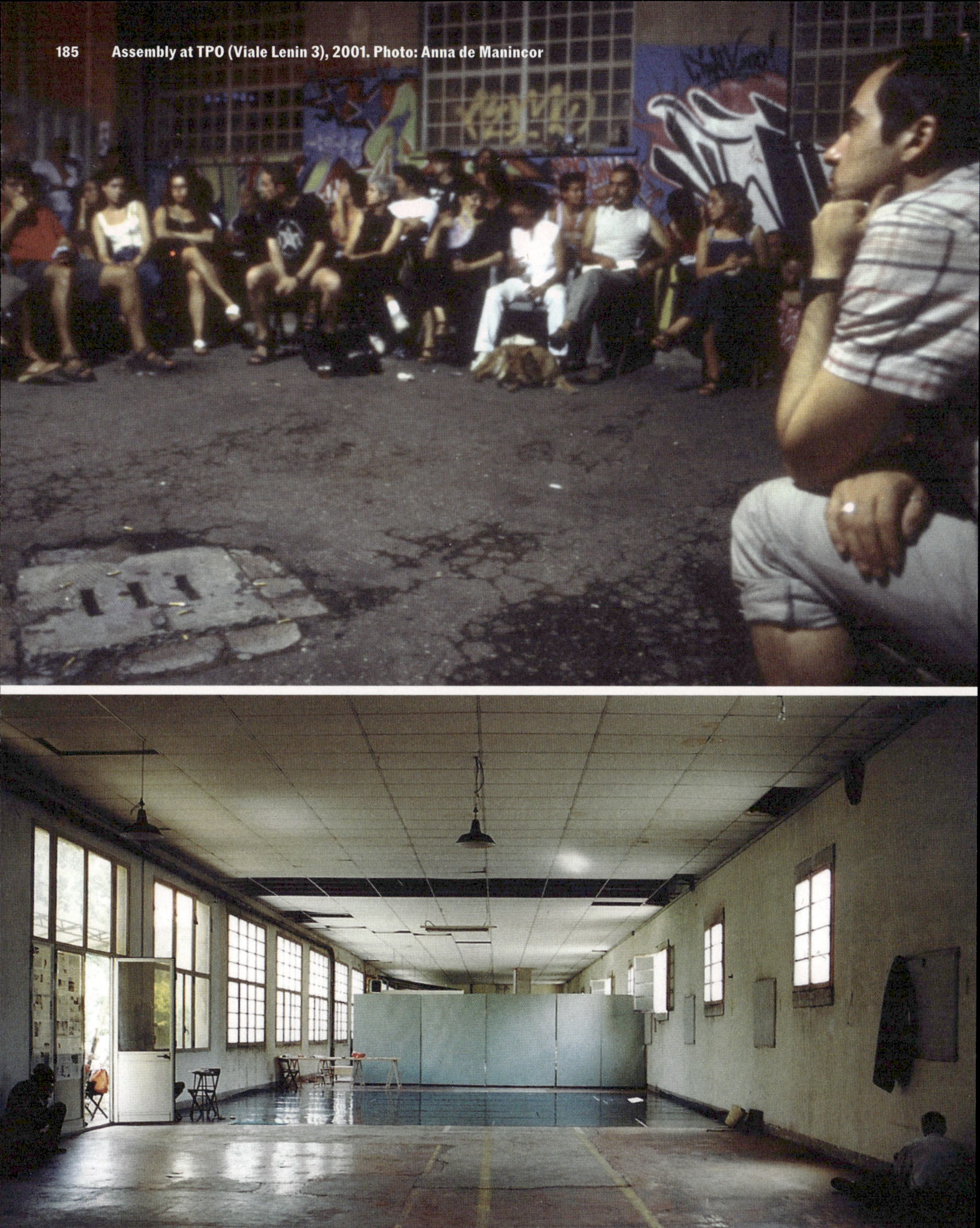

Assembly at TPO (Viale Lenin 3), 2001. Photo: Anna de Manincor

Rehearsal rooom at TPO (Viale Lenin 3), 2001. Photo: Anna de Manincor

Atlantide

1999–2015

Memories Of Apocalypse, merchandise table, 2005. Photo: Stefano Belacchi

The Atlantide occupied space was founded in the late 1990s to meet the needs of some of the main Bolognese feminist and queer collectives of the period. Established illegally inside one of the two buildings that constitute Porta Santo Stefano, one of the gates of the ancient city walls of Bologna, the internal organization was regulated by a collective assembly that defined and assigned a variety of tasks.

In its fifteen years of operation, the space hosted more than 250 concerts by Italian and foreign bands, becoming a reference point for the punk/hardcore scene and various other underground movements with an international flavor. Underpinning these events were the constant intersections between music and other forms of expression such as comics, street art, performing arts, photography, audiovisual media and independent publishing. The marches organized by Atlantide had a strong performative character and included concerts, art installations, and photography exhibitions, with a focus on trans and queer artists.

Atlantide was self-funded through entrance fees for events and concerts, managing to subsidize even activities outside the collective, such as MIT – Movimento d'Identità Transessuale. The importance of this space in the urban fabric of Bologna was linked to the need to have a physical place capable of offering non-mainstream cultural programming.

Atlantide's political action was carried out in a direct, independent and self-managed manner. The city's cultural realities acknowledged the presence and role of this space within the Bolognese context, as a workshop of cultural production and independent music promotion. Relations with local institutions changed over time.

Atlantide's experience ended in 2015 with the violent eviction of the space by law enforcement.

ADDRESS Piazza di Porta Santo Stefano 6, Bologna. FOUNDERS Clitoristrix, Quelle che non ci stanno, Antagonismogay, Smaschieramenti, NullaOsta

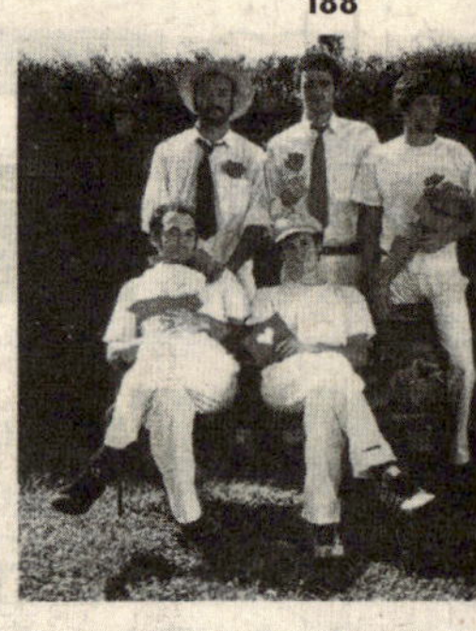

I paladini di Atlantide

La storia. I sette anni del centro sociale di Porta S. Stefano raccontati da chi l'ha occupato e da chi lo ha visto crescere come «uno spazio unico per la musica». E ora artisti e volontari danno il via alla mobilitazione

Marco Merlini

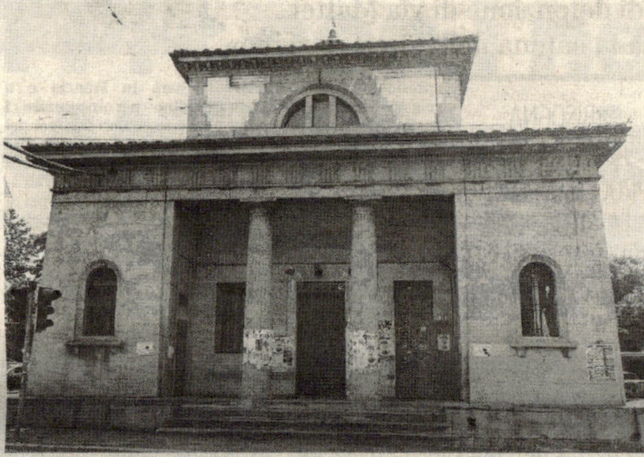

Correva l'anno 156 dalla costruzione del Cassero di Porta Santo Stefano. Per tutti, bolognesi e non, era semplicemente il 20 febbraio 1999: un gruppo di appartenenti a organizzazioni informali della sinistra movimentista, intorno alle quattro del pomeriggio, dopo aver sfilato in corteo, si ferma davanti all'edificio, alza una saracinesca, entra e si riunisce in assemblea. È il primo atto di una occupazione a cui oggi l'amministrazione comunale intende porre fine.

A dare il via all'azione da cui prese le mosse l'esperienza di Atlantide, furono gruppi come le Tute bianche, Giovani comunisti e alcuni col-

spiega Enrico Cacciari dei Sumo - Qui non suoneranno mai gruppi con testi razzisti o che dichiaratamente vogliono fare carriera». L'uscita di scena di Ya Basta, che sul finire del 2000 si trasferisce al Tpo di viale Lenin, sguarnisce la programmazione del centro sociale, nel quale tuttavia si affacciano altri gruppi come Antagonismo Gay e Clitoristrix.

Dal 2001 Atlantide si conforma come uno dei luoghi dove poter offrire quella musica, tutta rigorosamente dal vivo e legata al mondo delle etichette indipendenti, che non trova spazio nei circuiti più noti della città. Emblematica, in questo senso, l'esperienza dei Settlefish che a Porta Santo

sta della band - cresciuti tanti rag siamo formati all abbiamo potuto gruppi che ci han tantissimo e che a Bologna non potuto ascoltare»

È anche un luo l'elemento uman pre giocato un f cisivo: ed in qu partito un tam-ta per chiamare a ra ha conosciuto e fr negli anni il cent E proprio i Sett escludono iniziat tanti. «Quello ch cedendo è scand cheremo di mobi le realtà musical noscono Atlantid pedirne la chius parla come fosse

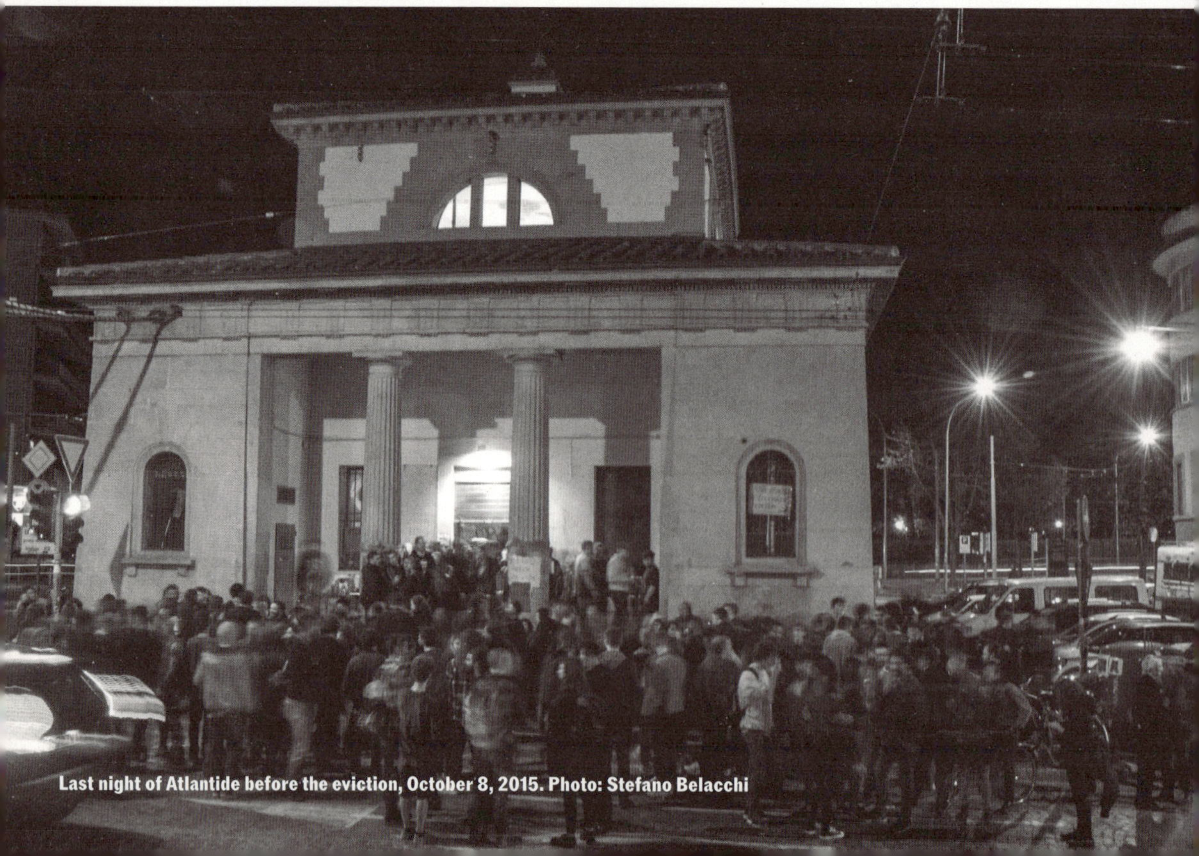

Last night of Atlantide before the eviction, October 8, 2015. Photo: Stefano Belacchi

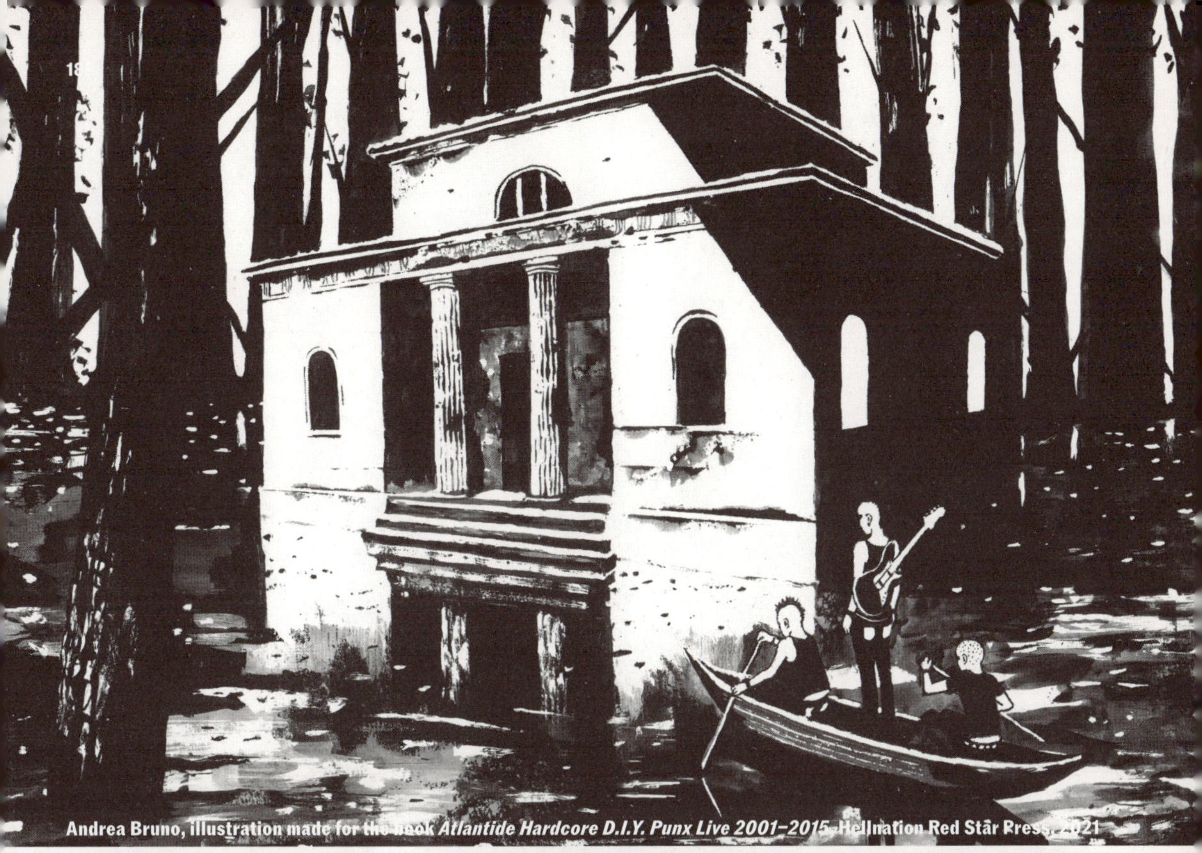

Andrea Bruno, illustration made for the book *Atlantide Hardcore D.I.Y. Punx Live 2001–2015*, Hellnation Red Star Press, 2021

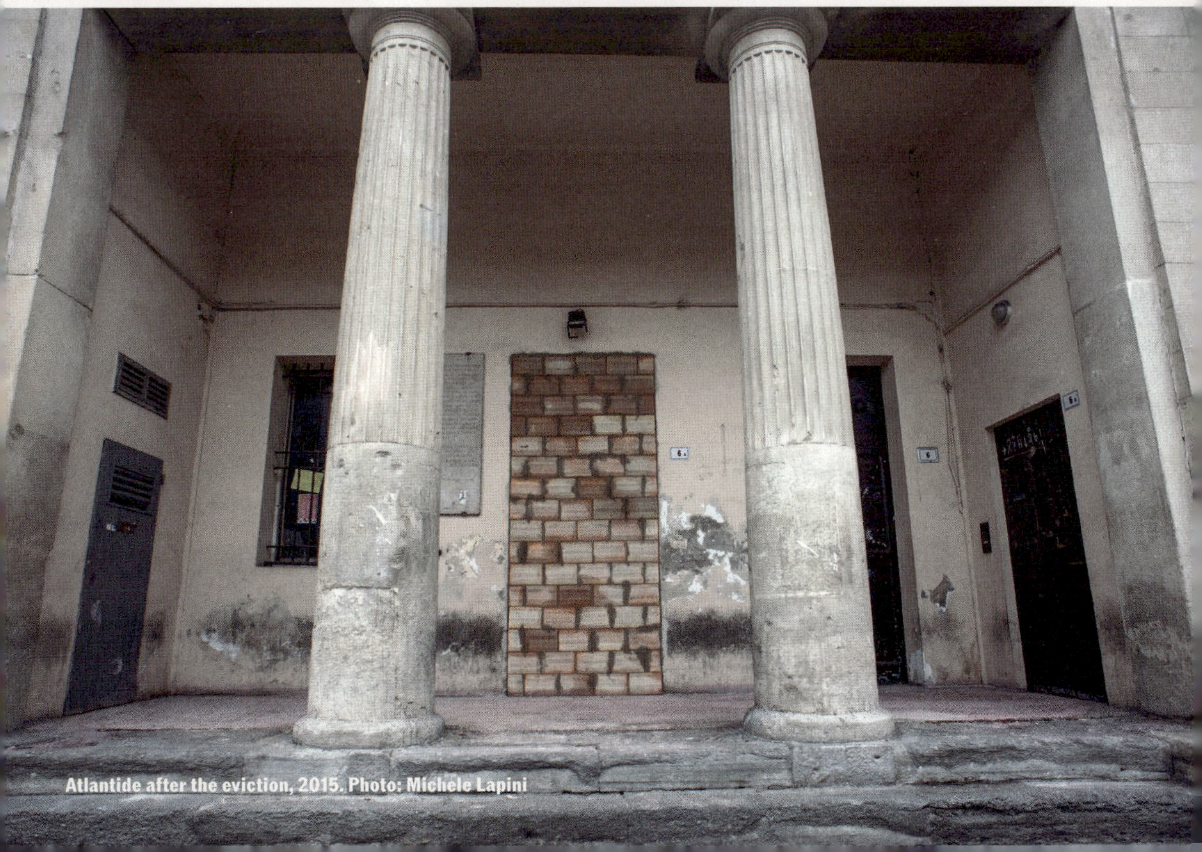

Atlantide after the eviction, 2015. Photo: Michele Lapini

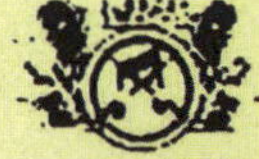

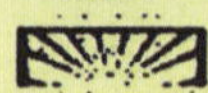

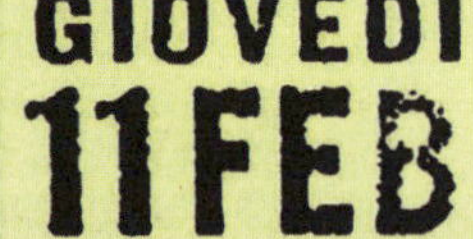

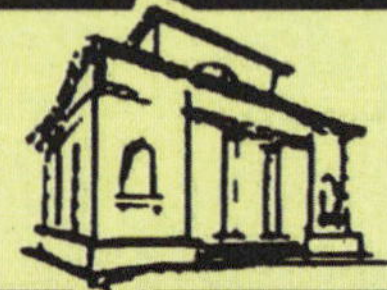

Cannabis Corpse feat. Philip Hall, flyer, February 11, 2010

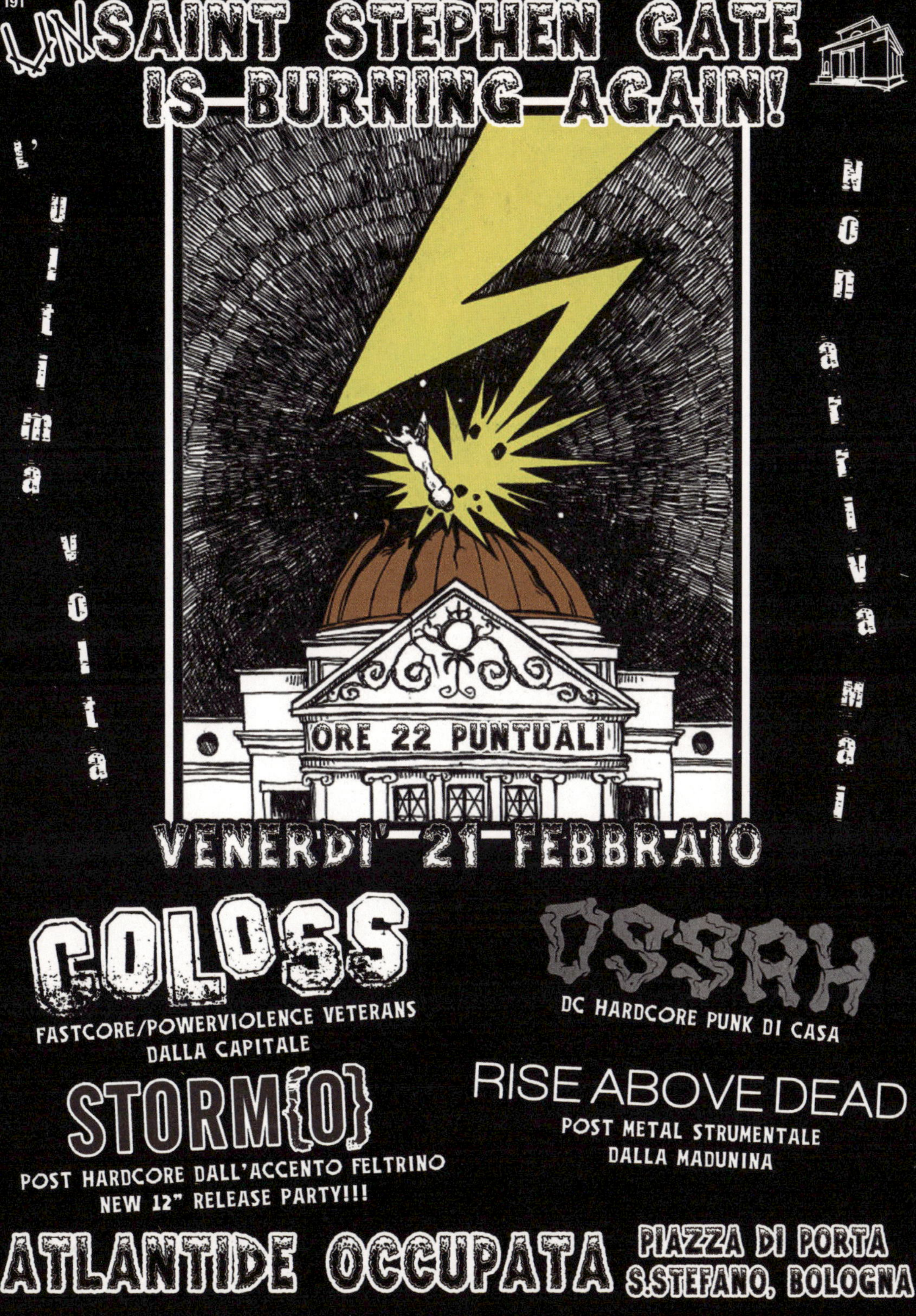

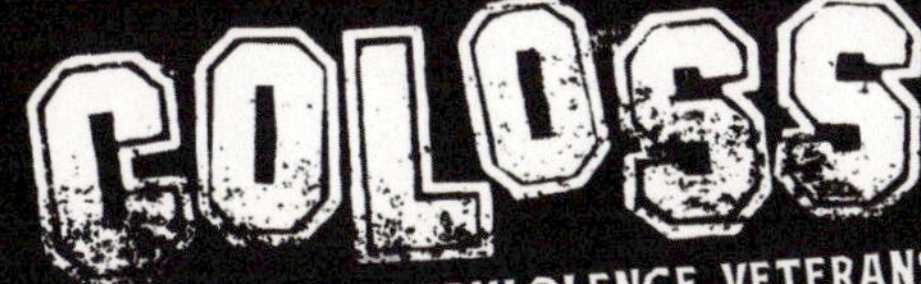

Un-Saint Stephen Gate is Burning Again!, flyer, February 21, 2014

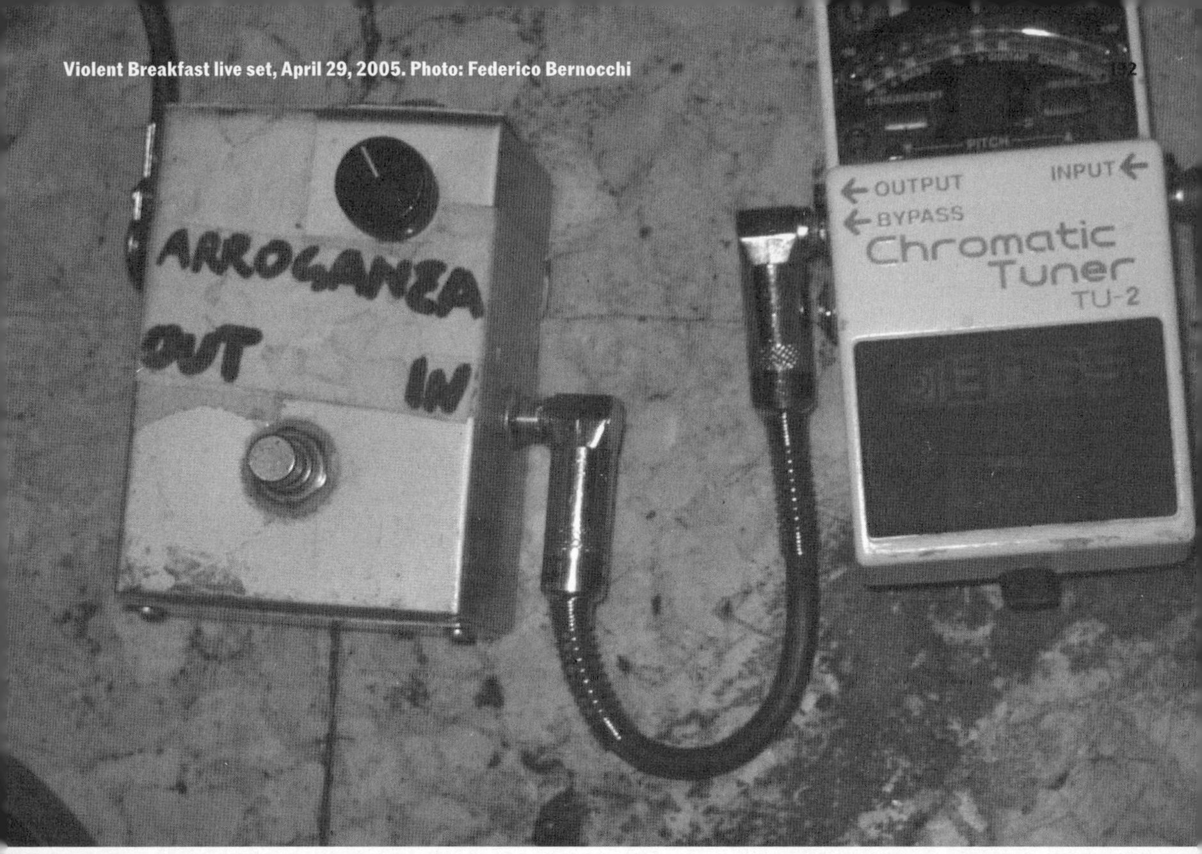

Violent Breakfast live set, April 29, 2005. Photo: Federico Bernocchi

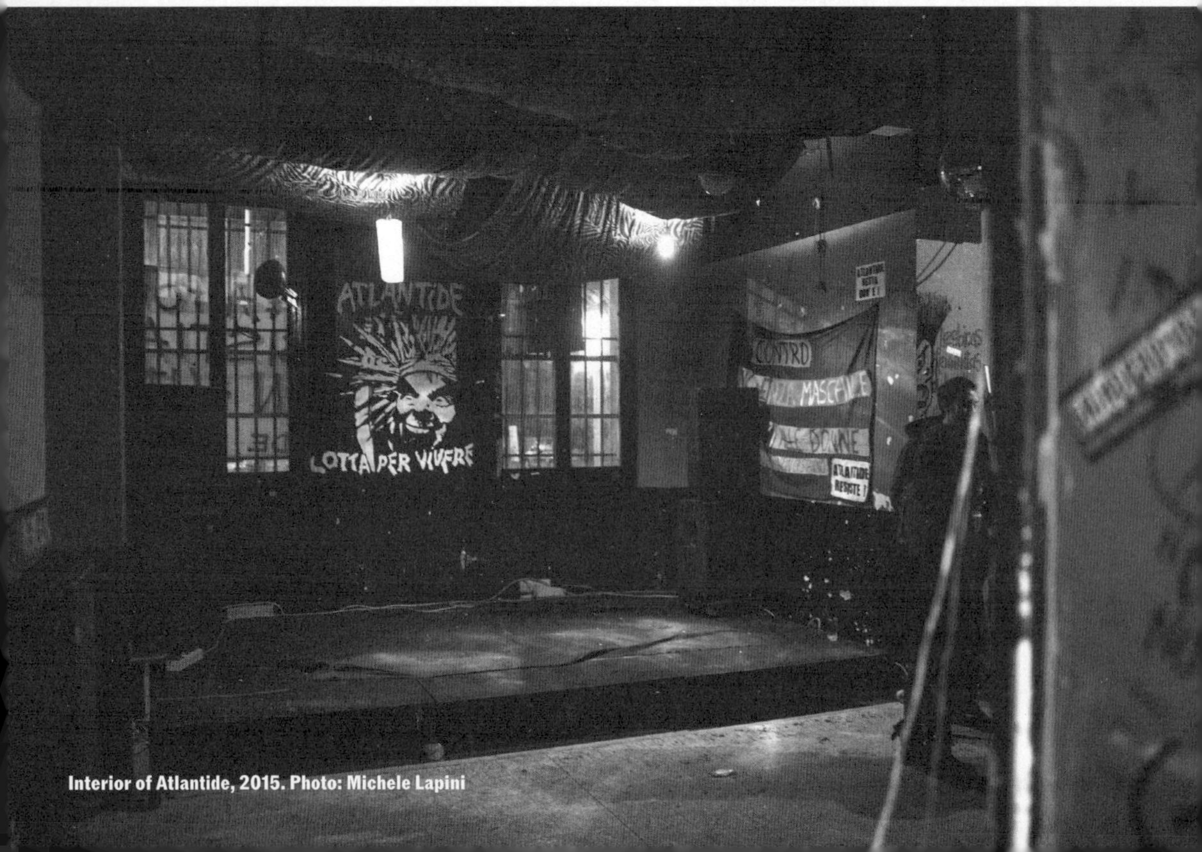

Interior of Atlantide, 2015. Photo: Michele Lapini

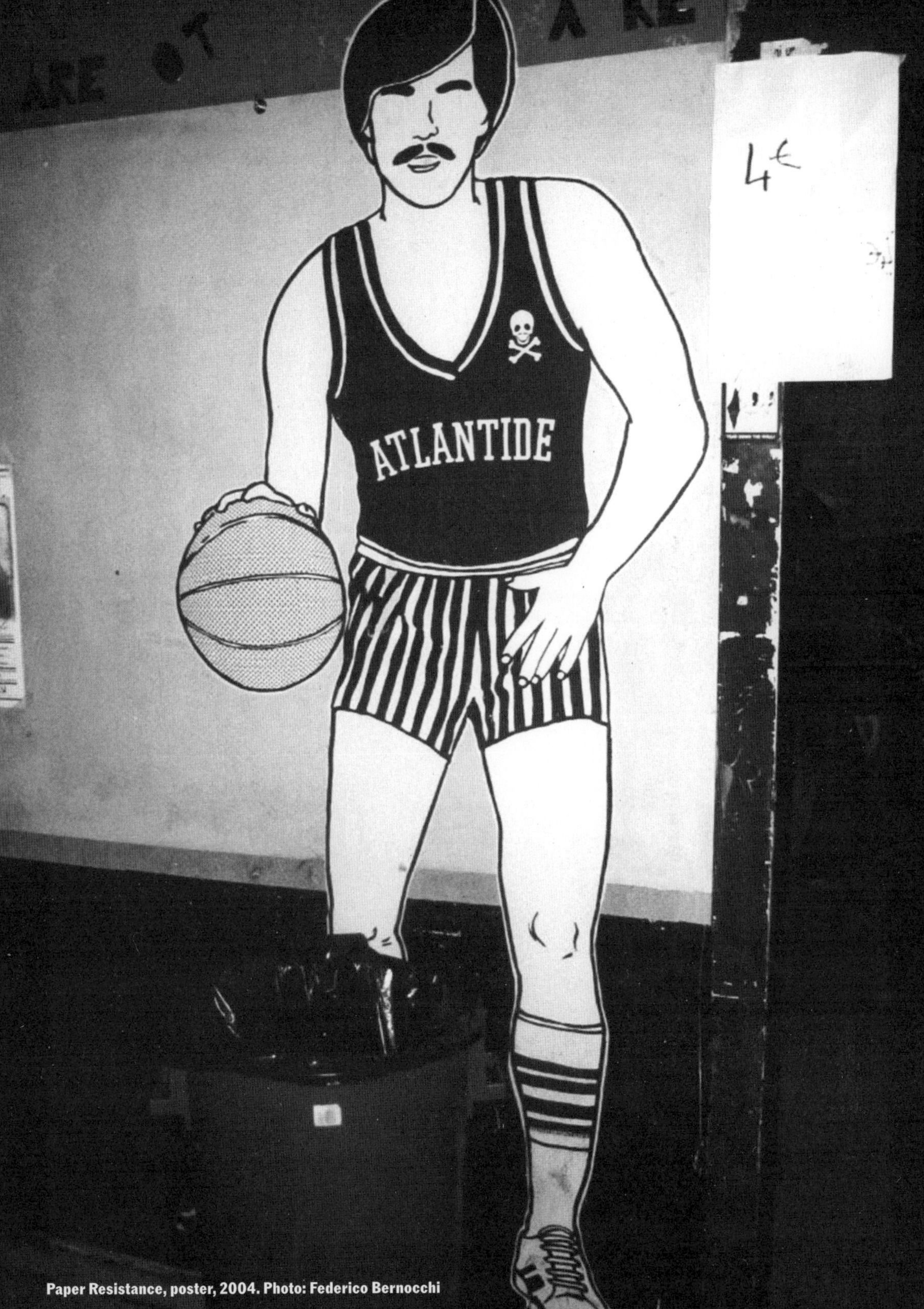

Paper Resistance, poster, 2004. Photo: Federico Bernocchi

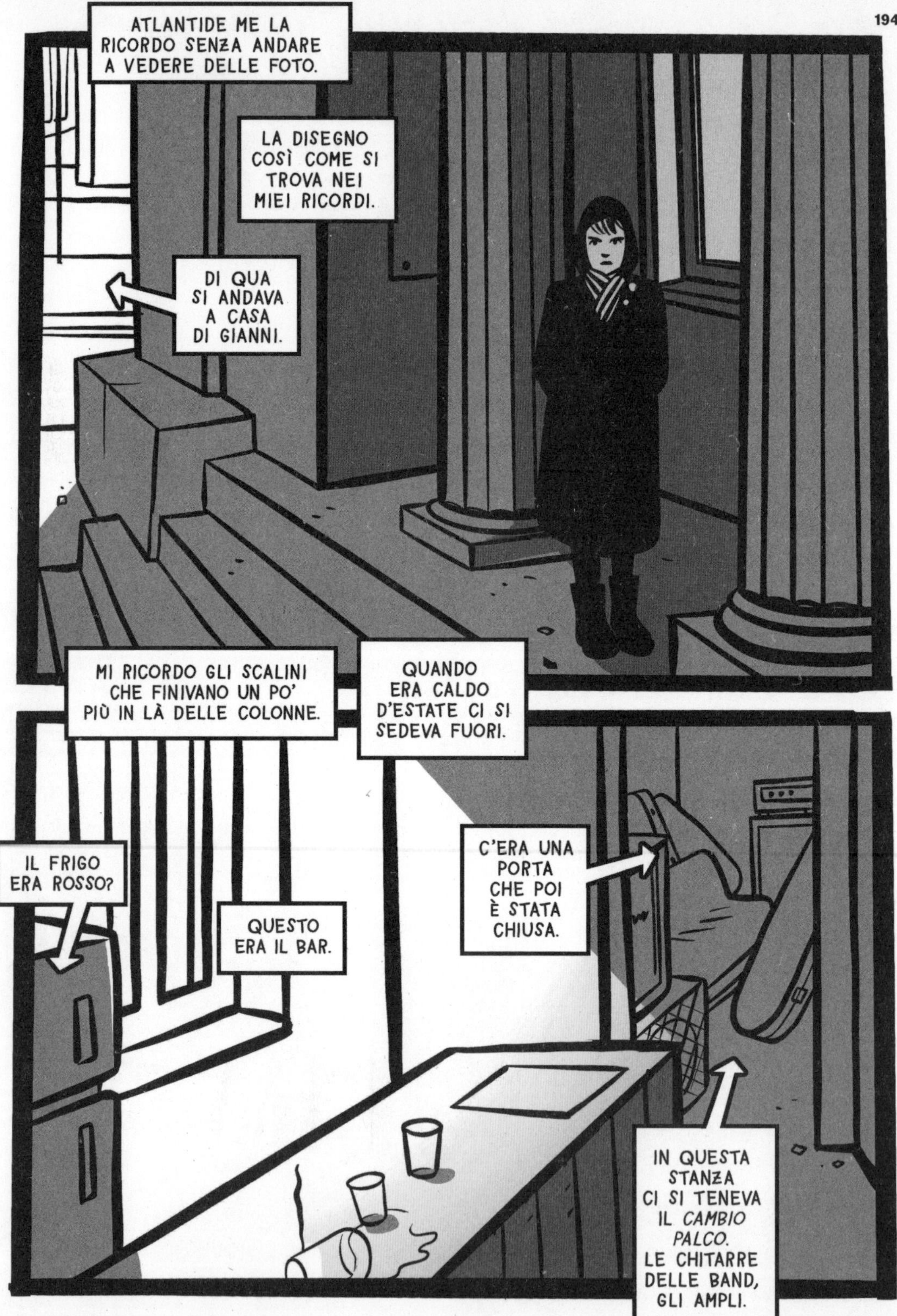

Alessandro Baronciani, illustration made for the book *Atlantide Hardcore D.I.Y. Punx Live 2001–2015*, Hellnation Red Star Press, 2021

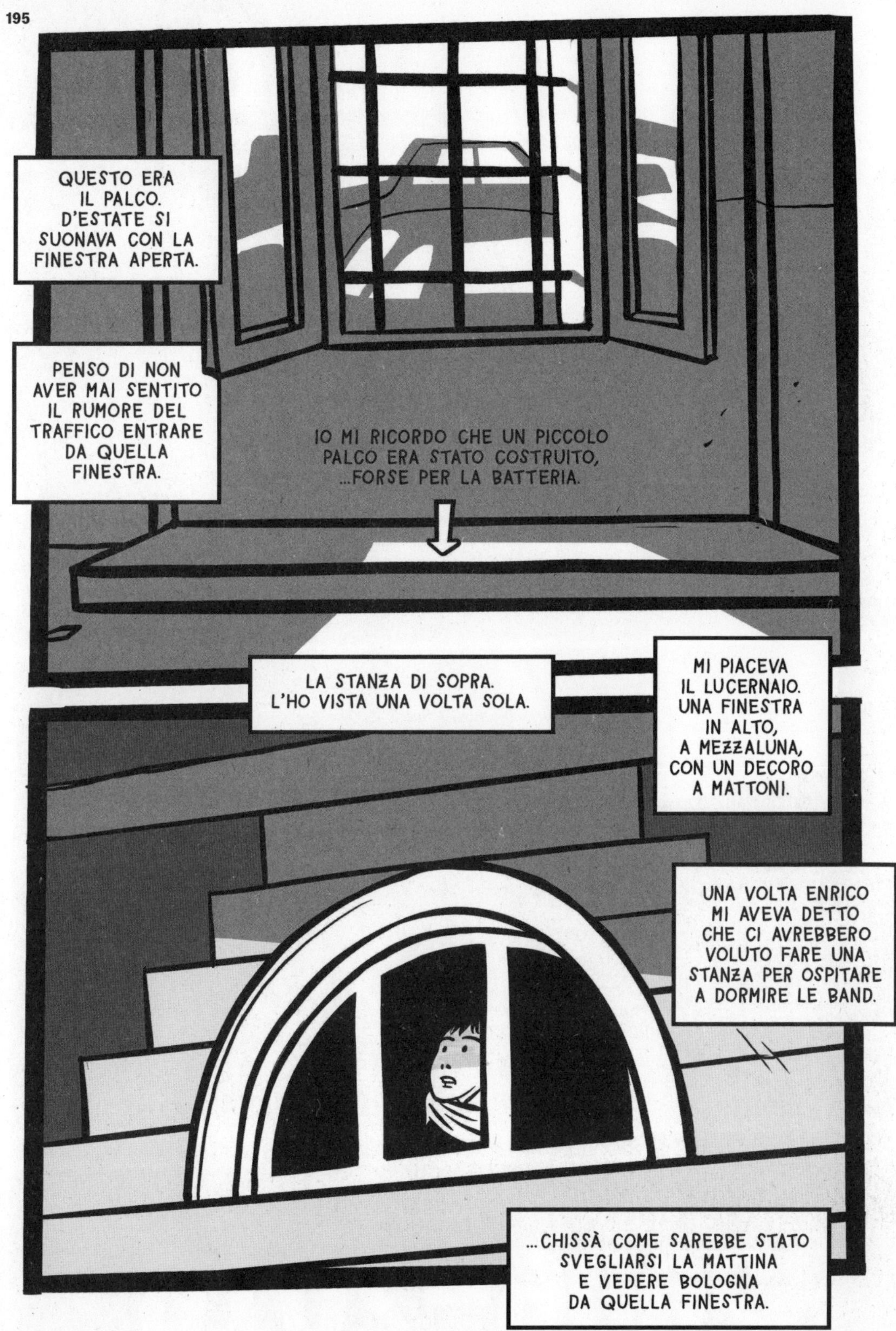

QUESTO ERA IL PALCO. D'ESTATE SI SUONAVA CON LA FINESTRA APERTA.
PENSO DI NON AVER MAI SENTITO IL RUMORE DEL TRAFFICO ENTRARE DA QUELLA FINESTRA.
IO MI RICORDO CHE UN PICCOLO PALCO ERA STATO COSTRUITO, ...FORSE PER LA BATTERIA.
LA STANZA DI SOPRA. L'HO VISTA UNA VOLTA SOLA.
MI PIACEVA IL LUCERNAIO. UNA FINESTRA IN ALTO, A MEZZALUNA, CON UN DECORO A MATTONI.
UNA VOLTA ENRICO MI AVEVA DETTO CHE CI AVREBBERO VOLUTO FARE UNA STANZA PER OSPITARE A DORMIRE LE BAND.
...CHISSÀ COME SAREBBE STATO SVEGLIARSI LA MATTINA E VEDERE BOLOGNA DA QUELLA FINESTRA.

Nosadella.due

2006–2016

Nosadella.due was founded in 2006 due to Elisa del Prete's desire to propose an art residency program in Bologna—one of the first in Italy—inspired by the residency as a curator she had done in Austria through an association based in Milan. The project, designed to facilitate the creative processes of the international artists invited, found space inside Del Prete's family home: an apartment at Via Nosadella 2, inside a building overlooking Piazza Malpighi.

In the undertaking of this cultural proposal, Del Prete collaborated with a variety of curators including Lelio Aiello, Giusy Checola and Francesca Cigardi. The need on the part of artists to work closely with the Bolognese territory through site-specific projects also led Nosadella.due to forge relationships and build networks with other entities around the city, such as MAMbo and Xing/Raum. Starting in 2012, Nosadella.due came into contact with Urban Center, becoming the exhibition space for a number of city festivals. A key aspect of this reality was the informality given by the domestic dimension of the place, which is why the audience of Nosadella.due was not only specialized but also made up of local citizens.

The Nosadella.due experience came to an end in 2016, when the founder decided to close the space due to the lack of any fruitful exchange with other territorial realities and the unsustainable increase in external demand.

ADDRESS Via Nosadella 2, Bologna. FOUNDERS Elisa Del Prete. COLLABORATORS Lelio Aiello, Giusy Checola, Francesca Cigardi, Chiara Tinonin, Francesca Polico, Gabriele Tosi

Bartleby

Bartleby occupiers hoisting banner, n.d.

Social breakfast in front of Bartleby (Via Capo di Lucca 30) to protest against threat of eviction, June 30, 2009

2008–2012

The Bartleby collective was founded in 2008 as a result of the mobilization of the student movement Onda Anomala against the Gelmini–Tremonti school and university reform, characterized by a series of massive cuts to the employment of young people in education.

Bartleby was made up of students, artists, temporary workers and entertainment workers who, under the motto "Spazi, Saperi e Reddito" ("Spaces, Knowledge and Income"), organized occupations and demonstrations in collaboration with other collectives around the city that shared their political ideals. The choice to struggle within and against the university institution allowed the collective to engage with the younger generation of students, proposing theoretical and political reasoning about the structure and management of the university within its spaces. Both of Bartleby's locations, in fact, were buildings owned by the University of Bologna: the first illegally occupied and the second obtained through an agreement with the University itself.

The convergence of artistic and political aspects was the basis of Bartleby's cultural programming and led to the creation of self-education seminars, events, concerts, exhibitions, comics festivals, and book presentations. These events were based on the involvement of widely recognized intellectuals, artists, filmmakers, musicians, cartoonists, and writers, including Gianni Celati, Wu Ming, Paper Resistance, Blu, Ericailcane, and Tuono Pettinato, as well as emerging artists, including students from the Academy of Fine Arts.

The Bartleby experience came to an end in 2012 due to the lack of any clear planning and the increasing difficulty in getting its cultural offerings acknowledged within a wider city context.

ADDRESS Via Capo di Lucca 30, Bologna (2008–10); Via San Petronio Vecchio 30/a, Bologna (2010–12). FOUNDERS Simone Addessi, Antonio Alia, Marzio Cavicchini. COLLABORATORS Kinodrome, Concor

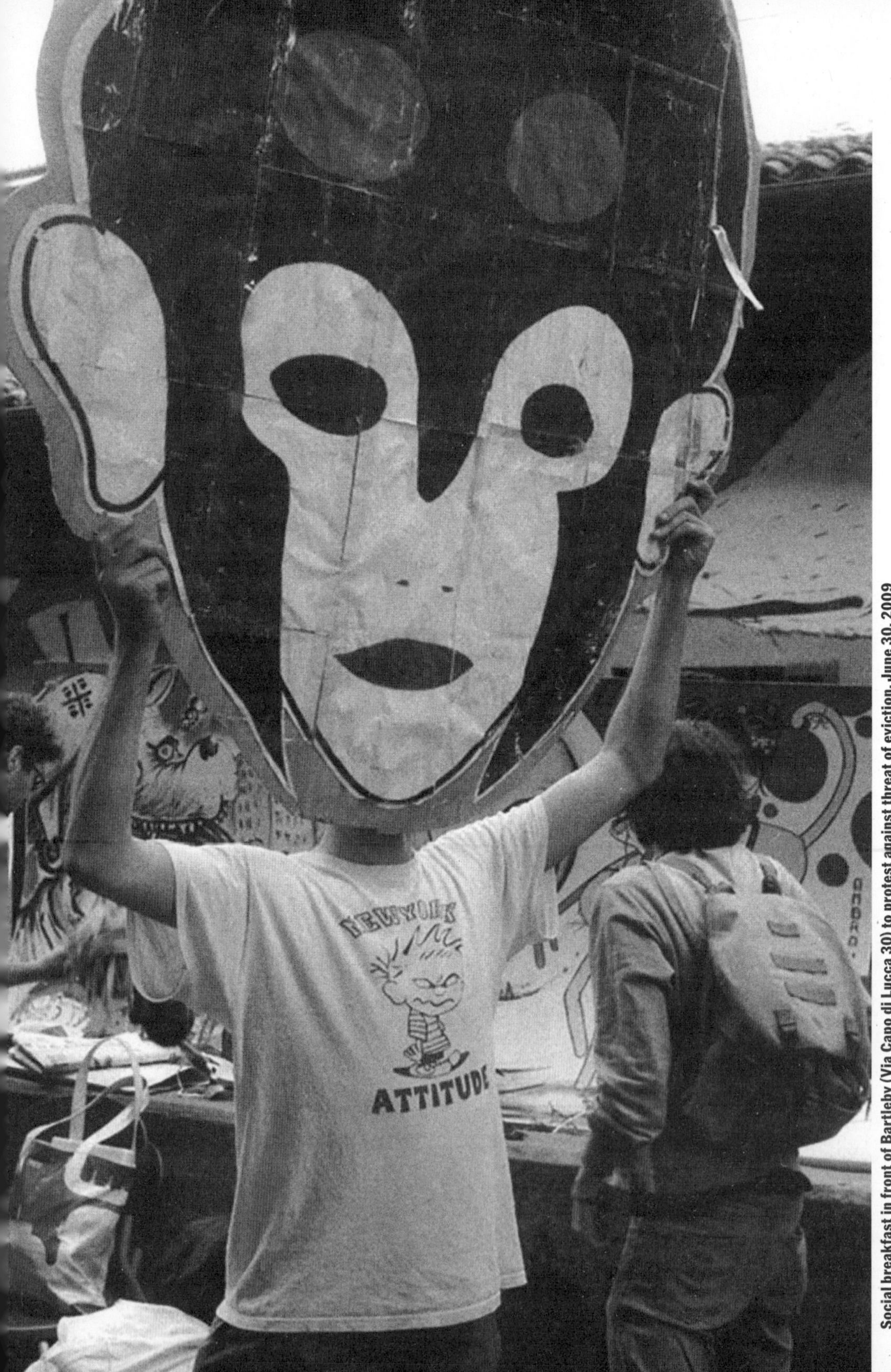

Social breakfast in front of Bartleby (Via Capo di Lucca 30) to protest against threat of eviction, June 30, 2009

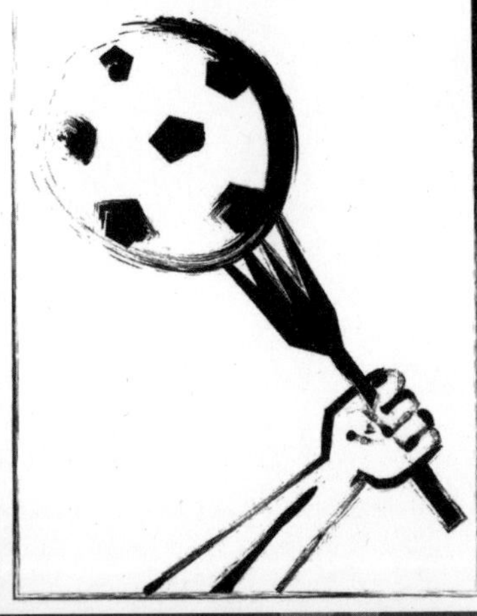

Artist unknown, *Kick the Rich*, sticker, n.d.

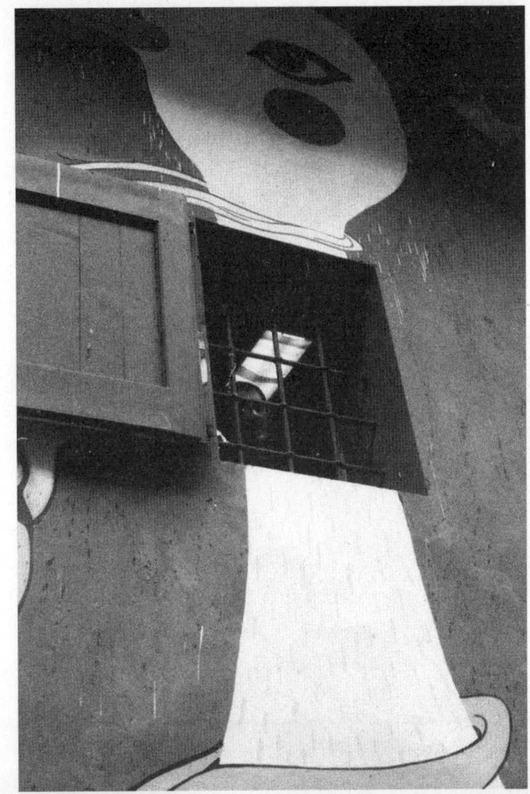

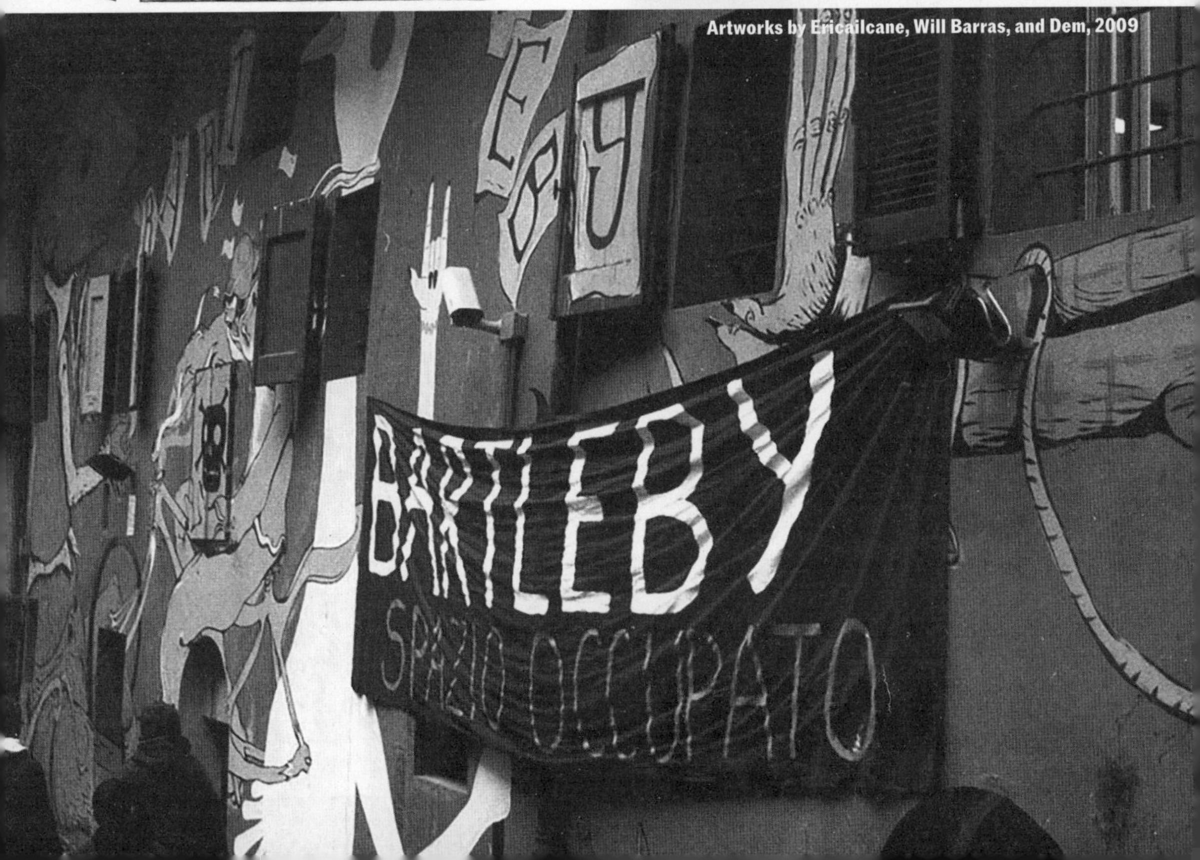

Artworks by Ericailcane, Will Barras, and Dem, 2009

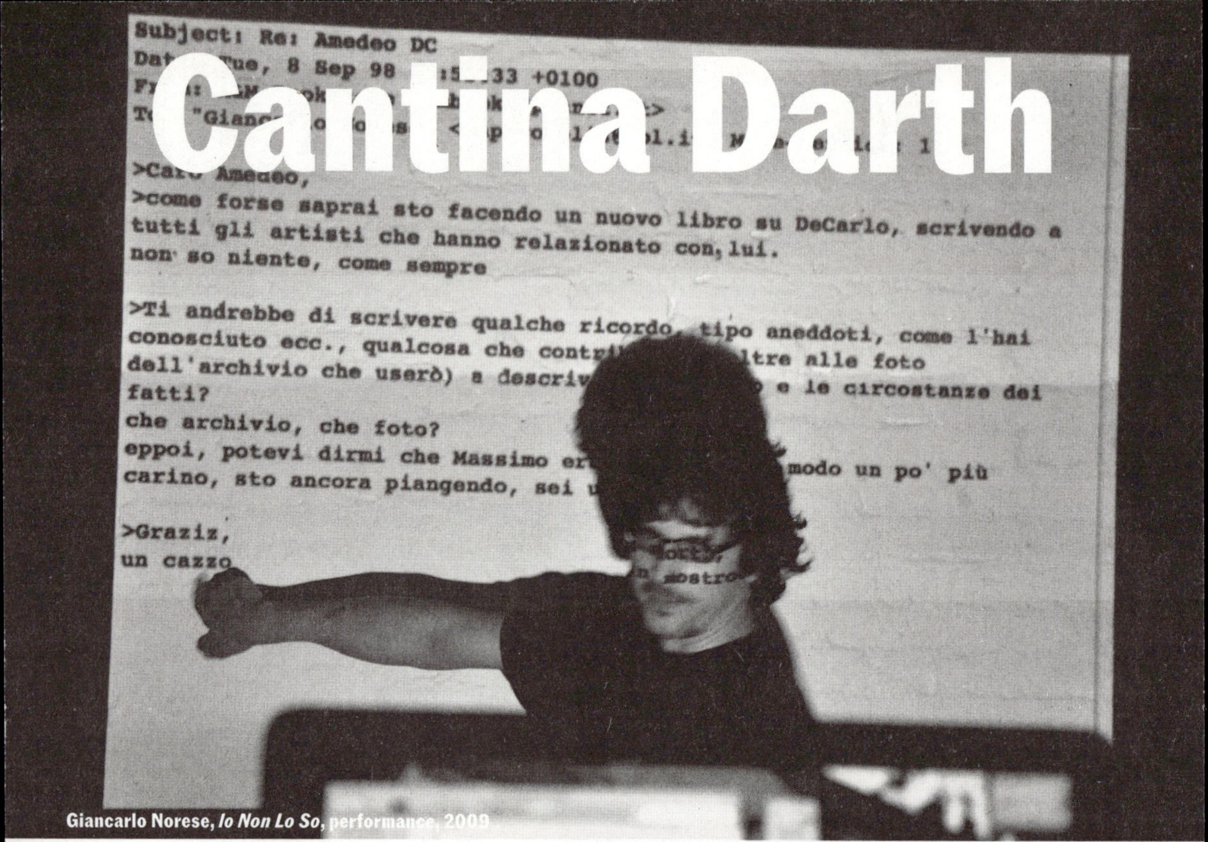

Giancarlo Norese, *Io Non Lo So*, performance, 2009

Emilio Fantin, *TU*, installation view, 2009

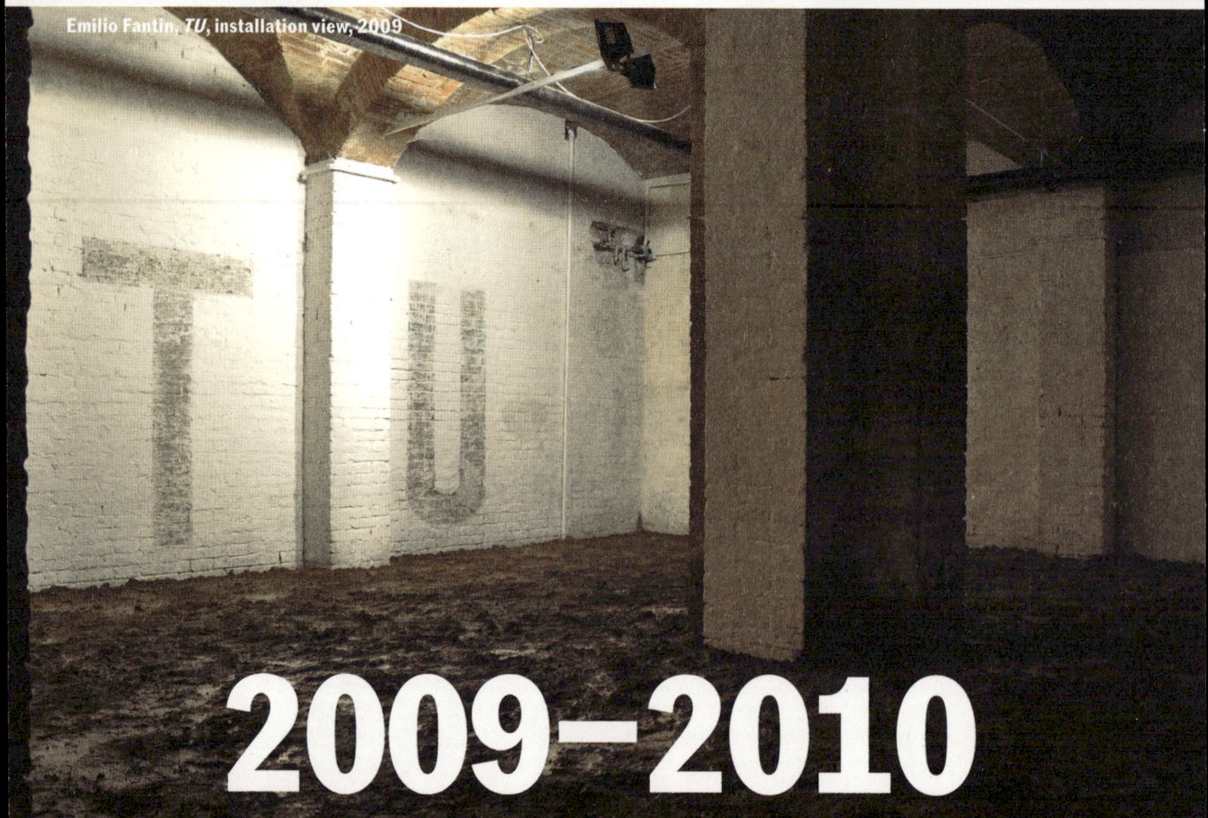

The Darth association was founded in 2003 from the union of a number of artists and curators active in Bologna, as a group for sharing individual experiences. Starting in 2009, the need emerged to find a space that would be a place for communal experimentation. Relationships with the territory and its constituent realities were solid, but relationships with political institutions remained scarce. For this reason, the association was unable to obtain funding, leaving cultural programming to rely on self-support as its only source of income.

The main purpose of Cantina Darth was to extend the interest in contemporary art to a wider audience through the organization of meetings, exhibition events, seminars, and round tables, capable of creating moments of discussion and confrontation. On the occasion of the Faenza Contemporary Art Festival, Darth organized *Ottimi rapporti* (2010), an informal conversation table between artists working for other artists. Another format conceived by Darth was *Peresempio* (2009), in which for two editions, artists and curators were invited to talk about their personal research including Emilio Fantin, Giancarlo Norese, Ferdinando Mazzitelli, Luca Panaro, Chiara Pergola, Diego Zuelli, and Anteo Radovan.

The previous experience of Annalisa Cattani and Adriana Torregrossa with Progetto Oreste 0 provided the collective with a major legacy of contacts from which several collaborations began. The discussion on contemporary art and its workings constituted the strength of the association, contributing to the creation and dissemination of active cultural policies.

The Darth experience ended due to lack of time and resources on the part of the collective's members, but Cattani's Novella Guerra space in Imola can be seen as a natural continuation of this Bologna-based experimentation.

ADDRESS Via dello Scalo 21, Bologna (2009); Via Berretta Rossa 25, Bologna (2010). FOUNDERS Annalisa Cattani, Dragoni-Russo, Francesco Finotto, Massimo Marchetti, Sabrina Muzi, Fabrizio Rivola, Petar Stanovic, Adriana Torregrossa. COLLABORATORS Stefano W. Pasquini

Casabianca

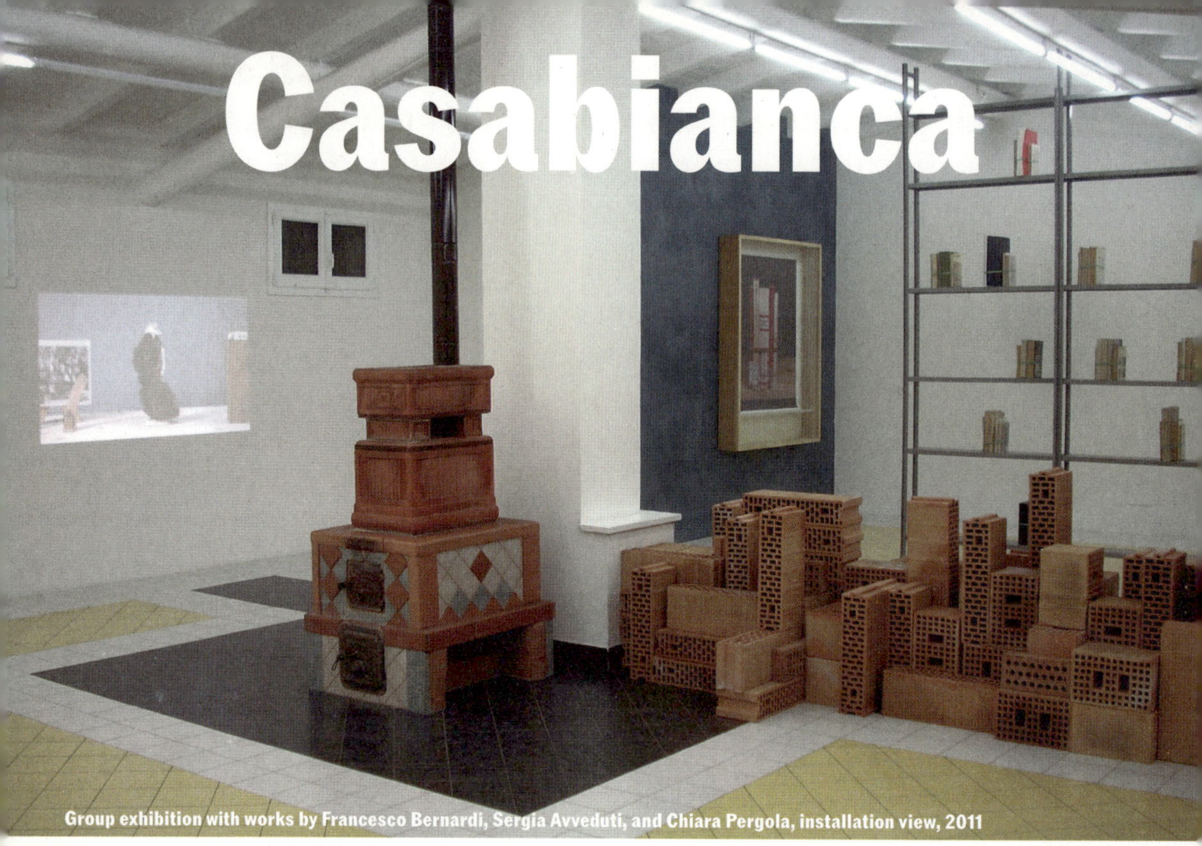

Group exhibition with works by Francesco Bernardi, Sergia Avveduti, and Chiara Pergola, installation view, 2011

Group exhibition with works by Fabrizio Basso, Silvia Cini, Gedske Ramlov, and Giorgia Severi, installation view, 2013

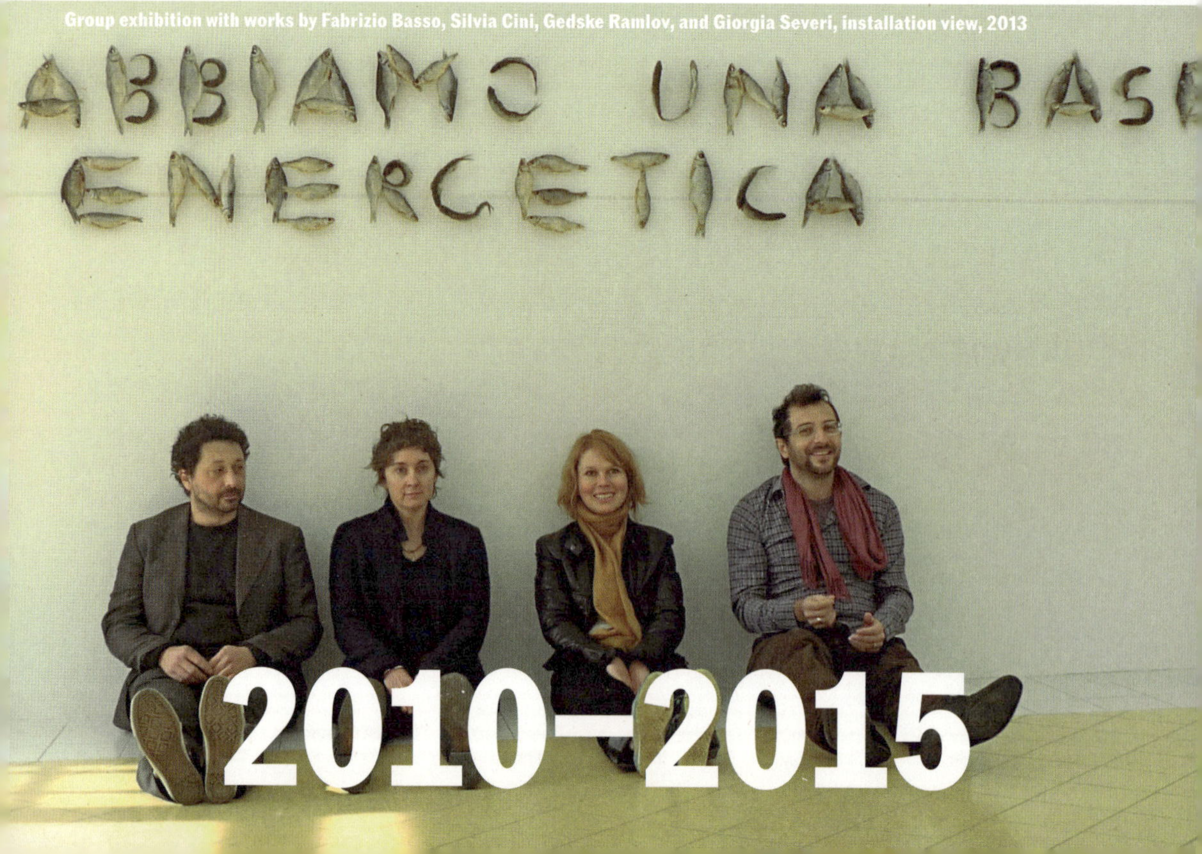

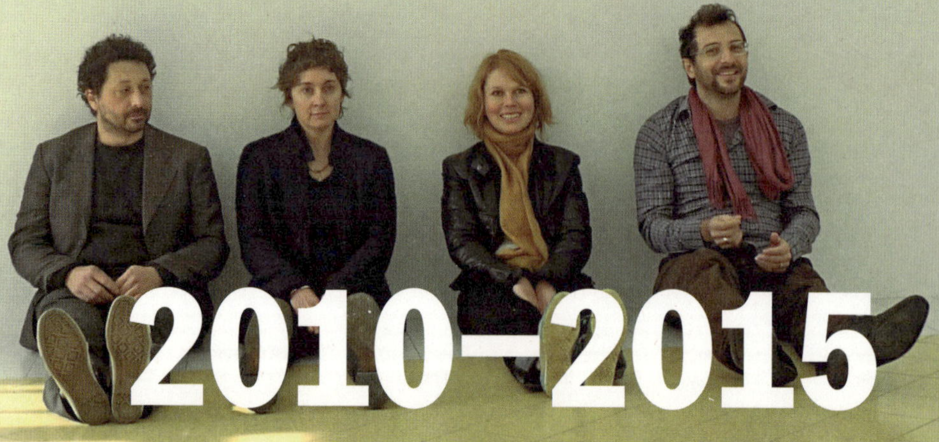

2010–2015

Casabianca was founded in 2010 in Zola Predosa, a small town that is part of the metropolitan area of Bologna, with the aim of bringing different generations of artists and curators into dialogue.

The founder of this space, Anteo Radovan, came from previous collective and non-profit experiences, such as Il Graffio space and the Oreste group, through which he had created contacts with the DAMS and other Academy communities. Fundamental was his collaboration with Massimo Marchetti, a member of the Darth collective, who was mainly in charge of communication and exhibition organization, while Radovan selected the projects to be proposed.

Cultural programming included exhibitions that developed out of proposals from outside artists and curators. Over the years, Casabianca hosted both established and emerging artists, including Francesco Bernardi, Luca Vitone, Giulia Cenci, Irene Coppola, Irene Fenara, and Ornaghi e Prestinari. Curatorship was usually external, entrusted to figures such as Gino Gianuizzi, Guido Molinari and Lelio Aiello, who had already been involved in other similar experiences.

Relationships and collaborations with local institutions were perceived as unnecessary, while the relationship with the local area was determined by the appeal given by the location, nestled in the countryside. Casabianca's experience ended in 2015 due to self-financing difficulties.

ADDRESS Via Pepoli 12, Zola Predosa. FOUNDERS Anteo Radovan. COLLABORATORS Massimo Marchetti

Adiacenze

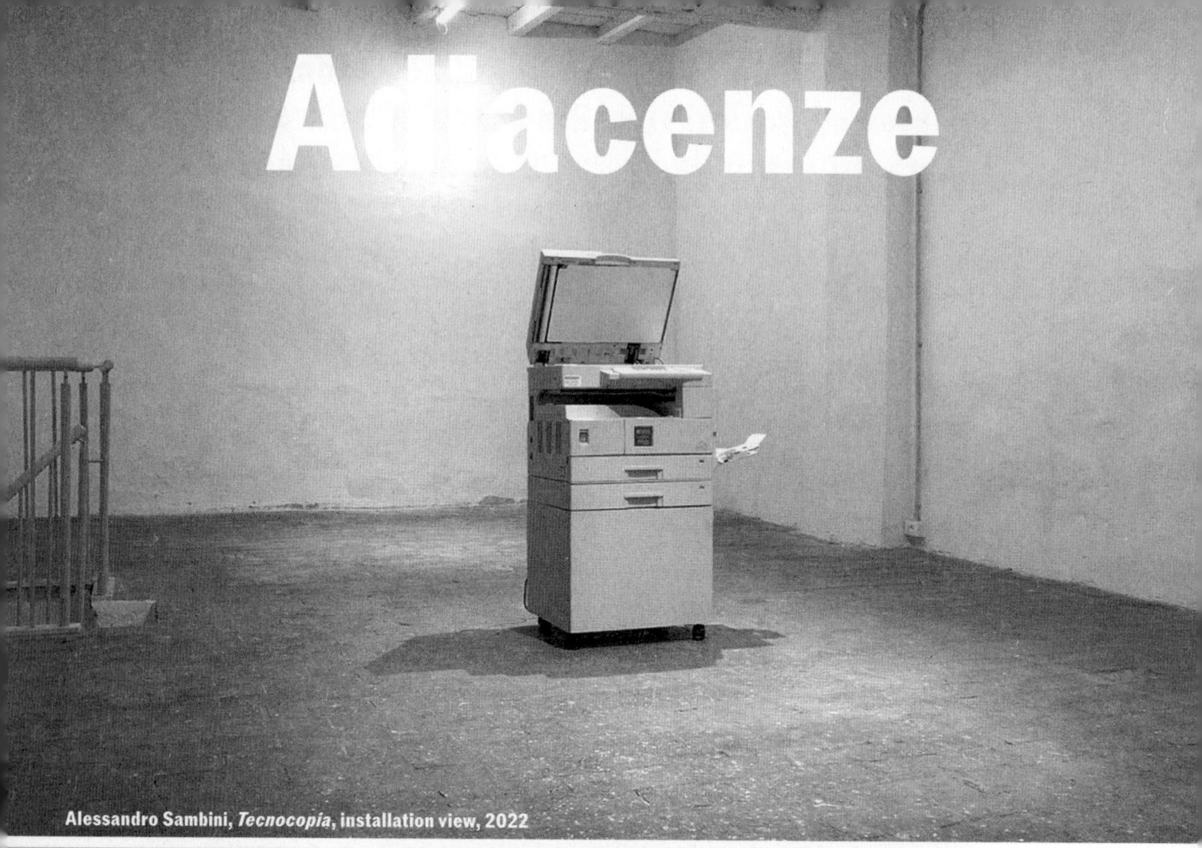

Alessandro Sambini, *Tecnocopia*, installation view, 2022

Martina Zena, *INTERPLAY*, performance, 2016

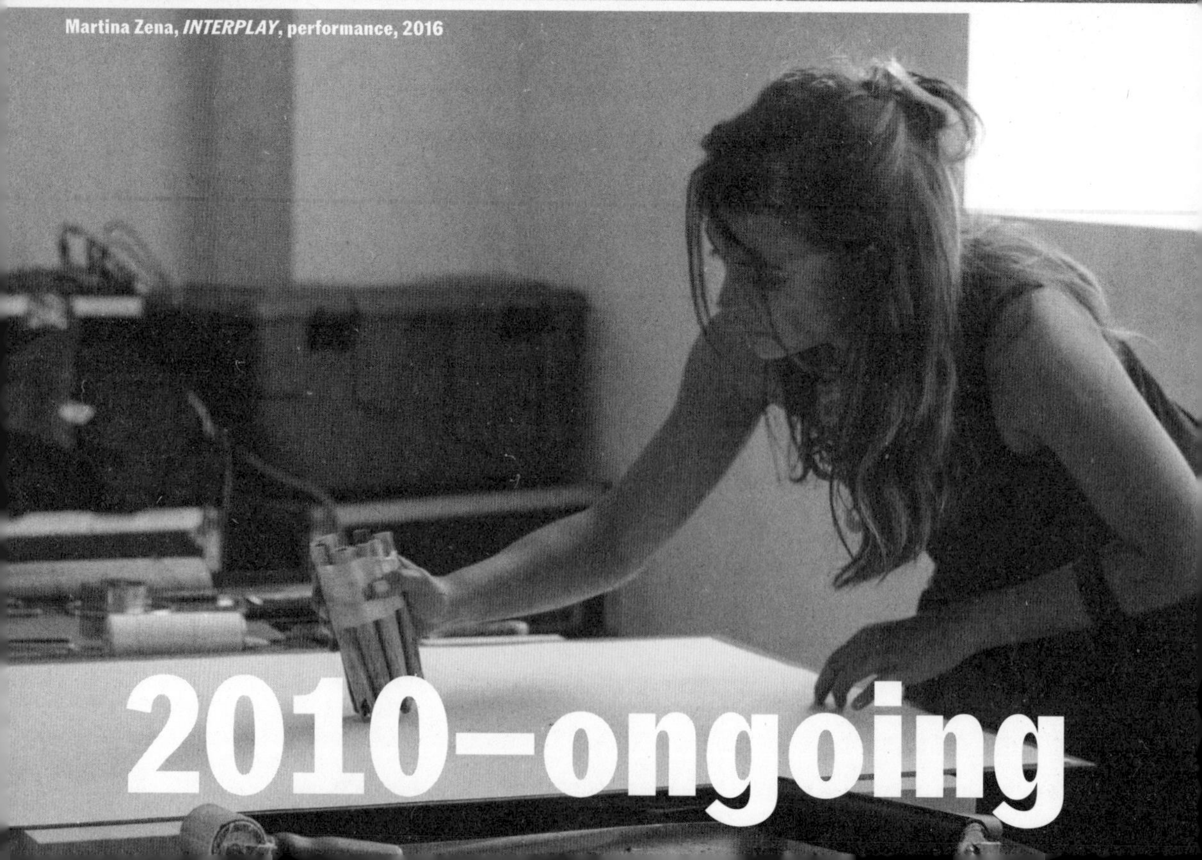

2010–ongoing

Adiacenze is an independent exhibition space dedicated to the visual arts, hosting exhibitions and projects by artists working with both traditional media and forms of multimedia experimentation. Under the artistic direction of the founders, Amerigo Mariotti, Giorgia Tronconi, and Daniela Tozzi, the cultural programming includes the organization of several exhibitions a year and a series of fringe events such as meetings, performances, presentations of editorial projects, and workshops.

Adiacenze was created to give visibility to emerging artists based in Bologna, but the programming also welcomes established national and international artists. Increasingly, Adiacenze's artistic program has taken on international connotations, thanks in part to the artist residency project in collaboration with the Casa della Cultura Italo Calvino in Calderara di Reno, which allows artists from other countries to spend periods of time working in Bologna. At the same time, the SWAP residency project aims to take Italian artists abroad.

Adiacenze represents a space for research and experimentation of fundamental importance within today's Bologna art scene, particularly considering the focus on digital technologies and their relationship to the body and relational dynamics.

ADDRESS Via San Procolo 7, Bologna (2010–12); Piazza San Martino 4/f, Bologna (2012–16); Vicolo Spirito Santo 1, Bologna (2016–).
FOUNDERS Amerigo Mariotti, Daniela Tozzi, Giorgia Tronconi. COLLABORATORS Diletta d'Angelo, Zhora Luce Mazzucato, Giuseppe Spataro

Elastico

Valeria Talamonti, *Processo Fragile*, installation view, 2012

Valentina Beotti and Claudia Pajewski, *La Nobile Arte*, performance, Gender Bender festival, 2012

2011–2021

Elastico grew out of FragileContinuo's previous experience (2008–11) and involved a collective of women artists interested in offering diverse programming focused on music and the visual arts.

Over its ten years of activity, the project changed locations several times, adapting to various contexts. Spazio Elastico, in Vicolo de' Facchini, included a space for exhibitions and musical performances and a boutique where publications, records and self-produced objects were sold. ELaSTiCo faART on Via dell'Arcoveggio, founded as a result of the encounter between the artistic duo TO/LET and Marzia Stano, Ilaria Mancosu and Luca Musilli, was instead a "factory" with ateliers, laboratories, workshops and training courses.

Right from its founding, Elastico wove relationships with the Academy of Fine Arts, where the founders and several of the artists involved in the exhibitions come from. Fundamental was the relationship with CRACK!, an international comics and print art festival that helped position Elastico in a circuit of independent spaces dedicated to sequential art and illustration.

Elastico was self-funded through membership subscriptions, the sale of self-productions, the staging of workshops, grants obtained via municipal calls for tender, and, depending on the venue, bar revenues during events. Elastico's experience as a space ended with the arrival of the pandemic, but the collective continued to shape its activities through Elastico Records: an avowedly "gender free" record label, and other forms of project planning while waiting for a new venue.

ADDRESS Spazio Elastico: Vicolo de' Facchini 2/a, Bologna (2011–13) | Elastico Studio: Via Porta Nova 12, Bologna (2013–14) | eLaSTiCo faART: Via Dell'Arcoveggio 49, Bologna (2016–21). FOUNDERS TO/LET (Sonia Piedad Marinangeli/Elisa Placucci), Elisa Visentini. COLLABORATORS Marzia Stano, Ilaria Mancosu, Luca Musilli, Dario Alejandro Barletta, Salvatore Morelli (Visual Lab), Marcella Ricciardi (Be My Delay), Alessio Bevilacqua

Novella Guerra

2011–ongoing

Emanuela Ascari, *Ciò che è vivo ha bisogno di ciò che è vivo*, performance, 2014

Novella Guerra was founded in the light of the dream of finding a *locus amoenus* in which to rediscover the pleasure of meeting and exchange between visual artists, through exhibitions, events, and a residency program. The space is located inside a farmhouse in the province of Imola, a municipality lying in the metropolitan area of Bologna. Its name is dedicated to the memory of the mother of Annalisa Cattani, the founder. In 2018, with Maura Banfo and Susanna Ravelli, Novella Guerra changed its name to Novella Guerra In\Out. Cattani's background as a lecturer at the Academy of Fine Arts in Bologna is largely related to Oreste, and her curatorial practice was refined as part of another independent space, Cantina Darth. Over the years, Novella Guerra has witnessed contributions form a variety of artists and curators, cooperatively involved on the decision-making level of its cultural programming.

Novella Guerra has developed a series of projects in collaboration with other national entities dedicated to alternative production in the visual arts, such as NESXT – Independent Art Festival, staged with the association Leggermente Fuori Sede. The space also offers a residency program that has seen the participation of both Italian and international artists.

Cultural programming focuses on exhibitions and interventions that are often site-specific in nature, rooted in personal and collaborative relationships. Projects include the "pigiama party luddista" ("Luddite sleepover") held in 2019 in collaboration with Stefania Galegati: an event during which the Gina X group of female artists and curators was founded.

Novella Guerra represents a space of great interest because of its ability to produce events and projects capable of gaining wide reception despite its outlying location and apparent distance from the Bologna and national art community.

ADDRESS Via Bergullo 15, Imola. FOUNDERS Annalisa Cattani. COLLABORATORS Dragoni-Russo, Massimo Marchetti, Marco Orazi, Stefano Pasquini, Fabrizio Rivola, Adriana Torregrossa

Senza Filtro

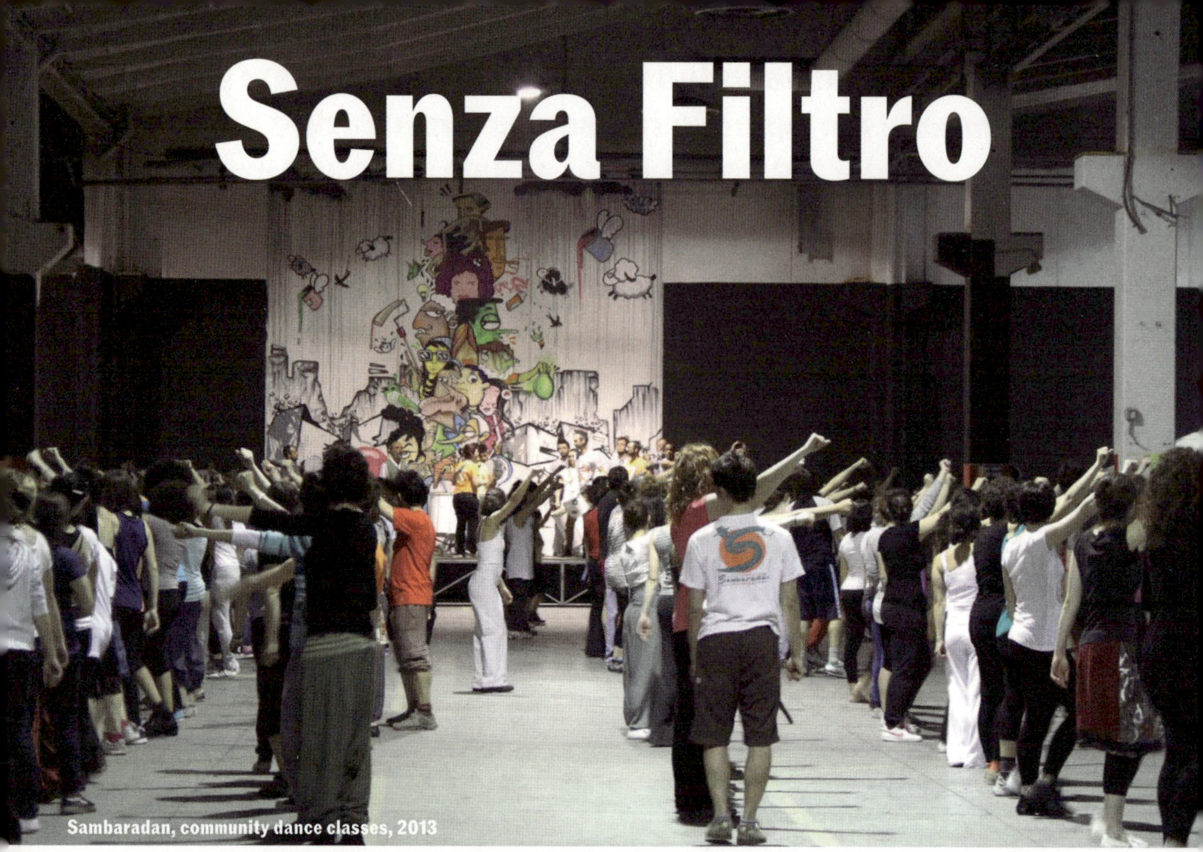

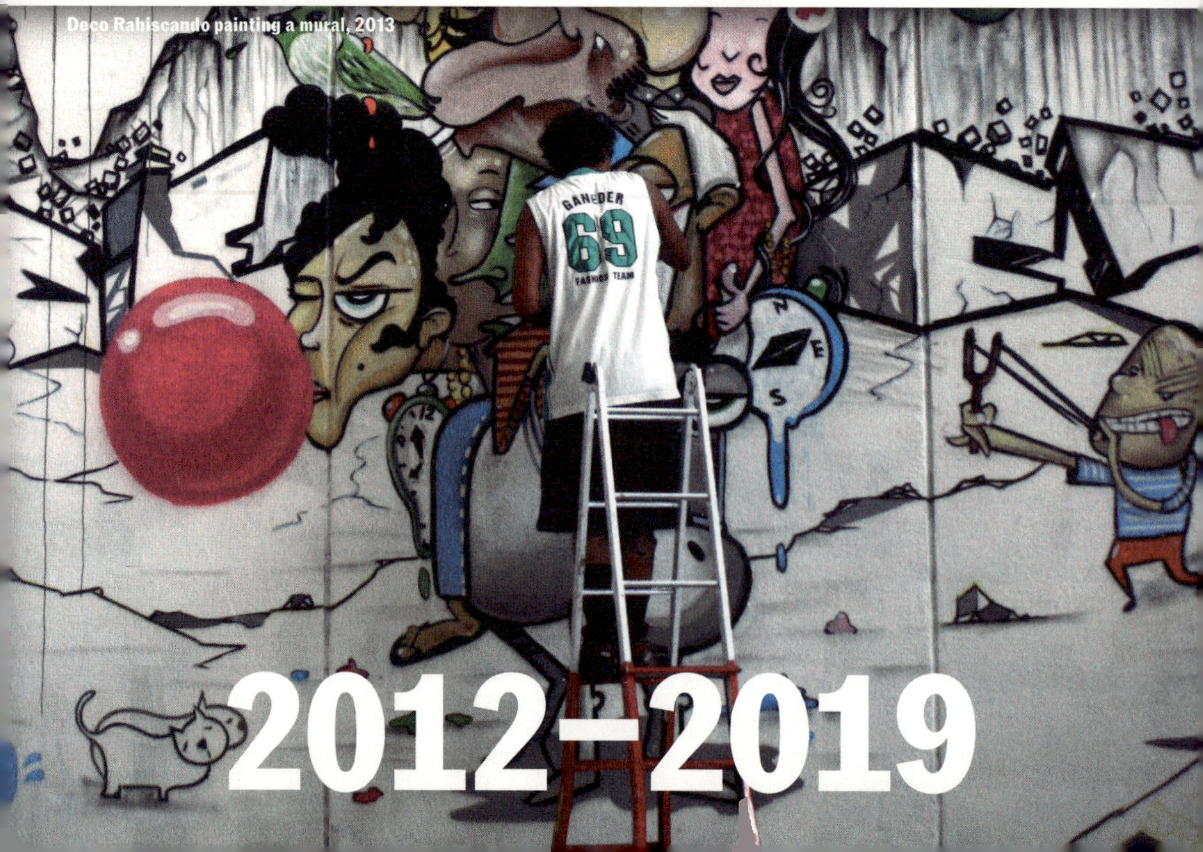

2012–2019

The abundance of disused spaces in the urban fabric and the desire for a place dedicated to the intersection of self-produced social, artistic and cultural activities led to the founding of Senza Filtro, also known as the "Sorting For Different Arts Center," in 2012.

The Planimetrie Culturali Association, responsible for founding this space, had been involved in mapping abandoned spaces to be revitalized through civic participation since 2000, and was led by informal groups and associations, such as Ca.Cu.Bo. (Cantiere Culturale Bolognese) and Scalo San Donato. Planimetrie Culturali's projects were dedicated to the temporary use of disused and—until their reassignment— abandoned spaces. In 2012, the association signed a contract with the owner of the building at Via Stalingrado 59, becoming de facto directly responsible for it.

Senza Filtro's desire was to give space to independent Bolognese realities dedicated to the arts, recreational activities and social integration. The approximately 6,000 square meters of the area managed by Senza Filtro accommodated: the Museo del Flipper ("Flipper Museum") of Associazione Tilt, the hostel of the Associazione Use-it, the spaces of Associazione Fuoricampo, the photography center of Associazione Piccolo Formato, the exhibition space managed by the VVVB collective, an educational space for teaching Italian to foreigners as part of the Associazione SEMinARIA, and the warehouse dedicated to sports activities such as skating, parkour and BMXing. The relationship with the local area and community was of paramount importance, fueled both by the involvement of individuals and collaboration with associations, and by addressing an extremely diverse audience. Senza Filtro's experience came to an end when the building was auctioned by the bankruptcy court.

ADDRESS Via Stalingrado 59, Bologna. FOUNDERS Werther Albertazzi, Piergiorgio Rocchi, Nicola Marzot, Elia De Caro, Andrea Carnoli, Maurizio Corrado, Diego Dal Moro

Làbas

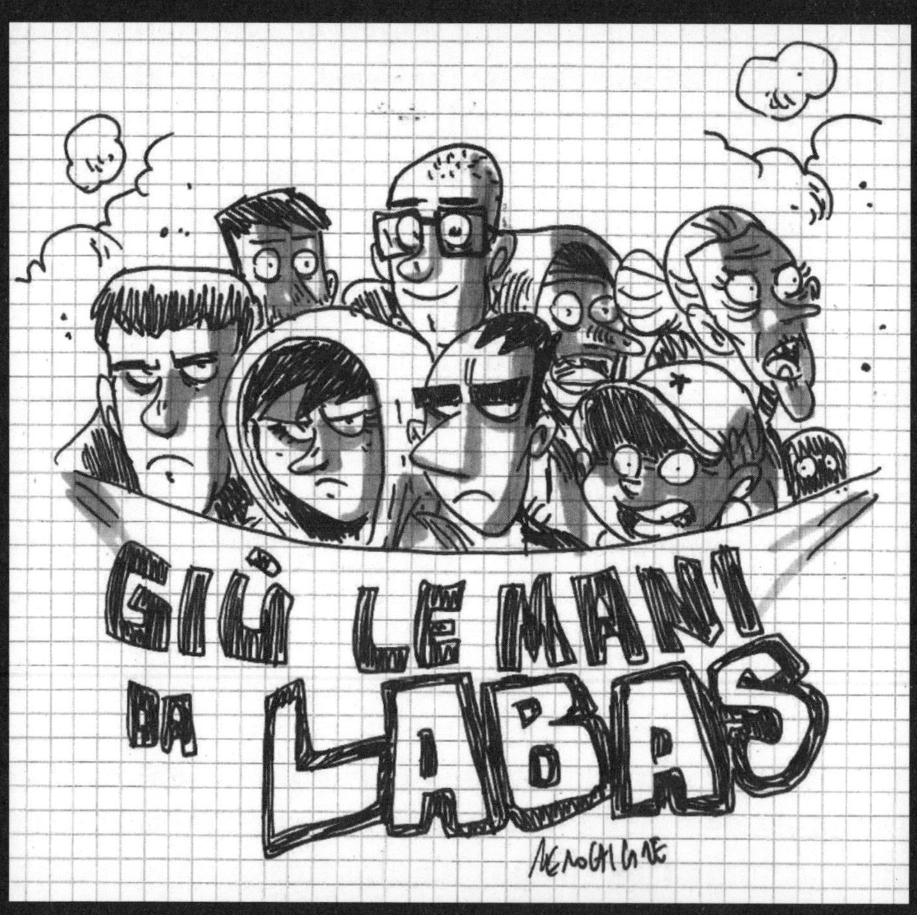

2012–ongoing

Zerocalcare, *Giù le mani da Làbas*, drawing, 2016

Làbas, an acronym for "Laboratorio d'assalto" ("Assault Laboratory"), was born from the desire to reappropriate a piece of public property that had been abandoned, the former Caserma Masini on Via Orfeo, and to open it to the public as a multipurpose center with diverse and inclusive cultural programming. From the outset, the goal was in fact to relate with the neighborhood and with other associations, informal groups and other spaces dedicated to the arts in the area. Contamination and external stimuli have been of fundamental importance to this reality, but this has not limited its freedom of movement.

To this day, roles and tasks are defined during assemblies, based on the availability of the individuals and groups that frequent the space. All activities are carried out through self-funding and volunteer work and, in some cases, through participation in citywide calls for tender.

The result of politically motivated stances, Làbas's cultural program includes interventions and exhibition projects by artists using comics and street art, as well as musicians and producers, with a focus on hip hop and electronic music.

Art projects are chosen for their ability to embody the collective experience and enrich it with new personal contributions, thus succeeding in involving as diverse an audience as possible. More than a "social center," in fact, Làbas defines itself as a "social town hall," i.e. a shared, autonomous, and inclusive space where anyone can feel like an active participant.

ADDRESS Ex Caserma Masini, Via Orfeo 46, Bologna (2012–17); Vicolo Bolognetti 2, Bologna (2017–). FOUNDERS Làbas Collective

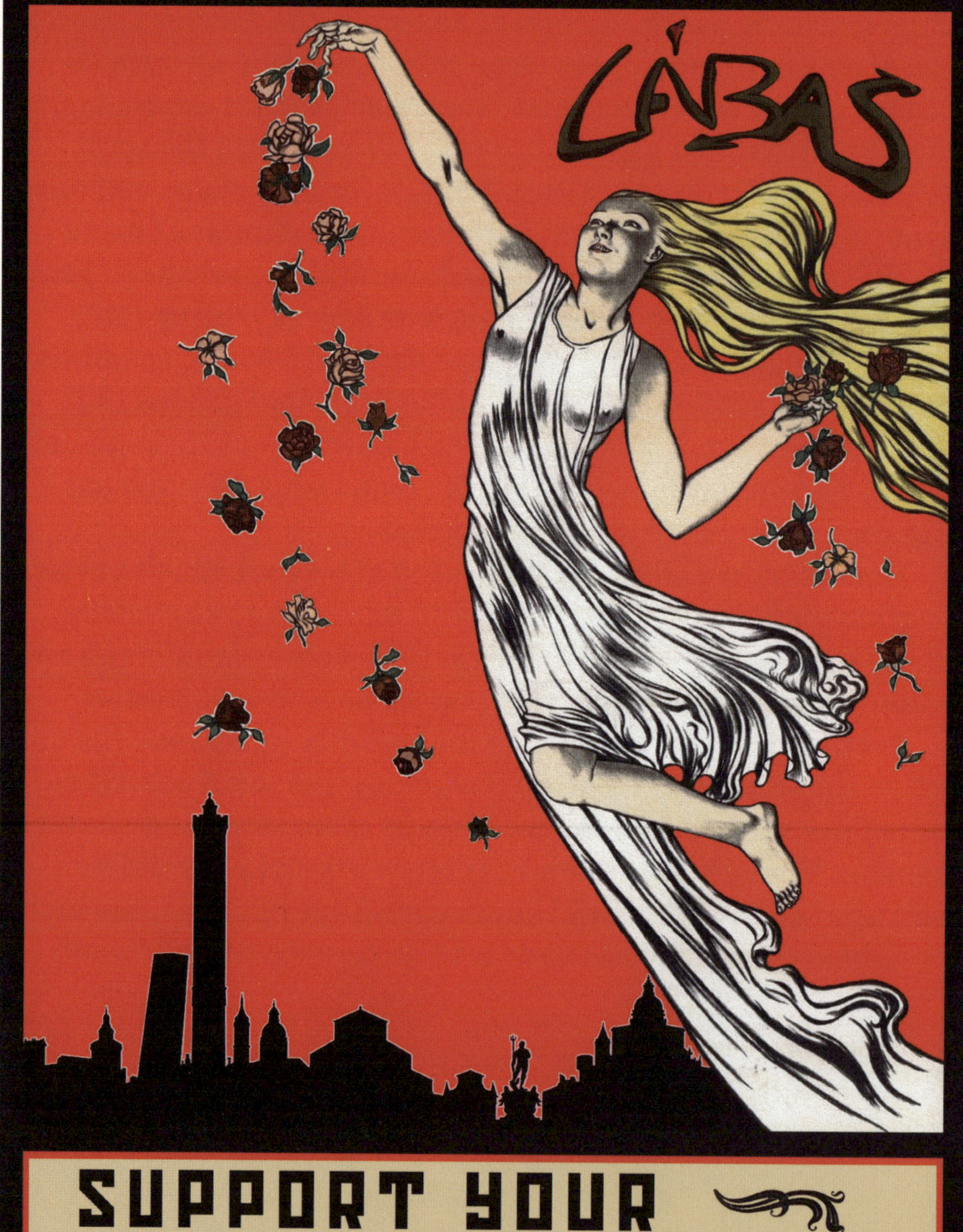
CÁBAS
SUPPORT YOUR
LOCAL ANTIFA

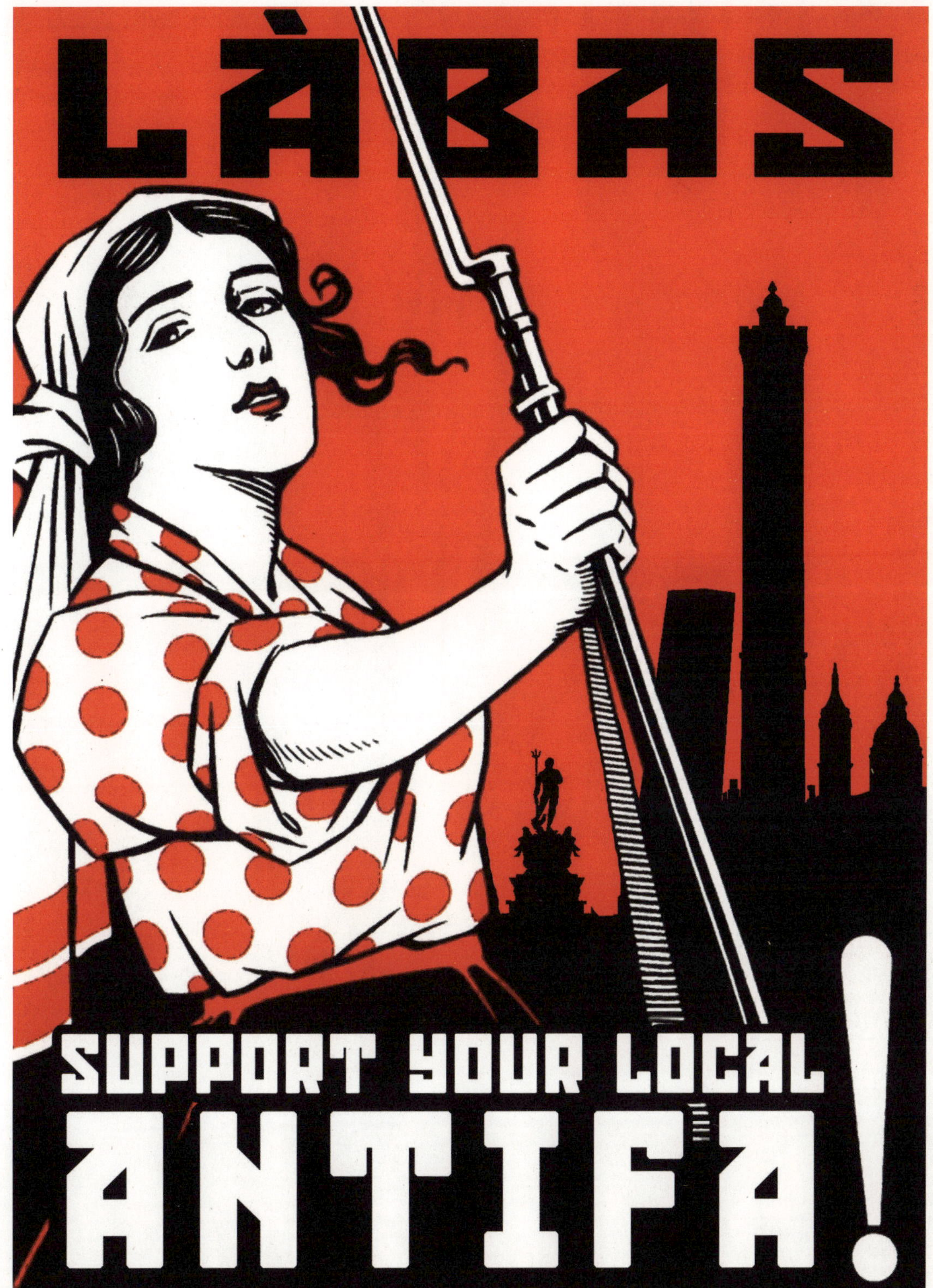
LÀBAS
SUPPORT YOUR LOCAL
ANTIFA!

Studio Cloud 4

2013–2016

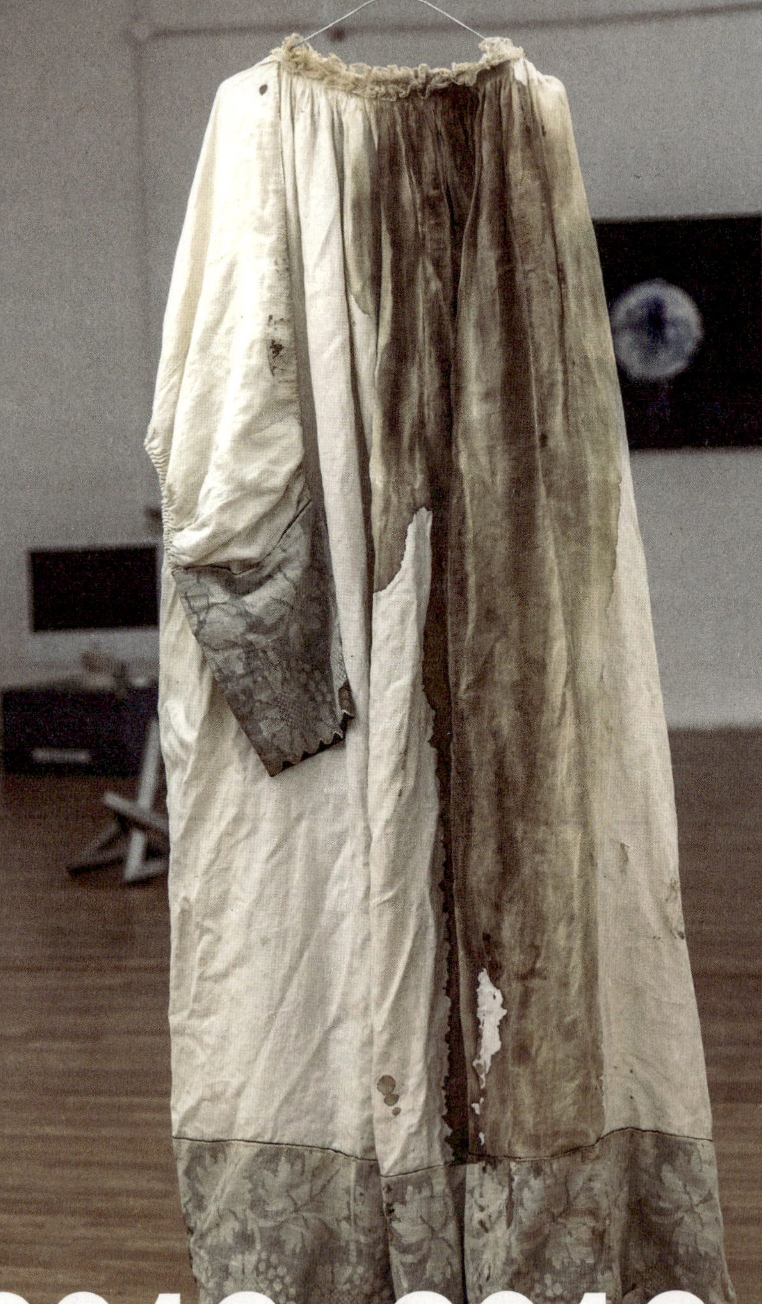

Driven by a desire to develop a dialogue on contemporary art, artist and lecturer Stefano Pasquini founded Studio Cloud 4 as part of the photography studio of Stefano Stagni and Paolo Frascaroli. The workshop of the two photographers thus became an eclectic exhibition space characterized by total freedom to experiment, without having to resort to compromises with the commercial dynamics of the art system. In fact, the proposed activities were financed entirely by the photography studio, and aspired to involve as wide an audience as possible.

In its three years of operation, Studio Cloud 4 mainly proposed thematic collective exhibition projects curated by Pasquini. *Venti Leggeri* (2013), for example, featured artists whose works were accumulated by the theme of lightness. In one case, works from a private collection, that of Tiberio Catelani, were exhibited. Other times, projects arose from direct relationships with artists, as in the case of the solo exhibitions of Angelo Pretolani and Eva Marisaldi.

The closure of the photography studio, following Frascaroli's retirement and Stagni's move to Canada, marked the end of Studio Cloud 4 in 2016.

ADDRESS Via Giuseppe Parini 4/a, Bologna. FOUNDERS Stefano W. Pasquini. COLLABORATORS Stefano Stagni, Paolo Frascaroli

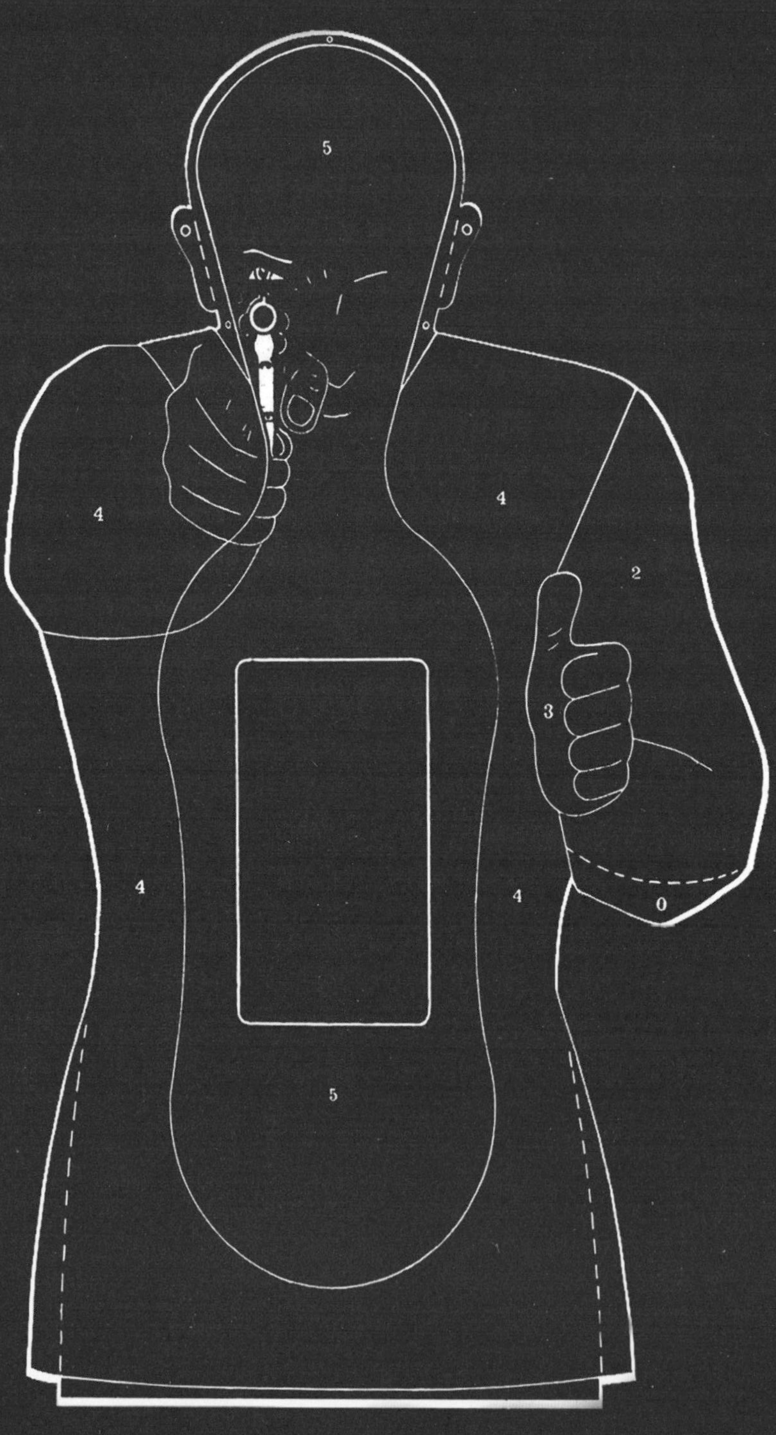

Giovanni Mundula, *Sedizioni*, artwork included in the group exhibition curated by the artist, 2013

221   Claudio Serrapica, *Untitled*, photograph, ca. 1970. From the solo exhibition *Di solito così non si fa*, 2015

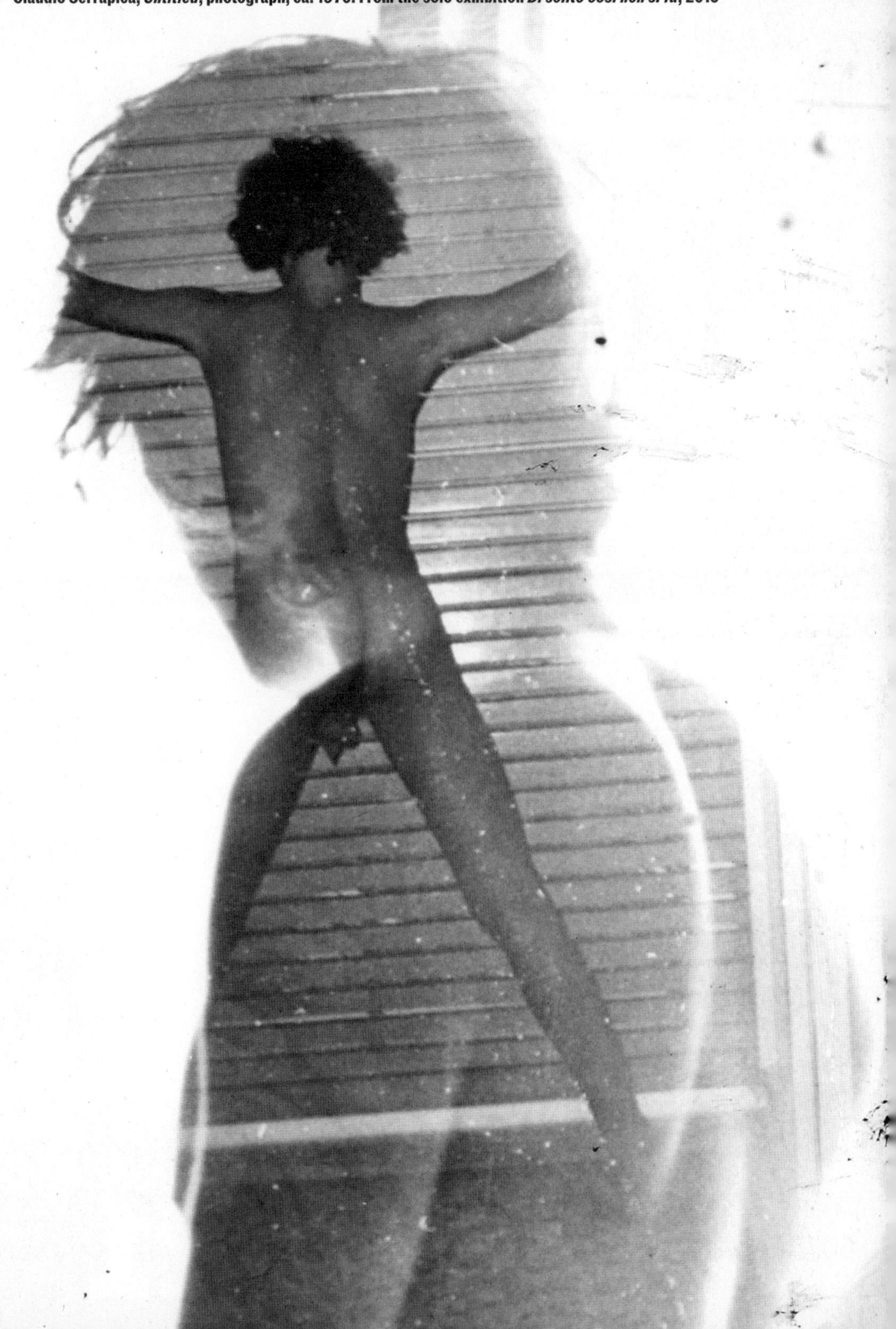

Localedue

Dina Loudmer, Giulia Poppi, Cuoghi Corsello, *MEDUSA MEDUSA MEDUSA*, performance, 2017

Matteo Coluccia, *Fare un'immagine di tanto in tanto*, performance, 2018

2013–2021

Localedue was founded by Fabio Farnè and Gabriele Tosi to provide an exhibition space for emerging artists and curators by offering them technical, curatorial, and communication support.

Founded in 2013 as an independent space, in 2016 it became a non-profit association. Until 2019, Localedue was based in Via Azzo Gardino in a space granted in management by Manifattura delle Arti, and subsequently operated nomadically, being hosted by other entities.

Cultural programming involved nationally established artists as well as emerging artists from the Academy of Fine Arts in Bologna, particularly through collaboration with lecturer and curator Lelio Aiello. Localedue was committed to experimentation, study and confrontation, offering solo and group exhibitions, special projects, performances, and workshops, as well as producing publications.

For the two founders, being independent meant experimenting without rigid planning and proposing non-commercial models that did not entail a dialogue with political and artistic institutions. Localedue thus appealed to a specialized and niche audience, but without the slightest commercial logic.

Having discontinued the informal agreement with the Manifattura delle Arti to grant the venue, Localedue remained active as a traveling reality until 2021, when the two founders decided to end its activity in order to devote themselves to other initiatives.

ADDRESS Via Azzo Gardino 12/c, Bologna (2013–19); traveling (2019–21). FOUNDERS Fabio Farnè, Gabriele Tosi

Ateliersi

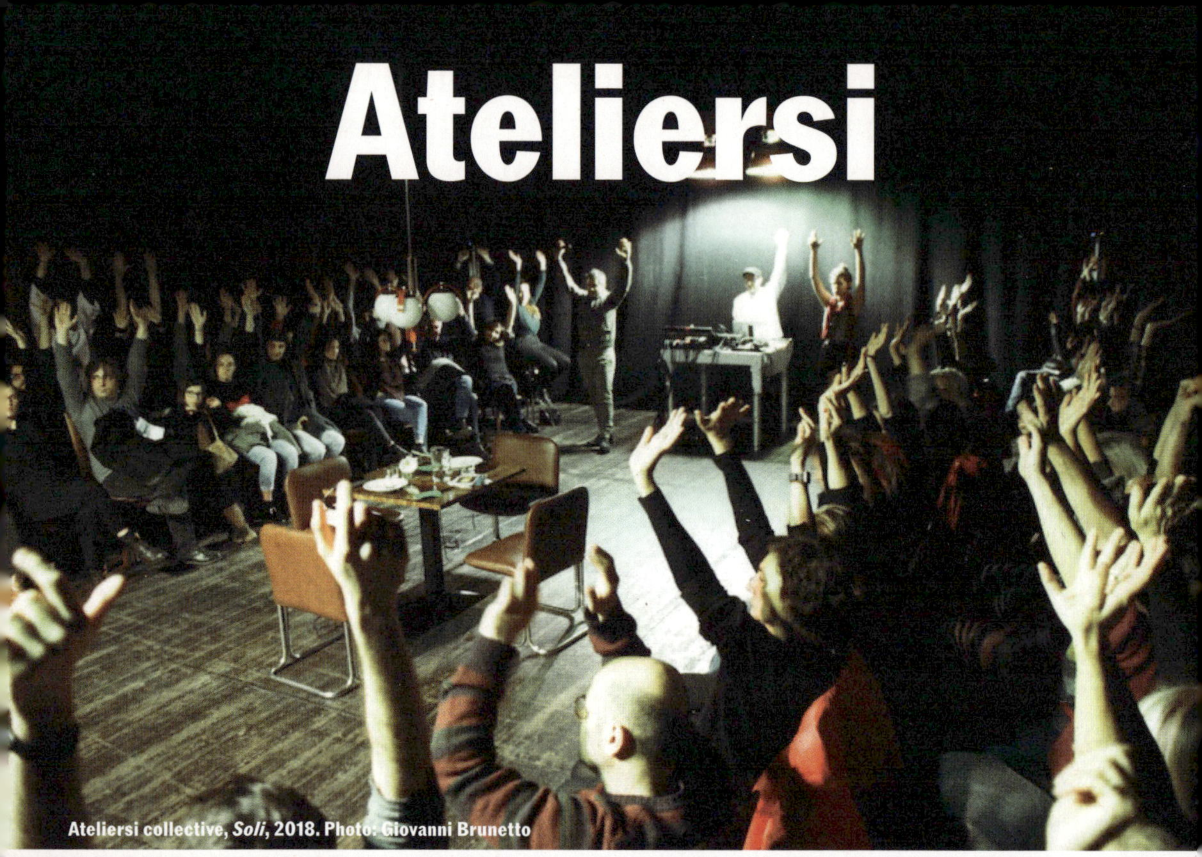

Ateliersi collective, *Soli*, 2018. Photo: Giovanni Brunetto

Alivelab event, 2019

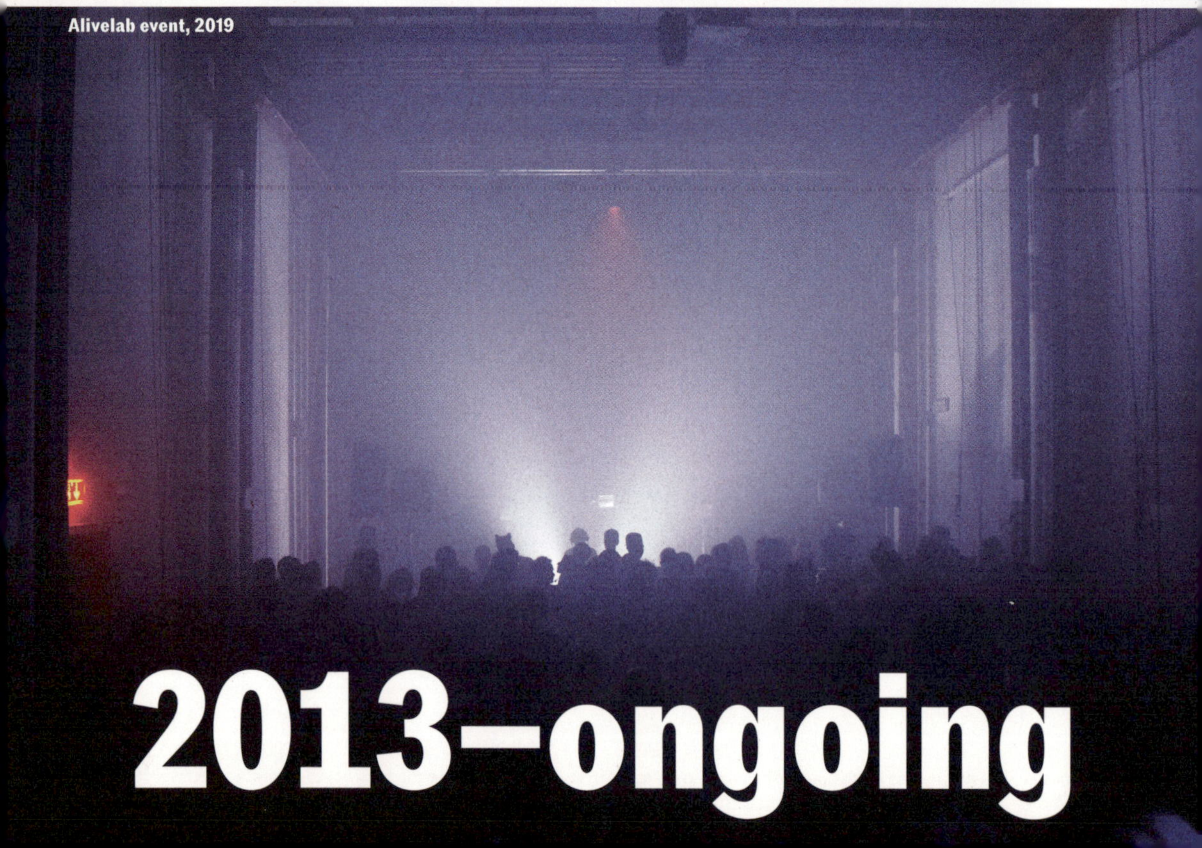

2013–ongoing

Experimentation with the languages of the performing arts and attention to the relationship between process and product are the focuses around which Ateliersi's artistic production is built.

This cultural space was founded in 2013, thanks to a collective made up of artists and curators. The venue on Via San Vitale connotes itself as a space dedicated primarily to artistic production, with a focus on the relationship between the processual dimension and that of the presentation of the artistic product. Ateliersi welcomes both artists from the theater and the performing arts, as well as visual and sound artists whose production involves performative modes. In addition, the cultural programming includes an articulated residency activity to which artists selected for their quality of innovation and experimentation are invited.

As part of Ateliersi, works are produced that then circulate both in Italy and abroad, at the same time bringing international stimuli to Bologna. The European dimension of this space is also made possible thanks to its membership in two cultural production networks—the Trans Europe Halles and Lo Stato dei Luoghi—and two *coordinamenti*, the C.Re.S.Co (Coordinamento delle Realtà della Scena Contemporanea, i.e. the "Supervision of Organizations on the Contemporary Scene") and the Coordinamento Nazionale dei Centri di Residenza per Artisti nei Territori ("National Coordination of Artists' Residency Centers throughout the Territory").

Ateliersi is an artistic and cultural hub of fundamental importance for the Bologna area, and is set up as a place to host a range of bodies working in the artistic, performing, educational and social fields. This need to relate stems from the awareness that it is through dialogue that culture can be generated.

ADDRESS Via San Vitale 69, Bologna. FOUNDERS Fiorenza Menni, Andrea Mochi Sismondi, Giovanni Brunetto, Tihana Maravić, Elisa Marchese, Diego Segatto. COLLABORATORS Greta Fuzzi, Silvia Guescini, Antonella Babbone, Chiara Mancini, Vincenzo Scorza, Eugenia Delbue, Margherita Kay Budillon, Alessandro Iannetti

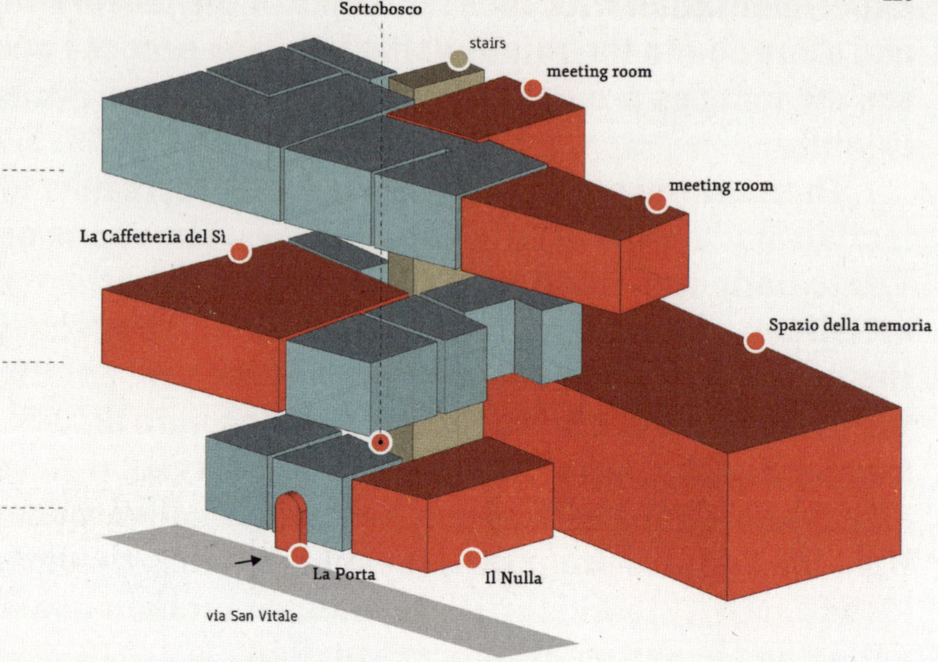

Ateliersi 3D architectural floor plan

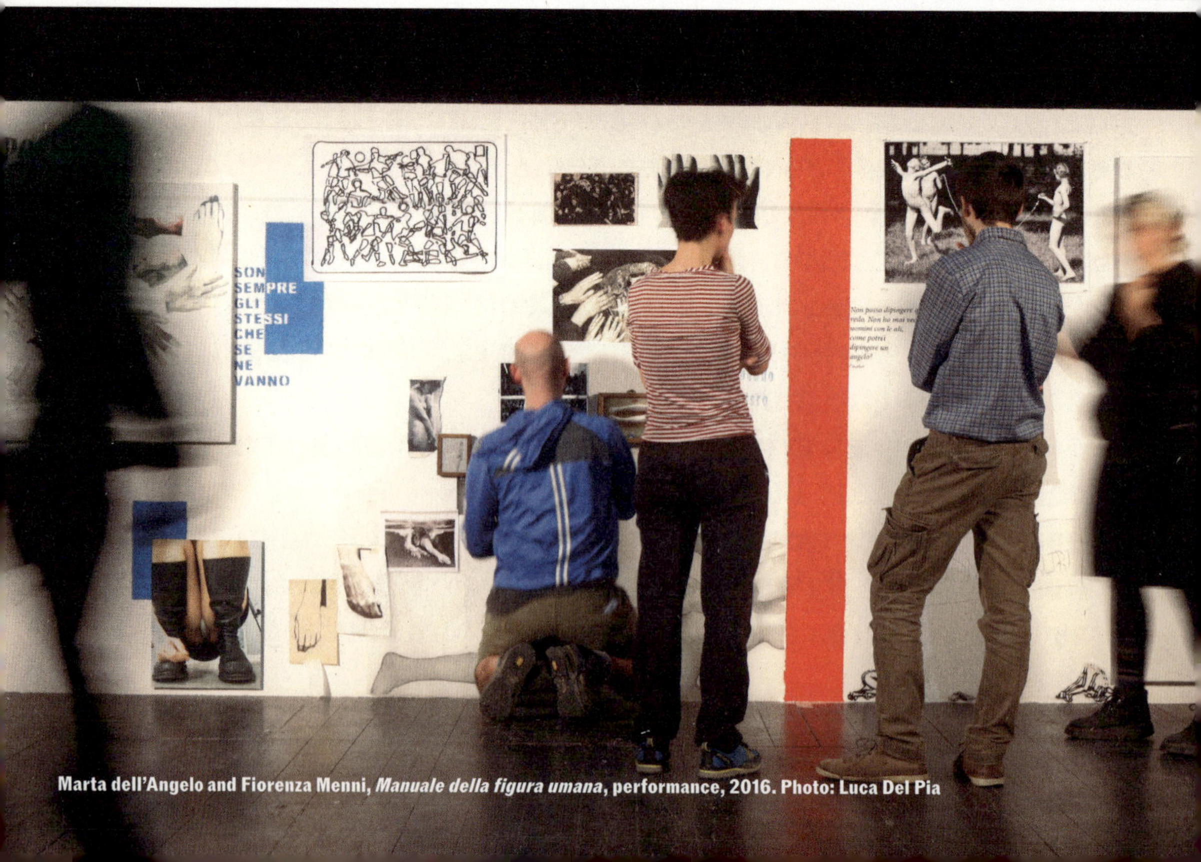

Marta dell'Angelo and Fiorenza Menni, *Manuale della figura umana*, **performance, 2016. Photo: Luca Del Pia**

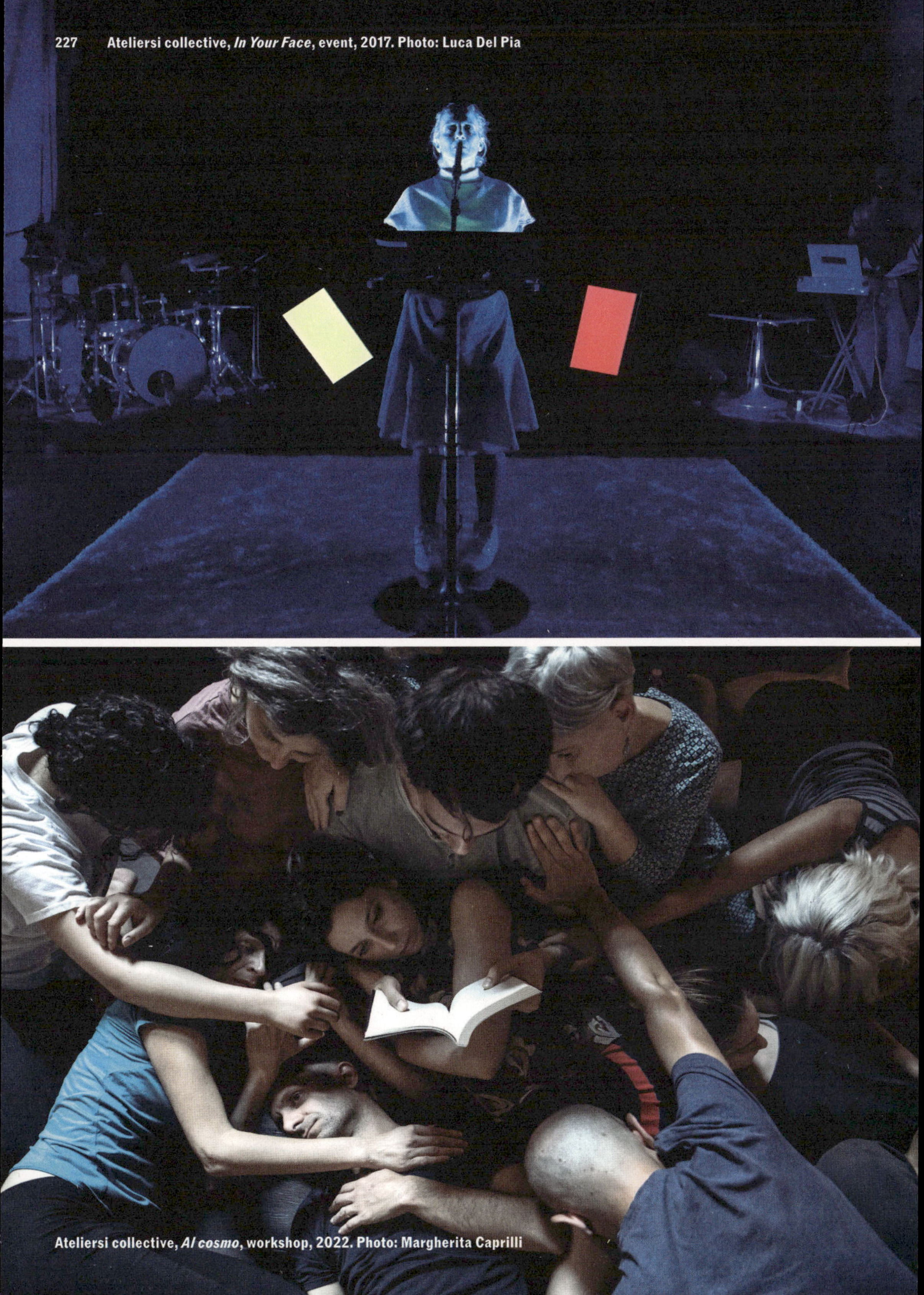

 Ateliersi collective, *In Your Face*, event, 2017. Photo: Luca Del Pia

Ateliersi collective, *Al cosmo*, workshop, 2022. Photo: Margherita Caprilli

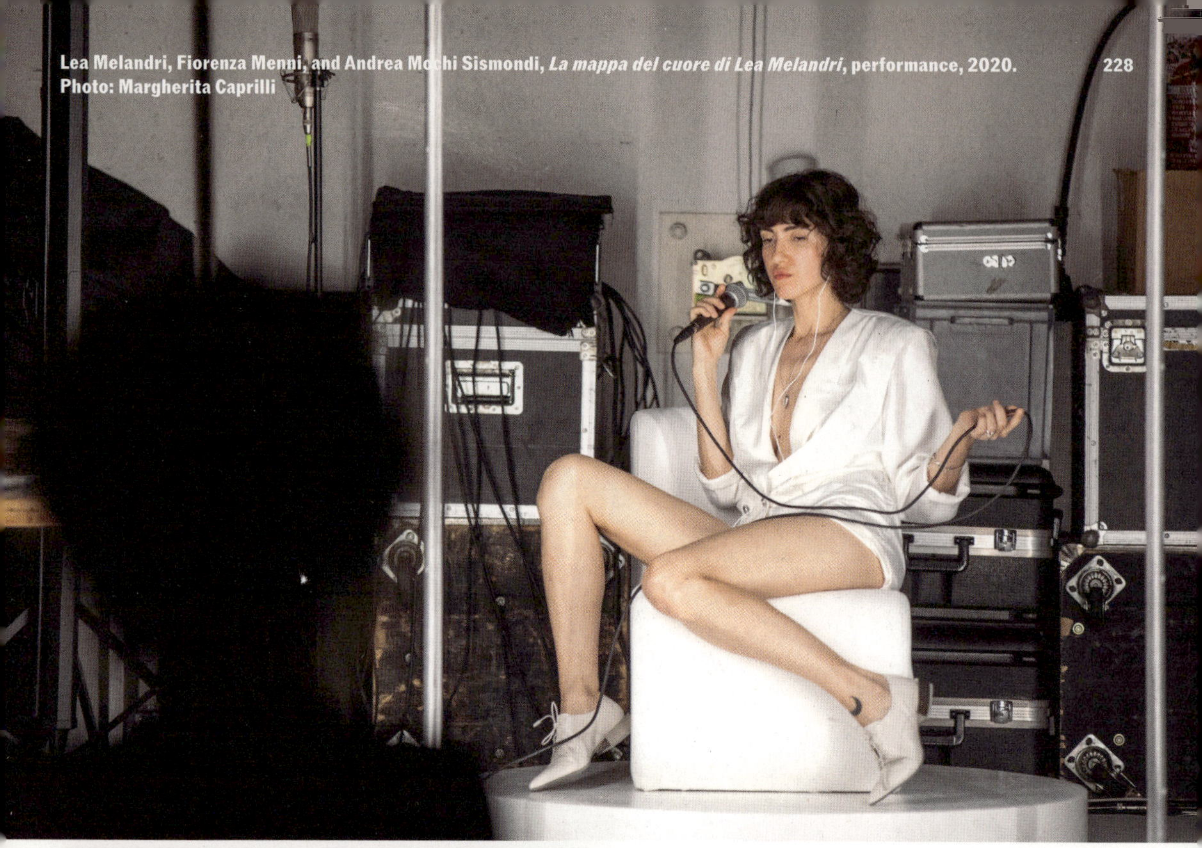

Lea Melandri, Fiorenza Menni, and Andrea Mochi Sismondi, *La mappa del cuore di Lea Melandri*, performance, 2020.
Photo: Margherita Caprilli

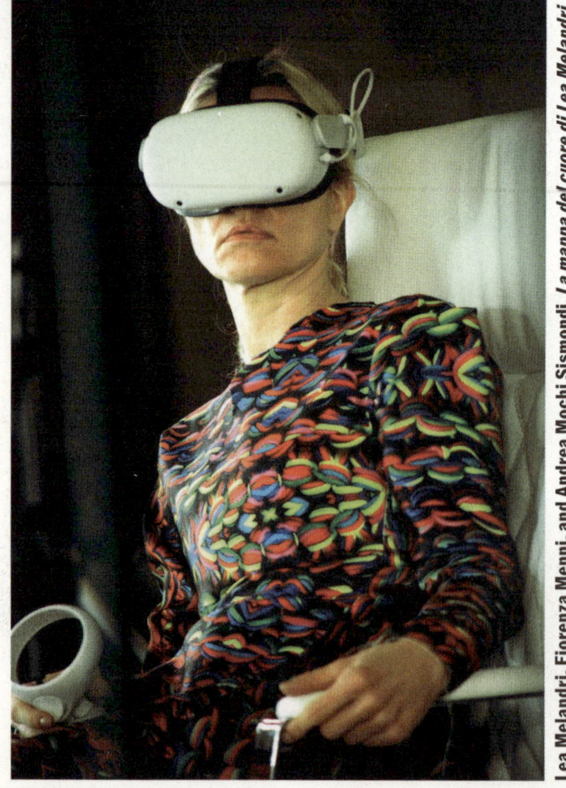

Lea Melandri, Fiorenza Menni, and Andrea Mochi Sismondi, *La mappa del cuore di Lea Melandri*, VR set, 2020. Photo: Giovanni Brunetto

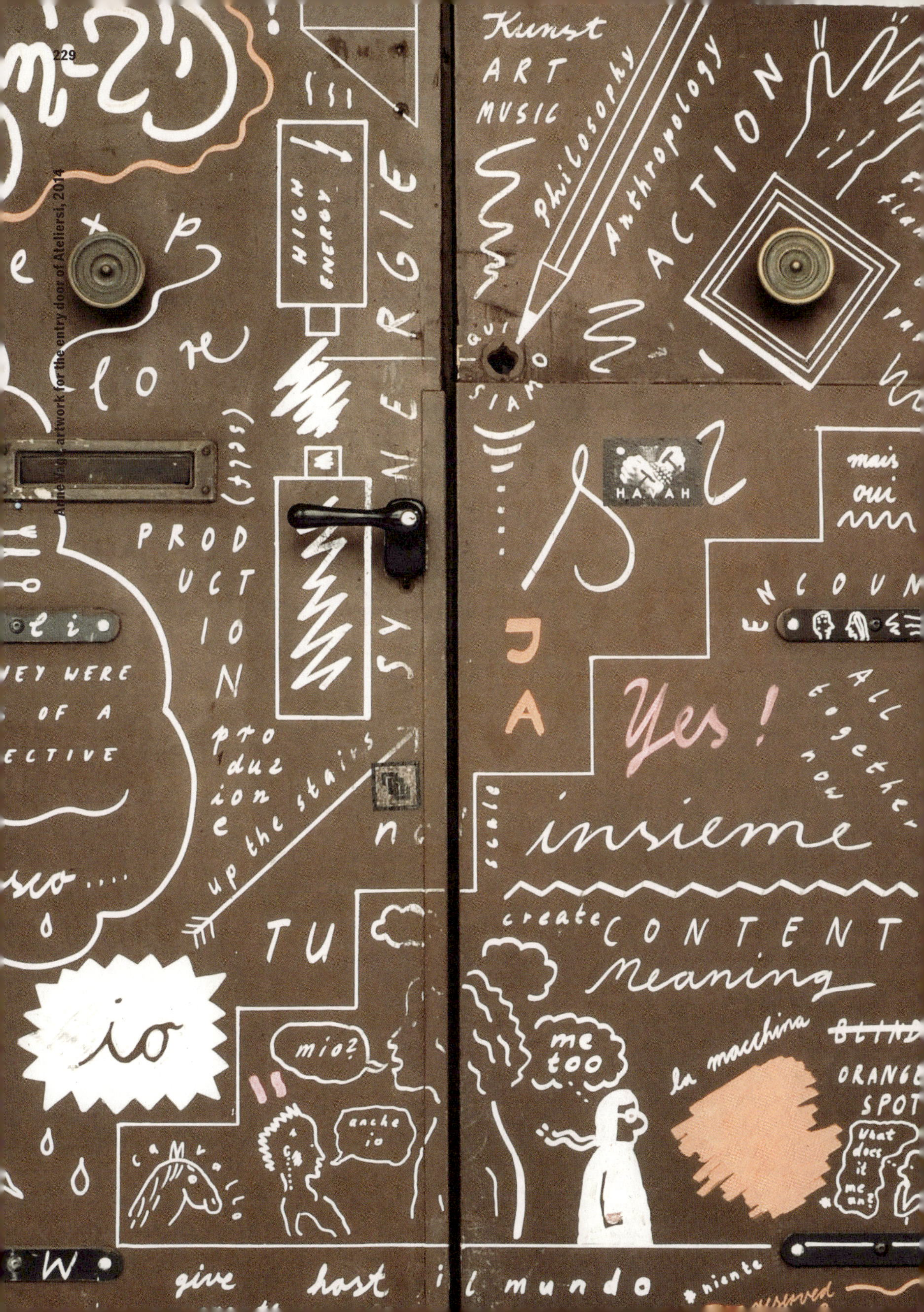

Kunst
ART
MUSIC
Philosophy
Anthropology
ACTION
HIGH ENERGY
ENERGIE
love
PRODUCTION
produzione
up the stairs
SYNERGIE
(3795)
WEY WERE
OF A
ECTIVE
co....
TU
io
mio?
anche io
came
give host il mundo
niente
SIAMO
HAYAH
JA
Yes!
insieme
create CONTENT meaning
mais oui
ENCOUN
ALL together now
scala
me too
la macchina
BLIND
ORANGE SPOT
Wat does it mean?

Maison Ventidue

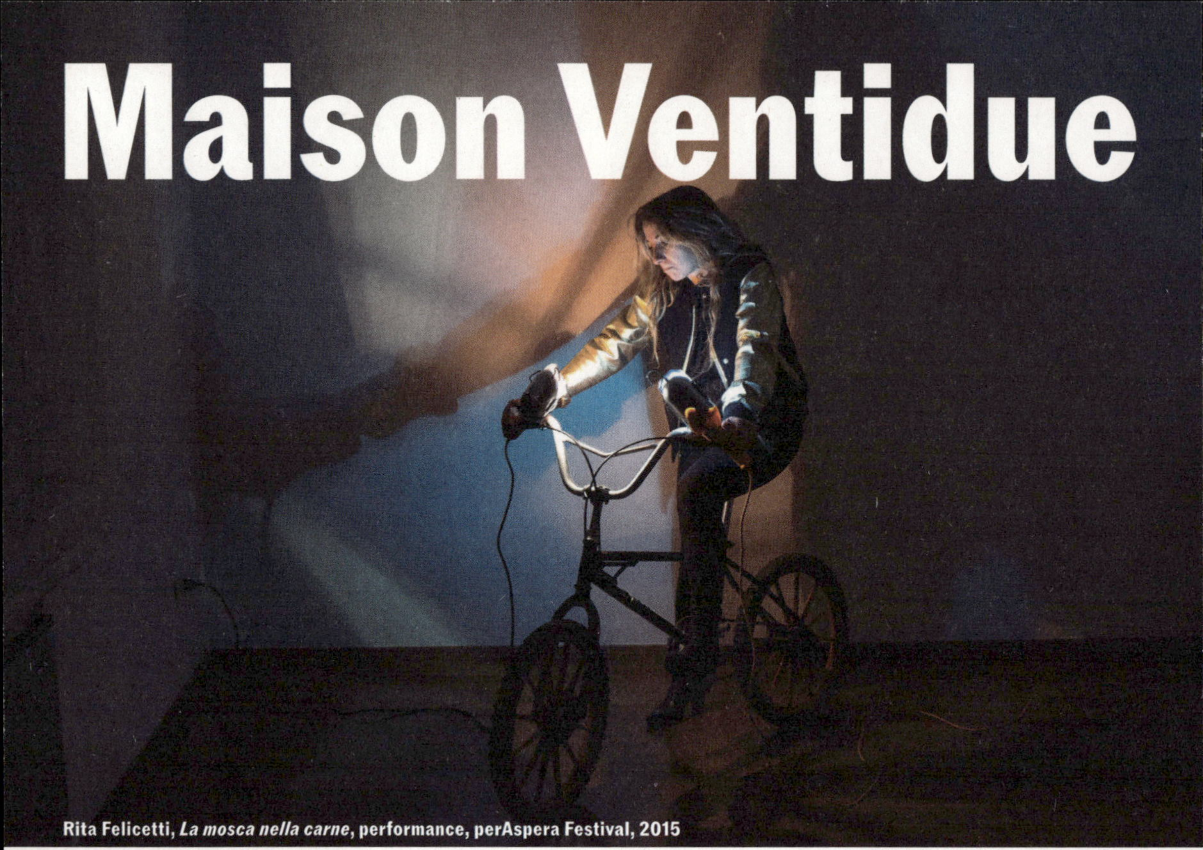

Rita Felicetti, *La mosca nella carne*, performance, perAspera Festival, 2015

I Sacchi di Sabbia, *Don Giovanni di W. A. Mozart (Opera d'appartamento)*, performance, 2015

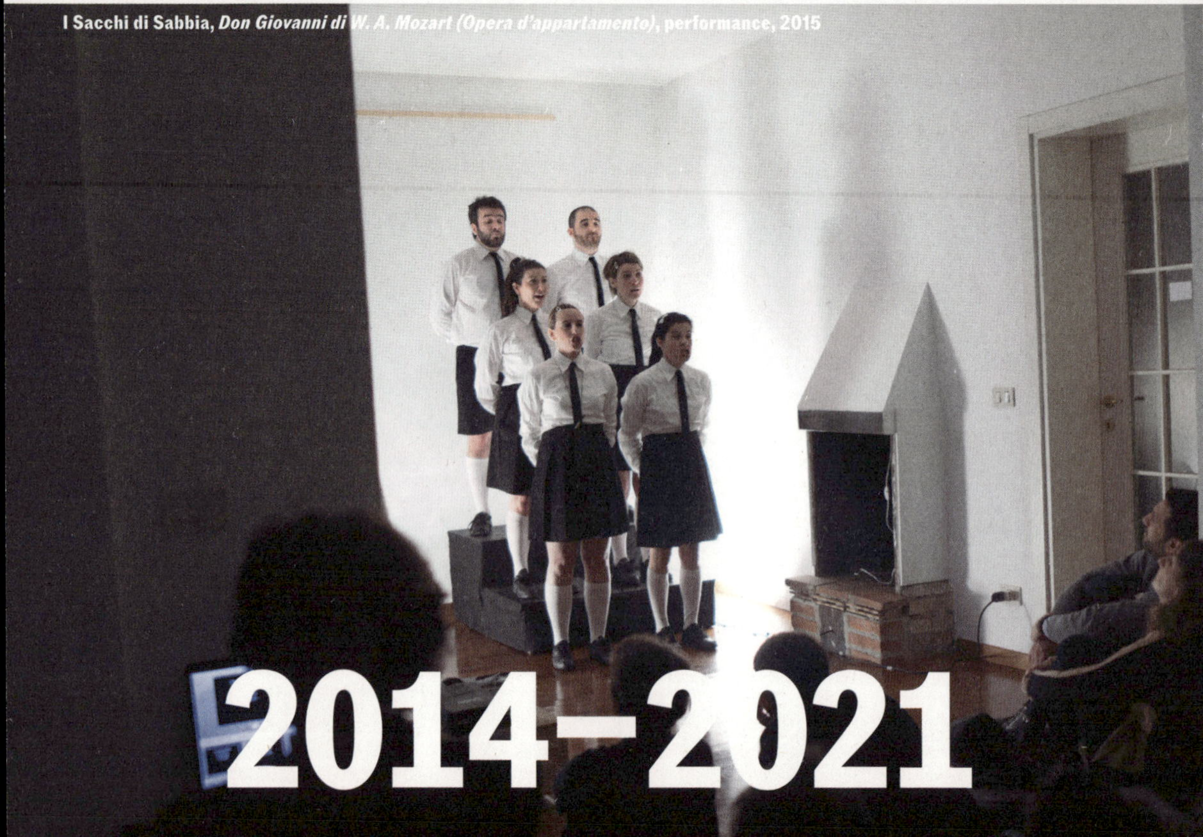

2014–2021

Under the artistic direction of the founder, Mariarosa Lamanna, Maison Ventidue's cultural programming involved the collaboration of curators and artists, including Marco Mastroianni, Serena Facioni, and Mariolino Guida. The activities of this space consisted mainly of organizing exhibitions of visual artists, initially invited by the curators and later selected through open calls. Relational installations, multimedia projects, and performances, as well as painting and drawing exhibitions were offered in the Maison Ventidue spaces.

Maison Ventidue maintained various kinds of relationships with the city's cultural institutions, which helped the project grow while allowing it to maintain its freedom in terms of decision-making and experimentation. Activities were self-financed, from forms of donation to membership fees. In 2021, the Maison Ventidue experience came to a natural end, having run out of energy after years of experimentation and growth.

ADDRESS Via dell'Indipendenza 22, Bologna (2014–20); Via Miramonte 4/6, Bologna (2019–21). FOUNDERS Mariarosa Lamanna. COLLABORATORS Marco Mastroianni, Serena Facioni, Mariolino Guida

TRIPLA

2016–2019

Founded by three students of the Academy of Fine Arts in Bologna, TRIPLA occupied three storefronts facing Via dell'Indipendenza, one of the city's main streets stretching from the Central Station to Piazza Maggiore. Given the peculiar location of the space, which was obtained under a temporary and free concession from the City of Bologna, the artists made it an opportunity for dialogue with a wide and general public, often questioning the commercial nature of the street itself.

In its three years of operation, TRIPLA proposed twenty-nine exhibitions, inviting local and international artists to work within a space connoted by the limited depth of the shop windows. The particularity of the space obliged the artists to create site-specific projects that could not be replicated elsewhere, which were also determined by the immediate enjoyment of an audience made up mainly of passersby.

Numerous relationships have been woven with local cultural institutions such as MAMbo (on the occasion of Art City), and with other non-profits such as Xing/Raum, Gelateria Sogni di Ghiaccio and Localedue.

TRIPLA, whose name and symbol are a reference to the everyday electric outlet adapter, closed in 2019 due to the city's failure to renew its concession.

ADDRESS Via dell'Indipendenza 71/f, Bologna. FOUNDERS Luca Bernardello, Paolo Bufalini, Filippo Cecconi

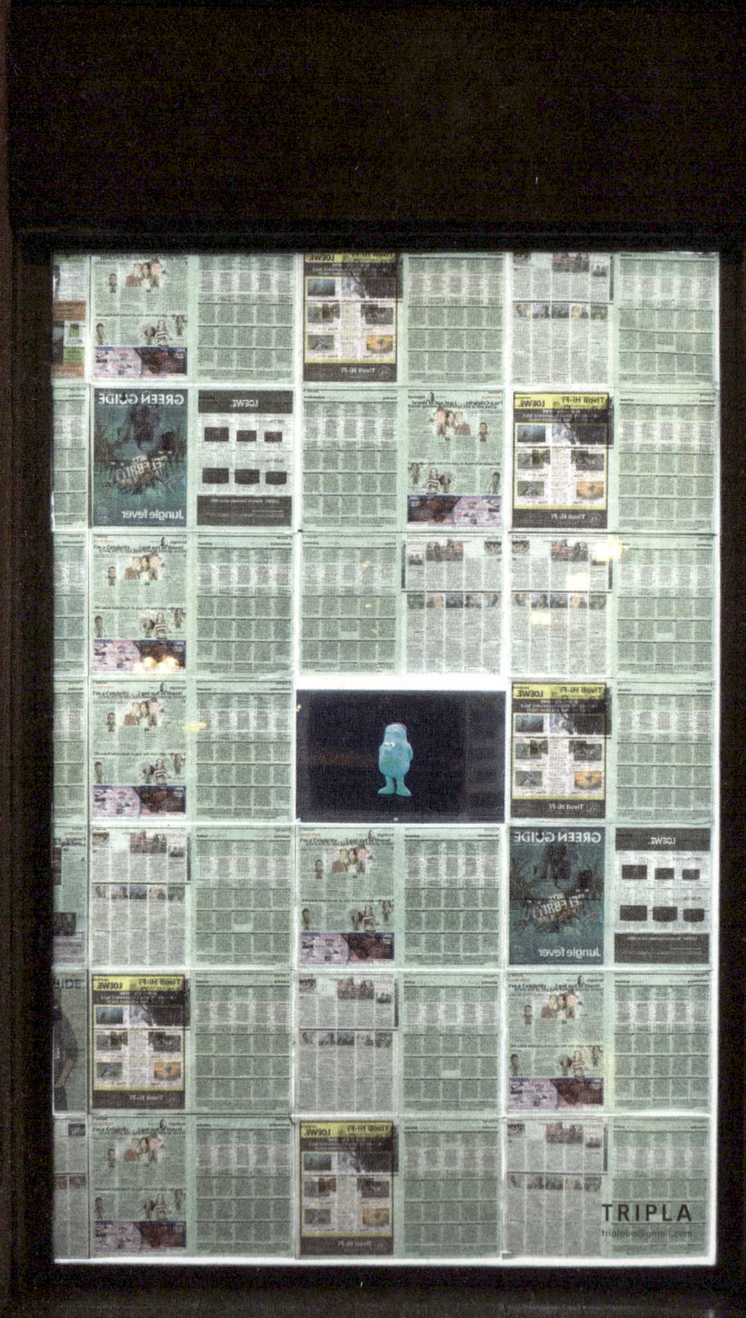

 Untitled Event #1, dome projection of the TRIPLA symbol, 2016

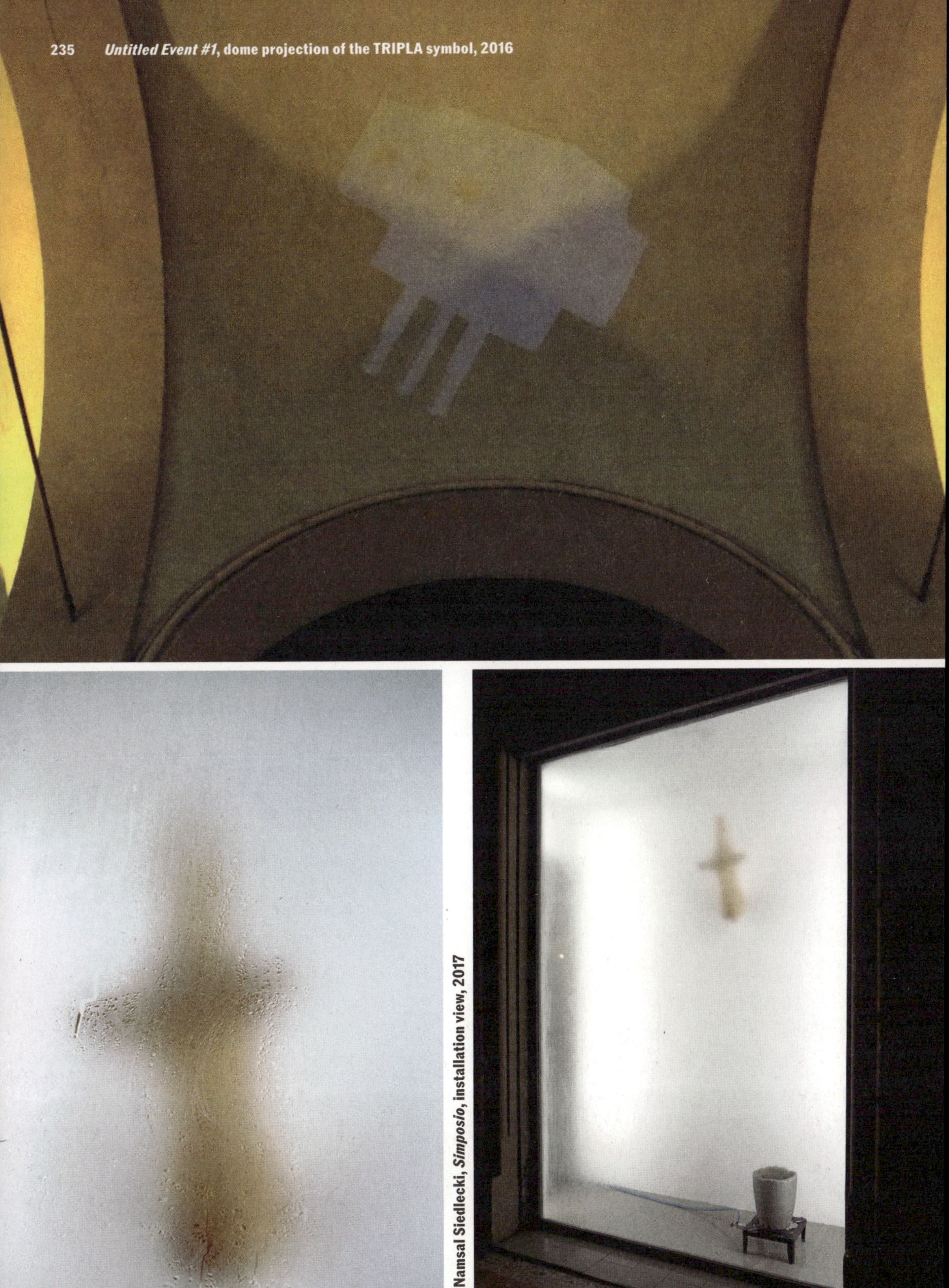

Namsal Siedlecki, *Simposio*, installation view, 2017

Gelateria Sogni di Ghiaccio

Gianluca Concialdi, *Ogni anno è il mio anno*, installation view, 2020

Stefano Cagol, *BANAL LOLA PARTY*, installation view, 2018

2016–ongoing

Gelateria Sogni di Ghiaccio was founded in 2016 by Mattia Pajé, Filippo Marzocchi and Marco Casella, three young artists who had just graduated from the Academy of Fine Arts in Bologna, to offer other emerging artists a space for experimentation where they might have fun and learn without having to deal with the commercial side inherent to contemporary art galleries. In addition to being an exhibition and design space, Gelateria Sogni di Ghiaccio was also the art studio and workplace of the three founders. From 2016 to 2019, the exhibition program was run by Pajé and Marzocchi, and from 2020 by Pajé alone. Currently, the space and the program are collectively managed by a group of twelve people.

Numerous collaborations were established over the years with city institutions such as Arte Fiera and MAMbo, but also with other non-profit spaces and organizations such as Xing, TRIPLA and Localedue.

Being independent meant this space could afford not to have a definite curatorial program. Its programming usually followed a spontaneous process, linked to personal frequentations with Italian and international artists, whose solo exhibitions were developed on a dialogic and cooperative basis. Installations and site-specific interventions with references to subcultures and Pop imagery were among the most recurrent forms of artistic expression in the programming of Gelateria Sogni di Ghiaccio.

ADDRESS Via Tanari Vecchia 5/a, Bologna. FOUNDERS Mattia Pajé, Filippo Marzocchi, Marco Casella

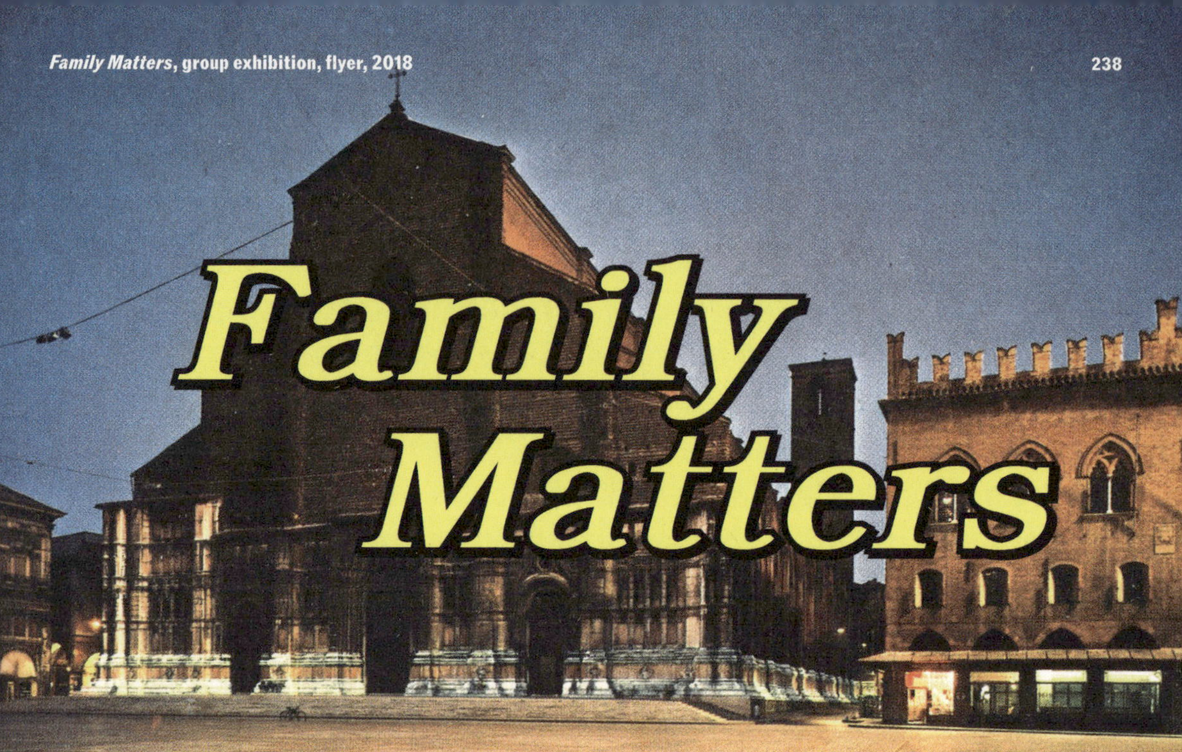

Family Matters 2, group exhibition, flyer, 2021

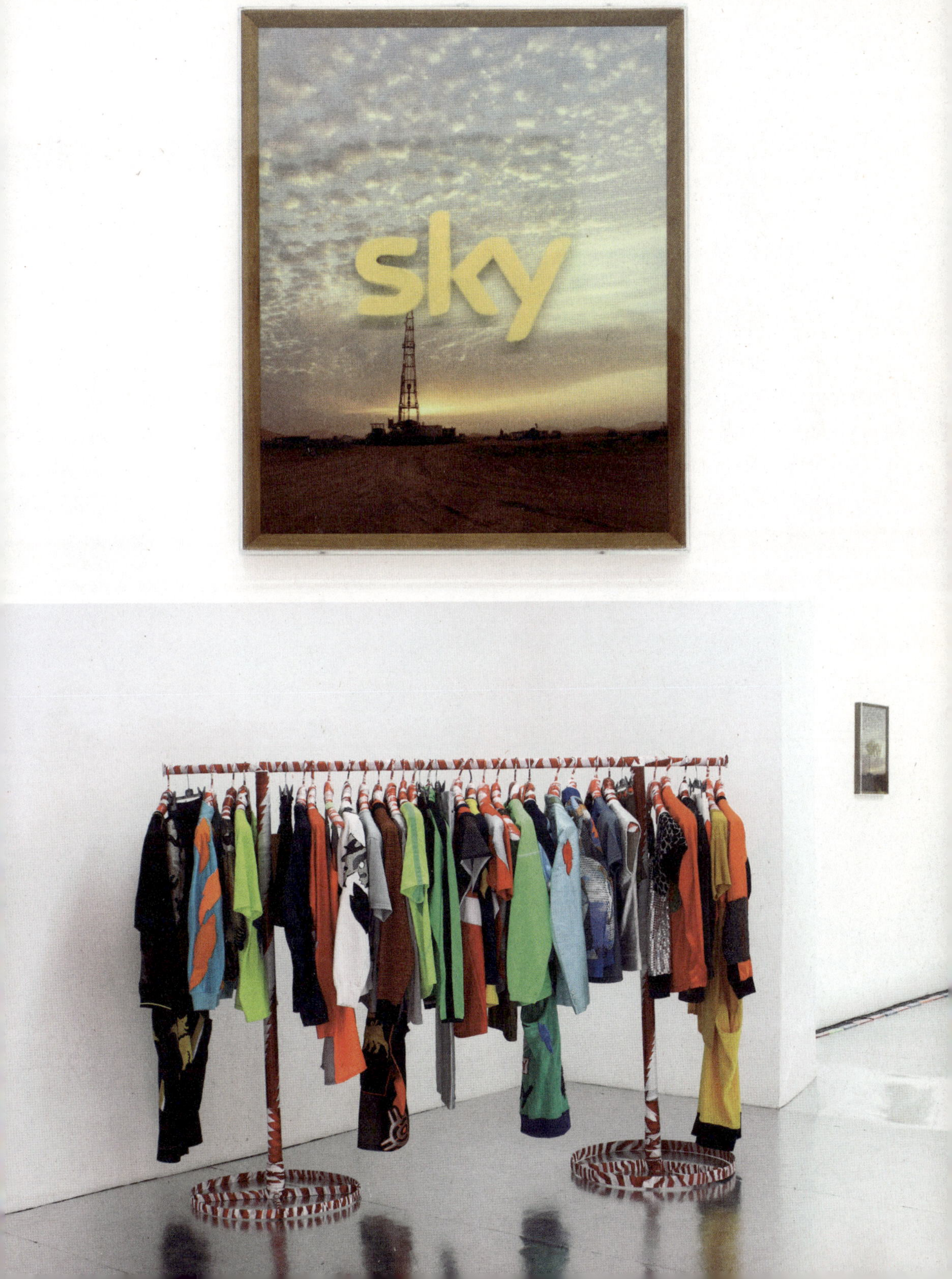

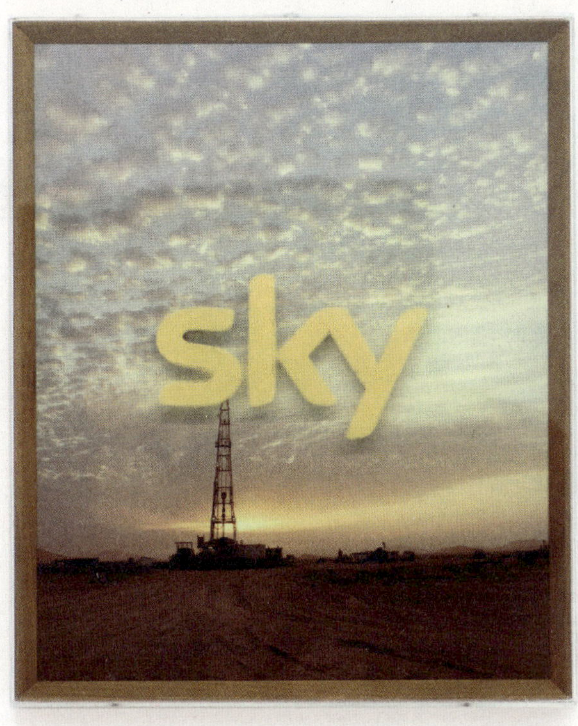

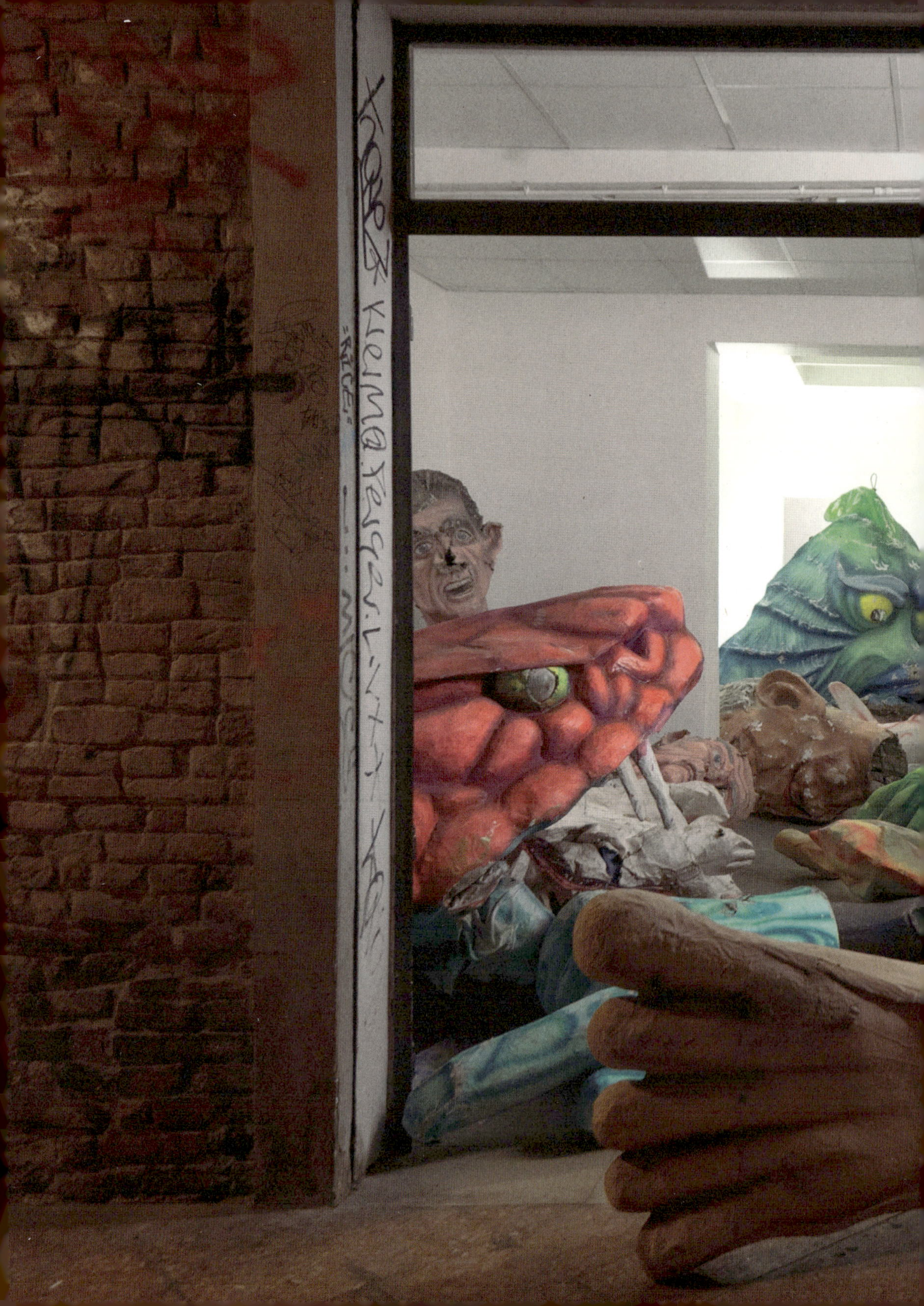

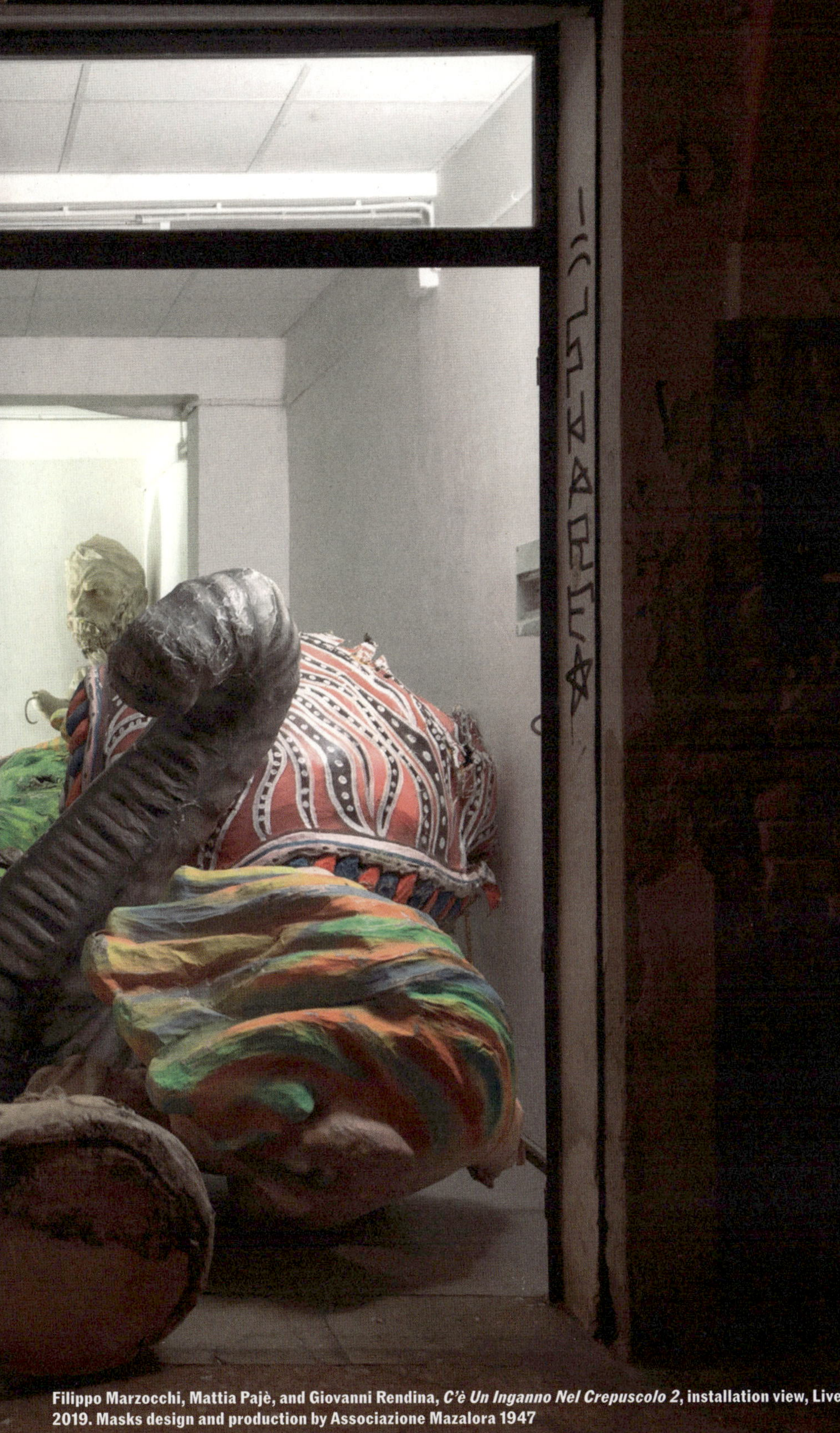

Filippo Marzocchi, Mattia Pajè, and Giovanni Rendina, *C'è Un Inganno Nel Crepuscolo 2*, installation view, Live 2019. Masks design and production by Associazione Mazalora 1947

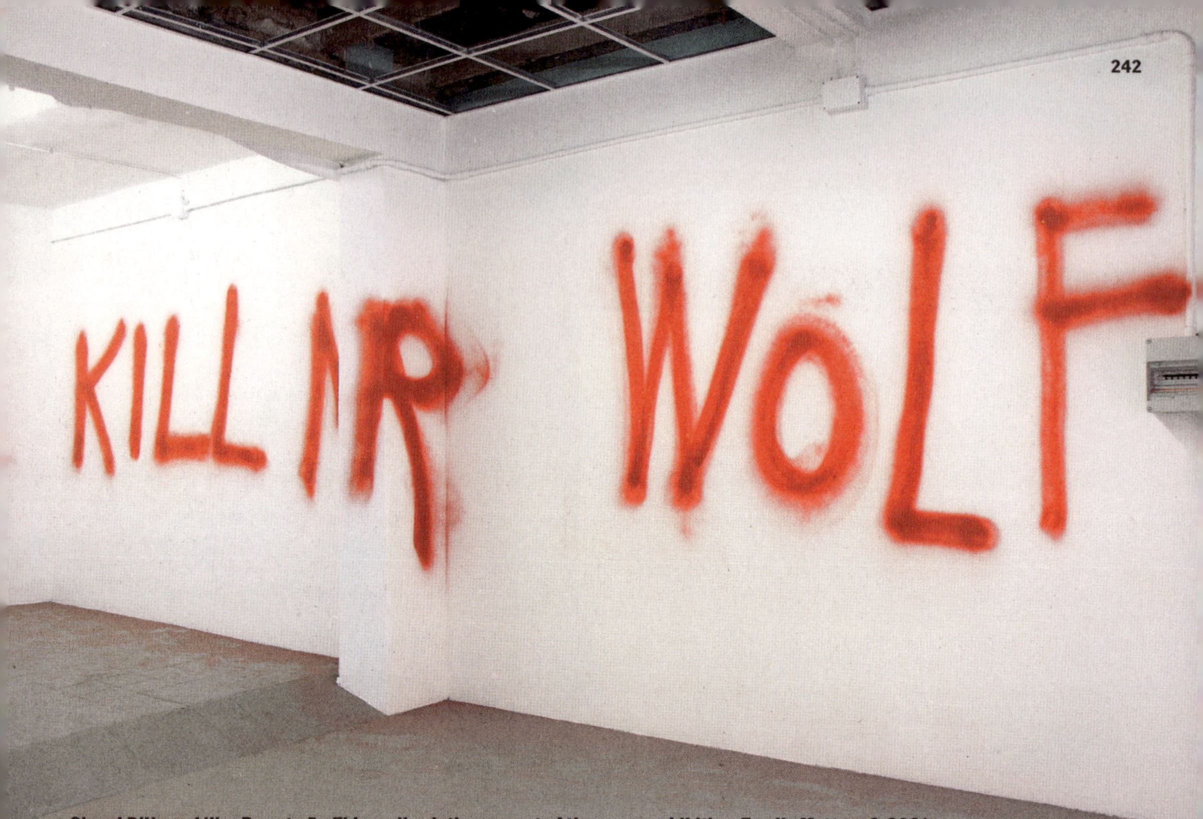

Gianni D'Urso, *I Was Born to Do This*, wall painting as part of the group exhibition *Family Matters 2*, 2021

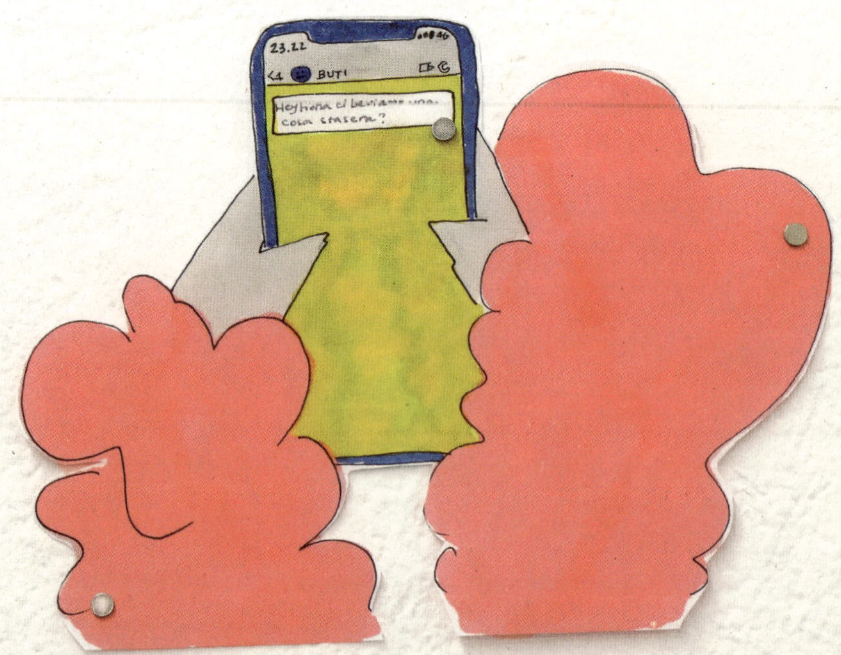

Valentina De Zanche, *Fiona, Fiona!*, curated by Lucrezia Galeotti, installation view, 2022

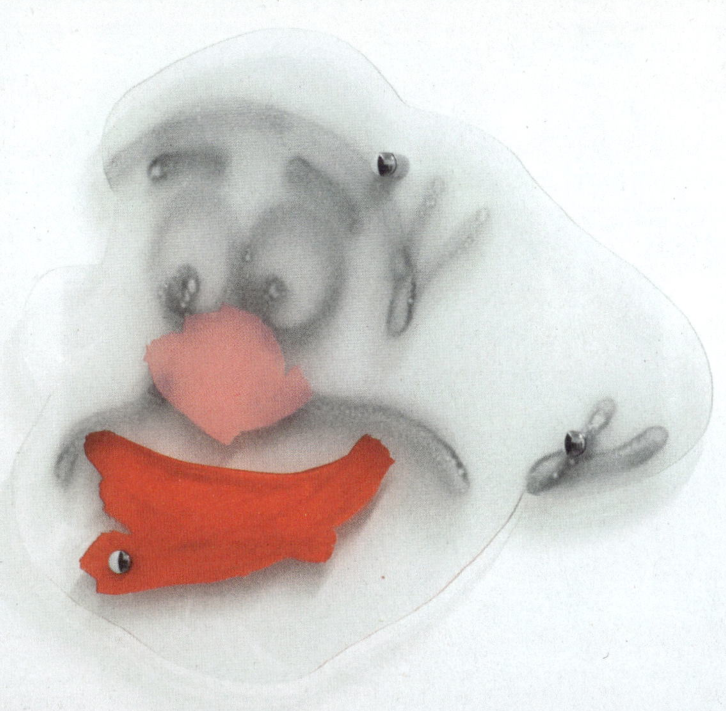

Pau Sampera, *Cucciolo*, installation view, 2018

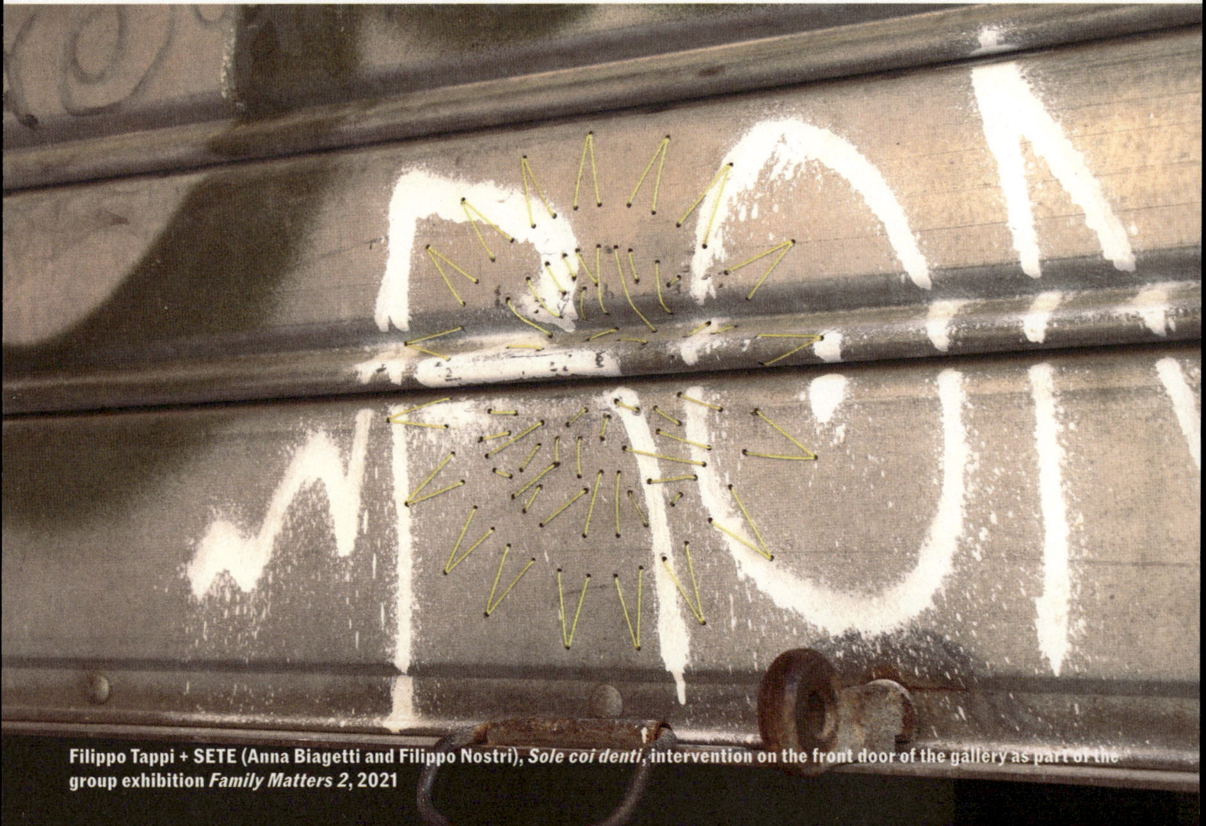

Filippo Tappi + SETE (Anna Biagetti and Filippo Nostri), *Sole coi denti*, intervention on the front door of the gallery as part of the group exhibition *Family Matters 2*, 2021

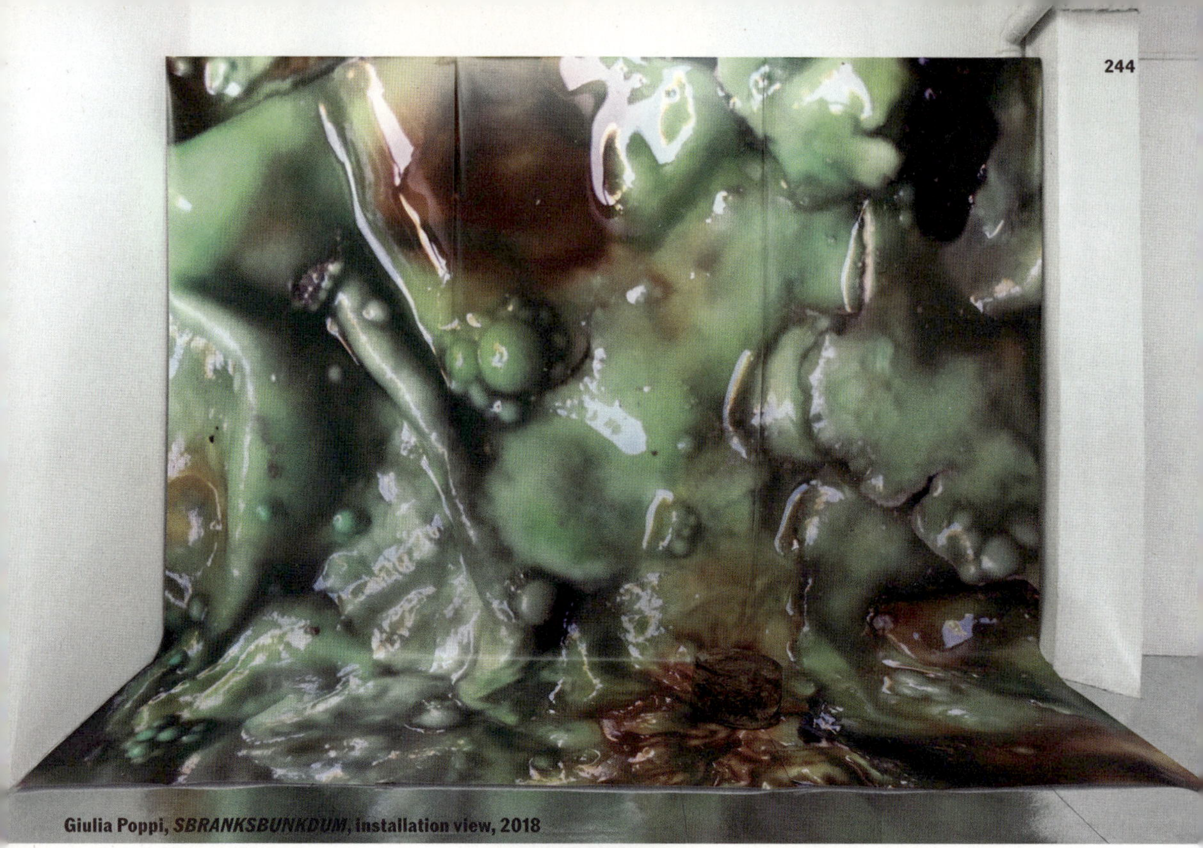

Giulia Poppi, *SBRANKSBUNKDUM*, installation view, 2018

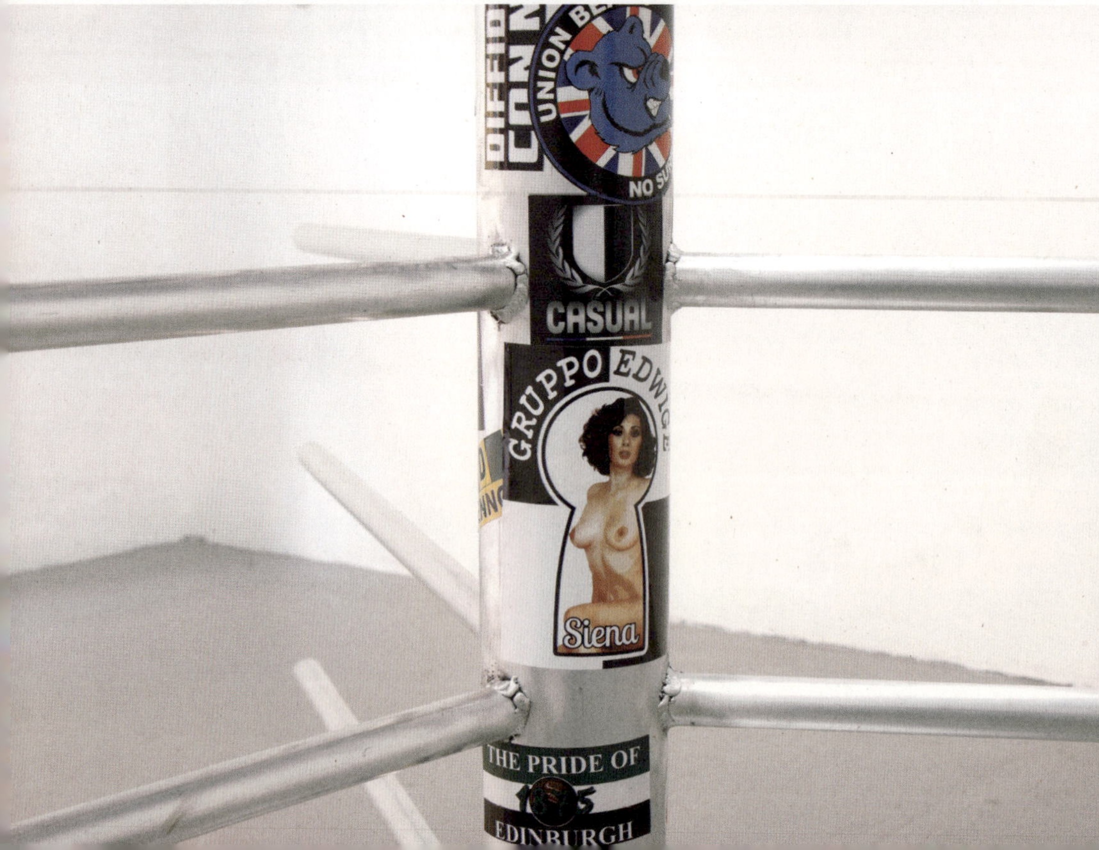

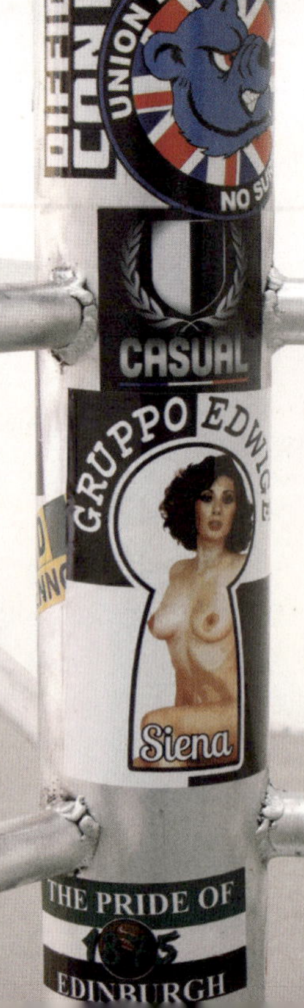

Giovanni De Cataldo, *L'isola dei cani*, curated by Saverio Verini, installation view, 2021

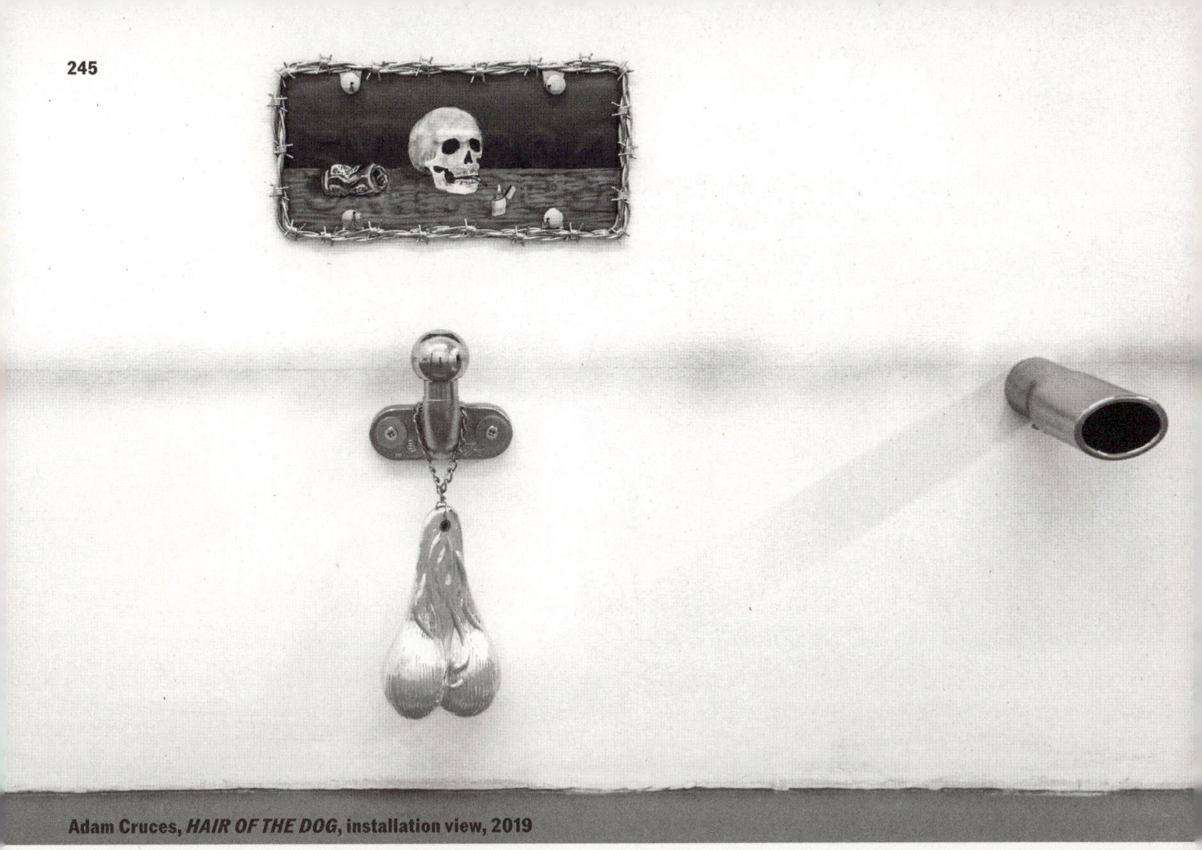

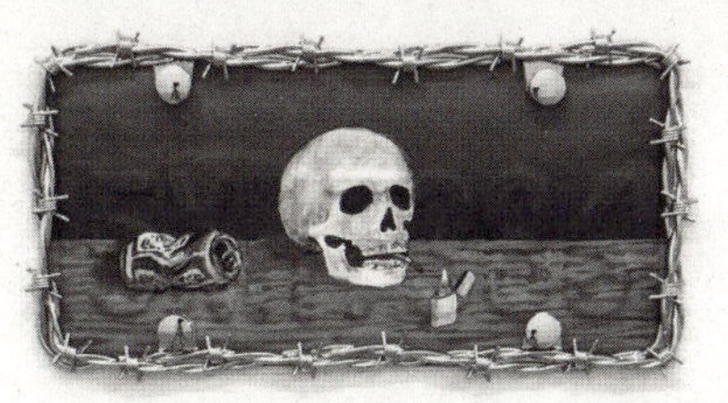

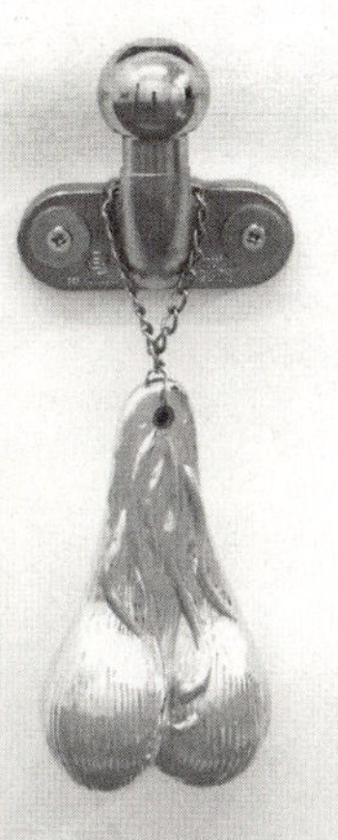

Adam Cruces, *HAIR OF THE DOG*, installation view, 2019

Alessandro Di Pietro, *HOBOBOLO*, installation view, 2021

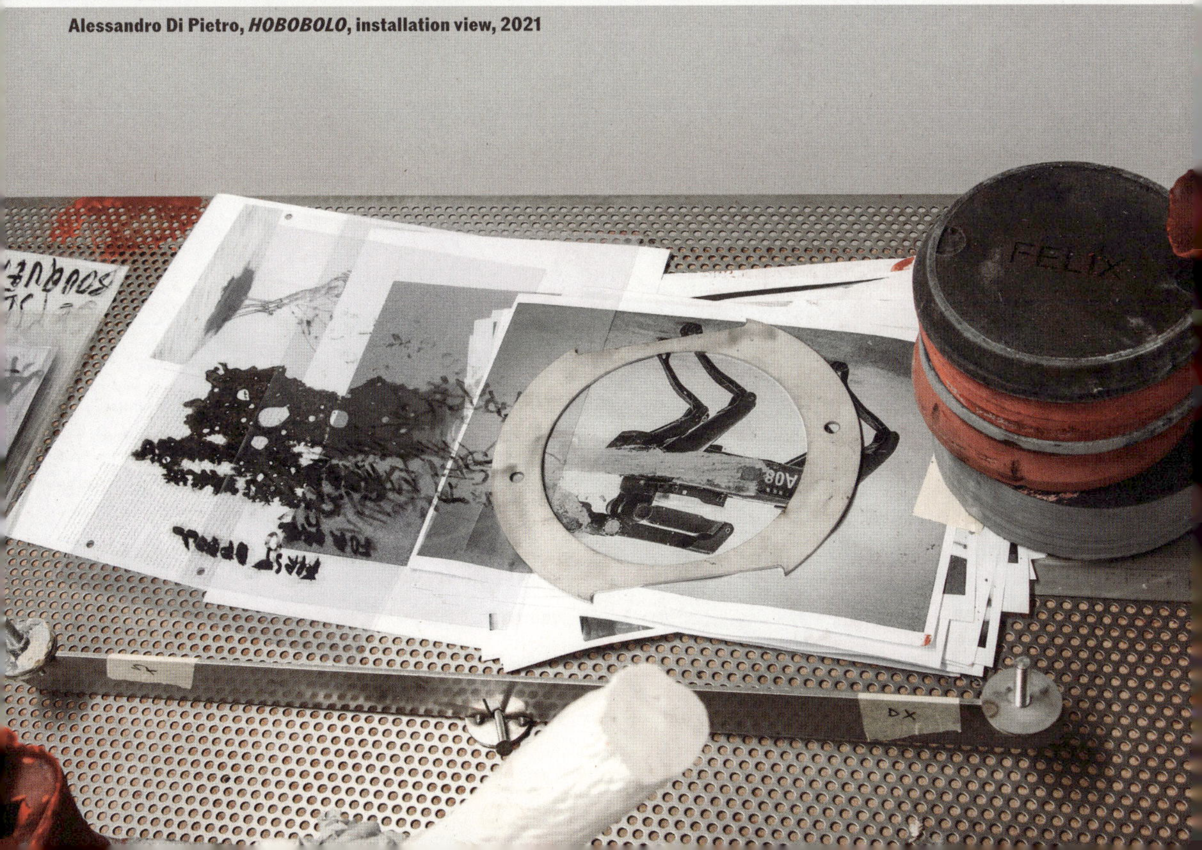

Alchemilla

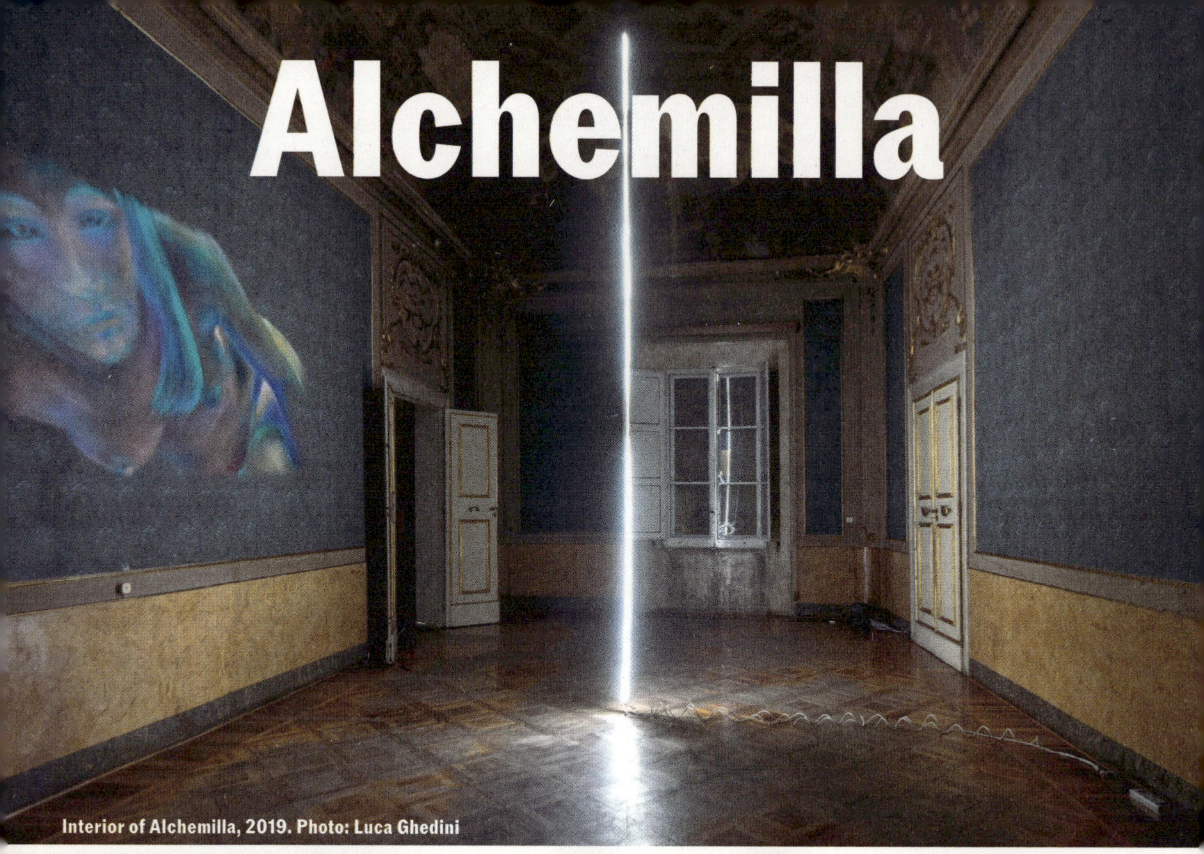

Interior of Alchemilla, 2019. Photo: Luca Ghedini

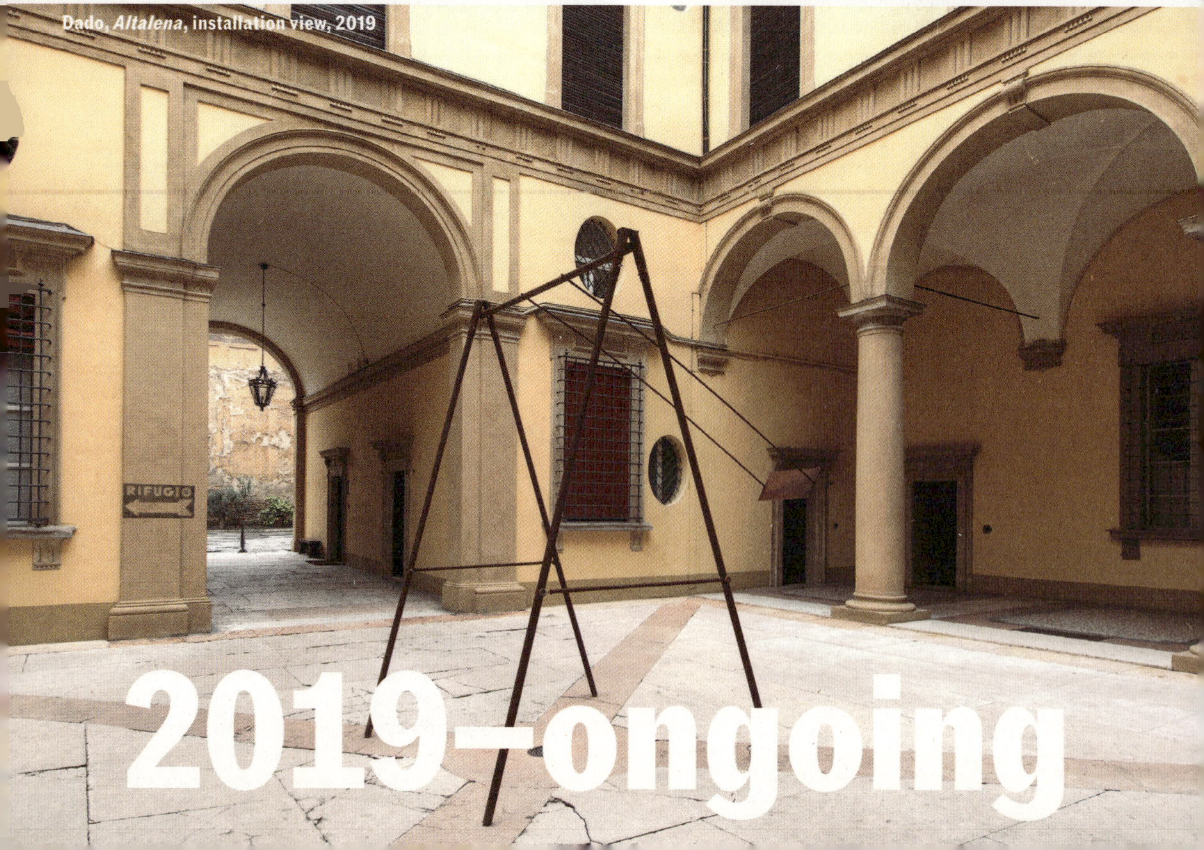

Dado, *Altalena*, installation view, 2019

2019–ongoing

Alchemilla is a cultural association based inside the historic Palazzo Vizzani on Via Santo Stefano, in an apartment owned by the family of Camilla Sanguinetti, one of the founders and head artistic director. The idea of an exhibition space that was also a place for research arose from the synergies among the founders, developed over previous curatorial projects.

Over the first three years, the curatorship of the projects was entrusted to Fulvio Chimento, who proposed exhibitions by Italian artists that emerged in the 1990s such as Stefano Arienti, Alessandro Pessoli, Cuoghi Corsello, and Pierpaolo Campanini. Later, curators from outside the board were involved, organizing exhibitions by younger artists such as Mattia Pajè, Roberto Fassone, and the Slug collective. Most of the projects explore site-specificity dynamics, be they installations or performances, either in dialogue or in contrast with the interior and exterior courtyard spaces of this sumptuous 1560 building.

Alchemilla relates with various institutions and artistic realities in the area, and since 2022 has been part of K.I.N. – Keep In Network, which unites independent cultural associations operating in Bologna and elsewhere. The space is partly self-financed, partly subsidized through public calls and private sponsors, involved depending on the projects. Alchemilla has also started a membership drive with the idea of involving members as active participants in decision-making processes, through annual assemblies and other meetings.

ADDRESS Palazzo Vizzani, Via Santo Stefano 43, Bologna. FOUNDERS Camilla Sanguinetti, Claudia Baccarani, Ragia Kaja A., Elisa Campagnaro, Fulvio Chimento, Antonella Malaguti, Andrea Panzavolta. COLLABORATORS Veronica Santi, David Casini, Cuoghi Corsello, Giulia Bardelli, Andrea Guccini

TU MI CHIAMI A COMPIERE UN ATTO D'AMORE

Veronica Santi, *Tu mi chiami a compiere un atto d'amore*, flyer, 2023

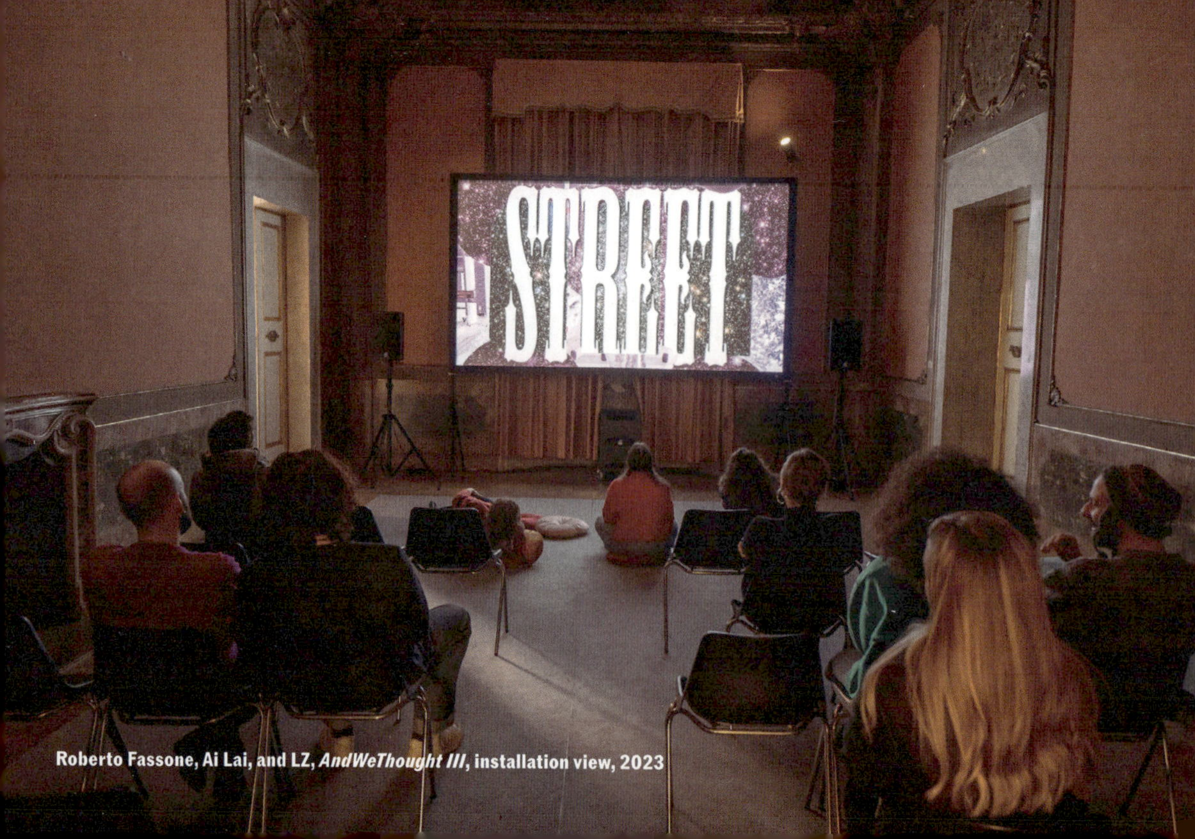

Roberto Fassone, Ai Lai, and LZ, *AndWeThought III*, installation view, 2023

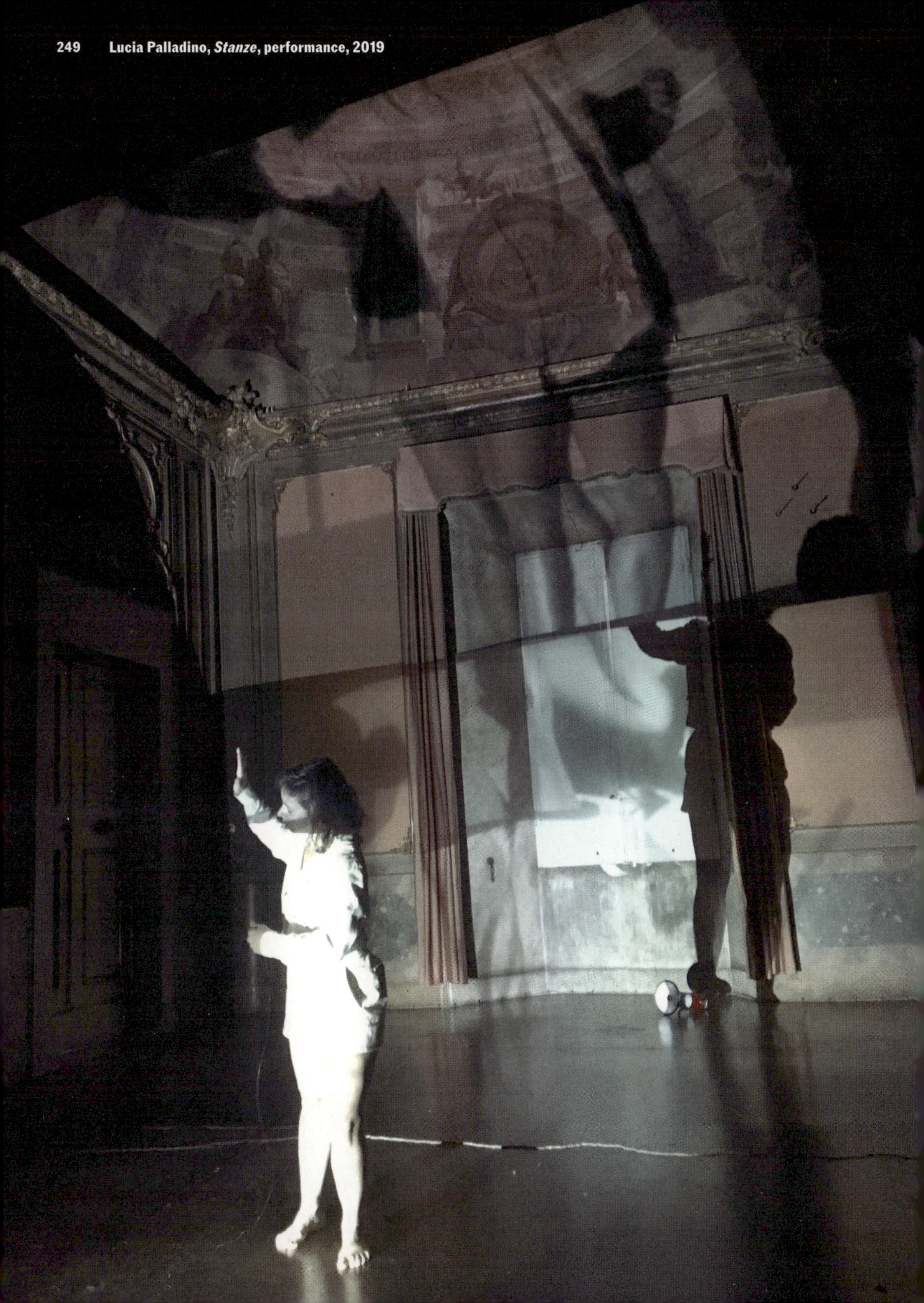

Parsec

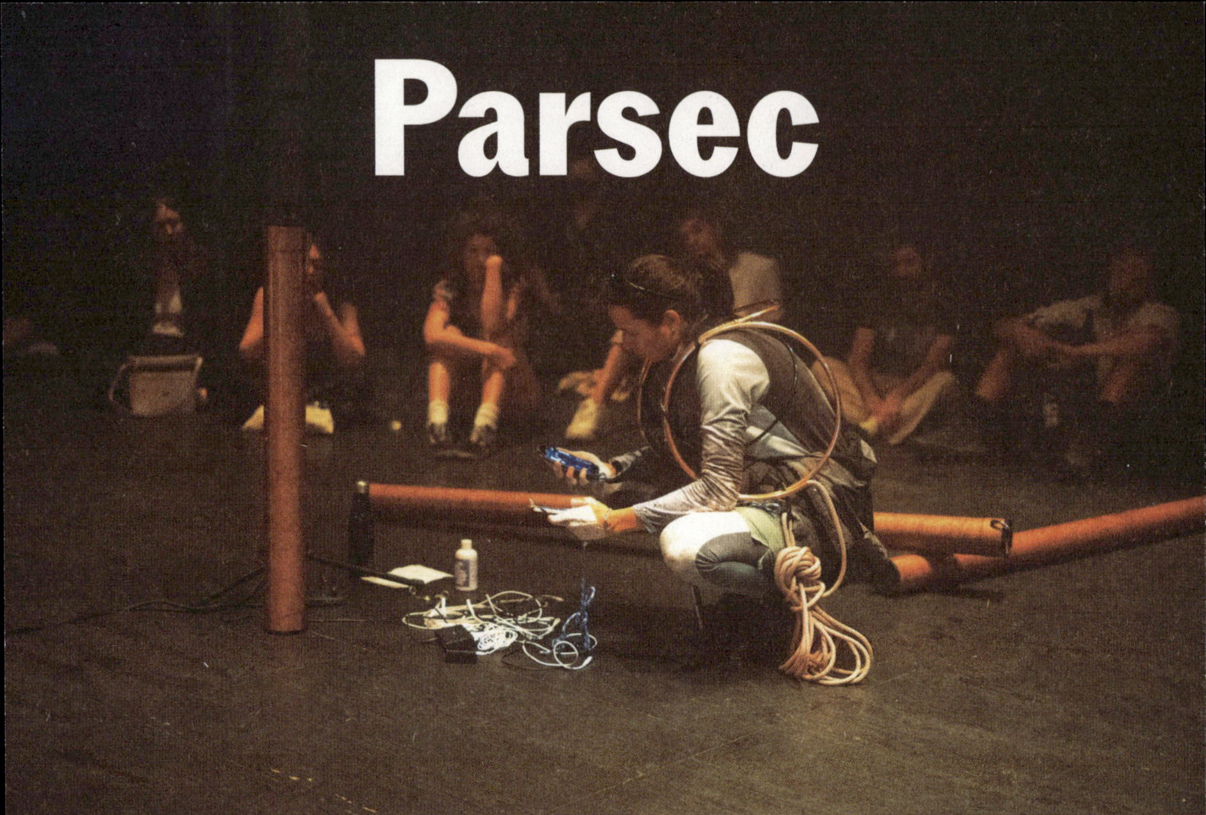

Caterina Gobbi (in collaboration with Ombre Lunghe), *Had There Been Anyone to Listen*, performance at Ateliersi, Art City, 2022

Enzo e Barbara, *Veleno Veneto*, installation view, 2023

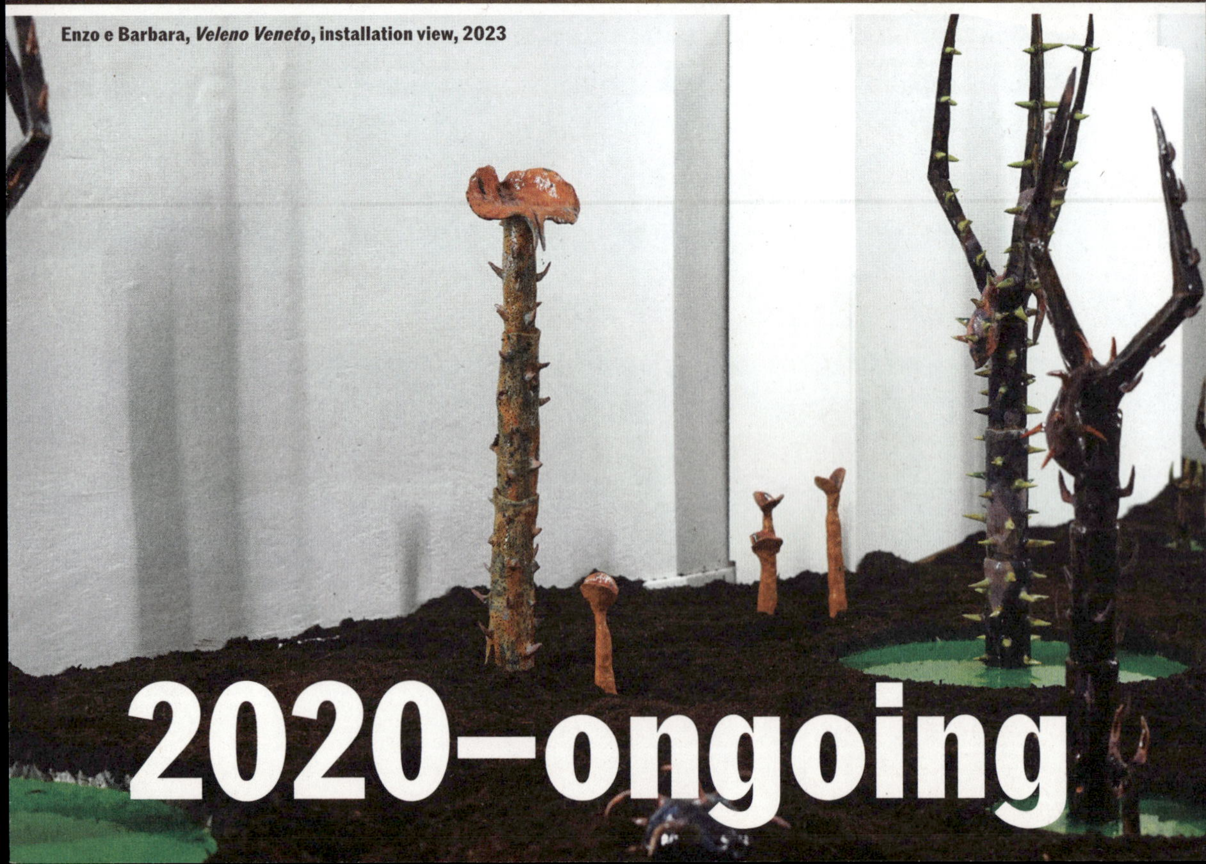

2020–ongoing

Parsec was born in 2020 out of the personal need of the founders to deploy the passions and skills gained during their formative years, convinced of the social value of art as a tool to reflect and discuss the present, from a cultural and political perspective.

Parsec's goal is to bring different perspectives into dialogue, involving local as well as national and international artists. The need to provide a heterogeneous offer influences the cultural programming, which mainly consists of the PARSEC RESIDENCY project and the staging of exhibitions on an annual basis, but is also enriched by other events and activities, such as two festivals focused respectively on the relationship between art and ecology and on the moving image. The curatorial program also consists of workshops, crits (i.e. moments when artists open themselves up to public discussion), talks, and performances. Artists are selected through direct searches, external collaborative proposals and open calls. In all three cases, the curatorial team prefers to collaborate and work directly with the artist involved, favoring content elements to aesthetic ones.

Collaboration with other entities in the area is of fundamental importance, as evidenced by membership to K.I.N. – Keep In Network, a network of independent spaces in Bologna. There is also a close dialogue with the Municipality of Bologna and the neighborhood around the space.

Parsec continues to operate independently, involving local artists and realities, with an awareness of how crucial this kind of approach is to keeping the art system alive by offering a viable alternative to mainstream channels.

ADDRESS Via del Porto 48 c/d, Bologna. FOUNDERS Irene Adorni, Silvia Calderoni, Daria Casadio, Matilde Cassarini, Francesca Dondi, Norina Iezzi, Margo Lengua, Giulia Monte, Arianna Pasini, Judith Inglavaga Pedros, Ginevra Romagnoli

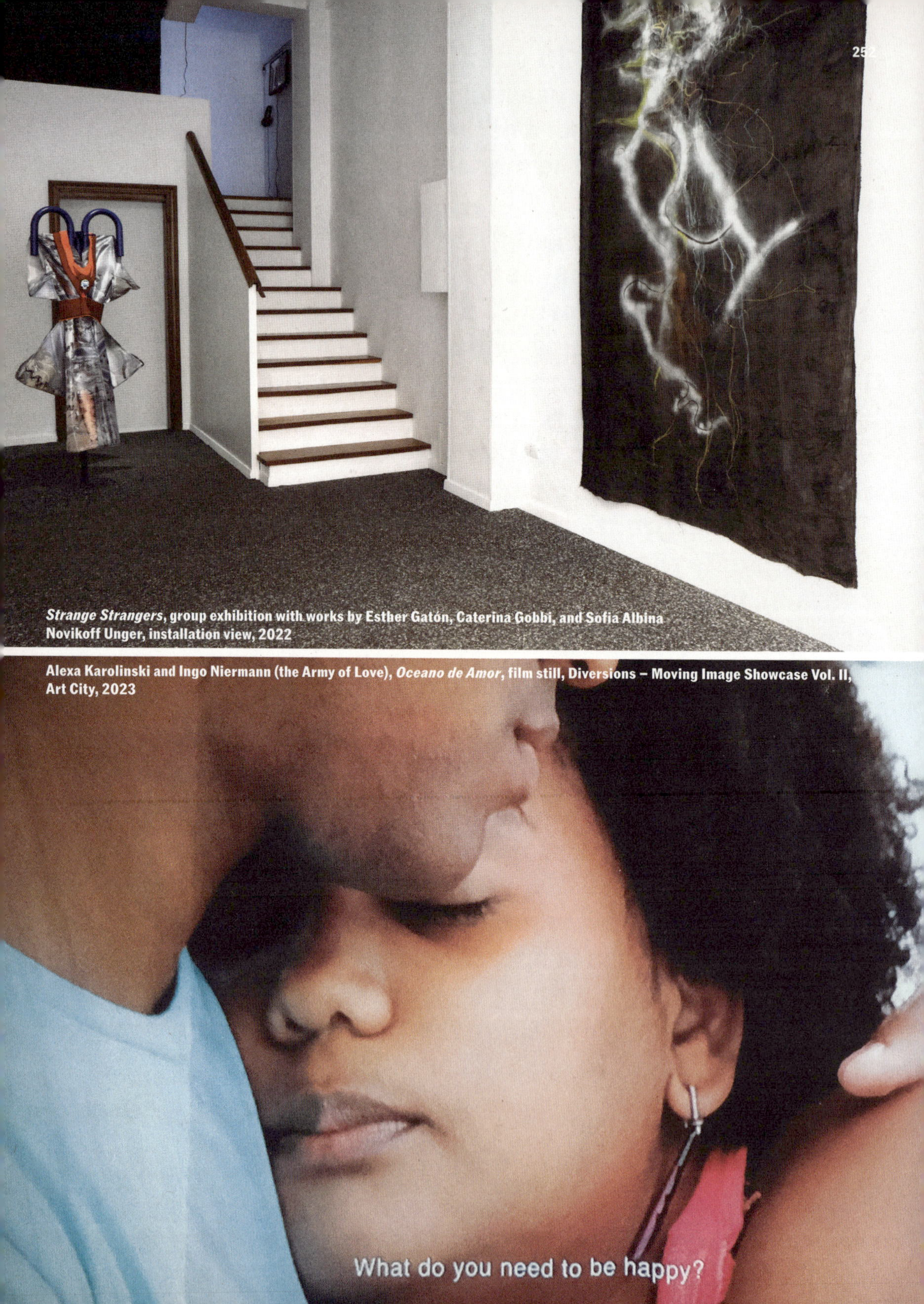

Strange Strangers, group exhibition with works by Esther Gatón, Caterina Gobbi, and Sofia Albina
Novikoff Unger, installation view, 2022

Alexa Karolinski and Ingo Niermann (the Army of Love), *Oceano de Amor*, film still, Diversions – Moving Image Showcase Vol. II,
Art City, 2023

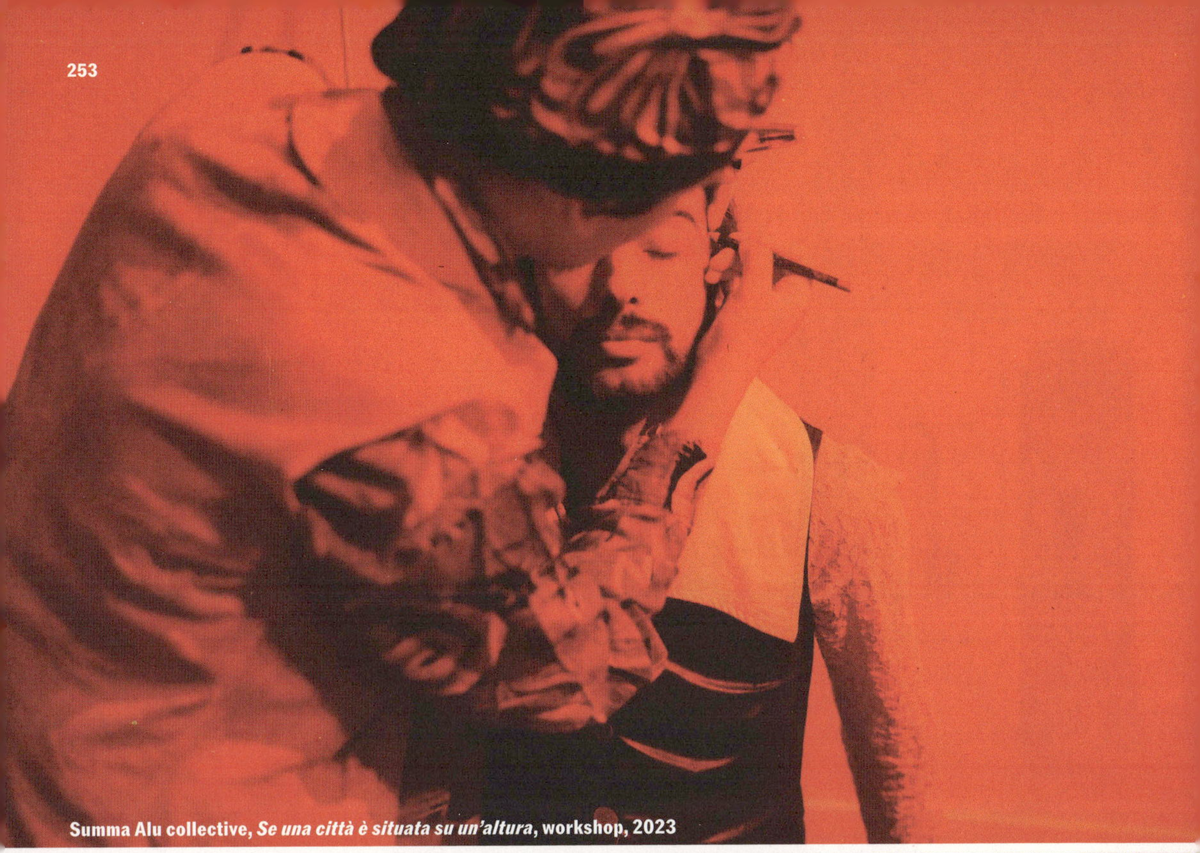

Summma Alu collective, *Se una città è situata su un'altura*, workshop, 2023

Neutopica, *This Manifesto Is A Place To Be*, performance, Terrapolis II – Festival, 2022

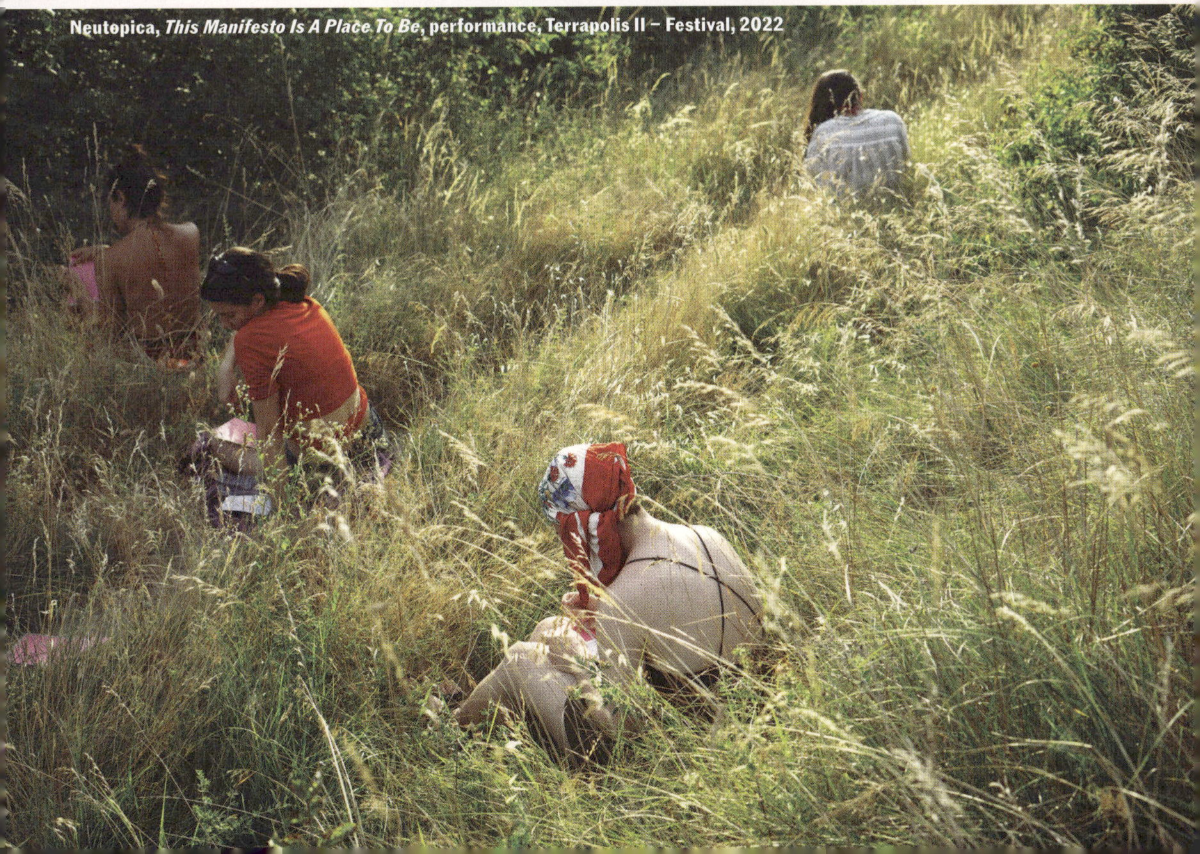

TIST

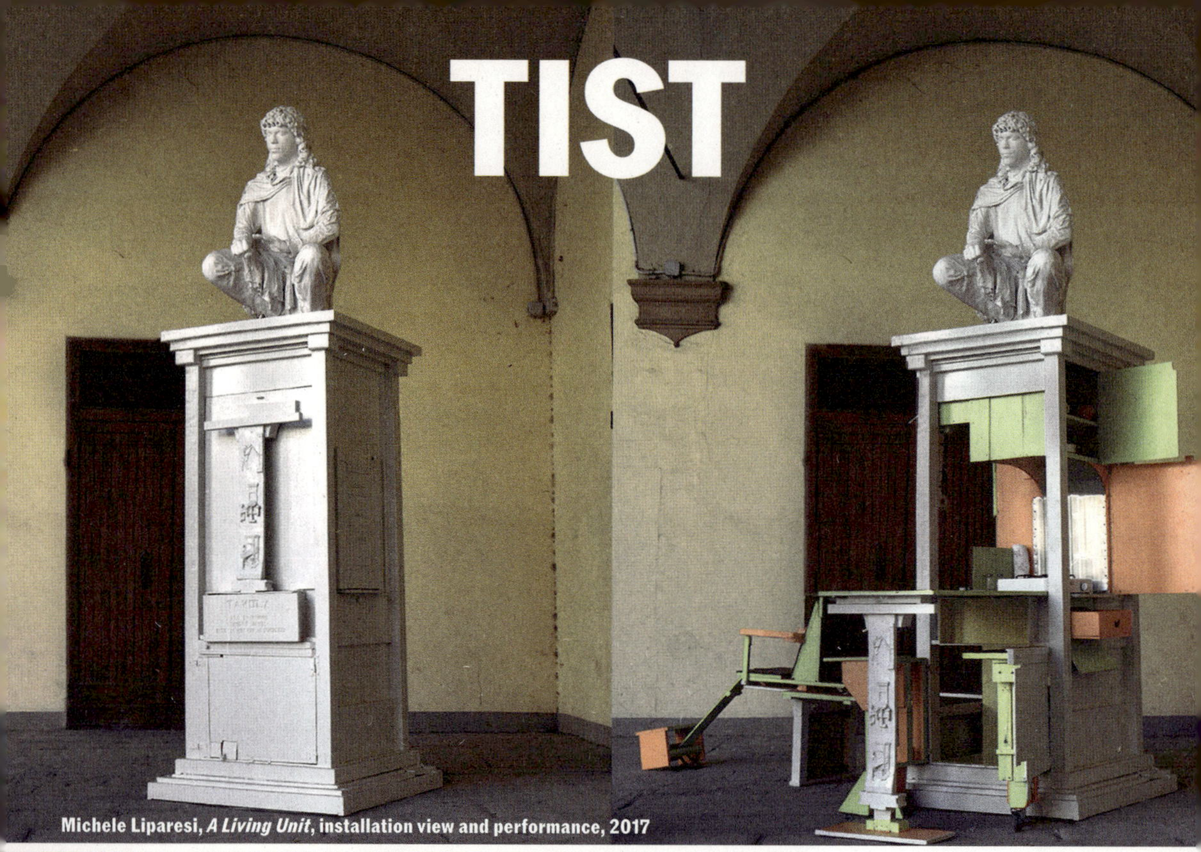

Michele Liparesi, *A Living Unit*, installation view and performance, 2017

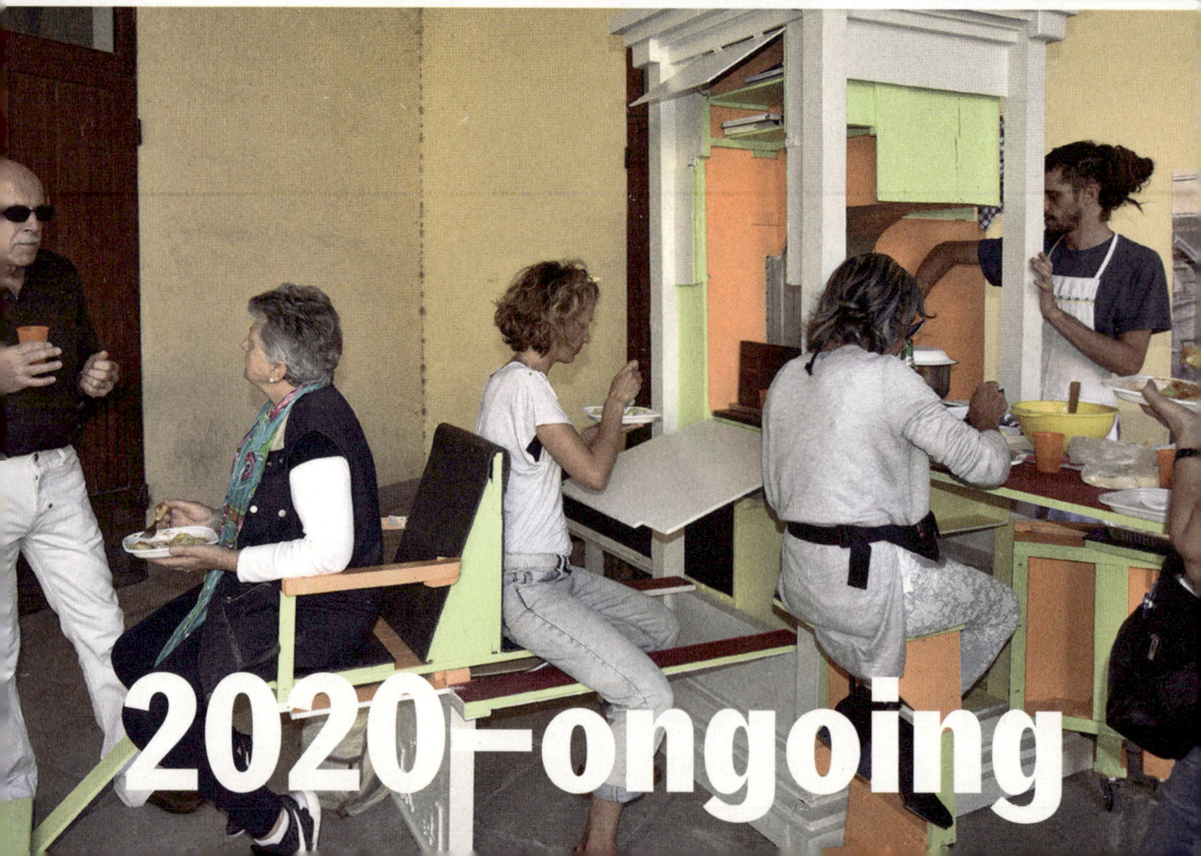

2020–ongoing

TIST – This Is So Temporary was founded in 2020 in response to the Italian government's decision to exclusively support commercial activities during the pandemic: a situation that led the collective founded by Michele Liparesi and Yulia Tikhomirova—soon after joined by Samir Sayed Abdellattef and Enrico Vassallo—to ponder the social and political role of art within contemporary society.

TIST is based in a warehouse in the industrial area of Rastignano, on the immediate outskirts of Bologna, and houses several ateliers, social venues, an indoor and an outdoor exhibition space. Reasoning on projects and the distribution of various tasks takes place during internal meetings and on the basis of horizontal logics.

An element of fundamental importance to TIST is institutional independence, as the collective imagines a different future, in which the art system—the relationships of which it deems to be based on forms of dependency, where art institutions appropriate the work of others—is a thing of the past: being independent therefore also means moving toward the future.

TIST's cultural production consists of a series of exhibition projects and interventions by artists related to the collective, the organization of festivals and the periodical publication of *FARò. Pratiche Estetiche Politiche*. These activities aim to reflect on the intersection between art and politics, considering art as a tool for social transformation. Among the main themes addressed by TIST are anti-monumentality in public space, the construction of collective memory on the basis of recent logics of decolonization—one gaining international momentum yet little practiced in Italy—the impact of the media, and the relationship with the social fabric and surrounding natural area.

ADDRESS Via Vincenzo Bellini 1, Rastignano. FOUNDERS Michele Liparesi, Yulia Tikhomirovax. COLLABORATORS Samir Sayed Abdellattef, Enrico Vassallo

ITALIAN TRANSLATIONS

TRA IMPEGNO POLITICO E SPAZIO DI LIBERTÀ: L'IMPORTANZA DI ESSERE ALTERNATIVI E AUTOGESTITI
Roberto Pinto

Bologna ha ricoperto un ruolo importante nel contesto artistico e culturale dell'Italia post Sessantotto. Nonostante sia solo la settima città italiana per popolazione, è riuscita a colmare alcune delle distanze che la separavano da Roma o Milano attraverso un suo modo peculiare di intervenire in profondità sulle questioni politico-culturali, acquisendo un peso e una visibilità internazionale che altre città italiane non hanno raggiunto. Per raggiungere tale obiettivo, il capoluogo dell'Emilia Romagna si è avvalso dello storico ruolo ricoperto dall'Università che, oltre ad assolvere ai suoi compiti istituzionali, ha funzionato da incubatore all'interno del quale sono nate, o si sono sviluppate, numerose ondate di movimenti antagonisti – nel 1968, ma soprattutto nel 1977 e all'inizio degli anni Novanta – che hanno funto da motori culturali della città. Molti dei promotori degli spazi autogestiti di cui ci stiamo occupando hanno fatto parte di tali movimenti, spesso si sono conosciuti proprio all'interno di essi e si sono aggregati con l'intenzione di costruire una società nuova anche – a volte soprattutto – attraverso la possibilità di lavorare insieme, senza regole imposte dall'alto e con la libertà di affermare sé stessi. Non sono state soltanto la comune militanza politica e la frequentazione del DAMS[1] o dell'Accademia di Belle Arti a spingere i giovani a costruire questa rete culturale alternativa. È importante, infatti, non sottovalutare che tutto il territorio bolognese è stato spesso caratterizzato dall'attenzione all'inclusione sociale e allo sviluppo comunitario, possibili anche grazie a un modello di lavoro e di impresa cooperativo che in questa regione ha avuto inizio già a metà dell'Ottocento[2]. Tale modello, che si avvicina a quello configuratosi in molti degli spazi indipendenti, in questo territorio si è sviluppato in maniera più massiva che in altre parti d'Italia ed è, tuttora, un sistema molto strutturato e capillare.

Un ruolo essenziale per la crescita e lo sviluppo dell'effervescenza culturale che ha caratterizzato la città alla fine del XX secolo è stato quindi svolto dall'azione capillare dell'"associazionismo" o, più in generale, da un lavoro di collaborazione. A partire dall'unione formale in associazioni legalmente costituite, o più semplicemente muovendo da un interesse comune – che spesso rispondeva alla necessità di appropriarsi di luoghi (anche tramite occupazioni illegali di spazi vuoti o temporaneamente non utilizzati)[3] in cui fare non solo politica, ma organizzare concerti, esporre opere, creare spettacoli teatrali – proliferano i centri sociali[4], gli spazi alternativi, le associazioni non-profit e gli *artist-run space*, la vera ossatura della creatività diffusa manifestatasi a Bologna in quegli anni. Non c'è dubbio che il lavoro svolto da questi spazi indipendenti e autogestiti sia stato senz'altro (almeno percentualmente) più importante rispetto a quello che si faceva nel resto d'Italia[5]. Circostanze così peculiari impongono, dunque, di allargare la nostra prospettiva d'analisi per rileggere la situazione artistica italiana di fine Millennio da un punto di vista diverso rispetto alla versione ufficiale che la vorrebbe dominata dall'Arte Povera, dalla Transavanguardia e dalle loro conseguenze. Questa prospettiva mira pertanto a concentrare l'attenzione su un filone di sperimentazione artistica più politico, che, pur transitando solo saltuariamente all'interno del circuito ufficiale di gallerie e musei, ha costruito una storia parallela che è necessario far riemergere[6].

Le proteste politiche – soprattutto post Sessantotto – nate a Bologna sono, dunque, un elemento imprescindibile per capire il ruolo assunto da questi spazi. I movimenti, sviluppatisi nel 1977 nelle scuole e nelle università, si sono presentati con una doppia anima: la prima strettamente politica, strutturata secondo la logica marxista della lotta di classe, e la seconda, altrettanto importante e nel tempo destinata a un successo più ampio, che metteva prioritariamente tra gli obiettivi un'azione politica agita attraverso i media e la cultura. Idea – per alcuni aspetti utopica e condivisa da teorici, artisti e scrittori, basti pensare alle figure di Andrea Pazienza o a Pier Vittorio Tondelli – ancora fortemente radicata nella scena culturale attuale, e basata sulla convinzione che la libertà passasse anche attraverso la trasformazione degli individui, la conquista di una più ampia autonomia personale e la possibilità di seguire i propri desideri. Con queste parole lo spiega Franco "Bifo" Berardi, uno dei protagonisti e dei teorici del movimento, in un libro dall'emblematico titolo *1977 l'anno in cui il futuro cominciò*:

> Il 1977, dunque, può essere descritto come il punto di separazione tra l'epoca industriale e delle grandi formazioni politiche, ideologiche e statali – e quella successiva, l'epoca proliferante delle tecnologie digitali, della diffusione molecolare dei dispositivi trasversali del potere. In questo quadro occorre comprendere anche il rapporto conflittuale tra il movimento e la sinistra tradizionale, che ereditava i suoi rituali e le sue ideologie dalla storia passata dell'epoca industriale. Il distacco poté apparire una delle tante, interminabili dispute dottrinarie e politiche interne al movimento operaio di cui la storia del ventesimo secolo è costellata [...] ma non era così. Non si trattava di una delle discussioni dogmatiche in cui ci si disputava l'egemonia sul movimento comunista, perché il movimento comunista si fondava su premesse che la generazione del '77 liquida nel momento stesso del suo costituirsi in movimento. [...] Immaginazioni schizoidi prendono il posto delle rappresentazioni disciplinari di tipo paranoico: il movimento del '77 non vuole essere ossessionato dalla centralità politica dello stato, del partito, dell'ideologia. Preferisce disperdere la propria attenzione, la propria azione trasformativa,

la propria comunicazione su territori molto più sfrangiati: le forme abitative, le droghe, la sessualità, il rifiuto del lavoro, la sperimentazione di forme lavorative eticamente motivate, la creatività. Per tutte queste ragioni quel movimento sfugge definitivamente alla presa concettuale e politica del movimento operaio terzinternazionalista, sia nella sua variante riformista del PCI, sia nella sua variante rivoluzionario-leninista. Quel movimento non aveva più niente a che fare con quelle vecchie storie[7].

Uno dei simboli di quella stagione è stato anche la nascita delle radio libere, che fioriscono spontaneamente e illegalmente in tutta Italia finché non vengono regolate da un decreto della corte costituzionale del 1976 che sancisce la liberalizzazione dell'etere. Radio Alice[8] è stata sicuramente una delle più attive, anche se le sue trasmissioni sono state diffuse soltanto per poco più di un anno, ed è assurta a simbolo della creatività giovanile, dell'attivismo politico e della rivoluzione musicale di quegli anni[9]. Un vero e proprio social media ante litteram[10], dato che la gente poteva telefonare e interloquire in diretta di tutto ciò che voleva, affrontando temi politici, musicali o, più semplicemente, raccontando i propri problemi o desideri. Radio Alice spesso ha saputo anche raccontare in diretta lo svolgersi di manifestazioni politiche e proteste, e persino gli scontri con la polizia. L'ultima diretta di Radio Alice, prima di una lunga chiusura, fu proprio la testimonianza dal vivo dell'ingresso delle forze dell'ordine nella storica sede in via del Pratello, il 12 marzo 1977, che mise fine alle trasmissioni[11]. La repressione di quei movimenti di piazza, narrata a più voci dall'emittente, segnò in modo evidente il progressivo distanziarsi delle ricerche individuali e creative dalla trama politica, così chiaramente unite prima di quel momento.

Un simile intreccio, politico e culturale, connota in modo preciso il momento storico che stiamo ricostruendo e infatti, gran parte degli spazi e delle comunità che li hanno creati, si sono formati proprio in reazione a quella stagione e alla successiva ondata arrivata all'inizio degli anni Novanta[12].

Spesso, però, tali segnali di protesta e di attività giovanili si sono scontrati con l'incapacità delle istituzioni di comprendere le esigenze e le tante e differenti sensibilità di quella nuova generazione. Le strutture esistenti hanno per lo più ignorato queste nuove forme espressive. Va tuttavia riconosciuto che la tendenza a non lasciare spazio e a non valorizzare i giovani portatori di nuove forme artistiche, non riguarda solo il panorama italiano e non è tipica solo degli ultimi decenni del Novecento. I musei, come le altre istituzioni il cui compito è conservare, tendono a rimanere legati al proprio patrimonio, alle loro collezioni e agli artisti già conosciuti e apprezzati. Molti dei movimenti e degli artisti ora riconosciuti come pietre miliari nella storia dell'arte, facevano fatica a mostrare le proprie opere già nell'Ottocento,

e organizzarono le proprie mostre in spazi alternativi che offrivano loro la libertà di proporre nuove letture. Solo per citare qualche caso possiamo ricordare il Padiglione del Realismo di Courbet (e ci sono esempi anche precedenti), la prima mostra degli Impressionisti nello studio di Nadar, oppure i Salon des Indépendants, creati per evitare le commissioni che selezionavano gli accessi alle altre esibizioni. Solo agli artisti consolidati e accettati dai canali ufficiali era garantito l'ingresso ai palcoscenici più importanti. E la situazione non cambia neanche nel periodo delle avanguardie storiche, come ricorda Amelia Jones sottolineando come anche nell'ambiente newyorkese dadaista venissero privilegiate le letture dominanti:

> In art history this tendency to privilege the cultural "victors"—those artists whose reputation has already been solidified or whose work in one way or another serves the purposes of the discourses that comprise the discipline and its institutional support structures (including the university, the museum, and the art market)—is even more striking, perhaps because of the strong ties between the discipline and the art market's penchant for, and commodification of, "unique" objects that seem inexorably to point to "unique" subjects as their makers and origins. In a mutually sustaining circuit of value, the art market and its institutional corollaries, the art gallery and museum, draw on the insights of art-historical scholarship and art-critical writing to legitimate the value (economic and otherwise) of the objects they display, which in turn are the "object" of art history's narratives of progress and critique[13].

Certamente, come ricordavamo, l'attivismo culturale nasce non soltanto contro un sistema dell'arte troppo "accademico" o troppo mercantile, ma, soprattutto, come ricerca di uno spazio di libertà politico-sociale in cui abbandonare i vecchi modelli da seguire, le regole da rispettare, i concetti tradizionali da conservare, per poter sperimentare liberamente anche mettendo in crisi l'idea tradizionale di autore e di opera[14]. Che l'importanza degli spazi indipendenti in Italia, e a Bologna in particolare, sia stata molto maggiore rispetto alla percezione che se ne aveva sul finire del Novecento, lo si deduce da quanto poco è stato scritto sulla loro attività[15] e su quanto ancora rimane da fare per valorizzare non soltanto il loro ruolo ma anche tutta la sperimentazione che è passata nelle loro sale. Al contrario, la centralità della loro funzione, legata certamente a uno stretto rapporto con i processi democratici di una cultura costruita dal basso, negli Stati Uniti è testimoniata da numerosi scritti al riguardo e persino da mostre come *Cultural Economies: Histories from the Alternative Arts Movement, NYC*, curata da Julie Ault presso uno dei più importanti spazi indipendenti newyorkesi, The Drawing Center[16]. Proprio in occasione di questo evento l'artista e teorica americana ha avuto modo di spiegare:

> Invention and reinvention are always possible, despite the Right, despite the culture wars, despite temporarily curtailed government funding, despite the stealthy and speedy privatization of the public realm. Looking back, and ahead, at the tremendously rich environment of structures, venues, support, and community produced by initiatives answering (or not) to the name alternative, one finds infinite exemplary acts and art. The result is countless models for practices that try to, and in some instances do, effectively transcend and challenge the established system. The individuals who come together around ideas of cultural democracy, working experimentally and taking risks, offer examples for others to emulate and improve on.

Commento che potremmo calare perfettamente per la descrizione di quegli anni di ricerca a Bologna.

Rimanendo in Europa, per studiare l'impatto dei nuovi centri autonomi, nella maggior parte dei casi gestiti da artisti, vale la pena di citare "The Glasgow Miracle" denominazione usata da Hans Ulrich Obrist per sottolineare l'importanza ricoperta da un sistema che vedeva la Transmission Gallery come esempio per i centri di ricerca e di produzione[17]. Ma, forse più di ogni altra città in Europa, è stata Berlino, soprattutto a partire dagli anni immediatamente successivi alla caduta del muro e alla riunificazione della Germania, a riconoscere la centralità degli spazi indipendenti. L'identità consolidatasi a Berlino Ovest durante la Guerra Fredda, quale luogo privilegiato di incontro e di ritrovo delle realtà giovanili e delle sperimentazioni artistiche, si estende immediatamente dopo il 1989 anche alla Berlino ex-Est. Numerosi sono gli spazi e gli episodi significativi, il più eclatante dei quali prende le mosse dalla mostra di Klaus Biesenbach *Berlin 37 Räume*[18], realizzata nel 1992 con la collaborazione del Kunst-Werke Institute for Contemporary Art (da lui co-fondato l'anno precedente)[19]. Proprio il Kunst-Werke, infatti, nato come una occupazione di spazi abbandonati, dal 1998 diventa anche sede della Berlin Biennale, che nel tempo si è guadagnata un ruolo importante nella programmazione internazionale. A Berlino e Glasgow, dunque, al contrario di quanto accaduto in Italia, piccole realtà autogestite come quelle appena citate, in virtù del loro innegabile ruolo pubblico e di servizio per la città (e non soltanto), sono state aiutate a crescere con l'apporto diretto o indiretto delle istituzioni locali che ne hanno colto le potenzialità e hanno dato loro fiducia e supporto. Parliamo certamente di un sistema culturalmente ed economicamente diverso, ma in Italia, al contrario, i centri indipendenti sono stati tutt'al più tollerati e quasi mai aiutati.

In generale in Italia, nel secondo dopoguerra, l'arte contemporanea ha avuto uno sviluppo più lento rispetto ad altri Paesi europei. Sotto il profilo della produzione artistica – pensando ad Alberto Burri e Lucio Fontana, all'Arte Povera o a fenomeni internazionali come Maurizio Cattelan – abbiamo senza dubbio registrato presenze importanti, ma i nostri artisti hanno avuto più difficoltà ad essere riconosciuti e sostenuti rispetto ai loro colleghi europei. Analogo discorso si potrebbe fare per il mercato dell'arte: spesso i collezionisti italiani, da Giuseppe Panza di Biumo a Miuccia Prada, da Giuliana e Tommaso Setari ad Achille Maramotti, hanno avuto una funzione importante nel sostegno delle ricerche più attuali; e le gallerie, come Massimo De Carlo o Continua, negli ultimi decenni sono state in grado di aprire sedi in altri centri nevralgici per il commercio dell'arte come Londra, Parigi, Hong Kong o Shanghai. Se però concentriamo la riflessione sul ruolo culturale, politico e sociale che l'arte ha assunto nella società, dobbiamo convenire che è stato quasi irrilevante. Il problema principale, segnalato da tutti gli operatori del settore, è legato alla mancanza (o alla scarsità) di investimenti pubblici destinati a sostenere l'attività di musei e spazi espositivi e a commissionare progetti di arte negli spazi pubblici, nelle strade o nelle piazze. Il risultato della cronica mancanza di finanziamenti ha comportato una serie di conseguenze dirette e indirette. Tale politica, infatti, è responsabile non solo dell'assenza di una rete di istituzioni e della limitata possibilità di programmazione dei pochi spazi espositivi e museali esistenti, ma anche dello scarso e intermittente interesse che il pubblico ha rivolto a questa attività. Persino il dibattito culturale, in un mondo in cui il ruolo delle immagini si è fatto sempre più importante, ha costantemente ignorato lo sviluppo delle ricerche artistiche e del discorso critico a esse legato, anche per una sostanziale mancanza di occasioni in cui presentare tali investigazioni.

Nonostante l'importantissimo ruolo assunto dalla Biennale di Venezia e, pur in maniera minore, dalla Triennale di Milano e dalla Quadriennale di Roma, i musei italiani dedicati al contemporaneo sono pochi e finanziati meno rispetto a quelli di altri Paesi europei. La Galleria Nazionale di Arte Moderna a Roma, nata – come la Biennale – alla fine dell'Ottocento, è stata per lungo tempo l'unica istituzione per continuità e ruolo dedicata alle esperienze artistiche recenti[20], ma la sua rilevanza internazionale è tuttora molto marginale rispetto agli altri grandi musei pubblici o privati[21] europei. L'apertura negli anni Ottanta del Castello di Rivoli e, successivamente, del Centro Pecci di Prato[22] sono stati fenomeni isolati e anche il sistema delle Gallerie Civiche, ovvero di spazi per l'arte legati e supportati dalle singole città, raramente ha fornito programmi interessanti e internazionali.

Solo nel 2010, il 28 maggio, è stato aperto il MAXXI – Museo nazionale delle arti del XXI secolo, e tale inaugurazione è sicuramente da annoverare come sforzo per de-provincializzare la situazione italiana: con un edificio progettato dall'archistar Zaha Hadid, dedicato all'arte e all'architettura, nei primi dieci anni di funzionamento ha visto la presenza complessiva di 3.328.000 visitatori[23], più o meno il flusso annuale di pubblico della Tate Modern o del Centre Pompidou. Il costante aumento degli spettatori negli anni rimarca quanto sia importante (anche per la ricaduta qualitativa nella produzione artistica) che si creino luoghi di conoscenza e sperimentazione. Anche solo, paradossalmente, per avere qualcosa su cui discutere o criticare. Per tutte queste ragioni e perché l'offerta espositiva italiana di fine Novecento era presentata nell'ambito delle gallerie private, l'arte (e gli artisti) di cui le riviste si sono occupate era soprattutto quella che il mercato dell'arte veicolava, che negli anni Ottanta e (in parte) Novanta, riguardava soprattutto la pittura, penalizzando le sperimentazioni che producevano poco dal punto di vista mercantile, e che erano spesso legate a una critica della mercificazione dell'arte.

Il ricco patrimonio artistico-culturale italiano quindi, quello che ogni governo in carica afferma di voler valorizzare, non ha mai fatto da volano per investimenti in questo settore; piuttosto, a livello ministeriale (e più in generale pubblico), la mancanza di fondi sufficienti per conservare il patrimonio archeologico e artistico esistente è stato l'argomento ricorrente per giustificare un sostanziale disinteresse nei confronti dell'arte contemporanea, che è rimasta a lungo senza supporto, priva di istituzioni e con una scarsa legittimazione nei contesti scolastici o universitari.

Ne consegue che il sistema artistico bolognese, così come quello italiano, si è dovuto costruire, almeno inizialmente, su una struttura decisamente asimmetrica e su una solida base fatta di gallerie private. Negli anni Ottanta, infatti, in giro per l'Italia aprono un gruppo di gallerie molto più agguerrite e attente alle nuove produzioni. Soprattutto Milano svolge un ruolo centrale nel lancio di una nuova generazione artistica che, dopo le sperimentazioni degli anni Sessanta (in cui spiccano le attività di Galleria Notizie a Torino e Sargentini a Roma), manca di punti di riferimento. A Milano nascono dunque gallerie che spostano l'attenzione generale verso forme d'arte più attuali e internazionali: accanto alle storiche Studio Marconi, e Diagramma di Luciano Inga Pin, aprono realtà quali Le Case d'Arte, Studio Casoli, Massimo De Carlo, Studio Guenzani, Fac Simile, a cui si successivamente si aggiungono gli spazi di Emi Fontana e Raffaella Cortese che rendono la struttura di gallerie milanese uno dei sistemi europei più importanti in tal senso. Anche a Bologna si registra un analogo crescente interesse: accanto alla Galleria de' Foscherari, nata nel 1962, sorgono a partire dagli anni Settanta numerosi altri spazi commerciali, come lo Studio G7, che tuttavia non sempre raggiungono la fortuna commerciale e la notorietà dei corrispettivi milanesi. Dal 1974, anche grazie alla spinta di Arte Fiera[24], si registra un'attenzione crescente nei confronti delle nuove forme artistiche. La fiera, oltre a essere un momento topico per il mercato, ha dunque svolto un ruolo importante per ridurre il gap informativo con l'estero e per configurarsi come luogo di confronto per l'Italia, anche attraverso una serie di eventi collaterali, quali per esempio le Settimane internazionali della performance[25] – con interventi, tra gli altri, di Marina Abramović e Ulay, Hermann Nitsch, Vito Acconci – nate in collaborazione con la Galleria Civica, che in gran parte le ospitava.

Nonostante la relativa effervescenza, anche se episodica, in questo panorama hanno fatto molta fatica a emergere esperienze legate alla performatività, all'arte relazionale, alle sperimentazioni digitali, a tutti quei territori di confine tra danza, musica, video, teatro e arti visive. In altre parole, ciò che non rientrava nella macro categoria "oggetti" – da produrre, esporre, vendere e conservare – non era quasi mai esposto in musei e gallerie, e tali sperimentazioni diventavano raramente tema di dibattito critico. I tanti spazi bolognesi che si sono sviluppati nel tempo, come per esempio neon, hanno sicuramente aperto le loro porte ai giovani – come Maurizio Cattelan o Eva Marisaldi che vi hanno fatto le loro prime personali – che non erano interessati soltanto a realizzare opere tradizionalmente intese. Del tutto simile era la situazione per quanto riguarda le contaminazioni tra arti visive e performative, che hanno trovato in Link Project, con il suo sguardo rivolto anche verso le tecnologie innovative, uno dei più importanti centri non solo a livello italiano, ma internazionale.

Accanto a questa modalità di costruzione di realtà indipendenti, più votate alla produzione e all'esposizione, va notato anche lo sviluppo parallelo di spazi (come pure di associazioni e di istituzioni) che hanno concentrato la loro attenzione sulla necessità di aiutare la mobilità artistica, e si sono pertanto dedicati a favorirla tramite spazi indipendenti deputati a configurarsi come residenze temporanee per artisti[26]. Nosadella.due è stato forse il luogo più attivo sotto questo punto di vista, contraddistinguendosi come centro di scambio per la mobilità internazionale degli artisti e per le nuove produzioni, che l'hanno reso uno dei nodi italiani di una rete molto ampia. Inoltre, non bisogna dimenticarlo, soprattutto se si pensa all'eredità dei movimenti del Settantasette, ci sono luoghi che hanno usato le loro energie e i loro spazi per costruire un'altra visione politica e una cultura più inclusiva e aperta, come il Cassero, che dal 1982 è un "circolo politico che si batte per il riconoscimento dei diritti delle persone LGBTQIA+"[27] in cui trovano cittadinanza laboratori, rassegne artistiche e attività di aggregazione sociale. Il modello culturale e politico che l'insieme di questi spazi ha offerto è stato fatto proprio dalla nuova generazione. Molte di queste attività sono, infatti, ancora in essere e i loro frutti hanno germinato in altri spazi indipendenti che abbracciano ideali e pratiche simili: ne è un esempio K.I.N.[28] un network di realtà indipendenti nato nel 2021 che permette di creare sinergie tra tredici diversi spazi artistici bolognesi.

Il grande fermento, al contempo sociale e culturale, di questi luoghi alternativi ha promosso quindi un attivo disordine[29] rispetto al sistema dell'arte e della cultura ufficiali, e ha anche portato all'elaborazione di proposte politiche e sociali alternative alla monolitica strutturazione imposta dai sistemi convenzionali di gestione della cultura. Proprio in virtù del fatto che queste realtà si fondano sul principio della collaborazione e della partecipazione, la loro programmazione non è stata sempre regolare e la gestione economica non ha avuto un modello collaudato: nella maggior parte dei casi questi spazi sono diventati strutture flessibili, in grado di trasformarsi secondo le esigenze dei singoli progetti o delle mutate condizioni. In questi luoghi le gerarchie sono dettate dalle esigenze e i ruoli possono essere facilmente mescolati tra loro: un artista può improvvisarsi curatore (o anche redattore, organizzatore, ecc.) e, viceversa, chiunque può partecipare attivamente ai processi creativi di opere e azioni che di abitudine erano di pertinenza esclusiva dell'artista. Finanche il ruolo dello spettatore può mutare in quello di partecipante attivo e talvolta anche di attivista. In sintesi, quella degli spazi indipendenti, è una storia che inaugura una forma (e una concezione) dell'arte più che mai attuale. L'ultima edizione di documenta[30], curata dal collettivo ruangrupa, indirettamente testimonia la sua importanza e attualità.

1   Il corso DAMS è nato agli inizi degli anni Settanta con l'intenzione di intercettare la necessità da parte delle giovani generazioni di approfondire gli studi sulle arti, la musica e lo spettacolo. Si veda Claudio Marra, Arianna Casarini, *NO DAMS. 50 anni del corso di laurea in discipline delle arti, della musica e dello spettacolo*, Pendragon, Bologna 2021.

2   Si veda https://www.legacoopemiliaromagna.coop/storia-e-valori/.

3   Una ricerca storico-critica sull'arte che oltrepassa i limiti delle vigenti normative è stata realizzata da Rebecca Zorach (a cura di), *Art Against the Law*, School of the Art Institute of Chicago, Chicago 2014, volume uscito all'interno della collana "Chicago Social Practice History Series" curata da Mary Jane Jacob e Kate Zeller.

4   Una serie di storie sui e intorno ai centri sociali si possono trovare in Serafino D'Onofrio e Valerio Monteventi, *Berretta Rossa. Storie di Bologna attraverso i centri sociali*, Pendragon, Bologna 2011.

5   Per approfondire sulla diffusione di pratiche partecipative a Bologna si veda Roberta Paltrinieri, Giulia Allegrini, *Partecipazione, processi di immaginazione civica e sfera pubblica. I laboratori di quartiere e il bilancio partecipativo a Bologna*, Franco Angeli, Milano 2020; e il successivo Roberta Paltrinieri (a cura di), *Culture e pratiche di partecipazione. Collaborazione civica, rigenerazione urbana e costruzione di comunità*, Franco Angeli, Milano 2020.

6   In questo senso sono numerosi i tentativi per ricostruire la scena più nascosta dell'arte contemporanea italiana. Tra gli altri segnalo Cecilia Guida, *Spatial Practices. Funzione pubblica e politica delle arti nella società delle reti*, Franco Angeli, Milano 2012; Emanuele Rinaldo Meschini, *Comunità, spazio, monumento. Ricontestualizzazione delle pratiche artistiche nella sfera urbana*, Mimesis, Milano 2021; Jacopo Galimberti, *Immagini di classe. Operaismo, Autonomia e produzione artistica*, DeriveApprodi, Roma 2023; ma anche la mostra e il relativo catalogo Lara Conte e Francesca Gallo (a cura di), *Territori della performance: percorsi e pratiche in Italia (1967-1982)*, Roma: MAXXI, 21 ottobre 2022–11 giugno 2023.

7   Franco "Bifo" Berardi e Veronica Bridi (a cura di), *1977 l'anno in cui il futuro cominciò*, Fandango Libri, Roma 2002, p. 24–25; si veda anche Franco "Bifo" Berardi, *Dell'innocenza. 1977*, Ombre Corte, Verona 1997.

8   Quanto sia importante nell'immaginario comune il ruolo svolto da questa radio, quasi un elemento fondativo di un certo modo di fare azione politica e culturale, lo si può evincere dal fatto che ci sono ben due film di fiction e un documentario il cui intreccio narrativo ruota attorno a Radio Alice. Nel 1991 Renato De Maria gira *Il trasloco*; nel 2002 Guido Chiesa realizza il documentario *Alice è in Paradiso*, e a distanza di due anni torna sull'argomento (con un copione scritto assieme al gruppo Wu Ming) con il film *Lavorare con lentezza. Radio Alice 100.6 MHz.*

9   Per le vicende musicali di Bologna (e in parte di Radio Alice) si veda Oderso Rubini e Andrea Tinti (a cura di), *Non Disperdetevi. 1977–1982. San Francisco, New York, Bologna, le città libere del mondo*, Shake edizioni, Milano 2009.

10 Franco "Bifo" Berardi, nell'introduzione a *Skizomedia. Trent'anni di mediattivismo*, DeriveApprodi, Roma 2006, spiega che "La diretta telefonica, come la usavano le radio libere di quegli anni, fu un'anticipazione del modello reticolare: perciò l'esplosione di internet all'inizio degli anni Novanta non mi colse impreparato" (p. 3).

11 La Radio rimase chiusa per circa un mese e fu poi riaperta senza l'apporto dei fondatori alle prese con l'accusa, poi rivelatasi infondata, di avere diretto i violenti scontri del giorno prima, conseguenti l'uccisione di uno studente, Francesco Lo Russo, morto durante uno scontro con i Carabinieri. Per una bibliografia su Radio Alice si veda https://www.radioalice.org/libri.

12 Molte testimonianze al riguardo (anche se prevalentemente nel campo musicale) sono raccolte in Rubini, Tinti, *Non Disperdetevi*, che si occupa prevalentemente della fine degli anni Settanta; per quanto riguarda il movimento studentesco della Pantera nato nel 1989 si veda Luciano Nadalini, *La Pantera a Bologna*, Agalev, Bologna 1990.

13 Amelia Jones, "New York Dada: Beyond the Readymade" in Leah Dickerman (a cura di), *The Dada Seminars*, The National Gallery, Washington 2005.

14 Ricordo che Umberto Eco, insegnante del DAMS, aveva da poco scritto *Opera Aperta. Forma e indeterminazione nelle poetiche contemporanee*, Bompiani, Milano 1962.

15 Per approfondire la storia del ruolo degli spazi non-profit milanesi si veda Patrizia Brusarosco e Milovan Farronato, *Souvenir d'Italie. A Nonprofit Art Story*, Mousse Publishing, Milano 2010.

16 La mostra si è tenuta nella sede di Wooster Street dal 24 febbraio al 6 aprile del 1996. Per l'occasione è stato anche stampato un catalogo a cura di Julie Ault in collaborazione con il magazine *Real Life*.

17 Si vedano: https://www.transmissiongallery.org/about; Hans Ulrich Obrist, "Ars (Artist Run Spaces)" in *…dontstopdontstopdontstopdontstop* (2006), Postmedia Books, Milano 2010, p. 20–21.

18 La mostra è stata allestita per una solo settimana (dal 14 al 21 giugno del 1992) in trentasette diverse case in Augustenstrasse, con la collaborazione di 31 diversi curatori. Si veda Klaus Biesenbach, *Berlin 37 Räume*, Graetz, Berlino 1992.

19 Il Kunst-Werke Berlin, è stato fondato da Klaus Biesenbach, Alexandra Binswanger, Clemens

Homburger, Philipp von Doering e Alfonso Rutigliano in una ex fabbrica in disuso, all'inizio degli anni Novanta.

20 Sul sito ufficiale del museo è ancora rivendicata la sua unicità nel panorama: "Si tratta dell'unico museo nazionale dedicato interamente all'arte moderna e contemporanea", https://lagallerianazionale.com/museo.

21 I visitatori della Galleria Nazionale nel 2021 sono stati, anche a causa della pandemia, 81.021; nel 2019 sono stati 190.604, di cui 88.676 paganti, http://www.statistica.beniculturali.it/rilevazioni/musei/Anno%202021/MUSEI_TAVOLA9_2021.pdf; http://www.statistica.beniculturali.it/rilevazioni/musei/Anno%202019/MUSEI_TAVOLA9_2019.pdf. I confronti con le istituzioni straniere sono impietosi – sia Tate Modern, sia Centre Pompidou viaggiano, non contando gli anni della pandemia, costantemente sopra i tre milioni di presenze annue – ma è chiaro che una valutazione comparativa avrebbe bisogno anche di un confronto tra le cifre investite in queste istituzioni dagli enti governativi.

22 Aprono rispettivamente nel 1984 e nel 1988.

23 I dati sono stati forniti dall'allora Ministro della Cultura Dario Franceschini e dalla Presidente della Fondazione MAXXI, Giovanna Melandri nel corso di una conferenza stampa celebrativa.

24 Arte Fiera Bologna è stata la prima fiera d'arte moderna e contemporanea in Italia e tra le prime in Europa. Inaugura infatti nel 1974, subito dopo quelle di Colonia (1967) e Basilea (1970).

25 Si veda Uliana Zanetti (a cura di), *La performance a Bologna negli anni '70*, Edizioni MAMbo, Bologna 2023.

26 Su questo argomento si veda Taru Elfving, Irmeli Kokko, Pascal Gielen (a cura di), *Contemporary Artist Residencies. Reclaiming Time and Space*, Valiz, Amsterdam 2019. Mentre, in ambito italiano, segnalo Caterina Angelucci e Giulio Verago (a cura di), *Endless Residency. Un osservatorio sulla mobilità artistica*, Postmedia Books, Milano 2023.

27 "La nostra storia inizia sullo sfondo dei moti studenteschi del '77, quando i movimenti di liberazione omosessuale cominciano a spogliare l'omosessualità delle etichette forzatamente imposte di vizio elitario, sensibilità e artisticità a tutti i costi", https://cassero.it/chi-siamo/.

28 https://keepinnetwork.com.

29 Si veda Richard Sennett, *The Uses of Disorder: Personal Identity & City Life*, Knopf, New York, 1970 (trad. it. *Usi del disordine. Identità personale e vita nella metropoli*, Costa & Nolan, Milano, 1999); e Pablo Sendra e Richard Sennett, *Progettare il disordine, Idee per la città del XXI secolo*, Treccani, Roma 2022, in cui il sociologo americano aggiunge: "Il bello del vivere in città è che sei libero e non più controllato da un *nomos,* una cultura del corretto comportamento. Preferisco che in strada ci siano più persone a fare casino che non occhi per controllarle. È un'esperienza molto diversa di corpo collettivo. Il primo ordina, il secondo riunisce. Se c'era qualcosa di originale nel mio libro, era la proposta di radunare le persone, non importa di quanto fossero indisciplinate nei loro raduni" (p. 163).

30 ruangrupa (a cura di), *documenta fifteen*, Hatje Cantz, Berlino 2022.

MODELLO BOLOGNA:
GLI SPAZI ALTERNATIVI PER L'ARTE COME LABORATORI DI INTERDISCIPLINARITÀ E PROFESSIONALIZZAZIONE
Francesco Spampinato

> "Someone's got a question but there's
> Nothing left to do [...]
> The Skank Bloc Bologna keeping us all alive
> Something in Italy [...]
> Now they're livin' on a notion and
> They're working on a hope
> A Euro vision and a skank in scope"[1]
>
> Scritti Politti, "Skank Bloc Bologna", 1978

Brano fondativo del post-punk inglese, "Skank Bloc Bologna" è anche tra i più esemplificativi omaggi con cui, durante gli anni Settanta, intellettuali e artisti da tutto il mondo hanno decantato Bologna come laboratorio di agitazione politica e innovazione culturale. La band che lo ha composto, gli Scritti Politti, un gruppo di militanti marxisti e studenti d'arte presso il Politecnico di Leeds, prese il nome dagli *Scritti Politici* (1967) di Antonio Gramsci, storpiandone il titolo. Un altro esempio, nello stesso periodo, è il numero speciale di *Semiotext(e)* dedicato ad "Autonomia" (1980) che conferma l'infatuazione, in questo caso della comunità artistica di Downtown New York, per Bologna come epicentro del Movimento del '77. Renato Zangheri, che come sindaco di Bologna dal 1970 al 1983 ne ha consolidato l'immagine di una città progressista, ha dichiarato come Bologna fosse, in effetti, "esemplare della esperienza di un governo comunista in Occidente [...] un banco di prova di molte idee, dei partiti, delle istituzioni, e anche degli individui"[2].

Lo spirito di quella Bologna, che i nostalgici decretano come ormai perduta e in parte dimenticata, continua ad aleggiare anche alla soglia di questo primo quarto di nuovo secolo, sotto i portici del centro come nei quartieri di periferia, nei progetti di rigenerazione urbana e negli ingranaggi di una comunità umana che, pur sedotta dalle logiche globali di automazione e virtualità – come dimostra la presenza di eccellenti industrie nei settori del packaging e dei motori, nonché di uno dei cinque più potenti supercomputer al mondo – riconosce ancora il valore dell'andare con lentezza, della prossimità e dello scambio. Di questo spirito sono incarnazione gli spazi artistici alternativi che hanno proliferato a Bologna dalla fine degli anni Settanta, un fenomeno che qui ha assunto proporzioni e caratteri talmente peculiari da consentirci di parlare di un "modello Bologna". Il presente volume mira a ricostruire una sommaria genealogia di questo fenomeno, passando per punti – ovvero spazi – salienti, ricostruendo microstorie e macroreti, restituendo dati, forzando porte e scoperchiando vasi colmi di preziosi documenti visivi.

Riprendendo una definizione tentata da Julie Ault, co-fondatrice del collettivo statunitense Group Material, in un'antologia che esplora il fenomeno degli spazi alternativi a New York dagli anni Sessanta agli Ottanta, queste:

> alternative enterprises shape and position themselves in relation to that for which they are an alternative: on understanding the relationships and interdependencies between profit and non-profit sectors of the cultural economy, how "mainstream" and "alternative" determine and influence one another, and how they blend[3].

Più in generale, per spazi alternativi per l'arte si intendono quegli spazi indipendenti dalle istituzioni e dal mercato, il più delle volte avviati e gestiti da artisti, che si configurano come luoghi di sperimentazione interdisciplinare, ma anche come spazi liberati in cui è possibile, attraverso le arti, ridefinire codici identitari, sociali e culturali. Un fenomeno, questo, le cui origini risalgono all'avvento della modernità, ma che si consolida durante il Novecento nel solco delle avanguardie, delle sottoculture e delle controculture, della critica istituzionale e delle varie forme di arte politica, relazionale, partecipativa e pedagogica.

In questa parabola, che si estende dal Cabaret Voltaire di Zurigo, dove nel 1916 nasce Dada, agli spazi nomadi avviati dagli anni Duemila dal collettivo ruangrupa, da Giacarta a documenta fifteen, un momento decisivo sono gli anni Sessanta. In questo decennio si manifestano i primi segnali di crisi della democrazia rappresentativa, di pari passo con quello che Jean-François Lyotard ha definito un crollo di fede nei confronti delle grandi narrazioni del passato, ovvero l'avvento del postmodernismo[4]. Gli spazi artistici alternativi, pertanto, non sono altro che un sintomo di un processo molto più vasto, di ribilanciamento degli equilibri interni alla società postindustriale. Giocano, però, un ruolo decisivo in quanto, se è vero che le arti esercitano una profonda influenza sul piano dell'immaginario, ovvero hanno il potere di suggerire cambi di prospettiva e prefigurare trasformazioni, in questi spazi le arti danno forma a istanze e soggettività che si pongono in alternativa alla società "ufficiale" e che, in qualche modo, ne rappresentano un tangibile ribaltamento.

In termini topografici, per mappare questi spazi si potrebbero richiamare l'immaginaria isola di *Utopia* (1516) di Thomas More, la psicogeografia situazionista, le micronazioni e tutti quei luoghi fittizi che stimolano l'umanità a immaginare che potrebbero esistere luoghi ideali: giusti, pacifici, democratici. Per restare legati all'epoca in cui il fenomeno degli spazi alternativi prende consistenza, invece, delle corrispondenze si potranno rintracciare con alcune metafore filosofiche proposte nell'alveo dello strutturalismo, come il concetto di "piega" di Gilles Deleuze[5], intesa come indefinita zona d'ombra, ma ancor di più quello di "eterotopia" di Michel Foucault che si riferisce a "delle specie di contro-spazi, delle specie di utopie effettivamente realizzate in cui gli spazi reali [...] sono, al contempo, rappresentati, contestati e rovesciati, delle specie di luoghi che stanno al di fuori di tutti i luoghi, anche se sono effettivamente localizzabili"[6]. Così come gli spazi alternativi per l'arte, luoghi sì, forse utopici, ma rispondenti a precisi numeri civici.

In cosa consiste, dunque, il "modello Bologna" se non innanzitutto nella sua stretta relazione con il tessuto sociale e culturale della città in cui ha preso forma? Alcuni caratteri fondamentali del fenomeno, inevitabilmente, sono comuni agli spazi artistici alternativi *tout court*: l'inclusività, l'interdisciplinarità, l'indipendenza. Quello che contraddistingue la storia degli spazi bolognesi, semmai, è che hanno elaborato modelli di professionalizzazione *bottom up* nei più svariati settori delle arti, dello spettacolo e della comunicazione, a volte in sinergia con le istituzioni e l'amministrazione locale, ma senza mai dipenderne. A differenza dell'evoluzione di questo fenomeno a New York o in certe città del Nord Europa, del resto, gli spazi di Bologna non hanno mai goduto di finanziamenti pubblici se non in sporadiche occasioni. Eppure, idealisti ed eroici, sono stati in grado di esistere e resistere, alcuni per pochi mesi, altri per decenni, formando generazioni di professionisti di quelle che oggi chiamiamo ICC – Industrie Culturali e Creative.

Sebbene molti di questi spazi si siano posti rispetto alla città su un piano conflittuale, acuitosi durante certe fasi amministrative, è indubbio che abbiano trovato a Bologna un terreno fertile, dal punto vista sia sociale che culturale. L'Università di Bologna è stata un incubatore formidabile in questo senso, in particolare il DAMS, l'innovativo corso di laurea in Discipline delle Arti, della Musica e dello Spettacolo nato nel 1971 come costola della Facoltà di Lettere e Filosofia. Al DAMS presero vita insegnamenti innovativi che guardavano alle arti visive, alla musica e allo spettacolo, inteso come teatro e cinema, da una prospettiva contemporanea, ibridandosi con la sociologia e la filosofia, alla luce del crescente impatto dei media e delle trasformazioni dell'industria culturale e della comunicazione. Fucina di energie confluite negli spazi alternativi è stata anche la locale Accademia di Belle Arti, a conferma del bisogno da parte dei giovani artisti di superare il modello solipsistico dello studio a favore di dinamiche pluralistiche di creazione.

All'interno del DAMS sono state generate ibride entità collettive, nate dal confronto tra docenti visionari e studenti desiderosi di mettere in pratica il sogno della "immaginazione al potere", motto di una controcultura che in Italia si è estesa dagli anni Sessanta a tutto il decennio successivo. Un caso esemplare è stato quello del Gruppo di Drammaturgia 2 coordinato da Giuliano Scabia, da cui nel 1972 è nato il *Gorilla Quadrumano*, uno spettacolo di teatro di strada che ha visto la partecipazione attiva degli abitanti di svariati quartieri italiani, a partire dal Pilastro di Bologna. Altro esempio significativo è stato quello del Gruppo A/Dams responsabile del testo collettivo *Alice disambientata: materiali collettivi (su Alice) per un manuale di sopravvivenza* (L'Erba Voglio, 1978), nato da un seminario su Lewis Carroll tenuto da Gianni Celati. Del romanzo di Carroll, evidentemente, a Celati e i suoi studenti non interessava solo la dimensione psichedelica del "paese delle meraviglie", ma che il buco nero in cui cade Alice la conducesse a una vera e propria eterotopia.

Grazie a iniziative come queste, nelle aule e nei corridoi di Strada Maggiore e via Guerrazzi, allora sedi del DAMS, prese forma quella che molti incominciarono a definire l'ala creativa del Movimento del '77. Le performance carnevalesche degli Indiani Metropolitani durante i cortei, i murales, e così le iniziative "mao-dadaiste" di controinformazione avviate da Franco "Bifo" Berardi, anima del Movimento, ovvero Radio Alice (esatto, la stessa Alice!) e la rivista *A/traverso*[7], risentirono di una temperie controculturale in qualche modo ispirata anche dai docenti del DAMS: Scabia, Celati, Umberto Eco, Renato Barilli, Luciano Anceschi e tanti altri "indisciplinati" intellettuali. L'influenza del DAMS non si limita alle origini del fenomeno che stiamo trattando, ma si estende fino a oggi, ed è da questa consapevolezza, e in parte senso di responsabilità, che la ricerca alla base di questo volume ha preso forma proprio all'interno del DAMS e di altri corsi di studio dell'attuale Dipartimento delle Arti dell'Università di Bologna.

I primi spazi con cui si apre questa rassegna, La Tregenda e Traumfabrik, avevano già alcune caratteristiche del "modello Bologna". Entrambi nati nel 1976, il primo durato alcuni mesi e il secondo sette anni, sono stati laboratori di pratiche interdisciplinari frutto di una spontanea trasposizione della vita nell'arte e viceversa. Le fondatrici de La Tregenda, una cantina in via San Vitale, hanno fatto la scelta radicale di aprire lo spazio a sole donne, in linea con la frangia femminista del Movimento. La Traumfabrik, ovvero "fabbrica dei sogni" in tedesco, fu invece un appartamento in via Clavature 20 – a riprova di quanto l'intreccio tra arte e vita fosse indissolubile – occupato illegalmente da Filippo Scozzari, Gianpietro Huber e Dadi Mariotti. In una città che nel 1977 fu segnata dall'uccisione di uno studente, Francesco Lorusso, dal Convegno contro la repressione e dai carri armati sotto le due torri, tra le pareti de La Tregenda e di Traumfabrik il Movimento si esprimeva in nuove forme, che ne coglievano le contraddizioni e ne indicavano un superamento.

La Traumfabrik fu un esempio pionieristico del "modello Bologna", come centro di aggregazione e laboratorio polifunzionale improntato sul rifiuto delle logiche dominanti del mercato e della cultura. Alla Traumfabrik si formarono band come il Centro d'Urlo Metropolitano, presto ribattezzatosi Gaznevada, e gli Stupid Set, per i quali il collettivo Grabinski realizzò proto-videoclip e installazioni multimediali che allegorizzavano la televisione e i sistemi di video-sorveglianza. Scozzari e Andrea Pazienza, allora studente DAMS, qui disegnarono alcune delle loro più importanti storie a fumetti, ma alla Traumfabrik "disegnavano tutti, alla selvaggia"[8], ricorda Scozzari in un suo memoir: illustrazioni, collage, sceneggiature per fumetti e film. Realizzati sotto l'effetto di sostanze stupefacenti, questi lavori su carta rappresentano oggi, insieme alle fotografie di Emanuele Angiuli, un corpus imprescindibile per ricostruire l'epopea di uno spazio totalizzante, vero contraltare al coevo sistema dell'arte contemporanea.

A fare della Traumfabrik un prototipo degli spazi alternativi bolognesi non sono solo la dimensione politica (in quanto parte del milieu movimentista del '77), l'approccio interdisciplinare alle arti e il nesso arte/vita, ma anche la sua connotazione come officina di attività professionalizzanti fondate sulle ibridazioni. Oltre agli inclassificabili oggetti intermediali dei Grabinski, altri esempi furono le attività grafiche e i progetti editoriali del collettivo Topographic, che videro la frequente collaborazione di Anna Persiani, da copertine di dischi e locandine a vere e proprie riviste come *L.U.X. Electric!* e *Musica80*. A questo proposito, bisognerà ricordare anche altre rivoluzionarie riviste che, sebbene nate altrove, videro coinvolti alcuni membri della Traumfabrik, Scozzari in primis, ovvero *Cannibale* e *Frigidaire*. Per non parlare degli svariati progetti musicali. Più che asservirsi alla cultura consumistica dominante, questi esempi di professionalizzazione finivano, in parte inconsciamente, per infiltrarla ed eroderne le fondamenta dall'interno.

Lo stesso Bifo ne riconobbe l'importanza come superamento dei sogni traditi del Movimento, come scrisse su *A/traverso* nel 1981:

> Una generazione di proletari sperimentatori si definisce sul terreno "artistico", perché l'arte si dà insieme come terreno metaforico e sperimentale. Metafora di concatenazioni sociali e tecnologiche che eccedono l'esistente e prefigurano un'organizzazione del Sapere e della produzione che l'esistente mira a distruggere. [...] Ripensiamo al '77 di Bologna: avevamo accumulato per anni sperimentazione e l'avevamo spesa tutta nella rivolta. Oggi si tratta di rovesciare il procedimento[9].

Questo numero della rivista, intitolato "Game Over", fu dedicato a sperimentazioni sonore e visive con interventi di Grabinski e di Renato De Maria, uno dei membri del gruppo, il quale nel tempo si confermerà come l'unico, insieme a Scozzari, a essere stato in grado di trasformare l'esperienza Traumfabrik in un mestiere, contando oggi su un'onorabile carriera nel mondo del cinema.

Alcune iniziative scaturite all'interno della Traumfabrik si configurarono come pseudo-imprese a partire da una sorta di marchio di fabbrica, "Traumfabrik Productions", che comparve sui flyer dei Gaznevada, sulle tavole di *Pentothal* (1977–1981) di Pazienza e nei progetti di *art direction* di Topographic. Gran parte delle band formatesi in Clavature trovarono il supporto della Italian Records, etichetta discografica guidata da Oderso Rubini nata dalla cooperativa bolognese Harpo's Bazaar, un esempio lungimirante di produzione dal basso che ha fatto delle band della Traumfabrik gli esempi più eccelsi della new wave italiana. Come scrisse l'Unità, la Harpo's Bazaar "tenta di porsi concorrenzialmente ai grandi monopoli discografici, piuttosto che demonizzarli. [...] Il risultato è una 'azienda economica' florida, che si è guadagnata credibilità culturale anche presso gli enti locali"[10]. L'idea era di fare dell'autoproduzione discografica un modello imprenditoriale di matrice politico-culturale, facendo leva sulle energie del territorio.

Nell'ambito della cultura punk e post-punk le iniziative discografiche indipendenti rappresentavano un contraltare ai colossi della musica pop, non solo in termini di stile e contenuti, ma soprattutto in ragione del bisogno di un artista di mantenere autonomia rispetto al mercato di massa. Gli stessi Scritti Politti nel 1980 pubblicarono "How To Make a Record", un manuale di discografia *do-it-yourself* imbevuto di messaggi militanti. Più che il Regno Unito, però, maggiori affinità legarono la comunità artistica bolognese a quella di New York che gravitava attorno a *Semiotext(e)* e alla scena No Wave[11]. A fare da ponte furono, dal fronte bolognese, i già citati Bifo e De Maria, insieme a Francesca Alinovi e Mariuccia Casadio, rispettivamente ricercatrice ed ex-studentessa del DAMS. Edit DeAk, Diego Cortez, Lydia Lunch, Jean-Michel Basquiat, Arto Lindsay e Keith Haring furono, invece, tra gli intellettuali e artisti newyorkesi coinvolti nella bolognese Settimana Internazionale della Performance, in concerti, produzioni discografiche e progetti espositivi.

In coincidenza con quanto accadeva in alcuni locali notturni di Downtown Manhattan come il Mudd Club e il Club 57, all'interno della ghiacciaia di un ex-macello di Borgo Panigale, nell'immediata periferia di Bologna, nacque Segreto Pubblico. Nel 1981 Bifo vi organizzò una versione performativa di "Game Over", mettendo in scena il processo di Pechino alla Banda dei Quattro in un ambiente da sala giochi. A segnare la breve storia di Segreto Pubblico furono, però, due progetti espositivi in forma di party, entrambi del 1982. Per *Frontiera Party*, a cura di Alinovi, lo spazio fu trasformato in ambiente preistorico in chiave postmoderna, con murales di Ivo Bonacorsi, cocktail colorati serviti da un gruppo di artisti legati a neon – altro neonato spazio alternativo cittadino – e l'esibizione di una band dall'esotico nome di Eterodattili. L'altro progetto fu il *Grabinsky TV Party*, un ambiente caratterizzato dall'inquietante presenza di telecamere di sorveglianza e schermi, ma finalizzato similmente al divertimento: la vita come festa, l'arte come allegoria.

Con Segreto Pubblico si consolidano altri due elementi chiave del "modello Bologna": lo spazio che diventa ambiente immersivo grazie ad allestimenti e impianti audiovisivi, e la possibilità di coniugare istanze partigiane alla musica e al ballo, intesi come strumenti di liberazione dei corpi, senza incorrere nel rischio dell'edonismo disimpegnato a cui solitamente si riconduce lo stile di vita postmoderno. Tutt'altro che disimpegnate, infatti, sono le iniziative collettive che, sulla scorta degli esempi storici fin qui discussi, nacquero a Bologna tra la fine degli anni Ottanta e i primi anni Novanta, in particolare Isola Nel Kantiere,

Livello 57, Link Project e il TPO – Teatro Polivalente Occupato. Si tratta di centri sociali nati da occupazioni illegali (tranne nel caso del Link) di edifici dismessi, gestiti da collettivi non a scopo di lucro, un modello che aggiornò la tradizione delle Case del Popolo di origine operaia e socialista al fenomeno internazionale dello *squatting* che emerse in quegli anni all'interno del movimento anticapitalista e antiglobalizzazione.

Per Serafino D'Onofrio e Valerio Monteventi, che del fenomeno qui discusso hanno fornito preziose chiavi di lettura con il loro libro del 2011 *Berretta Rossa*, questi spazi sono stati "Laboratori di politica e cultura, fucine di lotte e di forme alternative di svago, ma anche, in primo luogo, aggregazioni di individui che hanno deciso di aderire a un comune insieme di valori"[12]. E ancora: "vere e proprie fabbriche del lavoro postindustriale, luoghi di innovazione e di produzione creativa, dove sono stati elaborati tendenze e modelli comunicativi sui quali poi l'industria milanese, romana, e magari internazionale ha proceduto, utilizzando energie che qui a Bologna si erano formate"[13]. Anche in questa fase l'approccio in termini artistici fu fortemente interdisciplinare e votato alla esplorazione delle convergenze tra linguaggi visivi, performativi e mediali che fossero diretta estensione di un lifestyle di matrice sottoculturale, ovvero strumenti che consentissero a un gruppo di individui di identificarsi con una cultura alternativa a quella dominante.

La sottocultura per eccellenza, il punk, nella sua declinazione hardcore, è alla base della nascita dell'Isola Nel Kantiere, uno *squat* anche noto come Isola o I.N.K., all'interno di un edificio alle spalle di via Indipendenza e del Teatro Arena del Sole. Riccardo Pedrini, chitarrista della band bolognese dei Nabat, ha scritto che per lui "essere punk aveva significato recidere i rapporti con buona parte del cosiddetto *mondo circostante*. [...] era una fortissima tensione verso un *altrove*, politico, sociale o stilistico, musicale oppure comportamentale, o tutte quante queste cose assieme"[14]. All'Isola questo sembra essere l'assunto, anche se il punk e l'hardcore, qui suonato anche da figure internazionali come Fugazi, Henri Rollins e NOFX, presto cedette il passo a una nuova sottocultura, quella hip hop. Come il punk, anche l'hip hop è un movimento interdisciplinare: musica, graffiti, danza, autoproduzioni editoriali e mediatiche. E come il punk, anche l'hip hop è importato in Italia da altri paesi e altre culture ma viene qui declinato in modi originali.

L'Isola Nel Kantiere divenne una delle culle dell'hip hop italiano grazie alla nascita qui di collettivi quali Isola Posse All Stars, a cui si deve "Stop al Panico" (1991), inarrivabile archetipo di rap nostrano, marchio di fabbrica "Isola Nel Kantiere Production". Il brano fece da cassa di risonanza della diffidenza del coevo movimento studentesco della Pantera nei confronti delle istituzioni e del clima di terrore generato a Bologna dalle stragi della Uno Bianca. Con l'Isola Nel Kantiere, Bologna divenne l'epicentro di un nuovo movimento di disobbedienza civile, anche questo rafforzato, come nel '77, da tattiche artistiche. La strofa di "Stop al Panico" che meglio descrive questo sentimento è quella cantata da DeeMo, uno dei rapper del gruppo: "Bologna è rossa di vergogna e sangue, non sogna più. Anni e anni, anni di cazzate tipo 'isola felice' non han fatto che danni. Bologna è solo il buco del culo del mondo. C'è chi ha avuto, ha avuto e chi ha dato e va a fondo"[15]. Come per Alice, ancora una volta un buco, per accedere a un'altra eterotopia.

L'Isola Nel Kantiere venne sgomberata nel 1991, lo stesso anno in cui l'informatico inglese Tim Berners Lee pubblicò il primo sito web, rendendo così disponibile all'umanità l'accesso a quell'universo ancora inesplorato e da cui in gran parte oggi dipendiamo che è Internet. Del web allora inteso come luogo di possibilità e re-immaginazione della società, gli spazi alternativi di quegli anni furono una trasposizione tangibile. Una versione del concetto di eterotopia aggiornato alle novità dell'epoca in corso fu quello di T.A.Z., ovvero zone temporaneamente autonome, elaborato da Hakim Bey proprio nel 1991. Si tratta di luoghi che per periodi limitati divengono autonomi rispetto al contesto sociale, politico e culturale, in cui le arti esercitano un ruolo fondamentale. Addirittura, per Bey:

> la TAZ è l'unico possibile "luogo" e "tempo" per l'accadere dell'arte, per il puro piacere del gioco creativo, e come tangibile contributo alle forze che permettono alla TAZ di aggregarsi e manifestarsi. Nella TAZ l'arte come merce sarà semplicemente divenuta impossibile; sarà invece una condizione di vita [nella quale] "l'artista non è un tipo speciale di persona, ma ogni persona è un tipo speciale di artista"[16].

Nella Bologna dei primi anni Novanta esempi di T.A.Z. non furono solo gli spazi, ma anche le aree della città in cui i germi coltivati nei loro laboratori trovavano disseminazione virale. Si pensi ai cortei carnevaleschi e alle parate techno organizzati dall'Isola o dal Livello 57, capaci di rendere temporaneamente autonome arterie del tessuto urbano, piazze, parchi e portici, con carri, casse, cartelli e creature antropomorfe realizzate con materiale di riciclo, magari dagli inglesi Mutoid Waste Company che a Bologna e poi in Romagna trovarono casa. In parallelo a queste forme d'arte anonime, pensate come strumenti di contro-discussione, furono lanciate missioni esplorative in rete. Isola, Livello 57 e Link si dotarono di postazioni con personal computer connessi a Internet e proposero varie occasioni di discussione sui temi cardine della cultura cyberpunk, dalle BBS alla contro-informazione, dalla realtà virtuale alla Net.Art, prima che Internet venisse irrimediabilmente privatizzato e le nostre soggettività fagocitate dai social media.

All'indomani dello sgombero dell'Isola Nel Kantiere, il collettivo Damsterdamned – che negli anni della Pantera gestiva la programmazione culturale del DAMS occupato in via Guerrazzi – fu, insieme ad altre associazioni e gruppi, al centro di un patteggiamento con il Comune di Bologna per l'individuazione di un nuovo spazio. La scelta ricadde sull'ex-deposito delle Farmacie Comunali in via Fioravanti, dietro la stazione dei treni, all'interno del quale sorse il Link Project. Quintessenza del modello Bologna, al Link le energie della comunità artistica *off* di Bologna hanno dato forma a una fabbrica culturale, articolata in divisioni con compiti specifici, come dimostra un "organigramma" in apertura del secondo numero della sua omonima rivista. Le diciture generiche riportate nello schema corrispondono a entità professionali come Officine Alchemiche (allestimenti), Opificio Ciclope (produzioni multimediali), Loew & Associati (reparto grafico), e altre responsabili per la programmazione teatrale, musicale, relative alle arti visive, al cinema, ai servizi, ecc.

La rivista del Link è oggi una preziosa cartina tornasole per comprendere la natura polivalente e interdisciplinare del centro che, come ha ricordato in un testo recente Daniele Gasparinetti, una delle figure centrali nella storia del Link, era pensato come:

> un mondo-di-redazioni (mondo-di-relazioni), per dare vita a una "rivista vivente". Le redazioni sono le unità minime di raccordo, confronto e ordinamento delle linee. [...] non è la famiglia (padre-madre-progenie), ma un procedimento dialettico che può assumere molte forme di combinazione. L'oltre di queste unità di conto è già un'"assemblea". [...] Le assemblee rappresentano i luoghi delle confluenze-divergenti, e sono gli organi della non-totalizzabilità[17].

Dalle parole di Gasparinetti, però, traspare anche una contraddizione in termini degli spazi alternativi: se da un lato queste esperienze poggiano su dinamiche di condivisione e collettivizzazione, sono anche incubatori di divergenze e frustrazioni che ne mettono a repentaglio la sussistenza e rischiano anche di inficiarne la memoria.

La cultura elettronica, nelle sue più diverse sfumature, è stato il collante del Link, che grazie ad allestimenti permanenti e scenografie provvisorie si è configurato come ambiente immersivo e intermediale, fondato sulla convergenza di suoni, luci e schermi. La programmazione musicale – il principale strumento di sostentamento economico – comprendeva performance di esponenti di generi "storici", dal post-punk all'hip hop alla techno, insieme ai migliori rappresentanti di generi di quegli anni quali IDM, post-rock e trip hop. Rassegne monografiche sono state dedicate a protagonisti del cinema sperimentale e dell'arte video, tra cui Marcel Broodthaers, Chris Marker, Bill Viola, Gary Hill e gli italiani canecapovolto. Ruolo di primo piano ha avuto la sperimentazione teatrale con performance di compagnie italiane come Socìetas Raffaello Sanzio, Kinkaleri e Teatrino Clandestino. Attraverso incontri e interventi sulla rivista, questi prodotti alternativi dell'industria culturale venivano anche contestualizzati e discussi da artisti e accademici.

Il Link ha rappresentato un punto di snodo epocale, non solo perché ha messo a sistema elementi già emersi nei precedenti spazi – come fucina di attività interdisciplinari e professionalizzanti, motore di energie sottoculturali e spazio totalizzante – ma anche per la sua capacità di tessere rapporti, per quanto altalenanti, sia con l'amministrazione pubblica, che ne ha legittimato l'esistenza, sia con il mondo accademico, il sistema dell'arte e l'industria culturale. Riguardo al sistema dell'arte, molti spazi precedenti avevano ignorato o si erano opposti alle attività del territorio. La prima iniziativa dell'Isola Nel Kantiere, per esempio, fu la "manifestazione dei rubinetti", una contestazione alla Biennale dei Giovani Artisti dell'Europa e del Mediterraneo, la cui quarta edizione fu organizzata dal Comune di Bologna nel 1988. Armati di rubinetteria, un gruppo di "isolani" sfilarono tra le strade del centro per lamentare come, conclusa la Biennale, l'amministrazione avrebbe nuovamente "chiuso i rubinetti" dei finanziamenti per l'arte.

Altri spazi nati prima del Link, invece, avevano dimostrato una capacità di dialogo con il mondo dell'arte contemporanea cittadino, diventando luoghi in cui gli artisti avevano la possibilità di sperimentare con le tecniche e i linguaggi delle arti visive ma senza necessariamente incorrere in logiche di mercificazione. Fu il caso di neon e de Il Campo delle Fragole, il primo uno spazio dedicato principalmente ad espressioni di natura concettuale e relazionale, il secondo più interessato a pratiche pittoriche e di installazione. Entrambi questi spazi e gli artisti che ne hanno animato le attività hanno partecipato a mostre in gallerie e iniziative istituzionali, stabilendo un rapporto anche con la locale Arte Fiera. Nata nel 1974, Arte Fiera fu una delle prime fiere dedicate all'arte contemporanea di levatura internazionale, e contribuì alla percezione di Bologna come luogo di innovazione anche in termini di economia culturale. Oggi per Arte Fiera realtà profit e non-profit contribuiscono in modo sinergico a un programma fitto di eventi chiamato Art City.

Per diversi anni, all'interno del Link, nei giorni di Arte Fiera l'artista Luca Vitone, exstudente DAMS, ha organizzato Incursioni, un progetto espositivo che comprendeva installazioni, performance e incontri, ricordando al pubblico che l'arte può essere processo senza diventare prodotto. Al Link nacquero anche diversi festival dedicati alle ibridazioni tra arti visive e altri linguaggi espressivi come Hops! e Suoni visivi e immagini sonore. Il primo fu presentato come un progetto "in cui convivono produzioni liminali e zone interstiziali che ospitano a loro volta ricerche sui o sub generis: rappresentative schegge creative di contemporaneità, di rado portate sullo stesso terreno di gioco fuori dalle rispettive cliniche estetiche"[18]. Da queste esperienze e da un gruppo di membri del Link nascerà poi Netmage. International Live Media Festival, rassegna dedicata alle contaminazioni e convergenze tra il visivo e l'aurale in performance e progetti intermediali, itinerante di anno in anno in diverse sedi della città.

Il fenomeno dei festival, che da solo meriterebbe una ricerca e un volume dedicati, si è sviluppato in modo considerevole a Bologna a partire dagli anni Novanta, come estensione di attività nate negli spazi alternativi o da associazioni e organizzazioni legate a questi. In particolare, come sostiene Paolo Magaudda, i festival sono stati il risultato di "una certa 'istituzionalizzazione' di alcuni centri sociali cittadini, che vanno anche nell'ottica di una normalizzazione dell'offerta culturale. La sovvenzione delle istituzioni ha modificato alcune esperienze di rottura estrema in centri di produzione culturale"[19]. Oltre a Netmage, si pensi al festival Gender Bender prodotto dal Cassero, che da oltre vent'anni vanta una programmazione artistica di primo piano, internazionale e interdisciplinare, con un focus su questioni di identità di genere. A normalizzare la propria offerta culturale sono stati anche numerosi spazi attivi oggi che, su modello di neon e Il Campo delle Fragole, sono votati principalmente alle arti visive, come Adiacenze e Ateliersi.

A New York, additata come luogo di elezione per gli spazi alternativi per l'arte, queste esperienze hanno goduto di sovvenzioni ingenti da parte dello stato e di privati. Alcuni spazi nati negli anni Settanta sono diventati vere e proprie istituzioni come il New Museum of Contemporary Art e il PS1, oggi succursale del MoMA. A Bologna, invece, questo supporto è stato limitato a poche iniziative o riguarda la concessione di spazi di proprietà del Comune. Il caso del Cassero è di particolare importanza, in quanto si tratta del primo spazio gestito da un'associazione omosessuale in Italia a essere stato legittimato dall'amministrazione pubblica mediante la concessione di un edificio. Il principio di intersezionalità, ovvero l'inclusione di gruppi solitamente discriminati e marginalizzati, con attenzione per la comunità LGBTQIA+, è un altro carattere fondamentale degli spazi alternativi bolognesi, soprattutto Cassero, TPO e Atlantide. Al contrario del primo, però, le vicende degli altri due sono state segnate da conflitti e sgomberi.

Ricapitolando, i seguenti possono essere indicati come i caratteri fondamentali del "modello Bologna", variamente applicabili agli spazi alternativi per l'arte che sono stati oggetto di questa ricerca:

- il mito di Bologna come luogo di agitazione politica e innovazione culturale
- le rispondenze con il milieu accademico cittadino, in particolare il DAMS
- le convergenze tra vita, politica e produzione artistica
- il carattere sperimentale come laboratori di interdisciplinarità
- il ruolo di incubatori di professionalizzazione *bottom up* in relazione alle ICC
- la dimensione totalizzante attraverso ambienti immersivi e intermediali
- l'indipendenza rispetto alle istituzioni e al mercato
- lo sviluppo di pratiche artistiche di stampo sottoculturale
- il rapporto ambiguo, ora sinergico ora conflittuale, con il sistema dell'arte
- il rapporto ambiguo, ora sinergico ora conflittuale, con l'amministrazione pubblica
- il principio di intersezionalità e inclusione, che ne determina il valore sociale

Più che spazi che stanno *altrove*, da questa ricerca emerge come questi siano spazi che stanno *tra* e che producono iniziative, eventi, progetti e soggettività che stanno *tra*. Non a caso, alcune parole chiave ricorrenti nell'esplorazione di questo fenomeno hanno in comune il prefisso *inter-*, il quale indica appunto una posizione intermedia o un rapporto di reciprocità: interdisciplinare, intermediale, intersezionale, a cui potremmo aggiungere interstiziale, intertestuale e altri termini che alludono allo stare nel mezzo. Nel mezzo a cosa, però, esattamente? Nel mezzo dei processi di significazione, tra i meccanismi di costruzione del senso nell'economia culturale e nei media, nelle zone d'ombra in cui produzione artistica e comunicazione si confondono, e nell'indeterminazione tra arte e vita. Il valore di questi spazi, pertanto, risiede proprio nella loro posizione, nella città ma al contempo tra le maglie che ne determinano il funzionamento, come specchi deformanti su cui le arti consentono di ridefinire i codici della società postindustriale.

1 Estratti dal testo del brano "Skank Bloc Bologna" degli Scritti Politti, St. Pancreas Records, Leeds 1978.

2 Renato Zangheri, *Bologna '77. Comunisti, potere, dissenso: analisi di un'esperienza dal vivo. Intervista di Fabio Mussi*, Editori Riuniti, Roma 1978, p. 14, 101.

3 Julie Ault, "For the Record" in *Alternative Art New York, 1965–1985*, University of Minnesota Press, Minneapolis 2002, p. 4.

4 Si veda Jean-François Lyotard, *La condizione postmoderna. Rapporto sul sapere*, Feltrinelli, Milano 1981.

5 Si veda Gilles Deleuze, *La piega. Leibniz e il Barocco*, a cura di D. Tarizzo, Einaudi, Torino 2004.

6 Michel Foucault, "Eterotopie" (1984) in *Estetica dell'esistenza, etica, politica. Archivio Foucault 3. Interventi, colloqui, interviste. 1978–1985*, a cura di Alessandro Pandolfi, Feltrinelli, Milano 1998, p. 310.

7 Si veda Klemens Gruber, *L'avanguardia inaudita. Comunicazione e strategia nei movimenti degli anni Settanta*, Costa & Nolan, Genova 1997.

8 Filippo Scozzari, *Prima pagare poi ricordare. Da 'Cannibale' a 'Frigidaire'. Storica di un manipolo di ragazzi geniali*, Coniglio Editore, Roma 2007, p. 58.

9 Franco "Bifo" Berardi, "Il movimento. La sperimentazione", *A/traverso*, estate 1981.

10 Filippo Bianchi, "Un business chiamato movimento. La felice esperienza della cooperativa bolognese 'Harpo's Bazaar'", *l'Unità*, 22 aprile 1981, in Oderso Rubini e Anna Persiani (a cura di), *Pensatevi Liberi. Bologna Rock 1979*, Beatstream, Bologna 2019, p. 81.

11 Si veda Francesco Spampinato, "No Bologna No New York: il network No Wave tra le due città 1977–1983", in Uliana Zanetti (a cura di), *La performance a Bologna negli anni '70*, MAMbo – Museo d'Arte Moderna di Bologna, Bologna 2023, p. 184–93.

12 Serafino D'Onofrio e Valerio Monteventi, *Berretta Rossa. Storie di Bologna attraverso i centri sociali*, Pendragon, Bologna 2011, p. 10.

13 *Ibid.*, p. 28.

14 Riccardo Pedrini, *Ordigni. Storia del Punk a Bologna*, Castelvecchi, Roma 1998, p. 91.

15 Isola Posse All Stars, "Stop al Panico", vinile, 12", Isola Nel Kantiere Production, 1991.

16 Hakim Bey, *T.A.Z. Zone Temporaneamente Autonome*, Shake, Milano 2007, p. 54–55.

17 Daniele Gasparinetti, "Knil/Link. Una inversione del link in forma trans-storica", *Quaderni d'arte italiana*, no. 2, La Quadriennale di Roma e Treccani, 2022, p. 103–04.

18 Descrizione del festival Hops!, in occasione della sua prima edizione, sulle pagine della rivista *Link Project*, gennaio–febbraio 2000. Testo non firmato. Pagine non numerate.

19 Paolo Magaudda, "Sottoculture e creatività urbana. Le traiettorie, i luoghi e i miti della cultura giovanile a Bologna" in Piero Pieri e Chiara Cretella (a cura di), *Atlante dei movimenti culturali dell'Emilia-Romagna 1968–2007: III. Arti, Comunicazione, Controculture*, Clueb, Bologna 2007, p. 52.

L'ODORE DEL PRESENTE ASSOLUTO. DOPOTUTTO, NON ERA BOLOGNA
Andrea Lissoni

Un'immagine non basta, sono troppe immagini. Nemmeno un suono, troppo suono, troppi suoni. Certamente c'è un odore, molto specifico, l'odore del giorno dopo. Questa non è Bologna comunque, è il Link Project, dalle scale del sottopassaggio della stazione nella direzione opposta a quella dove tutti vanno, verso la Bolognina invece che verso il centro. L'odore è rimasto lì e riaffiora, molto occasionalmente: fumo, corpi, umani e non, macchine, birra, e molto altro.

Bologna per me era un nodo. Era il posto dove tutto quello che mi appassionava accadeva. Tutto quello che rappresentava il presente assoluto era lì, e non potevo mancarlo. Dopo quindici anni da pendolare inverso – viaggiando verso Bologna per il weekend e non nei giorni lavorativi – posso dire di non averla mai conosciuta davvero.

Ma cos'era il presente assoluto? Era la percezione di una condizione, l'essere connessi, l'essere nel mondo, l'essere nel flusso, l'essere parte della rivoluzione epocale che stava accadendo contribuendo a condividerla localmente, disseminandola, immaginando che potesse germogliare. Per me, questo era Bologna. Certamente una Bologna specifica, quella del Link, quella del Cassero, prima, e dei festival Netmage, F.I.S.Co., poi, e per aspetti completamente diversi, anche del Cinema Ritrovato. La Bologna fra 1996 e 2013 circa.

Solo tornando ancora ed ancora altre e fondamentali traiettorie sono emerse: la presenza e l'importanza di Bifo, la linea diffusa del pensiero post-operaistico, la straordinaria e direi unica rete di realtà performative eterodosse disseminate in Romagna, fra Cesena, Ravenna, Rimini e Riccione, aggregatori e diffusori di schegge di cultura audiovisuale anglosassone come il Riccione TTV Festival, i ponti con Firenze e Prato, soprattutto con il CPA, e con Kinkaleri, Virgilio Sieni e Ogino:knauss in particolare. E poi c'era neon, successivamente campobase.

Ricordo andarci di sabato, prima di cena. Incontrare ogni volta qualcosa estremamente sincero, contenuto nelle forme, spesso caricato emotivamente, mai drammatico, mai smargiasso, mai modesto nell'ampiezza dei gesti o nell'estensione della portata concettuale. Qualcosa di diverso, ma stranamente familiare. Diverso principalmente da ciò che potevo incontrare a Milano, la vivacità eterodossa a Viafarini, l'energia dell'altrove e mai percepita prima da Emi Fontana, l'eleganza da Guenzani, la provocazione ambiziosa da De Carlo, la visionarietà leggera da Fac-Simile di Horatio Goni. Neon era l'impressione di una comunità a cui tutti coloro che entravano appartenevano a prescindere, senza scrutinio o valutazione, a cui gli artisti offrivano senza mediazioni, compromessi, strategie, senza pelle.

Nelle viscere del Link, a fianco della libreria – Modo Infoshop, un riferimento essenziale per la cultura del tempo presente – prima che quell'odore si formasse, c'erano le cene, dove tutti, artisti, tecnici, lavoratori, collaboratori si incontravano. Ci ripenso come un momento unico e straordinario, in parte un'occasione persa, per sovraimpegno, densità di conversazione, timidezza.

Inevitabilmente, un primo viaggio c'è stato. Ma come ci ero arrivato, e perché?

Studiavo arte moderna all'Università di Pavia, dopo il movimento studentesco La Pantera e le connessioni interuniversitarie via fax, le esperienze più interessanti avvenivano nelle intersezioni fra on e offline ed io le seguivo pendolando fra bus e treni: a Milano e frequentando la Calusca ed il Conchetta, guardando a "Gomma" Guarneri e Raf Valvola, leggevo tutto Decoder, le pubblicazioni di ShaKe, la collana Interzone, avidamente tutto di Gibson, Haraway, Lanier, Sterling. Ascoltavo e ballavo tutto quello che non si era mai sentito prima e che stava accadendo in quel momento, elettronica in generale, fra jungle, broken beat, trance, hip hop distorto, trip-hop, illbient, ma anche la nuova scena indie e tutte le sue radici. Avevo lavorato su Studio Azzurro per la mia tesi e lì incontrato una rete di persone che mi avrebbero accompagnato ovunque, fra festival in cui ho sempre aiutato (Taormina Arte Video, con Valentina Valentini, che già aveva diretto la mia tesi) e altri in cui mi sono mosso fra i pochi specialisti. A Milano c'era Invideo, ma non bastava, la vera energia veniva da Mudima dove attraverso il formidabile programma dedicato a presentare i protagonisti di Fluxus vedevo forme d'arte radicalmente non convenzionali, performance, musica, video rigore nelle forme, libertà nei comportamenti. Avevo aiutato e collaborato con all'epoca vivacissimo Progetto Giovani, spinto dalla dedicata motivazione alla qualità delle voci internazionali di Roberto Pinto, soprattutto grazie al ciclo di incontri *La generazione delle immagini*. A Pavia, facendo colazione alla Casa dello Studente avevo preso l'abitudine di leggere *il manifesto*, divoravo *Alias*, ma non potevo mancare la rubrica del venerdì di Ninì Candalino sulle visioni elettroniche. Lì avevo incontrato il nome Damsterdamned ed avevo cominciato a seguire le prime onde da Bologna, fino a quando non sono diventati segnali e, successivamente, intrecci. Vari collettivi nati all'interno del DAMS (ma non solo) si fondevano – così leggevo – e nasceva il Link. Io mi occupavo sempre più di arte video, affascinato dalla formidabile transizione che stava rivoluzionando la tradizione della cultura analogica ed elettronica insieme, sciogliendosi in quella digitale. Lavoravo a Parigi nel Dipartimento Nuovi Media del Musée National d'Art Moderne/Centre Georges Pompidou con una borsa di studio e tutto quello che sognavo era vedere una situazione museale sperimentale, di ricerca ma anche di produzione, manifestarsi anche in Italia. Sembrava impossibile, le istituzioni erano ferme. Le onde vitali venivano solo da Bologna, dal Link, inevitabilmente, che non solo dedicava alle opere filmiche e video eterodosse, estreme, underground, regolari serate originali, ma anche sembrava programmare sempre più arte e, in particolare, film e video d'artista. Link era anche sede di Rifrazioni, una casa di distribuzione di video d'autore e d'artista dal catalogo davvero inusuale, con una connessione forte alla scena tedesca e al mondo artistico controculturale più in generale, co-diretta da Daniele Gasparinetti e Rainer Bumke, attivo anche come producer a Studio Azzurro. Credo che il primo passo fisico sia stato la mia attrazione per Romeo Castellucci/Socìetas Raffaello Sanzio, nell'autunno 1995, ancora durante il mio servizio militare, quando per la prima volta entrai nel mondo notturno Link, rimanendone catturato per sempre. In quello stesso periodo aveva suonato Aphex Twin, per la prima volta in Italia e il mio mondo cambiò per sempre. Ricordo avere incontrato per la prima volta il nome di Raphael Montañez Ortiz, un artista che mi ha accompagnato lungo venti anni, fino a quando l'ho finalmente incontrato in New Jersey. E a Jürgen Reble, con cui avremmo collaborato. Ma, ugualmente essenziale fu ritrovare opere e nomi come Nan Goldin, Rebecca Horn, Angela Melitopoulos e, non a caso, Emi Fontana.

Credo di essermi soffermato su Montañez Ortiz e Reble perché per me rappresentano in un certo senso l'anima, o meglio, l'immaginario Link: l'approccio basato su tagliare, incollare, ricombinare e generare vita nuova e un mondo di trasformazione alchemiche, di alterazioni della materia, di alchimia. Un artista visionario, che aveva fondato il Museo del Barrio a New York, un protagonista del Destruction in Art Symposium a Londra nel 1966, un rivoluzionario della storia del video, una figura centrale nell'estetica *cut 'n' mix*, una pratica gioiosa ma rigorosa che avremmo eletto a filosofia curatoriale. Un cineasta sperimentale che non conosceva limiti, né della sala – produceva soprattutto performance di expanded cinema – né del trattamento della pellicola, che recuperava usata, colorava, seppelliva, nascondeva in alberi e lasciava esposta alle intemperie, per poi condividerne le alterazioni in indimenticabili e sempre differenti proiezioni, spesso cooperando con amici musicisti elettronici come Thomas Köner.

L'anima plunderphonica di Montañez Ortiz, Dara Birnbaum, Alberto Grifi, Chris Cutler, Terre Thaemlitz, Coldcut e molto altro, veniva spontaneamente programmata fra video, film e soprattutto musica e si alternava a mondi astratti, visionari, alchemici e alla deriva: insieme, nel 2000, in occasione di Bologna Capitale Europea della Cultura avrebbero generato la prima versione del festival Netmage (il titolo veniva dalla domanda "cosa sono le immagini all'epoca della rete?"), la vita di una ancora piccola comunità creativo-curatoriale dopo il Link, che intitolammo *Media Magica*, seminando per creare una comunità, questa volta anche ambiziosamente internazionale, rinnovata. Mentre Bologna sembrava diventare rilevante nella scena artistica – il MAMbo apriva nei nuovi edifici giusto a fianco ai Magazzini del Sale, sede di un vivacissimo Cassero LGBTQIA+ Center e a pochi passi dalla Cineteca, potenzialmente un distretto creativo unico in Italia – con un picco simbolico e di energie per Arte Fiera prima che Artissima prendesse una forma esplicitamente curatoriale a metà anni 2000, ancora al Link Luca Vitone aveva dato

vita ad Incursioni nei giorni della fiera prima, invitandomi poi a co-curare Hops!: la visione di fondo consisteva nel presentare tutto ciò che in fiera non avrebbe trovato spazio, offrendo un'alternativa notturna e soprattutto performativa, sempre e urgentemente con un'attenzione speciale per i percorsi locali o italiani in erba più irrequieti, innanzitutto coloro che apparivano, si manifestavano, si proponevano come pubblico appassionato e curioso. Una linea sarebbe rimasta in F.I.S.Co., il festival internazionale sullo spettacolo contemporaneo ideato e guidato da Silvia Fanti, che fin dal 2000 aveva scombinato tutte le carte della scena italiana, combinando le eccellenze "locali" di Kinkaleri e mk con autori irrequieti e poi compagni di strada come Jérôme Bel, Myriam Gourfink, Maria Hassabi, Xavier Le Roy, Eszter Salamon. In tutto questo gli autori e le pratiche erano quasi infiniti, al punto da generare nuovi paradigmi, dal VJing al Live Media.

Le memorie successive sono associate al cercare e trovare spazi. Uno permanente, Raum, un attrattore selettivo di pratiche di ricerca eterodosse, in realtà un centro permanente di formazione eclettica dagli eccellenti risultati, visto da una prospettiva internazionale, forse il primo vero *independent art center* in Italia. E molti temporanei, specie per Netmage: giardini non noti, sotterranei, sottopassi, tunnel, edifici in trasformazione, ex-teatri, cinema in disuso, scali ferroviari, palazzi comunali, fino all'installazione nel centrale e maestoso Palazzo Re Enzo.

Questo nomadismo annuale, che seguivo con rispetto, corrispondeva nella mia memoria all'immagine del "recupero rinnovato" con cui ero così familiare e che in realtà mi aveva per sempre formato. Un recupero di fonti preziose in cui, appunto, "cerca, individua, seleziona, e ricombina, accogliendo, ascoltando e alchemicamente trasformando", erano ormai una visione di programmazione culturale, se non già di vita.

Le memorie sono di esplorazioni, molta umidità, pavimenti bagnati, pozzanghere, mancanza di luce, odore di chiuso, e finalmente qualche giorno di magia pura.

Quella magia pura di un ulteriore ricordo non più personale, ma del futuro, che la musicista Caterina Barbieri ha recentemente condiviso con me. Passando giovanissima un tardo pomeriggio da Piazza Maggiore in bicicletta di ritorno da una lezione di conservatorio, Caterina vede Palazzo Re Enzo illuminato all'interno con luci e colori mai viste: la curiosità, l'ingresso, i suoni, il numero di persone e un duo di ragazze suonare musica elettronica sedute a terra. Erano le sorelle Byrne, le Ectoplasm Girls, un giovanissimo duo artistico svedese di elettronica *noise*. Per Caterina Netmage è una scintilla: due ragazze suonano di fronte ad un pubblico concentrato ad un festival fra arte e musica elettronica, lo può decisamente fare anche lei.

Ecco, questo, al momento è il mio ricordo più toccante di Bologna, quello di frammenti di passato ricombinati con visione, con dedizione, con un senso della trasformazione fondato su un potenziale sempre innescato. E in fondo questo è anche il presupposto sui cui si fondano le giornate estive di Cinema Ritrovato, un evento che abita il distretto ma che da tempo trasforma Piazza Maggiore in una piattaforma internazionale di assoluta qualità e rilevanza.

E a proposito, ho ritrovato il comunicato/lettera aperta di chiusura a tutti coloro coinvolti in Link Project e penso che un estratto dica più di tutto di quel periodo e rappresenti i canali acquatici sotterranei su cui navigano le mie memorie:

> The Link Project has certainly been something more than just a cultural association, both in a formal way and at a more substantial level.
> We believe that it has represented a very important stage in Bologna's cultural life, having had the capability to go well beyond its original role.
> It is not yet possible to summarize in a few lines what the whole experience was about, either from a personal point of view nor from any other perspective, be it long-term and historical.
> It certainly turned out to be a vital experience. An organism, for better or worse, invaded by thousands of streams and currents of thought. This was its strange energy.
> We are dealing with an energy that surely has not failed and will not fade now with the close of its historically associated structure.
> The nature of vital worlds has this prerogative: extinction followed by rebirth.
> It may have been paradoxical to institutionalize this experience by crystallizing its features.
> Networks have fortunately become realities on a wide scale. Perhaps this was paramount In our minds when we undertook this route years ago.
> Another series of ups, then, because it is in this cycle of rebirth and renewal, which we have wanted to believe in, that we chose to involve ourselves and others on this strange adventure.
> We want to thank all the people who, for different reasons, have participated and were connected with the project.
> We wish all Link-thinkers a very exciting future.

Più buio e luce artificiale che luce del sole, più odore che aria tersa, più iperattività e conversazioni che pensieri e contemplazioni, più azione che documentazione, più azioni che derive. Trasformare. E molto di più.

GLI SPAZI ESPOSITIVI INDIPENDENTI DA UNA PROSPETTIVA DI GENERE
Lara De Lena

Con questo saggio, si intende analizzare la dimensione femminista degli spazi bolognesi in rapporto al contesto italiano e il ruolo delle donne all'interno di questi e, più in generale, nel mondo dell'arte istituzionale e non, tra gli anni Settanta e gli anni Novanta.

Come sostiene Linda Nochlin[1], l'arte è sempre il risultato di una situazione sociale, sia per quanto riguarda l'evoluzione dell'artista, sia per la natura e la qualità dell'opera in sé. Il suo intervento del 1971 in *ARTnews*, dal provocatorio titolo "Why Have There Been No Great Women Artist?", denuncia l'assenza della componente femminile nella storia dell'arte, causata dal perseverare di criteri di giudizio falsamente universali che hanno ignorato da sempre le artiste donne e ogni loro forma di creatività. Sebbene non esista uno stile riconoscibile come femminile qualcosa, per la studiosa americana, accomuna le artiste di successo: il senso di colpa per essere uscite dalla trama delle aspettative sociali, dato che – inevitabilmente – tutto quel che è abituale sembra anche naturale[2].

Come racconta Maria Antonietta Trasforini, i dizionari dell'arte prodotti negli anni Cinquanta non citano quasi nessuna artista, mentre a partire dagli anni Settanta i numeri aumentano considerevolmente: sono circa 500 quelle menzionate nel 1976, che diventeranno 21.000 nel 1984[3]. Alla riscoperta delle artiste dimenticate del passato, si accompagna una fioritura di artiste che operano nel contemporaneo. La spinta del neofemminismo scuote il mondo dell'arte e della cultura, e porta a quello che Chiara Zamboni definisce "momento radiante"[4], in cui si manifesta un'urgenza condivisa di un nuovo linguaggio che adotti parole che possano, come ha rilevato Mariella Pasinati "sovvertire lo sguardo maschile sulle donne, sull'arte, sul mondo, per affermare una propria, autonoma visione"[5].

In Italia, il primo passo del medesimo processo avviato da Nochlin arriva qualche anno più tardi, nel 1976, ad opera dell'artista Simona Weller, che pubblica *Il complesso di Michelangelo, ricerca sul contributo dato dalla donna all'arte italiana del Novecento* per La Nuova Foglio Editrice di Macerata. Con questo testo, Weller vuole smantellare l'atavico senso di inferiorità delle artiste nei riguardi del genio maschile creatore, e lo fa attraverso un'indagine sul campo, una sorta di censimento sulla condizione professionale e sociale delle donne che operano nel mondo dell'arte in Italia. Il libro porterà, nella primavera dell'anno successivo, alla realizzazione di una mostra dall'omonimo titolo presso la galleria di via Giulia a Roma, che presentava il lavoro di quaranta artiste romane sviluppato in ordine cronologico, dal primo Novecento fino alle più recenti tendenze degli anni Settanta[6]. Come dimostra l'operazione di Weller, mentre per gli artisti uomini vi era una certa facilità nell'ottenere visibilità e riconoscimento negli spazi istituzionali e accademici, per le donne l'accesso alle opportunità di esposizione era più problematico. Se è vero che, come sostiene Virginia Woolf, "se vuole scrivere romanzi una donna deve avere del denaro e una stanza tutta per sé"[7], per entrare nel mondo dell'arte da protagoniste è invece necessario uscire dal proprio spazio domestico e conquistare gli spazi espositivi, la stampa e il dibattito critico, il tutto mantenendo credibilità sociale e autorevolezza. Ma come possono artiste, critiche e curatrici, conquistare spazi se trovano ogni ingresso sbarrato da una lunga e resistente egemonia maschile? Da qualche parte è necessario partire, e lo si fa dagli interstizi, dalle piccole realtà e da sporadiche ma fondamentali visioni illuminate. I circuiti indipendenti, in questo contesto, diventano per le artiste un luogo di espressione e visibilità: meno istituzionali, più informali e antigerarchici, offrono un ambiente accogliente e inclusivo, in cui condividere esperienze e supportarsi a vicenda nella lotta per l'emancipazione, tanto nell'arte quanto nella società. In una prima fase, i dati non sono certo incoraggianti. Nell'ambito della situazione bolognese è utile menzionare che anche nel caso di realtà come Galleria Studio G7 e Studio Cavalieri – fondate da pioniere come Ginevra Grigolo e Adriana Cavalieri, che entravano all'inizio degli anni Settanta nel mondo delle gallerie private non senza difficoltà – la presenza femminile in mostra appare davvero esigua: tra il 15 e il 20% dei molti artisti che vi hanno esposto nel corso degli anni. E parliamo di esempi virtuosi legati al mondo delle gallerie private bolognesi, di luoghi che fin dalla loro apertura si sono rivolti a un mercato internazionale piuttosto che a un collezionismo locale, e che a una logica di mercato hanno preferito l'attenzione alle istanze più innovative, anche quando non facilmente mercificabili.

Nella temperie del movimento femminista Bologna, negli anni Settanta, vede proliferare – tra militanza, gioco e provocazione – le performance di strada e piccoli fenomeni editoriali come il numero unico della fanzine di impronta dadaista *Siamo isteriche...*, pubblicato nel 1976 a cura del Collettivo femminista bolognese, come racconta il documentario *Io sono femminista!*, realizzato nel 2019 da Teresa Rossano e promosso dal Centro di documentazione dei movimenti "Francesco Lorusso – Carlo Giuliani" di Bologna[8].

In questi anni nascono in città spazi indipendenti gestiti da donne, come La Tregenda e la libreria La Librellula. Fondata nel 1976 da Syusy Blady, La Tregenda ha vita molto breve (circa sei mesi) ma fa in tempo a realizzare serate culturali di alto livello tra musica, teatro e performance, a cui avevano accesso solo le donne. Racconta la fondatrice: "organizzavamo spettacoli e feste e il locale era nato grazie a una mia precedente esperienza politica e femminista. Cercammo di sviluppare un luogo dove le donne potevano incontrarsi, fare autocoscienza e sviluppare [...] la propria vena creativa"[9]. Fondamentale è anche il contributo della Librellula, storica libreria delle donne di Bologna, costituitasi nel marzo 1977 in Strada Maggiore per iniziativa di un gruppo di donne appartenenti all'esperienza dei collettivi femministi bolognesi, che nello stesso anno della sua apertura organizza Il festival del teatro femminista – tra i primi eventi culturali al femminile – e tiene presentazioni e dibattiti su produzioni corali nate da gruppi di autocoscienza, come *Equilibrismi*, raccolta documentale e fotografica legata al travestimento come forma di scoperta, a cui Donatella Franchi lavora con il proprio collettivo tra il 1977 e il 1981 e che, per una serie di vicissitudini, non vedrà mai una pubblicazione.

Si tratta di operazioni prive di un'idea di autorialità, in cui ogni forma di creatività era accolta senza gerarchie di valore[10]. Nel frattempo nei circuiti istituzionali vige ancora una ostinata resistenza a parlare di arte al femminile: emblematico il caso della celebre mostra *L'altra metà dell'avanguardia*, proposta da Lea Vergine a Franco Solmi per la GAM di Bologna già nel 1975, e che vedrà invece la luce a Milano solo nel 1980[11].

L'incontro tra arte e temi di genere si risolve spesso in conflitti e contraddizioni: pur ragionando sempre in un'ottica della differenza e contestualizzando ogni esperienza e tendenza, è un dato di fatto che, in buona parte, le artiste donne che operano negli anni delle lotte per l'emancipazione si differenziano dagli artisti uomini nei temi che caratterizzano il loro lavoro, tendendo a concentrarsi maggiormente sulle esperienze femminili e includendo temi legati all'identità di genere, alle questioni sociali e ai ruoli tradizionali delle donne nella società[12]. Pensiamo alle modalità di espressione, esposizione (o lacerazione) del corpo stesso dell'artista in lavori come quelli di Renate Bertlmann, Gina Pane o Marina Abramović, artiste passate alla Settimana Internazionale della Performance e sicuramente fonti di ispirazione per la comunità artistica bolognese e la nascita di nuove pratiche in città. Un esempio abbastanza recente di come queste abbiano contribuito a una lettura di genere della performance è rappresentato da *Significato*, azione inaugurale del Musée de L'OHM, fondato da Chiara Pergola nel 2009, in cui l'opera "diventa" il corpo di Abramović nella celeberrima performance *Rhythm 0* (1974)[13].

Costruite sui limiti della resistenza fisica, psicologica ed emotiva, in questo tipo di operazioni l'utilizzo del corpo serve a svelare le ambiguità della sua lettura nella sfera sociale e il rapporto diretto tra arte, desiderio e violenza. Sono questi temi a trovare spazio e a diventare il dispositivo di queste artiste che, unite dallo stesso substrato sociopolitico, cercano semplicemente di dare voce alle proprie esperienze personali, ponendosi domande su sé stesse, la loro identità e il loro posto nella società. Secondo Raffaella Perna, in questi anni le artiste "impiegano il corpo non soltanto come veicolo espressivo, ma come strumento attivo di azione politica, operando una simbiosi tra etica ed estetica volta a una completa ridefinizione del concetto di genere"[14].

Facciamo un passo indietro. Negli anni Sessanta e Settanta, come è noto, l'Italia era un terreno fertile per i movimenti femministi. Come ha rilevato Fiamma Lussana, il femminismo in Italia è un fenomeno sociale e culturale che si oppone al contesto politico da cui attinge. Le organizzazioni politiche femminili nate durante la Resistenza, sulla scia di una tendenza condivisa con buona parte dei movimenti femministi americani ed europei, promuovevano parità formale tra i sessi e, di conseguenza, applicavano leggi di tutela delle donne: ne è un esempio la Legge 1204 del 30 dicembre 1971, che prevede per le lavoratrici donne e madri orari ridotti e mansioni specifiche. Questo tipo di provvedimenti, per le femministe italiane non facevano altro che legittimare un ordine politico maschile "neutro e universale per definizione"[15] e avallare stereotipi già più che consolidati, imprigionando le donne nei consueti ruoli sociali. Bisognerà aspettare la seconda metà degli anni Settanta per vedere i collettivi femministi avvicinarsi alle istituzioni e alla sinistra radicale, non senza difficoltà e inconciliabilità di visioni[16]. Il binomio uguaglianza/omologazione è la base sulla quale si declinano i movimenti femministi italiani in quegli anni, anche nell'ambito della ricerca (e della critica) artistica. Non parliamo però di una linea comune ma bensì antitetica, almeno nella maggior parte dei casi.

Carla Lonzi – per fare l'esempio più noto ed emblematico – cristallizza una discontinuità radicale tra arte e femminismo, sia attraverso i suoi scritti (da cui emerge inesorabilmente il legame represso tra le due cose), sia nella decisione di abbandonare la critica d'arte per l'impegno sociale. Secondo Giovanna Zapperi, per Lonzi "l'autonomia del soggetto femminista si fonda sul rifiuto della cultura in quanto ideologia e potere che ingloba tutti gli aspetti delle relazioni sociali, in particolare per quanto riguarda il modo in cui queste contribuiscono a imprigionare la soggettività femminile in un insieme di ruoli e di identità"[17]. Il collettivo Rivolta Femminile e la relativa casa editrice Scritti di Rivolta Femminile – che la critica fonda a Roma nel 1970 con Elvira Banotti e Carla Accardi – nascono dalla difficoltà (con conseguente frustrazione) delle tre a posizionarsi esclusivamente e professionalmente nel mondo dell'arte, e promuovono il rifiuto radicale delle nozioni dominanti di creatività come pratica liberatoria per le donne[18].

Nella sua professione di critica d'arte, Lonzi aveva maturato un'insofferenza crescente nei confronti del distacco, del paternalismo e dell'idea di autorità caratteristiche dei colleghi uomini. Un rifiuto già esternato anni prima con l'articolo "La solitudine del critico" pubblicato sull'*Avanti!* nel 1963, che la porta a interessarsi agli artisti intesi come persone, piuttosto che alle opere che producono[19]. La partecipazione – come per le interviste di *Autoritratto* (1969) – diventa allora una modalità che le permette di oltrepassare il ruolo dell'osservatrice passiva, spettatrice esclusa dal processo creativo che si può identificare in modo ambivalente sia con il critico che con la donna, dato che, come osserva Donatella Franchi, nella società patriarcale in cui trova nutrimento anche il mondo dell'arte "[l]a donna ha il ruolo della controparte neutrale per eccellenza. Essa assiste ai gesti creativi dell'uomo che ha bisogno di lei come specchio del proprio io creativo senza riconoscergliene uno proprio, e cerca il partner maschile, l'artista uomo, come vero interlocutore"[20].

Ma perché per le donne è così difficile raggiungere la stessa notorietà e credibilità dei colleghi uomini? Cosa crea questo divario tra i due generi? Su questo, come sappiamo, si sta ancora dibattendo apertamente. È interessante, ad esempio, che Emanuela De Cecco abbia posto l'attenzione su come negli anni Settanta il privilegiare le istanze più partecipative in arte abbia svantaggiato le donne, quando è proprio grazie a queste che da decenni fioriscono pratiche artistiche relazionali e collettive. È ormai possibile affermare che, se l'arte propende sempre meno verso una visione unilaterale del mondo a vantaggio di una molteplicità di visioni in relazione tra loro, lo si deve alla presenza delle donne, al loro perseverare in pratiche che non puntano solo al risultato finale, ma danno valore al percorso, sempre condiviso. Allo stesso tempo è possibile affermare che, una certa parte di arte legata al comportamento si sia, proprio in quegli anni, fortemente politicizzata e legata ad aspetti di "spettacolarità", creando un divario con l'espressione della soggettività e dell'introspezione a totale svantaggio delle artiste, soprattutto quelle che utilizzavano temi, tecniche e materiali tipicamente femminili e affettivi.

Questo pregiudizio, radicato da sempre in una lettura che De Cecco ritiene ancora vasariana, ovvero basata sull'interpretazione della storia dell'arte dal punto di vista del "genio", ha fatto sì che calasse un velo censorio sull'opera di artiste la cui portata è stata rivalutata solo a posteriori (come è accaduto, ad esempio, per Maria Lai e Marisa Merz). La studiosa scrive:

> Il clima degli anni Settanta, trasferito all'ambito dell'arte, ha privilegiato artisti interessati a coinvolgere il pubblico, a lavorare sulla dimensione sociale e ha aperto alle artiste, per cultura e tradizione più sensibili alla sfera soggettiva, due strade entrambe accidentate. Artiste interessate a dinamiche dell'esperienza personale e alla dimensione quotidiana sono state relegate in un ruolo di secondo piano; altre, invece, si sono concentrate su problematiche relative al proprio ruolo nella società spostando l'interesse più sul contenuto che sullo sviluppo linguistico del lavoro[21].

In quegli anni non si riesce insomma a uscire dal "complesso di Michelangelo" di cui parlava Simona Weller. Nessuna strada si presenta sicura per le artiste, e i femminismi, nelle loro complesse declinazioni, si rivelano l'altra faccia dell'ostracismo da combattere per trovare un proprio posto nel mondo. Posizioni decisamente meno antagoniste e repulsive di quelle di Lonzi e più propense a favorire un'arte "di genere" sono rappresentate in quel decennio da autorevoli protagoniste della storia dell'arte al femminile. Tra queste vale la pena citare la gallerista Romana Loda e le artiste Anna Oberto e Mirella Bentivoglio (ma l'elenco

sarebbe molto più lungo), tra le promotrici più attive dell'arte femminista a cui va il merito di aver teorizzato e realizzato mostre di sole artiste donne che, indipendentemente dalla risposta del pubblico e della critica, hanno saputo evidenziare il forte divario tra la presenza maschile e femminile nella scena artistica di allora, in un momento storico in cui, a differenza del mondo anglosassone che conosceva già i *Women's Studies*, in Italia mancava quasi totalmente un dibattito teorico sul tema. Loda, gallerista e curatrice bresciana, sfortunatamente è ancora semi sconosciuta e oggetto di poche menzioni nell'attività critica legata a questi temi (fra queste spicca l'interesse mostrato negli ultimi anni da studiose come Perna)[22]. La stessa Lea Vergine riferisce di aver attinto da lei l'idea di dedicarsi a una rilettura della storia dell'arte in chiave femminile, come racconta nel 2001 a Ester Coen: "[h]o cominciato a notare con maggiore attenzione il lavoro delle donne finché a una mostra fatta da Romana Loda, a Brescia, una mostra storica, qualcuno dei presenti – forse la moglie di Boetti – mi disse hai scritto tante volte di artiste, perché non ti occupi seriamente di questo problema?"[23]. La mostra a cui fa riferimento Vergine è *Magma. Rassegna internazionale di donne artiste* realizzata al Castello di Oldofredi, vicino Brescia, in tre edizioni svoltesi tra il 1975 e il 1977. Nel catalogo della terza edizione, la curatrice definisce questa mostra e la precedente, *Coazione a mostrare* del 1974, da non considerare meramente come mostre femministe *tout court* poiché le artiste coinvolte rispondevano a precisi criteri selettivi. D'altro canto, Bentivoglio specifica di non essere contraria alle mostre femministe ma semplicemente di avvertirne i facili rischi[24]. Il problema dei "ghetti rosa" è un punto nodale. Come già detto, poiché alle artiste in quegli anni è precluso un ruolo attivo nel mondo istituzionale dell'arte e un pieno riconoscimento del loro lavoro, la reazione a questa censura rende molto complesso il loro rapporto con il movimento legato all'emancipazione delle donne e, paradossalmente, spesso le allontana da questo. Prevale quindi una chiusura nei confronti di una lettura di genere nell'arte da parte di alcune artiste che temono di essere tagliate fuori da un dibattito artistico alto. È ad esempio il caso della mostra curata da Bentivoglio nel 1972 al Centro Tool di Milano, dal titolo *Esposizione Internazionale di Operatrici Visuali*. Anna Oberto è chiamata a scrivere un testo introduttivo alla mostra, pubblicato come testo-cartolina nel decimo numero della rivista *Ana Eccetera* nel "Manifesto Femminista Anaculturale". Racconta l'autrice:

> Ugo Carrega del Centro Tool di Milano da tempo pensava di ospitare una mostra di sole donne. Quando nel 1971 Bentivoglio gli propose questa straordinaria raccolta di opere di artiste internazionali, Carrega, che era stato nostro redattore, mi chiese di scrivere il testo di presentazione. Era l'occasione, con il titolo *Perché una mostra di sole donne?*, per dichiarare il mio atteggiamento, non solo ideologico, contro l'arte

come merce di scambio, contro l'emarginazione della donna in cultura, ma anche le mie elaborazioni sul linguaggio al femminile, mettendo in parallelo il movimento politico di liberazione delle donne che iniziava a manifestarsi in quegli anni con la liberazione dal linguaggio codificato al maschile della nuova scrittura visuale, per segnificare la propria identità[25].

Nonostante *Esposizione Internazionale di Operatrici Visuali* si integrasse alla perfezione con la volontà di sensibilizzare sul tema della discriminazione delle artiste donne, fu contestata dalle stesse, buona parte delle quali, chiamate a esporre, declinarono l'invito e apostrofarono l'esposizione come "sessista", sostenendo – come riferisce Anne Marie Sauzeau Boetti – che "l'arte è buona o cattiva, ma non ha sesso"[26]. Se quello che obiettavano queste artiste è vero, è opportuno contestualizzare tale affermazione attraverso quello che scriveva nel 1976 la critica femminista statunitense Lucy Lippard:

> "La mia arte non ha genere" è un'affermazione comune. Naturalmente l'arte non ha genere, ma gli artisti sì. Stiamo accorgendoci solo adesso che questi "stereotipi" che mettono sull'esperienza femminile sono caratteristiche positive, non negative. Non è la qualità della nostra femminilità che è inferiore, ma la qualità di una società da cui è generato un simile punto di vista[27].

Il progetto di Bentivoglio fu in seguito replicato in diverse gallerie d'Italia, alla Columbia University a New York e al Museo d'arte di San Paolo in Brasile, fino ad approdare alla Biennale di Venezia del 1978 con l'esposizione *Materializzazione del linguaggio* presso i Magazzini del Sale alle Zattere, dove si presentava il lavoro di ottanta artiste italiane e internazionali. Secondo Arianna Di Genova, Bentivoglio "rivendicò in quella sede la primogenitura delle donne nel plasmare il mondo, nel sancire la realtà attraverso la manipolazione e la capacità semantica. Nella particolarissima rassegna innestò le sperimentazioni delle autrici a trascrizioni grafiche e prove anonime, procedendo verso la ricognizione di un 'metalinguaggio' presente nella produzione femminile"[28]. La mostra in Biennale ebbe una genesi piuttosto travagliata: poco tempo per organizzarla, difficoltà nella ricezione delle opere da esporre (in particolare dal blocco sovietico, da dove provenivano lavori di artiste emergenti grazie alle quali la curatrice intendeva dare voce a chi viveva una situazione di repressione) e subì anche la scelta di una sede piuttosto defilata. Inoltre, la critica tese a ignorarla a causa del suo carattere considerato separatista. In realtà, l'esperienza segna una tappa fondamentale verso l'evoluzione dell'incidenza femminile nel mondo dell'arte perché è di fatto il primo riconoscimento dato alle artiste militanti negli spazi e nei circuiti istituzionali. Non a caso è stata recentemente omaggiata da Cecilia Alemani nella Biennale di Venezia del 2022, *The Milk of Dreams*, in occasione della quale è stata pubblicata anche la ristampa anastatica del catalogo dell'edizione del 1978[29].

Superati gli anni Settanta, arriviamo a quella che la stessa Bentivoglio ha definito "la decade del riflusso"[30]. Negli anni Ottanta il tema dei femminismi sembra infatti avere una battuta d'arresto. Come rileva Francesca Della Ventura:

> Con il dissolversi della seconda ondata femminista e con i cambiamenti politici avvenuti tra la fine degli Settanta e i primi anni Ottanta – non solo in Italia con il consolidarsi del Partito Socialista di Bettino Craxi, ma anche nel resto dell'attuale Europa con François Mitterrand in Francia, Margaret Thatcher in Inghilterra e Helmut Kohl in Germania – si ritiene che la questione della partecipazione attiva dei cittadini, anche delle donne, nella politica passi in secondo piano e che di conseguenza anche la ricerca artistica che nei decenni precedenti si era nutrita delle contestazioni sociali venga meno, soprattutto dal punto di vista femminista[31].

Si tratta di un periodo storico che, rispetto al decennio precedente, cambia rotta riguardo a molti aspetti del fare artistico. In particolare, negli spazi espositivi istituzionalizzati, cambiano gli equilibri tra critici, curatori, galleristi e artisti (con netto svantaggio per gli ultimi). Il critico d'arte tende a essere un tutt'uno con il prodotto che intende vendere al pubblico, ne fa una emanazione di sé stesso: ne è un esempio l'articolo che Achille Bonito Oliva pubblica nel novembre del 1979 su *Flash Art*, identificandosi con la "sua" transavanguardia come Gustave Flaubert s'identificava con *Madame Bovary* ("La Transavanguardia cest'moi!"). Il successo planetario del suo progetto non può che confermare che, in quel periodo, questa era ancora la formula giusta in termini di mercato, visto il tramonto dell'arte ideologica e l'avvio dell'edonismo reaganiano. Se la transavanguardia è frutto di un matrimonio "morganatico" fra Pablo Picasso e Marcel Duchamp figuriamoci cosa possano mai entrarci le donne.

Tuttavia, gli anni Ottanta non rappresentano solo un passo indietro per i *Gender Studies*. Gli spazi non-profit riescono, ancora una volta, a mettere su piazza una possibilità alternativa e Bologna, in questo contesto, fa da pioniera. La città, anche grazie al contributo dei movimenti studenteschi e a un'amministrazione comunale compiacente, vive nel passaggio dagli anni Settanta agli anni Ottanta un periodo tanto difficile sul lato politico e sociale, quanto magico nella costruzione di una sorta di mitologia urbana che la vede crocevia delle istanze culturali più innovative. Fondato nel 1978, il Cassero è stato uno dei primi centri alternativi in Italia, affermandosi come un importante punto di incontro e supporto per la comunità LGBTQIA+ bolognese e oltre[32]. L'ottenimento, nel 1980, di una sede ufficiale in città grazie al sindaco Renato Zangheri, è un momento senza precedenti, perché segna l'uscita da una condizione di invisibilità a cui la comunità LGBTQIA+ era abituata da sempre. Come racconta Daniele Del Pozzo "[i] le militanti performavano pubblicamente – in piazza, sui giornali, negli uffici del Comune – la propria identità e il proprio desiderio, mettendoci le loro facce e i corpi. Questo uso consapevole, pubblico e politico, del proprio corpo non nasce a caso e discende senza dubbio dalle precedenti manifestazioni femministe"[33].

Nato come luogo di rifugio e solidarietà per le persone LGBTQIA+ dalle discriminazioni e dall'ostracismo imperanti, il Cassero è stato anche un punto di riferimento attivo sul ruolo della prevenzione e contro la stigmatizzazione dell'AIDS, quando il tema era ancora avvolto nella censura del perbenismo. Ha inoltre avuto da subito – e questo non è un aspetto secondario – anche un ruolo documentale: la costruzione di un archivio e una biblioteca era già nei primi verbali del direttivo, a riprova della ferrea volontà di raccontare una storia nella storia in cui i cittadini potessero rispecchiarsi. "Oggi parliamo di decolonizzazione – dice Sara De Giovanni – ma si cercava già allora, in una qualche maniera, di decolonizzare i contesti culturali della città da una idea etero-normativa"[34]. Questa realtà bolognese, prima e unica nel suo genere in Italia, ha effettivamente utilizzato la cultura per avvicinare la cittadinanza a quella che fino ad allora era considerata solo una minoranza, una realtà nomade che pian piano conquista un posto fra le mura cittadine. Ci vorranno due anni perché la comunità LGBTQIA+ espugni la storica sede di Porta Saragozza: lo farà in grande stile il 26 luglio 1982 con un corteo inaugurale fatto di girotondi, distribuzione di caramelle e un memorabile ballo in terrazza con Sandra Soster, allora Assessora alla Cultura in città.

Come ha osservato Stefano Casi: "la nascita del Cassero avvenne sull'onda di quel pensiero fantasioso, alternativo, volontaristico e talvolta pasticcione degli anni '70, ma conteneva già il senso e l'oggetto di quel che solo negli ultimi anni si è sempre più chiarito: il ritorno dall'insurrezione all'integrazione, sia come idea che come obiettivo"[35].

A Bologna, nel 1981, nasce dall'idea di un gruppo di giovani studenti anche la galleria neon, uno spazio espositivo indipendente che, nei suoi trent'anni di storia, ha creato un modello senza uguali di scambio e promozione culturale fuori dai circuiti (e dalle logiche) istituzionali. Pur sentendo sulle proprie spalle il peso del "post '77" bolognese, neon è stata capace da subito di rivolgersi al presente, virando sempre verso la sperimentazione. Più che una semplice galleria è stata una vera e propria comunità in cui interagivano allo stesso livello artisti, critici, curatori e collaboratori. Gino Gianuizzi, tra gli ideatori del progetto, racconta come il tutto sia nato dall'amicizia con Stefano Delli, Valeria Medica, Antonia Ruggeri, e Maurizio Vetrugno "perché ci piacevamo e ci piaceva stare insieme e ci volevamo bene e immaginare un luogo e un progetto condiviso ci sembrava una prospettiva entusiasmante"[36]. Neon diventa da subito la cassa di risonanza di molti artisti emergenti, tra i quali si annoverano voci femminili poi consolidate anche negli ambienti espositivi istituzionali. È il caso, tra le altre, di Eva Marisaldi, Antonella Mazzoni, Patrizia Giambi, Mili Romano senza contare che, per lo spazio, la critica Francesca Alinovi funge – utilizzando le parole del suo fondatore – da "catalizzatore" dalla fondazione e fino alla sua prematura scomparsa. Racconta Gianuizzi: "Francesca è entrata a neon il giorno dell'inaugurazione e ci siamo piaciuti immediatamente. Ha riconosciuto la stessa aria che respirava nei suoi primi viaggi di esplorazione della scena newyorkese"[37]. E partendo da Alinovi, saranno tantissime le curatrici che vi si avvicenderanno negli anni[38].

Per quanto riguarda le artiste, è in particolare Marisaldi ad avere con neon una sorta di sodalizio: partecipa nel 1987, ancora studentessa all'Accademia di Belle Arti di Bologna, a una serie di collettive dedicate alle nuove generazioni di artisti italiani e internazionali, con cui neon inaugura la sua nuova stagione seguita al trasferimento nella nuova sede di via Avesella. Nel 1990 tiene la sua prima personale, *ee*, a cura di Roberto Daolio e con quest'ultimo, che era stato anche il suo professore in Accademia, partecipa l'anno dopo alla mostra *Nuova Officina Bolognese* alla GAM di Bologna, presentando l'istallazione *Scatola di Montaggio*, opera rimasta emblematica per i modi peculiari usati dall'artista per raccontare le difficoltà e, contemporaneamente, l'urgenza nel comunicare con gli altri[39]. Nel 1993 Marisaldi realizza negli spazi di neon *La portata umana è nulla*, producendo un pozzo profondo tre metri incastonato tra i due piani della galleria e riempito di sabbie mobili. Un allestimento tanto ardito quanto suggestivo, che prova ancora una volta come questo spazio espositivo fosse pronto a "osare", creando situazioni al limite della sicurezza, spiazzanti ma estremamente suggestive. Per Elisabetta Modena, che ne dà un racconto entusiasta nel catalogo *NO, NEON, NO CRY*, osservare questo abisso all'interno di uno spazio espositivo ha "rappresentato un momento fondamentale non solo nella storia dell'artista e della galleria, ma anche in quella dell'arte italiana"[40].

Le modalità espressive in cui questa artista e i colleghi della sua generazione operano, riconducono al clima tipico degli anni Novanta, dato dal superamento dell'estetica postmoderna a vantaggio di un ritorno all'oggetto e all'interesse nei confronti della comunicazione massmediale. Utilizzando le parole di Gianni Romano "[s]e i numerosi movimenti artistici sorti all'inizio del Novecento sono caratterizzati da una volontà di rottura con il passato, i non-movimenti di fine Novecento sembrano caratterizzati da una decisa volontà di apertura verso il futuro"[41]. A progredire è anche il dibattito teorico tra arte e femminismo che, alla vigilia del nuovo millennio, arriva finalmente a istituzionalizzare gli studi sulle donne artiste, pur con tutte le difficoltà che il mondo accademico ha da sempre nei confronti delle novità. A Bologna sono gli anni degli *artist-run space*, spazi indipendenti, non-profit e dalla natura ibrida, come Il Graffio di via Sant'Apollonia, frequentato dai gruppi di autocoscienza femministi dalla fine degli anni Settanta e che dal 1994 viene gestito dall'artista e docente Anteo Radovan. Fino alla chiusura, avvenuta nel 2002, Il Graffio è stato una palestra per giovani esordienti, spesso studenti dell'Accademia. Tra questi Claudia Losi, artista e curatrice dall'approccio multidisciplinare che affronta questioni legate alla natura, al corpo e alla sfera femminile. In perfetta sintonia con le creative del ventennio precedente, l'artista adotta pratiche partecipative e utilizza materiali organici come lana, pelliccia o pelle, per indagare le relazioni con gli spazi privati e i luoghi intimi. Losi, come altre artiste della sua generazione (penso a Sabrina Mezzaqui con cui ha condiviso l'esperienza de Il Graffio), sfida le convenzioni culturali e sociali e incoraggia una riflessione sulla femminilità e sulla sua relazione con la natura e l'ambiente circostante.

Spesso i progetti realizzati dalle artiste in questo spazio si basano sull'idea dello scambio come forma di liberazione, esattamente come accadeva nei circoli femministi di autocoscienza. Ne è un esempio *Andata e Ritorno*, mostra collettiva realizzata in occasione di Bologna 2000 Capitale Europea della Cultura: pensata da Federica Manfredini e Donatella Franchi nel 1997, questa *mail art* al femminile in cui una scatola da imballaggio viaggia tra artiste che la usano per scambiarsi opere, è stata un'esperienza utile a intrecciare rapporti con artiste di altre città.

Anche le associazioni culturali e residenze d'artista Nosadella.due[42] di Elisa Del Prete, e Novella Guerra di Annalisa Cattani hanno sempre prediletto pratiche discorsive più che oggettuali, e processi creativi condivisi, come *To walk is easy. Just go*, realizzato in occasione di Art City Bologna nel 2014, a conclusione del programma di residenza dell'artista e attivista sudafricana Kyla Davis sui temi della giustizia sociale e ambientale. Questo tipo di approccio alla produzione artistica, finalmente sdoganato, dimostra che attraverso lo scardinamento delle categorie prestabilite che avevano egemonizzato i decenni precedenti, si incentiva la diversità e l'eterogeneità di voci femminili che ancora una volta guardano all'attivismo di coloro che le avevano precedute. Tuttavia, il discorso femminista non è più quello praticato negli anni della contestazione sociale e, pur prendendo le mosse dal pensiero della generazione di vent'anni prima, si rimette in gioco guardando al presente, alla globalizzazione e alle imperanti forme di ibridazione da cui ogni espressività non può più prescindere. Finalmente, parlando di generi come frutto di sovrastrutture, e quindi senza negarli né enfatizzarli, possiamo guardare in modo più trasparente alla produzione artistica femminile e fare nostre le parole dell'artista Mona Lisa Tina:

Gli approcci artistici e le possibilità espressive dell'arte delle donne, come sappiamo, sono tanto numerosi quanto le artiste.

La cosa interessante è che i critici del femminismo, che preferiscono evitare il dibattito sui meccanismi della società e della "guerra" tra i sessi, sostengono che la "buona arte" non ha genere; al contrario, i critici contemporanei sottolineano come il genere, che ha comunque un ruolo, non debba essere considerato un dato di fatto ma una sovrastruttura sociale. Forse nessuno dei punti di vista ha avuto o ha un'influenza di rilievo sulla consapevolezza e sui meccanismi emotivi e psichici che spingono una donna a essere artista e non a diventare un'artista[43].

1. Linda Nochlin, "Why Have There Been No Great Women Artists?", *ARTnews* 69, no. 9, gennaio 1971.

2. Per una rilettura del testo di Nochlin si veda la prefazione di Maria Antonietta Trasforini all'edizione italiana (*Perché non ci sono state grandi artiste?*, trad. Jessica Perna, Castelvecchi, Roma 2015); si veda anche Giovanna Zapperi, "L'Arte non è neutra", *Il Manifesto*, 27 febbraio 2015, https://ilmanifesto.it/larte-non-e-neutra.

3. Maria Antonietta Trasforini, "Lontane da dove. Artiste fra centri e periferie nei mondi dell'arte", in *Arte-mondo. Storia dell'arte, storie dell'arte*, a cura di Emanuela De Cecco, Postmedia Books, Milano 2010, p. 48.

4. Chiara Zamboni, "Momenti radianti", in Luisa Muraro, Wanda Tommasi, Chiara Zamboni, *Approfittare dell'assenza. Punti di avvistamento sulla tradizione*, Liguori, Napoli 2002, p. 171–85.

5. Mariella Pasinati, "Grandi artiste, ipotesi di genealogie femministe", *Letterate Magazine, SIL – Società Italiana delle Letterate*, no. 104, 4 agosto 2014, https://www.societadelleletterate.it/2014/07/5995.

6. Si veda Laura Iamurri, "Femmes artistes italiennes du XXe siècle: Il complesso di Michelangelo, Rome 1977", *Artl@s Bulletin* 8, no. 1, primavera 2019, https://core.ac.uk/reader/220148380.

7. Virginia Woolf, *A Room of One's Own* (1974), trad. Maria Antonietta Saracino, Einaudi, Torino 2020, p. 5. Il riferimento alla scrittrice inglese, ormai pietra miliare del femminismo, non è casuale perché si collega ai rapporti tra scrittura e arti visive che prendono vita dalle pratiche collettive. I circoli di conversazione che Woolf, sua sorella, l'artista Vanessa Bell e i due fratelli Thoby e Adrian Stephen tengono nel loro salotto londinese a inizio Novecento sono una forma di avanguardia artistica in netta contrapposizione con gli altri movimenti coevi e rappresentano un esempio di ascolto reciproco senza gerarchie di genere, inteso sia come genere maschile e femminile che come gerarchie di forme d'espressione artistica. Si veda Donatella Franchi, "La novità fertile", in *Matrice. Pensiero delle donne e pratiche artistiche*, a cura di Donatella Franchi, Libreria delle donne di Milano, Milano 2004, p. 13–32.

8. Si veda l'intervista alla regista in: Serenella Calderara, "Perché dire 'Io sono femminista' fa ancora paura", in *Left*, 30 Ottobre 2019, https://left.it/2019/10/30/perche-dire-io-sono-femminista-fa-ancora-paura/. Sul tema dell'isteria si veda anche: Maria Antonietta Trasforini, "Costruzioni nell'isteria", in Uliana Zanetti (a cura di), *Autoritratti. Iscrizioni del femminile nell'arte italiana contemporanea*, catalogo della mostra, Bologna: MAMbo, 2013, p. 139–41.

9. Oderso Rubini, Andrea Tinti (a cura di), *Non disperdetevi. 1977–1982. San Francisco, New York, Bologna, le zone libere del mondo*, Arcana Libri, Roma 2003, p. 326.

10. L'attività dei centri di autocoscienza femministi di allora ruotavano tra la Librellula, il Centro di documentazione delle donne di Bologna (CDD) e la Libreria delle donne di Milano. Attualmente il CDD si trova in via del Piombo 5 a Bologna, e comprende la Biblioteca italiana delle donne, l'Archivio di storia delle donne e il Centro di iniziativa politica e culturale. Dal 1983 è in convenzione tra l'associazione Orlando e il Comune di Bologna. La Libreria delle Donne ha invece sede in via San Felice 16/a ed è gestita dall'Associazione femminista e trans femminista Non Una di Meno Bologna.

11. Si veda Maria Antonietta Trasforini, "Luoghi del femminismo, sconfinamenti e azioni 'performative'. Bologna anni '70", in *La performance a Bologna negli anni '70*, a cura di Uliana Zanetti, Edizioni MAMbo, Bologna 2023, p. 226–35.

12. Sul tema della difficoltà per le artiste che operano negli anni delle lotte sociali a trovare un legame proficuo tra arte e femminismo si vedano: Maria Antonietta Trasforini, "A paso distinto. Arte y feminismo en Italia desde los años setenta", *MODOS: Revista de Història da Arte* 7, no. 2, maggio 2023; l'intervista all'artista Suzanne Santoro in Marta Seravalli, *Arte e femminismo a Roma negli anni Settanta*, Biblink, Roma 2013, p. 217–24.

13. L'azione *Significato* si è svolta alla galleria neon>campobase a Bologna il 29 settembre 2009. Per l'occasione, ai presenti sono stati offerti strumenti da incisione (attualmente conservati nella secreta del Musée de l'OHM) con cui intervenire sul piano del mobile. Per una descrizione delle intenzioni dell'artista si veda Chiara Pergola, "La forza fisica. Per un#arte femminista globale", *Manastabal. Femminismo materialista*, 27 ottobre 2019, https://manastabalblog.wordpress.com/2019/10/27/la-forza-fisica-per-un-arte-femminista-globale/.

14. Raffaella Perna, *In forma di fotografia. Ricerche artistiche in Italia dal 1960 al 1970*, DeriveApprodi, Roma 2009, p. 71.

15. Fiamma Lussana, *Il movimento femminista in Italia. Esperienze, storie, memorie*, Carocci, Roma 2012, p. 33.

16. Si veda, soprattutto per il tema dell'aborto legato alla Legge 194, Raffaella Perna, *Arte, fotografia e femminismo in Italia negli anni Settanta*, Postmedia Books, Milano 2013, p. 7–11.

17. Giovanna Zapperi, "Dialoghi tra creatività e femminismo: letture di Carla Lonzi nell'arte contemporanea", *Narrativa*, no. 37, 2015, p. 53, http://journals.openedition.org/narrativa/970.

18. Anne Marie Sauzeau Boetti parte dagli stessi presupposti di Carla Lonzi ma giunge a una conclusione diversa pochi anni più tardi: per lei il potere creativo della donna artista implica di fatto il tradimento dei meccanismi espressivi della cultura maschilista e patriarcale e porta quindi verso una sua radicale ri-significazione. Si veda Anne Marie Sauzeau Boetti, "Negative Capability as Practice in Women's Art", *Studio International* 191, no. 979, 1976, p. 24–25.

19. Si vedano Laura Iamurri, *Un margine che sfugge. Carla Lonzi e l'arte in Italia 1955–1970*, Quodlibet Studio, Macerata 2016; Mariasole

Garacci, "Sputare sulla critica d'arte. Carla Lonzi e il soggetto imprevisto contro la dialettica", *OperaViva*, 19 settembre 2016, https://operavivamagazine.org/sputare-sulla-critica-darte/.

20 Franchi, "La novità fertile", p. 28.

21 Emanuela De Cecco, "Trame: per una mappa transitoria dell'arte italiana femminile degli anni Novanta e dintorni", in Emanuela De Cecco, Gianni Romano (a cura di), *Contemporanee. Percorsi e poetiche delle artiste dagli anni Ottanta a oggi*, Postmedia Books, Milano 2009, p. 16.

22 Si veda Raffella Perna, "Mostre al femminile: Romana Loda e l'arte delle donne nell'Italia degli anni Settanta", *Ricerche di S/Confine* VI, no. 1, 2015, p. 143–54.

23 Ester Coen, *Schegge. Lea Vergine sull'arte contemporanea. Intervista di Ester Coen*, Skira, Milano 2001, p. 38. Mi interessa porre l'attenzione all'accenno da parte di Lea Vergine alla moglie dell'artista Alighiero Boetti: si tratta della già citata Anne-Marie Sauzeau, impegnata in quegli anni nell'indagine e nella promozione della produzione femminile, interessi che non a caso si riflettono in alcune opere del marito come *Maschio Femmina* (1973–74), in cui l'indagine sulla differenza sessuale lo allontana da temi e approcci "al maschile" consueti in quegli anni. Anche la tendenza di Boetti a operare in collettività e a demandare a terzi la produzione fattuale dei propri lavori è in linea con il rifiuto dello stereotipo dell'artista-genio a favore di una concezione dell'operazione artistica come fatto sociale.

24 Si veda Romana Loda (a cura di), *Magma: rassegna internazionale di donne artiste*, catalogo della mostra, Iseo: Castello Oldofredi; Verona: Museo di Castelvecchio, 1975–77.

25 Anna Oberto, Raffaella Perna, "Dare corpo alla parola. Intervista ad Anna Oberto", *OperaViva*, 18 luglio 2016, https://operavivamagazine.org/dare-corpo-alla-parola/.

26 Sauzeau Boetti, "Negative Capability as Practice in Women's Art", p. 24.

27 Lucy Lippard, *From the Center. Feminist Essays on Women's Art*, Dutton, New York 1976, p. 147–48.

28 Arianna Di Genova, "Mirella Bentivoglio, il corpo delle parole", in Maura Pozzati (a cura di), *Artiste della critica*, Corraini Edizioni, Mantova 2015, p. 50.

29 La presenza dell'artista alla Biennale di Venezia 2022 era all'interno della capsula chiamata *Corpo orbita*, in cui Cecilia Alemani ha inserito l'opera *Storia del monumento* che Mirella Bentivoglio realizzò con Annalisa Alloatti nel 1968. L'opera consiste in una cartella di sei litografie definita dall'autrice il simbolo stesso della "caduta del feticcio" inteso come il simbolo maschile del logos.

30 *Post Scriptum. Artiste in Italia tra linguaggio e immagine negli anni '60 e '70 (VIII Biennale Donna di Ferrara)*, a cura di Anna Maria Fioravanti Baraldi, catalogo della mostra, Ferrara: Padiglione d'Arte Contemporanea, 1998, p. 4.

31 Francesca Della Ventura, "Gli anni Ottanta e il lento revisionismo dei femminismi: l'Italia transavanguardista e la *Subkultur* tedesca", *Flash Art*, 20 Maggio 2021, https://flash---art.it/2021/05/gli-anni-ottanta-e-il-lento-revisionismo-dei-femminismi/.

32 Si veda Stefano Casi (a cura di), *Teatro in delirio: la vera storia del K.G.B. & B.-Kassero gay band & ballet*, Quaderni di critica omosessuale, no. 7, Centro di Documentazione Cassero, Bologna, 1989; per una ricostruzione della storia del Cassero si veda anche il documentario realizzato da Andrea Adriatico nel 2015, *Torri, checche e tortellini. Appunti per una storia senza storia dell'omosessualità del '900*.

33 "Il Cassero. Performare il genere, conversazione con Sara De Giovanni e Daniele del Pozzo", in Zanetti, *La performance a Bologna negli anni '70*, p. 330.

34 *Ibid.*

35 Stefano Casi, "Le checche di Bologna che cambiarono la storia", *casicritici*, 14 giugno 2015, https://casicritici.com/2015/06/14/le-checche-di-bologna-che-cambiarono-la-storia/.

36 Valentina Rossi, "Gino Gianuizzi racconta la galleria neon e la mostra che ne ripercorre la mitica storia", *ZERO Bologna*, 20 luglio 2022, https://zero.eu/it/persone/gino-gianuizzi-neon/.

37 Gino Gianuizzi, Eleonora Mariani (a cura di), *NO, NEON, NO CRY*, catalogo della mostra, Bologna: MAMbo, 2022, p. 5.

38 Su circa 300 eventi tra azioni, mostre e rassegne, nell'elenco completo disponibile nella cronologia in appendice al catalogo si contano 83 curatrici.

39 Di quest'opera ne dà un significativo ricordo il collezionista Giorgio Fasol, che era entrato in contatto con l'artista proprio grazie a neon e che comprò l'opera. Si veda Gianuizzi, Mariani, *NO, NEON, NO CRY*, p. 99.

40 *Ibid.*, p. 137. Sul lavoro di Eva Marisaldi si veda anche: Elisabetta Modena, "Eva Marisaldi, Dopolavoro. Frammenti di realtà al Premio Suzzara (1948–2013)", *Ricerche di S/Confine* VII, no. 1, 2016, p. 110–30.

41 Romano, "Pratiche mediali nell'arte delle donne: 1977–2000", in De Cecco, Romano, *Contemporanee*, p. 46.

42 Nel corso del suo decennio di attività (tra il 2006 e il 2016) Nosadella.due ha portato a Bologna oltre sessanta tra artisti e curatori e offerto eventi, performance, laboratori, proiezioni e conferenze focalizzate soprattutto sui processi da cui l'opera d'arte ha origine prima che sulla sua finalizzazione. Si veda http://www.nosadelladue.com.

43 Mona Lisa Tina, "Il linguaggio transgender dell'arte e il suo eterno femminino", in Lori Adragna, *Il corpo delle donne #1 [Archivio di una curatrice di performance]*, Inside Art Autori, Roma 2018, p. 117.

LA *MISE EN SCÈNE* DELL'INDIPENDENZA
Davide Da Pieve

Il rapporto di amore e odio che i cosiddetti spazi indipendenti intrattengono con le istituzioni ufficiali potrebbe essere il minimo comune denominatore di una categoria ampia e sfaccettata, sebbene ancora molto poco studiata. Che si tratti di un sentimento più simile all'odio o all'amore poco importa perché, in entrambi i casi, ne scaturisce quel tipo di rapporto e relazione che determina la ragion d'essere di questi luoghi che, più proviamo a osservare da vicino, meno ci sembrano essere realmente indipendenti e distaccati dall'intricata matassa su cui crescono i mondi dell'arte. A partire dal modo di "porsi, parlare e gesticolare" degli spazi indipendenti bolognesi e di coloro che li frequentavano tra gli anni Settanta e i primi decenni del nuovo millennio, sulla scorta dell'approccio sociologico elaborato da Erwin Goffman[1], presenteremo in questo testo alcuni esiti e teorie derivate dallo studio delle interazioni tra i gruppi che animavano alcuni di questi spazi, per provare a capire quale fosse il loro ruolo nella società e, in particolare, nel mondo dell'arte. Tale esercizio è particolarmente complesso in quanto le fonti a nostra disposizione sono molto poche: di fatto, il presente volume vuole proprio andare a riempire in modo sistematico questo grande vuoto, fino a oggi parzialmente colmato dai video documentari realizzati da Emanuele Angiuli[2] e da un numero esiguo di pubblicazioni ed esposizioni. Le nostre fonti consistono per lo più in racconti personali, autoproduzioni e VHS, non sono in grado di restituirci un quadro completo e veritiero in quanto inevitabilmente parziali. Uno degli aspetti più interessanti e originali di questa ricerca consiste proprio nel doversi confrontare con documenti inusuali, tipici di quel periodo storico – come flyer, locandine scritte a mano, opuscoli e fanzine – attraverso cui è possibile percepire il clima del tempo dal punto di vista visivo e linguistico, ma che lascia numerosi interrogativi alla ricostruzione dei fatti.

Pochissimi di questi luoghi hanno conservato e riordinato archivi, soprattutto se risalenti al periodo pre-digitale. Si pensi per esempio alla Traumfabrik, casa occupata nell'aprile 1976 che, nel giro di pochi anni, è diventata un punto di riferimento per molti in città e alla quale, nel 2007, è stata dedicata un'esposizione negli spazi di neon – all'epoca già neon>campobase – grazie al ritrovamento fortuito di uno scatolone contenente 400 disegni realizzati da coloro che attraversavano questo luogo. "Una mattina Piera [Zaganelli] arriva in ufficio e mi consegna uno scatolone su cui era scritto a pennarello *Disegni di Huber* e mi dice che gliel'ha dato Alessandra Andrini" dichiara Gianpietro Huber, uno dei principali protagonisti dello spazio insieme a Filippo Scozzari e Giorgio Lavagna, nello spezzone di un articolo[3]. Con questo scatolone si riapre "il file TRAUMFABRIK. Il caos creativo di Via Clavature 20, [...] dove Huber e Lavagna riportano in vita il progetto mettendolo a disposizione di una nuova generazione di creativi

estremisti"[4], si legge nelle battute finali del comunicato stampa dell'esposizione organizzata da neon>campobase.

Queste due brevi citazioni ci mostrano che in alcuni casi nemmeno i fondatori degli spazi sono a conoscenza di dove si trovino i loro materiali, ma soprattutto ci fa rendere conto di quanto i testi che accompagnano le esposizioni alimentino una certa narrazione che, inevitabilmente, influenza la percezione e il significato di ciò che osserviamo: per esempio, cosa significa esattamente "creativo estremista"?

In questo studio non adotteremo un approccio ontologico, cercheremo piuttosto di capire in che modo tali definizioni contribuiscano alla creazione del ruolo di questi spazi, e quale sia l'influenza esercitata da tali significati sulla percezione delle attività artistiche che essi propongono. Il focus sarà quindi sui materiali di mediazione prodotti dagli spazi indipendenti bolognesi: non ci limiteremo al materiale di accompagnamento delle esposizioni, ma ci rivolgeremo a tutta quella documentazione – prevalentemente testuale nel nostro caso, ma che può anche non esserlo, come nel caso di video, registrazioni audio, ecc. – disponibile e prodotta dagli spazi espositivi soprattutto a scopo di promozione e che, inevitabilmente, aggiunge senso e arricchisce l'esperienza del pubblico all'interno dello spazio.

Nel caso appena citato, nel breve testo di comunicazione di lancio dell'esposizione *Traumfabrik* da neon>campobase, siamo di fronte a quelle che Jérôme Glicenstein definisce "mediazioni costituenti", ovvero "tutti gli scritti preliminari che portano alla realizzazione di un'esposizione"[5] e che ne influenzano la percezione dei contenuti. Già Howard S. Becker aveva rilevato come tutti i lavoratori culturali contribuiscano alla creazione dell'opera d'arte, soprattutto da un punto di vista pratico[6]. Attraverso una riflessione mirata sulla mediazione, possiamo renderci conto che anche il ruolo che uno spazio ha nella società e soprattutto il tipo di interazione che esso ha con le istituzioni contribuisce alla costruzione del significato di ciò che presenta ed espone.

Il primo momento in cui uno spazio esprime se stesso, ciò che potremmo definire la prima "mediazione costituente", è inevitabilmente il documento relativo al suo atto di nascita. Mettersi alla ricerca di tal documento significa ritrovarsi di fronte a qualcosa di diverso in base al tipo di spazio che l'ha prodotto. Di fatto esistono due possibilità: nel caso di spazi occupati, molto probabilmente, si tratterà di documenti che non hanno valore legale, di testimonianze effimere prodotte dagli occupanti (opuscoli, fanzine, locandine, striscioni, ecc.); se invece abbiamo a che fare con uno spazio a cui fa capo un'associazione dobbiamo tenere conto che quest'ultima, per definirsi tale e distinguersi da ciò che viene definito "gruppo informale", può essere costituita solo attraverso un *atto pubblico*[7]. Chiaramente, ai materiali lasciati dai fondatori si somma tutto un corollario di fonti che provengono dall'esterno, quali articoli di giornale, interviste, memorie, ricerche e studi condotti a posteriori, attraverso cui è possibile risalire a date e fatti specifici.

È importante soffermarsi sulla natura dei documenti di mediazione perché, ad esempio, neon in quanto associazione culturale ha dovuto redigere un atto costitutivo[8], il quale comporta la costituzione di un gruppo formale e il consenso nei confronti di tutta una serie di aspetti legali da rispettare. Un altro dettaglio da non sottovalutare è che, grazie a questo documento, sappiamo con certezza che Gino Gianuizzi, Valeria Medica, Stefano Delli, Antonia Ruggeri e Maurizio Vetrugno sono i fondatori dello spazio e che i primi tre facevano parte del comitato direttivo, informazioni importanti per la ricostruzione storica, ma anche per sapere chi aveva la responsabilità legale di quel luogo. Questo tipo di documentazione non esiste ovviamente nel caso di spazi occupati e, anzi, la dinamica delle responsabilità è totalmente invertita: coloro che occupano tendono a nascondere le proprie identità perché stanno facendo qualcosa di evidentemente illegale. Di conseguenza, anche gli artisti che espongono in questi spazi stanno in qualche modo infrangendo la legge. La definizione di "creativo estremista" potrebbe forse ora risultare già più chiara, dato che, essendo stata la Traumfabrik una casa occupata, tale binomio indica non solo un tipo di creatività particolare dal punto di vista estetico, ma anche l'incidenza delle peculiarità dello spazio nel tipo di creatività esercitata in questo luogo.

A partire da tali aspetti – per certi versi scontati, ma fondamentali per entrare nel merito degli argomenti che si intende affrontare – il ruolo che gioca uno spazio occupato è certamente molto fascinoso, assolutamente autentico e genuino, perché delle persone, in nome delle loro urgenze e ideali, prendono una posizione netta e si mettono in qualche modo in pericolo, usando coerentemente parole come indipendenza, autonomia o alternativa. Più nello specifico, per tali spazi è possibile assumere questo ruolo di autentica indipendenza, in quanto organizzati attraverso la formulazione di regole costitutive, ovvero ciascuno di essi risponde a una propria legge e non a quella dello Stato. Come spiega John Searle, le regole degli scacchi – e, più in generale, le regole elaborate per un gioco – sono istituite appositamente per quello scopo specifico, e sono quindi definibili regole costitutive; differenti da queste sono invece le regole normative, ovvero quelle regole che configurano qualcosa che già di per sé ha un funzionamento stabile[9]. Nonostante le associazioni culturali e, in modo simile, i musei e le gallerie, abbiano la facoltà di costituire il proprio regolamento interno e di concedere ampi spazi di libertà agli artisti e ai soggetti ospitati, organizzandosi internamente nel modo in cui preferiscono (anche sulla base del numero di personale e delle proprie necessità), in Italia il loro funzionamento resta disciplinato dal Codice Civile: sono quindi obbligate a conformarsi a norme legali precostituite, che ne definiscono in parte entità, identità e ruolo. Le associazioni culturali hanno ad esempio una serie di obblighi e di limiti in relazione alle attività commerciali[10], il cui rispetto o controllo può dipendere da numerosi fattori.

Le vere differenze tra queste due tipologie di luoghi (legali e non) non sta tanto nei gradi di libertà artistica che è possibile esprimere al loro interno, quanto piuttosto nelle espressioni o nella facciata che ciascuno di questi luoghi mostra di sé, e nel modo in cui essi vengono percepiti dal pubblico.

A tal proposito è interessante leggere che uno dei fondatori di neon, Gino Gianuizzi, dichiara: "Quando abbiamo deciso di iniziare neon non sapevamo davvero che cosa avremmo voluto fare"[11] e che neon corrisponde a "un'azione dadaista/situazionista/anarchica"[12]. Dede Auregli ricorda "quello spazio piccolo ma molto alternativo"[13] ed è molto semplice trovare testimonianze di questo tipo tra le pagine del catalogo dell'esposizione *NO, NEON, NO CRY*, tenutasi al MAMbo – Museo d'Arte Moderna di Bologna nel 2022, o in pubblicazioni più datate dedicate ai "luoghi d'opposizione"[14]. Neon è tratteggiata a tutti gli effetti come luogo alternativo e indipendente, sia negli atteggiamenti, sia nelle proposte artistiche.

Ricorda Angelo Candiano che "si sentiva la necessità di nuovi spazi espositivi per dare voce a una generazione, la nostra, che potesse dissentire criticamente da alcune posizioni stereotipate e obsolete, pur nella continuità di un'ottica costruttiva e comunque aderente alla realtà decisamente cambiata. Fu la giovanissima galleria neon di Bologna, insieme a poche altre in Italia, a svolgere questa funzione"[15]. Questa citazione è molto interessante perché evidenzia il carattere di rottura di questo luogo e, al contempo, è uno dei pochi testi presenti nel catalogo della mostra del MAMbo che parla di neon come "galleria". Di fatto, già intorno agli anni Novanta neon comincia a essere definita galleria. Uno dei tanti motivi di tale riconoscimento deriva da una serie di ambigue partecipazioni che vedono neon prendere "parte ad Art Basel, Art Frankfurt, Arte Fiera, Artissima, ecc."[16] In primis fu certamente la partecipazione ad Arte Fiera a Bologna, avvenuta nel 1990[17], a modificare la percezione e il ruolo di quello spazio. L'attitudine era evidentemente diversa da quella di una tradizionale galleria:

> si partiva in camper imbarcando le opere e gli artisti, arrivati a Basel il camper diventava la base per altri artisti, immaginavamo la fiera come un luogo in cui intessere relazioni e non come un'articolazione del sistema di mercato. [...] Stare dentro il sistema per inserire elementi di disturbo, senza rispettarne le regole. Inutile dire che fosse una posizione perdente[18].

La partecipazione a tali eventi fa sì che neon cominci a essere "inserita fra le prime gallerie in una delle periodiche classifiche di *Flash Art*, inclusa in un documentario Rai dedicato alle più interessanti gallerie d'arte italiane," proponendo "artisti che poi entrano nell'orbita di gallerie di mercato"[19]. La vicinanza al mercato, anche se effettivamente molto singolare e mai realmente commerciale, consente a neon di essere legittimata nel mondo dell'arte, nonostante la proposta di giovani artisti allora sconosciuti e l'urgenza di attraversare lo spazio e il mondo dell'arte in modo nuovo e alternativo.

Lasciando per il momento da parte giudizi di valore, vogliamo piuttosto sottolineare che, al contrario di quanto appena visto, non si registrano partecipazioni di uno spazio occupato alle fiere d'arte. Questo non perché i giovani degli spazi occupati fossero meno meritevoli ma, molto probabilmente, sia perché gli occupanti non avevano tale desiderio, sia perché per un luogo che vive nell'illegalità è più facile creare la *propria* fiera con chi condivide le stesse regole del gioco – con coloro che definiremo del "medesimo circuito" – piuttosto che mettersi in regola, istituzionalizzarsi e avere la possibilità di essere invitato all'interno di un circuito fieristico ufficiale. Un cambiamento così repentino svaluterebbe inevitabilmente il *self* – per dirla con Erving Goffman[20] – ovvero la personalità, la facciata e quindi il ruolo di un luogo occupato.

Ed è questo il bivio che accomuna numerosi di questi spazi occupati: restare all'interno del proprio circuito, e quindi distaccati e "non pervenuti" all'interno nel mondo dell'arte? Oppure piegarsi, accettarne le regole e vedere legittimate le proprie istanze alternative per poter istituire nuove pratiche riconosciute?

Ovviamente non esiste un'unica risposta a tali domande. Come ricorda DeeMo, uno degli occupanti dell'Isola Nel Kantiere, spazio allestito all'interno del cantiere del Teatro Arena del Sole, nel quale nel 1991, dopo tre anni intensi di attività, si erano create due possibilità:

> la prima era accettare la proposta del Comune, di prendere in dotazione uno spazio, sottostando alle sue regole, quindi istituzionalizzandosi. Istituire un'associazione culturale, con dei nomi, dei riferimenti, etc. Ovviamente a molti non andava giù l'idea di istituzionalizzarsi a prescindere. L'altra possibilità era quella di occupare un altro spazio. L'Isola lì non si divise esattamente in due, ma alcuni isolani raccolsero l'offerta del Comune insieme ad altri che avevano militato assieme ai giri del DAMS, etc., ed aprirono questo spazio che poi si chiamerà Link [Project][21].

A partire da queste parole si potrebbe pensare che l'esperienza che segue, quella del Link Project, sia qualcosa di istituzionalizzato, e quindi di meno interessante, con un *self* svalutato.

Nell'editoriale del primo volume, uscito nel 1994, dell'opuscolo *Link Project House Organ* – lo strumento di comunicazione attraverso cui il Link Project informerà il suo pubblico per tutta la durata della sua esistenza – leggiamo: "assenza di inaugurazione, di quel momento tra ufficializzazione e il rito sociale [...]. Parliamo piuttosto di un primo atto di volontà di esistenza [...]. Non un

centro sociale, neanche un centro culturale, tantomeno un centro giovanile o post-adolescenziale o post senile. Potremmo parlare di piano quinquennale, sì di quelli che si usavano 'ai bei tempi'". E ancora scrivono in conclusione: "[la nascita del Link Project] è un atto di volontà, e aggiungiamo, nei confronti del mostro burocratico con il quale si è finiti per confrontarci. Un atto che non rispecchia un'idea conclusa, una posizione precisa che ci situi nel panorama già saturo del consumo culturalcomportamentale bolognese e italiano"[22]. Già in queste poche righe troviamo tutte le contraddizioni e le ambiguità necessarie per la creazione di una personalità fortissima e imprevedibile, che ci fa presumere un carattere tutt'altro che addomesticato all'interno delle poche – ma determinanti – regole che una associazione culturale deve rispettare. Il *self* di questo luogo, stando alle teorie di Goffman, può essere colto ancora attraverso gli aspetti non intenzionali di un'espressione, elementi che ci danno un'idea più realistica del nostro interlocutore. Come spiega il sociologo canadese:

> gli osservatori, sapendo che l'individuo [gli spazi nel nostro caso, oppure l'identità di un collettivo] tende a presentarsi sotto una luce favorevole, possono dividere la scena a cui assistono in due parti: l'una, che l'individuo può facilmente controllare a piacere e che riguarda in massima parte le sue affermazioni verbali; l'altra che sembra sfuggire al controllo dell'individuo e che consiste in massima parte nelle espressioni che "lascia trasparire"[23].

Gli autori dell'editoriale negano di appartenere a tutte le configurazioni più note fino ad allora, ed è importante che nella lista compaiano tutte tipologie di spazi in qualche modo legittimati dalla burocrazia. Invece, al contrario, non sono menzionati gli spazi occupati: è evidente che non lo sono più in quanto esiste una convenzione tra il Comune di Bologna e i fondatori del Link Project[24], ma la mancata menzione degli spazi occupati tra cosa non è il Link Project "lascia trasparire" scarsa avversità nei confronti di tale modello e, forse, la volontà di continuare a perseguirlo nonostante gli accordi con le istituzioni. Link Project cerca piuttosto di aprire una terza via sia da un punto di vista artistico, sia da un punto di vista politico. Troviamo nel Link Project un vero e proprio rifiuto di realizzare esposizioni artistiche in senso tradizionale e, al contempo, l'urgenza di aprirsi all'accadimento e alle relazioni per dare vita a una programmazione unica, nella quale veniva dato spazio ad artisti e produzioni che non avvenivano in altri luoghi bolognesi o addirittura italiani. Il Link Project, sul modello degli spazi occupati, riesce comunque a comportarsi come luogo costitutivo e istituente di nuove esperienze, lottando in tutti i suoi anni di attività con l'amministrazione, con le regole che gli si prova ad imporre e, di fatto, anche con sé stesso. È un'istituzione alternativa e socialmente riconosciuta che non riesce a digerire aspetti che le vanno stretti, perché "il problema sempre più centrale delle identità è un problema di sostanze pesanti. Precipitano. [...] Ma come mantenere insieme sostanza e leggerezza? [...] Come non perdere la sostanza, tutta, depurandola da ciò che di veramente sgradevole appartiene al nodo dell'identità, delle appartenenze di clan, sub-etnia, casta..."[25].

Leggendo queste parole, gli altri volumi dell'opuscolo, e consci del calibro delle sperimentazioni e delle attività proposte al Link Project, possiamo finire per pensare che, paradossalmente, il ruolo di uno spazio occupato sia molto più connotato rispetto a quello di uno spazio associativo, perché, al contrario di quanto ci si possa aspettare, possiede dei confini molto più rigidi, un ruolo sociale più chiaro e per tanti aspetti chiuso nella sua definizione, nelle sue urgenze e necessità: la sua identità dura e pura gli lascia meno margine di cambiamento. Gli spazi associativi invece sono luoghi eterogenei per eccellenza, in quanto avevano e hanno la possibilità di negoziare e ibridarsi con le definizioni che più preferiscono, in cambio del rispetto di alcune regole basilari e poco connotanti.

Un modo alternativo di porsi lo troviamo anche nel linguaggio adottato dal Link Project, che parla di sé alla prima persona plurale, come se lo spazio parlasse sempre a nome di una collettività, diventando in qualche modo un'entità a sé stante. Difficile trovare documenti simili per musei e gallerie dell'epoca, i quali producono per lo più testi di sala o cataloghi, e più raramente degli editoriali in cui si raccontano. In ogni caso, gallerie e musei sono luoghi di lavoro molto diversi, che possono avere storie molto lunghe, e sono quindi spesso entità separate dalle persone che li animano. Nei testi del Link Project possiamo invece cogliere che le persone, o meglio l'intelligenza collettiva che lo conduce, è tutt'uno con lo spazio: "noi abbiamo fatto", "noi siamo..."[26].

La sovrapposizione tra il luogo e le persone che lo gestiscono è un fenomeno in realtà piuttosto comune tra questo tipo di spazi, che si verifica certamente con maggiore facilità quando sono diretti per molti anni da una stessa figura. Per esempio, basta sfogliare rapidamente il recente catalogo dell'esposizione *NO, NEON, NO CRY* per capire che tale "personificazione dello spazio" non si limiti solo ai testi: "ho scoperto non molto tempo fa che 'Gino-Neon', come veniva chiamato da tutti, è in verità Gino Gianuizzi"[27], dichiara Giorgio Fasol e, di fatto, Alberto Balletti del duo Balletti e Mercandelli utilizza lo stesso binomio: "'Gino Neon' è per me ancora oggi sinonimo di libertà", sotto intendendo un riferimento sia alla persona, sia allo spazio[28]. Anche Elisa Del Prete ricorda che "neon e 'Gino' veniva usato quasi come sinonimo"[29] e addirittura lo stesso Gianuizzi dichiara che "parlare di neon equivale a parlare di me"[30].

A questo punto notiamo che tra tutti questi luoghi ci sono tante differenze, quante similitudini. Neon è qualcosa di molto diverso da Link Project, ma nonostante questo, le due realtà hanno almeno quattro elementi in comune (e forse anche di più): sono entrambe associazioni culturali; hanno spazi assegnati dal Comune; la partecipazione giovanile (sia tra gli organizzatori, che nel pubblico) è centrale; ambedue cercano di porsi al di fuori del mondo dell'arte, pur essendo più o meno consapevoli di non esserlo.

Quest'ultimo aspetto è forse l'elemento chiave per comprendere la centralità delle esperienze di questi due spazi e di come grazie a essi è forse possibile parlare di una sorta di "modello bolognese" per lo sviluppo degli spazi alternativi italiani e, chissà, stranieri. Tale collisione, tale incontro-scontro, tale amore e odio, fa sì che a partire dagli anni Novanta per gli spazi indipendenti e alternativi dedicati all'arte sia sempre più comune stipulare convenzioni con le pubbliche amministrazioni, pur dichiarandosi indipendenti. Il ruolo di tali spazi si caratterizza sempre più attraverso un dialogo con il mondo dell'arte e, al tempo stesso, un rifiuto di quest'ultimo.

Nel suo libro *La vita quotidiana come "gioco di ruolo"*, Giovanni Balducci scrive che "la vita sociale dell'individuo, secondo Goffman, si svolgerebbe, dunque, proprio tra 'palcoscenico' ('frontstage') e 'retroscena' ('backstage'), per cui all'attore sociale' è richiesto di non confondere i due contesti, in quanto ciò potrebbe ingenerare fraintendimenti sul suo 'ruolo' e, persino, una 'svalutazione' del suo 'self'"[31]. Forse sta proprio qui la difficoltà nel descrivere e afferrare in modo definitivo il comportamento (e la natura stessa) degli spazi alternativi nella società: questi sono *attori* e contemporaneamente *spettatori* del mondo dell'arte, sono entità dalla natura ambigua, in quanto la loro facciata contiene una contraddizione irrisolta che può essere più o meno evidente. Già nel 1995, in un opuscolo del Link Project, viene esplicitata la coscienza di tale conflitto in un trafiletto del Teatrino Clandestino: "[...] ma non è che qui io voglia riproporre tesi di inconsapevolezze ormai fin troppo consapevoli di esserlo o giustificanti teorie dell'antiteoria – siamo venuti qui alla rincorsa del nostro anacronismo del nostro romanticismo pateticamente cullati dall'illusione di afferrare il sublime"[32]. Forse, l'unico modo per andare avanti è quello di illudersi, continuare a lottare e non perdere quella spinta istituente capace di ampliare le programmazioni culturali di una città e, magari, rendere un posto migliore questa società.

Al di là di buoni propositi e speranze, possiamo quindi rilevare una chiara ed effettiva mutazione, una trasformazione del ruolo degli spazi indipendenti attraverso delle fratture che si vengono a creare all'interno delle tradizioni o delle abitudini implicite che caratterizzano il ruolo di qualsiasi attore sociale.

Le abitudini di un attore sociale, quelle che Goffman definisce *routine*, sono quegli elementi impliciti che ci fanno associare un *self* a una certa categoria o a un certo comportamento: un taglio di capelli, ad esempio, può farci pensare che la persona che lo porta segua una certa moda. La poliedricità e le numerose sfaccettature che caratterizzano gli spazi indipendenti, congiuntamente all'affermarsi di politiche neoliberali sempre più aperte, hanno fatto sì che uno spazio autogestito che muove dal basso, possa essere in qualche modo sovrapposto e confuso con l'ideale liberale dell'autoaffermazione individuale. È certamente possibile rilevare una svalutazione generale dei *self* più idealistici e che, molto probabilmente, al giorno d'oggi l'agire in modo indipendente e alternativo vada inteso più come uno *stile* che come un'*urgenza*, un modo di porsi e di presentare le cose, un ruolo ben preciso da recitare all'interno della società, piuttosto che come un circuito artistico parallelo nel quale vengono presentate pratiche che si scostano dal modo di fare delle istituzioni e dell'egemonia dominante.

Il caso limite e paradigmatico di tale ipotesi proviene dai numerosi casi in cui le istituzioni hanno cominciato a utilizzare il binomio "spazi indipendenti" come etichetta, come se si trattasse di un genere musicale, piuttosto che di un ideale alternativo o addirittura avverso alle istituzioni stesse.

Nel 2003 il Ministero della Cultura Italiano, allora presieduto da Giuliano Urbani, lanciò il progetto Luoghi del Contemporaneo "per la mappatura e la promozione della rete dei luoghi dell'arte contemporanea in Italia"[33]. Nel 2012, con l'allora ministro Lorenzo Ornaghi, il progetto venne radicalmente aggiornato dal Servizio Architettura e Arte Contemporanee della Direzione Generale per il Paesaggio, le Belle Arti, l'Architettura e l'Arte Contemporanee e reso disponibile online.

Con questa nuova piattaforma la Direzione Generale Creatività Contemporanea vuole raccontare i cambiamenti intervenuti nella distribuzione geografica dei Luoghi del Contemporaneo. Allo stesso tempo la mappatura è stata effettuata organizzando i Luoghi secondo una suddivisione tipologica che include, oltre agli spazi già tradizionalmente riconosciuti, anche gli spazi indipendenti, i musei d'impresa e una selezione di interventi artistici inseriti negli spazi pubblici e urbani[34].

Il corto circuito è tanto lampante quanto interessante e disastroso. Ancora oggi possiamo consultare la piattaforma e vedere che nelle schede degli spazi indipendenti bolognesi – tra cui figurano Raum, Adiacenze, Localedue, Gelateria Sogni di Ghiaccio – tre volte su quattro è indicata la parola "giovani" e in nessun caso la parola indipendenza. Tale operazione non fa altro che legittimare l'esistenza di questi luoghi, ridimensionarne il *self* e trattarli come luoghi importanti per i giovani e per il potenziale di innovazione culturale che essi portano con sé. Come vuole la tradizione di questi luoghi, devono essere i giovani ad attraversarli; tuttavia, legittimarli e trattarli al tempo stesso come indipendenti significa forse elevarli a spazi ufficiali del precariato: luoghi sospesi tra sperimentazione artistica e ricerca di un riconoscimento professionale. Tale azione ha avuto una sorta di effetto boomerang per quanto riguarda il ruolo di queste realtà, soprattutto per quelle gestite e fondate dai più giovani, in quanto legittimarli in

questo modo è probabilmente equivalso a creare una competizione interna tra spazi indipendenti, dove l'autonomia è qualcosa di più simile a uno stile comportamentale, a un'etichetta di cui fregiarsi, piuttosto che a una necessità o una ragion d'essere.

In realtà, sono stati coinvolti e invitati spazi indipendenti all'interno di fiere ufficiali (come ad ArtVerona[35]) e gli è stato permesso di esporre la loro facciata non corrotta, nonostante venissero presentati all'interno della gabbia dell'indipendenza. Interessante notare che in questa maniera riemerge il modo di porsi e di agire tipico degli spazi occupati – ovvero quello di crearsi un proprio circuito – ma con un senso completamente opposto: non un modo di agire che intende liberarsi attraverso la costituzione di nuove e proprie regole del gioco, ma, al contrario, partecipare al gioco di qualcun altro, acconsentendo alla strumentalizzazione e alla trasformazione di un ideale in etichetta o in mero esercizio di stile.

Il paragone con la musica è esemplare per mostrare come il ruolo degli spazi indipendenti o alternativi che dir si voglia, consenta anche agli artisti e alle proprie realizzazioni di acquisire un certo status o assorbire un certo stile da tutte le mediazioni linguistiche e simboliche da cui sono circondati. Prendiamo per esempio Aphex Twin, musicista che ha svolto un live anche negli spazi del bolognese Link Project nel 1995[36], e oggi artista e brand di fama mondiale. Il musicista inglese, cresciuto professionalmente tra la sua stanza e Londra, città underground per eccellenza, è stato capace di portare alla ribalta la sua sperimentazione senza mai perdere quella sorta di stigma e stile alternativo, tanto da diventare lui stesso emblema di tale atteggiamento. Nonostante l'enorme successo, Aphex Twin sarà sempre parte di quel mondo underground e alternativo che aveva in realtà concettualmente abbandonato già con il suo primo successo planetario, nel 1992, quando diffuse in tutto il mondo il logo del suo progetto, trasformando sé stesso in un brand – proprio come andavano facendo in quegli anni artisti come Jeff Koons o Damien Hirst, oppure le diverse personalità, da Michael Jordan a Puff Daddy, elencate da Naomi Klein nel libro *No Logo*[37].

Forse sarebbe più opportuno dire che gli spazi indipendenti sono luoghi che hanno creduto di essere tali recitando alla perfezione questo ruolo nella società, fino a quando non si sono resi conto che proprio le loro sperimentazioni e le loro urgenze stavano interagendo con quelle dinamiche alimentando proprio quel sistema da cui volevano rifuggire. Di conseguenza tale approccio è diventato un esercizio di stile capace di far percepire non solo un dato luogo, ma anche tutto ciò che veniva presentato al suo interno, come qualcosa in grado di mantenere alta l'illusione di essere riconosciuti, pur stando al di fuori del mondo dell'arte.

L'arte, che nasca nei musei o fuori di essi, è di per sé un bene – materiale o immateriale che sia – che ha bisogno di essere riconosciuto: l'essere artistico è lo status che un oggetto può acquisire o perdere[38]. Per cui, la legittimazione è un'arma a doppio taglio: da un lato consente di vedere prese sul serio le sperimentazioni condotte, dall'altro di essere svalutati in quanto si diventa parte di ciò che inizialmente non si voleva essere.

Forse l'importanza del ruolo degli alternativi o indipendenti, va ricercato nella loro capacità di essere epicentro istituente di novità artistica e sociale, fucine di sperimentazione che mettono a nudo problemi e urgenze che spesso rinnovano anche il modo di agire e comportarsi delle istituzioni. Nella capacità di aprire nuove utopie e orizzonti sta forse la chiave degli spazi indipendenti, nella loro possibilità di rompere i confini, andare oltre i generi e soprattutto oltre l'idea di conservare, scegliendo piuttosto di rinnovare e progredire. Nel secondo fascicolo della rivista del Link Project[39], in un trafiletto concesso alla redazione di Usmis per la presentazione del suo progetto e del suo spazio friulano Cjanive – spazio sensibile soprattutto a questioni di immigrazione oltreché artistiche – si legge infatti: "non possiamo cambiare il mondo, e nemmeno salvarlo, ma dal perduto si può andare verso l'impossibile". Ci troviamo di fronte a due facce della stessa medaglia: se non esistesse un mondo dell'arte egemone non potrebbe nemmeno esistere la sua alternativa.

1   Erving Goffman, *La vita quotidiana come rappresentazione* (1959), Il Mulino, Bologna 1969.

2   Mi riferisco in particolar modo a: *Traumfabrik – Via Clavature 20* (2009), *Piccolo gruppo in moltiplicazione* (2015) e *NEON 1981 – 2011* (2017).

3   Valerio Vigliar, "La Fabbrica dei sogni nella Bologna '77", *XL Repubblica*, 20 febbraio 2012, https://videodrome-xl.blogautore.repubblica.it/page/111/.

4   *Traumfabrik*, comunicato stampa della mostra, Bologna: neon>campobase, 2007, disponibile al link: https://1995-2015.undo.net/it/mostra/58634.

5   "[…] médiations constituantes […] tous les écrits préalables conduisant à la réalisation d'une exposition". Jérôme Glicenstein, *L'Art contemporain entre les lignes*, PUF, Paris 2013, p. 11.

6   Howard S. Becker, *I mondi dell'arte* (1982), Il Mulino, Bologna 2012.

7   L'atto pubblico per la costituzione di una associazione culturale negli anni Ottanta doveva essere registrato da un notaio, al giorno d'oggi deve essere invece registrato presso l'Agenzia delle Entrate.

8   L'atto costitutivo di neon è un documento che ho potuto visionare grazie a Gino Gianuizzi che lo conserva nel suo archivio privato.

9   Si vedano John Searle, *Atti linguistici* (1973), Bollati Boringhieri, Torino 2009, e John Searle, *La costruzione della realtà sociale* (1995), Einaudi, Torino 2006.

10 Si vedano gli Articoli 14–42 del Codice Civile, nei quali è possibile trovare la Disciplina delle associazioni, riconosciute e non, delle fondazioni e dei comitati.

11 Santa Nastro, "Neon a Modica. La storia della gloriosa galleria bolognese in mostra a LaVeronica", *Artribune*, 29 dicembre 2018, https://www.artribune.com/arti-visive/arte-contemporanea/2018/12/neon-a-modica-la-storia-della-gloriosa-galleria-bolognese-in-mostra-a-laveronica/.

12 *Ibid*.

13 Gino Gianuizzi, Eleonora Mariani (a cura di), *NO, NEON, NO CRY*, catalogo della mostra, Bologna: MAMbo, 2022, p. 23.

14 Si veda a tal proposito la sezione "Indirizzario e elenco di alcuni luoghi delle opposizioni", in Tommaso Tozzi, *Opposizioni '80. Alcune delle realtà che hanno scosso il villaggio globale*, Edizioni Amen, Milano 1991, p. 287.

15 *Ibid.*, p. 56.

16 *Ibid.*, p. 5.

17 *Ibid.*, si trova alla fine del libro l'elenco completo delle partecipazioni di neon alle fiere d'arte.

18 *Ibid.*, p. 5.

19 *Ibid.*

20 Goffman, *La vita quotidiana come rappresentazione*, p. 33.

21 Sonia Garcia, "Spazi di comunione: Isola Nel Kantiere", *Vice*, 12 ottobre 2015, https://www.vice.com/it/article/6exq3k/spazi-comunione-isola-nel-kantiere-deemo.

22 "Tanto per cominciare…", *Link Project House Organ*, no. 1, aprile–maggio 1994, p. 1.

23 Goffman, *La vita quotidiana come rappresentazione*, p. 17.

24 La convenzione stipulata tra il Comune di Bologna e il Link Project è un documento che ho potuto visionare grazie a Daniele Gasparinetti e Silvia Fanti, che lo conservano nel loro archivio privato.

25 "Tanto per cominciare…", *Link Project House Organ*, no. 1, p. 1–2.

26 *Ibid.*

27 Gianuizzi, Mariani, *NO, NEON, NO CRY*, p. 99.

28 *Ibid.*, p. 25.

29 *Ibid.*, p. 83.

30 *Ibid.*, p. 11.

31 Giovanni Balducci, *La vita quotidiana come "gioco di ruolo". Dal concetto di face in Goffman alla labeling theory della scuola di Chicago*, Mimesis, Milano 2021, p. 42.

32 Teatrino Clandestino, "L'idealista magico", *Link Project House Organ*, no. 13, 1997, p. 6.

33 https://luoghidelcontemporaneo.beniculturali.it/progetto.

34 *Ibid.*

35 Claudia Giraud, "10 anni di indipendenti: ecco i progetti di 14 project space italiani selezionati per ArtVerona", *Artribune*, 15 agosto 2019, https://www.artribune.com/arti-visive/arte-contemporanea/2019/08/10-anni-di-indipendenti-ecco-i-progetti-dei-14-project-space-italiani-selezionati-per-artverona/.

36 "Rephlex -Rephlex -Rephlex …… loop rave", *Link Project House Organ*, no. 5, 1995, p. 30.

37 Naomi Klein, *No logo* (2000), Baldini & Castoldi, Milano 2001.

38 Nigel Warburton, *La questione dell'arte* (2003), Einaudi, Torino 2004.

39 Usmis, "Benandants electronics", *Link Project House Organ*, no. 2, 1994, p. 17.

LA TREGENDA
1976–1977

La Tregenda è stato uno dei primi e rari spazi in Italia ad essere aperti a sole donne, che qui potevano incontrarsi, fare autocoscienza ed esprimersi attraverso le arti, in linea sia con l'ala femminista che con quella creativa del Movimento del 1977. La Tregenda aveva sede all'interno di una cantina in via San Vitale, parte di una serie di cantine "storiche" che negli stessi anni erano frequentate da creativi di ogni sorta, inclusi gruppi musicali come gli Skiantos che lì avevano una sala prove.

Nei pochi mesi di attività, presso La Tregenda sono stati organizzati diversi eventi legati a molteplici forme di espressione artistica: mostre, performance, incontri e proiezioni di film. Vi sono inoltre state ospitate performance di artiste già affermate, come la cantautrice etnomusicale e folk Giovanna Marini, la musicista jazz Patrizia Scascitelli e la danzatrice Valeria Magli. Lo spazio era aperto, però, anche a contributi di difficile classificazione, proposti da anonime frequentatrici, tra cui si ricorda la surreale installazione di una culla da bambini ma a dimensione di adulto, su cui era possibile stendersi e dormire.

La Tregenda ha fortemente perseguito un modello di autonomia e autogestione, potendo contare solo su forme di autofinanziamento e sulla collaborazione volontaria della propria comunità di appartenenza.

La connotazione peculiare di questo spazio, e l'aspetto che ancora oggi lo rende un modello radicale e irripetibile di autonomia politica e culturale, è stata la sua destinazione esclusiva a un pubblico di sole donne. Agli uomini fu garantito l'accesso solo in rare occasioni, inclusa una festa di Carnevale, ricordata dalle fondatrici come momento di liberazione e spensieratezza, in contrapposizione all'atteggiamento rabbioso e di assoluto separatismo perseguito dalle frange più estreme del movimento femminista.

La Tregenda chiuse nel 1977, quando la repressione del Movimento bolognese da parte dell'amministrazione locale e delle forze dell'ordine pose fine a un'epoca di sperimentazione in cui istanze politiche e comportamentali avevano preso forma e assunto una voce attraverso le arti.

TRAUMFABRIK
1976–1983

Esperienza emblematica della creatività bolognese a cavallo tra gli anni Settanta e Ottanta, la Traumfabrik raccoglieva l'essenza di una generazione tradita dalle promesse disattese della rivoluzione del Settantasette e abbagliata dai fasti dell'epoca del riflusso, gli anni Ottanta.

La "fabbrica dei sogni" fu fondata da Gianpietro Huber, Filippo Scozzari e Dadi Mariotti nel 1976 all'interno di un appartamento da loro occupato in via Clavature, nel Quadrilatero del centro cittadino, immaginata come un luogo in cui poter evadere dagli schemi imposti dalla società e percepiti come autentiche prigioni della creatività. Nei sette anni di attività, la Traumfabrik non ha proposto mostre o performance, ma è diventata uno spazio di incontro aperto, in cui divertirsi suonando e ascoltando musica, realizzando film sperimentali e disegnando, un'eterotopia condivisa con amici e compagni del Movimento, laboratorio di produzioni culturali alternative.

Arredato da Huber con mobili e oggetti di recupero, l'appartamento in via Clavature si connotava come spazio di creazione poliedrico, tra i cui frequentanti figuravano alcuni tra i principali esponenti del Nuovo Fumetto Italiano come Scozzari e Andrea Pazienza. Altri erano coinvolti in band post-punk quali Gaznevada, Stupid Set e Confusional Quartet, collaborando con la Harpo's Bazaar, poi Italian Records, anche alla realizzazione delle cover dei loro dischi e flyer. Riuniti sotto la sigla Topographic, alcuni di loro pubblicarono il numero zero di una rivista, *L.U.X. Electric!*, e contribuirono alla grafica e redazione dei primi numeri di *Musica80*. Altri, sotto il nome di Grabinski, avviarono una produzione audiovisiva sperimentale che consisteva in proto-videoclip e installazioni multimediali fondate sull'utilizzo del found footage. Diversi membri della Traumfabrik furono coinvolti nella IV (1980) e nella VI (1982) Settimana Internazionale della Performance a Bologna, un evento a cura di Francesca Alinovi, Renato Barilli e Roberto Daolio. A parte questo, furono pochi i casi in cui il loro lavoro fu presentato nel contesto dell'arte contemporanea.

La proficua produzione culturale della Traumfabrik comprendeva, oltre a fumetti, cover di dischi, volantini e fanzine, alcuni oggetti realizzati modificando materiali di riciclo e centinaia di lavori su carta: disegni, acquerelli, collage, fotomontaggi. Dopo essere passato da una cantina all'altra, di quel corpus è rimasta solo una scatola di lavori su carta, "salvati" da un'artista, Alessandra Andrini, che sebbene non avesse partecipato alle vicende della Traumfabrik per ragioni anagrafiche, scoprì di essere l'unica custode di questo prezioso ritrovamento, subito battezzato "reperto 1", il cui contenuto è stato presentato presso la galleria neon a Bologna nel 2007.

Il dilagare dell'eroina e la diffusione di un'epidemia di Epatite C hanno pesantemente influito sul decadimento della Traumfabrik, la cui storia si conclude con lo sgombero dell'edificio nel 1983. Di quell'esperienza, tanto spontanea quanto eroica se ne consideriamo la longevità e le dinamiche di autosostentamento, hanno raccontato alcuni protagonisti, come Scozzari nel suo memoir *Prima pagare poi ricordare* (2004) e Emanuele Angiuli dei Grabinski con il documentario *Traumfabrik Via Clavature 20* (2009), ma è il "reperto 1" a costituire la vera eredità della fabbrica dei sogni e solo il suo studio e valorizzazione potrà rendere giustizia a questa esperienza come esempio pionieristico di spazio artistico liberato e luogo di ripensamento del fare artistico in chiave interdisciplinare e democratica.

NEON
1981–2011

La volontà di aprire uno spazio di dialogo sull'arte all'interno del quale proporre pratiche innovative e mettere in discussione lo statuto di opera, di artista e di sistema, portò nel 1981 Gino Gianuizzi, Stefano Deli, Antonia Ruggeri, Valeria Medica e Maurizio Vetrugno alla fondazione di neon. Nato come esperimento aperto e fondato sulla confusione tra i ruoli di artista, gallerista e critico-curatore, di spirito punk e situazionista, la spinta iniziale di neon fu caratterizzata dal desiderio di inoculare elementi di disturbo in un sistema sclerotizzato. Numerosi progetti dei primi anni furono affidati a Francesca Alinovi, studiosa e curatrice in grado di catalizzare intuizioni ed energie di portata internazionale in attività di origine locale come nel caso dell'Enfatismo, micro-movimento artistico da lei teorizzato che rimase attivo fino al 1983, anno della sua morte. Dopo alcuni anni di pausa, neon riprese l'attività nel 1987 vedendo coinvolti in particolare Gianuizzi e, più tardi, Roberto Daolio, che condividevano l'attenzione per gli artisti emergenti. Dalla sede originaria in via Solferino, neon ha cambiato denominazione e location più volte – fondando anche due sedi a Milano nell'ultimo periodo di attività – ma senza mai venire meno al desiderio di supportare artisti per lo più all'inizio della loro carriera.

La libertà assoluta rispetto alle convenzioni del sistema commerciale dell'arte contemporanea si traduceva in un'attività scomposta e difficile da inquadrare, in cui gli artisti esposti erano legati principalmente all'arte concettuale, ma anche alla performance e alle sperimentazioni video. Inizialmente, Gianuizzi invitava artisti con cui aveva relazioni di empatia come Marco Lavagetto, Fathi Hassan, Maurizio Cattelan e Croce Taravella. Successivamente, con Daolio neon diventò la galleria dei giovani emergenti, esponendo tra gli altri Roberto Orlandi, Antonella Mazzoni, Eva Marisaldi, Alessandro Pessoli, Luca Vitone e Monica Cuoghi. Dopo il trasferimento nella sede di via Zanardi, neon>campobase si interessò in particolare alla ricerca sonora e alla sperimentazione video, proponendo un flusso continuo di eventi capace di costituirsi come un laboratorio permanente di ricerca e confronto.

Nei contesti istituzionali – come, per esempio, quelli delle fiere d'arte contemporanea a cui di tanto in tanto lo spazio ha partecipato – neon rappresentava un elemento di disturbo che non rispettava le regole codificate, ponendosi con attitudine situazionista. Rari sono stati i finanziamenti pubblici da parte delle istituzioni che non riconoscevano le potenzialità di questa realtà, ma neon era interessata soprattutto a instaurare un rapporto osmotico con la città, come è evidente nei due progetti *Container* e *Fuori contesto* che proponevano interventi diretti nell'ambiente cittadino. Il pubblico di neon era composto da una comunità di artisti, di studenti dell'Accademia di Belle Arti cittadina e del DAMS e, negli ultimi anni, da qualche avventuroso collezionista.

L'esperienza di neon si è conclusa nel 2011 a causa dell'aumento dei problemi finanziari e del disinteresse a diventare una vera e propria galleria d'arte commerciale.

SEGRETO PUBBLICO
1982–1985

Segreto Pubblico nacque dal legame di amicizia tra Ginetto Campanini e Francesco Tabarrini, entrambi trasferitisi a Bologna nel 1982 dopo un periodo di studi a Trento. Luogo di sperimentazione e ricerca, questo spazio mirava a sviluppare contaminazioni virali tra i diversi linguaggi artistici e performativi. La prima sede fu la vecchia ghiacciaia di un macello nella periferia bolognese di Borgo Panigale, uno spazio inusuale e affascinante, la cui conformazione si prestava in particolare a sperimentazioni sonore. La cupola dell'interno della ghiacciaia, infatti, fungeva da cassa armonica producendo un leggero ritardo nella propagazione del suono. Successivamente, la necessità di trasformare Segreto Pubblico in una realtà economicamente sostenibile, portò i membri del collettivo a trasferirsi dalla periferia al centro di Bologna, all'interno di una nuova sede più funzionale in via San Carlo.

Il programma culturale era caratterizzato da eventi, mostre, performance, rassegne di musica, teatro e poesia, e mirava ad aprire il mondo dell'arte contemporanea a nuove suggestioni, anche grazie al coinvolgimento di esponenti del contesto cittadino come Francesca Alinovi e Gino Gianuizzi e svariati protagonisti di altri spazi bolognesi quali Traumfabrik e neon.

Di particolare interesse furono due progetti artistici del 1982 presentati sotto forma di party, un modello, quello della festa, che rispondeva alle istanze edonistiche tipiche dell'epoca postmoderna, in linea con una tendenza caratteristica della coeva scena artistica di Downtown New York. Per *Frontiera Party*, a cura di Alinovi, lo spazio fu ricoperto da graffiti di natura tribale di Ivo Bonacorsi – fiori e dinosauri – mentre sul palco si esibiva la band art rock degli Eterodattili. Per il *Grabinsky TV Party*, invece, il gruppo di sperimentazioni audiovisive Grabinski, nato tra le pareti della Traumfabrik, posizionò una telecamera alla base della scala di accesso al locale, le cui registrazioni mostrano una lunga fila di tipici avventori del Segreto Pubblico, tra cui Jean-Michel Basquiat, amico del gruppo e spesso a Bologna in quel periodo. Lo spazio ospitò anche performance musicali post-punk con band italiane emergenti, come i Neon, e figure della scena newyorkese come Steve Piccolo, nonché un progetto performativo a cura di Franco "Bifo" Berardi fondato sulla trasposizione del numero "Game Over" (1981) della sua rivista *A/traverso*, una messa in scena del processo di Pechino alla Banda dei Quattro in un ambiente caratterizzato dalla presenza di quattro arcade games.

CASSERO
1982–in corso

Spazio polivalente divenuto simbolo delle rivendicazioni politiche e civili della comunità LGBTQIA+ a livello nazionale e internazionale, il Cassero è dalle sue origini promotore di una programmazione culturale di estrema importanza a livello artistico e sociale.

Nel 1982, data fondamentale per la città di Bologna e per l'Italia, il sindaco Renato Zangheri assegnò il Cassero di Porta Saragozza – una delle piccole torri dell'antica cinta muraria della città di Bologna – al Circolo XXVIII Giugno, gruppo omosessuale già attivo da diversi anni nel capoluogo emiliano: nacque così il Cassero. Fu la prima volta in Italia che un'istituzione pubblica riconobbe valore sociale e culturale a un'associazione apertamente omosessuale, assegnandole una sede di proprietà comunale. La giunta prese questa decisione nonostante il malumore della curia bolognese e di una parte della cittadinanza, contraria al fatto che questo tipo di realtà avesse dimora in un edificio originariamente dedicato alla Madonna di San Luca. La visibilità del circolo e la portata delle proprie attività aumentarono nel 2002, con il trasferimento del Cassero all'interno della Manifattura delle Arti presso la Salara del Parco del Cavaticcio, per volere del sindaco di centro destra Giorgio Guazzaloca che volle così riconsegnare simbolicamente il Cassero di Porta Saragozza alla comunità religiosa, considerando la centralità dell'edificio durante la processione dedicata alla Madonna.

Nato da esigenze di rivendicazione identitaria da parte di una minoranza, il Cassero ebbe, sin dai suoi primi anni di fondazione, un approccio culturale e artistico significativamente legato alle rivendicazioni politiche e sociali della comunità LGBTQIA+. Diverse iniziative negli anni hanno permesso al circolo di aumentare il proprio peso sociale e culturale attraverso l'arte, la musica, il teatro, il cinema, la letteratura e le arti performative, tutte forme di espressione artistica a cui si è dato spazio grazie a eventi di natura interdisciplinare come Il Festival del Cinema Gay e Lesbico di Milano e Bologna, Blowing Bubbles, la Libera Università Omosessuale, il Gender Bender festival, Teatro Arcobaleno e Performing Gender. Nonostante i quarant'anni di attività – e in particolare l'ultimo ventennio – siano stati caratterizzati da un intenso lavoro di costruzione di relazioni e di reti con altre realtà cittadine, nazionali e internazionali, il Cassero ha sempre mantenuto un aspetto di indipendenza intesa come autonomia decisionale. È proprio questa libertà a permettere ancora oggi al Cassero di rivolgersi a un pubblico diversificato, divenuto negli anni post-identitario, in quanto non composto unicamente da persone appartenenti alla comunità LGBTQIA+ ma alla collettività in senso lato, incluso il pubblico delle arti.

Le manifestazioni culturali del Cassero rispondono, infatti, alla necessità di fornire letture alternative a quelle mainstream proposte dai mass media, proponendo visioni non stereotipate.

Il Cassero oggi mantiene a livello nazionale e internazionale una posizione di rilievo politico e culturale, per la sua capacità di cambiamento e adattamento ai nuovi bisogni della società, facendo dell'arte uno strumento politico e di liberazione identitaria.

NOWALL
1985–1988

Nowall (No wall/Now all) fu fondato nel 1985 all'interno di un edificio precedentemente occupato dal circolo Arci di via delle Moline 2. L'ampia sede era composta da due sale, al piano terra e al secondo piano, ma i progetti culturali contaminavano a volte anche l'esterno del locale. Le decisioni venivano prese collettivamente, mentre l'organizzazione degli eventi era affidata ai singoli membri che avevano piena autonomia decisionale, sebbene Alberto Masala fosse responsabile della direzione artistica. Lo spazio era economicamente supportato dai ricavi del bar che si trovava al suo interno e dalle sponsorizzazioni esterne. Con il tempo e l'avanzare dei progetti, oltre al sostegno di Arcimedia, iniziarono anche le relazioni con l'Assessorato alle Politiche Giovani del Comune di Bologna.

Le attività di Nowall erano ispirate da alcune neo-avanguardie artistiche europee e statunitensi, come la Beat Generation, Fluxus, l'Art Brut parigina, i Provos di Amsterdam, ma anche da pratiche contemporanee come il Neo-espressionismo e il Punk berlinese. Nel 1986 Nowall è entrato nel network internazionale di centri culturali indipendenti Trans Europe Halles. In collaborazione con questa rete, sono stati realizzati eventi tra cui due edizioni del Festival d'Art Room, che metteva in contatto diverse situazioni di ricerca incentrate su nuove poetiche e azioni culturali a partire dal contesto sociale, due edizioni della Biennale dei Giovani Artisti dell'Europa e del Mediterraneo, un'edizione del festival AFA e le mostre *Landjuveel* (1987) e *Berlino Capitale europea della cultura* (1988).

L'esperienza di Nowall si è conclusa dopo tre anni di attività a causa della stanchezza del collettivo e per l'avanzare di nuovi progetti paralleli. A rileggere oggi l'esperienza di Nowall, emerge un chiaro allineamento con lo spirito della cultura post-punk, anche considerando l'attenzione per le pratiche performative, per i temi di identità di genere, l'approccio interdisciplinare e l'estetica decadente e a tratti nichilista tipica della cultura goth.

ISOLA NEL KANTIERE
1988–1991

All'interno della scena punk bolognese della fine degli anni Ottanta, da un nucleo legato al centro anarchico di Porta Santo Stefano e responsabile dell'occupazione di alcune abitazioni in via Galliera, nacque la necessità di dare vita a uno spazio culturale autogestito che rispecchiasse le istanze politiche di una nuova generazione che voleva dare forma al proprio dissenso attraverso le arti. Sebbene la scena punk di ispirazione anarchica fosse all'origine della nascita di Isola Nel Kantiere, questo spazio divenne in breve un incubatore per la cultura hip hop italiana.

La scoperta di un ex magazzino di ceramiche affacciato sulla Piazzetta San Giuseppe, alle spalle del Teatro Arena del Sole e dell'affollata e commerciale via dell'Indipendenza, dotato di un seminterrato isolato acusticamente particolarmente adatto alle performance musicali, portò nel settembre del 1988 alla fondazione di I.N.K. L'Isola prese forma su modello di iniziative simili, come Virus a Milano e numerosi altri spazi occupati a Berlino, Amsterdam e Copenhagen.

All'interno del collettivo si delinearono da subito una serie di ruoli sulla base delle competenze individuali: tecnico, grafico, promoter, cuoco, ecc. L'organizzazione era gestita in maniera orizzontale e l'unico organo decisionale era l'assemblea.

L'Isola ha inaugurato con una contestazione alla Biennale dei Giovani Artisti dell'Europa e del Mediterraneo che quell'anno aveva Bologna come sede, dimostrando il disinteresse del collettivo a confrontarsi con il sistema dell'arte ufficiale, se non su base conflittuale. Al contrario, il gruppo entrò subito in relazione con un network internazionale di etichette discografiche e band punk, hardcore e industrial provenienti da Stati Uniti, Germania e Olanda, interessate a suonare in spazi autogestiti. A questo proposito, si ricordano ad esempio le performance di Henry Rollins, Fugazi e Test Dept.

L'indipendenza dalle istituzioni pubbliche e dalle logiche di produzione commerciale fu un aspetto fondamentale di Isola Nel Kantiere, che si espresse soprattutto attraverso l'autoproduzione di dischi, fanzine e attività artistiche interdisciplinari, da una rassegna cinematografica curata, alla grafica e ai graffiti; da operazioni scultoree fondate sull'utilizzo di materiale di scarto a progetti multimediali.

Lo spirito *do-it-yourself* e antiautoritario del punk fu incanalato presto in una nuova serie di energie creative, in particolare nelle prime jam hip hop della città, dove i membri dell'Isola Posse All Stars hanno sviluppato il proprio stile, essendo tra i primi in Italia a usare la lingua italiana per fare rap. Questa crew si è formata proprio tra le pareti dell'Isola Nel Kantiere, dove produsse il brano-manifesto "Stop al panico" (1991), come colonna sonora di un'imponente manifestazione contro lo sgombero forzato dei centri sociali attivi a Bologna in quel periodo, in un clima sociale influenzato dai massacri della Uno Bianca. Tra i vari pionieri dell'hip hop italiano e di generi affini come il raggamuffin che esordirono all'Isola si ricordano anche Sud Sound System, DeeMo, Deda, Gopher D e Papa Ricky.

Il ciclo di vita dell'Isola è stato breve, ma carico di molte iniziative ed eventi culturali. Gli ultimi mesi sono stati caratterizzati da proposte più articolate, come la tre giorni INK3D, e da manifestazioni pubbliche per le strade del centro storico bolognese a bordo di sound system mobili, riuscendo a portare all'esterno i contenuti e lo spirito dello spazio occupato.

L'Isola Nel Kantiere fu sgomberata nel 1991 per volontà dell'Assessorato alla Cultura e lo spazio venne destinato ad area di carico-scarico dell'Arena Del Sole, nonostante la proposta di modifica del progetto presentata al Comune dal collettivo in collaborazione con un architetto.

DEPOT
1992–1995

L'attività di Depot, anche conosciuta come Depot and Hip Hop Gallery, sebbene non ci fossero evidenti legami con la cultura hip hop, cercava di proporre un nuovo modo di fare cultura sovvertendo l'elitarismo e le dinamiche commerciali che caratterizzano il mondo dell'arte.

Nei tre anni di attività, Depot ha organizzato mostre con cadenza settimanale all'interno di un bar in via del Pratello, coinvolgendo artisti emergenti e in collaborazione con studiosi e curatori attivi in città come Silvia Grandi, Michele Mariano, Roberto Daolio, Gino Gianuizzi, Guido Molinari, Vittoria Coen, Gilberto Pellizzola, Valerio Dehó e Claudio Marra. I progetti espositivi si concentravano sulle sperimentazioni nell'ambito della performance, della video arte e delle installazioni.

Uno dei progetti più ambiziosi è stata la mostra open air *ARS LUX* (1995), che ha visto il coinvolgimento di Roberto Daolio, Giacinto di Pietrantonio, Gabriele Perretta, Roberto Pinto, Gianni Romano, Marco Senaldi e Silvia Grandi. Si trattò di una mostra itinerante composta da 150 opere di artisti provenienti da tutto il mondo, stampate in PVC e collocate sulle piattaforme luminose utilizzate per la pubblicità, che sono state esposte in diciassette città italiane nell'arco di tre mesi.

L'avventura di Depot, realtà culturale innovativa ed emblematica del fervore bolognese dei primi anni Novanta, si è conclusa nel 1995 a causa di problemi legati all'inquinamento acustico.

IL CAMPO DELLE FRAGOLE
1992–2002

Il Campo delle Fragole fu fondato da un gruppo di artisti visivi e curatori denominatosi C-Voltaire, a partire dalla necessità di colmare la mancanza di uno spazio in cui esporre le proprie opere e in cui poter discutere e progettare eventi, senza dovere incorrere in dinamiche commerciali o in logiche individualiste di affermazione e riconoscimento. I membri del gruppo formalizzarono l'idea di aprire uno spazio a fronte di esperienze di collaborazione e dialogo che li aveva visti coinvolti all'interno dell'osteria La Vereda, un luogo di incontro frequentato da diversi esponenti della comunità artistica bolognese.

Coordinatrice dello spazio era Tiziana Ramponi, a cui si affiancò in certi periodi Luisa

Castagnoli, ma Il Campo delle Fragole vide la partecipazione di tutti i membri di C-Voltaire. Le decisioni venivano prese in maniera circolare, le proposte venivano discusse insieme e realizzate grazie a una collaborazione collettiva. I ruoli non erano mai definiti, ed è interessante pensare come degli artisti visivi si siano ritrovati ad assumere il ruolo di curatori o a elaborare progetti di comunicazione e promozione culturale che fino a quel momento esulavano dalla formazione tradizionale propria di un artista.

Con il trasferimento nella sede di via Polese, più grande rispetto alla precedente di via del Pratello, e disposta su due piani, Il Campo delle Fragole cominciò ad accogliere mostre di pittura e scultura, installazioni, performance, eventi di musica, teatro, cabaret e danza, incontri, reading e rassegne di film. Ramponi si è occupata con attenzione del rapporto con critici e curatori, a volte con il sostegno di Luigi Mastrangelo. La scelta degli artisti e dei progetti avveniva in maniera collettiva, sulla base di rapporti personali del gruppo o attivando collaborazioni con spazi simili di altre città come Roma, Torino, Milano e Trieste.

L'indipendenza fu un elemento fondamentale per avere spazio di progettazione e libertà nell'espressione artistica, nelle scelte della programmazione culturale e nelle collaborazioni con altre realtà dentro e fuori dall'Italia. L'importanza di C-Voltaire nel contesto locale e nazionale fu riconosciuta da svariati critici che ne recensirono le attività sulle principali riviste di arte contemporanea, e da ricercatori e docenti dell'Accademia di Belle Arti e del DAMS che vi collaborarono per vari progetti. Tra le produzioni più importanti de Il Campo delle Fragole vanno ricordate le dodici edizioni della rassegna Exit patrocinata dal Comune e dall'Arci, che ha portato all'organizzazione di mostre annuali in diversi luoghi della città nei giorni di Arte Fiera.

Le principali fonti economiche sono state l'autofinanziamento, le donazioni esterne e sporadiche forme di sostentamento istituzionale (tra cui si ricorda la collaborazione con l'Arci per la stampa dei cataloghi), ma soprattutto i ricavi del bar presente all'interno dello spazio.

L'esperienza de Il Campo delle Fragole si esaurì in modo naturale, a conclusione di un'evoluzione personale che spinse i membri di C-Voltaire a proseguire il proprio lavoro individualmente. Questo spazio indipendente è ricordato nella storia bolognese per la sua capacità di operare dentro e fuori dal sistema dell'arte, in opposizione a scuole, tendenze e alla natura imprenditoriale dell'arte mainstream.

LIVELLO 57
1993–2006

Il Livello 57 venne fondato all'inizio degli anni Novanta, in un periodo in cui Bologna era caratterizzata dalla presenza di vari altri centri sociali autogestiti. Luogo di sperimentazione di nuove forme di convivenza mirate a superare la normalità codificata dalla cultura di massa attraverso l'arte e la socialità, gran parte delle attività proposte dal Livello 57 furono legate alle culture cyberpunk e hip hop. Il centro sociale fu avviato all'interno di un edificio occupato in via dello Scalo da ex membri del centro sociale Pellerossa (da poco sgomberato dalla sede di Piazza Verdi), da diversi studenti universitari fuori sede appartenenti al movimento della Pantera, e da figure coinvolte in Radio K Centrale e nel progetto editoriale Grafton9, quest'ultimo oggi prezioso organo di archivio e diffusione di pubblicazioni underground e autoprodotte di ambito cyberpunk di quel periodo.

La programmazione culturale andava dall'organizzazione di eventi collettivi molto partecipati come la Festa della Semina e la Street Rave Parade Antiproibizionista, alla realizzazione di fanzine, ad autoproduzioni discografiche come il progetto *Livello 57 Zona a Rischio*. Lo spazio si configurò in breve come luogo di liberazione e fervido centro di sperimentazioni nell'ambito della musica, delle arti performative e della graffiti art, sebbene raramente le attività fossero presentate come mostre o come attività culturali, perché etichettarle come tali avrebbe inficiato il loro carattere spontaneo e anticonvenzionale.

Nella sua sede più caratteristica, quella di via Muggia, sotto il ponte di via Stalingrado e adiacente ai binari della ferrovia, fu centrale la presenza di una rampa da skateboard – una delle più grandi in Italia – a conferma della natura disobbediente di questa pratica in quegli anni, nonché le lunghe pareti orizzontali che delimitavano il complesso e che diventarono supporto di opere realizzate da alcuni dei principali artisti dei graffiti italiani e internazionali.

Nel 1995 emerse la necessità di realizzare un progetto di sensibilizzazione sul consumo consapevole delle sostanze stupefacenti e il Livello 57 propose il Laboratorio Antiproibizionista, che si connotò come uno spazio di elaborazione politica sulle droghe e sul loro consumo, il primo in Italia a produrre opuscoli informativi sulle nuove droghe sintetiche come ecstasy e ketamina. Nonostante una breve fase di dialogo avviata dal sindaco di centro destra Giorgio Guazzaloca nel 1999, il rapporto del Livello 57 con le istituzioni cittadine era di carattere conflittuale. La sua storia si conclude infatti il 25 luglio del 2006, in seguito al sequestro giudiziario degli immobili di via Battirame (la sua ultima sede) autogestiti dal centro sociale, con l'accusa di essere luogo di produzione e di spaccio di sostanze stupefacenti.

LINK PROJECT
1994–2001

Il Link Project, anche conosciuto come Link, nacque nel 1994 a seguito dell'occupazione autorizzata del deposito delle Farmacie Comunali in via Fioravanti 14, dietro la stazione dei treni di Bologna. Il collettivo che vi si instaurò era composto da figure che avevano partecipato a esperienze precedenti come l'Isola Nel Kantiere e il movimento della Pantera. Fondato a conclusione di un ciclo di occupazioni illegali e storie di conflittualità con le amministrazioni locali, le vicende del Link godettero di un inedito dialogo con le istituzioni.

Cardini dello spirito di indipendenza del collettivo erano l'autodeterminazione e l'autocostruzione, a partire dal modo in cui è stato trasformato internamente lo spazio. In linea con l'estetica post-industriale che in quegli anni caratterizzava locali notturni di Berlino e di Londra, un gruppo di artisti diede forma a interni e sculture riutilizzando materiale di scarto, in particolar modo rottami metallici.

Il lavoro, di cui gli aspetti gestionali venivano discussi e pianificati in modo democratico durante le assemblee settimanali, era organizzato in vari sottogruppi che si dedicavano a diversi aspetti dell'attività, proponendo un'articolata programmazione di eventi. Lo spazio accoglieva inoltre vari laboratori di autoproduzione, diventati in seguito case di produzione specializzate in diversi linguaggi artistici, dal video al graphic design alla musica (Opificio Ciclope, Loew, Officine Alchemiche, Century Vox Records, Massimo Volume, Fastilio, Splatterpink, Notte Vidal, TurbanZ e Shado).

Più che progetti espositivi in senso tradizionale, le attività del Link erano caratterizzate da un interesse per le pratiche performative e multimediali, spesso frutto di un approccio interdisciplinare. Che si trattasse di installazioni immersive, live-set di matrice musicale o produzioni teatrali relazionali, l'intreccio tra le arti e l'utilizzo intermediale di più dispositivi tecnologici erano elementi caratteristici della proposta del Link. Al centro di interesse dello spazio, infatti, vi era la cultura elettronica, ripensata, nel momento della sua diffusione di massa, come strumento di liberazione ed emancipazione dell'individuo. Fulcro del Link era, non a caso, un internet point dove veniva garantito l'accesso libero al web in anni in cui ancora si guardava alla rete con atteggiamento utopico.

L'intero ambiente era concepito come luogo di accadimenti e relazioni in cui gli artisti avevano la possibilità di sperimentare e ridiscutere i parametri della loro stessa attività.

Il Link era economicamente indipendente, autofinanziandosi tramite i biglietti di ingresso, il bar e il bookshop. Di particolare richiamo erano i DJ set e le performance musicali, principalmente legate alla musica elettronica di quegli anni e a musicisti e produttori provenienti dal Regno Unito e dalla Germania, da Aphex Twin alla nuova scena berlinese. Il Link fu uno straordinario laboratorio di sperimentazioni culturali innovative e interdisciplinari, slegate dalle consuete logiche commerciali. Uno strumento utile per capire quello che questo luogo ha rappresentato è l'omonima rivista prodotta al suo interno, ma le sue vere ricadute riguardano la professionalizzazione di molte persone che oggi lavorano in ambito culturale, tecnico, amministrativo, gestionale e creativo a Bologna e nel resto del mondo, figure per le quali questo spazio è stato una vera e propria scuola.

Il Link chiuse nel 2001 e il complesso venne raso al suolo come parte di un progetto di riqualificazione del quartiere. Nel 2004 alcuni membri del Link Project diedero vita a Link Associated, instaurandosi in una nuova sede e proponendo quasi esclusivamente una programmazione musicale con un'attenzione rivolta alle varie forme di electronic dance music.

FIORILE ARTE
1995–2005

Questo piccolo locale di 20 m² su via Nosadella, ha ospitato mostre di artisti sia emergenti che conosciuti. Le fondatrici, Mariangela Bacega e Patti Campani, erano responsabili della direzione artistica e della gestione dello spazio, ma le scelte venivano prese all'unisono con i diversi collaboratori di volta in volta coinvolti. Il pubblico era eterogeneo, composto sia da persone del settore che da individui estranei al mondo dell'arte che si trovavano a passare di fronte allo spazio in questa caratteristica strada del centro di Bologna.

Fiorile era in contatto con diverse associazioni e realtà locali come il circuito Arci, l'Osteria del Montesino e il collettivo C-Voltaire, responsabile de Il Campo delle Fragole. Negli anni, diverse sono state le collaborazioni con curatori tra cui Roberto Vitali, con cui Campani realizzò la trasmissione radiofonica Kactus, Edoardo Di Mauro, Valerio Dehò e Gabriele Perretta. Il Comune ha riconosciuto allo spazio il patrocinio di alcune delle attività, ma in termini economici l'associazione si basava sull'autofinanziamento.

Dopo la chiusura dello spazio, determinata da difficoltà economiche e organizzative, Campani continuerà a curare mostre in vari spazi espositivi con il nome di Fiorile+.

TPO
1995–in corso

Le origini del Teatro Polivalente Occupato, meglio conosciuto con l'acronimo di TPO, risalgono a un'assemblea tenutasi all'interno della sede di Radio K Centrale nel 1995, in un cui un gruppo di giovani esponenti del mondo del teatro ipotizzò la creazione di uno spazio aperto e di sperimentazione. Questo spazio divenne realtà qualche mese dopo, il 6 novembre 1995, quando alcune compagnie di attori indipendenti – tra cui Amadossalto, Teatro dell'Infetto e il Teatro Situazionautico Luther Blissett – riunite sotto l'etichetta di Teatranti Occupanti, invasero il Teatro di Scenografia in via Irnerio, di proprietà dell'Accademia di Belle Arti di Bologna, progettato dallo scultore e architetto Farpi Vignoli trentacinque anni prima e poco utilizzato fino a quel momento.

Sin dall'inizio, il TPO si è connotato come un centro sociale inclusivo, diffuso e partecipato, di natura antifascista e antisessista. Le varie figure e gruppi che vi hanno partecipato hanno rivendicato i diritti alla libera espressione attraverso dichiarazioni, manifestazioni e una programmazione culturale innovativa e spesso provocatoria, secondo un'idea dell'arte come strumento di costruzione sociale e di critica ai sistemi di potere. Il TPO è, infatti, un laboratorio di pratiche culturali allargate e di linguaggi interdisciplinari, oltre che uno spazio di conoscenza diffusa e cooperazione.

Sin dal primo anno di attività, l'occupazione ha riscosso l'approvazione di diversi docenti dell'Accademia, incluso Concetto Pozzati, all'epoca assessore alla cultura del Comune di Bologna, nonché di Vignoli, entusiasta di questa inaspettata destinazione d'uso dello stabile da lui progettato. Il rapporto con altre realtà del territorio si è sempre manifestato proficuo, soprattutto nelle relazioni con spazi e organizzazioni vicini in termini di identità e similmente votati alla produzione artistica indipendente.

Non vi è mai stata un'organizzazione rigida degli eventi e della programmazione culturale interna, e ogni importante decisione gestionale o politica viene presa durante riunioni periodiche. L'essere indipendenti si esprime ancora oggi nella massima libertà di azione sia nella programmazione che nelle posizioni politiche dell'associazione, ma anche in termini economici, considerando che le attività del TPO sono in gran parte autofinanziate.

La programmazione culturale del TPO è stata sempre estremamente diversificata e riesce ad accogliere pubblici diversi attratti da eventi specifici, che all'interno di questo spazio sanno di poter trovare un programma multidisciplinare. Negli anni, il TPO ha proposto progetti performativi e musicali, proiezioni di film, festival, incontri e workshop nell'ambito del teatro e dell'audiovisivo, seguendo un approccio interdisciplinare e una vocazione per la multimedialità. Di particolare importanza è stato il ruolo del TPO nella nascita di una nuova ondata di teatro d'avanguardia negli anni Novanta, con progetti di gruppi quali Motus, Teatrino Clandestino e Fanny & Alexander, tra gli altri.

Il TPO è rimasto nella sede di via Irnerio fino al 2000, anno in cui le pressioni da parte dell'Accademia di Belle Arti e la politica del sindaco di centro destra Giorgio Guazzaloca hanno portato allo sgombero del locale e al trasferimento all'interno dell'ex-Euraquarium di viale Lenin, un complesso industriale abbandonato. Il passaggio alla nuova sede, immediatamente fuori dal centro di Bologna, ha provocato una scissione nel gruppo originario destinata a non rimarginarsi. Costretto a lasciare lo stabile di Viale Lenin, demolito per fare posto a un residence e un parcheggio, dal 2007 il TPO ha sede in via Casarini 17/5.

ATLANTIDE
1999–2015

Lo spazio occupato Atlantide nacque alla fine degli anni Novanta dalle istanze di alcuni dei principali collettivi femministi e queer bolognesi del periodo. Insediatisi illegalmente all'interno di uno dei due edifici che costituiscono Porta Santo Stefano, una delle porte dell'antica cinta muraria della città di Bologna, l'organizzazione interna era regolata da un'assemblea collettiva che definiva e assegnava i diversi compiti.

Nei suoi quindici anni di attività, lo spazio ha ospitato oltre 250 concerti di gruppi italiani e stranieri, diventando punto di riferimento per la scena punk/hardcore e vari altri movimenti underground di stampo internazionale. Alla base di questi eventi vi erano i continui incroci tra musica e altre forme espressive come il fumetto, la street art, le arti performative, la fotografia, l'audiovisivo e l'editoria indipendente. I cortei organizzati da Atlantide avevano un forte carattere performativo e includevano concerti, installazioni artistiche e mostre fotografiche, con un'attenzione particolare per artisti trans e queer.

Atlantide si autofinanziava grazie ai biglietti di ingresso per eventi e concerti, riuscendo a sovvenzionare anche attività esterne al collettivo, come il MIT – Movimento d'Identità Transessuale. L'importanza di questo spazio nel tessuto urbano bolognese era legata alla necessità di avere un luogo fisico capace di offrire una programmazione culturale non mainstream.

L'agire politico di Atlantide era portato avanti in maniera diretta, indipendente e autogestita. Le realtà culturali cittadine riconoscevano la presenza e il ruolo di questo spazio all'interno del contesto bolognese, come laboratorio di produzione culturale e di promozione musicale indipendente. I rapporti con le istituzioni locali sono cambiati nel tempo.

L'esperienza di Atlantide si è conclusa nel 2015 con lo sgombero violento dello spazio da parte delle forze dell'ordine.

NOSADELLA.DUE
2006–2016

Nosadella.due nasce nel 2006 dalla volontà di Elisa del Prete di proporre a Bologna un programma di residenze artistiche, uno dei primi in Italia, ispirata da una residenza in qualità di curatrice che aveva avuto l'opportunità di svolgere in Austria attraverso un'associazione di Milano. Il progetto, nato con la volontà di facilitare i processi creativi degli artisti internazionali che vi venivano invitati, trovava spazio all'interno della casa di famiglia di Del Prete, un appartamento in via Nosadella 2, all'interno di un edificio con affaccio su Piazza Malpighi.

Nella realizzazione di questa proposta culturale, Del Prete ha collaborato con svariati curatori tra cui Lelio Aiello, Giusy Checola e Francesca Cigardi. Il bisogno da parte degli artisti di lavorare a stretto contatto con il territorio bolognese attraverso progetti site specific, ha inoltre portato Nosadella.due a stringere relazioni e costruire reti con altre realtà cittadine, come il MAMbo e Xing/Raum. A partire dal 2012, Nosadella.due è entrata in contatto con Urban Center, diventando lo spazio espositivo per alcuni festival cittadini. Un aspetto fondamentale di questa realtà era l'informalità data dalla dimensione domestica del luogo, motivo per cui il pubblico di Nosadella.due non era solo specializzato, ma anche cittadino.

L'esperienza di Nosadella.due si è conclusa nel 2016, quando la fondatrice ha deciso di chiudere lo spazio per via della mancanza di un rapporto proficuo di scambio con altre realtà territoriali e per l'aumento insostenibile delle richieste esterne.

BARTLEBY
2008–2012

Il collettivo Bartleby nasce nel 2008 in seguito alla mobilitazione del movimento studentesco Onda Anomala contro la riforma della scuola e dell'università Gelmini-Tremonti, caratterizzata da una serie di tagli ingenti ai danni dell'occupazione dei giovani nell'ambito dell'istruzione.

Bartleby era composto da studenti, artisti, precari e lavoratori dello spettacolo i quali, al motto "Spazi, Saperi e Reddito", organizzavano occupazioni e manifestazioni in collaborazione ad altri collettivi cittadini che ne condividevano gli ideali politici. La scelta di lottare dentro e contro l'istituzione universitaria ha permesso al collettivo di coinvolgere le giovani generazioni di studenti, proponendo un ragionamento teorico e politico sulla struttura e la gestione dell'università all'interno dei suoi stessi spazi. Entrambe le sedi di Bartleby, infatti, erano edifici di proprietà dell'Università di Bologna, la prima occupata illegalmente e la seconda ottenuta grazie a un accordo con l'Ateneo.

La convergenza dell'aspetto artistico e di quello politico era alla base della programmazione culturale di Bartleby e ha portato alla realizzazione di seminari di autoformazione, eventi, concerti, mostre, festival di fumetto e presentazioni di libri. Questi eventi si basavano sul coinvolgimento di intellettuali, artisti, cineasti, musicisti, fumettisti e scrittori ampiamente riconosciuti, tra cui Gianni Celati, Wu Ming, Paper Resistance, Blu, Ericailcane e Tuono Pettinato, ma anche di artisti emergenti, inclusi gli studenti dell'Accademia di Belle Arti.

L'esperienza di Bartleby si è conclusa nel 2012 per la perdita di una progettualità definita e le crescenti difficoltà a vedere riconosciuta la propria proposta culturale nel contesto cittadino.

CANTINA DARTH
2009–2010

L'associazione Darth nacque nel 2003 dall'unione di alcuni artisti e curatori attivi a Bologna, come gruppo di condivisione di esperienze individuali. A partire dal 2009 emerse l'esigenza di trovare uno spazio che fosse luogo di sperimentazione condivisa. I rapporti con il territorio e le realtà che lo compongono erano solidi, ma le relazioni con le istituzioni politiche rimanevano scarse. Per questo motivo, l'associazione non riuscì a ottenere finanziamenti, lasciando che la programmazione culturale fosse affidata all'autosostentamento come unica fonte economica.

La finalità principale di Cantina Darth era quella di estendere l'interesse per l'arte contemporanea a un pubblico allargato, attraverso l'organizzazione di incontri, eventi espositivi, seminari e tavole rotonde, capaci di creare momenti di discussione e confronto. In occasione del Festival dell'Arte Contemporanea di Faenza, Darth ha organizzato *Ottimi rapporti* (2010), una tavola di conversazione informale tra artisti che lavorano per altri artisti. Altro format ideato da Darth è stato *Peresempio* (2009), nel quale per due edizioni sono stati ospitati artisti e curatori chiamati a raccontare la loro ricerca personale tra cui Emilio Fantin, Giancarlo Norese, Ferdinando Mazzitelli, Luca Panaro, Chiara Pergola, Diego Zuelli e Anteo Radovan.

L'esperienza pregressa di Annalisa Cattani e Adriana Torregrossa con il Progetto Oreste 0 portava all'interno del collettivo un'eredità importante di contatti da cui sono nate diverse collaborazioni. Il confronto sull'arte contemporanea e i suoi funzionamenti costituiva il punto di forza dell'associazione, contribuendo alla creazione e alla diffusione di politiche culturali attive.

L'esperienza di Darth si è conclusa per la mancanza di tempo e di risorse da parte dei membri del collettivo, ma lo spazio Novella Guerra di Cattani a Imola può essere considerato come la naturale prosecuzione di questa sperimentazione bolognese.

CASABIANCA
2010–2015

Casabianca nacque nel 2010 a Zola Predosa, un piccolo comune che fa parte della città metropolitana di Bologna, con la volontà di mettere in dialogo generazioni diverse di artisti e curatori.

Il fondatore di questo spazio, Anteo Radovan, proveniva da esperienze collettive e non-profit precedenti, come lo spazio Il Graffio e il gruppo Oreste, attraverso cui aveva creato contatti con le comunità del DAMS e dell'Accademia. Fondamentale è stata la sua collaborazione con Massimo Marchetti, membro del collettivo Darth, che si occupava principalmente della comunicazione e dell'organizzazione delle mostre, mentre Radovan selezionava i progetti da proporre.

La programmazione culturale comprendeva mostre che nascevano dalle proposte di artisti e curatori esterni. Negli anni Casabianca ha ospitato sia artisti affermati che emergenti, tra cui Francesco Bernardi, Luca Vitone, Giulia Cenci, Irene Coppola, Irene Fenara e Ornaghi e Prestinari. La curatela era solitamente esterna, affidata a figure quali Gino Gianuizzi, Guido Molinari e Lelio Aiello, già coinvolti in altre esperienze simili.

Le relazioni e le collaborazioni con le istituzioni locali erano percepite come non necessarie, mentre il rapporto con il territorio era determinato dal fascino dato dalla location immersa nella campagna.

L'esperienza di Casabianca si concluse nel 2015 a causa delle difficoltà di autosostentamento.

ADIACENZE
2010–in corso

Adiacenze è uno spazio espositivo indipendente dedicato alle arti visive, che ospita mostre e progetti di artisti che lavorano sia con medium tradizionali che con forme di sperimentazione multimediale. Sotto la direzione artistica dei fondatori, Amerigo Mariotti, Giorgia Tronconi e Daniela Tozzi, la programmazione culturale prevede l'organizzazione di diverse mostre all'anno e di una serie di eventi collaterali come incontri, performance, presentazioni di progetti editoriali e workshop.

Adiacenze è nato per dare visibilità ad artisti emergenti di stanza a Bologna, ma la programmazione accoglie anche artisti già affermati a livello nazionale e internazionale. Sempre di più, il programma artistico di Adiacenze ha assunto una connotazione internazionale, anche grazie al progetto di residenze d'artista in collaborazione con la Casa della Cultura Italo Calvino di Calderara di Reno, che consente ad artisti di altri paesi di passare periodi di lavoro a Bologna. Al contempo, il progetto di residenza SWAP ha lo scopo di portare artisti italiani all'estero.

Adiacenze rappresenta uno spazio di ricerca e di sperimentazione di fondamentale importanza all'interno dell'odierno panorama artistico bolognese, in particolare considerando l'attenzione nei confronti delle tecnologie digitali e la loro relazione con il corpo e le dinamiche di relazione.

ELASTICO
2011–2021

Elastico è nato dalla precedente esperienza di FragileContinuo (2008–11) e ha visto coinvolto un collettivo di artiste interessate a proporre una programmazione diversificata incentrata sulla musica e sulle arti visive.

Nei suoi dieci anni di attività, il progetto ha cambiato più volte sede adattandosi a diversi contesti. Spazio Elastico, in vicolo de' Facchini, comprendeva uno spazio per mostre e performance musicali e una boutique in cui erano venivano vendute pubblicazioni, dischi e oggetti autoprodotti. ELaSTiCo faART in via dell'Arcoveggio, nato in seguito all'incontro tra il duo artistico TO/LET e Marzia Stano, Ilaria Mancosu e Luca Musilli, è stato invece una "factory" con atelier, laboratori, workshop e corsi di formazione.

Dalla sua fondazione, Elastico ha intessuto relazioni con l'Accademia di Belle Arti, da cui provengono le fondatrici e diversi degli artisti coinvolti nelle mostre. Fondamentale è stato il rapporto con CRACK!, festival internazionale di fumetto e arte stampata che ha contribuito a posizionare Elastico all'interno di un circuito di spazi indipendenti dedicati all'arte sequenziale e all'illustrazione.

Elastico si autofinanziava tramite il tesseramento dei soci, la vendita di autoproduzioni, la realizzazione di laboratori, grant ottenuti attraverso bandi comunali e, a seconda delle sedi, i ricavi del bar durante gli eventi. L'esperienza di Elastico come spazio si è conclusa con l'arrivo della pandemia ma il collettivo ha continuato a dare forma alle proprie attività attraverso Elastico Records, una casa discografica dichiaratamente "gender free", e altre forme di progettualità in attesa di una nuova sede.

NOVELLA GUERRA
2011–in corso

Novella Guerra nasce dal sogno di trovare un "locus ameno" dove riscoprire il piacere dell'incontro e dello scambio tra artisti visivi, attraverso mostre, eventi e un programma di residenza. Lo spazio sorge all'interno di un casolare nella provincia di Imola, comune compreso nell'area metropolitana di Bologna. Il suo nome è dedicato alla memoria della madre di Annalisa Cattani, la fondatrice. Nel 2018, con Maura Banfo e Susanna Ravelli, Novella Guerra cambia nome diventando Novella Guerra In\Out. La formazione di Cattani, docente presso l'Accademia di Belle Arti di Bologna, è legata principalmente ad Oreste e la sua pratica curatoriale si è affinata all'interno di un altro spazio indipendente, Cantina Darth. Negli anni, Novella Guerra ha visto la collaborazione di svariati artisti e curatori, coinvolti in maniera cooperativa sul piano decisionale della programmazione culturale.

Novella Guerra ha sviluppato una serie di progetti in collaborazione con altre realtà nazionali dedicate alla produzione alternativa nell'ambito delle arti visive, come NESXT – Independent Art Festival realizzato con l'associazione Leggermente Fuori Sede. Lo spazio propone anche un programma di residenze che ha visto la partecipazione di artisti italiani e internazionali.

La programmazione culturale è incentrata su mostre e interventi spesso di natura site-specific, nati da rapporti personali e di collaborazione. Tra i progetti, si ricorda il "pigiama party luddista" realizzato nel 2019 in collaborazione con Stefania Galegati, evento durante il quale fu fondato il gruppo di artiste e curatrici Gina X.

Novella Guerra rappresenta uno spazio di grande interesse per la sua capacità di produrre eventi e progetti in grado di ottenere vasta ricezione nonostante la posizione decentrata rispetto alla città e l'apparente distanza dalla comunità artistica bolognese e nazionale.

SENZA FILTRO
2012–2019

L'abbondanza di spazi dismessi presenti nel tessuto urbano e il desiderio di un luogo dedicato all'intersezione tra attività sociali, artistiche e culturali autoprodotte, ha portato nel 2012 alla fondazione di Senza Filtro, anche noto come "centro smistamento delle arti differenti" (Sorting For Different Arts Center).

L'Associazione Planimetrie Culturali, responsabile della fondazione di questo spazio, si occupa dal 2000 della mappatura degli spazi abbandonati da rivitalizzare attraverso percorsi di partecipazione civica condotti da gruppi informali ed associazioni, come Ca.Cu.Bo. (Cantiere Culturale Bolognese) e Scalo San Donato. I progetti di Planimetrie Culturali sono dedicati all'uso temporaneo di spazi dismessi e, fino alla loro risignificazione, abbandonati. Nel 2012, l'Associazione ha firmato un contratto con la proprietà dello stabile in via Stalingrado 59, divenendone di fatto diretta responsabile.

La volontà di Senza Filtro è stata di dare spazio a realtà indipendenti bolognesi dedicate alle arti, ad attività ricreative e all'integrazione sociale. Nei circa 6000 metri quadrati dell'area gestita da Senza Filtro sono stati accolti: il Museo del Flipper dell'Associazione Tilt, l'Ostello dell'Associazione Use-it, lo spazio dell'Associazione Fuoricampo, il centro fotografico dell'Associazione Piccolo Formato, lo spazio espositivo gestito dal collettivo VVVB, lo spazio didattico per l'insegnamento della lingua italiana a persone straniere dell'associazione SEMinARIA, e il capannone dedicato ad attività sportive come skate, parkour e bmx.

La relazione con il territorio e la comunità è stata di fondamentale importanza, alimentata sia dal coinvolgimento di singoli che dalla collaborazione con le associazioni, e dal rivolgersi un pubblico estremamente diversificato. L'esperienza di Senza Filtro si è conclusa quando l'edificio è stato messo all'asta dal Tribunale fallimentare.

LÀBAS
2012–in corso

Làbas, acronimo di Laboratorio d'assalto, è nato dalla volontà di riappropriarsi di un bene comune che era stato abbandonato, l'ex Caserma Masini in via Orfeo, e di aprirlo alla cittadinanza come centro polifunzionale con una programmazione culturale diversificata e inclusiva. Dal primo momento, l'obiettivo fu infatti quello di relazionarsi con il quartiere e con associazioni, gruppi informali e altri spazi dedicati alle arti presenti nella zona. Le contaminazioni e gli stimoli esterni sono stati di fondamentale importanza per questa realtà, ma non ne hanno limitato la libertà di movimento.

Ancora oggi, i ruoli e i compiti vengono definiti durante le assemblee, in base alle disponibilità dei singoli e dei gruppi che frequentano lo spazio. Tutte le attività sono realizzate grazie all'autofinanziamento e al volontariato e, in alcuni casi, mediante la partecipazione a bandi cittadini.

Frutto di istanze di natura politica, il programma culturale di Làbas comprende interventi e progetti espositivi di artisti che utilizzano il fumetto e la street art, ma anche di musicisti e produttori, con particolare attenzione all'hip hop e alla musica elettronica.

I progetti artistici sono scelti per la loro capacità di incarnare il vissuto collettivo e arricchirlo di nuovi apporti personali, riuscendo in questo modo a coinvolgere un pubblico il più eterogeneo possibile. Più che "centro sociale", infatti, Làbas si autodefinisce come un "municipio sociale", ovvero uno spazio condiviso, autonomo e inclusivo, dove chiunque si possa sentire un partecipante attivo.

STUDIO CLOUD 4
2013–2016

Mosso dal desiderio di sviluppare un dialogo sull'arte contemporanea, l'artista e docente Stefano Pasquini ha fondato Studio Cloud 4 all'interno dello studio fotografico di Stefano Stagni e Paolo Frascaroli. Il laboratorio dei due fotografi è diventato così un eclettico spazio espositivo caratterizzato da una totale libertà di sperimentare, senza dover scendere a compromessi con le dinamiche commerciali del sistema dell'arte. Le attività proposte erano infatti totalmente finanziate dallo studio fotografico e aspiravano a coinvolgere un pubblico più vasto possibile.

Nei tre anni di attività, Studio Cloud 4 ha proposto principalmente progetti espositivi collettivi tematici a cura di Pasquini. *Venti Leggeri* (2013), per esempio, presentava artisti i cui lavori erano accumunati dal tema della leggerezza. In un caso, sono state esposte opere provenienti da una collezione privata, quella di Tiberio Catelani. Altre volte, i progetti nascevano da rapporti diretti con artisti, come nel caso delle mostre personali di Angelo Pretolani e Eva Marisaldi.

La chiusura dello studio fotografico, in seguito al pensionamento di Frascaroli e al trasferimento in Canada di Stagni, ha segnato la fine di Studio Cloud 4 nel 2016.

LOCALEDUE
2013–2021

Localedue fu fondato da Fabio Farnè e Gabriele Tosi per fornire uno spazio espositivo ad artisti e curatori emergenti offrendo loro supporto tecnico, curatoriale e comunicativo.

Nato nel 2013 come spazio indipendente, nel 2016 diventa associazione non-profit. Fino al 2019, Localedue ha avuto sede in via Azzo Gardino in uno spazio concesso in gestione dalla Manifattura delle Arti, e successivamente ha operato in modo nomade, ospite di altre realtà.

La programmazione culturale coinvolgeva artisti già affermati a livello nazionale, ma anche artisti emergenti provenienti dall'Accademia di Belle Arti di Bologna, in particolare grazie alla collaborazione con il docente e curatore Lelio Aiello. Localedue si impegnava nella sperimentazione, nello studio e nel confronto, proponendo mostre personali e collettive, progetti speciali, performance, workshop e realizzando pubblicazioni.

Per i due fondatori, essere indipendenti significava sperimentare senza una progettualità rigida e proporre modelli non commerciali che non prevedessero un dialogo con le istituzioni politiche e artistiche. Localedue si rivolgeva quindi a un pubblico specializzato e di nicchia, ma senza la minima logica commerciale.

Interrotto l'accordo informale con la Manifattura delle Arti per la concessione della sede, Localedue è rimasto attivo come realtà itinerante fino al 2021, quando i due fondatori hanno deciso di terminarne l'attività per potersi dedicare ad altre iniziative.

ATELIERSI
2013–in corso

La sperimentazione dei linguaggi delle arti performative e l'attenzione alla relazione tra processo e prodotto sono i focus attorno ai quali si costruisce la produzione artistica di Ateliersi.

Questo spazio culturale nasce nel 2013, dalla volontà di un collettivo composto da artisti e curatori. La sede di via San Vitale si connota come spazio dedicato principalmente alla produzione artistica, con un'attenzione particolare alla relazione tra la dimensione processuale e quella di presentazione del prodotto artistico. Ateliersi accoglie sia artisti provenienti dal teatro e dalle arti performative, che artisti visivi e sonori, la cui produzione prevede modalità performative. La programmazione culturale comprende, inoltre, un'articolata attività di residenze in cui vengono invitati artisti selezionati per la loro qualità di innovazione e sperimentazione.

Nell'ambito di Ateliersi vengono realizzate opere che arrivano a circolare in Italia e all'estero, portando contemporaneamente stimoli internazionali a Bologna. La dimensione europea di questo spazio è anche dovuta alla sua adesione a due reti di produzione culturale, la Trans Europe Halles e Lo Stato dei Luoghi, e a due coordinamenti, il C.Re.S.Co (Coordinamento delle Realtà della Scena Contemporanea) e il Coordinamento Nazionale dei Centri di Residenza per Artisti nei Territori.

Ateliersi è un hub artistico e culturale di fondamentale importanza per il territorio bolognese e si configura come luogo di accoglienza di diverse realtà attive in ambito artistico, performativo, educativo e sociale. Questo bisogno di mettersi in relazione nasce dalla consapevolezza che tramite il dialogo si possa generare cultura.

MAISON VENTIDUE
2014–2021

Sotto la direzione artistica della fondatrice, Mariarosa Lamanna, la programmazione culturale di Maison Ventidue ha visto la collaborazione di curatori e artisti, tra cui Marco Mastroianni, Serena Facioni e Mariolino Guida. Le attività di questo spazio consistevano principalmente nell'organizzazione mostre di artisti visivi, inizialmente invitati dai curatori e successivamente selezionati mediante delle open call. Negli spazi di Maison Ventidue sono state proposte installazioni relazionali, progetti multimediali, performance e mostre di pittura e disegno.

Maison Ventidue ha intrattenuto varie relazioni con istituzioni culturali cittadine, che hanno aiutato il progetto a crescere, pur permettendogli di mantenere la propria libertà decisionale e di sperimentazione. L'attività si è autofinanziata, anche grazie a forme di donazione e tesseramento. Nel 2021 l'esperienza di Maison Ventidue si è conclusa in modo del tutto naturale, per esaurimento di energie dopo anni di sperimentazione e crescita.

TRIPLA
2016–2019

Fondato da tre studenti dell'Accademia di Belle Arti di Bologna, TRIPLA occupava tre vetrine affacciate su via dell'Indipendenza, una delle vie principali della città, che si estende dalla Stazione Centrale a Piazza Maggiore. Vista la peculiare posizione dello spazio, ottenuto in concessione temporanea e gratuita dal Comune di Bologna, gli artisti ne hanno fatto un'occasione di dialogo con un pubblico vasto e generico, spesso mettendo in discussione la natura commerciale della strada.

Nei tre anni di attività, TRIPLA ha proposto ventinove mostre, invitando artisti locali e internazionali a lavorare all'interno di uno spazio connotato dalla ridotta profondità delle vetrine. La particolarità dello spazio obbligava gli artisti a realizzare dei progetti site specific non replicabili altrove, determinati anche dalla fruizione veloce di un pubblico composto principalmente da passanti.

Numerose sono state le relazioni intessute con le istituzioni culturali del territorio come il MAMbo (in occasione di Art City), e con altre realtà non-profit come Xing/Raum, Gelateria Sogni di Ghiaccio e Localedue.

TRIPLA, il cui nome e simbolo sono un richiamo all'adattatore elettrico di uso quotidiano, ha chiuso nel 2019 a causa del mancato rinnovamento della concessione da parte del Comune.

GELATERIA SOGNI DI GHIACCIO
2016–in corso

Gelateria Sogni di Ghiaccio nasce nel 2016 dal desiderio di Mattia Pajé, Filippo Marzocchi e Marco Casella, tre giovani artisti appena diplomati presso l'Accademia di Belle Arti di Bologna, di offrire ad altri artisti emergenti uno spazio di sperimentazione in cui divertirsi e imparare senza dovere incorrere nelle logiche commerciali caratteristiche delle gallerie d'arte contemporanea. Oltre a spazio espositivo e di progettazione, Gelateria Sogni di Ghiaccio è stato anche lo studio artistico e luogo di lavoro dei tre fondatori. Dal 2016 al 2019 lo spazio è stato diretto da Pajé e Marzocchi, mentre dal 2020 dal solo Pajé. Attualmente lo spazio e il programma espositivo sono collettivamente gestiti da un gruppo di dodici persone.

Numerose sono state le collaborazioni avviate negli anni con istituzioni cittadine quali Arte Fiera e MAMbo, ma anche con altri spazi e organizzazioni non-profit come Xing, TRIPLA e Localedue.

Essere indipendente ha consentito a questo spazio di non avere un programma curatoriale definito. La sua programmazione seguiva solitamente un processo spontaneo, legato alle frequentazioni personali con artisti italiani e internazionali, le cui mostre personali si sono sviluppate su un principio dialogico e cooperativo. L'installazione e gli interventi site-specific con riferimenti a sottoculture e immaginario pop, erano tra le forme di espressione artistica più ricorrenti nella programmazione di Gelateria Sogni di Ghiaccio.

ALCHEMILLA
2019—in corso

Alchemilla è un'associazione culturale che ha sede all'interno dello storico Palazzo Vizzani in via Santo Stefano, in un appartamento di proprietà della famiglia di Camilla Sanguinetti, una delle fondatrici e responsabile per la direzione artistica. L'idea di uno spazio espositivo che fosse anche un luogo di ricerca nasce dalle sinergie tra i fondatori, sviluppatesi durante precedenti progetti curatoriali.

Nei primi tre anni la curatela dei progetti è stata affidata a Fulvio Chimento, che ha proposto mostre di artisti italiani emersi negli anni Novanta come Stefano Arienti, Alessandro Pessoli, Cuoghi Corsello e Pierpaolo Campanini. Successivamente, sono stati coinvolti curatori esterni al direttivo, i quali hanno organizzato mostre di artisti più giovani come Mattia Pajè, Roberto Fassone e il collettivo Slug. Gran parte dei progetti esplorano dinamiche di site-specificity, che si tratti di installazioni o performance, ora in dialogo ora in contrapposizione con gli ambienti interni e con la corte esterna dei questo sontuoso edificio del 1560.

Alchemilla si relaziona con diverse istituzioni e realtà artistiche del territorio, e dal 2022 fa parte della rete K.I.N. – Keep In Network che unisce associazioni culturali indipendenti che operano su Bologna e altrove. Lo spazio è in parte autofinanziato, in parte sovvenzionato attraverso bandi pubblici e sponsor privati coinvolti a seconda dei progetti. Alchemilla ha anche avviato un tesseramento con l'idea di coinvolgere i soci come parte attiva nei processi decisionali, attraverso assemblee annuali e altri momenti di incontro.

PARSEC
2020—in corso

Parsec nasce nel 2020 dall'esigenza personale delle fondatrici di mettere in pratica le passioni e le competenze maturate durante gli anni di formazione, convinte del valore sociale dell'arte come strumento per riflettere e discutere sul presente, in chiave culturale e politica.

L'obiettivo di Parsec è quello di far dialogare prospettive differenti, coinvolgendo artisti locali, ma anche nazionali e internazionali. La necessità di fornire un'offerta eterogenea influenza la programmazione culturale che si compone principalmente del progetto di residenza PARSEC RESIDENCY e dell'organizzazione di mostre con cadenza annuale, ma si arricchisce anche di altri eventi e attività, come due festival incentrati rispettivamente sul rapporto tra arte ed ecologia e sull'immagine in movimento. Il programma curatoriale è inoltre composto da laboratori, crit (ovvero momenti in cui gli artisti si aprono a un confronto con il pubblico), talk e performance. La selezione degli artisti avviene tramite ricerche dirette, proposte di collaborazione esterne e open call. In tutti e tre i casi, il gruppo curatoriale preferisce collaborare e lavorare attivamente con l'artista coinvolto prediligendo l'aspetto contenutistico a quello estetico. La collaborazione con altre realtà del territorio è di fondamentale importanza, come testimoniato dall'adesione a K.I.N. – Keep In Network, rete di spazi indipendenti bolognesi. Vi è inoltre uno stretto dialogo con il Comune di Bologna e con il quartiere in cui ha sede lo spazio.

Parsec continua a operare in maniera indipendente, coinvolgendo artisti e realtà locali, con la consapevolezza di quanto questo tipo di approccio sia fondamentale per continuare a tenere vivo il sistema dell'arte, proponendo un'alternativa valida al mainstream.

TIST – THIS IS SO TEMPORARY
2020—in corso

TIST – This Is So Temporary nasce nel 2020 in risposta alle decisioni del governo italiano di sostenere esclusivamente le realtà commerciali durante la pandemia, situazione che porta il collettivo fondato da Michele Liparesi e Yulia Tikhomirova, ai quali ben presto si uniscono Samir Sayed Abdellattef ed Enrico Vassallo, a ragionare sul ruolo sociale e politico dell'arte all'interno della società contemporanea.

TIST ha sede in un capannone nella zona industriale di Rastignano, nell'immediata periferia bolognese, e accoglie diversi atelier, luoghi di socialità, uno spazio espositivo interno e uno esterno. Il ragionamento riguardo ai progetti e la distribuzione delle varie mansioni avvengono durante le riunioni interne e secondo logiche orizzontali.

Elemento di fondamentale importanza per TIST è l'indipendenza istituzionale, poiché il collettivo immagina la possibilità di un futuro diverso, in cui il sistema dell'arte – del quale considera le relazioni come basate su un rapporto di tipo dipendente, in cui le istituzioni artistiche si appropriano del lavoro altrui – appartiene al passato: essere indipendenti significa quindi andare verso il futuro.

La produzione culturale di TIST si articola in una serie di progetti espositivi e interventi di artisti affini al collettivo, nell'organizzazione di un festival e nella pubblicazione periodica di *FARò. Pratiche Estetiche Politiche*. Queste attività hanno lo scopo di riflettere sull'intersezione tra arte e politica, pensando all'arte come strumento di trasformazione sociale. Tra le tematiche principali affrontate da TIST vi sono l'anti-monumentalità nello spazio pubblico, la costruzione della memoria collettiva secondo recenti logiche di decolonizzazione di matrice internazionale ancora poco praticate in Italia, l'impatto dei media, e il rapporto con il tessuto sociale e la natura circostante.

ACKNOWLEDGMENTS

Thanks to all the students who, under the supervision of Roberto Pinto and Francesco Spampinato, from 2021 to 2023 participated in the academic internship dare_SPAZI at the Department of the Arts of the University of Bologna, conducting interviews and collecting information and documents that constituted the starting point for the construction of this book: Beatrice Baistrocchi, India Caiozzo, Claudia Virginia Caporusso, Nicole Costella, Nikolaos Katsivelakis, Carlotta Morselli, Luca Paoletti, Jingge Ren, Nadia Salamino, Beatrice Sartori, Martina Trocano. Along with them, interviews with the founding members of the spaces featured in the book have been conducted also by Lara De Lena, Pasquale Fameli, Nicola Manzoni, Francesco Spampinato.

Thanks to all those involved in the spaces included in the book who shared with us their memories, perspectives, information and visual documents: Simone Addessi, Irene Adorni, Werthèr Albertazzi, Antonio Alia, Antonella Babbone, Franco "Bifo" Berardi, Enrico Biagini, Syusy Blady, Ivo Bonacorsi, Laura Bolandrini, Mauro "Boris" Borella, Giovanni Brunetto, Margherita Kay Budillon, Paolo Bufalini, Silvia Calderoni, Enrico Campagna, Patti Campani, Ginetto Campanini, Totò Cariello, Mariuccia Casadio, Marzio Cavicchini, Massimo Carozzi, Daria Casadio, Matilde Cassarini, Annalisa Cattani, Bettina Cottone, Rossella Chirizzi, Collettivo Làbas, Nicola Carlo Costantino, Francesco "Ratigher" D'Erminio, DeeMo, Sara De Giovanni, Valerio Dehò, Renato De Maria, Eugenia Delbue, Elisa Del Prete, Mirko Donati, Francesca Dondi, Donatella Franchi, Greta Fuzzi, Gino Gianuizzi, Silvia Grandi, Silvia Guescini, Gianpietro Huber, Alessandro Iannetti, Ioannis Kopsinis, Mariarosa Lamanna, Margo Lengua, Norina Lezzi, Damiano Le Rose, Michele Liparesi, Massimo Lorenzani, Chiara Mancini, Graziano Mannu, Tihana Maravic, Elisa Marchese, Massimo Marchetti, Amerigo Mariotti, Eva Marisaldi, Alberto Masala, Michail Mauracher, Mauro Meneghelli, Fiorenza Menni, Raffaele Messuti, Guido Molinari, Giulia Monte, Stefano Opipari, Mattia Pajè, Arianna Pasini, Stefano W. Pasquini, Judith Inglavaga Pedros, Gianni Pedullà, Anna Persiani, Jurate Piacenti, Anteo Randovan, Ginevra Romagnoli, Oderso Rubini, Camilla Sanguinetti, Vincenzo Scorza, Diego Segatto, Enrico Serotti, Andrea Mochi Sismondi, Enrico Sumo, Texas, Yulia Tikhomirova, TO/LET (Sonia Piedad Marinangeli / Elisa Placucci), Gabriele Tosi, Maria Antonietta Traforini, Giorgia Tronconi, Uliana Zanetti and many others who asked to remain anonymous.

Special thanks to the following photographers whose pictures represent today an invaluable time machine for breathing again the air of those spaces that are no longer active: Nanni Angeli, Emanuele Angiuli, Stefano Belacchi, Federico Bernocchi, Giovanni Brunetto, Anna de Manincor, Luca Del Pia, Giorgio Di Trapani, Margherita Caprilli, Luca Ghedini, Mathias Gumprich, Michele Lapini, Valentina Morandi, Sergio Perini, Gianluca Perticoni, Massimo Sciacca, Aldo Sorriso, Texas, Alessandro Zanini.

Thanks also to those who helped with the book's production at various stages, from the early steps of the Italian Council proposal to its release, including those who kindly granted us cultural partnership way before the book started taking shape: Valeria Baruzzi, Stefano Boeri, Sandra Costa, Pasquale Fameli, Ana Maria Guash Ferrer, Keith Gray, Damiano Gullì, Jennifer Malvezzi, Giacomo Manzoli, Sara Molho, Adrian e Melisa Paci, Matteo Piccioni, Dominique Poulot, Julia Ramírez-Blanco, Anna Rosellini, Caterina Sinigaglia, Bruno Soro, Lucio Spaziante, Nicola Trezzi.

We are deeply grateful to the Mousse team involved in the production of this book, for their professionalism, dedication, and precious feedback along the way. In particular, we'd like to thank Alessandro Schino, who has given shape and legibility to such a multiform iconographic corpus, Emma Passarella for checking and proofreading all the texts and information included in the book with commitment and enthusiasm, and Ilaria Bombelli for believing in this editorial project with passion since the very first moment and supervising its evolution with imagination and firmness.

And an extended gratitude to all those who animated these spaces over the past almost fifty years, be they directly involved, collaborators or simply attendees, making Bologna a hub for independent art practices and innovative cultural economies.

Skank Bloc Bologna
Alternative Art Spaces since 1977

Edited by
Roberto Pinto
Francesco Spampinato

Texts by
Roberto Pinto
Francesco Spampinato
Andrea Lissoni
Lara De Lena
Davide Da Pieve

Introductory texts to the spaces by
Nicola Manzoni and Francesco Spampinato

Publishing Editor
Ilaria Bombelli (Mousse)

Editorial Coordinator
Emma Passarella (Mousse)

Graphic Design
Alessandro Schino (Mousse)

Translations
Ben Bazalgette

Proofreading and copyediting
Emma Passarella (Mousse)

Printed in Italy by
Industrie Grafiche Pacini, Pisa

© 2024 Mousse Publishing, the authors of
the texts

Cover: Livello 57 (Via A. Muggia, 6), ca. 2000–04
Photo: Valentina Morandi
Back cover: Isola Nel Kantiere, February 1991
Photo: Massimo Sciacca

First edition
2024

ISBN 978-88-6749-624-2

€ 30 / $ 35

Published and distributed by
Mousse Publishing
Contrappunto s.r.l.
via Pier Candido Decembrio 28,
20137, Milan–Italy
moussemagazine.it

The publisher would like to thank all those who
have kindly given their permission for the repro-
duction of material for this book. Every effort has
been made to obtain permission to reproduce the
images and texts in this book. However, as is stan-
dard editorial policy, the publisher is at the disposal
of copyright holders and undertakes to correct
any omissions or errors in future editions.

Interviews with the founders of the spaces featured in this book are collected in a file available in open access through a web page of the
Department of the Arts, University of Bologna.

Project supported by Italian Council program
(2022), promoted by the Directorate-General
for Contemporary Creativity within the Italian
Ministry of Culture.

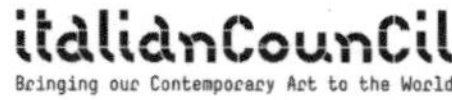

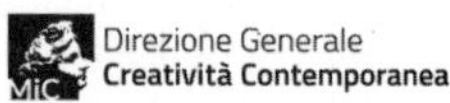